Advance Praise for *The Cambridge Handbook of Public-Private Partnerships, Intellectual Property Governance, and Sustainable Development*

"At a time in which prospects for normative and technical assistance initiatives to address access to public goods have been overwhelmed by new challenges arising from globalization, digitization, and the failure of multilateralism, this book offers a careful study of public-private partnerships (PPPs) in a variety of sectors, using case studies that offer guidance to policymakers, raise new questions for scholars, and, collectively, outline the contours of new pathways in the design and governance of PPPs, with a distinctive path to advancing access to knowledge and access to technology. The book is a should have — and a must read."

Ruth Okediji,
Harvard Law School and the Berkman Klein Center

"We cannot realistically approach attainment of the Sustainable Development Goals (SDGs) without transformative innovation in public health, energy, and agriculture, and without effective and equitable dissemination of the fruits of this innovation. The SDGs recognize the vital contribution of innovation and of partnership between public and private actors for sustainable development: indeed, the SDGs in a sense epitomise the pressing need for public–private partnership on a grand scale. At another level, each intellectual property (IP) right can be construed in itself as a kind of public–private partnership, devised in principle to harness private capacities and resources to deliver welfare-enhancing public goods. This timely publication explores the complex linkages between the broad policy context defined by the SDGs, and the concrete task of using the intellectual property system to forge practical partnerships that yield tangible results, examined through the lens of how intellectual property rights are managed within a diverse selection of public–private partnerships. In distilling practical and policy insights from this rich vein of experience, and analysing equally diverse approaches to managing intellectual property rights to leverage public benefit, this landmark volume opens up possibilities for a more nuanced, more grounded, and more enabling understanding for policymakers of the complex roles and potential contributions of the intellectual property system in efforts to achieve the SDGs; and it equally provides direct guidance for those engaged in the practical planning and management of knowledge-based programmes for sustainable development. In illuminating and documenting the linkages between the wider policy context and actual programme design and delivery, it marks a substantial advance towards the informed and empirically grounded inquiry that is sorely needed if we are to ensure that the intellectual property system fulfils its potential contribution to the SDGs."

Antony Taubman,
World Trade Organization

"This timely book covers a very important trio of topics, and is a 'must-read' for anyone interested in current issues relating to intellectual property and its broader social and developmental goals."

Edward Kwakwa,
World Intellectual Property Organization

"The twenty first century will be increasingly driven by the globalization of knowledge goods. How should intellectual property be governed in public–private partnerships if they are to comply with sustainable development goals? This impressive collection brings together concrete experiences to draw lessons for future directions in global governance of knowledge."

Sakiko Fukuda-Parr,
The New School

"This book makes a long overdue contribution to the understanding of public–private partnerships (PPPs) and their role in global knowledge governance. PPPs are often found on the intersection of private intellectual property and public interest. Their variety is as plentiful as the views expressed in this book which makes it a must read for anyone interested in the question of whether PPPs address intellectual property and development challenges effectively or worsen them."

Ellen 't Hoen,
Medicines Law & Policy and Global Health Unit,
University Medical Centre Groningen

THE CAMBRIDGE HANDBOOK OF PUBLIC–PRIVATE PARTNERSHIPS, INTELLECTUAL PROPERTY GOVERNANCE, AND SUSTAINABLE DEVELOPMENT

Public–private partnerships (PPPs) play an increasingly prominent role in addressing global development challenges. United Nations agencies and other organizations are relying on PPPs to improve global health, facilitate access to scientific information, and encourage the diffusion of climate change technologies. For this reason, the 2030 Agenda for Sustainable Development highlights their centrality in the implementation of the Sustainable Development Goals (SDGs). At the same time, the intellectual property dimensions and implications of these efforts remain under-examined. Through selective case studies, this illuminating work contributes to a better understanding of the relationships between PPPs and intellectual property considered within a global knowledge governance framework that includes innovation, capacity-building, technological learning, and diffusion. Linking global governance of knowledge via intellectual property to the SDGs, this is the first book to chart the activities of PPPs at this important nexus.

Margaret Chon is the Donald & Lynda Horowitz Professor for the Pursuit of Justice, and former Associate Dean for Research, at Seattle University School of Law, where her current research explores the relationship of intellectual property to human and sustainable development.

Pedro Roffe is a Senior Fellow at the International Centre for Trade and Sustainable Development, where his work focuses on intellectual property, foreign investment, transfer of technology, and international economic negotiations.

Ahmed Abdel-Latif is the Chief, Office of the Director General, at the International Renewable Energy Agency. Previously, he was Senior Programme Manager for Innovation, Technology and Intellectual Property at the International Centre for Trade and Sustainable Development.

The Cambridge Handbook of Public–Private Partnerships, Intellectual Property Governance, and Sustainable Development

Edited by
Margaret Chon
Seattle University School of Law
Pedro Roffe
International Centre for Trade and Sustainable Development
Ahmed Abdel-Latif
International Renewable Energy Agency

SEATTLEU
SCHOOL OF LAW

ICTSD
International Centre for Trade and Sustainable Development

CAMBRIDGE
UNIVERSITY PRESS

CAMBRIDGE
UNIVERSITY PRESS

University Printing House, Cambridge CB2 8BS, United Kingdom

One Liberty Plaza, 20th Floor, New York, NY 10006, USA

477 Williamstown Road, Port Melbourne, VIC 3207, Australia

314–321, 3rd Floor, Plot 3, Splendor Forum, Jasola District Centre, New Delhi – 110025, India

79 Anson Road, #06–04/06, Singapore 079906

Cambridge University Press is part of the University of Cambridge.

It furthers the University's mission by disseminating knowledge in the pursuit of education, learning, and research at the highest international levels of excellence.

www.cambridge.org
Information on this title: www.cambridge.org/9781107175839
DOI: 10.1017/9781316809587

First published 2018

Printed in the United States of America by Sheridan Books, Inc.

A catalogue record for this publication is available from the British Library.

Library of Congress Cataloging-in-Publication Data
Names: Chon, Margaret, editor. | Roffe, Pedro, editor. | Abdel-Latif, Ahmed, editor.
Title: The Cambridge handbook of public–private partnerships, intellectual property governance, and sustainable development / edited by Margaret Chon, Pedro Roffe and Ahmed Abdel-Latif.
Other titles: Handbook of public–private partnerships, global intellectual property governance and sustainable development
Description: Cambridge, United Kingdom ; New York, NY : Cambridge University Press, 2018. | Includes bibliographical references and index.
Identifiers: LCCN 2018010103 | ISBN 9781107175839 (hardback)
Subjects: LCSH: Public–private sector cooperation. | Intellectual property–International cooperation. | Sustainable development. | BISAC: LAW / Intellectual Property / General.
Classification: LCC HD3871 .C36 2018 | DDC 658/.046–dc23
LC record available at https://lccn.loc.gov/2018010103

ISBN 978-1-107-17583-9 Hardback

Contents

Figures

Tables

Contributors

Frederick M. Abbott is Edward Ball Eminent Scholar Professor of International Law at Florida State University College of Law. He has served as expert consultant for numerous international and regional organizations, governments, and nongovernmental organizations, mainly in the fields of intellectual property and technology transfer, public health, trade, competition, and sustainable development. He recently served on the Expert Advisory Group to the United Nations Secretary-General's High Level Panel on Access to Medicines. He is Co-Chair of the Committee on Global Health Law of the International Law Association, having served as Rapporteur for the Committee on International Trade Law from the inception of its work in 1993 to its conclusion in 2014. He regularly serves as a panelist for the WIPO Arbitration and Mediation Center. He has served as counsel to governments in WTO dispute settlement proceedings, and in national court proceedings. He is the author of many books and articles in the fields of international intellectual property rights law, public health, international economic law, and competition law.

Ahmed Abdel-Latif is Chief of the Office of the Director General at the International Renewable Energy Agency. Previously, he was Senior Programme Manager for Innovation, Technology and Intellectual Property at the International Centre for Trade and Sustainable Development. As an Egyptian career diplomat, he worked at the Permanent Mission of Egypt to the United Nations and the World Trade Organization in Geneva, where he was a delegate to the TRIPS Council and to the World Intellectual Property Organization. He has taken an active part in international discussions on intellectual property, innovation, and development. Recent publications include *Protecting Traditional Knowledge: The WIPO Intergovernmental Committee on Intellectual Property and Genetic Resources, Traditional Knowledge and Folklore* (2017, edited with D. Robinson and P. Roffe). He holds an LLM in public international law from the London School of Economics, a BA in political science from the American University in Cairo, and the Diplôme of the Institut d'Etudes Politiques de Paris.

Jens Bammel is an international publishing industry consultant. Having studied law, he has worked as a legal advisor to the United Kingdom magazine industry before joining the Publishers Licensing Society of the United Kingdom as CEO from 1998 until 2003. From 2003 until 2015 he represented the international publishing industry as Secretary General of the International Publishers Association. Since then, he has worked as a consultant to publishers, publishers' associations, and international organizations.

Sara Bannerman is Canada Research Chair in Communication Policy and Governance and an associate professor of communication studies at McMaster University in Canada. She has published two books on international copyright: *International Copyright and Access to Knowledge* (2016) and *The Struggle for Canadian Copyright: Imperialism to Internationalism, 1842–1971* (2013). She has also published numerous peer-reviewed articles and book chapters on international copyright, international copyright history, and other topics. She is a vice chair of the Law Section of the International Association for Media and Communication Research.

Thomas Bombelles is Head of NGO and Industry Relations in the Department for Transition and Developed Countries at the World Intellectual Property Organization (WIPO). He is a principal liaison for WIPO, with a range of external stakeholders representing civil society and the private sector. From 2013 to 2017 he was Head of Global Health in WIPO's Global Challenges Division. Before joining WIPO, he worked as an international policy analyst and government relations professional based in Washington, DC, for the Pharmaceutical Research and Manufacturers of America, and also for Merck & Co., Inc. During his career in the pharmaceutical industry, he devoted much of his time to addressing the issue of intellectual property protection and access to medicines. He has honors degrees from the University of Michigan, Ann Arbor, and the Johns Hopkins School of Advanced International Studies, Washington, DC.

Esteban Burrone is Head of Policy of the Medicines Patent Pool (MPP), where he oversees partnerships with a wide range of external organizations including governments, intergovernmental organizations, and civil society organizations. He has been with the MPP since its establishment in 2010 and is part of the senior management team. Before that he worked at the World Intellectual Property Organization and at UNITAID. He has more than fifteen years' experience working in the field of innovation, intellectual property rights, and access to medicines with a focus on developing countries. He holds a Master of Science in development studies from the London School of Economics and a Master in Business Administration from the International University in Geneva.

Irene Calboli is Professor of Law at Texas A&M University School of Law, Lee Kong Chian Fellow and Visiting Professor at Singapore Management University School of Law, and Transatlantic Technology Law Forum Fellow at Stanford Law School. She is an elected member of the American Law Institute. She currently serves as the Chair of the Art Law Section of the Association of American Law Schools. She is a member of the Board of the European Policy for Intellectual Property Law Association and the Legislation and Regulation Committee of the International Trademark Association. Her most recent books include *Diversity in Intellectual Property* (2015) and *Geographical Indications at the Crossroads of Trade, Development, and Culture: Focus on Asia Pacific* (2017).

Margaret Chon is the Donald & Lynda Horowitz Professor for the Pursuit of Justice and former Associate Dean for Research at Seattle University School of Law. She is the author of numerous articles, books, book chapters, and review essays on intellectual property, as well as on race and law. Her current research explores the relationship of global intellectual property legal frameworks to distributive justice and human development. A member of the Seattle University faculty since 1996, she has visited at many law schools, teaching classes on international intellectual property as well as other innovation and technology law subjects. An alumna of Cornell University College of Arts and

Science (AB Biology), the University of Michigan School of Public Health, and the University of Michigan Law School, she clerked with the US Court of Appeals for the Third Circuit and practiced intellectual property law before joining the academy.

Jeremy de Beer is an award-winning professor at the University of Ottawa's Faculty of Law and a cofounding director of the Open African Innovation Research network (Open AIR). He is a senior research associate at the IP Unit, University of Cape Town, and a senior fellow at the Centre for International Governance Innovation. He shapes ideas about innovation, intellectual property, global trade, and development. As a practicing lawyer and expert consultant, he has argued numerous cases before the Supreme Court of Canada, advised large and small businesses and law firms, and consulted for agencies from national governments and the United Nations.

Jennifer Dent has more than twenty years of broad-based pharmaceutical and biotechnology experience, including negotiation and structuring of deals, and management of global discovery and commercial alliances. Jennifer began her career as a sales representative in Canada working in a variety of positions for Parke Davis/Pfizer and Genentech. Following the acquisition of Genentech Canada by Roche, Jennifer held a number of senior management positions in marketing, lifecycle management, global product strategy, business development, and alliance management at Roche and Genentech in Canada, Switzerland, New Jersey, and south San Francisco. Jennifer cofounded Sound Biotechnology. Before that, she served as Vice President, Business Development, Marketing, and Sales at CombiMatrix Corporation in Washington. Jennifer graduated with a BSc from the University of Western Ontario and received her executive MBA at Western's Richard Ivey School of Business.

Padmashree Gehl Sampath works in the team at the United Nations Conference on Trade and Development (UNCTAD) that produces their flagship publication, the *Trade and Development Report*. Previously she led the Technology and Innovation Report Series of UNCTAD for several years. She is Adjunct Professor at the Faculty of Social Sciences, University of Aalborg, and a professorial fellow at the United Nations University-MERIT, where previously she worked as a researcher from 2002 to 2007. She was a lecturer on tenure for international development and innovation at the Open University, United Kingdom, from 2007 to 2009. She has published five books as well as several journal articles and chapters in books. She is on several boards, including the reviewing board of the Swiss Research Council. She received awards from the Rockefeller Foundation in 2009 and the Rotary International in India in 2010.

Katy M. Graef obtained her Bachelor's degree in microbiology from the University of Washington. She completed her PhD in virology at the University of Oxford, through the NIH Oxford-Cambridge Scholars Program. She became a postdoctoral research fellow at the Rocky Mountain Laboratories in Montana. She taught an undergraduate microbiology course and mentored numerous laboratory students during her undergraduate and graduate studies.

Isabelle Huys is a pharmacist and doctor in pharmaceutical sciences with further specialization in intellectual property rights (IPR) and regulatory sciences. She is a full-time professor at the Faculty of Pharmaceutical Sciences of KU Leuven, Belgium. Her research and teaching focus on IPR and legal and regulatory strategies in the drug life cycle, including biobanking, clinical research pathways, and market access, with the aim to promote access to safe, effective, and affordable therapies, including personalized treatments.

Susan Isiko Štrba is a visiting senior research fellow at the University of the Witwatersrand School of Law, where she lectures on intellectual property, cosupervises PhD students, and conducts research on topics related to intellectual property, trade, and development. She is a tutor at the WIPO Academy. She has been a visiting lecturer at the Graduate Institute of International and Development Studies in Geneva, and the Boston University International Campus in Geneva. She has extensive policy, legislative, and technical advising experience for the world's leading international organizations, including WHO, ILO, UNCTAD, WIPO, and the EU. She has been an advisor to the African Union, COMESA, a number of African governments, and various NGOs. Before joining the international arena, she was a practicing lawyer with firms in Nairobi, Kenya and Kampala, Uganda. She is the author of *International Copyright Law and Access to Education in Developing Countries: Exploring Multilateral Legal and QuasiLegal Solutions* and has published numerous journal articles in the field of IP and development. She is a member of the International Association for the Advancement of Teaching and Research in Intellectual Property and a member of the Executive Council of the Society of International Economic Law.

Ania Jedrusik is currently Intellectual Property Policy Manager at the European Federation of Pharmaceutical Industries and Associations. At the time of contribution to this book, she worked as an independent consultant with the Global Challenges Division of the World Intellectual Property Organization.

Anatole Krattiger is a Founding Partner of Prisma Innovations LLC, Geneva, Switzerland and an adjunct professor at Cornell University. He was Director of the Global Challenges Division at the World Intellectual Property Organization (WIPO), where he worked at the intersection of intellectual property policy and management, leading a multidisciplinary team that developed. He also managed two multi-stakeholder platforms in global health (WIPO Re:Search) and on green technologies (WIPO GREEN), both leveraging intellectual property for technology transfer and international development. Before joining WIPO in 2010, he served as Executive to the Humanitarian Board for Golden Rice, published over 130 monographs and chapters, edited several books, and was editor-in-chief of the *IP Handbook of Best Practices* (www.ipHandbook.org). He started his career as a farmer and agronomist in Switzerland and earned a Master's degree in genetics and a PhD in biotechnology, both from the University of Cambridge. He worked at one of the CGIAR centers, CIMMYT, in Mexico on food security, and worked with a colleague on the creation of ISAAA in 1991 (which he led as Executive Director until 2000), a nonprofit international broker of ag-biotech applications for developing countries with programs in a dozen countries in Africa, Asia, and the Americas.

Melissa Levine is the lead copyright officer and director of the University of Michigan Library Copyright Office. Her research centers on culture, law, and policy in cultural institutions, higher education, scholarly communication, and publishing. She provides support to the HathiTrust Digital Library on copyright and related matters. She has worked at the Smithsonian Institution, the Library of Congress, and the World Bank Art

Program. She is an adjunct professor at the University of Michigan School of Information and the Johns Hopkins University Master of Arts in Museum Studies program. She earned her JD from the University of Miami School of Law and her BA in art history from Emory University.

Delphine Marie-Vivien is Researcher in Law at the Centre de Coopération Internationale en Recherche Agronomique pour le Développement (CIRAD). Since 2012 she has been based in Vietnam. From 2005 to 2008 she was a visiting researcher at the National Law School, Bangalore. She has written extensively on comparative aspects of geographical indications (GIs) between EU and Asian countries, the issue of the public–private governance of GIs, the link to the origin for handicraft goods, the certification mechanism, and the use of GIs to protect biodiversity. Her current research focuses on comparing GIs with other food standards and safety regulations. Her recent publications include *The Protection of Geographical Indications in India: A New Perspective on the French and European Experience* (2015).

David J. Maurrasse is the founder and president of Marga Incorporated, a consulting firm founded in 2000 providing strategic advice and research to philanthropic initiatives and community partnerships. Since 2000, he has been affiliated with Columbia University, where he currently serves as an adjunct associate professor and adjunct research scholar. He was an assistant professor at Yale University and a senior program advisor at the Rockefeller Foundation. He has published numerous books, including *Strategic Public Private Partnerships: Innovation and Development* (2013); *Listening to Harlem* (2006); *A Future for Everyone: Innovative Social Responsibility and Community Partnerships* (2004); *Beyond the Campus: How Colleges and Universities Form Partnerships with Their Communities* (2001); and *Philanthropy and Society* (2018).

Ayşem Mert is an associate senior lecturer at the Department of Political Science, Stockholm University, Adjunct Faculty at the VU University Amsterdam, and a research fellow at the Earth System Governance Research Programme. Her research focuses on discourses of democracy and environment at transnational and global levels, political storytelling, and public–private cooperation/partnerships, using mixed and/or interpretive methods (particularly poststructuralist discourse theory and ecocriticism). She is the author of *Environmental Governance through Partnerships: A Discourse Theoretical Study* and coeditor of *Public–Private Partnerships for Sustainable Development: Emergence, Influence and Legitimacy*, and has published articles in *Environmental Values*, *Journal of Environmental Policy and Planning*, and *Global Policy*.

Chidi Oguamanam is a professor of law at University of Ottawa, Canada, a cofounder of the Open African Innovation Research (Open AIR) and the initiator of the ABS Canada project. His research engages the dynamics of knowledge transformations and intersections with focus on traditional knowledge, Western science, the intellectual property system, and the innovation landscape within the framework of global knowledge governance and development. He is affiliated with the Centre for Law, Technology and Society, the Centre for Environmental Law and Global Sustainability, and the Centre for Health Law, Policy and Ethics at the University of Ottawa. Widely published in law and interdisciplinary platforms, he is the author of *International Law Indigenous Knowledge: Intellectual Property, Plant Biodiversity and Traditional Medicine* (2010) and *Intellectual Property in Global Governance* (2012). He is a coeditor of *Innovation and Intellectual*

Property: Collaborative Dynamics in Africa (2013), and *Knowledge and Innovation in Africa: Scenario for the Future* (2014). He is a senior fellow at the Centre for International Governance Innovation (CIGI), Waterloo, and the Centre for International Sustainable Development Law (CISDL) at McGill University, Montreal.

Philipp Pattberg is Professor of Transnational Environmental Governance and Policy and Head of the Department of Environmental Policy Analysis, Institute for Environmental Studies (IVM), VU Amsterdam. He specializes in the study of global environmental politics, with a focus on private transnational governance, multi-stakeholder partnerships, network theory, and institutional analysis. His work has been published in *Annual Review of Environment and Resources, European Journal of International Relations, Global Environmental Politics, Governance,* and *Science*. He is coeditor of the *Encyclopedia of Global Environmental Governance and Politics* (2015).

Pedro Roffe is Senior Fellow at the International Centre for Trade and Sustainable Development. Mr. Roffe joined ICTSD with thirty years of experience with the United Nations Conference on Trade and Development (UNCTAD) where his work focused on international aspects of transfer of technology, intellectual property, and foreign direct investment. Most recently, his published contributions include: *The ACTA and the Plurilateral Enforcement Agenda: Genesis and Aftermath; Protecting Traditional Knowledge: The WIPO Intergovernmental Committee on Intellectual Property and Genetic Resources, Traditional Knowledge and Folklore*; and *Current Alliances in International Intellectual Property Lawmaking: The Emergence and Impact of Mega-Regionals*. Mr. Roffe graduated from the Faculty of Law of the Universidad de Chile with postgraduate studies at New York University, Europa Institute (University of Amsterdam), and the Graduate Institute of International Studies (Geneva).

Joshua D. Sarnoff is a professor of law at DePaul University College of Law, where he teaches patent law, advanced patent law, administrative law, law and climate change, and other courses. His scholarship focuses on the history and theory of patent law, environmental law, and innovation policy. From 2014 to 2015, he was a Thomas A. Edison Distinguished Scholar at the United States Patent and Trademark Office. He is a registered patent attorney. He is the editor of and a contributing author to the *Research Handbook on Intellectual Property and Climate Change* (2016).

Amy Starr obtained her Bachelor's degree in public health and international studies from the University of Washington. She completed her Master of Public Health and Graduate Certificate in Health Informatics from the University of Michigan. Her graduate studies focused on health behavior, health education, and health communications. She has been an associate at a digital health company reviewing mobile health applications and devices through behavioral science and usability lenses.

Hilde Stevens holds the Fund Baillet Latour supported Chair in Translational Medicines at the Institute for Interdisciplinary Innovation in healthcare (I^3h) and is Associate Professor at the Université libre de Bruxelles (ULB). Her research includes collaborative innovation models, intellectual property (IP), and mechanisms governing access to medicines for poverty-related and neglected (tropical) diseases. She focuses on the governance and performance of public–private partnerships (PPPs) and their added value in the acceleration of innovative therapy development. She is Educational Officer in

EUPATI BE, the Belgian Patient Platform, supported by EUPATI (European Patients' Academy on Therapeutic Innovation). She holds a Master's degree in biomedical science from Ghent University, Belgium, a Master's degree in general management from Vlerick Business School, Belgium, a Master's degree in intellectual property law from HUB-KUBrussel, Belgium, and a PhD in biomedical sciences from the University of Leuven, Belgium. She worked as a science consultant and was a patent engineer for several years.

Peter K. Yu is Professor of Law, Professor of Communication, and Director of the Center for Law and Intellectual Property at Texas A&M University. Before joining Texas A&M University, he held the Kern Family Chair in Intellectual Property Law and was the founding director of the Intellectual Property Law Center at Drake University Law School. He served as Wenlan Scholar Chair Professor at Zhongnan University of Economics and Law in Wuhan, China, and as a visiting professor of law at Hanken School of Economics, the University of Haifa, the University of Helsinki, the University of Hong Kong, and the University of Strasbourg.

Foreword

The book I am pleased to introduce is the first in-depth consideration of the connections between intellectual property (IP) and public–private partnerships (PPPs), which have become an important feature of the global development landscape. The Sustainable Development Goals (SDGs) affirm the unique role of partnerships in the implementation of the 2030 Agenda for Sustainable Development adopted by members of the United Nations in September 2015. In particular, SDG 17 addresses partnerships to achieve the aims of the other SDGs, under the assumption that PPPs have great potential as a means of implementation to contribute to many areas of sustainable development. Nonetheless, despite their growing importance in global governance for sustainable development, PPPs remain under-examined, under-evaluated, and under-researched.

The United Nations' experience with partnerships was acknowledged and endorsed by the Millennium Development Goals (MDGs), in effect from 2000 to 2015, and gained prominence as well from work undertaken in connection with the 2002 World Summit on Sustainable Development. Since then, the role of the private sector in development-oriented activities has expanded enormously. But it is only more recently that IP issues have taken prominence in the PPP discourse. In this context, this book is a pioneering attempt to have a closer look at PPPs and IP operating in different development domains, including public health, education, information and communication technologies (ICTs), agriculture, and climate change.

The book's primary goal is to contribute toward a better understanding of the diversity of partnerships operating at the juncture of IP and sustainable development, and to build a larger picture of their knowledge governance activities through case studies and analysis. In this regard, it examines innovation activities across a variety of development fields, assesses the current landscape of illustrative PPPs, and suggests possible directions for future policy and research. As explored by different experts in this book, various benefits and costs of partnership-driven knowledge governance strategies can already be perceived. The book's final section contains perspectives on institutional design and global knowledge governance. Situated within a larger knowledge governance framework, its concluding chapter synthesizes findings regarding whether and how PPPs encourage innovation, build innovation capacity, engage in technology sharing, or otherwise ensure wide dissemination and diffusion of innovation results across borders toward the advancement of the SDGs.

Taken together, the contributions to this book discern many significant practical, policy, and conceptual dimensions of the relationship between IP, PPPs, and the SDGs. It is deliberately designed to consider and better understand different perspectives, whether generally supportive or critical, of the nexus between these areas. With this view in mind it brings together authors from different backgrounds, representing a mixture of views on the issues at hand.

The contents of this book build on the initiative taken by the International Centre for Trade and Sustainable Development (ICTSD), in collaboration with Seattle University School of Law, to convene in 2013 and 2016 two dialogues with experts and practitioners to explore emerging issues at the interface of PPPs, knowledge governance, and sustainable development. The initiative is also in line with ongoing work by ICTSD to explore the contributions that both trade and trade policy could make to key objectives of the 2030 Agenda for Sustainable Development.

The collaboration between ICTSD, Seattle University School of Law, and the authors in this volume builds on our long-standing efforts to help achieve progress in various international processes and frameworks at the intersection of trade, IP, and sustainable development. ICTSD has been actively engaged in these areas since its establishment more than twenty years ago. We continue to pursue concrete responses to the challenges and opportunities posed by rapidly advancing technologies and emerging global policy frameworks, through multi-stakeholder dialogues and targeted policy-oriented research.

The backdrop to ICTSD's work in this area is the conviction that, in a knowledge-driven global economy, a better understanding of IP-related issues is the key to guaranteeing informed policymaking in virtually all areas of development. This is particularly important in an area as underresearched as PPPs. The editorial focus of the book has been on ensuring that international processes take into account a diversity of perspectives and strive toward designing appropriate policies and norms that are supportive of sustainable development objectives and international commitments.

We hope that you find this publication to be a useful contribution – in the well-established tradition of ICTSD – to building bridges between different stakeholders and to advancing mutually acceptable solutions to complex issues.

Ricardo Meléndez-Ortiz
Chief Executive Officer, International Centre for Trade and Sustainable Development (ICTSD)

Acknowledgments

This project would not have been possible without crucial support and input. Two events stand out. In July 2013, the International Centre for Trade and Sustainable Development (ICTSD), together with Seattle University School of Law, cosponsored a Dialogue on Public–Private Partnerships in Intellectual Property Governance, where early discussions of this topic took place among various representatives of public–private partnerships (PPPs), foundations, United Nations agencies, and delegates. In a second workshop held in July 2016, Public–Private Partnerships, Global Intellectual Property Governance, and Sustainable Development, many of the book's contributors discussed the specific impacts PPPs could have on the promotion of the United Nations Sustainable Development Goals (SDGs). These two dialogues not only shaped the major themes and particular case studies contained in this book but also advanced the sharing of knowledge about this emerging yet underanalyzed area more generally. Both events were undertaken jointly with ICTSD's Programme on Innovation, Technology and Intellectual Property and supported capably by numerous ICTSD staff members. In addition, Fabrice Lehmann, Emily Bloom, Jimena Sotelo, and Colette Holden were instrumental in making sure that all the important and minute details of book production were completed.

At Seattle University School of Law, we were fortunate to be able to rely on the expert administrative support of Nora Santos, as well as research assistance and cite-checking by law students Mio Asami, Natasha Khanna, Jeanna McClellan, and Lauren Sewell. Reference librarians Kerry Fitz-Gerald and LeighAnne Thompson provided much-needed assistance when needed. Dean Annette Clark and other senior administrative and faculty colleagues provided an environment strongly conducive to sustained research and scholarship.

The book's contents are the culmination of many other dialogues with supporters too numerous to thank individually but whose genuine interest and generous input have been critical over the last several years. In Seattle, which has become a hub for nonprofit involvement in biomedical research and development, conversations between Margaret Chon and Curt Malloy (then at Infectious Disease Research Institute) about the ways in which intellectual property law can impact global health via PPPs sparked an initial interest in exploring this complex area further. A subsequent residence by Chon as a senior fellow at the Jean Monnet Center for International and Regional Economic Law and Justice at New York University in 2011–2012 provided timely incubation for the concepts and theories underlying the nexus of PPPs, knowledge governance, and sustainable development. During that period, many kind colleagues at NYU and elsewhere shared their thoughts about the project. Since then, various international conferences supplied additional opportunities for exploring this intersection, including those sponsored by the Congress of the Association for the Teaching and Research of Intellectual Property, the International Intellectual Property Roundtable, and the Global Congress on Intellectual Property and the Public Interest. At one of these Global Congresses, Chon and Ahmed Abdel-Latif (then at ICTSD) concurred that this topic of growing importance merited further inquiry and ultimately pursued this book project together with Pedro Roffe, who has a long and distinguished track record of work and advocacy at the intersection of intellectual property, trade, and development. The book project benefited from the encouragement and support of ICTSD's senior management team, in particular, Chief Executive Ricardo Meléndez-Ortiz as well as Managing Directors Andrew Crosby and Deborah Vorhies. Our editor at Cambridge University Press, Matt Gallaway, was immediately supportive as well.

It has been an honor and pleasure for the three editors (Chon, Roffe, and Abdel-Latif) to work with the various contributors to this book. Together, these authors have created a substantial collective body of work that advances knowledge in an area that has not been well understood and that bears far greater exploration than has been undertaken to date. Their diligence, expertise, and intellectual and personal generosity – not to mention patience – has resulted in the substantive chapters contained here, which are the primary rewards for their editors (and hopefully also for their readers). Many thanks are due to all who supported this project, but mostly to these expert contributors.

Glossary

2030 Agenda	United Nations 2030 Agenda for Sustainable Development
AAAA	Addis Ababa Action Agenda
AAP	American Association of Publishers
ABC	[WIPO] Accessible Books Consortium
Agenda 21	a nonbinding, voluntarily implemented action plan for sustainable development, adopted by more than 178 governments at the United Nations Conference on Environment and Development held in Rio de Janeiro in 1992
AIPPI	International Association for the Protection of Intellectual Property
ALAI	Association Littéraire et Artistique Internationale
AMR	antimicrobial resistance
ANDI	African Network for Drugs and Diagnostic Innovation
AO	appellation of origin
APCs	advance purchase commitments
API	Angola Partnership Initiative
ARDI	Access to Research for Development and Innovation
BIO	Biotechnology Innovation Organization
BVGH	BIO Ventures for Global Health
CARB-X	Combating Antibiotic Resistant Bacteria Biopharmaceutical Accelerator
CASP	Core Agriculture Support Program
CDA	confidential disclosure agreement
CERC	US–China Clean Energy Research Center
CEWG	[WHO] Consultative Expert Working Group on Research and Development: Financing and Coordination
CGIAR	Consultative Group of International Agricultural Research Centers
CIC	Committee on Institutional Cooperation
CIPIH	[WHO] Commission on Intellectual Property Rights, Innovation and Public Health
COP	[UNFCCC] Conference of the Parties
CPC	Centre Pasteur du Cameroun
CRADA	cooperative R&D agreement
CRMS	Copyright Review Management System
CSR	corporate social responsibility
CTCN	[UNFCCC] Climate Technology Centre and Network

CTR	clinical trials regulation
DfID	Department for International Development
DNDi	Drugs for Neglected Diseases Initiative
DTA	data transfer agreement
EML	[WHO] Essential Medicines List
EST	environmentally sound technology
EU	European Union
FAO	Food and Agriculture Organization
FDI	foreign direct investment
FIND	Foundation for Innovative New Diagnostics
FIT	funds-in-trust
FTA	fair trade agreement
GAVI	GAVI Alliance (previously Global Alliance for Vaccines and Immunisations)
GCF	Green Climate Fund
GEF	Global Environment Facility
GFATM	Global Fund to Fight AIDS, Tuberculosis and Malaria
GHIT	Global Health Innovative Technology Fund
GIs	geographical indications
GPS	global positioning satellite
GSK	GlaxoSmithKline
GSPD	Global Sustainability Partnerships Database
GSPOA	[WHO] Global Strategy and Plan of Action on Public Health, Innovation and Intellectual Property
HCV	hepatitis C virus
HDL	HathiTrust Digital Library
HHS	[US] Department of Health and Human Services
HINARI	Health InterNetwork Access to Research Information
HIV	human immunodeficiency virus
IAVI	International AIDS Vaccines Initiative
ICCPR	International Covenant on Civil and Political Rights
ICESCR	International Covenant on Economic, Social and Cultural Rights
ICI	International Cooperative Initiative
ILO	International Labour Organization
IMI	Innovative Medicines Initiative
INAO	Institut National de l'Origine et de la Qualité (previously Institut National des Appellations d'Origine)
INBio	Instituto Nacional de Biodiversidad
INGO	intergovernmental organization
IP	intellectual property
IPCC	Intergovernmental Panel on Climate Change
IPOS	Intellectual Property Office of Singapore
IPR	intellectual property right
JTI	joint technology initiative
KPI	key performance indicator
L&E	limitations and exception to copyright
LAMP	loop-mediated isothermal amplification

LDCs	least developed countries
LMIC	low- and middle-income country
Marrakesh Treaty	Marrakesh Treaty to Facilitate Access to Published Works for Persons Who Are Blind, Visually Impaired or Otherwise Print Disabled (also known as the VIP Treaty)
MDG	Millennium Development Goal
MEA	multilateral environmental agreement
MI	mission innovation
MMV	Medicines for Malaria Venture
MOU	memorandum of understanding
MPP	Medicines Patent Pool
MSF	Médecins Sans Frontières (also known as Doctors without Borders)
MTA	material transfer agreement
NCD	noncommunicable disease
NCE	new chemical entity
NGO	nongovernmental organization
NIH	National Institutes of Health
NII	National Institute of Immunology
NINA	noninstrumented nucleic acid amplification
NMIMR	Noguchi Memorial Institute for Medical Research
NPO	nonprofit organization
NREL	National Renewable Energy Laboratory
NTDs	neglected tropical diseases
Open AIR	Open African Innovation Research
OSF	Open Society Foundations
P3s4HR	PPPs for Human Rights
PACE	United States–India Partnership to Advance Clean Energy
PDO	protected denomination of origin
PDP	product development partnership
PGI	protected geographical indication
POC	proof of concept
POINT	Pool for Open Innovation against Neglected Tropical Diseases
PPP	public–private partnership
PRND	poverty-related neglected disease
R&D	research and development
RMI	rights management information
ROI	return on investment
SALB	South African Library for the Blind
SARS	severe acute respiratory syndrome
SCCR	[WIPO] Standing Committee on Copyright and Related Rights
SDG	Sustainable Development Goal
SME	small- and medium-sized enterprise
STEM	science, technology, engineering, and mathematics
STM	scientific, technical, and medical
TB	tuberculosis
TB Alliance	Global Alliance for TB Drug Development
TEC	[UNFCCC] Technology Executive Committee

TFM	technology facilitation mechanism
TIGAR	Trusted Intermediary Global Accessible Resources
TM	Technology Mechanism
TMP	technology management plan
TNC	transnational corporation
TPM	technological protection measure
TPP	Trans-Pacific Partnership
TRIPS	Agreement on Trade-Related Aspects of Intellectual Property (Annex 1C of the Marrakesh Agreement Establishing the World Trade Organization)
UCSD	University of California, San Diego
UDHR	Universal Declaration of Human Rights
UML	University of Michigan Library
UN	United Nations
UNCED	United Nations Conference on Environment and Development (also known as the Earth Summit or the Rio Summit)
UNCSD	United Nations Commission on Sustainable Development
UNDP	United Nations Development Programme
UNEP	United Nations Environment Programme
UNFCCC	United Nations Framework Convention on Climate Change
UNOP	United Nations Office for Partnerships
USAID	United States Agency for International Development
USPTO	United States Patent and Trademark Office
VIPs	people who are blind, visually impaired, or otherwise print-disabled
WBU	World Blind Union
WCT	WIPO Copyright Treaty
WEMA	Water Efficient Maize for Africa
WHA	World Health Assembly
WHO	World Health Organization
WIPO	World Intellectual Property Organization
WSSD	World Summit on Sustainable Development
WTO	World Trade Organization

Introduction

1 Charting the Triple Interface of Public–Private Partnerships, Global Knowledge Governance, and Sustainable Development Goals

Margaret Chon, Pedro Roffe, and Ahmed Abdel-Latif*

In less than two decades, public–private partnerships (PPPs) have become an essential feature of the global development landscape and a fixation in development discourse and practice. The Sustainable Development Goals (SDGs) affirm their centrality in the implementation of the UN's 2030 Sustainable Development Agenda (2030 Agenda).[1] However, it is only more recently that PPPs have emerged in intellectual property (IP) domains, primarily in relation to public health.

In this context, this book is the first attempt to have a closer look at PPPs and IP within a more capacious knowledge governance framework, not only in relation to public health but also in connection to other fields such as education, information and communications technologies (ICTs), libraries, agriculture, and climate change. Its chapters explore the relationship among three broad subjects: IP, PPPs, and the 2030 Agenda's SDGs. Each area by itself would be a major undertaking. Analyzing all three simultaneously might be considered a long and possibly unmanageable reach. Yet it is the premise of this book that understanding the growing impacts at the interface of these three heretofore distinct areas is critically important. As argued recently:

> [s]imilar to human rights, SDGs should be taken into account in shaping intellectual property rights, in the process of interpretation and compliance. SDGs today provide the most important contemporary standards of justice and equity in international economic law. ... Many of their goals cannot be achieved without enhancing the effort, and new tools need to be developed, such as ... framework rules for the operation of public–private partnerships (PPPs).[2]

To make the case for a thoughtful (and overdue) treatment of this triple interface, this chapter first canvasses relevant aspects of each of these three topics – IP, PPPs, and the SDGs – and the significance of their growing connections. It then examines more closely each of the "Ps" in PPPs, flagging the many unresolved issues and questions about these types of joint governance arrangements or collaborative partnerships, at the practical,

* This chapter is coauthored by Abdel-Latif in a personal capacity. The views expressed are those of the author and do not necessarily reflect the views of any institution with which he is affiliated.

1 G.A. Res. 70/1, Transforming Our World: The 2030 Agenda for Sustainable Development (October 21, 2015; hereinafter 2030 Agenda) *available at* https://sustainabledevelopment.un.org/post2015/transformingourworld.

2 Thomas Cottier, *Embedding Intellectual Property in International Law, in* CURRENT ALLIANCES IN INTERNATIONAL INTELLECTUAL PROPERTY LAWMAKING: THE EMERGENCE AND IMPACT OF MEGA-REGIONALS 33 (Pedro Roffe and Xavier Seuba eds. 2017).

policy, and conceptual levels. Finally, it situates each of the other chapters, providing brief synopses and locating their diverse perspectives within an emerging conceptual map of the triple interface.

I Unwinding the Triple Interface

IP systems and legal regimes are experiencing enormous challenges and change in a period that some are starting to call the fourth Industrial Revolution.[3] Many converging factors are forming this proverbial perfect storm. These include the acceleration of technological development overall, the appearance of "disruptive" business models,[4] the manifestation of wholly new technological realms such as artificial intelligence, block chain technology, the so-called Internet of things, nanotechnology, robotics, and analytics driven by "big data," as well as digitally driven developments in biology and the life sciences. This current technological lunge is taking place parallel with the rapid and controversial expansion of core functions of IP, from incentive to commodity to asset,[5] combined with numerous challenges to the multilateral IP legal regime by a burgeoning number of bilateral, mega-regional, and plurilateral treaties.[6]

In addition, IP must cope with the rapid emergence of hybrid forms of governance, which involve not only agreements and actions coordinated among states but also among multi-stakeholder partnerships within transnational legal frameworks. These partnerships among intergovernmental organizations and/or their member states with the private sector – whether nonprofit or for-profit – are now rampant and embedded within the global IP landscape. The historical and too often still prevailing attitude of IP's "splendid isolation"[7] seems increasingly obsolete in this era characterized by extreme technological development, rapid globalization, hybrid governance arrangements, and cross-cutting regime linkages.

[3] *See generally* Klaus Schwab, The Fourth Industrial Revolution (2016), *available at* www.weforum.org/about/the-fourth-industrial-revolution-by-klaus-schwab.

[4] The term "disruptive innovation" has evolved in different directions. *See, e.g.*, Clayton M. Christensen & Derek van Bever, *The Capitalist's Dilemma*, 92 Harv. Bus. Rev. 61, 62 (Jun. 2014) ("The seminal concepts of *disruptive* and *sustaining* innovations were developed . . . studying competition among companies. They relate to the process by which innovations become dominant in established markets and new entrants challenge incumbents. The focus of this article, however, is the *outcome* of innovations – their impact on growth.").

[5] Rochelle Cooper Dreyfuss & Susy Frankel, *From Incentive to Commodity to Asset: How International Law is Reconceptualizing Intellectual Property*, 36 Mich. J. Int'l L. 557, 560 (2015); *see also* Cottier, *supra* note 2, at 22 ("Despite legal justification by the needs of innovation and consumer welfare, intellectual property protection is in reality as much motivated by market segmentation and the promotion and protection of investment. These motives have increasingly influenced the application and interpretation of intellectual property rights.").

[6] *See generally*, Pedro Roffe & Xavier Seuba eds., *Current Alliances in International Intellectual Property Lawmaking: The Emergence and Impact of Mega-Regionals* 2017 (Int'l Ctr. for Trade & Sustainable Dev. (ICTSD) & Ctr. for Int'l Intell. Prop. Studies (CEIPI), Ser. No. 4).

[7] Cottier, *supra* note 2, at 23 ("IPRs can no longer be dealt with in splendid isolation, but need to be construed and applied in the general context of law. . . . It is most difficult under the auspices of public international law – thus on the level where harnessing globalisation and effective checks and balances are most needed. The lack of a constitutional framework and the fragmentation of international law are major impediments in addressing balancing across different agreements."); *cf.* Graeme B. Dinwoodie & Rochelle C. Dreyfuss, A Neofederalist Vision of TRIPS: The Resilience of the International Intellectual Property Regime (2012).

More generally, the growing involvement of multiple stakeholders across public and private sectors in the form of PPPs and other multi-stakeholder partnerships illustrates the rise of more complex global governance dynamics[8] where global governance is:

> First, ... deliberately associated with globalization. ... Second, ... an ongoing conceptual and descriptive enterprise ... Third, ... enunciated against the backdrop of a perceived thinning of state sovereignty and *the emergence of multivalent non-state or sub-state entities and new networks of actors on the global stage that, together, have assumed the nature of disaggregated sovereignty*. ... Fourth, unfolds more in the sense of a concerted horizontal interaction of actors at the global level without the necessity of an overarching hierarchical authority.[9]

The discernible pivot toward PPPs in global governance generally can be traced to several factors. At a time when traditional sources of public funding are under strain, PPPs offer possible synergies among partners – leveraging their talents, technologies, resources, expertise, and convening power. These partnerships also respond to the current realities of the global development system, which has moved to frameworks "beyond aid" and is experiencing challenges in development funding, including overseas development assistance.[10] In short, PPPs can provide significant means of implementation for addressing development challenges not adequately covered by existing institutional arrangements, which may be constrained by finances, mission, or reach.

The partners within these global governance arrangements in turn impact global *knowledge governance*, whether by encouraging innovation, building innovation capacity,

[8] Gráinne de Búrca, *New Governance and Experimentalism: An Introduction*, 210 Wisc. L. Rev. 232 (2011); Benedict Kingsbury, Nico Krisch, & Richard B. Stewart, *The Emergence of Global Administrative Law*, 68 L. Contemp. Prob. 15, 20 (2005). These transnational legal orders or various forms of legal pluralism are characterized by "informal arrangements developed by ad hoc coalitions of powerful states and transnational governance networks [that] give rise to a new informality in governance." A. Claire Cutler, *Legal Pluralism as the "Common Sense" of Transnational Capitalism*, 3 *Oñati Socio-legal Series* 719, 725 (2013), *available at* http://ssrn.com/abstract=2327501.

[9] Chidi Oguamanam, Intellectual Property in Global Governance: A Development Question 27–28 (2012) (emphasis added) ("Fifth, of necessity and logic, the tensions ... implicated in globalization also unravel in global governance. Finally, like globalization, global governance cannot be wished away.") More recently, global governance has been summarized as "increasingly characterized by flexible structures, greater tolerance for informality, and, most strikingly, an openness to public–private partnerships and an increasingly active role for a wide range of nonstate actors. While the embrace of nonstate actors is not uniform – the governance of global trade differs markedly on this score from the governance of the global environment, for instance – many international regimes now feature substantial participation by private actors. In short, traditional multilateralism remains alive and well[, but] multilateral governance is increasingly supplemented, and in some cases even supplanted, by *multi-stakeholder* governance." Kal Raustiala, *Public Power and Private Stakeholders* (original emphasis), UCLA School of Law, Public Law Research Paper No. 17–26 (Aug. 21, 2017), *available at* https://ssrn.com/abstract=3023598.

[10] Jomo Kwame Sundaram, Anis Chowdhury, Krishnan Sharma, & Daniel Platz, *Public–Private Partnerships and the 2030 Agenda for Sustainable Development: Fit for Purpose?* 1 (UN Dept. of Econ. & Soc. Affairs, DESA Working Paper No. 148, ST/ESA/2016/DWP/148, February 2016) ("The Addis Ababa Action Agenda (AAAA) of the recently concluded Third International Conference on Financing for Development (Addis Ababa, 13–16 July 2015) recognizes that 'both public and private investment have key roles to play in infrastructure financing, including through (...) public private partnerships' ... However, the AAAA also highlights the need to 'build capacity to enter into PPPs, including as regards planning, contract negotiation, management, accounting and budgeting for contingent liabilities.' It further stresses the need to 'share risks and reward fairly, include clear accountability mechanisms and meet social and environmental standards'").

engaging in technology transfer, or otherwise ensuring dissemination and diffusion of the results of innovation across borders. Taken together, these important activities are referred to here as *knowledge governance* or *innovation activities*. PPPs often contend with the IP-intensive nature of these innovation activities.

Within knowledge economies, especially within IP-intensive industries, high uncertainty, risk, and cost are often associated with developing complex innovations, whether for industrialized or developing country sectors – thus PPPs may be a response to particular market failures, for example, in the area of poverty-related neglected diseases (PRNDs).[11] Moreover, the public sector may lack sufficient resources to provide full support for innovation activities – thus PPPs may also address insufficient government capacity and/or support for the production and dissemination of public goods, including many key innovation activities related to sustainable development.[12] Additionally, knowledge governance includes the growing participation of nonstate actors such as nongovernmental organizations (NGOs) or nonprofit organizations (NPOs), which may be primarily mission-driven rather than profit-driven. These newer stakeholders encourage innovation activities and knowledge governance goals traditionally associated with the public sector and the public interest. And the increasingly complex nature of knowledge production and sharing means that diverse partners in global collaborative networks can be essential to productive cross-border innovation activities.

But as part of a global innovation picture, IP-related partnerships are no longer narrowly confined to the research and development (R&D) of new technologies, nor to the development of national or local innovation capacities, nor even to technology transfer across borders. These partnerships also directly and indirectly impact myriad areas involved in the production and delivery of many global public goods[13] crucial for human flourishing and global sustainable development,[14] such as agriculture and food security, climate change adaptation and mitigation, knowledge provision through ICTs, and public health through the widespread dissemination of pharmaceuticals and vaccines. Thus, PPPs involved in innovation activities may address – while perhaps also simultaneously contributing to – the immense regulatory coordination issues inherent in the production and distribution of global public goods.[15]

The rise of cross-sector or multi-stakeholder partnerships such as PPPs is especially notable in the realm of global health, but these newer hybrid institutions have also

[11] Poverty-related neglected diseases are sometimes alternatively referred to as neglected diseases or neglected tropical diseases.

[12] For a succinct summary of the distinction in economic literature between public goods and private goods, see Brett M. Frischmann, INFRASTRUCTURE: THE SOCIAL VALUE OF SHARED RESOURCES 24–49 (2012).

[13] *See generally* GLOBAL PUBLIC GOODS: INTERNATIONAL COOPERATION IN THE 21ST CENTURY (Inge Kaul et al. eds., 1999); PROVIDING GLOBAL PUBLIC GOODS: MANAGING GLOBALIZATION (Inge Kaul et al. eds. 2003).

[14] The Brundtland Report defined sustainable development as "development that meets the needs of the present without compromising future generations to meet their own needs." UN WORLD COMMISSION ON ENVIRONMENT AND DEVELOPMENT, OUR COMMON FUTURE (1987). In doing so, it emphasized a "much greater recognition of the interdependence of environmental, social and economic systems." Norichika Kanie, Steven Bernstein, Frank Biermann, & Peter M. Haas, *Introduction: Global Governance Through Goal-Setting, in* GOVERNING THROUGH GOALS: SUSTAINABLE DEVELOPMENT GOALS AS GOVERNANCE INNOVATION 1, 9 (Norichika Kanie & Frank Biermann eds., 2017).

[15] Oguamanam, *supra* note 9, at 133–35 (discussing interventions of PPPs in the context of agricultural development and food security).

emerged decisively in other areas. Multilateral organizations have been increasingly relying on partnerships to tackle a number of issues and challenges they are facing. In the UN context, the World Health Organization (WHO) has been involved in the establishment of several PPPs to tackle communicable diseases such as malaria and tuberculosis (TB), for instance.[16] The World Intellectual Property Organization (WIPO) is aligning some of its strategic goals and activities within the institutional frameworks of PPPs.[17] And the UN Framework Convention on Climate Change has recognized the role of PPPs for purposes of encouraging technology transfer.[18] Outside of the UN system, other intergovernmental organizations (INGOs) and individual member states have multiple initiatives involving PPPs for development.[19] Additional stakeholders include philanthropic organizations, which also contribute to this trend by encouraging the formation of PPPs for purposes of product development as well as distribution of drugs for PRNDs and vaccines; in some cases, their budgets rival or even exceed those available in the public sector. As this book's chapters document and discuss, PPPs have a number of social purposes, including but not limited to capacity-building, technological learning, and technology sharing – and even the promotion of human rights – within global knowledge governance.[20]

PPPs have become an important feature of global regimes shaping sustainable development goals set forth in the 2030 Agenda and its seventeen accompanying SDGs.[21] As described in some chapters in this book, the role of partnerships had gained tremendous prominence from preparatory work undertaken in connection with the World Summit on Sustainable Development (WSSD), which took place in Johannesburg in 2002. At this conference, two hundred partnerships were launched as a so-called Type II outcome of this multilateral conference – a historic moment that is widely seen as ushering in the current era of development PPPs.[22] Commentators observe that "[j]ust as the [1992 United Nations Conference on Environment and Development, also known as the] Rio Conference was as much about the legitimizing of NGOs in global governance as it was about the environment, Johannesburg was about the legitimacy of the role of business in development."[23] Since then, the role of the private sector (whether for-profit or non-profit) in development-oriented activities has expanded enormously.

[16] See Frederick H. Abbott, Chapter 2, *infra*; Estaban Burrone, Chapter 5, *infra*.

[17] See Anatole Krattiger et al., Chapter 3, *infra*; Katy M. Graef et al., Chapter 4, *infra*; Jens Bammel, Chapter 7, *infra*; Sara Bannerman, Chapter 8, *infra*; Susan Isiko Štrba, Chapter 9, *infra*; and Ahmed Abdel-Latif, Chapter 11, *infra*.

[18] See Joshua D. Sarnoff & Margaret Chon, Chapter 12, *infra*; Ayşem Mert & Philipp Pattberg, Chapter 13, *infra*.

[19] See Hilde Stevens & Isabelle Huys, Chapter 6, *infra*; Melissa Levine, Chapter 10, *infra*; Irene Calboli & Delphine Marie-Vivien, Chapter 14, *infra*; and David J. Maurrasse, Chapter 16, *infra*.

[20] See Padmashree Gehl Sampath, Chapter 15, *infra*; Chidi Oguamanam & Jeremy De Beer, Chapter 17, *infra*; and Peter K. Yu, Chapter 18, *infra*.

[21] 2030 Agenda, *supra* note 1.

[22] Kanie et al., *supra* note 14 at 9; Felix Dodds, David Donoghue, & Jimena Leiva Roesch, NEGOTIATING THE SUSTAINABLE DEVELOPMENT GOALS: A TRANSFORMATIONAL AGENDA FOR AN INSECURE WORLD 142–43 (2017); Benedicte Bull, *Public–Private Partnerships: The United Nations Experience 480*, *in* INTERNATIONAL HANDBOOK ON PUBLIC–PRIVATE PARTNERSHIPS (Graeme A. Hodge, Carsten Greve, & Anthony E. Boardman eds., 2010).

[23] Benedicte Bull & Desmond McNeill, DEVELOPMENT ISSUES IN GLOBAL GOVERNANCE: PUBLIC–PRIVATE PARTNERSHIPS AND MARKET MULTILATERALISM 10 (2007) (quoting Zadek).

The UN also acknowledged and endorsed the importance of partnerships in its Millennium Development Goals (MDGs), in effect from 2000 to 2015.[24] Unlike the predecessor MDGs, which were formed rather quickly within a relatively closed process,[25] the current SDGs are the result of extensive input

> [t]hroughout 2012 and 2013, [in which] the United Nations facilitated what seemed like the first exercise in global participatory democracy, organizing fifty-plus country consultations, multiple global thematic consultations, and a worldwide online citizen survey – all of which were accompanied by numerous parallel NGO, expert, and state initiatives. Likewise, the General Assembly took seriously its deliberative task ...
>
> The open nature of the process also permitted civil society organizations, UN agencies, and private corporations to engage at multiple points and stages in the drafting. A staggering range of diverse interests were promoted and defended by these actors.[26]

The relatively participatory and open nature of this deliberative process has several consequences. One of these is the inclusion of international human rights measures, which is a significant evolution from the previous MDGs; another is the disruption of the MDG's distinction between developed and developing countries.[27] Broader stakeholder involvement also resulted in a proliferation of development metrics.[28] The end result is a surprisingly broad array of goals, targets, and indicators: 17 current goals (as opposed to 10 MDGs), 169 current targets (compared to 18, later expanded to 21, under the MDGs), and 232 current indicators (compared to 48, later expanded to 60, under the MDGs).[29]

Thus, the SDGs encompass a much broader and certainly much more detailed set of activities related to sustainable development, including the production of key global public goods impacted by IP and knowledge governance. They give global governance considerably more content, albeit in the language of goal-setting rather than norm-setting.[30] This decisive turn toward goals, targets, and indicators as benchmarks of progress toward sustainable development in turn raises profound questions of measurement, monitoring, and evaluation – all major topics beyond the scope of this book.[31] Many of the book's chapters do, however, seek to achieve a better understanding of

[24] MDG 8: Develop a Global Partnership for Development, UN Dep't of Econ. and Soc. Affairs, 2017, *available at* www.un.org/millenniumgoals/global.shtml.

[25] Ved P. Nanda, *The Journey from the Millennium Development Goals to the Sustainable Development Goals*, 44 Denv. J. Int'l L. & Pol'y 389, 398 (2016).

[26] Malcolm Langford, *Lost in Transformation? The Politics of the Sustainable Development Goals*, 30 Ethics & Int'l Aff., 167, 170–71 (2016); Kanie, et al., *supra* note 16 at 3, 16–17.

[27] Stephen Browne, Sustainable Development Goals and UN Goal-Setting 138–54 (2017) ("This larger movement away from a uni-directional transfer of development aid (from so-called 'developed' to 'developing' sectors) is also reflected in the emphasis on individual state accountability (of both developed and developing states) for the achievement of the SDGs").

[28] *Id.* at 171.

[29] For MDGs, see *Millennium Indicators*, UN, *available at* https://millenniumindicators.un.org/unsd/mi/pdf/mdglist.pdf. The total number of SDG indicators is 244, but some of those are repeated under several targets. *See SDG Indicators*, UN Dep't of Econ. & Soc. Aff., *available at* https://unstats.un.org/sdgs/indicators/indicators-list/. *See also* UN, Sustainable Development Report 2017, *available at* https://unstats.un.org/sdgs/files/report/2017/TheSustainableDevelopmentGoalsReport2017.pdf.

[30] Kanie et al., *supra* note 16 at 1–2.

[31] Browne, *supra* note 27, at 143–49; *see generally* Poverty and the Millennium Development Goals (Alberto D. Cimadamore, Gabriele Koehler, & Thomas Pogge eds., 2016).

Box 1.1. UN Sustainable Development Goal 17[32]
Strengthen the means of implementation and revitalize the global partnership for sustainable development.

[TARGETS:] Multi-stakeholder partnerships

- 17.16 Enhance the global partnership for sustainable development, complemented by multi-stakeholder partnerships that mobilize and share knowledge, expertise, technology, and financial resources, to support the achievement of the sustainable development goals in all countries, in particular developing countries
- 17.17 Encourage and promote effective public, public–private and civil society partnerships, building on the experience and resourcing strategies of partnerships

effective implementation, by discerning the characteristics of PPPs associated with constructive progress toward the goals.

Of key importance to this book, SDG 17 proposes to "[s]trengthen the means of implementation and revitalize the global partnership for sustainable development." (See Box 1.1 for the key relevant target and accompanying indicators.) This seventeenth goal is viewed as a cross-cutting goal, which encourages partnerships as a primary if not exclusive approach toward implementation of all the other sixteen goals. Several of SDG 17's targets are grouped under the rubric of "Technology," including a target to "[e]nhance North-South, South-South and triangular regional and international cooperation on and *access to science, technology and innovation and enhance knowledge sharing* on mutually agreed terms, including through improved coordination among existing mechanisms, in particular at the United Nations level, and through a global technology facilitation mechanism."[33]

The dynamics underlying the simultaneous emergence of partnerships for sustainable development and for knowledge governance can be attributed in part to the powerful need for linkages across different domains to effectuate development goals, and particularly innovation-related development goals. This is very apparent in the global fight against communicable diseases, which do not recognize borders. Partnerships could be described as "regime-straddling" because they cut across distinct development policy areas with their accompanying and typically siloed legal regimes, as well as across public and private sectors.[34]

Rather than treating each development issue (e.g., global health) as a self-contained problem, PPPs and other forms of multi-stakeholder governance anticipate that more inclusive collaboration, interdisciplinary cooperation, and multifaceted approaches are necessary to tackle complex, cross-border issues. The emphasis in the SDGs on the interdependence and interconnectedness of problems – that is, "how systems are coupled

[32] SDG 17, *supra* note 34.

[33] SDG 17: Revitalize the global partnership for sustainable development (emphasis added), UN, *available at* www.un.org/sustainabledevelopment/globalpartnerships/.

[34] Margaret Chon, *PPPs in Global IP (Public–Private Partnerships in Global Intellectual Property), in* Methods and Perspectives in Intellectual Property 296 (Graeme B. Dinwoodie ed., 2013). *Cf.* Laurence R. Helfer, *Regime Shifting: The TRIPS Agreement and New Dynamics of International Intellectual Property Lawmaking*, 29 Yale J. Int'l L. 1 (2004).

and the need for integrative policies"[35] – is another key difference between the prior MDGs and the current SDGs.[36] PPPs are situated across different disciplines, sectors, and regimes, including IP legal regimes. Regime straddling requires new and possibly out-of-the-box forms of governance disciplines and mechanisms, whether through management choices (in the private sector) or regulatory policies (in the public sector). This is all the more critical because the new benchmarks for progress on the SDGs are accompanied by very few binding commitments, not to mention "specific responsibilities, obligations, or associated compliance mechanisms."[37]

The relationship of PPPs to global governance, whether or not in the context of the SDGs, can be viewed along two or even three different dimensions: partnerships require some type of effective internal governance or management to coordinate the differing approaches of partners internally, and they also require mechanisms to interface with any external stakeholders within their immediate networks. Finally, individual PPPs are stakeholders themselves within decentralized governance models; as such, they necessarily contend with both national and multilateral funding and regulatory institutions. The interactions of the various actors, whether partners or stakeholders, are expected to result in specified outcomes, or goals, in the case of the SDGs.

Especially relevant to knowledge governance activities, the partnerships envisioned through SDG 17 are tied to the promise of greater innovation for sustainable development. SDG 9 directly addresses this linkage ("Build resilient infrastructure, promote inclusive and sustainable industrialization and foster innovation") with its accompanying targets.[38] As noted earlier, the early harbingers of this connection between sustainable development and IP were apparent in the global health policy space, which had been highly polarized because of differential access to treatment for global communicable diseases such as HIV/AIDs. Partners within public health-oriented PPPs are in the position to act instrumentally through their deployment of tangible and intangible proprietary rights for non-commercial ends.[39] These partners (often NGOs or NPOs) sometimes leverage IP for social mission either defensively ("to preclude commercial use of protected materials") or offensively ("to promote non-commercial creative exchange and adaptation"), as Antony Taubman observes, and "this is the essence of IP management in public–private partnerships."[40] A few of the SDGs reflect explicit affiliations

[35] *Id.* at 14.

[36] Kanie et al., *supra* note 16 at 10–11.

[37] Kanie et al., *supra* note 16 at 18; *see also* Oran R. Young, Conceptualization: Goal-Setting as a Strategy for Earth System Governance, *in* GOVERNING THROUGH GOALS: SUSTAINABLE DEVELOPMENT GOALS AS GOVERNANCE INNOVATION 31, 35–37 (Norichika Kanie and Frank Biermann eds., 2017) (describing pitfalls of a goal-setting approach to governance).

[38] SDG 9: Build Resilient Infrastructure, Promote Inclusive and Sustainable Industrialization and Foster Innovation, UN, *available at* https://sustainabledevelopment.un.org/sdg9.

[39] Chon, *supra* note 35, at 284; *see also* Steiner Andreson & Masahiko Iguchi, *Lessons from the Health-Related Millennium Development Goals, in* GOVERNING THROUGH GOALS: SUSTAINABLE DEVELOPMENT GOALS AS GOVERNANCE INNOVATION 165, 175–78 (Norichika Kanie & Frank Biermann eds., 2017) (outlining the achievements and criticisms of the GAVI Alliance).

[40] Antony Taubman, *A Typology of Intellectual Property Management for Public Health Innovation and Access: Design Considerations for Policymakers*, 4 THE OPEN AIDS J. 1, 12 (2010) (also discussing open innovation, open source, commons-based peer production and distributed innovation in drug development).

between IP and sustainable development;[41] many more of the connections between IP and the SDGs, however, are implicit.

While the SDGs have been sparsely analyzed so far, the rise of development partnerships has not gone unnoticed. Various critiques of what has been called "market multilateralism"[42] have articulated concerns about the financing of PPPs – whether the concern is with the defunding of public sector development, the lack of national capacity to effectively oversee transparent and efficient financing of PPPs, or the possibly self-interested priorities of the private sector.[43] Within multilateral institutions tasked with global knowledge governance, these add to long-standing concerns about possible multilateral priority-setting through funding influences by the private sector[44] as well as over-reliance on market mechanisms to optimize social welfare through innovation.[45] Observers of collaborative innovation state that while:

> increasing numbers of 'wicked problems,' which cannot be solved by standard solutions or by spending more money, call[] for innovative solutions. . . . [including] multi-actor collaboration in spurring innovation relating to public policies, organizations[,] and services . . .[,] many things can go wrong in the contingent process of networking, collaboration[,] and innovation and the precarious links between them. As such, some kind of innovation management is required in order to remove barriers, enhance drivers[,] and keep the process of collaborative innovation on track.[46]

Some observers voice skepticism about the ability of the SDGs to overcome deepening structural inequalities both within and across countries.[47] However, the current reality is that the SDGs represent part of a shift in the approach to development and development assistance, to emphasize greater private sector involvement (both nonprofit and

[41] SDG Target 3b, for example, states: "Support the research and development of vaccines and medicines for the communicable and non-communicable diseases that primarily affect developing countries, provide access to affordable essential medicines and vaccines, in accordance with the Doha Declaration on the TRIPS Agreement and Public Health, which affirms the right of developing countries to use to the full the provisions in the Agreement on Trade-Related Aspects of Intellectual Property Rights regarding flexibilities to protect public health, and, in particular, provide access to medicines for all." *See generally* Intellectual Property and International Trade: The TRIPS Agreement (Carlos M. Correa & Abdulqawi A. Yusuf, eds., 2016).

[42] Bull & McNeill, *supra* note 25.

[43] *See* Sundaram et al., *supra* note 12, at 12–19; María José Romero, What lies beneath? A Critical Assessment of PPPs and Their Impact on Sustainable Development (2016); Manuel F. Montes, *Public-Private Partnerships as the Answer . . . What was the Question?*, Inter Press Service 4 (Sep. 26 2017); Civil Society Reflection Group, *Spotlight on Sustainable Development 2017: Reclaiming Policies for the Public* (Report of the Reflection Group on the 2030 Agenda for Sustainable Development 2017) *available at* www.2030spotlight.org/sites/default/files/download/spotlight_170626_final_web.pdf.

[44] *Cf.* Carolyn Deere Birkbeck, The World Intellectual Property Organization (WIPO): A Reference Guide 184–85 (2016); *cf.* Carolyn Deere, *The Politics of Intellectual Property Reform in Developing Countries: The Relevance of the World Intellectual Property Organization, in* The Development Agenda: Global Intellectual Property and Developing Countries 111, 121–22 (Neil Netanel ed., 2008).

[45] Keith E. Maskus & Jerome H. Reichman, *The Globalization of Private Knowledge Goods and the Privatization of Global Public Goods, in* International Public Goods and Transfer of Technology Under a Globalized Intellectual Property Regime 3 (2005).

[46] Jacob Torfing, *Collaborative Innovation in the Public Sector, in* Handbook of Innovation in the Public Services 301 (2013) (emphasis added).

[47] Gillian MacNaughton, *Vertical Inequalities: Are the SDGs and Human Rights up to the Challenges?*, 8 Int'l J. Hum. Rts., 1050 (2017); *see also* Cimadamore, et al., *supra* note 33.

for-profit) and less reliance on overseas development assistance.[48] They are part and parcel of the trend in some countries towards shrinking the state and expanding the market. This movement in turn has major implications for IP regimes, whether national and international, which provide the basic rules and flexibilities for the deployment of market-based IP rights.

These larger trends are also accompanied by a greater emphasis in the SDGs on state responsibility for ensuring the human rights and other structural pre-requisites for successful development.[49] SDG 16, for example, declares that states should "[p]romote peaceful and inclusive societies for sustainable development, provide access to justice for all[,] and build effective, accountable and inclusive institutions at all levels."[50] This goal foregrounds the question of the kinds of knowledge governance policies that will contribute to this overall push towards just societies. As many IP scholars have argued elsewhere, the human rights and human development frameworks, among others, should guide global knowledge governance.[51]

How IP regimes participate in and are impacted by this multi-stakeholder governance approach within transnational legal ordering is the primary focus of this book. While governed by analytics such as goals, targets, and indicators, the SDGs also normatively represent "institutional cosmopolitanism"[52] whereby the

> [d]eveloped states and their citizens recognize their own contributions to global harm: for example, excessive consumption, secretive financial regimes, and harsh migration policies. Yet the approach the [SDGs] take is preventative rather than remedial. The root causes are identified in global structures and are to be tackled at the source. Some universal targets are also grounded instrumentally in the idea of global public goods. Global action to preserve and promote certain goods – such as the environment, health, economic growth, safe and secure migration – will benefit the citizens of all states.[53]

48 *See* Sundaram et al., *supra* note 12, at 12–19.

49 Langford, *supra* note 28, at 172 ("The SDGs thus recognize explicitly that progress on development will require internal and domestic institutional reform. By way of example, the target on enhanced foreign aid in Goal 17 is now preceded by a target on improved domestic tax and revenue collection. Legally, the human rights movement has demanded greater coherence between development policy and human rights treaties. This was acknowledged by states in the 2012 Rio Declaration, which set out the framework for drafting the agenda. The upshot is that international human rights law emerged as an important source of inspiration for new targets.")

50 SDG 16: Promote Peaceful and Inclusive Societies for Sustainable Development, Provide Access to Justice for all and Build Effective, Accountable and Inclusive Institutions at all Levels, UN (2017) *available at* https://sustainabledevelopment.un.org/sdg16. *See generally* Ingo Keilitz, *The Trouble with Justice in the United Nations Sustainable Development Goals*, 7 Wm. & Mary Pol'y Rev. 1–30 (2016).

51 *See, e.g.*, Laurence R. Helfer, *Toward a Human Rights Framework for Intellectual Property*, 40 U.C. Davis L. Rev. 971 (2007), *available at* https://ssrn.com/abstract=891303; J. Janewa Osei-Tutu, *Human Development as a Core Objective of Global Intellectual Property*, 105 Kentucky L.J. 1 (2016), *available at* https://ssrn.com/abstract=2896342; Brett M. Frischmann, *Capabilities, Spillovers, and Intellectual Progress: Toward a Human Flourishing Theory for Intellectual Property*, Cardozo Legal Stud. Res. Paper No. 442 (Sep. 23, 2014), *available at* https://ssrn.com/abstract=2500196; Aura Bertoni, *Research and "Development as Freedom" – Improving Democracy and Effectiveness in Pharmaceutical Innovation for Neglected Tropical Diseases*, 43 IIC: Intn'l Rev. of Indus. Prop. and Copyright L. 771–797, (Jan. 2012); Madhavi Sunder, From Goods to a Good Life: Intellectual Property and Global Justice (2012).

52 Langford, *supra* note 28, at 172.

53 *Id.*

Addressing the triple interface is certainly an ambitious scope. But recognizing the current role of IP in its movement from "splendid isolation" toward "institutional cosmopolitanism" is not only extremely timely but also essential to ensuring better knowledge governance management and policy decisions. Recognition, however, is just the first step. The next section of this chapter raises some of the conceptual challenges associated with a closer look at the interface.

II The Uncharted Territory: "Ps" in PPPs

This section grapples with the many omissions and refractions in our understanding of the PPPs that are tasked to implement the SDGs. Given the extraordinary reach of PPPs, it is indeed surprising how few systematic analyses or assessments exist of their impacts, outcomes, and outputs. As a UNDESA Working Paper recently pointed out, even the basic definitions and contours of development PPPs are without broad consensus.[54] One definition describes PPPs of a transnational character generally as:

> institutionalized cooperative relationships between public actors (both governments and international organizations) and private actors beyond the nation-state for governance purposes. By governance purposes, we mean the making and implementation of norms and rules for the provision of goods and services that are considered to be binding by [these actors].[55]

While this loosely fits many of the PPPs described in this book, PPPs are rapidly evolving hybrid institutions of global governance; their characteristics vary from partnership to partnership and from sector to sector. It is difficult to draw general conclusions about them, perhaps because they are ad hoc and flexible by design. PPPs are interventions that are unlike either market or hierarchy, and that is indeed one reason for their proliferation.

Each of the three "Ps" in PPPs (public, private, and partnership) have unresolved definitional and functional boundaries, with often intertwined descriptive and normative dimensions. They raise many questions of first impression or first principles. To begin with a foundational (and contested) question, how does (or should) the "P" representing the public – whether national governments or INGOs – participate as a "partner"?[56] No longer do states have exclusive power over norm-setting, norm interpretation, or even

[54] Sundaram et al., *supra* note 12, at annex 1.

[55] Tanja A. Börzel and Thomas Risse, *Public–Private Partnerships: Effective and Legitimate Tools of Transnational Governance?*, *in* Complex Sovereignty: Reconstituting Political Authority In The Twenty-First Century 195, 196 (Edgar Grande & Louis W. Pauly eds., 2005). See also Marco Schäferhoff, Sabine Campe, and Christopher Kaan, *Transnational Public–Private Partnerships in International Relations: Making Sense of Concepts, Research Frameworks, and Results*, 11 International Studies Rev. 451, 455 (2009) (defining "transnational PPPs as institutionalized transboundary interactions between public and private actors, which aim at the provision of collective goods."). This volume does not address PPPs within primarily domestic contexts even if they have impacts beyond borders. *See, e.g.*, Susan Ginsburg & Ann Davis, The Sourcebook of Public–Private Partnerships for Security and Resilience 2018: A Compendium of Laws and Policy Documents (ABA Publishing 2018).

[56] Economic Commission for Europe, Committee on Economic Cooperation and Integration, *Draft Guiding Principles on Good Governance in People-First Public–Private Partnerships for the UN Sustainable Development Goals*, ECE/CECI/PPP/2016/CRP.1 (Oct. 19, 2016).

norm implementation. As a consequence, what impact does this decentralized policy-making process have on the policy space of knowledge governance? Should the "P" in public include non-state actors with public interest-oriented missions, allowing states to cede their primary if not exclusive role in providing public goods? What is the role of individual states or INGOs in providing policy coordination among diverse and possibly fragmented PPP initiatives? And will effective functioning of PPPs require more regulatory streamlining across borders in order to decrease burdens and obstacles?

As to the second "P," what is or should be the ambit of the "P" representing the private? Does (or should) the "P" in private include nonprofit as well as for-profit partners? What are the differing motivations and strategies of NPOs and corporate partners? Within the for-profit "private" sector, what are the significant distinctions between the concerns over multinational involvement versus the activities of small and medium sized enterprises often associated with innovation? Within the nonprofit sector, is it fair to assume that the lack of a profit motive can be equated to the public interest? What is or should be the role or mission (as opposed to profit) in motivating nonprofit partners?

And finally, how do these first two "P"s relate not only to each other, but also to the third "P" of partnership? Is there an optimal point on the spectrum of collaboration or joint governance by the first two "P"s in any given partnership? Can the public partner effectively steer the partnership within a soft hierarchical, even regulatory, mode toward the production of public goods?[57] Should we anticipate and safeguard against private capture of the public interest within partnerships? Which policy flexibilities exercised within PPPs should be constrained, shaped, or steered within a larger multilateral framework? How do PPPs complement and enhance the development activities of the public sector, which all observers agree still have important roles within governance by goal-setting?[58] And within knowledge governance or innovation activities specifically, how does technology generation and sharing between partners occur? PPPs have at least two kinds of impacts: direct impacts by filling gaps where market distortions occur, and indirect impacts, by sharing technologies that can lead to further innovation. Under what conditions and when should a partnership be deployed to optimize these impacts?

Adding to the conceptual morass, PPPs do not operate on a blank slate but rather within multilateral legal and regulatory regimes where norm-setting and norm implementation are already rife with complex networks, relationships, and other forms of heterarchical, pluralistic governance – what some have referred to as the fragmentation of global governance.[59] Embedded within these distributed multilateral and multi-stakeholder governance regimes operating within transnational legal frameworks is a preexisting and arguably deep normative incoherence around the relationship of innovation activities to development, to wit, whether IP and innovation activities inevitably and "naturally" lead to development or whether, instead, development objectives should

[57] Steven Bernstein, *The United Nations and the Governance of Sustainable Development*, *in* GOVERNING THROUGH GOALS: SUSTAINABLE DEVELOPMENT GOALS AS GOVERNANCE INNOVATION 213 (Norichika Kanie & Frank Biermann eds., 2017) (describing steering by the UN).

[58] *Id.* at 218–20 (concluding that public partners have an important role to ensure coherence, orchestration, and legitimacy); *id.* at 228–30 (asserting that important direct government functions within goal-setting include the provision of science, monitoring, and review).

[59] *See* Dinwoodie and Dreyfuss, *supra* note 9; *see generally* Rakhyun E. Kim, *The Nexus Between International Law and the Sustainable Development Goals*, 25 REV. EUR. CMTY. & INT'L ENVTL. L. 15 (2016).

lead, shape, and steer IP norms.[60] One perspective could be characterized as a more categorical and formalistic – or even technocratic – approach towards IP's role within knowledge governance. The other perspective could be viewed as relying on the insight that IP cannot be viewed in "splendid isolation"[61] or as an end in itself, but is necessarily part of pluralistic dialogues across regimes so as to optimize social welfare through knowledge governance.[62]

Leading multilateral institutions such as WIPO and the World Trade Organization (WTO) have been grappling with this conceptual difficulty for decades, most recently through the so-called WIPO Development Agenda as well as the WTO Doha Development Round, respectively. The latest attempts at integrating development goals and initiatives within WIPO has resulted in significant structural changes since the Development Agenda was first implemented in 2007,[63] yet the integration of the 2030 Agenda's SDGs with the overall work plan at WIPO and/or its Development Agenda has been arguably sporadic so far rather than holistic.[64] Meanwhile, at the national level, both developing and developed country sectors are re-landscaping the geography of global intellectual property to meet domestic welfare demands more explicitly throughout the public law regimes. Ruth Okediji views these efforts as significant "legal innovations," which she describes as

> new techniques, institutions, or methods specifically designed in the light of [WTO] TRIPS obligations, and that facilitate implementation of those obligations in a manner consistent with or that reconcile national welfare goals as the primary justification for IP protection . . . Across developed and developing countries, legal innovation offers a fine instrument for defining sovereign responsibility for the effects of IP rights in society.[65]

How do or should PPPs fit into these policy debates about IP and sustainable development? Will PPPs address the policy incoherence around IP and development or worsen it? Can they advance effective, efficient, and equitable joint governance through partnerships engaged in innovation activities, or do they supplant more optimal forms of

[60] *See generally* Intellectual Property, Trade and Development: Strategies to Optimize Economic Development in a TRIPS-Plus Era (Daniel Gervais ed., 2d ed. 2014); Intellectual Property Rights: Legal and Economic Challenges for Development (Mario Cimoli, Giovanni Dosi, Keith E. Maskus, Ruth L. Okediji, Jerome H. Reichman, and Joseph E. Stiglitz eds. 2014); Intellectual Property and Sustainable Development: Development Agendas in a Changing World (Ricardo Meléndez-Ortiz & Pedro Roffe eds., 2009); Intellectual Property and Development: Lessons from Recent Economic Research (Carsten Fink & Keith E. Maskus, eds., 2005).

[61] Cottier, *supra* note 4.

[62] *See, e.g.*, Claudio Chiarolla, *The Work of the World Intellectual Property Organization (WIPO) and Its Possible Relevance for Global Ocean Governance, in* Comprehensive Study On Effective And Sustainable Global Ocean Governance: UN Specialized Agencies And Global Ocean Governance, (D.J. Attard & M. Fitzmaurice eds., 2016), *available at* https://ssrn.com/abstract=3002489.

[63] World Intellectual Property Organization, *Report on the Independent Review of the Implementation of the Development Agenda Recommendations*, at 27–28, WIPO Doc. CDIP/18/7 (Aug. 15, 2016); cf. Jeremy de Beer, *Defining WIPO's Development Agenda, in* Implementing the World Intellectual Property Organization's Development Agenda 1 (Jeremy de Beer ed., 2009); The Development Agenda: Global Intellectual Property and Developing Countries, (Neil Weinstock Netanel, ed., 2008).

[64] Peter K. Yu, *Five Decades of Intellectual Property and Global Development*, 8 WIPO J. 1–10 (2016), *available at* https://ssrn.com/abstract=2872682; *see also* WIPO Committee on Development and Intellectual Property (CDIP) Reports, *available at* www.wipo.int/policy/en/cdip/.

[65] Ruth Okediji, *Legal Innovation in International Intellectual Property Relations*, 36 U. Pa. J. Int'l L. 191 (2014).

knowledge governance? And how will overall policy coordination, either at the national or multilateral level, occur among these decentralized initiatives? PPPs can potentially play an important role in ensuring that norm-setting happens in a democratic fashion, by encouraging and integrating greater input from a broad range of stakeholders. But they can also fall prey to a number of different challenges, including potential policy capture, fragmentation, and/or laundering.

With regard to technology sharing, in particular, at least two types of potential obstacles can be discerned: first, within a PPP itself, among its partners, and second between a PPP and its broader environment. To overcome these obstacles, what are the major policy choices with respect to complementarity between public and private responsibilities, and what is the correct design mix of proprietary (exclusive) and open (inclusive) innovation access and use? Relatedly, what kinds of outcomes are expected with regard not only to the innovation activities of the three "P"s, but other public policy goals of IP, such as the related three "A"s of knowledge diffusion and dissemination, that is, availability, accessibility, and affordability?[66] Social licensing strategies to promote the three "A"s may matter much more to the NGO or NPO partner than to its other partners. And correspondingly, some partners within PPPs may not have sufficient leverage over the other PPP participants to push their partners toward social licensing goals outside of a short-term trajectory set by funding cycles for public agencies or private foundations, profit cycles for commercial partners, and/or budgetary concerns of governments.[67]

These definitional and functional ambiguities around PPPs involved in innovation activities reflect lack of consensus around basic goals and implementation practices. What we do know so far is far outweighed by what we do not know. We do know that on a *practical* level, PPPs vary in terms of their approaches to innovation activities and sustainable development more broadly. On a *policy* level, we know that PPPs have the potential to generate critical information regarding aspects of global knowledge governance, such as best practices for IP licensing, as well as for financing, regulatory coordination and oversight, and technology dissemination. And on a *conceptual* level, we know that knowledge governance arrangements involving PPPs in development inevitably raise issues around accountability, representation, and transparency – especially where the expected output is a development-oriented public good that is intended primarily to contribute to overall social welfare. All of these insights operate, however, at a very high level of abstraction.

III Rewinding the Triple Interface

The myriad unanswered questions in the previous section confirm that PPPs remain under-examined, under-evaluated, and under-researched, despite their growing importance in global governance for sustainable development generally, and knowledge

[66] Steve Brooke, Claudia M. Harner-Jay, Heidi Lasher, and Erica Jacoby, *How Public–Private Partnerships Handle Intellectual Property: The PATH Experience, in* INTELLECTUAL PROPERTY MANAGEMENT IN HEALTH AND AGRICULTURAL INNOVATION: A HANDBOOK OF BEST PRACTICES 1775 (Anatole Krattiger, Richard Mahoney, Lita Nelsen, Jennifer Thomson, Alan Bennett, Kanikaram Satyanarayana, Gregory Graff, Carlos Fernandez, and Stanley Kowalski eds., 2007), available at: www.iphandbook.org/.

[67] Chon, *supra* note 35, at 293.

governance specifically.[68] This book's primary goal is to contribute toward a better understanding of the diversity of multi-stakeholder partnerships, including PPPs, operating at the juncture of IP and sustainable development, and to build a larger picture of their knowledge governance activities through case studies and other analysis.

In this regard, the book's chapters examine innovation activities across a variety of development fields, assess the current landscape of exemplary PPPs, and suggest possible directions for future policy and research. Together, these chapters explore the various benefits and costs of partnership-driven knowledge governance strategies through a representative range of PPPs across various development domains. The book's four sections cover PPPs operating in public health, education, ICTs, and libraries; climate change-related technologies as well as agriculture. The final section presents perspectives on knowledge governance and institutional design of PPPs.

This book's chapters span many kinds of partnerships.[69] In order to address the diversity of PPPs in IP, we do not impose a common definition of PPPs upon the authors or readers. Nor do the chapters adhere to shared methodology regarding any aspect of the triple interface. In other words, the authors here engage with freedom to explore those facets of the triple interface they find most compelling to convey and analyse, and with whatever methodological tools they feel appropriate. Authors who are involved in the PPPs they present here were encouraged to take a critical approach towards them, beyond enumerating their achievements and successes. We leave it to the readers to assess the extent to which this has been the case.

In addition, this book is deliberately designed to stake out various perspectives, whether generally supportive or critical, of the triple interface. An important value added is that it brings together authors from various backgrounds, thus representing a broad diversity of views on the issues at hand. In this regard, we hope the book will ultimately foster a dialogue among key PPP stakeholders, policymakers, and scholars, with the goal of facilitating knowledge gap-filling, knowledge sharing, and possible knowledge levelling about this important arena of global governance and sustainable development. A brief description of each chapter follows.

A *Public Health*

The section on public health begins with a legal and policy overview of PPPs in global health by **Frederick Abbott**. He focuses on the role of PPPs in possibly transforming funding models for R&D of pharmaceuticals. His chapter explores the boundaries

[68] Analyses of the double interface of PPPs and development, or of PPPs and IP are few and far between. *See, e.g.*, David J. Maurrasse, STRATEGIC PUBLIC PRIVATE PARTNERSHIPS: INNOVATION AND DEVELOPMENT (2013); Philipp Pattberg, Frank Biermann, Sander Chan & Ayşem Mert (eds.), PUBLIC–PRIVATE PARTNERSHIPS FOR SUSTAINABLE DEVELOPMENT: EMERGENCE, INFLUENCE AND LEGITIMACY (2013). A literature search of SDGs and partnerships and/or SDGs and intellectual property revealed very few published materials on either topic. This scholarly gap is evident in the business and management literature as well. *See* Ans Kolk, Arno E. Kourula, and Niccolò Pisani, *Multinational Enterprises and the Sustainable Development Goals: What Do We Know and How to Proceed?*, 24 Transnational Corporations 9 (2017), *available at* https://ssrn.com/abstract=2988607 (analyzing the nature of the private for-profit partners in PPPs).

[69] Dodds, *supra* note 24, at 143 (Development partnerships can be categorized as those organized by the UN, those facilitated or supported by the UN, and those that have no involvement by the UN).

between public and private R&D, surveys key PPPs in the public health arena, describes the advantages and disadvantages of PPPs, and then proposes ways in which PPPs might lead into alternative models of funding pharmaceutical R&D. Abbott describes various contradictions of existing financial structures and emphasizes delinkage (defined as "separating the R&D function from the production, sale and distribution function") as an important fulcrum between public and private interests in generating R&D moving forward.

Anatole Krattiger, Thomas Bombelles, and Ania Jedrusik then present the INGO partner perspective on WIPO Re:Search. Their chapter reviews the multi-stakeholder partnership landscape for public health in the context of the SDGs as well as broader innovation incentive schemes for PRNDs (or what these authors call neglected tropical diseases). They then examine some economic determinants of innovation and how different partnership models such as PPPs endeavor to address related challenges. This case study includes a detailed examination of various characteristics of WIPO Re:Search, including its structure and governance, funding, and other critical components.

A complementary chapter follows about BIO Ventures for Global Health, co-authored by **Katy M. Graef, Jennifer Dent, and Amy Starr**. They explore two open innovation platforms co-led by BVGH – the Pool for Open Innovation against Neglected Tropical Diseases and WIPO Re:Search – that encourage and support biopharmaceutical companies' contributions to PRND R&D through PPPs. Their contribution also discusses the necessity of a partner responsible for proactively establishing collaborative projects between participating organizations and managing established alliances to ensure that challenges are addressed and projects are successful. It concludes with a description of how the WIPO Re:Search consortium governs the sharing of IP among organizations and the consortium's alignment with the SDGs.

The next contribution, by **Esteban Burrone**, provides a legal and policy case study of a specific PPP, the Medicines Patent Pool (MPP), which is the first patent pool in public health designed to enhance access to affordable medicines in developing countries through the negotiation of access-oriented and transparent voluntary licences with the pharmaceutical industry. His chapter outlines the concept of patent pooling as it has evolved over recent years in the public health field. He then reviews its practical application in HIV R&D through the establishment of the MPP, and its subsequent expansion into hepatitis C and TB research. Burrone ends with an analysis of the potential applicability of the patent pooling model to other pharmaceutical R&D areas, by identifying the kinds of public health challenges that such a model could address in the context of meeting the health-related SDGs.

The final chapter in the public health section of the book, co-authored by **Hilde Stevens and Isabelle Huys**, is based on an in-depth study of the Innovative Medicines Initiative, Europe's largest early-phase PPP. They map the ways in which IP is generated, protected, and managed within and beyond these types of research PPPs. The chapter reviews the relevant concepts and taxonomizes these PPPs as partnership-focused, open collaboration, or hybrid models. It then examines key issues, such as the boundaries of the precompetitive partnership, the role of trust within those PPPs, IP ownership and access rights (particularly with regard to foreground and background IP), the importance of transparent IP rules underlying knowledge sharing strategies, and the role of IP in the performance of PPPs. Their work also demonstrates the importance of acknowledging a broad range of IP performance measures related to knowledge sharing, including the sharing of know-how, show-how, databases, and protocols. The authors conclude with some recommendations for best practices to facilitate efficient and equitable knowledge sharing via PPPs.

B *Education, ICTs, and Libraries*

This section leads off with a chapter written by **Jens Bammel**, who presents a case study of the Health InterNetwork Access to Research Information (HINARI), which is the World Health Organisation's PPP for facilitating access to scientific information to researchers in developing countries. He describes how this access can at times be achieved within the constraints of copyright and licences, by taking advantage of the role that publishers play in knowledge distribution and harnessing their added value and expertise. Bammel concedes that collaborative partnerships based on licensing are not a complete panacea to unequal access to information, but concludes that the track record of this partnership (one of several partnerships in the "Research for Life" family) demonstrates that there is value in exploring PPPs that make use of the publishing industry's skills rather than to oppose them. The chapter examines some of HINARI's structural characteristics, including qualifying countries and institutions, organizational and technical set-up, and legal agreements. It not only delves into various success factors, such as those that were required to enable publishers to engage fully, but also describes solutions to key obstacles, including the challenge of the transition from aid to trade.

Sara Bannerman provides an information policy case study of WIPO's "Access to Research for Development and Innovation" (ARDI) program, also part of the Research4Life family of PPPs. She first reviews the history of networked governance and PPPs at WIPO and asks more broadly whether, and how, PPPs can best be structured to work for sustainable development. Bannerman then evaluates the WIPO Development Agenda project entitled *Specialized Databases' Access and Support* (Phase I and II) as a case study of PPPs as they currently operate in WIPO. This part of her chapter examines the extent to which the ARDI program – a part of this WIPO-based project – contributes to policy participation by the users most affected by the program, and to important goals of equity and access. Critically examining the concept of development embedded in the ARDI program, she argues that if WIPO is to adopt a sustainable development agenda in which partnerships play a major role, consistent with the intent of the SDGs, it must adopt higher and more inclusive standards for PPP governance.

Next, **Susan Isiko Štrba** explores the contribution of the Accessible Books Consortium (ABC), a PPP initiative based at WIPO, in providing greater access to published materials to communities of visually impaired persons (VIP). Based on interviews conducted in 2016 with participating stakeholders in the ABC (including WIPO, representatives of libraries, VIP communities, and publishers), the chapter first maps the challenge of access to information by VIPs, highlighting the role of copyright. She describes the ABC in detail, and follows this with a detailed evaluation of the ABC as a partnership. Her chapter ends by discussing the achievements, shortcomings, and challenges of the ABC, highlighting lessons for implementing the Marrakesh Treaty to Facilitate Access to Published Works by Visually Impaired Persons and Persons with Print Disabilities, and suggesting how the IP goals of innovation and access to information may be realized through partnerships implementing the SDGs. The author concludes that the public law treaty framework and private sector initiatives are interdependent; both are required to address issues of access.

From a US perspective, **Melissa Levine** provides a legal and information policy case study of HathiTrust, involving a partnership between Google Books and a consortium of university libraries, spearheaded by a public university, the University of Michigan. This case study demonstrates how PPPs can propel nonprofit mission, by helping libraries to better meet the informational needs implicit in the SDGs, and by improving global access to knowledge and information with more clarity for both copyright holders and cultural institutions. Following an exploration of the role of IP as a distinct challenge to the partnership goals, including the difficulties associated in locating the boundaries of the public domain, she concludes that similar PPPs cannot either form or function without an enabling environment of strong copyright exceptions and limitations. Levine provides some suggestions for adjusting both national and multilateral copyright legal and policy frameworks to better serve both public and private interests of PPPs with similar goals.

C *Environmental Issues: Green Technologies and Agriculture*

In the first of three chapters on climate change, **Ahmed Abdel-Latif** outlines how the multilateral regime governing climate change not only recognises the role of PPPs, but also seeks to enhance their contribution to global efforts to accelerate technology diffusion and innovation in green technologies. These efforts by PPPs connect the multilateral mechanisms for encouraging the production and dissemination of green technologies to the more comprehensive and holistic SDGs of the 2030 Agenda. He first summarizes the historical evolution of global climate and sustainable development discussions, then examines how climate change discussions have addressed IP issues to date. Following this examination, Abdel-Latif describes how PPPs in green technology have sought to approach IP matters in a pragmatic manner. He concludes with examples of PPPs at the multilateral level (WIPO GREEN) as well as at the bilateral level (the U.S.-China Clean Energy Research Center and the US-India Partnership to Advance Clean Energy).

The contribution by **Joshua D. Sarnoff** with **Margaret Chon** provides a taxonomy of innovation policy choices within climate change-related technology transfer, including legal, public policy, management policy, and government funding choices. Starting with a description of some global inequalities that likely will result from existing unequal patterns of creation and distribution of climate change technologies and associated ownership of IP rights, the chapter then explains how PPPs pose significant challenges for specific policy choices regarding innovation funding of climate change technologies and associated IP. It presents a typology of government choices in innovation funding and explains how these basic national policies may affect the nature, direction, and roles of PPPs in the climate change and energy development domains. In addition, it proposes several approaches to overcoming access and price constraints. These include both public sector policies and private sector (and/or governmental proprietary) choices to increase technology dissemination. The chapter concludes with a renewed call for greater public funding, and for more careful management of the innovation policy choices of climate change technology PPPs.

Ayşem Mert and Philipp Pattberg draw on a multiyear research project on the emergence and effectiveness of PPPs, which utilizes a large-N database called the Global Sustainability Partnerships Database, to understand better the role and relevance of PPPs in contemporary global environmental governance. The empirical focus in this chapter is on partnerships addressing climate change and/or energy. The chapter first defines partnerships as a case of network governance and briefly discusses the origins of partnerships for sustainable development. It then provides an overview of the status of technology innovation and technology transfer in multilateral environmental governance. After supplying this context, Mert and Pattberg present their findings from an empirical analysis of the performance of PPPs in the climate and energy subfield. The chapter concludes with suggestions for improving climate change-related partnerships moving forward as envisioned by the 2030 Agenda.

Irene Calboli and Delphine Marie-Vivien offer a comparative legal and policy study of agriculture-related geographical indications (GIs) in three jurisdictions: France, India, and Singapore. Agricultural GIs provide numerous public benefits through their contributions to agricultural and rural development. In their chapter, Calboli and Marie-Vivenne survey these different national approaches, to answer the following questions: What is the best GI governance model for achieving the public policy objectives of GI protection; specifically, should such a model be based primarily on state-driven action, or rather on the actions by the private sector? Ultimately, they conclude that a system in which either the state or the private sector has exclusive, or majoritarian, control may not be an optimal system for GI governance. Instead, coordination between both the state and private stakeholders work is a requirement – but not necessarily to the same degree, or even at the same time, given that national circumstances and needs may require different approaches. Thus, for successful shared governance between the public and private sectors, they posit that legal and policy flexibility is needed.

D *Governance and Institutional Design Perspectives*

Padmashree Gehl Sampath examines specific features of international PPPs, to characterise them within the broader landscape of PPPs and explain the key aspects that set them apart. Through a bibliometric review of the current state of existing empirical evidence on PPPs, IP, and technology transfer issues, she then evaluates the current state of empirical information available on these PPPs in the context of technological sharing and capacity building. Drawing on these results, Sampath critically analyses the treatment of technology transfer in PPPs, positing an urgent need to understand the ways in which technology-related objectives and achievements of existing PPPs differ as well as what precise advantages and limitations they pose in practice. Lastly, her chapter raises a set of critical issues on whether existing models and solutions devised thereunder address the question of technology transfer in a satisfactory manner. It concludes with some suggestions for future institutional design to address capacity-building, technological learning, and technology sharing goals, which the SDGs have prioritized for development.

With the Open African Innovation Research (Open AIR) network as a case study of a cross-regional research platform, **Chidi Oguamanam** and **Jeremy de Beer** link empirical and conceptual perspectives on PPPs to the key operational elements of this networked platform, including its core driving factors relevant to development issues associated with IP and knowledge governance in Africa. The chapter posits that insights from Open AIR's construct and research findings, which flow from its activities as a research-driven rather than a product-driven initiative, can shine light on how PPPs (or cross-sector partnerships in general) can be better exploited and reengineered beyond their current and ad hoc interventionist outlook, and therefore serve more effectively as sustainable development vehicles. It summarizes multiple examples of successful collaborative research fostered by Open AIR across different development domains.

Drawing on lessons from the MDGs and a case study of the Millennium Development Villages, **David J. Maurrasse** offers a policy study of PPPs. He situates what he calls cross-sector partnerships, including PPPs, in the context of their influence on the current SDGs and their former counterpart, the UN MDGs. Specifically, the chapter discusses the lessons learned from the involvement of cross-sector partnerships in the progress made towards the MDGs. In assessing the impact of partnerships on the implementation of both the SDGs and MDGs, the chapter draws on examples from agricultural and rural development for poverty reduction. While not discussing PPPs in relation to knowledge governance specifically, Maurrasse concludes by providing guidelines for future cross-sector partnerships in addressing global governance and development challenges generally.

Peter K. Yu closes this final section of the book with a key legal and policy exploration of human rights law and its relation to PPPs. The incorporation of human rights into the SDGs is an advance from the previous MDGs, but also raises new challenges in implementation through PPPs. Yu focuses on the roles and responsibilities of IP-related PPPs in the international human rights regime. In doing so, he examines the "protect, respect, and remedy" framework and the Guiding Principles on Business and Human Rights, which John Ruggie presented to the UN Human Rights Council in his capacity as the UN Secretary-General's Special Representative on the Issue of Human Rights and Transnational Corporations and Other Business Enterprises. After evaluating the strengths and weaknesses of Ruggie's proposed framework and the Guiding Principles, this chapter explains why partnerships should assume greater human rights responsibilities. This chapter concludes with three specific examples illustrating how PPPs can be utilized to foster a more appropriate balance between IP and human rights, including possibilities and constraints of private partner involvement in implementing the SDGs.

And in a concluding chapter to the entire volume, **Margaret Chon** synthesizes the lessons learned. She summarizes the chapters' findings according to four thematic sections: (1) aligning with public policy objectives; (2) coordinating with other knowledge governance efforts; (3) managing the partnership boundaries; and (4) enhancing sustainable development. Based on these findings, she then suggests multiple items for future policy analysis and scholarly research.

The chapters contained in this book provide early guideposts to the still largely uncharted territory of the triple interface of IP, PPPs, and sustainable development. They add scholarly inquiry and policy analysis from both private and public perspectives about and from governmental, INGO, NGO, NPO, as well as for-profit partners and stakeholders. Ultimately, the book provides a provisional but important map to the multiple roles of PPPs in global knowledge governance and sustainable development. It should generate further policy analysis and scholarly research about this rapidly emerging and evolving, yet already embedded and impactful, triple interface.

References

Andreson, Steiner and Masahiko Iguchi, *Lessons from the Health-Related Millennium Development Goals*, in GOVERNING THROUGH GOALS: SUSTAINABLE DEVELOPMENT GOALS AS GOVERNANCE INNOVATION (Norichika Kanie and Frank Biermann eds. 2017).

Bernstein, Steven, *The United Nations and the Governance of Sustainable Development, in* GOVERNING THROUGH GOALS: SUSTAINABLE DEVELOPMENT GOALS AS GOVERNANCE INNOVATION (Norichika Kanie and Frank Biermann eds. 2017).

Bertoni, Aura, *Research and "Development as Freedom" – Improving Democracy and Effectiveness in Pharmaceutical Innovation for Neglected Tropical Diseases,* 43 IIC: INTN'L REV. OF INDUS. PROP. AND COPYRIGHT L. 771 (Jan. 2012).

Birkbeck, Carolyn D., *The Politics of Intellectual Property Reform in Developing Countries: The Relevance of the World Intellectual Property Organization, in* THE DEVELOPMENT AGENDA: GLOBAL INTELLECTUAL PROPERTY AND DEVELOPING COUNTRIES (Neil Netanel ed. 2008).

Birkbeck, Carolyn D., THE WORLD INTELLECTUAL PROPERTY ORGANIZATION (WIPO): A REFERENCE GUIDE (2016).

Börzel, Tanja A. and Thomas Risse, *Public–Private Partnerships: Effective and Legitimate Tools of Transnational Governance?, in* COMPLEX SOVEREIGNTY: RECONSTITUTING POLITICAL AUTHORITY IN THE TWENTY-FIRST CENTURY (Edgar Grande and Louis W. Pauly eds. 2005).

Brooke, Steve, Claudia M. Harner-Jay, Heidi Lasher, and Erica Jacoby, *How Public–Private Partnerships Handle Intellectual Property: The PATH Experience, in* INTELLECTUAL PROPERTY MANAGEMENT IN HEALTH AND AGRICULTURAL INNOVATION: A HANDBOOK OF BEST PRACTICES 1775 (Anatole Krattiger, Richard Mahoney, Lita Nelsen, Jennifer Thomson, Alan Bennett, Kanikaram Satyanarayana, Gregory Graff, Carlos Fernandez, and Stanley Kowalski eds. 2007), *available at* www.iphandbook.org/ (last visited Nov. 19, 2017).

Browne, Stephen, SUSTAINABLE DEVELOPMENT GOALS AND UN GOAL-SETTING (2017).

Bull, Benedicte, *Public–Private Partnerships: The United Nations Experience 480, in* INTERNATIONAL HANDBOOK ON PUBLIC–PRIVATE PARTNERSHIPS (Graeme A. Hodge, Carsten Greve, and Anthony E. Boardman eds. 2010).

Bull, Benedicte and Desmond McNeill, DEVELOPMENT ISSUES IN GLOBAL GOVERNANCE: PUBLIC–PRIVATE PARTNERSHIPS AND MARKET MULTILATERALISM (2007).

Chiarolla, Claudio, *The Work of the World Intellectual Property Organization (WIPO) and Its Possible Relevance for Global Ocean Governance, in* COMPREHENSIVE STUDY ON EFFECTIVE AND SUSTAINABLE GLOBAL OCEAN GOVERNANCE: UN SPECIALIZED AGENCIES AND GLOBAL OCEAN GOVERNANCE (D. J. Attard and M. Fitzmaurice eds. 2016), *available at* https://ssrn.com/abstract=3002489 (last visited Nov. 19, 2017).

Chon, Margaret, *PPPs in Global IP (Public–Private Partnerships in Global Intellectual Property), in* METHODS AND PERSPECTIVES IN INTELLECTUAL PROPERTY (Graeme B. Dinwoodie ed. 2013).

Christensen, Clayton M. and Derek van Bever, *The Capitalist's Dilemma*, 92 HARV. BUS. REV. 61 (Jun. 2014).

Cimadamore, Alberto D., Gabriel Koehler, and Thomas Pogge (eds.), POVERTY AND THE MILLENNIUM DEVELOPMENT GOALS (2016).

Cimoli, Mario, Giovanni Dosi, Keith E. Maskus, Ruth L. Okediji, Jerome H. Reichman, and Joseph E. Stiglitz (eds.), INTELLECTUAL PROPERTY RIGHTS: LEGAL AND ECONOMIC CHALLENGES FOR DEVELOPMENT (2014).

Civil Society Reflection Group, *Spotlight on Sustainable Development 2017: Reclaiming Policies for the Public* (Report of the Reflection Group on the 2030 Agenda for Sustainable

Development 2017), *available at* www.2030spotlight.org/sites/default/files/download/spotlight_170626_final_web.pdf (last visited Nov. 19, 2017).

Cottier, Thomas, *Embedding Intellectual Property in International Law, in* CURRENT ALLIANCES IN INTERNATIONAL INTELLECTUAL PROPERTY LAWMAKING: THE EMERGENCE AND IMPACT OF MEGA-REGIONALS (Pedro Roffe and Xavier Seuba eds. 2017).

Correa, Carlos M., and Abdulqawi A. Yusuf (eds.), INTELLECTUAL PROPERTY AND INTERNATIONAL TRADE: THE TRIPS AGREEMENT (2016).

Cutler, A. Claire, *Legal Pluralism as the "Common Sense" of Transnational Capitalism,* 3 *Oñati Socio-legal Series* 719 (2013), *available at* http://ssrn.com/abstract=2327501 (last visited Nov. 19, 2017).

de Beer, Jeremy, *Defining WIPO's Development Agenda, in* IMPLEMENTING THE WORLD INTELLECTUAL PROPERTY ORGANIZATION'S DEVELOPMENT AGENDA 1 (Jeremy de Beer ed., 2009).

de Búrca, Gráinne, *New Governance and Experimentalism: An Introduction,* 210 WISC. L. REV. 232 (2011).

Dinwoodie, Graeme B. and Rochelle C. Dreyfuss, A NEOFEDERALIST VISION OF TRIPS: THE RESILIENCE OF THE INTERNATIONAL INTELLECTUAL PROPERTY REGIME (2012).

Dodds, Felix, David Donoghue, and Jimena Leiva Roesch, NEGOTIATING THE SUSTAINABLE DEVELOPMENT GOALS: A TRANSFORMATIONAL AGENDA FOR AN INSECURE WORLD (2017).

Dreyfuss, Rochelle C. and Susy Frankel, *From Incentive to Commodity to Asset: How International Law is Reconceptualizing Intellectual Property,* 36 MICH. J. INT'L L. 557 (2015).

Economic Commission for Europe, Committee on Economic Cooperation and Integration, *Draft Guiding Principles on Good Governance in People-First Public–Private Partnerships for the UN Sustainable Development Goals,* ECE/CECI/PPP/2016/CRP.1 (Oct. 19, 2016).

Fink, Carsten and Keith E. Maskus (eds.), INTELLECTUAL PROPERTY AND DEVELOPMENT: LESSONS FROM RECENT ECONOMIC RESEARCH (2005).

Frischmann, Brett M., *Capabilities, Spillovers, and Intellectual Progress: Toward a Human Flourishing Theory for Intellectual Property,* CARDOZO LEGAL STUD. RES. PAPER NO. 442 (Sep. 23, 2014), *available at* https://ssrn.com/abstract=2500196 (last visited Nov. 19, 2017).

FRISCHMANN, BRETT M., INFRASTRUCTURE: THE SOCIAL VALUE OF SHARED RESOURCES (2012).

Gervais, Daniel (ed.), INTELLECTUAL PROPERTY, TRADE AND DEVELOPMENT: STRATEGIES TO OPTIMIZE ECONOMIC DEVELOPMENT IN A TRIPS-PLUS ERA (2d ed. 2014).

Ginsburg, Susan and Ann Davis, THE SOURCEBOOK OF PUBLIC–PRIVATE PARTNERSHIPS FOR SECURITY AND RESILIENCE 2018: A COMPENDIUM OF LAWS AND POLICY DOCUMENTS (ABA Publishing 2018).

Helfer, Laurence R., *Regime Shifting: The TRIPS Agreement and New Dynamics of International Intellectual Property Lawmaking,* 29 YALE J. INT'L L. 1 (2004).

Helfer, Laurence R., *Toward a Human Rights Framework for Intellectual Property,* 40 U.C. DAVIS L. REV. 971 (2007), *available at* https://ssrn.com/abstract=891303 (last visited Nov. 19, 2017).

Kanie, Norichika, Steven Bernstein, Frank Biermann, and Peter M. Haas, *Introduction: Global Governance Through Goal-Setting, in* GOVERNING THROUGH GOALS: SUSTAINABLE DEVELOPMENT GOALS AS GOVERNANCE INNOVATION (Norichika Kanie and Frank Biermann eds., 2017).

Kaul, Inge, Isabelle Grunberg, and Marc Stern (eds.), GLOBAL PUBLIC GOODS: INTERNATIONAL COOPERATION IN THE 21ST CENTURY (1999).

Kaul, Inge, Pedro Conceição, Katell Le Goulven, and Ronald U. Mendoza (eds.), PROVIDING GLOBAL PUBLIC GOODS: MANAGING GLOBALIZATION (2003).

Keilitz, Ingo, *The Trouble with Justice in the United Nations Sustainable Development Goals,* 7 WM. AND MARY POL'Y REV. (2016).

Kim, Rakhyun E., *The Nexus Between International Law and the Sustainable Development Goals*, 25 Rev. Eur. Cmty. and int'l Envtl. L. 15 (2016).

Kingsbury, Benedict, Nico Krisch, and Richard B. Stewart, *The Emergence of Global Administrative Law*, 68 L. Contemp. Prob. 15 (2005).

Kolk, Ans, Arno E. Kourula, and Niccolò Pisani, *Multinational Enterprises and the Sustainable Development Goals: What Do We Know and How to Proceed?*, 24 Transnational Corporations 9 (2017), *available at* https://ssrn.com/abstract=2988607 (last visited Nov. 19, 2017).

Langford, Malcolm, *Lost in Transformation? The Politics of the Sustainable Development Goals*, 30 Ethics and Int'l Aff. 167 (2016).

MacNaughton, Gillian, *Vertical Inequalities: Are the SDGs and Human Rights up to the Challenges?*, 8 Int'l J. Hum. Rts. 1050 (2017).

Maskus, Keith E. and Jerome H. Reichman, *The Globalization of Private Knowledge Goods and the Privatization of Global Public Goods*, *in* International Public Goods and Transfer of Technology Under a Globalized Intellectual Property Regime 3 (Keith E. Maskus and Jerome H. Reichman eds., 2005).

Maurrasse, David J., Strategic Public Private Partnerships: Innovation and Development (2013).

Meléndez-Ortiz, Ricardo and Pedro Roffe (eds.), Intellectual Property and Sustainable Development: Development Agendas in a Changing World (2009).

Montes, Manuel F., *Public–Private Partnerships as the Answer ... What was the Question?*, Inter Press Service 4 (Sep. 26, 2017).

Nanda, Ved P., *The Journey from the Millennium Development Goals to the Sustainable Development Goals*, 44 Denv. J. Int'l L. and Pol'y 389 (2016).

Netanel, Neil Weinstock (ed.), The Development Agenda: Global Intellectual Property and Developing Countries (2008).

Oguamanam, Chidi, Intellectual Property in Global Governance: A Development Question (2012).

Okediji, Ruth, *Legal Innovation in International Intellectual Property Relations*, 36 U. Pa. J. Int'l L. 191 (2014).

Osei-Tutu, J. Janewa, *Human Development as a Core Objective of Global Intellectual Property*, 105 Kentucky L.J. 1 (2016), https://papers.ssrn.com/sol3/papers.cfm?abstract_id=2896342 (last visited Nov. 19, 2017).

Pattberg, Philipp, Frank Biermann, Sander Chan, and Ayşem Mert (eds.), Public–Private Partnerships for Sustainable Development: Emergence, Influence and Legitimacy (2013).

Raustiala, Kal, *Public Power and Private Stakeholders*, UCLA School of Law, Public Law Research Paper No. 17–26 (Aug. 21, 2017), *available at* https://ssrn.com/abstract=3023598 (last visited Nov. 19, 2017).

Roffe, Pedro and Xavier Seuba eds., *Current Alliances in International Intellectual Property Lawmaking: The Emergence and Impact of Mega-Regionals* 2017 (Int'l Ctr. for Trade and Sustainable Dev. (ICTSD) and Ctr. for Int'l Intell. Prop. Studies (CEIPI), Ser. No. 4).

Romero, María J., What lies beneath? A Critical Assessment of PPPs and Their Impact on Sustainable Development (2016).

Schäferhoff, Marco, Sabine Campe, and Christopher Kaan, *Transnational Public–Private Partnerships in International Relations: Making Sense of Concepts, Research Frameworks, and Results*, 11 International Studies Rev. 451 (2009).

Schwab, Klaus, The Fourth Industrial Revolution (2016).

Sundaram, Jomo K., Anis Chowdhury, Krishnan Sharma, and Daniel Platz, *Public–Private Partnerships and the 2030 Agenda for Sustainable Development: Fit for Purpose?* 1 (UN Dept. of Econ. and Soc. Affairs, DESA Working Paper No. 148, ST/ESA/2016/DWP/148, Feb. 2016).

Sunder, Madhavi, FROM GOODS TO A GOOD LIFE: INTELLECTUAL PROPERTY AND GLOBAL JUSTICE (2012).

Taubman, Antony, *A Typology of Intellectual Property Management for Public Health Innovation and Access: Design Considerations for Policymakers*, 4 THE OPEN AIDS J. 1 (2010).

Torfing, Jacob, *Collaborative Innovation in the Public Sector, in* HANDBOOK OF INNOVATION IN THE PUBLIC SERVICES (2013).

UN, General Assembly Resolution 70/1, Transforming Our World: The 2030 Agenda for Sustainable Development (October 21, 2015), *available at* https://sustainabledevelopment.un.org/post2015/transformingourworld (last visited Nov. 19, 2017).

UN, MDG 8: Develop a Global Partnership for Development, UN DEP'T OF ECON. AND SOC. AFFAIRS, 2017, *available at* www.un.org/millenniumgoals/global.shtml (last visited Nov. 19, 2017).

UN, *Millennium Indicators*, UN, *available at* https://millenniumindicators.un.org/unsd/mi/pdf/mdglist.pdf (last visited Nov. 19, 2017).

UN, SDG 9: Build Resilient Infrastructure, Promote Inclusive and Sustainable Industrialization and Foster Innovation, UN (2017), *available at* https://sustainabledevelopment.un.org/sdg9 (last visited Nov. 19, 2017).

UN, SDG 16: Promote Peaceful and Inclusive Societies for Sustainable Development, Provide Access to Justice for all and Build Effective, Accountable and Inclusive Institutions at all Levels, UN (2017), *available at* https://sustainabledevelopment.un.org/sdg16 (last visited Nov. 19, 2017).

UN, SDG 17: Revitalize the global partnership for sustainable development (emphasis added), UN (2017), *available at* www.un.org/sustainabledevelopment/globalpartnerships/ (last visited Nov. 19, 2017).

UN, *SDG Indicators*, UN DEP'T OF ECON. AND SOC. AFF., *available at* https://unstats.un.org/sdgs/indicators/indicators-list/ (last visited Nov. 19, 2017).

UN, Sustainable Development Report 2017, *available at* https://unstats.un.org/sdgs/files/report/2017/TheSustainableDevelopmentGoalsReport2017.pdf (last visited Nov. 19, 2017).

UN World Commission on Environment and Development, OUR COMMON FUTURE (1987).

World Intellectual Property Organization [WIPO], *Report on the Independent Review of the Implementation of the Development Agenda Recommendations*, WIPO Doc. CDIP/18/7 (Aug. 15, 2016).

WIPO Committee on Development and Intellectual Property Reports, *available at* www.wipo.int/policy/en/cdip/ (last visited Nov. 19, 2017).

Young, Oran R., *Conceptualization: Goal-Setting as a Strategy for Earth System Governance*, in GOVERNING THROUGH GOALS: SUSTAINABLE DEVELOPMENT GOALS AS GOVERNANCE INNOVATION (Norichika Kanie and Frank Biermann eds., 2017).

Yu, Peter K., *Five Decades of Intellectual Property and Global Development*, 8 WIPO J. (2016), *available at* https://ssrn.com/abstract=2872682 (last visited Nov. 19, 2017).

Part I

Public Health

2 Public–Private Partnerships as Models for New Drug Research and Development: The Future as Now

Frederick M. Abbott

I Introduction and Background

The international community is searching for ways to improve the system under which new pharmaceutical treatments, vaccines, and diagnostics are discovered, developed, and distributed. The predominant model relying on patents and regulatory market exclusivity, combined with pricing power, is creating enormous public and private budgetary pressures, and at least arguably is misallocating research and development (R&D) resources. The monolithic vertically integrated pharmaceutical originator is largely a myth. The drug discovery, development, and distribution process has long involved a wide range of participatory arrangements, with basic discovery, follow-on research, translation, and manufacturing technology functions distributed across in-house and external actors. A main distinguishing characteristic of the pharma originator company is its profit-driven motivation, as compared with alternative models such as public–private partnerships (PPPs) and product development partnerships (PDPs) that are motivated in other ways. Each of these models already has a substantial public or nonprofit financing component.

The question explored in this contribution is whether and how PPPs and PDPs should become a more significant part of the global pharmaceutical development and distribution system. The chapter begins by describing the current model of pharmaceutical R&D, including the blurry boundary between public and private R&D. Following this is a section surveying some current PPP and/or PDP models of R&D, and analyzing the advantages and limitations of PPPs and/or PDPs. The next part connects the R&D activities of these partnerships to capital markets and investment incentives in the R&D of public goods. This part of the chapter discusses the potential role of PPPs and/or PDPs as part of a delinkage of R&D from production and distribution functions. The chapter concludes that further experimentation with PPPs and PDPs is warranted.

II The Current Model of Pharmaceutical R&D

The world biomedical industry is generating innovative medical treatments. Much of this progress is based on the general advance of science. New research tools improve the capability of scientists to identify the causes of disease. As our understanding of biotechnological processes improves, so does the ability of researchers to create new types of intervention.

A vast "originator" industry,[1] chemical and biological, serves to channel capital toward potentially profitable pharmaceutical innovations. Key decisions are made by or through investment bankers.[2] Potential breakthroughs in treatment rely on a capital markets based pharmaceutical R&D framework to drive science forward. This predominant capital markets approach to innovation has drawbacks. Three are noteworthy: (1) the demand of capital markets for high rates of return impels originator (and also generic) companies to maximize profits, including by charging the highest possible price for drugs;[3] (2) the substantial premium on marketing and selling treatments demanded because profits depend on sales; and (3) the absence of attention to diseases or conditions for which there is a limited capacity to pay, which attract less investment in innovation because of limited prospect for profits.[4]

The originator industry and its drive for profits has been a long-standing target for criticism from public health-oriented groups. Nonetheless, the major originator pharmaceutical companies (pharma or pharma companies) do more than pay substantial salaries to officers and directors, distribute dividends, and repurchase shares. They support a complex infrastructure of universities, teaching hospitals, doctors, and researchers through contract and acquisition of technologies. The wealth generated by the pharma companies supports a network that provides much of the scientific backbone supporting and ultimately discovering new products. And it is worth noting that the major pharma companies are mainly owned by individuals through retirement, pension, and insurance plans, even if sometimes indirectly.[5] Wealthy hedge fund managers may benefit from increased shareholder value, but they own only a minor portion of these companies. These characteristics are important to consider in assessing the benefits and costs of the dominant capital markets driven model of R&D, and this chapter will revisit them in connection with alternative R&D models.

A *PPPs and PDPs Defined*

The terminology "public–private partnership" (PPP) and "product development partnership" (PDP) encompasses an extensive range of potential configurations. Their relationship to the profit-driven model described in the previous section has not been explored thoroughly. PPP suggests an institutional arrangement involving public funding, which is

1 The term "originator" is customarily used to refer to the party that first obtains approval from the drug regulatory authority for the commercial marketing of a new drug.

2 *See, e.g.*, Staff of S. Comm. on Fin., 114th Cong., The Price of Sovaldi and its Impact on the U.S. Health Care System, 106–10 (Comm. Print 2015).

3 *See, generally*, Frederick M. Abbott, *Excessive Pharmaceutical Prices and Competition Law: Doctrinal Development to Protect Public Health*, 6 U.C. Irvine L. Rev. 281 (2016).

4 *See, e.g.*, World Health Organization [WHO] – Special Programme for Res. and Training on Tropical Diseases [TDR], Health product research and development fund: a proposal for financing and operation, at, e.g., vii, 1 (2016); Bernard Pecoul et al., *Drugs for Neglected Diseases initiative [DNDi]*, U.N. High-Level Panel On Access to Meds. (Feb. 27, 2016), www.unsgaccessmeds.org/inbox/2016/2/27/bernard-pecoul.

5 *See, e.g.*, Sam Ro, *Here's Who Owns the Stock Market*, Bus. Insider, Mar. 13, 2013, www.businessinsider.com/chart-stock-market-ownership-2013-3.

typically associated with governments. But most self-described PPPs in the biomedical area secure a significant portion of their funding from nongovernmental organizations, including foundations.[6] While the latter may be nonprofit and/or charitable organizations, they are neither public in the traditional sense of being responsible to an electorate or other political institution, nor are they private in the sense of profit-seeking enterprises.

PDP could refer to almost any R&D effort involving more than one entity (i.e., a partnership). There is nothing in the term that suggests governmental or NGO participation, as such. In the common parlance, the terms PPP and PDP tend to be used interchangeably, although an R&D enterprise involving two private pharma companies is unlikely to be referred to as a PPP but rather as simply a partnership involving collaborative R&D.

B *Public versus Private R&D*

A key issue in thinking about alternative mechanisms for innovation is whether government-owned and/or -operated R&D would be as successful – or better – in generating outcomes than the private sector. From an historical standpoint, evidence cuts both ways. Many important innovations have resulted from government-funded research programs and, likewise, many important innovations have been generated by individuals and enterprises working largely without government support.[7] Both government and private sector institutions have their advantages and disadvantages. Government organizations provide incentives in terms of legitimacy and status; private sector organizations provide incentives in terms of power and financial resources.[8] Performance in government and private sector institutions is typically benchmarked or assessed by different types of criteria. Both types of organization are capable of generating successful outcomes. Both types of organization are subject to institutional failure.

In this regard, combining public and private approaches to new drug R&D may have advantages and disadvantages depending upon the specific organizational arrangement, the target that is addressed, and ultimately the management of the enterprise. It seems doubtful that a particular organizational structure can be identified that would optimize the outcome in all cases.[9] Instead, perhaps, it is important to maintain open-mindedness about how particular R&D enterprises should be structured, and not rigidly insist on one institutional approach.

6 *See infra* text accompanying notes 15–27.

7 *See, e.g.*, Fred Block & Matthew R. Keller, *Where Do Innovations Come From? Transformations in the U.S. National Innovation System, 1970–2006*, The Info. Tech. & Innovation Found. [ITIF] (Jul. 9, 2008), www.itif.org/files/Where_do_innovations_come_from.pdf. For earlier references regarding the sources of innovation, see Frederick M. Abbott, *Protecting First World Assets in the Third World: Intellectual Property Negotiations in the GATT Multilateral Framework*, 22 Vand. J. Transnat'l L. 689, 697–700 (1989).

8 For a discussion of this framework perspective, see Harold Lasswell & Abraham Kaplan, Power and Society: A Framework for Political Inquiry (Yale University Press 1950; New Haven Press (as assignee)).

9 *Accord*, Block & Keller, supra note 7. *See also* Ashish Arora, Wesley M. Cohen, & John P. Walsh, *The Acquisition and Commercialization of Invention in American Manufacturing: Incidence and Impact*, 45 Res. Pol'y 1113 (2016), www.nber.org/papers/w20264.

C *The Blurry Boundary Between Public and Private R&D*

As a factual matter, virtually all (if not all) enterprises developing pharmaceutical products (including small molecule, biologic, vaccines, and diagnostics) involve a combination of public and private funding. The mix is a matter of degree. For example, the development of a new drug by a large originator company based in the United States (US) commonly involves early-stage research conducted or funded by the National Institutes of Health (NIH), and possibly the patenting of technology under the terms of the Bayh-Dole Act.[10] If not within the NIH itself, some part of the R&D effort will almost certainly have been conducted at a university or teaching hospital, each of which would almost certainly have been supported by some public/government funding. There may from time to time be an exception where a private entity develops a new drug product wholly on its own initiative without any direct government support. But even in such case, the R&D would generate tax credits or deductions against income, another form of government support, and private sector companies generally depend on government institutions to provide the overall legal framework in which they can and do function.

A government insulates the originator from competition by copyists through the grant of patents and marketing exclusivity; it also provides considerable regulatory infrastructure support through the activities of the drug regulatory authorities, customs authorities, and so on. Originator companies raise funds through securities markets that are also supported in various ways by government insurance and regulation.

Incentives are often characterized as "push" or "pull." The former refers to subsidization or grant funding that pays for R&D up front, and the latter refers to advance offtake or procurement agreements that guarantee a return on the successful completion of R&D. When referring to nontraditional R&D models such as PPPs and PDPs, the practice of negotiating advance commitments is not uncommon as a means of providing security to up-front funding entities (i.e., a combination of push and pull).[11] As a practical matter, most R&D efforts undertaken by originator pharma companies also rely on publicly-funded offtake agreements as pull incentives.[12] For example, in the United States, the Veterans Administration, Medicare, and Medicaid programs provide a stable source of procurement or offtake for new drugs developed by the originator industry.[13] In fiscal

[10] *See, e.g.*, Frederick M. Abbott & Graham Dukes, Global Pharmaceutical Policy 16–85 (2009).

[11] For definitions, see Report of the United Nations Secretary General's High Level Panel on Access to Medicines 29 (2016).

[12] If a new drug has been approved by the FDA, it may be subject to some comparative efficacy assessment by governmental procurement authorities. In most cases a new drug will be added to one or more formularies, federal or state.

[13] According to Avelere Health, *Federal Spending on Brand Pharmaceuticals* (2015):

> "Health Federal Spending on Outpatient Prescription Drugs for Medicare and Medicaid in 2014
> Based on data from the Medicare Trustees Report, the National Health Expenditures (NHE) Accounts, the Centers for Medicare & Medicaid Services (CMS), and other sources, the federal government spent an estimated $127 billion on outpatient prescription drugs covered by Medicare, Medicaid, VA, and TRICARE in calendar year 2014:
>
> - Medicaid: $15 billion
> - Medicare Part D: $81 billion
> - Medicare Part B: $22 billion
> - VA: $3 billion
> - TRICARE: $5 billion" (at pg. 5)

year 2016, prescription drug spending in the United States amounted to $328.6 billion,[14] and at least half of that can be accounted for by government spending (federal and state combined).[15] Even in the traditional sense of originator new drug development, there is a major pull incentive in the form of budgeted government procurement expenditure.

The border or boundary line between private and public drug development is blurry and ever-shifting. It is different depending on the country where activities are taking place. Categorical distinction between public and private pharmaceutical development is mainly a fiction.

III Current PPP and/or PDP Models of R&D

As noted previously, virtually all new drug development can be characterized as involving a combination of public and private funding. One potential distinction between predominantly private sector enterprises and the institutions typically referred to as PPPs and PDPs is that the latter typically provide their products to procurement authorities at low prices, and are typically nonprofit. A nonprofit organizational character might well be the defining characteristic of a PPP or PDP. While most, if not all, originator pharma companies make some portion of their products available at low prices, or donate them at no cost, these activities are not a defining characteristic.

Major archetypes of existing PPPs/PDPs include (but are not limited to) Drugs for Neglected Diseases Initiative (DNDi), Global Health Innovative Technology Fund (GHIT), Medicines for Malaria Venture (MMV), GAVI Alliance, and Foundation for Innovative New Diagnostics (FIND). Each of these organizations includes governmental and nongovernmental funding sources, works in cooperation with private sector companies, and makes its products available on a low-cost/nonprofit basis. A new entry into the PPP environment is the Combating Antibiotic Resistant Bacteria Biopharmaceutical Accelerator, or CARB-X. Each of these examples is discussed briefly here.

A *DNDi*

DNDi (or Drugs for Neglected Diseases Initiative) was created in the early 2000s at the initiative of initiative of Médecins Sans Frontières (MSF or Doctors without Borders) to address a pronounced lack in funding for R&D efforts to address so-called neglected

See, e.g., U.S. Dep't of Veterans Affairs, *Doing Business with VA* (2015) (showing Veterans Administration expenditures on drugs, pharmaceuticals, and hematology in fiscal year 2014 (including through related programs), totaling $8.261 billion).

14 Cents. for Medicare and Medicaid Servs., *National Health Expenditure Data* (2016), available at: https://www.cms.gov/Research-Statistics-Data-and-Systems/Statistics-Trends-and-Reports/NationalHealthExpendData/NHE-Fact-Sheet.html (last visited June 12, 2018). Dollar ($) amounts mentioned in this chapter refer to U.S. dollars.

15 As states are major procurers of pharmaceutical products as well, combined federal and state expenditures certainly exceed one half of total pharmaceutical expenditures. *See Pharmaceuticals: Facts, Policies, and NCSL Resources*, National Conference of State Legislatures [NCLS] (Jul. 2, 2017), www.ncsl.org/research/health/pharmaceuticals-facts-policies-and-ncsl-resources.aspx. Total pharmaceutical expenditures exceeded $370 billion. *See* Richard Gauchi, PowerPoint presentation, Prescription Drugs: Overview and Update (Nov. 2, 2015).

diseases.[16] It is by now generally accepted that the predominant exclusivity based model for aggregating investment for R&D on new drugs fails to address diseases affecting patient populations with limited financial resources, because of the absence of sufficient financial demand. At the time DNDi was formed, its approach was pathbreaking.

DNDi relies on contributions from governments and foundations to finance its R&D efforts. It has been among the most successful of PPPs in its fund-raising efforts, and it has been notably successful in developing new therapies, including improved formulations, and recently new chemical entities. DNDi has successfully partnered with originator companies in making use of proprietary compound libraries, as well as in making use of high-throughput screening equipment. DNDi is able to enter into such favorable arrangements because it has not been in competition with the originators for lucrative markets.

DNDi is expanding its mandate to address neglected patients as well as neglected diseases.[17] For example, DNDi has recently entered into agreements under which it is working toward making available a very low cost alternative to the Hepatitis C treatments offered by the major originators; in particular, it has been working with an Egyptian generic company that is using a nonpatented compound similar to sofosbuvir. Although it remains to be seen, the alternative under development by DNDi and its partners would be an effective low-cost Hep-C treatment substitute that can be used in high income countries, assuming (and this is a major question) that governmental authorities (including judges) in the high income countries are willing to accept the nonpatented or noninfringing status of the drugs.

B *GHIT*

GHIT (or Global Health Innovative Technology Fund) is organized in a manner similar to DNDi.[18] Its main funding source is the government of Japan, and its private sector working partners are principally Japan-based originator companies. GHIT funding partners also include major foundations, and it works with UNDP on its access programs.

GHIT has targeted several diseases prevalent among low-income populations in sub-Saharan Africa, and is engaged in clinical trials of several of its drug candidates.[19] GHITs access policy indicates that it will make treatments available to low-income populations on a nonprofit basis.[20] GHIT and DNDi are partnering on certain projects, including

[16] *See* DNDi, www.dndi.org (last visited Jul. 14, 2017). DNDi is an acronym for "Drugs for Neglected Diseases initiative." *E.g.*, DNDi, From Neglected Diseases to Neglected Patients and Populations (2015), www.dndi.org/wp-content/uploads/2016/08/DNDi_AR_2015.pdf.

[17] The reference to patients is an acknowledgment that when new treatments are developed they may not be accessible even for patients in higher income countries. Making available lower-priced versions of existing drug treatments is now part of DNDi's mission.

[18] *See* Global Health Innovative Tech. Fund [GHIT], www.ghitfund.org.

[19] *See, e.g.*, Access and Delivery P'ship [ADP], Issue Brief: An Integrated Approach to the Discovery, Development and Delivery of New Health Technologies for Malaria, Tuberculosis, and Neglected Tropical Diseases: Tanzania (2016), http://adphealth.org/upload/resource/Issue_brief_case_study_of_Tanzania.pdf.

[20] GHIT Access Pol'y, www.ghitfund.org/afag/policies.

GHIT funding of DNDi/pharma projects to identify novel drug targets and to screen for potential treatments for leishmaniasis and Chagas disease.[21]

C *MMV*

MMV (or the Medicines for Malaria Venture) refers to itself as a PDP, although like DNDi and GHIT it is funded through a combination of governmental, foundation, and other philanthropic sources (including private sector companies), with a more specific focus on development of antimalarials.[22] In terms of access, MMV indicates that its objective is to assure that new medicines will be made available at an affordable price, typically with no profit and no loss, through public sector channels. It seeks to retain intellectual property rights to drugs developed through its funding, and a royalty-free license for use in its malaria programs in low resource countries.[23]

D *GAVI*

GAVI Alliance (formerly Global Alliance for Vaccines and Immunizations) is a PPP with the principal mission of providing access to low-cost vaccines to children in developing countries.[24] Principal seed funding for GAVI came from the Bill and Melinda Gates Foundation, and its main partners are the World Health Organization (WHO), UNICEF, and the World Bank. GAVI's business model involves pooling developing country demand for vaccines and establishing advanced market commitments to purchase,[25] thereby providing secure funding for vaccine producers.[26]

E *FIND*

FIND (or the Foundation for Innovative New Diagnostics) was founded to promote the development of diagnostic tests for poverty-related diseases, including tuberculosis, malaria, sleeping sickness, HIV, and Chagas disease. Using funding from foundations, governments, UNITAID, and working in cooperation with private sector companies, WHO TDR, and others, FIND has successfully developed low-cost diagnostics adapted to local conditions.

FIND negotiates preferential pricing arrangements from diagnostic suppliers for the public sector in low and middle income countries, and health providers must commit to

[21] *See, e.g.*, Press Release, DNDi, GHIT Fund Reinforces Its Support to DNDi Leishmaniasis and Chagas Disease Projects (Mar. 30, 2017), www.dndi.org/2017/media-centre/news-views-stories/news/ghit-reinforces-support-to-dndi-for-leish-and-chagas/.

[22] *See* Meds. for Malaria Venture [MMV], www.mmv.org/.

[23] *Socially Responsible Agreements*, MMV, www.mmv.org/partnering/socially-responsible-agreements, (last visited Nov, 5, 2016).

[24] *See* www.gavi.org (last visited Jul.16, 2017).

[25] *See, e.g.*, AMC Secretariat of Gavi, *Advance Market Commitment for Pneumococcal Vaccines Annual Report 1 January–31 December 2015*. Principal suppliers under this advance market commitment regime for pneumococcal vaccines in 2015 were GSK and Pfizer. *See Pneumococcal* AMC, Gavi www.gavi.org/funding/pneumococcal-amc/.

[26] A PPP primarily designed to secure affordable treatments developed by third parties is sometimes referred to as a product access PPP, to be contrasted with the PDPs such as DNDi, GHIT, and MMV.

low-margin markups.[27] With respect to intellectual property, industry partners must assign FIND a royalty-free license to use the technology in public and nonprofit sectors in high endemic countries; the industry partners retain rights for high income countries and in the private sector in developing countries.[28]

F *CARB-X*

A recent entry into the PPP sphere is Combating Antibiotic Resistant Bacteria Biopharmaceutical Accelerator, or CARB-X, which is housed at Boston University School of Law, and brings together the US Department of Health and Human Services (HHS), through its Biomedical Advanced Research and Development Authority, or BARDA, division, as well as the NIH NIAID, the UK Wellcome Trust, and the AMR Centre, (a new UK-based funder of biomedical research and accelerator). CARB-X will initially engage two R&D accelerators, Massachusetts Biotechnology Council in Cambridge, Mass., and the California Life Sciences Institute of South San Francisco.[29] CARB-X has commitments for over $40 million in funding for its first year of operation, and up to $350 million over a five-year period.

At this early stage, the licensing and access policies of CARB-X are being worked out.[30] Potential models include Wellcome Trust policies for antibiotics. The leadership of CARB-X also takes note of the Davos Declaration and accompanying Industry Roadmap for Progress on Combating Antimicrobial Resistance signed by thirteen pharma companies and that includes supporting affordable access.[31]

IV Advantages and Limitations of PPPs and PDPs

A *Current Limitations on Scope*

A defining characteristic – if not "the" defining characteristic – of each of the PPPs described earlier is that each was formed, and each operates, to address a situation of market failure. The R&D funding directed to these organizations in most cases comes from government or foundation sources that are addressing problems largely unrelated to domestic public health system needs of industrialized states, with the exception of the newly forming CARB-X. In this regard, the PPPs are addressing public health needs that are largely confined to low- and low-middle-income countries, although it is important to note that DNDi has recently shifted its focus toward neglected populations as well as neglected diseases so as to signal broader concern for low-income populations throughout the world.

[27] *Negotiated Product Pricing*, FIND, www.finddx.org/pricing/.
[28] *Business Model*, FIND, www.finddx.org/business-model/.
[29] *See* www.carb-x.org/ (last visited Jul. 16, 2017).
[30] Email from Kevin Outterson, Executive Director, CARB-X, to author (Oct. 31, 2016) (on file with author).
[31] *See* Rev. on Antimicrobial Resistance [AMR], Declaration by the Pharmaceutical, Biotechnology and Diagnostics Industries on Combating Antimicrobial Resistance (Jan. 2016), https://amr-review.org/sites/default/files/Industry_Declaration_on_Combating_Antimicrobial_Resistance_UPDATED%20SIGNATORIES_MAY_2016.pdf (last visited Jul. 16, 2017); *see also*, Int'l Fed'n of Pharm. Mfrs. & Ass'n [IFPMA], Industry Roadmap for Progress on Combating Antimicrobial Resistance – September 2016, www.ifpma.org/wp-content/uploads/2016/09/Roadmap-for-Progress-on-AMR-FINAL.pdf (last visited Jul 16, 2017).

None of the aforementioned PPPs assert as its mission a transformation of the global model for developing new drugs across the range of diseases, or for promoting access to them. And none of them involve self-sustaining revenue generation models.

B *Extending the Scope of PPPs as Alternative R&D Models*

With that said, however, DNDi may help to illustrate that it is possible to build a new drug development model that eliminates the for-profit intermediary financier from the process. In other words, DNDi serves as the nonprofit intermediary hub, performing the function that a major originator company typically performs, that is: (1) identifying disease targets; (2) engaging third parties to perform identification of promising compound candidates; (3) selecting candidates for clinical trials; and (4) managing the process of registration, and introduction of the product onto the market. DNDi has indicated that its costs of developing new drugs are substantially lower than those that are publicly suggested by the major originator companies (in the order of $150 million as compared with well over $1.5 billion).[32]

Nonetheless, DNDi has to date addressed only a small portion of the potential set of disease candidates that challenge global public health, and it has had the advantage of access to compound libraries already created by originator companies. At an expanded scale, could the DNDi type of "hub" operation work with the much larger capital requirements and expenditures, such as those involved in the development of new biologic drugs, and where the risks of failure are large? Is a nonprofit entity capable of administering large-scale funding in a manner that does not entail inefficiency and waste, or corruption?

These are not insignificant or merely speculative issues. While the profit motive may induce certain types of bad behavior, other motivations for bad behavior with respect to government/public and/or nonprofit administration may be equally problematic. The private sector is brutal at punishing unsuccessful actors. It may be more difficult to discipline entrenched nonprofit or public authorities.

C *Discipline and Incentive in R&D Models*

Introducing some type of performance-disciplining measures into a nonprofit hub model could guard against inefficiency, waste, and corruption, or more prosaically against poor decision-making. The management team of a PPP would need to be assessed against some criteria, and the system would need to be highly transparent. In some respects, PPP management would be in a position not entirely dissimilar from the officers of for-profit originator companies, but without the very high salaries and stock-option allocations. A major difference, however, would be that the performance indicator would not be profit; instead, it would be success in regard to addressing public health requirements.[33]

[32] For details regarding wide variations in estimates of funds needed to develop new drugs, *see* Abbott, *supra* note 3.

[33] The directors and officers of for-profit corporations have fiduciary duties to the corporation and its shareholders, and the directors and officers of nonprofit organizations have fiduciary duties to the organization. The text reference to the profit motive for the typical for-profit pharmaceutical enterprise is not directed to the legal standard under which organizational responsibility may be determined, but rather the internal and external assessment by which the success of a corporation and its ability to attract investment is evaluated by the financial community.

One could argue that the existing originator model assesses corporate officers and directors in relation to success in addressing public health requirements, with profit serving as a proxy. If a company does not develop successful new drugs, it does not profit. Therefore, the standard Wall Street model does what the nonprofit hub model would seek to do. The problem with this analogy is that things done in the pursuit of profit are not the same things that should be done in the pursuit of public health. For example, a public health approach would not encourage dispensing of drugs like antipsychotics or attention deficit disorder controllers to senior citizens or young patients for the sake of increasing sales. This type of excessive marketing and promotion is a common occurrence within the for-profit pharmaceutical sector, for which companies are only from time to time penalized.

What type of incentive/discipline structure would be appropriate to a PPP hub? The following guidelines are proposed as a starting point:

1. Salaries for senior officers/staff would need to be commensurate with high-paying university positions that are generally sufficient to attract talented scientists and managers.
2. Management would be required to lay out a business plan with defined targets, and such plan would be reviewed by an appropriate supervisory board, and perhaps a team of external expert reviewers. Management performance would then be assessed against success in achieving the goals laid out in the business plan. To the extent feasible, the plan would include objective indicators in the interest of reducing subjective judgment and bias on the part of all concerned.[34]
3. Financial dealings would be transparent and audited. Because the objective of the enterprise would be the advancement of science, the default position with respect to information concerning R&D would be transparency. This means that competing PPPs might make use of published information, which could theoretically lead to multiple efforts directed toward the same disease target. This risk, however, should be one that is shared among the various PPP hubs. If the possibility for patenting and market exclusivity claims on PPP innovation by originator for-profit entities exists, this might cause a reassessment of transparency policies, and might require defensive patenting of discoveries.

D *The Riddle of Capital Aggregation*

1 Financial Nature of Distinguishing Characteristics

At the outset of this chapter, it was noted that all or virtually all new drug R&D involves a combination of public and private funding. It has long been the case that major originator pharma companies essentially act as clearinghouses for third-party research, providing the function of analyzing and assessing external work, and making decisions regarding where to invest in clinical trials and subsequent approval processes. When you combine government R&D funding (as in the case of the US NIH) with the R&D clearinghouse function of the major originator company, the main distinctions between

[34] For example, the DNDi Business Plan 2015–2023 sets out a number of objective targets in terms of treatments and new chemical entities to be developed, and these objectives could be used as indicators against which the performance of the management team could be assessed. DNDi, DNDi Business Plan 2015–2023 (2015), www.dndi.org/wp-content/uploads/2009/03/DNDi_Business_Plan_2015-2023.pdf.

the for-profit R&D enterprise with the archetypal PPP like DNDi are financial in nature, specifically: (1) the source of external capital, which is raised through public securities markets (like the New York Stock Exchange); and (2) the for-profit firm's revenues, which are generated on behalf of private securities holders rather than some public fund.

To make matters a bit more confusing, as stated earlier, a large proportion of stock in the United States is owned by pension funds and retirement accounts, so that effectively the profits are returned to a fairly broad segment of the public.[35] In this regard, the originator pharma companies based in the United States (and analogously in Europe) could be viewed as the custodian of the assets of individuals living within the United States, who are investing those assets toward R&D. Other than the officers of the originator companies who may be taking a larger share of the revenues than appears socially responsible, one can argue that high pharmaceutical prices reflect that proportion of US individuals owning stock paying themselves. Those outside the United States who are adversely affected by high prices are those who do not own such assets.

E *Money in the System*

There are a substantial number of variations on proposals for aggregating R&D capital outside the current predominant model based on patents and regulatory exclusivity. Any alternative to the current model will require some means to aggregate capital, make determinations regarding where to invest that capital from the R&D standpoint, select among promising drug candidates regarding whether to move forward (including whether to initiate clinical trials), and initiating and supervising the registration and approval process before the relevant national drug authority. All of these today are functions that are largely performed by private sector originator pharma companies.

Probably the most compelling argument supporting alternative mechanisms for aggregating capital is the enormous amount of money in the current global pharmaceutical system that manifests annual sales revenues substantially greater than $1 trillion.[36] Using generous estimates, only about $150 billion of that revenue finds its way into private and public R&D efforts.[37] Of course there are costs attributable to producers and distributors of drugs over and above the R&D component, but even a generous accounting for costs probably gets to about $500 billion. The other 50 percent of sales revenue goes somewhere else. The challenge is to find a way to channel procurement demand into R&D

[35] According to Goldman Sachs: "Households directly own 38 percent of the US equity market," … "However, the total effective household ownership is closer to 80 percent when combined with indirect ownership in the form of mutual funds (20 percent), pension funds (16 percent), and insurance policy holdings (7 percent)." Sam Ro, *CHART OF THE DAY: Here's Who Owns the Stock Market*, Bus. Insider, March 13, 2013, www.businessinsider.com/chart-stock-market-ownership-2013-3 (last visited June 12, 2018).

[36] *See, e.g.*, IMS Inst., *The Global Use of Medicines: Outlook through 2016* (2016), www.imshealth.com/files/web/IMSH%20Institute/Reports/The%20Global%20Use%20of%20Medicines%20Outlook%20Through%202016/Medicines_Outlook_Through_2016_Report.pdf (last visited Jul. 16, 2017).

[37] US PhRMA estimates that its members spent $51.2 billion on R&D in 2014. Pharm. Res. and Mfrs. Of Am. [PhRMA], *2015 Profile Biopharmaceutical Research Industry* (2015), www.phrma.org/sites/default/files/pdf/2015_phrma_profile.pdf. Added to that would be approximately $30 billion in research funding from the US NIH. Rest of world pharmaceutical R&D is typically less than US private sector spending. *See* Org. for Econ. Cooperation and Dev.[OECD], *Research and Development in the Pharmaceutical Sector* (2015), www.oecd-ilibrary.org/docserver/download/8115071ec070.pdf?expires=1478360602&id=id&accname=guest&checksum=9DC067062F87B1CE6B0D0F72453F580F. Given that the industry figures are largely self-reported, $150 billion should be considered a generous estimate.

pools that are well managed and could substitute for originator companies that appear to charge a very large premium for their services.

F *Delinkage as a Key Concept*

Delinkage involves separating the R&D function from the production, sale, and distribution functions.[38] Under this model, the production, sale, and distribution of pharmaceuticals would be treated as competitive business unencumbered by market exclusivity. Delinkage is the situation largely present in the existing generic pharmaceutical industry. Generic pharma producers still must comply with a host of regulatory requirements, including compliance with GMP, registration, and so forth. Delinkage, therefore, does not presume unregulated pharmaceuticals markets.

Delinkage is designed mainly to protect the procurement authority and consumer from high pharmaceutical prices. The predominant model for R&D relies on patents and market exclusivity to generate high rates of return for originator companies that use some portion of profits to invest and reinvest in new drug development and other improvements.[39] The essential objective of delinkage is to isolate R&D costs, and pay for them *other than* through sales and distribution revenues. It does not necessarily follow that R&D costs will decline. It is generally assumed, however, that by removing the distortions in the current system stemming from the need to generate large profits, there will be systemic savings. It remains that capital for investment in R&D must come from somewhere, if it is not coming from high-margin pharmaceutical sales.

G *Government Taxing and Spending as a Source of Funding*

The government secures its financial resources from the collection of taxes, and taxes come from the same individuals and businesses that purchase pharmaceutical products. So, the government could establish a fund for pharmaceutical R&D, which is allocated to PPP hubs that are responsible for developing new drugs, taking them through the clinical trial phase, and making them available to generic producers. With regard to production, there may need to be limits on pricing even without market exclusivity if it appears that excessive prices are charged. In this model, margins should be low.

Using the United States as an illustration, the NIH already allocates a very large pool of R&D funds to pharmaceutical research, and has established methodologies for selecting R&D projects. It is not a stretch to suggest that these R&D projects move forward some

[38] *See, e.g.*, Michelle Childs, Director Policy Advocacy, Medicines Sans Frontieres [MSF], *The de-linkage of the cost of research and development and the price of health products*, Powerpoint presented at meeting of WHO Committee of Experts Working Group: Financing and Coordination (Nov. 16–19, 2011).

[39] As noted earlier, the system has its flaws, not the least of which is that much of the profit is used for purposes other than investment in R&D and production, including sometimes excessive executive salaries, buybacks of stock unsupported by sound business justification, and other means of allocating revenues that do not serve public health purposes. The poster child for excessive pharmaceutical salaries is the former CEO of Pfizer, Hank McKinnel, who walked away with approximately $180 million in compensation after leading the company through a string of R&D failures. *See* The Associated Press, *Pfizer's Ex-Chief to Get Full Retirement Package*, N.Y. Times, Dec. 22, 2006, at C2. Flaws include reliance on generation of high-margin sales to sustain the model. Sales promotion may perversely encourage overprescribing. *See* Abbott & Dukes, *supra* note 10, at 163–92.

additional steps, such as into the development of production process technologies, involved in the translation of basic discoveries into commercially marketable new drugs. Those additional steps could be undertaken through the PPP hub entities that would essentially be subcontractors to NIH.

Potential drawbacks are also foreseeable. While governments can be staffed with teams of experts, peer review, and so on, there remains the question whether bureaucracies are good at allocating capital. It is not clear that government bureaucracies are better institutions to pursue these tasks than private industry. Nonetheless, a system that relies on an NIH-type institution to identify targets of R&D and allocate government resources is an alternative to the existing model.

A model that moves from private sector funding through aggregation of risk capital to a public sector funding model that relies on funds from the government budget (taken from taxation) would presumably entail impact on the general economy of a country. Conceptually, employment might remain more or less stable, but whether inflows into the taxation pool would remain sufficient is a question. If indeed originator pharma companies pay fairly low taxes, this may undercut an argument in favor of maintaining the existing private sector model.[40] While employees of pharma companies presumably pay income taxes, these employees would similarly pay taxes if funded by the government budget.

Consider, for example, that a substantial part of the US government healthcare budget (state and federal) is devoted to the purchase of originator pharmaceuticals. If procurement outlays were cut substantially, federal and state tax requirements would correspondingly be lower. This shift in expenditure should not adversely affect existing nonprofit R&D entities that would continue to be relied upon for innovative endeavors even if their operating models might be more mainstream in a delinkage environment.

H *Insurance Pools*

An alternative to government funding is privately managed insurance pools.[41] Health insurers already aggregate the funding to address the demand for pharmaceutical products their patients require. Health insurers would have a vested interest in reducing incidence of disease since this would result in reduced outlays. Since the insurance companies already aggregate funds, conceptually these funds could be allocated to *ex ante* R&D as well as to *ex post* procurement. If R&D costs could be substantially reduced through some type of low-margin R&D hub facility, *ex post* expenditures could be substantially reduced. No doubt, this complex concept needs to be worked out in its details. Nonetheless, as private health insurers are the second largest funder of pharmaceutical procurement behind the federal and state governments, the pools of funds

[40] It appears, for example that Pfizer has paid almost no income taxes within the United States over the past several years, leaving most of its profits offshore. *10 Corporate Tax Dodgers You Should Know About*, Moyers & Company (May 29, 2014), http://billmoyers.com/2014/05/29/10-companies-that-dodge-corporate-taxes/; Chad Stone, *Reality Check on Corporate Income Tax Rates*, U.S. News, Nov. 13, 2015, www.usnews.com/opinion/economic-intelligence/2015/11/13/reality-check-on-corporate-income-tax-rates.

[41] For a proposal involving intergovernmental risk pools, see Jeffrey Mark Erfe, *Reducing Outbreaks: Using International Governmental Risk Pools to Fund Research and Development of Infectious Disease Medicines and Vaccines*, 87 Yale J. Biol. Med. 473, 473–479, (2014) www.ncbi.nlm.nih.gov/pmc/articles/PMC4257034/.

aggregated by these insurers are a logical possibility for repurposing. One foreseeable difficulty with such an idea is that insurers might elect to free-ride on each other's investments, so a mechanism would need to be organized to spread outlays through a major collective pool.

I *The WHO Consultative Expert Working Group (CEWG) R&D Treaty Proposal*

It should be evident that the idea of the PPP hub as implementing mechanism for R&D may be the type of arrangement contemplated by proposals at the WHO for an R&D Treaty.[42] The general aim of the R&D Treaty is to combine an interest in new models for R&D with some type of mechanism that ensures a base level of governmental funding, while at the same time guarding against the potential free-rider problem. More specifically, would taxpayers in the United States be willing to engage in nonprofit tax-payer based funding of R&D projects if the resulting new drugs were made freely available to a global population, including other countries and regions that are capable of investing their own resources in R&D?

J *Are Free Riders a Real Problem?*

It is not clear that the free-rider problem is the impediment it might be made out to be. The current global framework for biomedical R&D relies very substantially on investments undertaken in the United States, and to a somewhat lesser extent Europe and Japan. The balance of investment and purchasing power may be shifting, with China playing a growing role, and India presumably not far behind. Would these countries give up their scientific pursuits of new drugs because drugs might be available based on the efforts of US researchers? If there was a serious free-rider problem, could the United States take some type of trade-balancing action, such as the collection of R&D offset tariffs, to address the problem? Such an action might break the existing WTO mold, but the WTO mold is there to be broken as the circumstances may justify. It seems unlikely that the advanced negotiation of an R&D Treaty is a necessary prerequisite to a move toward different models in the United States.

K *Treatment of Disease and Lifestyle Drugs*

Although the system described earlier might result in substantially lower pharmaceutical prices for new discoveries of drugs to treat important diseases, this would nonetheless leave the market for nonessential drugs like beauty-enhancers, sometimes referred to as lifestyle drugs. The market for cosmetic medicines and other lifestyle drugs is a very large one, and it should not be dismissed as some kind of dysfunctional anomaly. Could a parallel system that addresses the development of new types of Botox work alongside an expanded PPP hub model?

[42] *See*, for description of proposals, Ryan Abbott, Opinion, *Inside Views: Potential Elements Of The WHO Global R&D Treaty: Tailoring Solutions For Disparate Contexts*, Intellectual Property Watch (Jan. 29, 2013), www.ip-watch.org/2013/01/29/potential-elements-of-the-who-global-rd-treaty-tailoring-solutions-for-disparate-contexts/

It is foreseeable that new drug development could move along different tracks depending upon the subject matter field of R&D. It is, however, important to note that the cost savings that might be generated by moving toward a PPP hub model for therapies to treat disease could be affected by a parallel system addressing lifestyle concerns if both systems were integrated in some type of pooled insurance arrangement. If lifestyle drugs are made available through a combined pool, and prices and demand are high, the result could be a similar one for end users of disease therapies if their insurance costs reflect pool demand.

V Conclusions: Innovation and Access

Forms of capital aggregation, institutional structure, and decision-making are fluid. A good argument can be made on behalf of each public and private sector R&D, or some combination of the two. At the end of the day, the fundamental question from the R&D side is whether progress will be made in preventing and treating disease, and at what cost. From the human rights and social impacts side, the question is whether the preventatives and treatments will be made available to those who need them. Ultimately, whether treatments will be made available depends upon the access policy. Unless we know what the access situation is going to be, which could be referred to as the downstream impact, it is difficult to make decisions regarding the optimal upstream model. If funds are not going to be available to purchase and distribute treatments, it is not particularly helpful to develop them. And, without knowing whether those funds will be available, it is difficult to make decisions regarding the amount of capital that should be aggregated and invested. The systemic issues are essentially circular.

By defining the patient access situation in advance, the public or private investor can better determine whether investment should be undertaken. There should be a largely predictable outcome in terms of sales and/or procurement costs. The distortion in the current system or model is that private investors can exploit vulnerable patient populations once treatments are developed. Though private investors assert that price controls are anathema because they limit the profitability of investment, and therefore the amount of risk that investors are willing to take, determining the size of the market and setting the price in advance would allow private investors to scale their investments to realistic market outcomes. If there is a lack of investment based on inadequate potential market, public funding in the form of subsidies or advance market commitment can step in to supplement with additional funding.[43]

Delinkage is likely to play a significant role in alternative models used for funding new drug R&D. It envisages generic competition in the downstream market for pharmaceuticals with concomitant low prices. Price regulation can possibly serve a function similar to that of delinkage. In other words, forms of market exclusivity can be used so long as

[43] It is an interesting to consider whether a governmental authority, such as the US Department of Health and Human Services, or the Centers for Disease Control, could calculate potential disease market baskets and maximum procurement costs, and limit medicines providers to that aggregate basket, including a set per treatment price. Advance commitments could be established with bids from the private sector, factoring in R&D costs. If sufficient interest is not shown in the bidding, government could step in to supplement the price.

there is an alternative mechanism for assuring that prices are affordable enough to promote optimal accessibility.

There are many potential alternatives to the predominant model under which new drugs are developed primarily by using patents and marketing exclusivity as means to aggregate capital through the promise of high prices. Leaders of the originator pharmaceutical industry not uncommonly express the idea that if the system is not broken, why fix it?[44] They point to the risk that attempts to modify the existing system will result in a shortfall of funds invested in R&D.

However, a mix of public and private funding of new drug R&D is an existing reality. The real issue is whether shifting control to models that reduce profit motivation and include more publicly oriented management would lead to better outcomes. Experimentation is warranted. Existing PPPs and PDPs are demonstrating that alternative models are workable in some contexts. The main question is whether and how their success can be scaled.

References

10 Corporate Tax Dodgers You Should Know About, MOYERS & COMPANY (May 29, 2014), http://billmoyers.com/2014/05/29/10-companies-that-dodge-corporate-taxes/ (last visited Nov. 17, 2017).

Abbott, Frederick M. and Graham Dukes, GLOBAL PHARMACEUTICAL POLICY 16–85 (Edward Elgar 2009).

Abbott, Frederick M., *Excessive Pharmaceutical Prices and Competition Law: Doctrinal Development to Protect Public Health*, 6 U.C. IRVINE L. REV. 281 (2016).

Abbott, Frederick M., *Protecting First World Assets in the Third World: Intellectual Property Negotiations in the GATT Multilateral Framework*, 22 VAND. J. TRANSNAT'L L. 689, 697–700 (1989).

Abbott, Ryan, Opinion, *Inside Views: Potential Elements of the WHO Global R&D Treaty: Tailoring Solutions for Disparate Contexts*, INTELLECTUAL PROPERTY WATCH (Jan. 29, 2013), www.ip-watch.org/2013/01/29/potential-elements-of-the-who-global-rd-treaty-tailoring-solutions-for-disparate-contexts/ (last visited Nov. 17, 2017).

ACCESS AND DELIVERY PARTNERSHIP [ADP], Issue Brief: An Integrated Approach to the Discovery, Development and Delivery of New Health Technologies for Malaria, Tuberculosis, and Neglected Tropical Diseases: Tanzania (2016), http://adphealth.org/upload/resource/Issue_brief_case_study_of_Tanzania.pdf (last visited Nov. 17, 2017).

AMC Secretariat of Gavi, *Advance Market Commitment for Pneumococcal Vaccines Annual Report 1 January–31 December 2015*.

Arora, Ashish, Wesley M. Cohen, and John P. Walsh, *The Acquisition and Commercialization of Invention in American Manufacturing: Incidence and Impact*, 45 RES. POL'Y 1113 (2016), www.nber.org/papers/w20264 (last visited Nov. 17, 2017).

Associated Press, *Pfizer's Ex-Chief to Get Full Retirement Package*, N.Y. TIMES, Dec. 22, 2006, at C2.

Block, Fred and Matthew R. Keller, *Where Do Innovations Come From? Transformations in the U.S. National Innovation System, 1970–2006*, The Info. Tech. & Innovation Found. [ITIF] (Jul. 9, 2008), www.itif.org/files/Where_do_innovations_come_from.pdf.

[44] *See* separate contribution of Andrew Witty, then president of GSK, to the Report of Secretary General's High Level Panel on Access to Medicines, *supra* note 11.

Carb-X, www.carb-x.org/ (last visited Jul. 16, 2017).
CENTS. FOR MEDICARE AND MEDICAID SERVS., *National Health Expenditure Data* (2016), https://www.cms.gov/Research-Statistics-Data-and-Systems/Statistics-Trends-and-Reports/National HealthExpendData/NHE-Fact-Sheet.html (last visited June 12, 2018).
Childs, Michelle, Director Policy Advocacy, Medicines Sans Frontieres [MSF], *The de-linkage of the cost of research and development and the price of health products*, Powerpoint presented at meeting of WHO Committee of Experts Working Group: Financing and Coordination (Nov. 16–19, 2011).
DNDi, DNDi BUSINESS PLAN 2015–2023 (2015), www.dndi.org/wp-content/uploads/2009/03/DNDi_Business_Plan_2015-2023.pdf (last visited Nov. 17, 2017).
DNDi, FROM NEGLECTED DISEASES TO NEGLECTED PATIENTS AND POPULATIONS (2015), www.dndi.org/wp-content/uploads/2016/08/DNDi_AR_2015.pdf (last visited Nov. 17, 2017).
Email from Kevin Outterson, Executive Director, CARB-X, to author (Oct. 31, 2016) (on file with author).
Erfe, Jeffrey Mark, *Reducing Outbreaks: Using International Governmental Risk Pools to Fund Research and Development of Infectious Disease Medicines and Vaccines*, 87 YALE J. BIOL. MED. 473, 473–479, (2014) www.ncbi.nlm.nih.gov/pmc/articles/PMC4257034/ (last visited Nov. 17, 2017).
FIND, *Business Model*, www.finddx.org/business-model/ (last visited Nov. 17, 2017).
FIND *Negotiated Product Pricing*, www.finddx.org/find-negotiated-product-pricing/ (last visited Nov. 17, 2017).
Gauchi, Richard, Powerpoint presentation, Prescription Drugs: Overview and Update (Nov. 2, 2015).
GAVI, www.gavi.org (last visited Jul. 16, 2017).
GHIT ACCESS POL'Y, www.ghitfund.org/afag/policies (last visited Nov. 17, 2017).
GLOBAL HEALTH INNOVATIVE TECH. FUND [GHIT], www.ghitfund.org (last visited Nov. 17, 2017).
IMS INST., *The Global Use of Medicines: Outlook through 2016* (2016), www.imshealth.com/files/web/IMSH%20Institute/Reports/The%20Global%20Use%20of%20Medicines%20Outlook%20Through%202016/Medicines_Outlook_Through_2016_Report.pdf (last visited Jul. 16, 2017).
INT'L FED'N OF PHARM. MFRS. & ASS'N [IFPMA], INDUSTRY ROADMAP FOR PROGRESS ON COMBATING ANTIMICROBIAL RESISTANCE – SEPTEMBER 2016, www.ifpma.org/wp-content/uploads/2016/09/Roadmap-for-Progress-on-AMR-FINAL.pdf (last visited Jul 16, 2017).
Lasswell, Harold and Abraham Kaplan, POWER AND SOCIETY: A FRAMEWORK FOR POLITICAL INQUIRY (Yale University Press 1950; New Haven Press (as assignee)).
MEDICINES. FOR MALARIA VENTURE, www.mmv.org/ (last visited Nov. 17, 2017).
Medicines for Malaria Venture, *Socially Responsible Agreements*, MMV, www.mmv.org/partnering/socially-responsible-agreements (last visited Nov. 5, 2016).
ORG. FOR ECON. COOPERATION AND DEV, *Research and Development in the Pharmaceutical Sector* (2015), www.oecd-ilibrary.org/docserver/download/8115071ec070.pdf?expires=1478360602&id=id&accname=guest&checksum=9DC067062F87B1CE6B0D0F72453F580F (last visited Nov. 17, 2017).
Pecoul, Bernard, et al., *Drugs for Neglected Diseases initiative [DNDi]*, U.N. HIGH-LEVEL PANEL ON ACCESS TO MEDS. (Feb. 27, 2016), www.unsgaccessmeds.org/inbox/2016/2/27/bernard-pecoul (last visited Nov. 17, 2017).
Pharmaceuticals: Facts, Policies, and NCSL Resources, NATIONAL CONFERENCE OF STATE LEGISLATURES [NCLS] (JUL. 2, 2017), www.ncsl.org/research/health/pharmaceuticals-facts-policies-and-ncsl-resources.aspx (last visited Nov. 17, 2017).
Pharm. Res. and Mfrs. Of Am. [PhRMA], *2015 Profile Biopharmaceutical Research Industry* (2015), www.phrma.org/sites/default/files/pdf/2015_phrma_profile.pdf (last visited Nov. 17, 2017).

Press Release, DNDi, GHIT Fund Reinforces Its Support to DNDi Leishmaniasis and Chagas Disease Projects (Mar. 30, 2017), www.dndi.org/2017/media-centre/news-views-stories/news/ghit-reinforces-support-to-dndi-for-leish-and-chagas/ (last visited Nov. 17, 2017).

REPORT OF THE UNITED NATIONS SECRETARY GENERAL'S HIGH LEVEL PANEL ON ACCESS TO MEDICINES 29 (2016).

REV. ON ANTIMICROBIAL RESISTANCE [AMR], DECLARATION BY THE PHARMACEUTICAL, BIOTECHNOLOGY AND DIAGNOSTICS INDUSTRIES ON COMBATING ANTIMICROBIAL RESISTANCE (Jan. 2016 https://amr-review.org/sites/default/files/Declaration_of_Support_for_Combating_AMR_Jan_2016.pdf (last visited Nov. 17, 2017).

Ro, Sam, *Here's Who Owns the Stock Market*, BUS. INSIDER (Mar. 13, 2013), www.businessinsider.com/chart-stock-market-ownership-2013-3 (last visited Nov. 17, 2017).

S. Comm. on Fin., 114th Cong., THE PRICE OF SOVALDI AND ITS IMPACT ON THE U.S. HEALTH CARE SYSTEM, 106–10 (Comm. Print 2015).

Stone, Chad, *Reality Check on Corporate Income Tax Rates*, U.S. NEWS (Nov. 13, 2015) www.usnews.com/opinion/economic-intelligence/2015/11/13/reality-check-on-corporate-income-tax-rates (last visited Nov. 17, 2017).

WORLD HEALTH ORGANIZATION – SPECIAL PROGRAMME FOR RES. AND TRAINING ON TROPICAL DISEASES, HEALTH PRODUCT RESEARCH AND DEVELOPMENT FUND: A PROPOSAL FOR FINANCING AND OPERATION, at, e.g., vii, 1 (2016).

3 Driving Innovation for Global Health through Multi-stakeholder Partnerships

Anatole Krattiger, Thomas Bombelles, and Ania Jedrusik*

Introduction

Health is recognized as a public good and governments have a responsibility to ensure equitable health care provision. Yet, disadvantaged populations in low- and middle-income countries (LMICs) are less likely than others to have access to public sector health services. Inadequate health care infrastructures, distance to health facilities, insufficient numbers of trained health care workers, and low diagnostic capacity are among some factors contributing to this situation. Access to health care is further reduced when diseases urgently require action, as is the case with malaria, and tuberculosis (TB), but for which treatment options are inadequate or do not exist.

Multisectoral and cross-organizational partnerships[1] play a growing role in health research and development (R&D) as they help share the burden, risk, and expenses required to effectively address global health challenges. Public–private partnerships (PPPs) in the health sector have been growing in popularity, both in the provision of services and in developing new technologies. Initiatives such as WIPO Re:Search connect private sector with public sector entities to facilitate R&D and technology transfer necessary to support the development of new medicines, vaccines, and diagnostics that address some of the most challenging issues in global health today such as "neglected tropical diseases" (NTDs).[2] While the various initiative have their own specific characteristics, they share in common a general approach that borrows from private sector business models of organization while being largely noncommercial (i.e., not seeking a profit).

This chapter will review the multi-stakeholder partnership landscape in the context of the United Nations (UN) 2030 Agenda for Sustainable Development (2030 Agenda),

* This publication is not intended to reflect the views of the Secretariat of WIPO or its Member States. The mention of specific companies or products of manufacturers does not imply that they are endorsed or recommended by WIPO in preference to others of a similar nature that are not mentioned. The designations employed and the presentation of material throughout this publication do not imply the expression of any opinion whatsoever on the part of WIPO concerning the legal status of any country, territory, or area or of its authorities, or concerning the delimitation of its frontiers or boundaries.

1 Multi-stakeholder, multisectoral, and cross-organizational partnerships can be public–private partnerships, but they do not necessarily include both public and private partners at the same time.

2 Terminology can vary regarding these types of diseases; for example, "poverty-related neglected diseases" (PRNDs) is a commonly used and overlapping term. In many cases, the PNRDs are also NTDs, but WIPO Re:Search is anchored in the WHO list of NTDs. Therefore, this chapter employs the term NTDs.

as well as broader innovation incentive schemes, namely for NTDs. The chapter looks at some economic determinants of innovation and studies how different partnership models endeavor to address related challenges. WIPO Re:Search is presented as one recent initiative with the potential to create partnership networks that catalyze R&D in NTDs, malaria, and TB.

I The UN Sustainable Development Goals (SDGs)

In September 2015, The UN General Assembly adopted the 2030 Agenda "Transforming our World: the 2030 Agenda for Sustainable Development."[3] The 17 new Sustainable Development Goals (SDGs) and 169 Targets thereunder aim to end by 2030 all forms of poverty, hunger, inequality, and injustice, and to take action on climate change, global health, and education. The SDGs build on the success of the earlier Millennium Development Goals (MDGs), and are even more ambitious than their predecessor. Two of these goals are particularly relevant in the context of this paper.

First, Goal 3[4], which is devoted specifically to health, is framed in broad terms that are relevant to all countries and all populations:[5] "Ensure healthy lives and promote well-being for all at all ages." SDG 3 is associated with 13 targets. Among other aspects, Goal 3 addresses the need to unite efforts to tackle NTDs.

The pressing need to address NTDs is reflected under Target 3.3, which calls on countries by 2030, "[to] end the epidemics of AIDS, tuberculosis, malaria and neglected tropical diseases and combat hepatitis, water-borne diseases and other communicable diseases." This is a significant widening of the focus relative to MDGs in two ways: a shift from control to elimination, and explicit reference to TB, NTDs, hepatitis, and water-borne diseases in addition to HIV/AIDS, malaria, and "other diseases."[6]

Second, Goal 17[7] recognizes that a successful sustainable development agenda requires global partnerships between governments, the private sector, and civil society. In particular, two targets encourage multi-stakeholder partnerships:

> "17.16 Enhance the Global Partnership for Sustainable Development, complemented by multi-stakeholder partnerships that mobilize and share knowledge, expertise, technology and financial resources, to support the achievement of the Sustainable Development Goals in all countries, in particular developing countries.
>
> 17.17 Encourage and promote effective public, public–private and civil society partnerships, building on the experience and resourcing strategies of partnerships."[8]

In 2005 and 2006, the term "neglected tropical diseases" began to appear in peer-reviewed papers[9] and has since come into popular use. Also in 2005, an original core

[3] G. A. Res. 70/1 (Sept. 25, 2015).
[4] *Id.*
[5] World Health Organization [WHO], *Health in 2015: from MDGs to SDGs* (2015) http://apps.who.int/iris/bitstream/10665/200009/1/9789241565110_eng.pdf?ua=1.
[6] *Id.*
[7] G. A. Res. 70/1 (Sept. 25, 2015).
[8] *Id.*
[9] Peter J. Hotez, *The Neglected Tropical Diseases and the Neglected Infections of Poverty: Overview of Their Common Features, Global Disease Burden and Distribution, New Control Tools, and Prospects for Disease Elimination, in* The Causes and Impacts of Neglected Tropical and Zoonotic Diseases: Opportunities for Integrated Intervention Strategies (Institute of Medicine (US) Forum on Microbial Threats ed., 2011).

group of the thirteen major NTDs was proposed, which has since been expanded by the World Health Organisation (WHO) to a list of seventeen diseases. In their 2005 paper, Molyneux, Hotez, and Fenwick listed the following common features of NTDs:

- ancient afflictions that have burdened humanity for centuries;
- poverty-promoting conditions;
- associated with stigma;
- rural areas of low-income countries and fragile states;
- no commercial markets for products that target these diseases; and
- interventions, when applied, have a history of success.[10]

According to WHO, neglect occurs at many different levels: at the community level because the NTDs inflict social stigmas and prejudice; at the national level because the NTDs occur in remote and rural areas, afflicting populations that are marginalized; and at the international level because they are not perceived as posing an immediate global health threat.[11]

The expressed consideration given to NTDs constitutes an opportunity to draw greater global attention and add them to a mainstream action plan. Since these targets cannot be achieved without R&D to develop new health technologies (e.g., new and improved medicines, vaccines, diagnostics),[12] multi-stakeholder partnerships are tools to achieve the objectives suggested in the Goal 17. These two goals should be seen as mutually reinforcing, especially because the burden of NTDs falls overwhelmingly in LMICs. In these countries, the commercial markets alone would not drive R&D for new products,[13] or incentivize the investments necessary to optimize the use of existing medicines or to develop readily available, easy-to-use, reliable, and low-cost diagnostic tools. In a broader context, reducing the burden of diseases will also directly and indirectly affect many of the other SDGs by improving people's well-being and reducing their level of poverty.

II The Innovation Cycle and Incentives

At the outset, there are various approaches to encourage innovation with no single policy instrument alone appropriate under all circumstances. Therefore, the considerations below, relating to incentives spurring innovation, are in no way exhaustive.

"Push and pull mechanisms" can provide incentives for R&D in NTDs. "Push mechanisms" can, in general, be defined as incentives before R&D has started, such as up-front public funding, while "pull mechanisms" provide rewards to the final outcome of R&D, such as certain products. In other words, one category "pushes" capital into R&D investment, while the second "pulls" products into the market. Push mechanisms include tools such as grants and tax credits for R&D spending, while pull mechanisms create purchase funds and other tools to support markets for new products, or provide

[10] David H Molyneux, Peter J Hotez, and Alan Fenwick, *"Rapid-Impact Interventions": How a Policy of Integrated Control for Africa's Neglected Tropical Diseases Could Benefit the Poor*, PLoS Med (2005).

[11] WHO, *Neglected Tropical Diseases, Hidden Successes, Emerging Opportunities* (2006) http://apps.who.int/iris/bitstream/10665/69367/1/WHO_CDS_NTD_2006.2_eng.pdf.

[12] Policy Cures, *Measuring Global Health R&D for the Post-2015 Development Agenda* (2015) www.ghtcoalition.org/pdf/Measuring-global-health-R-D-for-the-post-2015-development-agenda.pdf.

[13] *Id.*

incentives through streamlined regulatory review processes, such as priority review vouchers.[14] In developed countries, combinations of "push" (to reduce R&D costs and generate research) and "pull" (generating market demand for products that result from the research) mechanisms provide some incentive for investment in R&D.[15] The key difference is that, in the case of a "push" mechanism, innovation is supported at the outset, whereas in the latter case, it is the capacity of the market that is increased.[16] A combination of push and pull mechanisms, if designed and implemented properly should, in general, facilitate the development of new health innovations.[17] For example, pull mechanisms such as advance purchase commitments (APCs) have the potential to provide for a stable demand, thereby reducing risk and incentivizing investments in needed technologies. However, they also have their challenges since it is difficult to predict development in the future. To guarantee proper functioning, APCs require sometimes burdensome and bureaucratic monitoring mechanisms and they might still not be able to cope with changing market dynamics.[18]

The intellectual property (IP) rights system is considered a pull mechanism.[19] It is seen as a useful incentive mechanism for governments to mobilize market forces toward innovation in certain areas.[20] The research-based pharmaceutical industry uses IP as a tool to help create market conditions in which product prices can cover the costs of doing business (including R&D, productions and liability insurance), so that private sector stakeholders will invest resources in product development and the marketing of new technologies. Such incentives are considered essential, among other reasons, due to the considerable financial and technical resources required for new product development, coupled with the high risk of failure, even at a late stage.[21]

The IP system is a useful mechanism when private motivation to innovate aligns with society's preferences with regard to new technologies.[22] It is debatable, however, whether the IP system can contribute to incentivizing inventions in areas where there is no profitable market. The same IP protection that is beneficial where a market helps to obtain a reasonable return on investment does not necessarily support an environment for R&D in unprofitable markets, even when the social or human need is great.

In order to better understand the issues surrounding incentives for innovation, the development of new medicines requires a closer look. Innovation in health can be presented as a cycle, which goes from R&D of new, basic compounds to the testing and development of new products, up to the delivery of these products, and then

[14] WHO, World Intellectual Property Organization [WIPO] & World Trade Organization [WTO], *Promoting Access to Medical Technologies and Innovation: Intersections between Public Health, Intellectual Property, and Trade* (2012) www.wto.org/english/res_e/booksp_e/pamtiwhowipowtoweb13_e.pdf.

[15] OECD, Coherence for Health: Innovation for New Medicines for Infectious Diseases, The Development Dimension (2009).

[16] WIPO, *World Intellectual Property Report 2011: The Changing Face of Innovation* (2011) www.wipo.int/edocs/pubdocs/en/intproperty/944/wipo_pub_944_2011.pdf.

[17] OECD, *supra* note 12.

[18] Andrew Farlow, *The Global HIV Vaccine Enterprise, Malaria Vaccines, and Purchase Commitments: What is the Fit?* (2005) www.who.int/intellectualproperty/submissions/Farlow.pdf.

[19] WIPO, supra note 16.

[20] *Id.*

[21] WHO, WIPO & WTO, *supra* note 14.

[22] WIPO, *supra* note 16.

re-investing in R&D to start the cycle anew.[23] A well-functioning innovation cycle can be dynamic and self-sustaining.[24] In a highly profitable market there are continuous efforts to develop new products by multiple players. In less profitable markets, there may be fewer players but developers try to maintain a portfolio of candidates that they may push simultaneously depending on their priority setting system, including the availability of resources.

This scheme applies principally to developed countries and the diseases that are common among the global population.[25] The innovation cycle does not function optimally where the disease burden falls disproportionately on poor populations in developing and least developed countries. For these countries, where the economic demand is weak – but not the human need – there is little financial incentive to develop new or modified interventions appropriate to the disease burden.[26] As the WHO Commission on Intellectual Property Rights, Innovation and Public Health (CIPIH) describes it: for diseases that predominantly affect disadvantaged patients in developing countries, there is a critical gap in the availability of incentives that fuel the conventional innovation cycle.[27]

This illustrates a critical reality: the current market-driven innovation cycle works better for some countries and diseases than for others.[28] Incentive mechanisms need to be designed and deployed effectively to make the innovation cycle work for developing countries which will overcome the lack of market incentives.[29] IP rights will tend to be more important for highly profitable markets and less important for markets that depend on government procurement to meet the needs of the poor. In other words, the IP system is not in itself an incentive to innovate; the incentive for commercial investment in innovation stems from the existence of an economically viable market.[30]

This gap has inspired an array of practical initiatives across territorial boundaries to find new ways of combining the diverse inputs, infrastructure, and resources needed for product development, typically making use of collaborative structures.[31] Incentives for R&D vary with the nature of the market. There are six factors that affect success in new product innovation, of which IP is only one.[32] However, IP will almost always have some

[23] WHO Comm'n on Intellectual Prop. Rights, *Public Health: Innovation and Intellectual Property Rights* (2006) www.who.int/intellectualproperty/documents/thereport/ENPublicHealthReport.pdf?ua=1.

[24] Kamil Idris & Hisamitsu Arai, The Intellectual Property-Conscious Nation: Mapping the Path from Developing to Developed (2006).

[25] WHO, *supra* note 23.

[26] *Id.*

[27] *Id.*

[28] *Id.*

[29] *Id.*

[30] Roy Widdus, *Product Development Partnerships on "Neglected Diseases": Intellectual Property and Improving Access to Pharmaceuticals for HIV/AIDS, Tuberculosis and Malaria*, *in* Negotiating Health: Intellectual Property and Access to Medicines 205 (Pedro Roffe et al. eds., 2006).

[31] *Id.*

[32] Richard Mahoney, *Product Development Partnerships: Case Studies of a New Mechanism for Health Technology Innovation*, 9 Health Res. Pol'y and Sys. 33 (2011). The six factors are: 1. The design and execution of research and development programs from preclinical studies to licensure; 2. Analysis and planning for the marketing and distribution of new technologies in individual developing countries; 3. Analysis and planning for the procurement and supply of new health technologies by the global health community; 4. Planning and implementation of manufacturing capabilities; 5. Establishment and implementation of regulatory systems to ensure safe and effective products; 6. Establishment and implementation of intellectual property rights (IPR) management systems.

value, since new inventions may be useful not only for the target product but also for other products that may have highly profitable markets.

III Costs of R&D in Health

Developing a pharmaceutical product and bringing it from a laboratory to market takes a long time, is expensive, and involves the burden of complying with stringent regulatory approval processes, all of which result in a small number of successful outcomes.[33]

The topic of the true costs of medical research and development is much debated with numerous studies providing varying estimates, depending, in part, on what costs are included or excluded. The cost estimate of bringing a medicine to market will depend on, for instance, whether only the direct cost of developing an individual medicine is considered, or whether the global R&D costs of a company or institution are also considered.[34] For example, research by the Tufts Center for the Study of Drug Development[35] assessed the cost of developing a prescription medicine that gains market approval at US$2.6 billion.[36] Lower estimates were put forward by the Deloitte Centre for Health Solutions in the United Kingdom, which estimated the cost in 2014 at $1.4 billion[37] and the Drugs for Neglected Diseases initiative (DND*i*), a product development partnership (PDP), estimated its own costs of development to range from EUR 6–20 million for an improved treatment, and EUR 30–40 million for a new chemical entity (NCE).[38]

What is less controversial is that the cost model of pharmaceutical development represents a "J curve," i.e., the closer to registration the higher the costs.[39] Bringing the product to registration reflects not just direct costs but the risk of failure.[40] Traditionally, the costs have been borne by a company from revenues of existing products.[41] An entity without a formidable revenue stream could not support the risk of failure.

R&D costs also depend greatly on the type of medical innovation in question.[42] For example, there is a big difference between a medicine based on a new chemical entity (NCE) not previously used in any pharmaceutical product and an incremental modification of an existing medicine. However, even for NCEs the stated costs differ widely.

33 WHO, WIPO & WTO, *supra* note 14.

34 Clive Cookson, *Studies Fuel Criticism of High Drug Development Costs*, FIN. TIMES, April 9, 2015, www.ft.com/content/6a57fcd4-bdcd-11e4-8cf3-00144feab7de?mhq5j=e5.

35 Press Release, Tufts Ctr. for the Study of Drug Dev., Cost to Develop and Win Marketing Approval for a New Drug Is $2.6 Billion (November 18, 2014). http://csdd.tufts.edu/news/complete_story/pr_tufts_csdd_2014_cost_study.

36 Dollar ($) amounts mentioned herein refer to U.S. dollars.

37 Deloitte Centre for Health Solutions, *Measuring the Return from Pharmaceutical Innovation 2014*, DELOITTE (2014), https://www2.deloitte.com/uk/en/pages/life-sciences-and-healthcare/articles/measuring-the-return-from-pharmaceutical-innovation-2014.html.

38 Drugs for Neglected Diseases Initiative, *An Innovative Approach to R&D for Neglected Patients: Ten Years of Experience & Lessons Learned by DNDi* (2014), www.dndi.org/wp-content/uploads/2009/03/DNDi_Modelpaper_2013.pdf.

39 Thomas Bombelles et al., *Neglected Tropical Disease Research: Rethinking the Drug Discovery Model*, 7 FUTURE MEDICINAL CHEMISTRY 7, 693–700 (2015).

40 *Id.*

41 *Id.*

42 WHO, WIPO & WTO, *supra* note 14.

Often, on top of R&D, manufacturing facilities are costly. For instance, the production of vaccines and biologics includes significant fixed costs due to the very specific character of these products. The expenses linked to establishing and gaining regulatory approval for a manufacturing facility for products with a small profit margin will discourage companies from entering this domain.[43]

High costs of pharmaceutical innovation are confronted with the challenge of ensuring that these innovations reach those who need them. Affordability, acceptability, and accessibility are priorities for any public health policy.

Experience gained over the last few decades has shown that for products where there are no profitable markets that could justify R&D investments, collaborations between pharmaceutical companies and nonprofit entities are essential to progress. Such public–private partnerships are especially important for the development of products directed to neglected diseases.

IV Collaborative Models to Address NTDs

According to WHO, NTDs are communicable diseases[44] that prevail in tropical and subtropical conditions in 149 countries, affecting more than a billion people, who are mainly living in poverty and without adequate sanitation. NTDs cost developing countries billions of dollars every year.[45] Over the past twenty years, a range of new collaborative innovation models have been created to tackle the need for innovation in the field of NTDs.

In May 1974, the World Health Assembly (WHA) called upon the WHO to intensify activities in tropical disease research.[46] This WHA resolution eventually led to the creation of the Special Programme for Research and Training in Tropical Diseases, which is hosted at the WHO and is sponsored by the United Nations Children's Fund (UNICEF), the United Nations Development Programme (UNDP), the World Bank and WHO. This partnership is committed to R&D and a dynamic collaboration to achieve innovations for NTDs in a new environment of private and public partnerships.[47]

The emergence of donor organizations, such as the Global Fund to Fight AIDS, Tuberculosis and Malaria; the GAVI Alliance; and the Bill and Melinda Gates Foundation, led to an era of partnerships launched in the early 2000s.[48] New partnerships endeavored to address the mismatch between the need for health technologies for NTDs and the lack of engagement of the commercial sector that shied away from the costs and risks because of the low market potential.[49]

43 *Id.*
44 WHO, *Neglected Tropical Diseases Summary*, WHO (2017) www.who.int/neglected_diseases/diseases/summary/en/.
45 *Id.*
46 World Health Assembly Res. 27.52.
47 WHO, *Making a Difference: 30 Years of Research and Capacity Building in Tropical Diseases* (2007) http://apps.who.int/iris/bitstream/10665/43689/1/9789241595575_eng.pdf.
48 Mahoney, *supra* note 32.
49 Cheri Grace, *Product Development Partnerships (PDPs): Lessons from PDPs Established to Develop New Health Technologies for Neglected Diseases*, Human Dev. Res. Ctr. (2010).

The move toward a more cohesive international response to NTDs started to emerge in 2003 at WHO under the leadership of then Director General Dr. J. W. Lee.[50] A turning point in efforts against NTDs was achieved after the first Global Partners' Meeting convened by WHO in 2007[51] – an initiative outside any formally structured partnership that resulted in a shared commitment to support WHO's strategies, goals, and targets.[52]

In 2010, WHO released its first report on NTDs, entitled "Working to overcome the global impact of NTDs."[53] This paper has had a significant impact and since then the World Bank, pharmaceutical companies, philanthropic foundations, bilateral aid agencies, endemic countries, and other public and private sector organizations have increased their support to respond to the challenges posed by NTDs.[54]

In 2012, WHO published "Accelerating Work to Overcome the Global Impact of Neglected Tropical Diseases," a roadmap that sets out implementation targets for the control, elimination, or eradication of seventeen NTDs by 2020.[55] This gave rise to further strengthening global efforts in the field of NTDs.

Drawing inspiration from the WHO Roadmap and previous developments, the Bill and Melinda Gates Foundation, the United States Agency for International Development (USAID), the United Kingdom's Department for International Development, the WHO, DNDi, and the Governments of Mozambique, Tanzania, Brazil, as well as thirteen pharmaceutical companies met in 2012 in London, where they pledged to unite in their efforts in supporting the control, elimination, or eradication of ten NTDs.[56] The resulting London Declaration on Neglected Tropical Diseases (London Declaration)[57] was a significant step in the efforts to accelerate progress toward eliminating or controlling NTDs. It recognized that existing tools were having a major impact, but that several NTDs required new or improved medicines and diagnostics. Its partners committed to ensuring supplies of drugs, and to advancing R&D through partnerships, funding, and technical support. The London Declaration has been endorsed by 80 organizations, and led to the donation of 7.9 billion tablets and a pledge of more than $17.8 billion in drug

[50] Lorenzo Savioli et al., *Neglected Tropical Diseases: The Development of a Brand with No Copyright. A Shift from a Disease-Centered to a Tool-Centered Strategic Approach, in* THE CAUSES AND IMPACTS OF NEGLECTED TROPICAL AND ZOONOTIC DISEASES: OPPORTUNITIES FOR INTEGRATED INTERVENTION STRATEGIES: WORKSHOP SUMMARY (2011).

[51] Some 200 participants attended the meeting, including representatives of WHO Member States, United Nations agencies, the World Bank, philanthropic foundations, universities, pharmaceutical companies, international nongovernmental organizations, and other institutions dedicated to contributing to control neglected tropical diseases. WHO, *First Global Partners' Meeting on Neglected Tropical Diseases*, www.who.int/neglected_diseases/partners_meeting/en/.

[52] WHO, *Accelerating Work to Overcome the Global Impact of Neglected Tropical Diseases – A Roadmap for Implementation: Executive Summary* (2012) www.who.int/neglected_diseases/NTD_RoadMap_2012_Full version.pdf.

[53] *Id.*

[54] Amber Cashwell et al., *BRICS in the Response to Neglected Tropical Diseases*, 92 BULLETIN OF THE WORLD HEALTH ORG. 385 (2014).

[55] WHO, *supra* note 52.

[56] Uniting to Combat Neglected Tropical Diseases, *Country Leadership and Collaboration on Neglected Tropical Diseases: Third Progress Report of the London Declaration* (2015) http://unitingtocombatntds.org/sites/default/files/document/UTCNTD%20FULL%20REPORT.pdf.

[57] Uniting to Combat Neglected Tropical Diseases, *London Declaration on Neglected Tropical Diseases* (2012) http://unitingtocombatntds.org/sites/default/files/resource_file/london_declaration_on_ntds.pdf.

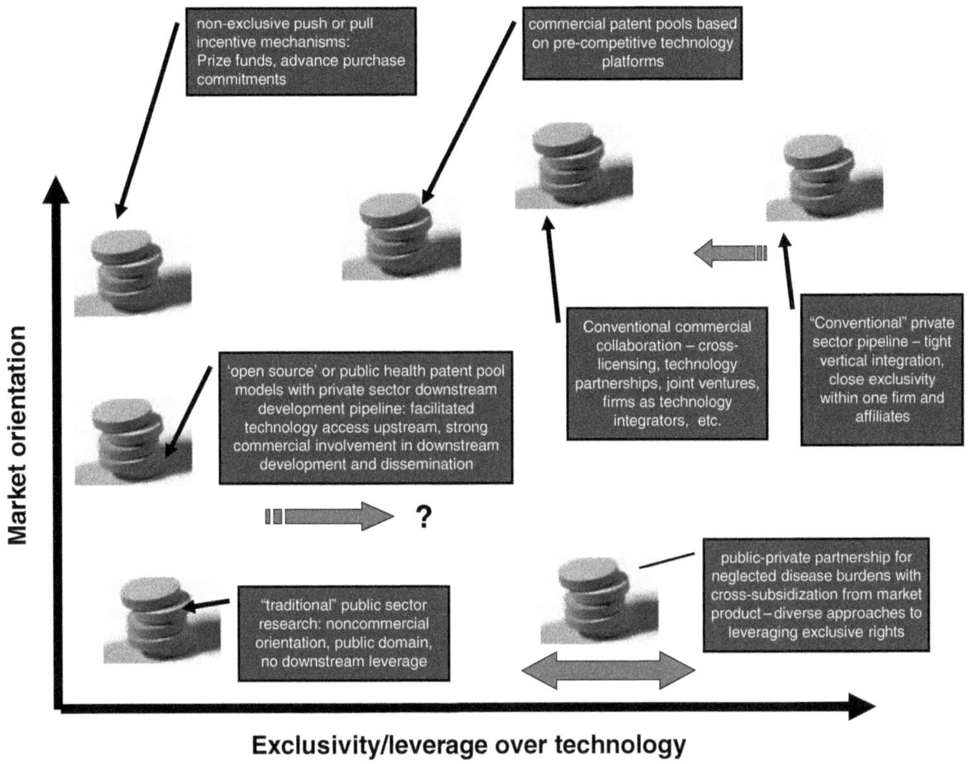

Figure 3.1. Mapping market incentives and leverage over technology in innovation structures. *Source*: Antony Taubman, *A Typology of Intellectual Property Management for Public Health Innovation and Access: Design Considerations for Policy Makers*, 4 Open Aids J. 1, 4 (2010).

donations by 2020.[58] The London Declaration in many ways confirms that the partnership route between industry, public sector, nonprofit, and philanthropic organizations is a key component in the arsenal of R&D.[59]

According to the eighth annual G-FINDER report, one of the most comprehensive reports on public and private funding into R&D for NTDs, $3.4 billion was invested in NTDs R&D in 2014.[60] This was the largest investment in NTDs R&D in the history of the G-FINDER survey.[61]

In sum, a variety of innovation models are used in the development of health technologies (see Figure 3.1). The London Declaration and WIPO Re:Search are just some of the examples of more novel structures which include a multitude of actors from public and private sectors. What they all have in common is that they are neither situated in an entirely noncommercial context nor do they apply a rigid, highly exclusive and entirely private model of technology development.

[58] Uniting to Combat Neglected Tropical Diseases, http://unitingtocombatntds.org/.

[59] David Torstensson, *Fighting Tropical Disease: It's Now a Common Cause*, PharmExec.com, (Feb. 8, 2012), www.pharmexec.com/fighting-tropical-disease-its-now-common-cause.

[60] *Global Funding of Innovation for Neglected Diseases: G-FINDER*, PolicyCures (2015) http://policycures.org/gfinder.html.

[61] *Id.*

What is clear in areas such as NTDs is that neither private nor public entities are capable of resolving global health challenges alone. Public institutions and research centers are sometimes confronted with limited financial resources. At the same time, private sector entities might be careful about initiating internal pharmaceutical R&D programs when there are no commercial prospects for such products. Industry can be expected to require some form of risk sharing before investing in such programs.

By contrast, partnerships such as Medicines for Malaria Venture (MMV), which have been generously funded are able to operate independently. They may cooperate with private companies as contractors and engage them for work, so that the companies take few risks and invest little themselves. These partnerships can use industry skills (especially in manufacturing, clinical trials, and regulatory affairs) that are important for progress and which the public sector may not wish to build up on its own. The key could be partnership and finding the right "meshing" of capabilities to make an effective mechanism.

Even though a lot of attention is given to the role of the industry, public sector entities continue to have a significant impact on the innovation cycle in health R&D.[62] Researchers from public sector organizations, including private universities and institutes, are usually involved in early-stage drug development, but they also play an important role in the innovation cycle at subsequent stages.[63] The public sector plays a critical role in the delivery phase of health products; governments are usually the main procurer as well as being involved in the distribution and delivery of such products.[64] Moreover, the private sector's expertise, know-how, state of the art facilities, networks, manufacturing capabilities, capital investment, and market development experience allow important projects to be undertaken or continued when, otherwise, they might not be possible. In that sense, the public and private sectors collaborate and interact throughout the product development and delivery cycles.

In recent years, there has been a rapid global expansion and acceleration of one of these forms of collaborations – PPPs for public health.

V Public–Private Partnerships (PPPs) for Public Health

Partnerships between public and private actors can lead to enormously positive outcomes for well-defined public health goals. They are a powerful mechanism for addressing difficult problems by leveraging the ideas, resources, networks and/or expertise of diverse partners[65] who engage in PPPs to make sure that health innovations are affordable, available, and accessible to people around the world.

Various definitions of "public–private partnerships" have been prepared but there does not seem to be a clear consensus around what a PPP really is (beyond the fact that public and private entities collaborate in some manner) and what its essential elements are.[66] However, four points stand out as broadly applied to all PPPs in health:

[62] WHO, WIPO & WTO, *supra* note 14.
[63] *Id.*
[64] *Id.*
[65] Michael R. Reich, *Public–Private Partnerships for Public Health*, 6 Nature Med. 617 (2000).
[66] Jeffrey Barnes, *Designing Public–Private Partnerships in Health*, SHOPS (2011), www.abtassociates.com/reports/PPP_Primer.pdf.

- they integrate public sector and private sector approaches, and generally use industry practices in their R&D activities;
- they manage neglected diseases R&D portfolios and target one or more neglected diseases;
- they are created to pursue public health objectives rather than commercial gains; and
- they ensure that the developed products are distributed at the lowest possible sustainable price.[67]

Another definition, which avoids the difficulty of having to judge the private partners' commitment to the social mission, was formulated by Jeffrey Barnes in his report for USAID: "A PPP in health is any formal collaboration between the public sector at any level (national and local governments, international donor agencies, bilateral government donors) and the nonpublic sector (commercial, nonprofit, and traditional healers, midwives, or herbalists) in order to jointly regulate, finance, or implement the delivery of health services, products, equipment, research, communications, or education."[68] This definition includes the elements of a formal agreement and recognizes the capacity of private partners to strengthen any health system component. Barnes argues that successful partnerships show that partnering must take account of, and accommodate, the profit motive.[69]

In the context of addressing health problems in LMICs, Roy Widdus and Pedro Roffe enumerate four main categories of such partnerships:

- product development partnerships (PDPs);
- partnerships for improving access to pharmaceuticals;
- global coordination and financing mechanisms; and
- partnerships for strengthening health systems.[70]

R&D supported by PDPs may lead to patentable inventions, proprietary (trade secret) data, and technical know-how, all of which the PDP needs to manage in its agreements with collaborators. Indeed, PDPs in general, have two interconnected long-term objectives: creating a new product and ensuring that it is as widely and affordably available as possible. It should be noted that PDPs apply different IP management strategies depending on the particular project in order to best advance their social and development missions.

PDPs, by working together, have the potential for exchanging and transferring valuable knowledge and skills. Robust exchanges of know-how among public and private sector players also expedites the translation of knowledge about diseases of the poor while also reflecting national sensitivities, changing contexts, and the concomitant desire for economic growth.[71] Dissemination of technology and knowledge provides opportunities for

[67] WHO, *Public Health, Innovation and Intellectual Property Rights; Report of the Commission on Intellectual Property Rights, Innovation and Public Health* (2006) www.who.int/intellectualproperty/documents/thereport/ENPublicHealthReport.pdf.
[68] Barnes, *supra* note 66.
[69] *Id.*
[70] Widdus, *supra* note 30.
[71] Carlos M. Morel et al., *Health Innovation Networks to Help Developing Countries Address Neglected Diseases*, 309 SCIENCE 401 (2005).

regions, firms, and institutions that are comparatively less developed to close the technology gap and to develop their own innovative capacity.[72]

Over the last two decades, many PDPs aiming to address gaps in health innovation have been established. The targeted commitments and investments from private and public partners have reduced the burden of several NTDs, but significant gaps remain. Concurrently, there have been profound changes in the world of intellectual property management[73] and research on NTDs, malaria, and TB over the last two decades, and these changes have led to the environment in which WIPO Re:Search was founded and currently operates.

VI WIPO Re:Search – Overview

The WIPO is one of a number of stakeholders contributing to the fight against NTDs, in areas where WIPO has a comparative advantage. A PPP-like structure was eventually chosen as the most effective form. The engagement is anchored in WIPO's role as the specialized agency of the UN serving as the global forum for IP services and information. As such, WIPO is uniquely positioned to help organizations work toward creating a truly global view and understanding of the IP system, including the flexibilities to implement the patent system at the national level, to provide information on patents (including information on the patent status of key medicines and vaccines in developing countries), and to lend its expertise on patent law and its interplay with public policy.[74] Most importantly, however, WIPO has been able to leverage a concerted approach by many pharmaceutical companies to openly share their intellectual property assets for the development of NTD, malaria, and TB solutions.

WIPO's Director General, Mr. Francis Gurry, considers PPPs to be most effective vehicles for implementing policies agreed to by WIPO Member States.

> "Public–private partnerships can deliver on the objectives set by member states. They provide access both to intellectual resources and to financial capital that do not exist in the public sector. [...] In each case the private sector is also contributing financial resources."[75]

Critically for a UN agency, public–private partnerships do not affect the Organization's intergovernmental character. Member States still drive the Organization and establish its normative program.[76]

In October 2011, a new Consortium of WIPO Re:Search – *Sharing Innovation in the Fight Against Neglected Tropical Diseases* – was launched by WIPO jointly with BIO Ventures for Global Health (BVGH) and thirty-one initial WIPO Re:Search Members. The World Health Organization (WHO) serves as a technical adviser to WIPO on

[72] Jennifer Brant and Balaji Parthasarathy, *The Dynamics of Global Technology and Knowledge Flows* (Innovation and Intellectual Prop. Series, Research Paper No. 4, 2015).

[73] Krattiger et al. (eds.), Intellectual Property Management of Health and Agricultural Innovation: A Handbook of Best Practices (2007).

[74] WHO, WIPO & WTO, *supra* note 14.

[75] Cathy Jewell, *Harnessing the Power of the Private Sector – An Interview with Francis Gurry*, 5 WIPO Mag., Oct. 2015, at 2.

[76] *Id.*

NTDs, malaria, and TB. The Consortium's goal is to catalyze the development of medical products for NTDs, malaria, and TB through innovative research partnerships and knowledge sharing. Central to the value of WIPO Re:Search is the sharing of IP assets in a highly efficient manner with low transaction costs. To this end, the Consortium has created an open innovation platform through which public and private sector entities can share IP to eventually benefit patients in LMICs.

WIPO Re:Search is a reflection of the hope of WIPO, BVGH, and its partners that public–private collaboration under the aegis of a UN agency can provide a valuable and concrete contribution to improving the R&D landscape for NTDs, malaria, and TB.[77] WIPO's sponsorship of this initiative supports WIPO's mandate from its Member States as expressed in the WIPO Development Agenda (DA) recommendations,[78] specifically:

- facilitating access to knowledge and technology for developing countries including Least Developed Countries (LDCs);
- promoting the transfer and dissemination of technology to the benefit of developing countries, including LDCs;
- encouraging Member States, especially developed countries, to urge their research and scientific institutions to enhance cooperation and exchange with research and development institutions in developing countries, especially LDCs; and
- cooperating with other intergovernmental organizations to provide developing countries, including LDCs, upon request, advice on how to gain access to and make use of intellectual property-related information on technology.[79]

Indeed, various WIPO DA recommendations under Cluster A ("Technical Assistance and Capacity Building") and Cluster C ("Technology Transfer, Information and Communication Technologies (ICT) and Access to Knowledge") are being realized in a tangible manner through this initiative. For instance, Recommendation 26 requires WIPO "to encourage Member States, especially developed countries, to urge their research and scientific institutions to enhance cooperation and exchange with R&D institutions in developing countries, especially LDCs." One of the key goals of WIPO Re: Search is to ensure such an ongoing exchange. Furthermore, WIPO DA recommendation 2 asks WIPO to establish voluntary funds specifically for LDCs, and accord high priority to finance activities in Africa to promote, *inter alia*, the legal, commercial, cultural, and economic exploitation of intellectual property in these countries. As we will see later in this chapter, WIPO Re:Search fellowships for researchers from LMICs, until now mainly from Africa, contribute to the implementation of this objective.

WIPO Re:Search is a voluntary endeavour open to all *bona fide* private and public entities, including intergovernmental institutions. It comprises institutions from all relevant sectors, including public, private, academic, and civil society. WIPO Re:Search has a cooperative, voluntary character, with various groups and institutions collaborating toward a common set of principles and objectives. Even though WIPO Re:Search

[77] *Id.*

[78] WIPO, *The 45 Adopted Recommendations under the WIPO Development Agenda* (last visited April 10, 2016), www.wipo.int/ip-development/en/agenda/recommendations.html.

[79] *WIPO Re:Search Guiding Principles* (June 8, 2011) www.wipo.int/export/sites/www/research/docs/guiding_principles.pdf.

enables partnerships between private and public institutions, it is not a PDP itself. To date, it has facilitated mainly early stage research and addresses possible barriers to products moving into PDPs, if the PDPs wish to develop them further.

As of December 2016, WIPO Re:Search has enjoyed more than five years of success and growth; it comprises 109 Members with BVGH having facilitated over 100 collaborations.[80]

VII Structure and Governance

The membership of WIPO Re:Search, includes three groups of key players: Providers, Users, and Supporters:

- "**Providers**" share their IP assets, materials, or services with other WIPO Re:Search Members for licence or use;
- "**Users**" are Members that have entered into licence agreements with Providers to utilize these IP assets (and/or materials and/or services) made available by Providers;
- "**Supporters**" are Members that encourage the facilitation of R&D of products for NTDs. Supporters may voluntarily offer to provide support, services, or assistance of any kind to the Consortium or its Members in order to facilitate achievement of the principles and objectives of the Consortium.

WIPO Re:Search is open to those that agree to the WIPO Re:Search Guiding Principles, as is mentioned in the opening lines: "The Consortium is a voluntary endeavour open to all *bona fide* private and public entities."[81] In addition to pharmaceutical companies, Members of WIPO Re:Search include universities, PDPs, research centers, associations and national IP offices from all over the world.[82] A notable component to the development of new and better treatments for NTDs is the emphasis on the inclusion of research centers in developing countries.[83]

Many of the Members participate both as a Provider and User, and have uploaded data in the database, participated in the hosting arrangements, and entered into collaborations.

The Consortium has three major components:

- The **Database**, hosted by WIPO, providing information about IP available for licensing from a Provider, as well as services, technology, or materials which can be accessed and/or licensed by anyone, anywhere, for free;
- The **Partnership Hub**, managed by the Partnership Hub Administrator (BVGH) in cooperation with WIPO, where Members and other interested parties can learn about the Consortium, available licensing and research collaboration opportunities, networking possibilities, and funding options;
- A range of specific **supporting activities**, led by WIPO in cooperation with BVGH, facilitate the negotiation of licensing agreements and address technical matters such as identifying research needs and opportunities, among others, with technical advice from WHO.

[80] *Id.*
[81] *Id.*
[82] *Id.*
[83] *WIPO Re:Search Members*, www.wipo.int/research/en/about/members.html.

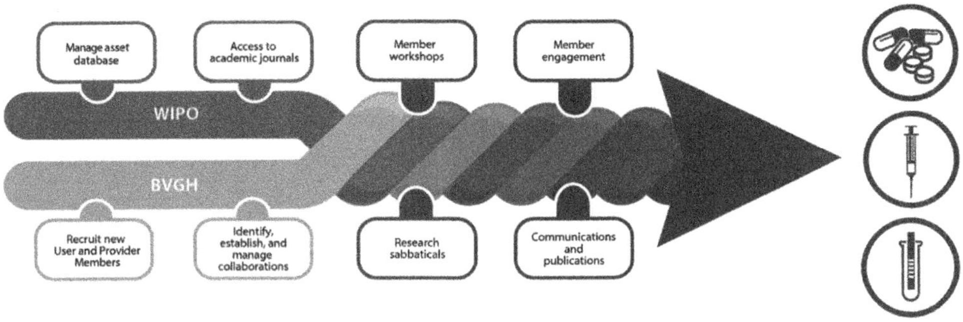

Figure 3.2. WIPO Re:Search based on the collaboration between WIPO and BVGH.
Source: BIO Ventures for Global Health.

As the Secretariat of WIPO Re:Search, WIPO manages the Database, coordinates regular communication between WIPO, BVGH, and Members, and organizes the annual or biennial meeting of members.[84] BVGH is the Partnership Hub Administrator and facilitates connections and collaborations between Members, recruits new Members, and communicates the Consortium's activities and achievements.[85] WIPO and BVGH work closely together as depicted in Figure 3.2.

VIII Funding

WIPO finances the WIPO Re:Search Secretariat function, whereas the Partnership Hub relies on funding from the private sector Members. To date, additional support for the Partnership Hub has not been obtained from other sources such as philanthropic foundations, nor from European and North American bilateral donors.

Additionally, WIPO Re:Search activities are supported by Funds-in-Trust (FIT) from the Government of Australia and Japan. Research fellowships for developing country scientists are supported by the government of Australia, while certain communications and training activities have been funded by the government of Japan.[86]

Beyond the funding for the fellowships, the FIT programs are also dedicated to supporting the capacity-building activities. For example, the Government of Japan has sponsored training programs on successful technology licensing for the African Network for Drugs and Diagnostic Innovation, which were offered to fourteen scientists and technology managers from research institutions from ten African countries.[87] The support of the government of Japan has also enabled the organization of other training activities for

[84] Thomas Bombelles et al., *WIPO Re:Search: Sharing Innovation in the Fight Against Neglected Tropical Diseases* (2015) www.wipo.int/edocs/pubdocs/en/wipo_pub_gc_8.pdf.

[85] Roopa Ramamoorthi et al., *WIPO Re:Search: Accelerating Anthelmintic Development through Cross-Sector Partnerships*, 4 Int. J. for Parasitology: Drugs & Drug Resistance 220 (2014); Symposium, *Anthelmintics: From Discovery to Resistance* (2016); Symposium, *Global Challenges for New Drug Discovery Against Tropical Parasitic Diseases* (2014).

[86] Bombelles et al., *supra* note 84.

[87] WIPO, *The First Five Years of the WIPO Japan Funds-in-Trust for Industrial Property (Japan FIT/IP) for Africa and Least Developed Countries (LDCs): A Productive Collaboration with the Japan Patent Office (JPO)* (2013) www.wipo.int/export/sites/www/cooperation/en/funds_in_trust/docs/japanfitip_jpo_firstfive years_en.pdf.

WIPO Re:Search members, particularly from LMICs, at the margins of annual meetings and elsewhere (Geneva in 2012, New York in 2014, as well as Manila in 2015 and 2016).

IX Database

One of the fundamental resources of WIPO Re:Search is its Database. The information therein on IP and other assets, which are available for licensing from the WIPO Re: Search partners, is intended to be of potential use for NTDs, malaria, and TB, or for application to related R&D.

Providers of uploads to the Database include pharmaceutical companies and many other public and private sector research institutions from all over the world. Interested researchers can access and use those resources to meet their needs. In particular, this can help scientists from developing countries to identify technologies that may be of interest to them.[88] The central element of WIPO Re:Search, however, is to provide a framework for building collaborations beyond the database, through the services of BVGH as an intermediary, bringing users and providers together.

X Services Beyond the Database

Over the years, WIPO Re:Search has expanded from its original ambition of facilitating research collaborations between pharmaceutical companies and academic researchers. The Consortium now also facilitates agreements between pharmaceutical companies and biotech startups, as well as bilateral collaborations between academic institutions.[89]

To establish a collaborative opportunity, BVGH (in its role as Partnership Hub Administrator) studies scientific literature published by Members' scientists, identifies areas of potential collaboration, and contacts the researchers to suggest partnership ideas.[90] In other words, it acts as a matchmaker that connects users who have specific research plans and needs with Provider Members holding assets that fulfil those needs (see Figure 3.3). After BVGH builds the initial link, Providers and Users must come together to define the conditions of the collaboration. A clearly defined mission becomes the critical underpinning of all collaborations.[91]

WIPO Re:Search may also help its Members at a later stage. Bringing a product through preclinical, clinical, and regulatory filing activities is an inherently expensive endeavour that requires significant expertise. As an exploratory possibility for further services, if a WIPO Re:Search partnership shows potential for future development, BVGH could help the participating Members identify sources of funding as well as support with the expertise needed to transit the potential product through the pipeline to the market and those who need it the most.[92]

88 Richard Mahoney, *Strategic Review of WIPO Re:Search*, Global Challenges Rep. (2015) www.wipo.int/export/sites/www/research/en/docs/wipo_research_external_review.pdf.

89 Ramamoorthi et al., *supra* note 85.

90 *Id.*

91 William B. Mattes, *Divided We Fall*, *in* Collaborative Innovation in Drug Discovery: Strategies for Public and Private Partnerships 11 (Rathnam Chaguturu ed., 2014).

92 Ramamoorthi et al., *supra* note 85.

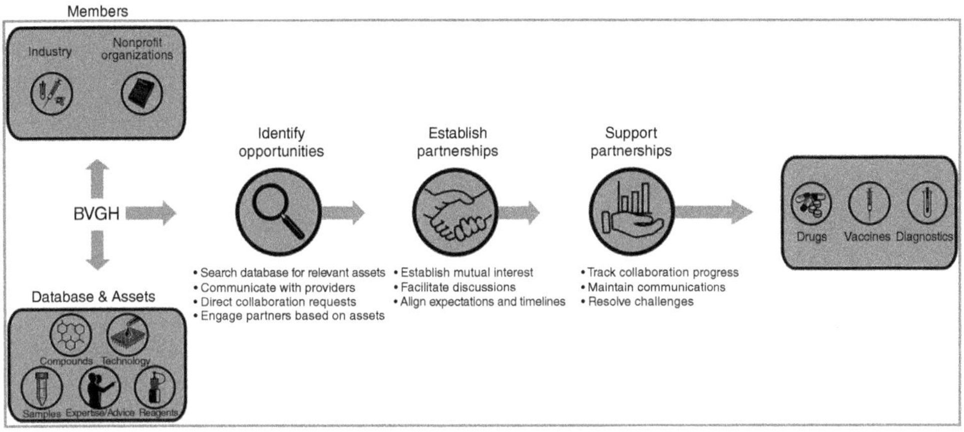

Figure 3.3. The Partnership Hub – facilitating collaborations.

XI Research Capacity Building and Knowledge Transfer

Collaborations built through WIPO Re:Search do not focus only on developing medicines, vaccines, or diagnosis. Of equal importance is capacity building, which is regarded as one of the important long-term contributions of the Consortium.

Capacity building can be defined as an approach to the development of sustainable skills, organizational structures, resources, and commitment to health improvement in health and other sectors, to prolong and multiply health gains many times over.[93] Building research capacities in LMICs is crucial to empowering individuals, institutions, organizations, and nations. This can be done, *inter alia*, by research and advanced training for individual researchers at state-of-the-art research institutions, usually located in developed countries. Potential gains from such partnerships have included increased access to new ideas and best practices, technical expertise, and resources; wider coverage and impact of research benefits; and an increased probability of sustainability, recognition, and advantage of the research partnerships.[94]

Moreover, building medical research capacity contributes to international development. A strong research base can help developing countries in various ways, including dealing with local health challenges such as NTDs that may be not otherwise be addressed by researchers from elsewhere. Further, this will strengthen their role in global research and reduce the need for future development assistance, developing health solutions that are more relevant to the local context, and encouraging scientists to stay and work in their home country rather than move abroad, thereby reducing "brain drain"[95]

WIPO Re:Search supports capacity building by providing opportunities for developing country scientists to work in laboratories of pharmaceutical companies and developed country research centres. To assist in the development of product development skills in the developing world, WIPO Re:Search has established several training opportunities for

[93] NSW Health Department, A Framework for Building Capacity to Improve Health (2001).

[94] Mary Ann Lansang and Rodolfo Dennis, *Building Capacity in Health Research in the Developing World*, 82 Bulletin of the World Health Org. 764 (2004).

[95] House of Commons Science and Technology Committee, Building Scientific Capacity for Development, 2012–13, HC 377 (UK).

researchers from African Member institutions, such as research fellowships described in the section below. Through such experiences, the participating scientists gain the skills and knowledge essential to move their projects forward. Such an approach helps to maximize existing investments in health research made by some developing countries.[96] (See Appendix 1.)

Indeed, these capacity-building opportunities facilitated through WIPO Re:Search foster international collaboration and cooperation, and increase the skills and capabilities of laboratories across the region, thus allowing these institutes and researchers to be active contributors to the global movement to eliminate the health inequalities of the developing world.[97]

Those Member institutions and companies that host researchers from LMICs can benefit in terms of knowledge and know-how transfer. Even though they may already have the assets and expertise needed to systematically discover and develop medicines, they can still benefit from the direct and in-depth knowledge of the pathogens' biology and understanding of disease mechanisms that NTD researchers have – expertise that is essential to develop treatments for these diseases.[98]

XII IP and Access

Effective IP management through voluntary licensing is an essential tenet of WIPO Re: Search. Because the sharing occurs in the framework of a formal agreement, more information, including patent and related registered rights, know-how, manufacturing processes, and regulatory data and the corresponding physical materials such as propriety compounds and technologies are shared within the collaboration. This vision is reflected in the WIPO Re:Search Guiding Principles, which stipulate, *inter alia*, that the Members believe there are opportunities to use IP innovatively and to encourage both public and private sector R&D of health solutions that are particularly needed by the world's poorest populations. Moreover, they are convinced that an open innovation framework for the sharing of IP, as well as technology and research materials not protected by IP rights, can facilitate such R&D into new products for NTDs.

Each WIPO Re:Search partnership is governed by its own specific agreement; however, it is expected that these agreements will embody the spirit of the WIPO Re:Search Guiding Principles. The Guiding Principles are incorporated into all collaboration agreements.

The WIPO Re:Search Guiding Principles can broadly be summarized as follows:

- Members will provide royalty-free licences for R&D related to NTDs, malaria, and tuberculosis;
- Members will provide a royalty-free licence for any product developed through WIPO Re:Search that is used and sold in LDCs;
- Members will consider the issue of access and affordability to these products for all developing countries, including those that do not qualify as LDCs; and
- Users will retain ownership of any new IP developed, but are encouraged to make new inventions available to other Members of WIPO Re:Search.

96 Morel et al., *supra* note 71.
97 Ramamoorthi et al., *supra* note 85.
98 Jennifer Dent, Katy M. Graef, and Paddy Shivanand, *Open Innovation to Bolster Research and Development for Neglected and Emerging Infectious Diseases*, 1 J. Med. Dev. (2015). Available at http://ojs.whioce.com/index.php/jmds/article/view/119/99.

XIII Status of Collaborations

By December 2016, 109 collaborations between WIPO Re:Search Members were established. The research collaborations covered fourteen diseases among which malaria is the most common focus of collaborations. While the collaborations focus on basic research and drug, vaccine, and diagnostic development, drugs are the most common focus of collaborations established each year, and compounds are the most commonly shared asset each year. During 2012–2013, the majority of established collaborations involved, respectively, a for-profit and nonprofit Member. Those involving only nonprofit Members became the majority from 2014 onward. Thirty-two collaborations include a Member from a developing country, among which twelve Members are African Members. A total of forty collaborations are ongoing and four collaborations have advanced to the next stage of development.

Conclusions: Successes and Challenges

WIPO Re:Search Members trust that partnerships will not only accelerate product development but are also a key means to ensure access. From the beginning, it was clear that significant scientific and technical know-how as well as IP that private partners bring to partnerships will be determining factors for the success of this initiative.

With over one hundred collaborations in four years,[99] WIPO Re:Search contributes to the important goal of tackling NTDs, malaria, and TB. In its short existence, the partnerships facilitated by WIPO Re:Search have focused on early stage research. However, the value a partnership delivers takes time to be fully realized. Considering that developing a medicinal product and bringing it to the market is a long and complex process, this should not be discouraging. In fact, many Member researchers are already seeing their product discovery projects advance due to access to industry assets.[100] The progress in the WIPO Re:Search mission can be traced via the monthly Partnership Hub's newsletter[101] and in its Annual Reports.[102]

The capacity-building experiences of the six selected researchers discussed above who participated in WIPO Re:Search fellowships are presented in a WIPO Global Challenges Report.[103] This paper highlights the long-term impact of such collaborations, and their potential to facilitate R&D in NTDs. In particular, the selected researchers from Africa have emphasized the empowering nature of the fellowships as well as the fact that skills, knowledge, and know-how gained have profoundly contributed to their research.

WIPO Re:Search currently faces a number of opportunities and challenges. In 2015, Dr. Richard Mahoney, an independent health specialist and researcher engaged by

[99] See the list of collaborations at www.wipo.int/research/en/collaborations/.

[100] *Id.*

[101] See, e.g., BIO Ventures for Global Health, Partnership Hub Mid-Year Report 2017, https://bvgh.org/wp-content/uploads/2017/09/2017-BVGH-Partnership-Hub-Mid-Year-Report.pdf.

[102] See, e.g., BIO Ventures for Global Health, *2015 Partnership Hub Mid-Year Report: Catalyzing Partnerships for Global Health* (2015), www.wipo.int/export/sites/www/research/en/docs/bvgh_midyear_research_report_2015.pdf.

[103] Ania Jedrusik, *Sharing Innovation and Building Capacity to Fight Neglected Tropical Diseases: A Selection of WIPO Re:Search Fellowship Stories*, Global Challenges Rep. (2016) www.wipo.int/edocs/pubdocs/en/wipo_pub_gc_11.pdf.

WIPO, prepared a report entitled "Strategic Review of WIPO Re:Search," that identified its successes and challenges and provided a set of recommendations for future action.[104] He found that WIPO Re:Search had emerged at a time when companies were willing to relax IP considerations in order to facilitate R&D. As a result, WIPO Re:Search was able to create new R&D markets for underutilized assets and a global network of stakeholders for technology R&D in the target fields. He recommended some areas for improvements to the network infrastructure and the funding base, as well as a strategic governance reorientation, through the creation of an Advisory Committee to assist WIPO, BVGH, and all Members to define the future direction and goals of the project.[105]

WIPO Re:Search was founded on the belief that the sharing of IP assets and knowledge transfer can be used creatively to stimulate research and development into new health solutions for NTDs, malaria, and TB, while ensuring access for the most disadvantaged populations. Indeed, with the effective structure of WIPO Re:Search, combining the strength of a UN agency with an energetic nonprofit, namely, BVGH, that manages the Partnership Hub, and coupled with vibrant members of the Consortium, WIPO Re:Search has demonstrated that IP does not have to be a barrier to research on NTD technologies.

As the understanding of the role of IP management evolves, industry has realized that it could do more to address the "access" side of the "innovation-access continuum."[106] Access essentially begins with the way IP is managed during the invention, research, and product development stages through creative licensing practices. Given that NTDs, malaria, and TB represent a noncompetitive space for companies' commercial interests, and given WIPO's expertise in IP, and its long-standing relations with private sector inventors, this specialized UN agency was a natural venue to establish the multisectoral, public–private sector Consortium. Finally, having "prenegotiated" the minimum licensing terms, enshrined in the Guiding Principles,[107] that any institution that joins the Consortium needs to endorse, the transaction costs of entering into IP and knowledge sharing have been reduced significantly. This is a particularly important component of the way the Consortium operates and explains, in part, why so many collaborations were initiated within the framework of WIPO Re:Search.[108]

Now that the Consortium has demonstrated its initial success, new questions arise to move into the next, more mature phase. What is the longer-term vision of WIPO Re:Search? What are the next steps to ensure that WIPO Re:Search is able to build on its successes? What resources are required, especially for WIPO and BVGH as the administrator of the Partnership Hub, to support the ongoing expansion of WIPO Re:Search? These topics will keep the WIPO Secretariat, BVGH, and the Members busy as they continue the efforts to identify ways of maintaining the Consortium's success while simultaneously enabling and driving its future evolution.

[104] Mahoney, *supra* note 88.
[105] *Id.*
[106] *Id.*
[107] *WIPO Re:Search Guiding Principles* (June 8, 2011) www.wipo.int/export/sites/www/research/docs/guiding_principles.pdf
[108] Collaboration agreements are the tangible results of WIPO Re:Search's work. The full list of collaboration agreements is available at www.wipo.int/research/en/collaborations/collaborationagreements.html.

Appendix A: WIPO Re:Search Fellowships

WIPO Re:Search has provided opportunities for research fellowships of six developing country scientists at Member facilities, supported by funds-in-trust from the Government of Australia. WIPO Re:Search sought gender balance in the fellowships and half of the fellows were women. This is especially important since in some LMICs, female scientists face social, cultural, and economic barriers to the participation in "Women in Science, Technology, Engineering and Mathematics (STEM)" fields. WIPO Re:Search supports women from such places in realizing their potential and gaining recognition in their field.

A short summary of each of the six fellows and their current research follows here.[109]

Dr. Fidelis Cho-Ngwa, Head of the Pan-African ANDI Centre of Excellence and Associate Professor of Biochemistry and Molecular Biology at the University of Buea in Cameroon, works on onchocerciasis (river blindness) which affects 25 to 40 percent of Cameroonians.

Dr. Cho-Ngwa developed an interest in onchocerciasis research and in 2013, Dr. Cho-Ngwa was invited to spend three months at Novartis facilities in Basel, Switzerland. Having extensive experience in onchocerciasis, he travelled to Basel with clear goals in mind. Dr. Cho-Ngwa wanted to acquire in-depth knowledge and skills required to use high-performance liquid chromatography and mass spectrometry techniques in order to extract, purify, and identify active natural product compounds for filarial diseases. Novartis' state-of-the-art equipment combined with the host's strong support made Dr. Cho-Ngwa's plan possible.

Dr. Wellington Oyibo, Director of Research and Innovation, University of Lagos, Nigeria, is a medical parasitologist who previously worked on onchocerciasis; however, during the past ten years he has focused on malaria. Dr. Obiyo's rich experience in malarial diagnostics includes his participation in a WHO platform focusing on the use of malaria rapid diagnostic tests (RDTs) together with quality assurance of these tests. Dr. Obiyo joined the program convinced about a possibility to merge his diagnosis-oriented approach and Novartis' expertise in drug development. "They are producing medicines, but you have to be able to test a patient before the treatment," he remarked. "I wanted to explore if as a pharma company they had an interest to get into diagnosis." Dr. Obiyo hopes to obtain a malaria antibody that is able to dislodge or disrupt the interaction in which malarial parasites attach to the blood vessels.

Dr. Olfat Hammam is a pathologist who specializes in schistosomiasis pathology. She works at the Theodor Bilharz Research Institute in Giza, Egypt and has academic training in Egypt and Germany. WIPO Re:Search supported Dr. Hammam in completing her fellowship at Stanford University, Palo Alto, California. Her choice was a result of a careful investigation and preparatory work by BVGH, and Dr. Hammam saw the Stanford lab as a perfect match. Dr. Michael Hsieh, with whom she was invited to work, has extraordinary expertise in schistosomiasis and otherNTDs. In addition, he specializes in animal models for research – something that she wanted to explore in depth. Dr. Hammam sees the fellowship at Stanford as having provided an important boost to her research.

[109] Jedrusik, *supra* note 104.

Dr. Christian Agyare is a professor at the Department of Pharmaceutics, Kwame Nkrumah University of Science and Technology (KNUST), Kumasi, Ghana, specializing in investigating medicinal plants for their potential to treat infectious, including neglected, diseases. In October 2013, Dr. Agyare travelled to the Center for Discovery and Innovation in Parasitic Diseases (CDIPD), University of California, San Francisco, to start a ten-month fellowship. "My collaboration started with Dr. Conor Caffrey from CDIPD, which was made possible by WIPO Re:Search. The collaboration has continued with a project on parasites responsible for NTDs," Dr. Agyare explained.

Dr. Agyare's initial idea was to perform the extraction and purification of compounds from the anti-parasitic products in Ghana and then to travel to California to further examine their activity. However, new demands on his time arose in Ghana, and instead of returning to California himself, one of his students, Ms. Gertrude Kyere-Davies, who at the time was pursuing a degree in pharmaceutical microbiology, was invited to the University of California to continue Dr. Agyare's research. While in the CDIPD labs, Ms. Kyere-Davies learned various methods for growing the organisms and how to safely store them. She was glad that she could continue the work with the same team because of the complexity of the research and the need for time to obtain tangible results.

Dr. Krupa Naran was a doctoral fellow at the Institute of Infectious Diseases and Molecular Medicine, University of Cape Town, South Africa. As she has stated, "At the time when I went to AstraZeneca our lab just started doing some initial drug discovery in tuberculosis. On the biology side, it meant setting up different assays [investigative procedures aimed at the assessment of the composition of a substance] to try to figure out which would be the best drug to treat TB." During the fellowship, the experts at AstraZeneca supported her in developing new skills and knowledge relating to assay development and beyond. Dr. Naran reported: "I have gained incredible knowledge and experimental skills in areas such as the culturing of nonreplicating bacteria, kill kinetics, and intracellular assays, all of which forms the basis of our drug discovery program."

References

Barnes, Jeffrey, *Designing Public–Private Partnerships in Health, SHOPS* (2011), www.abtassociates.com/reports/PPP_Primer.pdf.

BIO Ventures for Global Health, *2015 Partnership Hub Mid-Year Report: Catalyzing Partnerships for Global Health* (2015), www.wipo.int/export/sites/www/research/en/docs/bvgh_midyear_research_report_2015.pdf (last visited Nov. 18, 2017).

BIO Ventures for Global Health, Partnership Hub Mid-Year Report 2017, https://bvgh.org/wp-content/uploads/2017/09/2017-BVGH-Partnership-Hub-Mid-Year-Report.pdf (last visited Nov. 18, 2017).

Bombelles, Thomas (Interview by Hannah Coaker), *Neglected Tropical Disease Research: Rethinking the Drug Discovery Model*, 7 Future Medicinal Chemistry 7 (2015).

Bombelles, Thomas, Jennifer Dent, Meghana Sharafudeen, Philip Stevens, Katy M. Graef, and Anatole Krattiger, *WIPO Re:Search: Sharing Innovation in the Fight Against Neglected Tropical Diseases* (2015), www.wipo.int/edocs/pubdocs/en/wipo_pub_gc_8.pdf (last visited Nov. 18, 2017).

Brant, Jennifer and Balaji Parthasarathy, *The Dynamics of Global Technology and Knowledge Flows*, (Innovation and Intellectual Prop. Series, Research Paper No. 4, 2015).

Cashwell, Amber, Anupama Tantri, Ashley Schmidt, Greg Simona, and Neeraj Mistrya. *BRICS in the Response to Neglected Tropical Diseases*, 92 BULLETIN OF THE WORLD HEALTH ORG. (2014).

Cookson, Clive, *Studies Fuel Criticism of High Drug Development Costs*, FIN. TIMES, April 9, 2015, www.ft.com/content/6a57fcd4-bdcd-11e4-8cf3-00144feab7de?mhq5j=e5.

Dent, Jennifer, Katy M. Graef, and Paddy Shivanand, *Open Innovation to Bolster Research and Development for Neglected and Emerging Infectious Diseases*, 1 J. MED. DEV. (2015) Available at http://ojs.whioce.com/index.php/jmds/article/view/119/99 (last visited Nov. 18, 2017).

Deloitte Centre for Health Solutions, *Measuring the Return from Pharmaceutical Innovation 2014*, DELOITTE (2014) https://www2.deloitte.com/uk/en/pages/life-sciences-and-healthcare/articles/measuring-the-return-from-pharmaceutical-innovation-2014.html (last visited Nov. 18, 2017).

Drugs for Neglected Diseases Initiative, *An Innovative Approach to R&D for Neglected Patients: Ten Years of Experience & Lessons Learned by DNDi* (2014) www.dndi.org/wp-content/uploads/2009/03/DNDi_Modelpaper_2013.pdf (last visited Nov. 18, 2017).

Farlow, Andrew, *The Global HIV Vaccine Enterprise, Malaria Vaccines, and Purchase Commitments: What is the Fit?* (2005) www.who.int/intellectualproperty/submissions/Farlow.pdf. note 14.

Grace, Cheri, *Product Development Partnerships (PDPs): Lessons from PDPs Established to Develop New Health Technologies for Neglected Diseases*, HUMAN DEV. RES. CTR. (2010).

Hotez, Peter J., *The Neglected Tropical Diseases and the Neglected Infections of Poverty: Overview of Their Common Features, Global Disease Burden and Distribution, New Control Tools, and Prospects for Disease Elimination, in* THE CAUSES AND IMPACTS OF NEGLECTED TROPICAL AND ZOONOTIC DISEASES: OPPORTUNITIES FOR INTEGRATED INTERVENTION STRATEGIES (Institute of Medicine (US) Forum on Microbial Threats ed., 2011).

HOUSE OF COMMONS SCIENCE AND TECHNOLOGY COMMITTEE, BUILDING SCIENTIFIC CAPACITY FOR DEVELOPMENT, 2012–13, HC 377 (UK).

Idris, Kamil, and Hisamitsu Arai, THE INTELLECTUAL PROPERTY-CONSCIOUS NATION: MAPPING THE PATH FROM DEVELOPING TO DEVELOPED (2006).

Jedrusik, Ania, *Sharing Innovation and Building Capacity to Fight Neglected Tropical Diseases: A Selection of WIPO Re:Search Fellowship Stories*, GLOBAL CHALLENGES REP. (2016), www.wipo.int/edocs/pubdocs/en/wipo_pub_gc_11.pdf (last visited Nov. 18, 2017).

Jewell, Cathy, *Harnessing the Power of the Private Sector – An Interview with Francis Gurry*, 5 WIPO MAG., Oct. 2015.

Krattiger, Anatole, Richard T. Mahoney, Lita Nelsen, Jennifer A. Thomson, Alan B. Bennett, Kanikaram Satyanarayana, Gregory D. Graff, Carlos Fernandez, and Stanle P. Kowalski (eds.), INTELLECTUAL PROPERTY MANAGEMENT OF HEALTH AND AGRICULTURAL INNOVATION: A HANDBOOK OF BEST PRACTICES (2007).

Lansang, Mary Ann, and Rodolfo Dennis, *Building Capacity in Health Research in the Developing World*, 82 BULLETIN OF THE WORLD HEALTH ORG. (2004).

Mahoney, Richard, *Product Development Partnerships: Case Studies of a New Mechanism for Health Technology Innovation*, 9 HEALTH RES. POL'Y AND SYS. (2011).

Mahoney, Richard, *Strategic Review of WIPO Re:Search*, GLOBAL CHALLENGES REP. (2015), www.ip-watch.org/weblog/wp-content/uploads/2015/10/WIPO-GlobalChallenges-ReSearch-Review-Oct-2015.pdf (last visited Nov. 18, 2017).

Mattes, William B., (Rathnam Chaguturu ed.), *Divided We Fall, in* COLLABORATIVE INNOVATION IN DRUG DISCOVERY: STRATEGIES FOR PUBLIC AND PRIVATE PARTNERSHIPS (2014).

Molyneux, David H., Peter J Hotez, and Alan Fenwick, *"Rapid-Impact Interventions": How a Policy of Integrated Control for Africa's Neglected Tropical Diseases Could Benefit the Poor*, PLoS Med (2005).

Morel, Carlos M., Tara Acharya, Denis Broun, Ajit Dangi, Christopher Elias, N. K. Ganguly, Charles A. Gardner, R. K. Gupta, Jane Haycock, Anthony D. Heher, Peter J. Hotez, Hannah E. Kettler, Gerald T. Keusch, Anatole F. Krattiger, Fernando T. Kreutz, Sanjaya Lall, Keun Lee, Richard Mahoney, Adolfo Martinez-Palomo, R. A. Mashelkar, Stephen A. Matlin, Mandi Mzimba, Joachim Oehler, Robert G. Ridley, Pramilla Senanayake, Peter Singer, and Mikyung Yun, *Health Innovation Networks to Help Developing Countries Address Neglected Diseases*, 309 Science (2005).

NSW Health Department, A Framework for Building Capacity to Improve Health (2001).

OECD, Coherence for Health: Innovation for New Medicines for Infectious Diseases, The Development Dimension (2009).

Policy Cures, *Global Funding of Innovation for Neglected Diseases: G-FINDER* (2015) http://policycures.org/gfinder.html (last visited Nov. 18, 2017).

Policy Cures, *Measuring Global Health R&D for the Post-2015 Development Agenda* (2015) - www.ghtcoalition.org/pdf/Measuring-global-health-R-D-for-the-post-2015-development-agenda.pdf (last visited Nov. 18, 2017).

Ramamoorthi, Roopa, et al., *WIPO Re:Search: Accelerating Anthelmintic Development through Cross-Sector Partnerships*, 4 Int. J. for Parasitology: Drugs & Drug Resistance (2014).

Symposium, *Anthelmintics: From Discovery to Resistance* (2016); Symposium, *Global Challenges for New Drug Discovery Against Tropical Parasitic Diseases* (2014).

Reich, Michael R., *Public–Private Partnerships for Public Health*, 6 Nature Med. 617 (2000).

Savioli, Lorenzo, Antonio Montresor, and Albis F. Gabrielli, *Neglected Tropical Diseases: The Development of a Brand with No Copyright. A Shift from a Disease-Centered to a Tool-Centered Strategic Approach*, *in* The Causes and Impacts of Neglected Tropical and Zoonotic Diseases: Opportunities for Integrated Intervention Strategies: Workshop Summary (2011), www.ncbi.nlm.nih.gov/books/NBK62524/ (last visited Nov. 18, 2017)

Taubman, Antony, *A Typology of Intellectual Property Management for Public Health Innovation and Access: Design Considerations for Policy Makers*, 4 The Open AIDS J. 1 (2010).

Torstensson, David, *Fighting Tropical Disease: It's Now a Common Cause*, PharmExec.com (Feb. 8, 2012), www.pharmexec.com/fighting-tropical-disease-its-now-common-cause.

Tufts Ctr. for the Study of Drug Dev., Press Release, Cost to Develop and Win Marketing Approval for a New Drug Is $2.6 Billion (November 18, 2014), http://csdd.tufts.edu/news/complete_story/pr_tufts_csdd_2014_cost_study (last visited Nov. 18, 2017).

Uniting to Combat Neglected Tropical Diseases, *Country Leadership and Collaboration on Neglected Tropical Diseases: Third Progress Report of the London Declaration* (2015) http://unitingtocombatntds.org/sites/default/files/document/UTCNTD%20FULL%20REPORT.pdf.

Uniting to Combat Neglected Tropical Diseases, *London Declaration on Neglected Tropical Diseases* (2012) http://unitingtocombatntds.org/sites/default/files/resource_file/london_declaration_on_ntds.pdf (last visited Nov. 18, 2017).

Uniting to Combat Neglected Tropical Diseases, http://unitingtocombatntds.org/ (last visited Nov. 18, 2017).

World Health Organization [WHO], *Accelerating Work to Overcome the Global Impact of Neglected Tropical Diseases - A Roadmap for Implementation: Executive Summary* (2012), www.who.int/neglected_diseases/NTD_RoadMap_2012_Fullversion.pdf.

WHO, *First Global Partners' Meeting on Neglected Tropical Diseases*, www.who.int/neglected_diseases/partners_meeting/en/ (last visited Nov. 18, 2017).

WHO, *Health in 2015: from MDGs to SDGs* (2015), http://apps.who.int/iris/bitstream/10665/200009/1/9789241565110_eng.pdf?ua=1 (last visited Nov. 18, 2017).
WHO, *Making a Difference: 30 Years of Research and Capacity Building in Tropical Diseases* (2007), http://apps.who.int/iris/bitstream/10665/43689/1/9789241595575_eng.pdf (last visited Nov. 18, 2017).
WHO, *Neglected Tropical Diseases Summary*, WHO (2017), www.who.int/neglected_diseases/diseases/summary/en/ (last visited Nov. 18, 2017).
WHO, *Neglected Tropical Diseases, Hidden Successes, Emerging Opportunities* (2006), http://apps.who.int/iris/bitstream/10665/69367/1/WHO_CDS_NTD_2006.2_eng.pdf (last visited Nov. 18, 2017).
WHO, *Public Health, Innovation and Intellectual Property Rights; Report of the Commission on Intellectual Property Rights, Innovation and Public Health* (2006), www.who.int/intellectualproperty/documents/thereport/ENPublicHealthReport.pdf (last visited Nov. 18, 2017).
WHO Comm'n on Intellectual Prop. Rights, *Public Health: Innovation and Intellectual Property Rights* (2006), www.who.int/intellectualproperty/documents/thereport/ENPublicHealthReport.pdf?ua=1 (last visited Nov. 18, 2017).
WHO, WIPO & WTO, *Promoting Access to Medical Technologies and Innovation: Intersections between Public Health, Intellectual Property, and Trade* (2012), www.wto.org/english/res_e/booksp_e/pamtiwhowipowtoweb13_e.pdf (last visited Nov. 18, 2017).
World Intellectual Property Organization [WIPO], *The 45 Adopted Recommendations under the WIPO Development Agenda*, www.wipo.int/ip-development/en/agenda/recommendations.html (last visited April 10, 2016).
WIPO, *The First Five Years of the WIPO Japan Funds-in-Trust for Industrial Property (Japan FIT/IP) for Africa and Least Developed Countries (LDCs): A Productive Collaboration with the Japan Patent Office (JPO)* (2013), www.wipo.int/export/sites/www/cooperation/en/funds_in_trust/docs/japanfitip_jpo_firstfiveyears_en.pdf (last visited Nov. 18, 2017).
WIPO Re:Search, www.wiporesearch.org/ (last visited Nov. 18, 2017).

4 Creating, Managing, and Advancing Collaborations: The Road to Successful Partnerships

Katy M. Graef, Jennifer Dent, and Amy Starr

I BVGH history and Mission

In 2010, the World Health Organization (WHO) classified a group of seventeen (17) bacterial, viral, and parasitic diseases as "neglected" because they lacked safe, effective, and affordable drugs, vaccines, and diagnostics to prevent, diagnose, and treat them. Globally, over one billion people are directly affected by these diseases.[1] While these seventeen diseases often are not fatal, they can result in permanent disfigurement, disrupted childhood development, and increased work and school absenteeism. These neglected tropical diseases (NTDs) are endemic to over 140 countries worldwide, with the majority of infections occurring in low- and middle-income countries (LMICs) located in Africa, Asia, and Latin America. The economic effects of NTDs compound the financial challenges faced by these developing economies and stifle their growth. For example, the WHO has estimated that dengue virus infections alone directly and indirectly cost over US$2 billion annually.[2] Thus NTDs pose a crippling burden to some of the world's poorest nations.

The biopharmaceutical industry has historically paid little attention to NTDs and other diseases that predominantly affect the poor (poverty-related diseases [PRDs]). This inattention is primarily due to the lack of market opportunity and inability to secure a return on the large investment in research and development (R&D) that is needed to bring a medical product to the market. However, in 2004, driven by the growing need for the development of solutions to address the unmet medical needs of the developing world – including NTDs – the Biotechnology Innovation Organization (BIO), the world's largest biopharmaceutical, diagnostic, and life sciences trade organization, established BIO Ventures for Global Health (BVGH).[3] BVGH was created to develop and implement programs that engage BIO's stakeholders and leverage their assets to impact global health.[4] This included publishing business cases for the development of specific

[1] David H. Molyneux, Lorenzo Savioli, and Dirk Engels, *Neglected Tropical Diseases: Progress Towards Addressing the Chronic Pandemic*, 389 Lancet, 312 (2017).

[2] World Health Organization [WHO], *Investing to Overcome the Global Impact of Neglected Tropical Diseases* (2015) http://apps.who.int/iris/bitstream/10665/152781/1/9789241564861_eng.pdf.

[3] Justin Gillis, *Medical Aid on the Way for Poorer Nations*, Wash. Post, June 6, 2004, at A19.

[4] See, e.g., BIO Ventures for Global Health [BVGH], Tuberculosis Vaccines: The Case for Investment (2006).

products targeting PRDs,[5] and establishing partnerships to accelerate product development.[6] One such program was BVGH's Global Health Primer – a compilation of information about twenty-five PRDs and the products in use or in development for their management. Through these and other programs, BVGH initiated dialogue between BIO's stakeholders and the global health community and encouraged industry's involvement in R&D of products for the many unmet medical needs of the developing world.[7]

One major barrier hindering the development of products to prevent, diagnose, and treat NTDs is that the diseases' experts have had limited access to the biopharmaceutical industry's small molecules, technologies, and know-how. Conversely, the biopharmaceutical industry's lack of attention to and expertise in these diseases impedes their development of much needed products.[8] These challenges can be addressed by developing platforms through which disease experts can access industry's knowledge and assets and by creating strategic public–private partnerships (PPPs) that leverage the respective strengths of each sector.

The drivers of industry's attention to NTDs and PRDs are varied. Globalization over past decades has raised awareness of PRDs and the health care needs of the millions living in poverty. Through corporate social responsibility (CSR) programs, companies are contributing their resources to address these diseases. In addition, companies recognize that Africa, Latin America, and South Asia will become crucial markets and are investing significant capital in R&D of products for diseases affecting these regions. BVGH's programs encourage companies to recognize the benefits of addressing PRDs and the possibilities of building new partnerships within these regions to address health care needs.

This chapter will explore two open innovation platforms co-led by BVGH – the Pool for Open Innovation against Neglected Tropical Diseases (POINT) and WIPO Re:Search – that encourage and support biopharmaceutical companies' contributions to NTD R&D through PPPs. The necessity of a partner responsible for proactively establishing collaborative projects between participating organizations and managing established alliances to ensure challenges are addressed and projects are successful is discussed. This chapter concludes with a description of how the WIPO Re:Search Consortium governs the sharing of intellectual property between organizations and the Consortium's alignment with the United Nations Sustainable Development Goals (SDGs).

[5] BVGH & PATH, The Case for Investment in Enterotoxigenic *Escherichia coli* Vaccines (2011).

[6] Jennifer Dent, Katy M. Graef & Paddy Shivanand, *Open Innovation to Bolster Research and Development for Neglected and Emerging Infectious Diseases*, J. Med. Dev. (July 10, 2015), http://ojs.whioce.com/index.php/jmds/article/view/119/99.

[7] According to Carl Feldbaum, President Emeritus of the Biotechnology Innovation Organization and a member of the BVGH Board of Directors since its launch, "BVGH was established to help bridge a great divide between BIO's stakeholders – public and private companies, academic and research institutions – and approximately 6 billion people living in the developing world, especially those suffering from neglected tropical diseases." When interviewed in 2014, Mr. Feldbaum expressed his disappointment that industry's initial progress had been slow; however, he was encouraged by the shift in the pharmaceutical industry's perception of developing world markets.

[8] Dent, Graef, and Shivanand, *supra* note 6 at 1–5.

II Pool for Open Innovation against Neglected Tropical Diseases (POINT)

Established in February 2009 by GlaxoSmithKline (GSK) as part of the company's larger plan to aid the developing world, POINT was created to allow universities and government research institutes to access GSK's small molecules, patents, and know-how on favorable terms to bolster and accelerate their neglected disease drug development. Sir Andrew Witty, GSK's Chief Executive Officer, proposed the voluntary "patent pool" and called on other biopharmaceutical firms to open up access to their intellectual property (IP) assets relevant to NTDs. This proposal followed Witty's announcement that GSK would cap its prices for patented medicines in poor countries at 25 percent of what it charged in developed countries and reinvest 20 percent of the profit it made from selling medicines in poor nations into health care infrastructure projects in those countries.[9]

At its inception, the pool contained approximately eight hundred (800) patents. Within less than a year, Alnylam Pharmaceuticals, the Massachusetts Institute of Technology, and South Africa's Technology Innovation Agency announced their participation in POINT.[10] These organizations' contributions expanded the pool of IP assets to include over twenty-three hundred (2,300) patents.[11]

During the development of POINT, GSK engaged BVGH to manage the program and promote the program's independence from GSK.[12] Following POINT's launch, BVGH helped to facilitate POINT's first collaboration between GSK, iThemba, and Emory University. While this partnership demonstrated the impact an IP-sharing platform could have, and the value of company contributions, it was recognized that additional company assets would be beneficial. BVGH also recognized that a stagnant pool of IP assets does not attract researchers' interests. Instead, potential IP users must be proactively engaged and presented with novel partnership ideas based on the assets in the pool and aligned with the areas of interest and research needs of the IP users. A model involving thoughtful partnership development and alliance management would need to be employed to meet the program's objectives.

III WIPO Re:Search

POINT's demonstration of an IP-sharing, open innovation platform dedicated to accelerating product development for diseases of poverty began to garner the interest of a wider group of biopharmaceutical companies. As the world's leading institution in overseeing and shaping global IP policies, the World Intellectual Property Organization (WIPO) was an obvious partner in a new initiative. WIPO has a mandate to lead the development of a balanced IP system that enables innovation and creativity for the benefit of all.[13] When approached by interested companies in 2010, WIPO expressed an interest in exploring a new and broader model to exhibit this open access concept and to demonstrate that IP is not a barrier to research and development. WIPO, BVGH, and

[9] *GSK Backs Patent Pool for Neglected Diseases*, Nature (Feb. 18, 2009), www.nature.com/news/2009/090218/full/457949e.html.

[10] Heidi Ledford, *MIT and South African Research Agency Dive Into Industry Patent Pool*, Nature News-blog (May 6, 2017; 2:35 PM), http://blogs.nature.com/news/2010/05/mit_dives_into_industry_patent.html

[11] Dent, Graef, & Shivanand, *supra* note 6 at 1–5.

[12] Linda Nordling, *Patent Pool Starts to Attract Interest*, SciDev.net (Oct. 5, 2010), www.scidev.net/global/health/news/patent-pool-starts-to-attract-interest.html.

[13] *Inside WIPO*, www.wipo.int/about-wipo/en/.

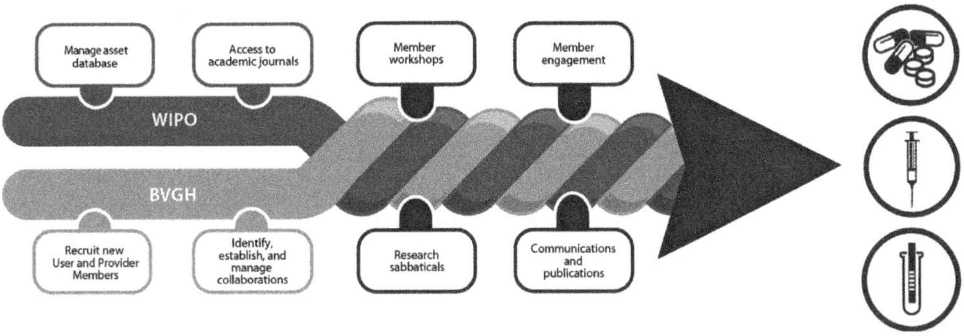

Figure 4.1. WIPO and BVGH are responsible for coordinating and leading WIPO Re:Search activities. WIPO manages the WIPO Re:Search Database and provides developing world organizations with access to academic journal articles. BVGH recruits new WIPO Re:Search Members and facilitates and manages partnerships between Members. Both BVGH and WIPO are responsible for engaging Members, coordinating Member workshops, and communicating the activities and successes of the Consortium.
Source: BIO Ventures for Global Health.

eight biopharmaceutical companies[14] (Alnylam, AstraZeneca, Eisai, GSK, MSD [known as Merck & Co., Inc. in the US and Canada], Novartis, Pfizer, and Sanofi) created a new platform that leveraged WIPO's infrastructure, built upon the ideas and momentum created by POINT, and expanded the scope of the pool to include diagnostics and vaccines. These efforts led to the establishment of the WIPO Re:Search Consortium, a platform through which the biopharmaceutical industry's IP assets and resources are connected to qualified academic and nonprofit neglected disease researchers through collaborative research agreements. The goal of the Consortium is to accelerate the development of new drugs, vaccines, and diagnostics for NTDs, malaria, and tuberculosis.[15]

The activities and administration of WIPO Re:Search are coordinated jointly by WIPO and BVGH. Each organization has distinct and complementary responsibilities within their respective roles as the Partnership Hub Administrator (BVGH) and the Secretariat (WIPO). Leveraging its IP expertise and authority, WIPO hosts IP training workshops for Consortium Members. WIPO is also responsible for organizing the WIPO Re:Search annual (or biennial) meeting, coordinating teleconferences between all Members, and managing the WIPO Re:Search Database,[16] an online database of IP assets made available by Provider Members.[17] Through its role as the Partnership Hub Administrator, BVGH is responsible for establishing research collaborations between

[14] As of 2016, ten companies are participating in WIPO Re:Search: Alnylam; Eisai; GSK; Janssen, the Pharmaceutical Companies of Johnson & Johnson; MSD; Merck KGaA, Darmstadt, Germany; Novartis; Pfizer; Sanofi; and Takeda.

[15] Jennifer Dent et al., *WIPO Re:Search: A Consortium Catalyzing Research and Product Development for Neglected Tropical Diseases*, 2 PHARMACEUTICAL PAT. ANALYST 591 (2013).

[16] Anatole Krattiger, Thomas Bombelles, and Ania Jedrusik, Driving Innovation for Global Health Through Multi-stakeholder Partnerships, Chapter 3, *supra* (in this volume).

[17] Institutions join the Consortium as "User," "Provider," and/or "Supporter" Members. Provider Members – most notably the Founding Pharmaceutical Members – are those organizations that have expressed a willingness to share their IP assets, such as know-how, expertise, materials, and services, with other Members. User Members subsequently utilize these contributed assets to accelerate their neglected disease R&D activities. Supporter Members join the Consortium to demonstrate their approval of the WIPO Re:Search mission and its innovative and open access to IP.

WIPO Re:Search Members and providing alliance management and support to all ongoing research projects. BVGH also leads the recruitment of new WIPO Re:Search Members. Both BVGH and WIPO are responsible for communicating the activities and achievements of WIPO Re:Search to Members and the greater global health and IP communities.

IV Targeted Recruiting

A Consortium membership composed of research organizations from different sectors and geographies ensures not only a diversity of collaborations, but also a variety of ideas and capacities directed toward the development of products for neglected infectious diseases. At its inception in 2011, thirty-two organizations were Members of WIPO Re:Search.[18] During the subsequent three years, BVGH focused a significant portion of its efforts toward expanding the WIPO Re:Search membership. This included a specific emphasis on recruiting User Members from Africa – where NTDs predominate. By the end of 2014, ninety-one organizations from twenty-six countries – including eighteen from Africa – were Members of WIPO Re:Search.

To have the greatest and most effective impact, WIPO Re:Search membership as a whole should have all the necessary assets, skills, and capabilities to move a product from discovery to the market. Furthermore, the membership should include organizations performing research and product development for all WIPO Re:Search diseases. As WIPO Re:Search entered its fourth year, BVGH honed its recruiting efforts toward those organizations that could bring key assets, skills, and capabilities to fill gaps in the WIPO Re:Search membership's competencies. In late 2016 BVGH began the process of systematically mapping the assets and research activities of WIPO Re:Search User and Provider Members. Identification and organization of Members' assets and capabilities will allow BVGH to manage the growing number of Members and resources while informing its approach to Member recruitment. By the end of 2016, a total of 109 organizations from 31 countries were WIPO Re:Search Members. These organizations include leading academic research centers with internationally renowned NTD experts, such as the University of California, San Diego (UCSD) and University of Georgia. They also include product development partnerships (PDPs), such as Medicines for Malaria Venture (MMV), Drugs for Neglected Diseases initiative (DNDi), and Foundation for Innovative New Diagnostics (FIND), as well as nonprofit organizations with experience conducting clinical trials in NTD-endemic regions, such as the Noguchi Memorial Institute for Medical Research. As BVGH continues to systematically map Members, it plans to recruit strategically relevant organizations to join and contribute to WIPO Re:Search.

[18] Alnylam Pharmaceuticals; Assoc. of University Technology Managers (AUTM); AstraZeneca, Biotechnology Innovation Organization (BIO); California Institute of Technology (Caltech); Center for World Health & Medicine (CWHM); Drugs for Neglected Diseases initiative (DNDi); Eisai Co., Ltd.; Emory University; Fundação Oswaldo Cruz (Fiocruz); GlaxoSmithKline (GSK); Indian Council for Medical Research (ICMR); International Federation of Intellectual Property Attorneys (FICPI); iThemba; Kenya Medical Research Institute (KEMRI); Mahidol University; Massachusetts Institute of Technology (MIT); Medical Research Council—South Africa; Medicines for Malaria Venture (MMV); MSD; National Center for Genetic Engineering and Biotechnology (BIOTEC); Novartis; PATH; Pfizer; Sabin Vaccine Institute; Sanofi; Swiss Tropical and Public Health Institute (Swiss TPH); National Institutes of Health (NIH); US Patent and Trademark Office; University of California, Berkeley; University of California, San Francisco (UCSF); University of Dundee.

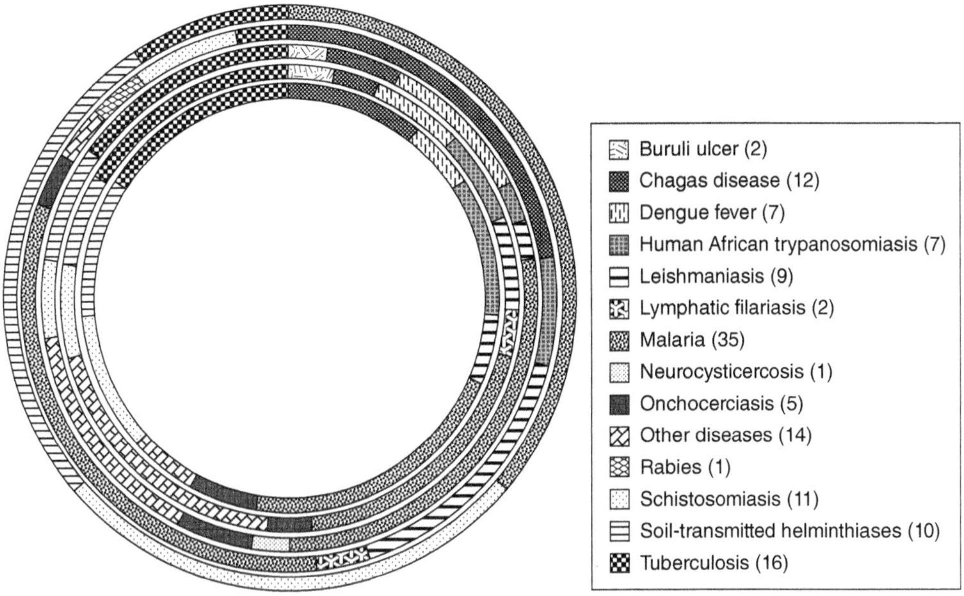

Figure 4.2. Through its proactive partnering approach, BVGH has established 108 research collaborations spanning 13 neglected infectious diseases.
Source: BIO Ventures for Global Health.

V Proactive Partnering

Proactive development and management of collaborations is key to the successful implementation of asset exchange programs. As the WIPO Re:Search Partnership Hub Administrator, BVGH is responsible for leveraging its close connection with WIPO Re:Search Members – including the participating biopharmaceutical companies – to establish and manage research partnerships.[19] BVGH accomplishes this by proactively examining Member scientists' research interests and needs and recommending collaborations with other Members that fulfill those needs. BVGH also fields asset requests from Members, identifies other Member organizations able to meet these requests, and then forges mutually beneficial collaborations with clearly defined roles, responsibilities, and objectives.[20]

By the end of the Consortium's first year, BVGH had established thirteen partnerships between Members. The partnership development momentum continued with twenty-eight and thirty-six collaborations established in 2013 and 2014, respectively. At the conclusion of its fifth year of operation, 108 collaborations, involving 56 members, had been established. Of these 108 partnerships, 25 were still ongoing at the end of 2016. These collaborations span thirteen different[21] diseases and involve the sharing of several classes of IP assets: compounds, data and reagents, expertise and advice, samples, and technologies and assays.

How BVGH establishes collaborations depends on the Member it is seeking to engage. A primary objective of WIPO Re:Search is to leverage biopharmaceutical companies'

[19] Dent, *supra* note 14, at 591.
[20] *Id.* at 593.
[21] Fourteen diseases, including "other."

assets to accelerate product development for neglected infectious diseases. Ten companies currently belong to WIPO Re:Search: Alnylam; Eisai; GSK; Janssen, the Pharmaceutical Companies of Johnson & Johnson; MSD; Merck KGaA, Darmstadt, Germany; Novartis; Pfizer; Sanofi; and Takeda. BVGH applies a customized approach to establishing partnerships for each of these companies. This customized approach includes the coordination of recurring discussions with each company, during which BVGH provides updates on the company's partnerships. BVGH also inquires about the company's current WIPO Re:Search partnership strategy: which assets it wishes to share, Members it is interested in engaging, and diseases it desires to focus on, as well as partnering bandwidth. Each company is encouraged to participate in WIPO Re:Search partnerships in a way that fits that company's goals, resources, and capacity. For example, a company may choose to limit its participation to sharing its assets, whereas a different company may be more actively engaged in a partnership, not only sharing assets, but also scheduling regular updates with its partners, and contributing to the analysis of the data. BVGH works with each company to determine the style of participation that suits that company's strategies and expectations.

BVGH applies a similar, customized approach to establishing collaborations with not-for-profit WIPO Re:Search Members. When a new Member joins WIPO Re:Search, BVGH reviews that Member's researchers' online profiles and publications, connects with those researchers to learn more about their interests, research plans, and needs, and suggests collaborations with other Members – both academic and for-profit – that could meet those needs.

VI Managing Alliances

WIPO Re:Search collaborations – as with other research endeavors – are planned and initiated with the best of intentions. A multitude of factors, including competing interests, funding changes, and lack of communication, can result in a collaboration not reaching its intended outcome. As the number and complexity of WIPO Re:Search collaborations expanded, BVGH augmented its partnering activities by creating a set of documents and implementing procedures to circumvent challenges before they can prevent a partnership from reaching a successful conclusion.

Before initiating discussions between potential collaborators, BVGH circulates its collaboration guidelines (Appendix A), which outline how BVGH will work with the potential collaborators to establish and track their WIPO Re:Search collaboration. This includes a description of the documents that must be completed prior to beginning and upon completion of a collaboration. The guidelines also describe the metrics that BVGH will track – such as project milestones reached, manuscripts published, and funding awards obtained. To further circumvent potential challenges and set expectations, BVGH has developed a collaboration outline document (Appendix B) that must be completed and approved by all participants of a WIPO Re:Search collaboration. This document requires a description of the research project and objectives, IP assets to be shared, expected timelines, and the source of funding for the project.

After establishing each collaboration, BVGH provides partnership support and alliance management – tracking each collaboration's progress, maintaining communications between all participants, and resolving any challenges and roadblocks that arise. BVGH also engages the collaborators to schedule timeline-appropriate check-in dates and recurring meetings to encourage continuous communication and early resolution of challenges. As needed, BVGH identifies and engages additional WIPO Re:Search Member scientists to add further resources and expertise in order to move the research project to the next stage of product development. For example, BVGH brought an additional partner with expertise in solving the structures of pathogens' proteins to a WIPO Re:Search schistosomiasis drug discovery project. This additional partner agreed to attempt to solve the structure of the *Schistosoma mansoni* protein targeted by the drug discovery project. With the structure in hand, the researchers will be able to perform rational drug design and synthesize compounds that preferentially interact with the *S. mansoni* protein over to the homologous human protein.

BVGH evolves and augments its partnering and alliance management procedures to meet the needs and goals of the Consortium and its Members. Upon reaching the completion of a WIPO Re:Search collaboration, BVGH requests that each collaborator complete a "collaboration close-out form," which requests feedback and impressions of the collaboration.

VII Evolving Outputs

Aligning with the Consortium's primary objective of engaging biopharmaceutical companies in neglected infectious disease research and product development, the majority of collaborations established by BVGH in the first two years after the Consortium's inception involved a for-profit Member contributing its assets – most often compound sets and libraries – to a nonprofit or academic Member researcher. As WIPO Re:Search membership grew and BVGH strengthened its relationships with User Members, the collaborations established by BVGH shifted to those solely involving nonprofit/academic Members. These nonprofit + nonprofit partnerships are often multifaceted, with both partners equally contributing assets and expertise to a research project. By the end of 2016, fifty-three of the collaborations included an industry and a nonprofit/academic partner. Forty-nine collaborations involved only nonprofit/academic partners.[22] Four collaborations between two for-profit entities were also established.

The diversity of projects stemming from WIPO Re:Search expanded as well. The overwhelming majority of collaborations established during the Consortium's first year focused on drug development. However, diagnostics discovery and basic research have become more prominent over time. Correlating with the changing landscape of Members participating in a collaboration, the majority of diagnostics and basic research projects have involved two nonprofit entities.

VIII Measuring Impact

The first WIPO Re:Search collaboration was established in early 2012. While a metric such as the number of diseases eradicated or number of lives saved will be the ultimate measure of the success of the Consortium, these metrics cannot yet reflect the early performance of the Consortium and its research projects. Current analyses estimate that

[22] *Accelerating R&D for Neglected Diseases through Global Collaborations: WIPO Re:Search Partnership Stories 2013–2015*, BVGH (2015) www.bvgh.org/LinkClick.aspx?fileticket=sbxNzyE6Xac%3d&tabid=277.

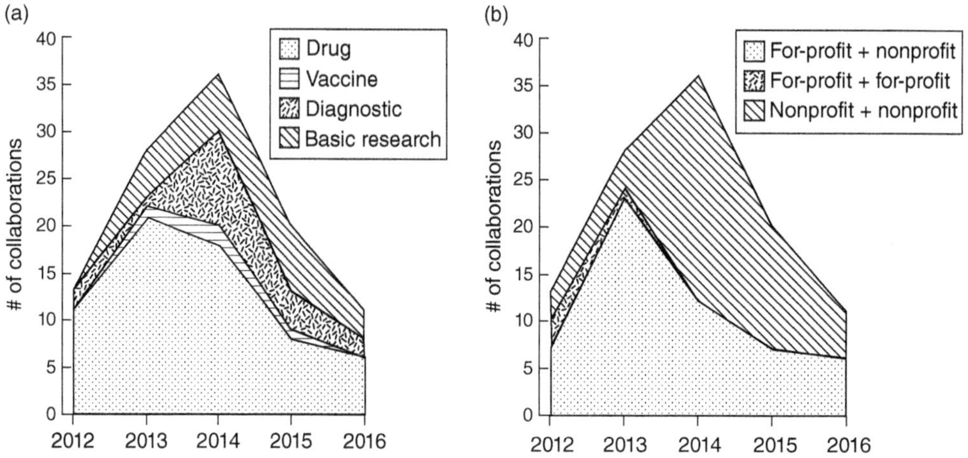

Figure 4.3. At the Consortium's inception, the majority of collaborations BVGH established focused on drug development. As time advanced, diagnostics development and basic research became more prominent (a). While the majority of collaborations established during the Consortium's first two years and to date involve a for-profit and nonprofit organization, in recent years, nonprofit + nonprofit partnerships have increased, outpacing for-profit + nonprofit collaborations in 2014 and 2015 (b).
Source: BIO Ventures for Global Health.

it can take upwards of ten years to move a drug from discovery to the market.[23] The majority of WIPO Re:Search collaborations were initiated at an early discovery stage and would thus require at least an additional six years to reach the market.

Until such a time when a product would be expected, BVGH has established alternative metrics to evaluate its performance as well as the impact of the collaborations it has established. Similar to the pharmaceutical industry, where the quality of a given company's pipeline may be measured by the number of viable candidates under development, BVGH measures its performance by the number of meaningful partnerships it has established between Members, the number of Members it has engaged in those collaborations, the diversity of research questions the collaborations were established to answer, and the variety of diseases and products those collaborations address.

To date, BVGH has engaged 65 percent of the WIPO Re:Search User and/or Provider Members in a research collaboration. Thirteen of the twenty-one WIPO Re:Search diseases have been the focus of a collaboration. Research projects focused on basic research as well as drug, vaccine, and diagnostic discovery and development have been established. These collaborations span the various stages of product development – from discovery to screening, hits identification to optimization, preclinical to clinical research.

While the depth of the WIPO Re:Search Partnership Pipeline[24] demonstrates BVGH's prolific partnering abilities, other metrics are more reflective of the collaborations' potential

[23] *Biopharmaceutical Research & Development: The Process Behind New Medicines*, PhRMA (2015), www.phrma.org/report/biopharmaceutical-research-and-development-the-process-behind-new-medicines.

[24] The full partnership pipeline can be viewed at: https://bvgh.org/bio-ventures-global-health/wipo-research/wipo-research-collaborations/,

impacts. The goal of the Consortium is to accelerate product development for neglected infectious diseases. A collaboration's movement into the next stage of development is a good indication of its quality and potential for impact. Of the 107 agreements established to date, 15 have met important development milestones, including 4 that are still active within the Consortium.[25] The number of peer-reviewed publications accepted and funding awards obtained also indicate the strength and potential for impact of a collaboration. Participants of a WIPO Re:Search collaboration are encouraged to publish the results of their collaborations, and to date, six articles have been published. Moreover, participants of two WIPO Re:Search collaborations have jointly applied for and received funding. These two funding awards totaled over US$380,000 (£250,000 GBP).

IX WIPO Re:Search Case Studies

A *GlaxoSmithKline and the University of California, San Diego*

Kinases are involved in many key cellular processes and are chemically tractable drug targets. However, less than 5 percent of the human kinome has been explored with selective small molecule inhibitors.[26] To enable research on this historically understudied portion of the kinome, GlaxoSmithKline (GSK) compiled two sets of kinase inhibitors, Published Kinase Inhibitor Set 1 (PKIS1) and Set 2 (PKIS2), and openly shared these sets with academic researchers to be used as tools to advance biological evaluation and pharmacological understanding of the unmapped human kinome.[27]

Polo-like kinases are important regulators of cell cycle progression and mitosis. In mammals there are five of these (Plk 1–5). SmPlk1 and SmSak – orthologous to human Plk1 and Plk4, respectively – are expressed in the parasitic worm, Schistosoma mansoni. Researchers at UCSD have evidence from whole-organism screens that specific inhibition of SmPlk1 by commercially available inhibitors of human Plk1 kills the helminth. To further the investigation of SmPlk1 as a potential target for disease intervention, BVGH connected UCSD and GSK. GSK agreed to provide the UCSD researchers with PKIS1 and PKIS2. The sets, which contain 367 and 539 compounds, respectively, include potent and selective inhibitors of human Plk1. Based on their studies of PKIS1 and PKIS2, the UCSD scientists have identified a number of potent anti-Schistosoma compounds as well as further demonstrated SmPlk1 as a potential schistosomiasis drug target.[28]

[25] Six collaborations involved AstraZeneca, which left the Consortium in 2014. At the time of AZ's departure, these six collaborations had progressed to the next stage of development. BVGH no longer tracks the outcomes of these collaborations, and as such, it is unknown whether these projects are still active. One collaboration involved 60 Degrees Pharmaceuticals (60P), which left the Consortium in 2015.

[26] *NIH Phase-II-UNCD as Bio-Inert Interface for Anti-Thrombogenicity Applications*, SBIR STTR, www.sbir.gov/sbirsearch/detail/677614.

[27] Thavy Long et al., *Structure-Bioactivity Relationship for Benzimidazole Thiophene Inhibitors of Polo-Like Kinase 1 (PLK1), a Potential Drug Target in Schistosoma mansoni*, PLOS NEGLECTED TROPICAL DISEASES (Jan. 11, 2016), www.ncbi.nlm.nih.gov/pmc/articles/PMC4709140/.

[28] *Id.*

B *Alnylam Pharmaceuticals/Northeastern University and the National Institute of Immunology*

With half of the world's population living in areas at risk for transmission, malaria is one of the most severe public health concerns worldwide.[29] The disease has two stages in the human host – an obligatory asymptomatic liver-stage followed by a symptomatic blood stage. Treating malaria symptoms requires clearing blood-stage parasites, and appropriately, most antimalarial drug discovery efforts have largely focused on developing therapeutics against blood-stage parasites. However, inhibiting the liver stage, when the lower parasite burden might delay resistance development, presents a more attractive approach for prophylaxis. Yet presently there are no approved liver-stage therapies with the exception of primaquine, which is contraindicated during pregnancy and in people with glucose-6-phosphate dehydrogenase (G6PD) deficiency, a widespread phenotype across malaria-endemic regions.[30]

Accordingly, a researcher at the National Institute of Immunology (NII) in Delhi, India is working to identify a drug target for liver-stage malaria. He has found four host-based transcription factors that he believes affect the severity of liver-stage malaria infection. In order to analyze their role, he is interested in knocking down these genes in the *in vitro* and *in vivo* models that he has developed. One approach to knocking down genes is through RNA interference. Given their expertise in this field, BVGH connected the NII researcher with scientists at Alnylam Pharmaceuticals in Cambridge, Massachusetts. Alnylam designed and synthesized optimized small interfering RNAs (siRNAs) against the four host transcription factor genes identified by the NII researcher.

Another challenge in getting efficient gene knockdown is the delivery and targeting of the siRNAs within the tissue. To complete this puzzle, BVGH introduced a third collaborator from Northeastern University in Boston, Massachusetts. The Northeastern University researcher, who is an expert in target-specific delivery systems, encapsulated the siRNAs in nanoparticles that target them to hepatocytes (liver cells). The NII researcher confirmed that the siRNAs knocked down expression of the target genes and subsequently assessed the effect this knock-down had on malaria parasite growth *in vitro*. Knock-down of three of the four transcription factors resulted in significant inhibition of the malaria parasite's growth in hepatocytes. The researcher will subsequently test the effect the siRNAs have on liver-stage malaria *in vivo*.

Ultimately these analyses will help the team identify host proteins that could then be targeted for novel drug development for liver stage-malaria thus addressing a significant therapeutic void.

C *McMaster University and University of South Florida*

Soil-transmitted helminths infect approximately 1.5 billion people worldwide, resulting in diarrhea, abdominal pain, general malaise, and weakness. The helminths responsible for these infections – roundworms (*Ascaris*), whipworms (*Trichuris*), and hookworms

[29] *Malaria Factsheet*, WHO (Dec. 2016) www.who.int/mediacentre/factsheets/fs094/en/.

[30] Rosalind E. Howes et al., *Spatial Distribution of G6PD Deficiency Variants Across Malaria-Endemic Regions*, Malaria Journal (Nov. 15, 2013), https://malariajournal.biomedcentral.com/articles/10.1186/1475-2875-12-418.

(*Necator* and *Ancylostoma*) – are transmitted through contact with or consumption of soil contaminated with parasite egg-ridden feces.[31] Improving sanitation in endemic regions can dramatically reduce the incidence of these infections.

Researchers at the University of South Florida (USF) have developed a solar-chemical toilet that sanitizes waste products; however, to determine the efficacy of the treatment, they need to assess the viability of parasite eggs post-treatment. The process of isolating eggs from sewage or environmental samples to assess their viability requires the filtration of large quantities of samples as well as multiple sedimentation and flotation steps. Due to the nature of these samples, the filters are easily and routinely clogged by solid debris and the process can take two days. An alternative device that could swiftly and cost-effectively isolate and concentrate helminth eggs from sewage and bio-solids samples would greatly aid the USF researchers' assessment of the solar-chemical toilet.

To assist the USF scientists with their work, BVGH connected them to a biomicro-fluidics expert at McMaster University in Canada. After several discussions the McMaster University researcher and his group developed a compact, portable, and low-cost tangential flow filtration device that separates particles according to their size without the use of any sophisticated instrumentation. The device can retain particulates as minute as two microns as well as worm eggs as large as 400 microns, and it is particularly useful in concentrating *Ascaris* eggs from a variety of samples. The USF and McMaster scientists have collaborated extensively over the past year on developing and testing various designs of this device. The USF scientists are already comparing an improved, second generation filtration device's ability to isolate eggs from environmental and fecal samples to that of the WHO-standard technique (Kato Katz). If successful, this device could become the routine method to use when testing clinical and environmental samples for the presence of parasite eggs, thus helping to detect the parasites at their source and stemming their transmission.

D *NINA Heater: Bringing Malaria Testing to the Field*

One of the main barriers to eliminating malaria is accurate and timely diagnosis of the disease. There are methods available to screen for *Plasmodium falciparum* infection; however, many are not affordable, are unable to detect asymptomatic cases, or have long turnaround times. These challenges often result in asymptomatic people not being diagnosed and treated, resulting in continued malaria transmission. Newer methods, such as loop-mediated isothermal amplification (LAMP), have been created with these challenges in mind. However, these are still dependent upon consistent electricity – something that is commonly unavailable in many malaria-endemic regions.

In order to address this issue, a team of researchers and engineers at PATH developed a technology known as a noninstrumented nucleic acid amplification (NINA) heater. The NINA heater uses an exothermic chemical reaction to generate the heat necessary for DNA amplification such that no external electricity source is needed. A malaria LAMP assay combined with the NINA heater is a tool suitable for field use.

[31] *Soil-Transmitted Helminth Infections*, WHO (Jan. 2017) www.who.int/mediacentre/factsheets/fs366/en/.

E *PATH and the University of Calgary*

BVGH connected the scientists at PATH with an infectious disease doctor and researcher at the University of Calgary in Canada, who works on implementing effective malaria diagnostics that can be used in low-resource settings.

The University of Calgary scientist tested a pan-*Plasmodium/Plasmodium falciparum*-specific LAMP assay with the NINA heater, first in his laboratory at the University of Calgary and then in the field in Ethiopia. The results of his studies demonstrated that the NINA-LAMP combination was more sensitive than microscopic diagnosis and comparable to a nested PCR test.[32]

F *PATH and the Centre Pasteur du Cameroun*

A researcher at the Centre Pasteur du Cameroun (CPC) developed two reverse transcription-LAMP-based assays (RT-LAMP) – one to detect gametocytes, the transmissible form of the *Plasmodium* parasite, and one to detect low-level parasitemia in malaria patients. Developing an assay to detect the gametocytes will help to determine the risk of transmission from humans back to mosquitoes. Detecting low-level parasitemia will help to minimize the number of false negative malaria diagnoses obtained using other available malaria diagnostics. Both of these are important factors as the world moves toward malaria elimination. BVGH connected the CPC researcher with the PATH scientists, who agreed to share their NINA heater. The CPC researcher assessed both of his RT-LAMP assays with the NINA heater. These tests have yielded encouraging results including a peer-reviewed publication describing the low-level parasitemia assay. The two groups also expect to publish the results of the gametocyte assay.

X Managing IP

Transparent management of IP rights is an important aspect of any collaborative project, including those established through WIPO Re:Search. Drawing on POINT's access and affordability principles, the Consortium and its activities are governed by the WIPO Re:Search Guiding Principles (Principles or Guiding Principles).[33] These Principles are incorporated into all collaboration agreements and dictate ownership of new IP and access and affordability of products resulting from a WIPO Re:Search collaboration.[34] The majority of partnerships established through WIPO Re:Search were initiated following the execution of a material transfer agreement (MTA). Other partnerships have been governed by a broader memorandum of understanding (MOU) or confidential disclosure agreement (CDA). Regardless of the type of agreement partners prefer to use, the Guiding Principles are expected to be incorporated.

[32] Meslo Sema et al., *Evaluation of Non-Instrumented Nucleic Acid Amplification by Loop-Mediated Isothermal Amplification (NINA-LAMP) for the Diagnosis of Malaria in Northwest Ethiopia*, MALARIA JOURNAL (Jan. 28, 2015), www.ncbi.nlm.nih.gov/pubmed/25626339.

[33] *WIPO Re:Search Guiding Principles*, World Intellectual Property Organization [WIPO] (June 8, 2011), www.wipo.int/export/sites/www/research/docs/guiding_principles.pdf.

[34] Krattiger et al., *supra* note 16.

XI Partnerships as Implementers of Sustainable Development Goals

The Sustainable Development Goals (SDGs) build on the momentum of the Millennium Development Goals (MDGs) and are designed to shape development, align stakeholders, and indicate global progress toward ending poverty, protecting the planet, and ensuring prosperity for all.[35] PPPs have historically been, and will continue to be, key instruments of delivery for development initiatives, such as the SDGs, due to their adaptability as well as shared risk and resources model.[36] Going forward, it will be essential for PPPs to align their strategies and activities to the SDGs to collectively make the greatest possible impact on development.

The WIPO Re:Search Consortium's core tenets align with the SDGs. WIPO Re: Search focuses its activities on malaria, tuberculosis, and NTDs. Along with HIV/AIDS, SDG Target 3.3 underscores the need to end the epidemics of tuberculosis, malaria, and NTDs, as well as combat hepatitis, water-borne illnesses, and other communicable diseases. Furthermore, SDG Target 3.b focuses on supporting R&D for health care products for communicable and noncommunicable diseases that particularly affect developing regions.[37] WIPO Re:Search is helping to meet this Target by establishing collaborations to stimulate and accelerate drug, vaccine, and diagnostic development for NTDs, malaria, and tuberculosis. The WIPO Re:Search Guiding Principles, which inform the Consortium's approach to IP ownership and product accessibility, require any product resulting from a WIPO Re:Search collaboration to be sold royalty-free in LDCs and that affordability should be considered in all other developing regions.[38] These principles further align with SDG Target 3.b, which emphasizes the need to ensure access to affordable medicines and vaccines.

SDG Goal 9 concentrates on promoting sustainable industrialization, resilient infrastructure, and innovation across the world, with an emphasis on developing countries. Target 9.5 calls for the enhancement of scientific research in developing countries.[39] Many of the diseases that WIPO Re:Search focuses on disproportionately – if not entirely – affect people living in Africa. In an effort to tap into the research interests and knowledge of Africa, while also providing opportunities for African researchers to connect with leaders in the biopharmaceutical sciences, BVGH – with the support of the Consortium – made a concerted effort to recruit research centers from Africa. In 2012 and 2013, twelve of the new Members recruited were based in Africa. Of the 107 collaborations established by BVGH, 28 include an African partner. In certain instances, the collaborations also provided the researcher with the opportunity to gain new skills. Three collaborations have involved a capacity-building or training aspect. For example, BVGH established a collaboration between researchers at the University of Ibadan in Nigeria and the National Institute of Parasitic Diseases (NIPD), Chinese Center for Disease

[35] *Sustainable Development Goals*, UN DEV. PROGRAM www.undp.org/content/undp/en/home/sustainable-development-goals.html.

[36] U.N.. DEPT. OF ECON. AND SOC. AFF., PARTNERSHIPS FOR SUSTAINABLE DEVELOPMENT GOALS (2016) https://sustainabledevelopment.un.org/content/documents/2329Partnership%20Report%202016%20web.pdf.

[37] *Sustainable Development Goal* 3, U.N. SUSTAINABLE DEV. KNOWLEDGE PLATFORM, https://sustainabledevelopment.un.org/sdg3.

[38] WIPO, *supra* note 33.

[39] *Sustainable Development Goal* 9, U.N. SUSTAINABLE DEV. KNOWLEDGE PLATFORM, https://sustainabledevelopment.un.org/sdg9.

Control and Prevention, in China to identify antigens from two *Schistosoma* species that could be incorporated into a diagnostic test. With funding from the Chinese government, a post-doctoral researcher from the University of Ibadan will travel to NIPD. While at NIPD, the scientist will work alongside his collaborators, receive training on NIPD's antigen discovery platform, and use schistosomiasis patient samples from Nigeria to discover new diagnostic *Schistosoma* antigens.

With funding from IP Australia, BVGH was also able to arrange research training sabbaticals for six scientists from WIPO Re:Search member organizations in Africa. These scientists, who ranged from graduate students to laboratory heads, spent three months to one year at a leading research university or multinational pharmaceutical company. These training opportunities were customized to meet the specific training needs and research interests of each participating scientist.[40] In 2015 IP Australia committed additional funding for research training sabbaticals. This second round of training opportunities will focus on building research capacity specifically in the Indo-Pacific region. Through these sabbaticals and research collaborations, WIPO Re:Search is actively promoting and augmenting scientific capacity in key developing regions.

SDG Goal 17 outlines the importance of PPPs as mechanisms for development that can unlock and mobilize private resources toward development issues. Goal 17 further emphasizes the need to create frameworks and incentives to support the establishment of PPPs to meet the other sixteen SDGs.[41] WIPO Re:Search is a timely and germane example of how PPPs can be established and managed to support and impact global health. WIPO Re:Search collaborations leverage knowledge and skills and mobilize IP assets from the private, public, and civil sectors. The track record of WIPO Re:Search demonstrates that PPPs not only work, but that individuals and organizations across the globe and within all sectors are eager to combine resources and share risk to address the world's greatest challenges.

Conclusion

Through globalization, the spread of people, ideas, and diseases is accelerating. Growing global interconnectedness is shedding light on diseases that have been neglected in the past and changing the ways society and the scientific community approach development. This is evident by the SDG Targets, which address tuberculosis, malaria, and NTDs, as well as through the global emphasis on PPPs as a means of implementation. Scientists and organizations are becoming less siloed in their infectious disease work. More collaborations, through PPPs and consortia, are directing R&D resources toward diseases historically neglected by the scientific community.

The biopharmaceutical industry is also recognizing the need for impactful global health efforts to relieve disease burden in developing countries and emerging markets. Through the creation of open innovation platforms, including POINT and WIPO Re:Search, as well as additional pragmatic approaches, the biopharmaceutical industry

[40] Ania Jedrusik, *Sharing Innovation and Building Capacity to Fight Neglected Tropical Diseases: A Selection of WIPO Re:Search Fellowship Stories*, Global Challenges Rep. (2016) www.wipo.int/edocs/pubdocs/en/wipo_pub_gc_11.pdf.

[41] *Sustainable Development Goal 17*, U.N. Sustainable Dev. Knowledge Platform, https://sustainabledevelopment.un.org/sdg17.

is contributing to the advancement of NTD R&D. WIPO Re:Search and other PPPs provide the framework through which the biopharmaceutical industry can share its IP assets and resources with qualified infectious disease researchers. Leveraging IP to stimulate rather than hinder R&D is achievable by having clear guidelines, documented expectations, and an understanding of ownership. Refuting arguments that IP is inherently restrictive and hinders access to health products, open IP innovation platforms, like WIPO Re:Search, encourage and support the use of IP – within the legal IP framework – to benefit public health.

In order for PPPs to be successful, it is crucial to develop a transparent framework for collaborations, thus ensuring a mutual understanding of expectations and ownership of resources. Equally important activities for effective PPPs include targeted recruitment to develop a well-rounded group of contributing members, proactive partnering engagement of members, alliance management, adaptability, and impact measurement. As the Partnership Hub of the WIPO Re:Search Consortium, BVGH is responsible for the aforementioned components of success. BVGH's active alliance management and expectation-setting help align Members' efforts to finding innovative solutions to advance product development for NTDs, malaria, and tuberculosis.

IP sharing and collaboration drive WIPO Re:Search activities. Given the growing interest in NTD, malaria, and tuberculosis research by PPPs and the global health community's emphasis on these diseases, it is essential for WIPO Re:Search to be scalable and flexible. With the right foundation through the Guiding Principles, and an active partnership manager, WIPO Re:Search will continue to be a conduit between pharmaceutical companies' assets and know-how and researchers' innovative infectious disease solutions.

Appendix A: BVGH Collaboration Guidelines

BVGH strives to build successful WIPO Re:Search collaborations that achieve their scientific objectives. To ensure efficient and effective use of resources and assets, BVGH asks that all parties participating in a WIPO Re:Search collaboration follow the guidelines below.

Research Project and Goals

Prior to initiating a WIPO Re:Search collaboration, BVGH will ask User Members to complete the "WIPO Re:Search Collaboration Outline." Each Outline should describe:

1. Clearly defined research objectives agreed upon by all collaborators
2. Key milestones (e.g., completion of first round of screening)
3. Go/no-go decision points, if applicable (e.g., funding requirements, meeting target IC_{50} values)
4. Project timelines based on availability of resources and other commitments

BVGH will use this information to facilitate communication between the partners and keep track of collaboration milestones and progress. Upon reaching a milestone, the BVGH team will work with collaborators to identify new partners and resources, if needed, to move the project forward.

Project Monitoring/Tracking and Close-out

After establishing a new collaboration, BVGH will schedule regular teleconferences with all project collaborators. The purpose of these discussions is to track project progress and resolve challenges.

All collaborators will be asked to complete the "WIPO Re:Search Collaboration Close-Out" document upon the conclusion of the project. This simple, half-page document provides collaborators with the opportunity to share their thoughts on the collaboration's successes and challenges. This feedback will also help the BVGH team improve their support and alliance management services.

Metrics

In order to monitor WIPO Re:Search statistics, BVGH asks collaborators to track project metrics including the following:

1. Research milestones achieved
2. Publications and presentations arising from the collaboration
3. Grants applied for and any funding received
4. Number of students or postgraduates that received training as part of the collaboration

Publications and Presentations

To raise awareness of the Consortium and its achievements, BVGH requests that all Members acknowledge WIPO Re:Search when presenting or publishing the results of their collaborations. BVGH suggests that the following or similar language be used in publications: "We thank BIO Ventures for Global Health (BVGH) for catalyzing this collaboration through WIPO Re:Search."

BVGH encourages Members to contact Katy Graef at kgraef@bvgh.org about any WIPO Re:Search-related publications or presentations so that they can be mentioned in an issue of the monthly BVGH Partnership Hub Snapshot newsletter.

Appendix B: BVGH Collaboration Outline Document

Requestor Information:	**Date:**
Name (s)	
Contact Information	*(provide full contact information including address, phone number, email address)*
Primary Organization	Organization: Scientific Lead:
Additional Organizations	*Note all other organizations associated with the proposed work plan*
Other Agreements	*Please describe any similar agreements or ongoing research projects.*
Request Overview	
Research Objectives	*Briefly describe the collaboration: Background summary, research objectives, specific goals, and the question you hope to answer. If relevant, please describe what problem you are trying to solve. Include relevant citations as necessary.* Background: Research objectives: Specific goals for this collaboration:
Description of Work	*Limit description to less than 100 words* *(Include experimental plan (assays), projected timeline, key project milestones, and go/no-go decision points, where applicable)*
Target Organisms	*List all organisms that will be tested, if applicable*
Asset(s) Requested/Shared	
Asset requested/shared	☐ Compounds *(provide description below)* ☐ Expertise ☐ Assay/Platform/Technology ☐ Other (please specify, see below)
For compound/chemical requests	☐ Compound library: *(provide description)* ☐ Compound class or series: ☐ Probe compounds for mechanism of action studies: ☐ Other:
Format for delivery of compounds	☐ Number of compounds: ☐ Format: *(in plates? Bold one: 96 / 384 / 1536 / 3456 well? Vials?)* ☐ Powder required? Y / N Quantity (mg):___ DMSO solution Y / N ____ µL ☐ Liquid stocks : Concentration : ___ Volume required : ___ mL ☐ Blinded as to structure acceptable? (Y/N): ☐ Other considerations (e.g.: special shipping/handling):
Other assets requested	*Please provide a description of requested asset if it is not a compound/chemical*
Project support	
Do you have the necessary capacity and resources to complete the project as outlined above? *If the research project involves multiple stages, do you anticipate the need for additional partners and/or resources? If so, please explain.* *How will this project be funded? Please provide the funding organization and grant type (e.g. NIH, Wellcome Trust)*	
Project timeline	
Timelines	➢ Estimated project initiation date:
	➢ Estimated project completion date:

References

BIO VENTURES FOR GLOBAL HEALTH, *Accelerating R&D for Neglected Diseases through Global Collaborations: WIPO Re:Search Partnership Stories 2013–2015* (2015), www.bvgh.org/LinkClick.aspx?fileticket=sbxNzyE6Xac%3d&tabid=277 (last visited Nov. 18, 2017).

BIO VENTURES FOR GLOBAL HEALTH, TUBERCULOSIS VACCINES: THE CASE FOR INVESTMENT (2006).

BIO VENTURES FOR GLOBAL HEALTH & PATH, THE CASE FOR INVESTMENT IN ENTEROTOXIGENIC *ESCHERICHIA COLI* VACCINES (2011).

Dent, Jennifer, Roopa Ramamoorthi, Katy Graef, Lisa Marie Nelson, and Johannes Christian Wichard, *WIPO Re:Search: A Consortium Catalyzing Research and Product Development for Neglected Tropical Diseases*, 2 PHARMACEUTICAL PAT. ANALYST (2013).

Dent, Jennifer, Katy M. Graef, and Paddy Shivanand, *Open Innovation to Bolster Research and Development for Neglected and Emerging Infectious Diseases*, J. MED. DEV. (July 10, 2015), http://ojs.whioce.com/index.php/jmds/article/view/119/99.

GSK Backs Patent Pool for Neglected Diseases, NATURE (Feb. 18, 2009), www.nature.com/news/2009/090218/full/457949e.html (last visited Nov. 18, 2017).

Gillis, Justin, *Medical Aid on the Way for Poorer Nations*, WASH. POST, June 6, 2004.

Howes, Rosalind E., Mewahyu Dewi, Frédéric B Piel, Wuelton M Monteiro, Katherine E Battle, Jane P Messina, Anavaj Sakuntabhai, Ari W Satyagraha, Thomas N Williams, J Kevin Baird, and Simon I Hay, *Spatial Distribution of G6PD Deficiency Variants Across Malaria-Endemic Regions*, MALARIA JOURNAL (Nov. 15, 2013), https://malariajournal.biomedcentral.com/articles/10.1186/1475–2875-12–418 (last visited Nov. 18, 2017).

Inside WIPO, www.wipo.int/about-wipo/en/ (last visited Nov. 18, 2017).

Jedrusik, Ania, *Sharing Innovation and Building Capacity to Fight Neglected Tropical Diseases: A Selection of WIPO Re:Search Fellowship Stories*, GLOBAL CHALLENGES REP. (2016), www.wipo.int/edocs/pubdocs/en/wipo_pub_gc_11.pdf (last visited Nov. 18, 2017).

Ledford, Heidi, *MIT and South African Research Agency Dive Into Industry Patent Pool*, NATURE NEWSBLOG (MAY 6, 2017; 2:35 PM), http://blogs.nature.com/news/2010/05/mit_dives_into_industry_patent.html (last visited Nov. 18, 2017).

Long, Thavy, R. Jeffrey Neitz, Rachel Beasley, Chakrapani Kalyanaraman, Brian M. Suzuki, Matthew P. Jacobson, Colette Dissous, James H. McKerrow, David H. Drewry, William J. Zuercher, Rahul Singh, and Conor R. Caffrey, *Structure-Bioactivity Relationship for Benzimidazole Thiophene Inhibitors of Polo-Like Kinase 1 (PLK1), a Potential Drug Target in Schistosoma mansoni*, PLOS NEGLECTED TROPICAL DISEASES (Jan. 11, 2016), www.ncbi.nlm.nih.gov/pmc/articles/PMC4709140/ (last visited Nov. 18, 2017).

Molyneux, David H., Lorenzo Savioli, and Dirk Engels, *Neglected Tropical Diseases: Progress Towards Addressing the Chronic Pandemic*, 389 LANCET (2017).

SBIR STTR, *NIH Phase-II-UNCD as Bio-Inert Interface for Anti-Thrombogenicity Applications*, www.sbir.gov/sbirsearch/detail/677614 (last visited Nov. 18, 2017).

Nordling, Linda, *Patent Pool Starts to Attract Interest*, SCIDEV.NET (Oct. 5, 2010), www.scidev.net/global/health/news/patent-pool-starts-to-attract-interest.html (last visited Nov. 18, 2017).

PHARMACEUTICAL RESEARCH AND MANUFACTURERS OF AMERICA, *Biopharmaceutical Research & Development: The Process Behind New Medicines* (2015), www.phrma.org/report/biopharmaceutical-research-and-development-the-process-behind-new-medicines (last visited Nov. 18, 2017).

Sema, Meslo, Abebe Alemu, Abebe Genetu Bayih, Sisay Getie, Gebeyaw Getnet, Dylan Guelig, Robert Burton, Paul LaBarre, and Dylan R Pillai, *Evaluation of Non-Instrumented Nucleic Acid Amplification by Loop-Mediated Isothermal Amplification (NINA-LAMP) for the Diagnosis of Malaria in Northwest Ethiopia*, MALARIA JOURNAL (Jan. 28, 2015), www.ncbi.nlm.nih.gov/pubmed/25626339 (last visited Nov. 18, 2017).

UN Dev. Program, *Sustainable Development Goals*, www.undp.org/content/undp/en/home/sustainable-development-goals.html (last visited Nov. 18, 2017).

U.N. Dept. of Social and Econ. Affairs, Partnerships for Sustainable Development Goals (2016) https://sustainabledevelopment.un.org/content/documents/2329Partnership%20Report%202016%20web.pdf.

U.N. Sustainable Dev. Knowledge Platform, *Sustainable Development Goal 3*, https://sustainabledevelopment.un.org/sdg3.

U.N. Sustainable Dev. Knowledge Platform, *Sustainable Development Goal 9*, https://sustainabledevelopment.un.org/sdg9.

U.N. Sustainable Dev. Knowledge Platform, *Sustainable Development Goal 17*, https://sustainabledevelopment.un.org/sdg17.

World Intellectual Property Organization, *WIPO Re:Search Guiding Principles*, (June 8, 2011) www.wipo.int/export/sites/www/research/docs/guiding_principles.pdf.

World Health Organization, *Investing to Overcome the Global Impact of Neglected Tropical Diseases* (2015) http://apps.who.int/iris/bitstream/10665/152781/1/9789241564861_eng.pdf.

World Health Organization, *Malaria Factsheet*, (Dec. 2016) www.who.int/mediacentre/factsheets/fs094/en/ (last visited Nov. 18, 2017).

World Health Organization, *Soil-Transmitted Helminth Infections*, (Jan. 2017), www.who.int/mediacentre/factsheets/fs366/en/ (last visited Nov. 18, 2017).

5 Patent Pooling in Public Health

Esteban Burrone*

In recent years, patent pooling has emerged as a mechanism to address some of the innovation and access challenges relating to health technologies. While patent pools have existed for several decades in other fields of technology, it is a relatively new concept in the biomedical and public health fields, where it has been adapted to pursue public health objectives. The patent pooling model represents a new type of public–private partnership (PPP) in health that relies on the licensing of patents on access-oriented terms to enable multiple third parties to develop and/or supply patented health technologies in a given geography.[1]

This chapter first outlines the concept of patent pooling as it has evolved over recent years in the public health field. It then reviews its practical application in HIV through the establishment of the Medicines Patent Pool (MPP), and its subsequent expansion into hepatitis C and TB. The MPP is the first patent pool in public health designed to enhance access to affordable medicines in developing countries through the negotiation of access-oriented and transparent voluntary licences with the pharmaceutical industry. The chapter concludes with an analysis of the potential applicability of the patent pooling model in other areas by identifying the kinds of public health challenges that such a model could contribute to addressing in the context of meeting the health-related sustainable development goals (SDGs).

I The Concept of Patent Pooling in Public Health

Patent pools have long existed in various fields of technology. Early examples of patent pools include one for sewing machines in the mid-nineteenth century and the aircraft patent pool established during World War I to ensure manufacturers could have the licences needed to manufacture new airplanes.[2] In recent decades, patent pools have prospered primarily in the information and communication technology field, where they have often been linked to technical standards negotiated under one of the major

* The views expressed in this article are those of the author and do not necessarily represent those of the Medicines Patent Pool.

[1] For an overview of different models of public–private partnerships in health, see Kent Buse & Gill Walt, *Global Public–Private Partnerships: Part II – What are the Health Issues for Global Governance?*, 78 Bull. World Health Organ. (2000).

[2] Robert P. Merges, *Institutions for Intellectual Property Transactions: The Case for Patent Pools* (1999).

standard-setting organisations. In such cases, patent pools have generally been established as private consortia of patent holders, each owning intellectual property on technology considered "essential" to the implementation of that standard. By participating in the patent pool, patent holders generally commit to licensing the technology to each other and to third parties on fair, reasonable, and nondiscriminatory terms to enable the manufacturing of products that comply with the standard in question. In some cases, the administration of the patent pools themselves has been delegated to specialized entities.[3]

Calls for patent pooling in the biomedical field began with the rise in biotechnology patenting in the early 2000s and focused on enabling access to intellectual property on key research tools or platform technology needed by other innovators to undertake further research and development. For example, in December 2000, the United States Patent and Trademark Office (USPTO) proposed the establishment of a patent pool as a possible solution to concerns about access to biotechnology patents. Despite attempts to ensure genomic sequences remained in the public domain,[4] the surge in patenting of genomic sequences raised some concerns that further pharmaceutical research and development could be hampered without widespread licensing of such research tools. A patent pool, it was argued, could "provide for greater innovation, parallel research and development, removal of patent bottlenecks, and faster product development."[5]

A specific example of the need for a patent pool-type mechanism to overcome multiple overlapping patents on genomic sequences emerged following the outbreak of severe acute respiratory syndrome (SARS) in 2002–2005. The filing of patent applications on the genomic sequence of the coronavirus responsible for SARS by several institutions led to discussions on the establishment of a patent pool.[6] The patent pool would issue licences on essential patents on a nonexclusive basis and enable developers to work on the development of vaccines for the benefit of all stakeholders.[7] It was also hoped that a patent pool for SARS could set a helpful precedent that might lead to the establishment of analogous pools for other disease areas, such as malaria, tuberculosis, or avian influenza. The subsequent end of the outbreak removed the sense of urgency and the patent pool was never established.

In 2006, the World Health Organization (WHO) Commission on Intellectual Property Rights, Innovation and Public Health (CIPIH) reviewed the arguments for the establishment of patent pools in public health and recognized that patent pools on upstream technologies could be useful to promote innovation relevant to developing countries.[8]

[3] *Id.*

[4] Jorge Contreras, *Bermuda's Legacy: Policy, Patents, and the Design of the Genome Commons*, 12 MINN. J. L. SCI. & TECH. 61 (2011).

[5] U.S. PATENT AND TRADE OFFICE [USPTO], PATENT POOLS: A SOLUTION TO THE PROBLEM OF ACCESS IN BIOTECHNOLOGY PATENTS? (2000), www.uspto.gov/web/offices/pac/dapp/opla/patentpool.pdf (last visited Nov. 23, 2017).

[6] See, e.g., James H.M. Simon et al., *Managing Severe Acute Respiratory Syndrome (SARS) Intellectual Property Rights: The Possible Role of Patent Pooling*, 83 BULL. WORLD HEALTH ORG. 707 (2005), www.who.int/bulletin/volumes/83/9/707.pdf (last visited Nov. 23, 2017).

[7] World Trade Organization [WHO], World Intellectual Property Organization [WIPO], World Health Organization [WHO], *Promoting Access to Medical Technologies and Innovation* 118 (2012).

[8] *Report of the Commission on Intellectual Property Rights, Innovation and Public Health*, WHO (2006).

The report suggested that the relative lack of market incentives for technologies that are particularly needed in developing countries could enable agreements that would otherwise be more difficult to achieve.

The subsequent WHO Global Strategy and Plan of Action on Public Health, Innovation and Intellectual Property (GSPOA) went further by recognizing the role patent pools could play not only to facilitate innovation, but also to promote access to new health products. In adopting the GSPOA, the World Health Assembly recommended the development of new mechanisms to promote access to key health-related technologies and specifically called for examining the "feasibility of establishing voluntary patent pools of upstream and downstream technologies to promote innovation of and access to health products and medical devices."[9]

To follow up on certain elements of the GSPOA, the WHO established a Consultative Expert Working Group on Research and Development (CEWG) that was to focus on issues relating to the financing and coordination of R&D for diseases that disproportionately affect developing countries. In reviewing proposals from various stakeholders, the CEWG noted the potential for combining patent pools with possible incentive mechanisms such as prize funds to promote innovation for new formulations needed in developing countries. Moreover, the CEWG recommended patent pools (and in particular downstream pools) as cost-effective approaches to improving access in developing countries and as a way of delinking the cost of R&D from the final price of products. The discussion on "de-linkage" is one that has gathered significant attention in international discussions on the financing of R&D for diseases that disproportionately affect developing countries and is discussed in some detail in the chapter by Frederick Abbott in this volume.[10]

The concept of patent pooling has therefore evolved significantly from the way it has been applied in other fields of technology, where it has often been implemented through private consortia to facilitate product development and enable interoperability between products. In public health, patent pooling has been put forward as a mechanism for public health management of IP through a partnership between an entity with a public health mandate, on the one hand, and private pharmaceutical companies, on the other. Public health patent pools aim to improve access to health technologies, particularly in developing countries, and facilitate further innovation through nonexclusive voluntary licensing.[11]

[9] *Global Strategy and Plan of Action on Public Health, Innovation and Intellectual Property*, WHO 13 (2011), www.who.int/phi/publications/Global_Strategy_Plan_Action.pdf (last visited Nov. 23, 2017).

[10] Frederick M. Abbott, Chapter 2, *infra*; see also WHO, *Research and Development to Meet Health Needs in Developing Countries: Strengthening Global Financing and Coordination. Report of the Consultative Expert Working Group on Research and Development: Financing and Coordination* (2012) [hereinafter WHO, Research and Development], http://apps.who.int/iris/bitstream/10665/254706/1/9789241503457-eng.pdf?ua=1 (last visited Nov. 23, 2017).

[11] Other initiatives to establish IP pooling-type mechanisms in the biomedical field include the Pool for Open Innovation against Neglected Tropical Diseases proposed by pharmaceutical company GSK; WIPO Research, a platform established in 2011 to enable access to IP, technology, and know-how for the development of medical products for neglected tropical diseases, malaria, and tuberculosis; and Librassay, a patent pool for diagnostics and tools in support of personalized medicine and health care administered by MPEG-LA.

II Patent Pooling in HIV

The first patent pool with a clear public health mandate was established in 2010 following a decision by the Executive Board of UNITAID, a publicly funded global health initiative that is housed by the WHO.[12] With its initial mandate in HIV, the Medicines Patent Pool's mission is "to improve health by providing patients in low- and middle-income countries with increased access to quality, safe, efficacious, more appropriate and more affordable health products, through a voluntary patent pool mechanism."[13]

A *The General MPP Model*

The Medicines Patent Pool (MPP) operates as a nonprofit voluntary licensing mechanism through partnerships with the pharmaceutical industry (originator and generic) that facilitate access and promote innovation. Specifically, the MPP aims to:

- Improve access to more affordable quality-assured HIV medicines in developing countries by enhancing competition among manufacturers
- Enable the development of formulations adapted to developing country needs, such as paediatric formulations
- Facilitate the development of fixed-dosed combinations or "three-in-one pills" that combine various active pharmaceutical ingredients into a single dosage form

It operates by negotiating licences with patent holders and in turn licensing those patents to multiple manufacturers. Such manufacturers are then able to develop the licensed medicine (including new formulations and combinations) and make it available in a defined set of developing countries in exchange for royalties. Figure 5.1 provides a visual overview of how the MPP operates.

B *Terms and Conditions in MPP Access-Oriented Licences*

Given its public health mandate, the MPP works to include terms and conditions in its licences that are important from a public health perspective. Examples of key terms and conditions in MPP access oriented licences include:

Broad geographical scope allowing sales by generic manufacturers in countries that are home to up to 94 percent of people living with HIV in low- and middle-income countries and 99 percent of children with HIV globally; this includes 55–80 percent of middle-income countries, depending on the licence;

Ability to sublicense in a nonexclusive and nondiscriminatory manner to multiple generic manufacturers;

Permission to develop new formulations of existing medicines (such as new paediatric formulations) and to combine several medicines into fixed dose combinations

[12] UNITAID is a global health initiative, established to provide sustainable, predictable, and additional funding to significantly impact on market dynamics to reduce prices and increase the availability and supply of high quality drugs and diagnostics for the treatment of HIV/AIDS, malaria, and tuberculosis for people in developing countries. It is hosted by the World Health Organization. On the establishment of the MPP, *see* Memorandum of Understanding, Jun. 8–9, 2010, MPP-UNITAID, EB12/R7.

[13] Memorandum of Understanding, Jun. 8–9, 2010, MPP-UNITAID, EB12/R7.

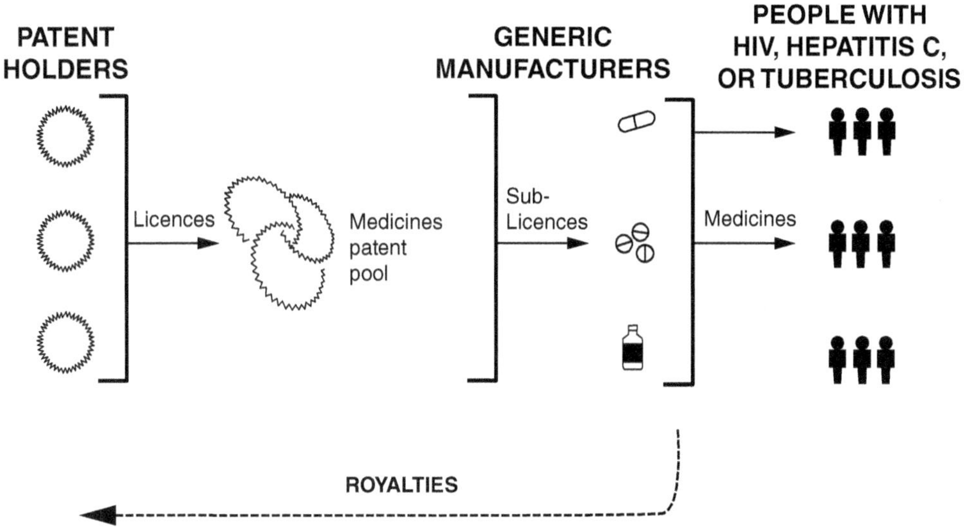

Figure 5.1. The Medicines Patent Pool model.

Flexibility for licensees to supply outside the licensed territory when no patents are being infringed or where countries outside the licensed territory issue compulsory licences;
Reasonable royalty rates, where necessary, to enable broad geographical scope, including differentiated royalties according to a country's per capita income;
Freedom by licensees to challenge any of the licensed patents;
Waivers on data exclusivity, where applicable;
Obligation to meet strict quality assurance requirements;

A key guiding principle for the MPP during its negotiations has been to enable access to new patented treatments in as many low- and middle-income countries as possible while ensuring that the licence itself does not constitute an additional barrier to access for countries not included in the licence. Hence provisions in many of MPP licences enabling supply by licensees outside the licensed territory if no patents are being infringed.

Concerns have sometimes arisen about MPP licences not including all middle-income countries. MPP licences are the result of negotiations between the MPP and patent holders and have enabled unprecedented geographical coverage for access-oriented licences. Certain countries, however, are perceived as significant commercial markets by the pharmaceutical industry and have remained outside many of the MPP licences. Exceptions have been for paediatric formulations for which geographical scope has often been greater, in view of its more limited commercial importance and key public health significance, or licences with certain public research organizations. In some cases, in order to expand the geographical scope of its licences, the MPP has agreed to focus on the public market only, while exclusivity remains in the more lucrative private market. Public national treatment programs generally provide treatment for the vast majority of people living with HIV, including many of the most vulnerable groups, in the countries included in MPP licences. The focus has therefore been in ensuring competitive supply and affordability in that segment for as many countries as possible.

C *Transparency*

A key characteristic of MPP licences is that they are all published in full form on the MPP website.[14] This has introduced unprecedented transparency in access-oriented licensing of pharmaceuticals.[15]

The decision to make all agreements public was made by the MPP Board early on in the existence of the MPP, as part of its transparency policy.[16] This precommitment to transparency of the licences it negotiates has enabled external third-party review of the terms and conditions of licences. Moreover, it has contributed to setting new standards in voluntary licensing by encouraging a healthy debate on terms and conditions that could or should be included in access-oriented licences.

The commitment to transparency is not limited to the MPP licences, but also applies to the patent data collected by the MPP. Understanding the patent status of priority HIV medicines in developing countries is complex, as many patent offices do not make such information available through online databases. At the time of its establishment, the MPP set out to collect patent status data for twenty-five HIV medicines in developing countries. Supported by the World Intellectual Property Organization (WIPO) and several other stakeholders, who collaborated in collecting the information from national patent offices, the MPP was able to collect the information for a large number of low- and middle-income countries and has made that information available in an online database now called MedsPaL. The database is an online tool that provides information on the patent and licensing status of over 100 formulations for HIV, hepatitis C, and tuberculosis in more than 110 countries.[17] Information on data exclusivity has recently also been added.

D *Governance*

In terms of governance, the MPP operates as an independent not-for-profit Swiss Foundation, linked to UNITAID via a Memorandum of Understanding (MOU) through which the operations of the MPP are funded. The first five-year MOU lasted from mid-2010 to end 2015, and was followed by a second five-year MOU from 2016 to 2020. The close link to UNITAID has been important to enable the MPP to become an integral part of the international response to HIV.

The governance board of the MPP is made up of independent experts that represent a broad base of stakeholders including members with past experience in the originator

[14] The full text of MPP licences, as well as summaries of key terms and conditions, are available at: *Licenses in the MPP*, Meds. Patent Pool, www.medicinespatentpool.org/current-licences/ (last visited Jun. 17, 2017).

[15] A recent analysis by the Access to Medicines Index concluded that "based on an analysis of the licences available for examination, those negotiated via the Medicines Patent Pool provide licensees with the highest level of flexibility and broadest geographic scope." ATM Index 2014, at 105, https://accessto medicinefoundation.org/media/atmf/2014-Access-to-Medicine-Index.pdf (last visited Nov. 23, 2017) (last visited Nov. 23, 2017).

[16] See *The Medicines Patent Pool Transparency Policy*, MPP, www.medicinespatentpool.org/wp-content/uploads/MEDICINES+PATENT+POOL+TRANSPARENCY+POLICY-1.pdf (last visited May 31, 2016).

[17] MedsPaL, www.medspal.org (last visited Oct. 14, 2016).

and generic pharmaceutical industry, civil society and patient groups, government, product development partnerships, and international organizations. In addition, an Expert Advisory Group composed of twenty-two experts is in charge of advising the MPP staff and the Board on the licences being negotiated. The group has played a central role in the MPP negotiations as part of the necessary checks and balances to ensure that licences negotiated by the MPP maintain high public health standards and are consistent with its mandate and objectives. It includes individuals with wide-ranging expertise (public health, intellectual property, economics, research and development, HIV, TB, and HCV) and with experience in organizations representing the communities of people with the three diseases (HIV, HCV, and TB).

E *Prioritizing Products for In-Licensing*

One of the first steps for the MPP was to establish a list of priority medicines for in-licensing based on medical and IP criteria. The idea was to ensure that the work of the MPP focuses on the licensing of products that are important from a medical perspective and that are patent-protected in developing countries with significant patent term left to expiry. The prioritization is repeated on an annual basis to ensure MPP priorities take into account the most recent clinical data, as well as changes in patent status.[18]

The medical prioritisation is undertaken in close collaboration with the WHO and with inputs from a group of experts with significant experience in resource-limited settings. The WHO treatment guidelines are the starting point for products that were already on the market. However, MPP's prioritization also assesses pipeline medicines that are still under development in order to accelerate generic availability of new medicines, shortly after they are approved.

The IP prioritization required collecting patent status data on twenty-five HIV medicines from a large number of developing countries. This information proved difficult to obtain and required direct interaction with many national and regional patent offices from around the world, particularly many that do not make such information regularly available through the Internet. Support from WIPO was important in establishing contacts with the national patent offices and collecting the necessary data. Having collected the patent data, several stakeholders, including procurement agencies purchasing medicines on behalf of developing country governments, requested the MPP to share that data, as it represented valuable information that was otherwise not available. The patent data was therefore published online in what has now become MedsPaL, an online tool that provides information on the patent and licensing status of over 100 formulations for HIV, hepatitis C, and tuberculosis in more than 110 countries.[19]

Based on the results of the prioritization, the MPP invites patent holders of priority medicines to consider licensing to the MPP on transparent and public-health oriented terms and conditions such as those outlined in part A.

[18] For the most recent version, *see Target Medicines*, MEDS. PATENT POOL, www.medicinespatentpool.org/ourwork/target-medicines/ (last visited Jun. 17, 2017).

[19] MedsPaL is available at www.medspal.org (last accessed on 14 October 2016).

F *MPP's Collaborative Partnerships*

At the time of the establishment of the MPP, the Human Rights Council "welcome(d) the creation of the Medicines Patent Pool Foundation by UNITAID, with a view to improving access to appropriate, affordable antiretrovirals in developing countries."[20] The resolution expressed its concern that, for millions of people throughout the world, the full realization of the right of everyone to the enjoyment of the highest attainable standard of physical and mental health, including through access to medicines that are safe, effective, and affordable, still remained a distant goal. The MPP was therefore viewed as a mechanism that could contribute to the realization of this human right, at least in relation to HIV.

During its first year in existence the MPP received similar endorsements from a number of other international organizations and international policy processes, which helped to establish its credibility and legitimacy, including with the pharmaceutical companies the MPP aimed to partner with.[21] For a nascent institution these endorsements were critical in signalling the expectation of the international community for key stakeholders to work with the Medicines Patent Pool.

In addition to high-level endorsements, the MPP also set out to forge partnerships with many of the leading organisations in the public health and IP fields in order to benefit from the institutional support, networks, and expertise of such organizations. This included, for example, collaboration with the WHO in many different areas (prioritisation of products for in-licensing; quality assurance; forecasting of ARV demand), which resulted in the establishment of a formal workplan of collaborative activities in 2014. MPP also sought out collaboration with the WIPO, in particular to collect patent information from developing countries, which was key for preparing for licensing negotiations. It also formed partnerships with other leading organizations working in the field of paediatric HIV through the establishment of the Paediatric HIV Treatment Initiative,[22] which is working with the pharmaceutical industry to accelerate the development of needed paediatric formulations. Additionally, it collaborated with the Global Fund in the context of the latter's market dynamics strategy to ensure that uptake of MPP licences is coordinated closely with the leading funders of the HIV response.

Significant efforts were also devoted to establishing and strengthening collaboration with governments, particularly those from countries with high HIV prevalence or where MPP licences could potentially achieve the greatest public health impact. A key objective was to gather data on treatment needs, prices, and procurement challenges being faced by governments that could be used to strengthen the case for the inclusion of additional countries in the geographical scope of MPP licences. Partnerships are also being established with national patent offices, some of which have formally committed to regularly providing the patent data needed by the MPP for inclusion in MedsPaL.

[20] Human Rights Council Res. 15/6, U.N. Doc. A/HRC/15/L.28 at 6 (Sep. 27, 2010).

[21] Thus, between May and July 2011, the MPP was mentioned as an important mechanism in the UN Political Declaration on HIV/AIDS of the UN General Assembly, the Deauville declaration of the G8 and the WHO Global Health Sector Strategy for HIV/AIDS 2011–16.

[22] This is an initiative launched by the MPP, the Drugs for Neglected Diseases initiative (DNDi), and UNITAID, later joined by the Clinton Health Access Initiative (CHAI) and the WHO as technical partner, which aims to accelerate the development and rollout of needed HIV pediatric formulations.

Furthermore, the establishment of consultative mechanisms with leading civil society institutions and community groups was essential in consolidating the legitimacy of the MPP, to better understand the needs on the ground, discuss possible licensing terms and conditions that could be used in licences, and advance the work of the MPP to addressing overall access challenges in different countries and complement other initiatives.

Last but not least, the MPP model itself is based on partnerships with the pharmaceutical industry with which the MPP signs licences and engages regularly to ensure new patented medicines become available in developing countries at affordable prices soon after their introduction in high income countries. Originator partners have included the leading pharmaceutical companies operating in the field of HIV such as AbbVie, Bristol-Myers Squibb, Gilead Sciences, MSD, Roche and ViiV Healthcare. On the generic side, twenty-five companies have partnered with the MPP to develop and supply the new ARVs. In some cases, this includes developing new formulations that address specific gaps.

G *Lessons from HIV for Other Diseases*

Since its establishment in 2010, the MPP has entered into voluntary licences with seven patent holders on thirteen HIV medicines and one technology that can be used for the development of nano-formulations of HIV medicines. It has sub-licensed to thirteen generic manufacturers who have already supplied 17 million patient/years of WHO-recommended HIV medicines to 127 developing countries.

By the end of 2017, the work of the MPP had enabled US$ 239 million in savings to the international community through the purchase of more affordable treatments. This is equivalent to one year of first-line treatment for over 6 million people. With the coming to market of generic versions of new ARVs, it is estimated that savings from MPP licences would reach US$ 2.3 billion over the coming years, enabling significantly more people to access needed HIV medicines in developing countries and contributing to the achievement of Sustainable Development Goal 3.[23]

A key objective of the MPP has also been to accelerate availability of quality assured generics of new HIV medicines for use in developing countries. This is achieved by negotiating voluntary licences with patent holders as early as possible in the lifecycle of the products, in some cases even before they receive regulatory approval, which enables generic manufacturers to begin development earlier. In the past, it has taken between five to ten years for new ARVs approved by the US Food and Drug Administration to become available as quality assured generics for use in developing countries.[24] And it took even longer to have more than two generic manufacturers competing on the market. Early licensing by the MPP, including the preparation of joint forecasts with the WHO and technical support to licensees where appropriate, is helping to facilitate and accelerate the development process.[25] This is contributing to significantly reducing this timeline and enable many developing countries to access new treatments at affordable prices sooner.

[23] Sandeep Juneja, et al., *Projected savings through public health voluntary licences of HIV drugs negotiated by the Medicines Patent Pool (MPP)*, PLoS ONE 12(5): e0177770 (2017), available at: https://doi.org/10.1371/journal.pone.0177770; *Five Years of Patent Pooling in Public Health*, MPP (2015); Esteban Burrone and Greg Perry, *Ensuring New Medicines Reach Those in Most Need*, 2 Lancet HIV e362 (2015).

[24] *Id.*

[25] *See also Progress and Achievements of the Medicines Patent Pool 2010–2015*, MPP (2015).

The experience of the MPP in HIV has provided a concrete example of how patent pooling can contribute to addressing some of the innovation and access challenges relating to health technologies more generally. While the design of the HIV patent pool was guided by the specific circumstances in HIV, some of these circumstances may also apply to other areas in public health.

From an access perspective, the model was predicated on new patented medicines already on the market and a need for access in developing countries that could best be met through competition among multiple manufacturers to reduce the price to affordable levels. From an innovation perspective, the model sought to address the need for follow-on innovation in relation to products needed mostly in developing countries (e.g., paediatric formulations for HIV treatment) and for products that require combining technology patented by more than one entity (fixed dose combinations).

In November 2015, following extensive consultations, the mandate of the MPP was expanded to hepatitis C and tuberculosis.[26] While there are significant differences between the two disease areas, in both cases there are new medicines that have recently obtained regulatory approval or are in late-stage development that have patents pending or filed in several developing countries. There are significant access needs in low-and middle-income countries, and sustainable supply through competition among manufacturers could contribute to addressing some of the access gaps. The specific circumstances, however, are very different between the two disease areas and these differences need to be reflected in the way the model is implemented and the kinds of provisions that may be included in the licences.

In terms of innovation, while there has been significant private investment in R&D for hepatitis C in recent years, leading to multiple new HCV treatments reaching the market, investments in tuberculosis R&D have been very limited, with only two new products have reached the market in the past forty years. Thus, while patent pooling in HCV will likely be primarily aimed at facilitating affordable access for products that are already on the market, patent pooling in the field of tuberculosis could be very important in relation to upstream technology to enable collaborative research and the development of new TB regimens. Hence, the first MPP licence in HCV was for a medicine already widely used in high income markets that had recently been included in the WHO Model Essential Medicines List (EML). The objective of the licence, therefore, was to enable manufacturing of generic versions of the medicines for the competitive supply in 112 low- and middle-income countries. The first MPP licence in TB, on the other hand, was for a medicine that has been stalled in clinical development for a number of years. The MPP licence is expected to contribute to accelerating its development by facilitating access to the IP by other potential developers.[27]

[26] *See* Press Release, *The Meds. Patent Pool Expands Mandate to Hepatitis C and Tuberculosis Treatment*, MPP (Nov. 6, 2015), www.medicinespatentpool.org/the-medicines-patent-pool-expands-mandate-to-hepatitis-c-and-tuberculosis-treatment/ (last visited Nov. 23, 2017).

[27] *See The Medicines Patent Pool Announces First License for Tuberculosis Treatment*, MPP (Jan. 25, 2017), www.medicinespatentpool.org/the-medicines-patent-pool-announces-first-licence-for-tuberculosis-treatment/ (last visited Nov. 23, 2017).

III Patent Pooling and its Potential Applicability to Other Public Health Challenges

While the previous section provides an overview of one specific experience in the implementation of patent pooling to address access and innovation challenges in public health, this part will look at its broader applicability. The following provides an overview of the kinds of challenges in public health that this new kind of PPP can contribute to address. These include:

(1) Patent pooling to enhance access to affordable health products in poor countries, sectors, and regions
(2) Patent pooling to facilitate follow-on innovation
(3) Patent pooling to facilitate R&D and access in combination with innovative incentives
(4) Patent pooling to overcome "patent thickets"

A *Patent Pooling to Enhance Access to Affordable Health Products in Poor Countries, Sectors, and Regions*

Underlying this model is the idea that competition between multiple manufacturers can be an effective way to bring prices down to affordable levels for many health products, therefore facilitating access, particularly for people, countries, sectors, or regions that would otherwise be unable to afford them. Access-oriented licensing to multiple manufacturers through a patent pool enables competition to take place where it may have otherwise not been possible and facilitates access to needed medicines to poor countries or poor sectors of society. The brokering role of a public health organization like a patent pool enables a reduction in transaction costs for all parties and ensures that licences include provisions that are key to ensure consistency with public health principles. This includes, for example, terms that enable broad access to as many people as possible, in particular, the most vulnerable, and that ensure that the licence removes as many barriers to access as possible without introducing new barriers or restrictions that may negatively affect the attainment of its public health goals.

While to date this has only been applied to HIV, and more recently to HCV, its application could potentially also be extended to other health technologies that are patented in developing countries and for which widespread nonexclusive licensing through a patent-pool-like mechanism could contribute to enable affordable access in developing countries. This could include, for example, patented health technologies needed to achieve the Sustainable Development Goals, such as certain medicines for other communicable diseases (SDG target 3.3), noncommunicable diseases (SDG target 3.4), essential medicines (SDG target 3.8), or vaccines (SDG target 3.8).

One specific area that may merit particular attention is patented medicines that are included in the WHO EML. In its submission to the UN High Level Panel on Access to Medicines, WHO recommended "the expansion of the MPP to all disease areas, and for all patented essential medicines on the WHO EML to be licensed into the Pool." Another example is a recent statement by pharmaceutical company GSK, of its intent to "commit its future portfolio of cancer treatments to patent pooling" and its interest in exploring this possibility with the MPP.

B *Patent Pooling to Facilitate Follow-on Innovation*

Licensing through a patent pool can provide a simple mechanism for entities engaging in follow-on innovation to obtain access to the necessary IP to undertake further research and development. This could be, for example, entities seeking to develop new formulations of patented medicines that address specific public health needs in developing countries for which there are limited market incentives.

In HIV, this model is being applied to the development of new adapted formulations of existing HIV medicines, such as paediatric formulations. With the MPP's entry into tuberculosis, the model could also be used to facilitate the re-purposing of certain antibiotics for use in TB. There may be many other opportunities in which follow-on innovation could be facilitated through nonexclusive voluntary licensing. In these instances, patent pooling can contribute to making patented medicines available to multiple developers on public health-oriented terms and contribute to further innovation and the development of new health products.

C *Patent Pooling to Facilitate R&D and Access in Combination with Innovative Incentives*

There are instances in which additional incentives are being considered as a manner to promote research and development in areas in which existing commercial incentives may be insufficient. Linking such incentives to licensing models that are clearly anchored in public health principles has been proposed as one approach in such circumstances. Two specific examples that have recently attracted significant attention in which such an approach could potentially be applied are (a) new antibiotics to combat antimicrobial resistance (AMR), and (b) new regimens for the treatment of tuberculosis.

1 The Case of Antimicrobial Resistance

The recent WHO Global Action Plan on Antimicrobial Resistance[28] describes the urgent need for new antibiotics and for increased investments in research and development. Discussions are ongoing on possible new incentive mechanisms that would contribute to strengthen the current antibiotic pipeline.[29] There is general agreement that incentives should be designed in a manner that de-links the financing of research and development from the sales of new antibiotics and for a need to consider innovation, access, and conservation holistically. There is also broad recognition that there may be a need for novel approaches to IP management in this area, including by the pharmaceutical industry in the 2016 Davos statement on combating antimicrobial resistance.[30]

[28] *Global Action Plan on Anti-Microbial Resistance*, WHO (2015), http://apps.who.int/iris/bitstream/10665/193736/1/9789241509763_eng.pdf?ua=1 (last visited Nov. 23, 2017).

[29] *See, e.g.*, *Securing New Drugs for Future Generations: The Pipeline Of Antibiotics*, Review on Antimicrobial Resistance [AMR] (2015); Maurie-Paule Kieny, *Creating and Intergovernmental Consortium for New Antibiotics: a New Development Model*, AMR Control 26 (2015); *Towards a New Global Business Model for Antibiotics: Delinking Revenue From Sales*, Chatham House (2015).

[30] *Declaration by the Pharmaceutical, Biotechnology and Diagnostics Industries on Combating Antimicrobial Resistance (AMR)*, Int'l Fed'n of Pharm. Mfrs. & Ass'n (Jan. 2016), www.ifpma.org/partners-2/declaration-by-the-pharmaceutical-biotechnology-and-diagnostics-industries-on-combating-antimicrobial-resistance-amr/ (last visited Nov. 23, 2017).

Public-health oriented patent pooling can contribute to de-link R&D funding from sales[31] and a number of proposals have identified patent pooling as a way in which IP on new antibiotics could be managed in a public health-oriented manner.[32] This can contribute to ensuring affordable access for those in need, within a global development and stewardship framework, such as the one discussed at the WHO.[33] Further analysis would be needed to explore its feasibility and understand how the model could be best adapted to fulfil this role.

2 The Case of Upstream Tuberculosis

Combining patent pooling with incentive mechanisms has also been proposed in the context of addressing some of the challenges in TB drugP development. The "3P: Pull, Pool, Push" project aims to improve financial incentives for TB drug development both at the pre-clinical and clinical stage and ensure access and affordability of new regimens once developed.[34] The "push" and "pull" incentives would be linked to the pooling of intellectual property in order to ensure open collaborative research can take place leading towards the development of new TB regimens. In terms of access, the project envisages licensing for the competitive production of the final products to ensure that new TB regimens become available at affordable prices. The initiative is already supported by several leading organizations in the field of tuberculosis, such as the Stop TB Partnership, the TB Alliance, the Union Against Tuberculosis and Heart Disease, and Médecins sans Frontières, and has met with significant interest from some high-burden TB countries.

IV Patent Pooling to Overcome "Patent Thickets"

In certain instances, patent thickets[35] on upstream technology can become a barrier to the development of health products. The SARS case mentioned above is one example where concerns were raised that many overlapping patent applications could become a barrier to the development of needed vaccines and diagnostics. Similar concerns have

31 WHO, *Research and Development*, *supra* note 10.
32 Kieny, *supra* note 29; Chatham House, *supra* note 29.
33 World Health Assembly [WHA], *Global Action Plan on Antimicrobial Resistance*, WHA68.7 (May 26, 2015).
34 For proposal selected by WHO European Region as a possible health R&D demonstration project, *see Summary Report on the nomination of Experts and the shortlisting of Health R&D Demonstration Projects*, WHO (2013), www.who.int/phi/implementation/EURO_procedure_for_selection_of_demo_projects.pdf (last visited Nov. 23, 2017); for a summary of the original proposal, *see Accelerating Innovation and Access to Medicines for Tuberculosis through Open Collaboration: A Push, Pull, Pool Approach ("the 3P Project")*, WHO (2010), www.who.int/phi/implementation/10_summary_EN.pdf (last visited Nov. 23, 2017); and for a more recent summary entitled, *see* 3P: Pull. Pool, Push, *Better TB treatment. Faster. Proposal to accelerate innovation and access to new treatment regimens for TB*, The Access Campaign, www.msfaccess.org/sites/default/files/TB_3P2pager_Dec-2015_ENG.pdf (last visited Jun. 18, 2017).
35 While there are many definitions of a "patent thicket," one that is widely cited definitions is "an overlapping set of patent rights requiring that those seeking to commercialize new technology obtain licenses from multiple patentees." Carl Shapiro, *Navigating the Patent Thicket: Cross Licenses, Patent Pools, and Standard-Setting*, 1 The Innovation Pol'y and the Econ. 119 (2011).

been raised in relation to other upstream technology (e.g., research tools, genomic sequences, vaccines),[36] leading to calls for collaborative licensing models such as patent pools to contribute to addressing them.[37] The objective in these cases is to facilitate access to research tools and early stage technology enabling further scientific development.

Conclusion

Public health patent pools represent an innovative type of PPP that can be used to manage privately held IP rights in the public interest. Article 7 of the TRIPS Agreement states that "the protection and enforcement of intellectual property rights should contribute to the promotion of technological innovation and to the transfer and dissemination of technology, to the mutual advantage of producers and users of technological knowledge and in a manner conducive to social and economic welfare, and to a balance of rights and obligations." Access-oriented and nonexclusive voluntary licensing through patent pooling mechanisms with a clear public health mandate can contribute to achieving this goal and overcoming a number of access and innovation challenges in the biopharmaceutical field.

As shown in the case of HIV, a patent pool can contribute to spurring further innovation (e.g., in relation to paediatric and fixed dose combinations) and to improve access in developing countries. While the design of the patent pool can vary depending on the specific public health challenge a patent pool is trying to address, a firm grounding in public health principles and close collaboration and partnership with key stakeholders seems central to ensuring that it responds to needs and attracts the interest of patent holders and other partners that need to contribute to its success.

While the patent pooling model has so far only been applied to specific diseases (HIV, HCV, TB), the new SDG framework, with its focus on universal health coverage, calls for consideration to be given to the potential applicability of the model beyond these specific diseases. In particular, it would be timely to explore its applicability in relation to other health technologies facing access and innovation challenges that could potentially be addressed (at least in part) through a PPP model based on licensing and patent pooling. This chapter provides several examples of the potential of public health-oriented patent pools to contribute to the implementation of the SDGs, such as in the field of antimicrobial resistance or in relation to patented essential medicines included in the WHO EML. While all such proposals would need to be studied in detail to explore their feasibility and potential public health impact, the experience in HIV, HCV, and TB provides an interesting model that may be applied or adapted to other circumstances.

[36] *See* Martin Friede et al., *Innovation for Vaccines Against Poverty Diseases: The Need for New Support Mechanisms*, WHO (2014); USPTO, *supra* note 5.

[37] *See, e.g.*, Cambridge University Press, Gene Patents and Collaborative Licensing Models: Patent Pools, Clearinghouses, Open Source Models and Liability Regimes (Geertrui van Overwalle ed., 2009).

References

3P: PULL. POOL, PUSH, THE ACCESS CAMPAIGN, *Better TB treatment. Faster. Proposal to accelerate innovation and access to new treatment regimens for TB*, www.msfaccess.org/sites/default/files/TB_3P2pager_Dec-2015_ENG.pdf (last visited Nov. 21, 2017).

ACCESS TO MEDICINES FOUNDATION, INDEX 2014, https://accesstomedicinefoundation.org/media/atmf/2014-Access-to-Medicine-Index.pdf. (last visited Nov. 21, 2017).

Burrone, Esteban and Greg Perry, *Ensuring New Medicines Reach Those in Most Need*, 2 LANCET HIV e362 (2015).

Buse, Kent and Gill Walt, *Global Public–Private Partnerships: Part II – What are the Health Issues for Global Governance?*, 78 BULL. WORLD HEALTH ORGAN. (2000).

Chatham House, *Towards a New Global Business Model for Antibiotics: Delinking Revenue From Sales* (2015).

Contreras, Jorge, *Bermuda's Legacy: Policy, Patents, and the Design of the Genome Commons*, 12 MINN. J. L. SCI. & TECH. 61 (2011).

Friede, Martin, Jean-Paul Prieels, Anneleen Spooren, and Mathieu Mottrie, *Innovation for Vaccines Against Poverty Diseases: The Need for New Support Mechanisms* (2014), www.who.int/immunization/research/forums_and_initiatives/02_Friede_Business_Model.pdf (last visited Nov. 23, 2017).

INT'L FED'N OF PHARM. MFRS. & ASS'N, *Declaration by the Pharmaceutical, Biotechnology and Diagnostics Industries on Combating Antimicrobial Resistance* (Jan. 2016), www.ifpma.org/partners-2/declaration-by-the-pharmaceutical-biotechnology-and-diagnostics-industries-on-combating-antimicrobial-resistance-amr/ (last visited Nov. 23, 2017).

Juneja, Sandeep, Aastha Gupta, Suerie Moon and Stephen Resch, *Projected savings through public health voluntary licences of HIV drugs negotiated by the Medicines Patent Pool (MPP)*, PLoS ONE 12(5): e0177770 (2017), available at: https://doi.org/10.1371/journal.pone.0177770.

Kieny, Maurie-Paule, *Creating and Intergovernmental Consortium for New Antibiotics: A New Development Model*, AMR Control (2015).

MEDICINES PATENT POOL, *Five Years of Patent Pooling in Public Health* (2015).

MEDICINES PATENT POOL, *Licenses in the MPP*, www.medicinespatentpool.org/current-licences/(last visited Nov. 23, 2017).

MEDICINES PATENT POOL, *The Medicines Patent Pool Announces First Licence for Tuberculosis Treatment*, MPP (Jan. 25, 2017), www.medicinespatentpool.org/the-medicines-patent-pool-announces-first-licence-for-tuberculosis-treatment/(last visited Nov. 23, 2017).

MEDICINES PATENT POOL, *The Medicines Patent Pool Expands Mandate to Hepatitis C and Tuberculosis Treatment* (Nov.6, 2015), www.medicinespatentpool.org/the-medicines-patent-pool-expands-mandate-to-hepatitis-c-and-tuberculosis-treatment/ (last visited Nov. 21, 2017) (last visited Nov. 23, 2017).

MEDICINES PATENT POOL, *The Medicines Patent Pool Transparency Policy*, MPP, https://medicinespatentpool.org/uploads/2017/07/MEDICINES-PATENT-POOL-TRANSPARENCY-POLICY-301014.pdf (last visited Nov. 23, 2017).

MEDICINES PATENT POOL, *Progress and Achievements of the Medicines Patent Pool 2010–2015* (2015).

MEDICINES PATENT POOL, *Target Medicines*, www.medicinespatentpool.org/ourwork/target-medicines/(last visited Nov. 23, 2017).

MEDSPAL, www.medspal.org (last visited Nov. 23, 2017).

Memorandum of Understanding, Jun. 8–9, 2010, MPP-UNITAID, EB12/R7.

Merges, Robert P., *Institutions for Intellectual Property Transactions: The Case for Patent Pools* (1999), www.law.berkeley.edu/files/pools%281%29.pdf (last visited Nov. 23, 2017).

REVIEW ON ANTIMICROBIAL RESISTANCE, *Securing New Drugs for Future Generations: The Pipeline of Antibiotics* (2015), https://amr-review.org/sites/default/files/SECURING%20NEW

%20DRUGS%20FOR%20FUTURE%20GENERATIONS%20FINAL%20WEB_0.pdf (last visited Nov. 21, 2017).

Shapiro, Carl, *Navigating the Patent Thicket: Cross Licenses, Patent Pools, and Standard-Setting*, 1 THE INNOVATION POL'Y AND THE ECON. 119 (2011).

Simon, James H.M., Eric. Claasen, Carmen E. Correa, and Albert D.M.E. Osterhaus, *Managing Severe Acute Respiratory Syndrome (SARS) Intellectual Property Rights: The Possible Role of Patent Pooling*, 83 BULL. WORLD HEALTH ORG. 707 (2005), www.who.int/bulletin/volumes/83/9/707.pdf (last visited Nov. 23, 2017).

UNITED NATIONS, Human Rights Council Resolution 15/6, U.N. D.oc. A/HRC/15/L.28 (Sep. 27, 2010).

U.S. PATENT AND TRADE OFFICE, PATENT POOLS: A SOLUTION TO THE PROBLEM OF ACCESS IN BIOTECHNOLOGY PATENTS? (2000), www.consultstanton.com/wp-content/uploads/2015/02/PATENT-POOL-WHITE-PAPER.pdf (last visited Nov. 23, 2017).

Van Overwalle, Geertrui (ed.), CAMBRIDGE UNIVERSITY PRESS, GENE PATENTS AND COLLABORATIVE LICENSING MODELS: PATENT POOLS, CLEARINGHOUSES, OPEN SOURCE MODELS AND LIABILITY REGIMES (2009).

WORLD HEALTH ASSEMBLY, *Global Action Plan on Antimicrobial Resistance*, WHA68.7 (May 26, 2015).

WORLD HEALTH ORGANIZATION, *Accelerating Innovation and Access to Medicines for Tuberculosis through Open Collaboration: A Push, Pull, Pool Approach ("the 3P Project")* (2010), www.who.int/phi/implementation/10_summary_EN.pdf (last visited Nov. 23, 2017).

WORLD HEALTH ORGANIZATION, *Global Action Plan on Anti-Microbial Resistance* (2015), http://apps.who.int/iris/bitstream/10665/193736/1/9789241509763_eng.pdf?ua=1 (last visited Nov. 23, 2017).

WORLD HEALTH ORGANIZATION, *Global Strategy and Plan of Action on Public Health, Innovation and Intellectual Property* (2011), www.who.int/phi/publications/Global_Strategy_Plan_Action.pdf (last visited Nov. 23, 2017).

WORLD HEALTH ORGANIZATION, *Report of the Commission on Intellectual Property Rights, Innovation and Public Health* (2006).

WORLD HEALTH ORGANIZATION, *Research and Development to Meet Health Needs in Developing Countries: Strengthening Global Financing and Coordination. Report of the Consultative Expert Working Group on Research and Development: Financing and Coordination* (2012), www.who.int/phi/CEWG_Report_5_April_2012.pdf (last visited Nov. 23, 2017).

WORLD HEALTH ORGANIZATION, *Summary Report on the nomination of Experts and the shortlisting of Health R&D Demonstration Projects* (2013), www.who.int/phi/implementation/EURO_procedure_for_selection_of_demo_projects.pdf (last visited Nov. 23, 2017).

WORLD TRADE ORGANIZATION, World Intellectual Property Organization, World Health Organization, *Promoting Access to Medical Technologies and Innovation* (2012).

6 Intellectual Property in Early-Phase Research Public–Private Partnerships in the Biomedical Sector

Hilde Stevens and Isabelle Huys*

Introduction

To assess the nature of intellectual property (IP) in early-phase research or precompetitive public–private partnerships (PPPs) in the biomedical field, more understanding is required of the ecosystem in which biomedical PPPs function. In essence, biomedical PPPs are knowledge communities. Pooling complementary resources and expertise, as well as sharing the risks and other (often administrative) burdens between the public and the private stakeholders, increases the effectiveness of PPPs.[1] But diverse social, economic, legal, regulatory, and scientific factors make the PPP model a rather complex collaborative one.

Depending on several criteria, (bio)pharmaceutical research and development (R&D) PPPs may be classified into four different types based on the type of projects they conduct. Upstream research projects entail precompetitive (or early-phase) research and the proof-of-concept (POC) phase. This chapter focuses primarily on these upstream PPPs. Downstream development projects include the Product Development (PD) and

* The authors gratefully acknowledge the Fonds Baillet Latour for supporting H.S. with the Chair in Translational Medicine as well as the Brocher Foundation for hosting H.S. as a visiting researcher (in 2013, 2015, and 2017). The dates in this chapter are based on the PhD research performed at KU Leuven, which was based on qualitative research (interviews, an IP policy analysis study, an IP valuation study in six precompetitive consortia). Several parts of this chapter are drawn from the following sources: Hilde Stevens et al., *Perspectives and Opportunities for Precompetitive Public–Private Partnerships in the Biomedical Sector*, 32 Biotechnology L. Rep. 131, (Jun. 2013) [hereinafter Stevens et al., *Perspectives*]; Hilde Stevens et al., *Intellectual Property Policies in Early-Phase Research in Public–Private Partnerships*, 34 Nature Biotechnology 504, (May 6, 2016) [hereinafter Stevens et al., *Intellectual Property Policies*]; Hilde Stevens, The Role of Intellectual Property in (Precompetitive) Public–Private Partnerships in the Biomedical Sector, ISBN 978–9-4619728–1-1, (2015) [hereinafter Stevens, The Role of Intellectual Property]; Hilde Stevens et al., *Innovative Medicines Initiative (IMI) Case Study Analysis Reveals the True Added Value of Early-Phase Public–Private Partnerships (PPPs)*, 34 Biotechnology L. Rep. 153, (Aug. 1, 2015) [hereinafter Stevens et al., *IMI Case Study*]; Hilde Stevens & Isabelle Huys, *Case study analysis on behalf of IMI JU Executive Office under a service contract procedure: SUMMIT – IMIDIA – Open PHACTS NEWMEDS – eTOX – U-BIOPRED Innovative Medicines Initiative Joint Undertaking (IMI), summary in* IMI, *Annual Activity Report 2013*, 25–27 (Feb. 14, 2014), www.europarl.europa.eu/document/activities/cont/201408/20140818ATT87695/20140818ATT87695EN.pdf [hereinafter Stevens & Huys, *Case Study Analysis*].

[1] Tanja A. Börzel & Thomas Risse, *Public–Private Partnerships: Effective and Legitimate Tools of International Governance?*, *in* Complex Sovereignty: On the Reconstitution of Political Authority in the 21st Century 195 (Edgar Grande & Louis W. Pauly Eds., 2002); Jennifer M. Brinkerhoff, *Government-nonprofit partnership: A defining framework*, 22 Public Admin. Dev. 19, 22 (2002).

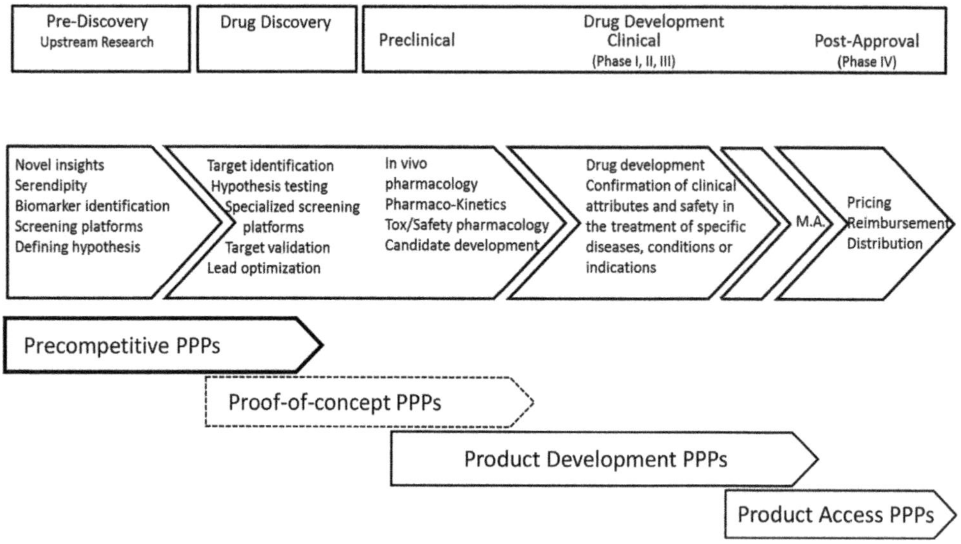

Figure 6.1. Classification of the different types of PPP along the discovery–development–delivery continuum in the biopharmaceutical sector.
Source: Hilde Stevens et al., *Perspectives and Opportunities for Precompetitive Public–Private Partnerships in the Biomedical Sector*, 32 BIOTECHNOLOGY L. REP. 131 (Jun. 2013), 135. Reprinted with permission from BIOTECHNOLOGY LAW REPORT, Volume 32, Issue 3, published by Mary Ann Liebert, Inc., New Rochelle, NY.

the Product Access (PA) phase. These four types are used as the basis for the classification of R&D PPPs in the biomedical sector: precompetitive or early-phase research PPPs, POC PPPs, PDPs, and PA PPPs (Figure 6.1).[2] Other criteria to define PPPs, such as geographic scope, mission and objectives, organizational structure, and/or funding source, can be used to further describe the PPPs within these four classes.

Knowledge development through sharing is enhanced in precompetitive partnerships. Taking into account the multifaceted partnering model of precompetitive PPPs and the heterogeneity of partners – including their often conflicting missions, objectives, and cultures – it is not surprising that IP plays a pivotal role and that intellectual property rights (IPRs) and trust issues are critical parts of the negotiation process.[3] In precompetitive PPPs, highly trained experts are offered a platform to explore the skills, knowledge,

[2] Stevens et al., *Perspectives*, *supra* note *, at 132–33; Kent Buse & Gill Walt, *Global Public–Private Partnerships: Part I – A New Development in Health?*, 78 BULL. OF THE WORLD HEALTH ORG. 549, 549–50 (2000); Warren Kaplan et al., WORLD HEALTH ORGANIZATION [WHO], *Priority Medicines for Europe and the World 2013 Update*, 186–87 (May 6, 2013), www.who.int/medicines/areas/priority_medicines/MasterDocJune28_FINAL_Web.pdf; Pieter Stolk, *Background Paper 8.1 Public Private Partnerships*, 5, 12, 13 (May 1, 2013), www.who.int/medicines/areas/priority_medicines/BP8_1PPPs.pdf.

[3] Bernard H. Munos, Can Open-Source R&D Reinvigorate Drug Research?, 5 NATURE REV. DRUG DISCOVERY 723, 6–7 (2006); Michel Goldman, Comment, *Reflections on the Innovative Medicines Initiative*, 10 NATURE REV. DRUG DISCOVERY 321, 322 (J2011); Gabriel Vargas et al., *Arguments Against Precompetitive Collaboration*, 87 CLINICAL PHARMACOLOGY & THERAPEAUTICS 527, 527–29 (2010); Asher Mullard, *Could Pharma Open its Drug Freezers*, 10 NATURE REV. DRUG DISCOVERY 399, 400, (2011); Jagadeesh Napa, Editorial, *Open Source Drug Discovery*, PHARMA FOCUS ASIA, www.pharmafocusasia.com/strategy/open-source-drug-discovery; Daniel Cressey, Comment, *Animal Research: Battle Scars*, 470 NATURE 452, (Feb. 23, 2011); Editorial, *Expanding Precompetitive Space*, 10 NATURE REV. DRUG DISCOVERY 833 (2011).

and collaborative behavior of researchers operating in the same field. As a result, precompetitive PPPs are perceived as a platform for partner scouting, networking, and selection.[4] Some early-phase research PPPs also perform downstream development of therapies, in which case the importance of IP as well as access to it increases. However, if competitors are working together, potentially conflicting goals and missions need to be put aside in order to increase the chances of the PPP's success.[5]

A complete, publicly available set of policies and procedures allows potential partners to assess their roles and responsibilities as well as gain insight into the rewards and expectations involved in participation.[6] We therefore recommend that biomedical PPPs include basic definitions and information regarding the framework for the management of IP, including IP use, access, and ownership. No single IP framework applies to every PPP in early-phase research. Variation in key IP elements depending on the PPP's focus and the objectives seems appropriate; customization of IP policy can help to incentivize participation in the PPP.[7]

The variation between a more restricted IP framework (what this chapter refers to as a partnership-focused strategy) and an open IP framework (referred to here as an open-collaboration strategy) seems justified given the heterogeneity of the partners and their respective objectives and needs. Tailoring is necessary to serve any particular PPP's mission and to obtain its objectives. PPPs targeting downstream development project results (drugs and diagnostic tests) tend to apply an IP sharing strategy where access to foreground IPRs[8] and freedom to operate are permission-constrained and preferably negotiated with the consortium partners. This is a type of partnership-focused strategy. By contrast, PPPs focused on upstream project results or on specific downstream products for neglected (usually tropical) diseases, HIV/AIDS and malaria (commonly referred to as poverty-related neglected diseases or PRNDs) are more likely to adopt an IP framework that allows more sharing of IPRs. This exemplifies an open-collaboration strategy. Both partnership-focused and open-collaboration models have benefits and drawbacks. Hybrid strategies are deployed when appropriate to advance the project. As such, we argue for a contingency approach, in which different frameworks for sharing knowledge are applied depending on the research focus, business strategy, and feasibility thereof. (See Table 6.1.)

It is estimated that only 10 percent of the resources spent on developing new drugs and therapies is spent on illnesses represented by 90 percent of the burden of disease.[9] Research areas such as PRNDs, which suffer from scarce R&D budgets could benefit

[4] Stevens et al., *Perspectives*, *supra* note *, at 138–39.

[5] *Id.* at 132.

[6] Elkins, Sean, Maggie A.Z. Hupcey, & Antony J. Williams (eds.), Collaborative Computational Technologies for Biomedical Research 42 (John Wiley & Sons, Inc. 2011).

[7] Stevens et al., *Intellectual Property Policies*, *supra* note *, at 509.

[8] "Foreground IP" means the *results of the research conducted during the project*, including (technological and commercial) knowledge, know-how, and data, as well IPRs pertaining to such knowledge, data, or know-how. The latter category will be referred to as "foreground IPRs" and includes patent rights, copyrights, database rights, and so on. Foreground IP is contrasted in this chapter to "background IP," which means preexisting (technological and commercial) knowledge, know-how, and data, as well as IPRs pertaining to such knowledge, data, or know-how. The latter category will be referred to as "background IPRs" and includes patent rights, copyrights, database rights, and so on. This background IP can potentially be included in the project at the start or during the project process.

[9] Munos, *supra* note 3, at 2.

Table 6.1. IP frameworks (knowledge sharing strategies) applied in biomedical PPPs.[†]

IP frameworks (knowledge sharing strategies) applied in biomedical PPPs

Conditions		Partnership-focused strategy	Hybrid strategy	Open-collaboration strategy
Possibility to patent		Yes	Yes, but results preferably in public domain	Yes, but with limitations specified
Access	Access mechanisms / legal basis	Contractual framework based upon IP rights: Contracts (e.g., Project Agreement) including different clauses regarding patents and other industrial rights	Contracts and IP in case of partnership-focused strategy, licenses in case of open-collaboration strategy	Contractual framework based upon IP rights: (viral) licenses (e.g., Open Access Protocol, Creative Commons or Copyleft Licenses), to help continue the virtuous cycle of research
	Target group	During project: project participants After project termination: project participants, affiliates and/or defined third parties	During project: project participants, consortium members or public After project termination: PPP participants, affiliates and/ or defined third parties	All
	Duration	Limited/defined	Limited to undefined	Undefined
Project focus		Profit- or nonprofit-driven research, mainly focusing on diseases of affluence	Nonprofit driven research, focusing on PRNDs	Profit- or nonprofit-driven research, focusing on NCDs and/or PRNDs
Envisioned project deliverables		– Biotechnology tools (upstream research results) – Drugs, therapies and diagnostic tests for NCDs (downstream research results) – A mix of tools and drugs for PRNDs and NCDs (downstream research results)	– Biotechnology tools (upstream research results) – Tools and drugs for PRNDs (upstream and downstream research results)	– Biotechnology tools (upstream research results) – Diagnostic tests and drugs for PRNDs (downstream research results)
PPPs wherein the strategy prevails		IMI, BioWin, The Biomarkers Consortium, FP7, SC4SM, CTMM, 3 PPPs that expressed for their IP policy to remain confidential	MMV, DNDi, OMOP, WIPO Re:Search	SGC, SAGE, TSC (HapMap), OSDD, OAI, TRC, ADNI

[†] Stevens et al., *Intellectual Property Policies, supra* note *, at 509.

Abbreviations:

NCDs: noncommunicable diseases or diseases of affluence

PRNDs: poverty-related and neglected (tropical) diseases, HIV/AIDS and Malaria

Source: Stevens, Hilde et al., *Intellectual Property Policies in Early-Phase Research in Public–Private Partnerships*, 34 Nat. Biotechnol. 509 (2016).

from the open-collaboration model. Further in-depth research to define success formulas and pitfalls can provide recommendations to leverage this PPP collaborative strategy to a higher level and provide more equitable access to medical care in low- and middle-income countries (LMICs). This benefits not only patients suffering from PRNDs, but also those increasingly affected by the rapidly growing noncommunicable diseases (NCDs) epidemic.

It is important to emphasize the broad definition of IP used in this chapter; IP as described here includes both the IPRs granted and protected by the IP laws, as well as know-how and other intangible assets. The use of the latter forms of IP is controlled by policies, contracts, protocols, and norms.[10] This chapter also considers knowledge sharing mechanisms as a key aspect of IP management for shared goals of any partnership involving multiple stakeholders. The role of IP in the broadest and most inclusive sense of the term is pivotal to deploying IP as a tool for collaboration, rather than as the centerpiece of it.[11] Performance of scientific research and in particular the evaluation of IP in PPPs is quantitatively demonstrated by key performance indicators (KPIs), for instance, the number of patents and patent applications, but increasingly by others measures as well.

This chapter aims to shed a light on the different aspects that come into play when mapping the way IP is generated, protected, and managed (e.g., shared) within and beyond early-phase research PPPs. In Part I, we focus on the relevant concepts and typology of early-phase research PPPs, including precompetitive PPPs.[12] Following this are sections focusing on key issues, including the boundaries of the precompetitive partnership (Part II); the role of trust within those PPPs (Part III); IP ownership and access rights (Part IV), including the importance of transparent IP rules underlying knowledge sharing strategies; and the role of IP in the performance of PPPs (Part V). Most of the content and examples are drawn from previous research on Europe's largest early-phase public–private partnership, the Innovative Medicines Initiative (IMI). We conclude in Part VI with some recommendations for best practices to facilitate efficient and equitable knowledge sharing.

I Early-Phase Research PPPs: Concepts and Typology

The PPP model in the pharmaceutical industry is not new. Initially, PPPs were set up in the late-stage drug development cycle for the poorest populations, often suffering from PRNDs, such as dengue, leprosy, and leishmaniasis.[13] The first PPP in life sciences dates

[10] Jaakko Paasi et al., BAZAAR OF OPPORTUNITIES FOR NEW BUSINESS DEVELOPMENT – BRIDGING NETWORKED INNOVATION, INTELLECTUAL PROPERTY AND BUSINESS 4 (Imperial College Press 2013).

[11] Stevens, THE ROLE OF INTELLECTUAL PROPERTY, *supra* note *, at 170–71.

[12] Early-phase research PPPs focus on developing joined projects that are in a preliminary stage of development. Projects are typically based on, e.g. basic research ideas or the need to develop a technology or data platform that could help to accelerate drug development. More specifically, projects in this phase of the drug development cycle are precompetitive. However, as will be explained further in this chapter, early-phase and precompetitive are not complete synonyms; what seems precompetitive for some stakeholders might just be the core business for others.

[13] Roy Widdus, *Public–Private Partnership*, 99 TRANSACTIONS OF THE ROYAL SOC'Y TROPICAL MED. & HYGIENE S1, S2, S4 (Supp.1 2005); Roy Widdus, *Public–Private Partnerships for Health: Their Main Targets, Their Diversity, and Their Future Directions*, 79 BULL. OF THE WORLD HEALTH ORG. 713, 716–17 (2001).

from 1987; the Merck Mectizan® Donation Program, a drug donation program set up by Merck, was aimed at improving the conditions for those suffering from onchocerciasis (or river blindness).[14] Later, Merck expanded this program and involved GlaxoSmithKline (GSK) to donate albendazole; co-administration of Mectizan® and albendazole can be used to treat co-endemic lymphatic filariasis and onchocerciasis in Africa and Yemen.[15] In the same decade, PPPs also targeted HIV/AIDS and malaria.

Big pharmaceutical companies came to realize that collaboration is in most instances the only effective way to bring inventions far enough in the value chain to become eligible for industrial take-up or to create interest by venture capitalists. With PPPs set up in the field of PRNDs and successfully performing early R&D projects in other sectors, the pharmaceutical industry began to tackle the innovation crisis in the drug sector through PPPs. These PPPs perform research at the precompetitive stage, and focus on diseases of affluence or NCDs, such as cancer, diabetes, and obesity.[16]

Basic knowledge of underlying disease mechanisms seems required to accelerate the development of the next-generation's drugs. This basic but complex knowledge generation requires interdisciplinary, translational research conducted by different experts from industry and academia. A shared stakeholder objective is to translate basic biological research into therapies serving patients. Industry realizes the potential of combining different ideas, skills, and expertise in technologically demanding areas and is increasingly tapping into early-phase research conducted at universities and small- and medium-sized enterprises specializing in biotechnology (biotech SMEs).[17] Thus, in the biomedical sector, stakeholders generally include pharmaceutical companies, biotech SMEs, academia, and nongovernmental organizations (NGOs). As the concept has evolved over time, PPPs today also involve other stakeholders in healthcare, such as patient organizations, private foundations, and regulatory bodies.[18]

These early-phase or precompetitive PPPs have emerged quite recently and are focused on optimizing the knowledge generation phase or the prediscovery stage in the drug development lifecycle. PPPs operating in a precompetitive phase start their activities before and at the early discovery of promising drug compounds or diagnostics, although some have led to the identification of potential drug compounds. Such PPPs attempt to answer fundamental research questions and generate technology platforms, research tools, shared databases, and predictive models to progress disease knowledge and enhance the development of safer and more effective drugs.[19] Their primary goal is not to discover or develop products or therapies; therefore it is not necessary for the consortium partners

[14] Widdus, *Public–Private Partnership*, *supra* note 15, at S7; Robert G. Ridley, *Putting the Partnership into Public–Private Partnerships*, 79 Bull. of the World Health Org. 694, 694 (2001).

[15] Mectizan Donation Program, www.mectizan.org/ (last visited Sep. 22, 2017).

[16] Teri Melese et al., *Open Innovation Networks Between Academia and Industry: An Imperative for Breakthrough Therapies*, 15 Nature Med. 502, 502–03 (2009); Janet. A. Wagner et al., *The Biomarkers Consortium: Practice and Pitfalls of Open-Source Precompetitive Collaboration*, 87 Clinical Pharmacology & Therapeutics 539, 539 (2010).

[17] Stevens et al., *Perspectives*, *supra* note *, at 131; Jim Kling, *Biotechs Follow Big Pharma Lead Back into Academia*, 29 Nature Biotechnology 555, 555–56 (2011).

[18] Stevens, The Role of Intellectual Property, *supra* note *, at 6.

[19] Janet Woodcock, *Precompetitive Research: A New Prescription for Drug Development?*, 87 Clinical Pharmacology & Therapeutics 521, 521 (2010).

to include valuable assets (such as candidate products) as background IP[20] to launch the project.[21] A number of early-phase research PPPs will also perform activities in the POC phase and aim at target identification and validation, assay development, screening hit identification, lead compound optimization, preclinical (in vivo animal) studies, and sometimes early clinical studies to establish first-in-human evidence. Both early-phase research PPPs and PDPs can focus on the POC whereby they increase the value of compounds, making them more attractive to pharmaceutical companies for further investment and entrance into expensive clinical trials.[22] In this way, PPPs focusing on the POC phase have a vital role in filling up the gray zone and bridging the so-called valley of death,[23] that is, the situation where risky projects are abandoned because of lack of funds required during extended time periods, rather than because of negative research outcomes. Other criteria to further specify early-phase research PPPs are the mission and objectives, organizational structure, funding source, and geographic scope.[24]

In contrast to most PDPs, which often focus on PRNDs or diseases affecting commercially unattractive target populations,[25] precompetitive PPPs are directed towards a broad range of topics identified as future priorities for health.[26] And as people in LMICs are increasingly affected by the epidemics of NCDs or so-called diseases of affluence, there is a need to investigate ways to adapt technologies developed for high-income countries for use in LMICs.[27] Having the potential to address broader population needs, such PPPs are therefore more attractive for investment. Governments look favorably on competitors joining forces in a precompetitive phase.[28] Initiatives such as the IMI in Europe and Critical Path Institute in the United States establish PPPs in a precompetitive field.[29]

II The Boundaries of Precompetitive Partnerships

It is not clear at what time the so-called competitive phase starts and for whom. Depending on the point in time, the organizational structure of the PPP, and the stakeholder perspective, the definition of what is considered precompetitive might differ. For academia, doing fundamental research and publishing in high-impact journals to build out a scientific reputation is a core activity and thus the moment to excel. By contrast, biotech SMEs develop and commercialize technology platforms and research

[20] For a definition of background IP, see, *supra* note 8.

[21] Woodcock, *supra* note 21 at 521.

[22] *What is CD3?*, Centre for Drug Design & Discovery, www.cd3.eu/about-cd3/about-cd3what-is-cd3.

[23] R. Sanders Williams and Susan Desmond-Hellman, *Making Translation Work*, 332 Science 1359 (2011); Arti K. Rai et al., *Pathways Across the Valley of Death: Novel Intellectual Property Strategies for Accelerated Drug Discovery*, *in* Gene Patents and Collaborative Licensing Models. Patent Pools, Clearinghouses, Open Source Models and Liability Regimes, 247, 248 (Geertrui Van Overwalle Ed., Cambridge University Press 2009).

[24] Stevens et al., *Perspectives, supra* note *, at 133; Stevens, The Role of Intellectual Property, *supra* note *, at 34.

[25] Widdus, *Public–Private Partnership, supra* note 14, at S2-S4.

[26] Goldman, *supra* note 3, at 321; Treaty on European Union [TEU], art. 129, Feb. 7, 1992, 1992 O.J. (C 191), 31 I.L.M. 253.

[27] World Health Organization [WHO], *Health in 2015: from MDGs, Millennium Development Goals to SDGs, Sustainable Development Goals*, 28 (2015), www.who.int/gho/publications/mdgs-sdgs/en/; see also Stevens et al., *Vaccines, supra* note *.

[28] Wagner, *supra* note 17, at 511.

[29] Vargas, *supra* note 3, at 527–28.

Box 6.1. The Innovative Medicines Initiative (IMI)

The IMI is a Joint Technology Initiative (JTI) between the European Union, represented by the EC, and the European Federation of Pharmaceutical Industries and Associations.[30] IMI is currently the world's largest PPP in the biomedical sciences. The PPP was launched in 2008 after identification of the key bottlenecks in research that need to be overcome to stimulate innovation in the drug development process. This PPP is situated at a prediscovery or POC stage and covers early research to improve needed and poorly understood science. The IMI Strategic Research Agenda (targeting key challenges such as safety and efficacy prediction, knowledge management, and education and training) was implemented to enhance the competitiveness of the pharmaceutical sector in Europe for the benefit of patients and scientists.[31] Consortia focusing on projects targeting the development of new methods and tools for safer and more effective drugs are inherently more prone to IP issues than consortia focusing on knowledge management projects. The former type of consortia represent the majority of the IMI consortia.[32]

tools; the related patents are at the core of their business portfolios. And large pharmaceutical companies refer to cooperation at this stage as being "noncompetitive" or "procompetitive."[33] NGOs often seek to control IPRs at an early stage to secure access to future developments for unmet needs. This might be perceived as ambiguous,[34] as their desire to control IPRs for philanthropic investment goals may exceed the interest in collecting royalties for profit aims.[35] Thus discrepancy in the definition of precompetitive research can exist between the different partners in the partnership, and among the stakeholders in general.

Precompetitive PPPs are relatively new in the biomedical sector. Hence, it remains to be seen if, and when, the precompetitive phase ends and when more product-oriented research objectives come into play. PPPs initially aimed at performing precompetitive research start to extend their successful projects. An example is the IMI, the world's largest precompetitive PPP. (See Box 6.1.) IMI has taken advantage of the most successful project outcomes to be further developed in its second phase IMI 2.[36] Therefore, precompetitive PPPs can be seen as performing open-ended research projects, which

[30] European Commission, *Commission Staff Working Document: Joint Technology Initiatives: Background, State-of-Play and Main Features*, SEC(2007) 692 (2007) 3, 12, https://ec.europa.eu/research/jti/pdf/background_jtis_en.pdf.

[31] The Innovative Medicines Initiative [IMI], *The Innovative Medicines Initiative (IMI) Research Agenda: Creating Biomedical R&D Leadership for Europe to Benefit the Patients and Society*, 3, 7 (Feb. 15, 2008), http://rp7.ffg.at/upload/medialibrary/IMI-GB-research-agenda-006v2–15022008.pdf; IMI, *The Innovative Medicines Initiative (IMI) Strategic Research Agenda: Revision 2011*, 3, 10, 25 (June, 16, 2011), www.imi.europa.eu/sites/default/files/uploads/documents/reference-documents/SRArevised2011.pdf (last visited Nov. 23, 2017).

[32] Stevens et al., *IMI Case Study*, *supra* note * at 154.

[33] Stevens et al., *Perspectives*, *supra* note *, at 136–37.

[34] Editorial, *With Strings – Researchers Should Shrug Off Their Fears and Welcome the Concept of Venture Philantrophy*, 475 Nature 266 (2011).

[35] Stevens et al., *Intellectual Property Policies*, *supra* note *, at 508.

[36] Michel Goldman et al., *The Innovative Medicines Initiative: An Engine for Regulatory Science*, 14 Nature Rev. Drug Discovery 1, 2 (2014).

might further be developed in more product-oriented development models after the projects end, whether via an R&D alliance or in private development.[37]

III The Importance of Trust

Precompetitive PPPs are platforms for scientists and industrial partners sharing thoughts and ideas, gaining more insight into scientific enigmas, as well as discovering breakthroughs and disruptive innovations. Leveraging complementarity and gaining expertise are common motives for all stakeholders participating in precompetitive PPPs.[38] Industry partners are highly interested in the scientific performance of universities as selection criteria for future collaborations.[39] Academic partners may fear they will miss out on visibility and potential collaboration opportunities if they do not participate in PPPs.[40] Thus precompetitive PPPs are perceived as opportunities for partner scouting, networking, and selection.[41]

The collaboration of competitors, sometimes referred to as coopetition, may raise suspicion regarding motives and therefore may contribute to the lack of trust between stakeholders.[42] Trust is based on a mutual understanding of the stakeholders' expectations and a shared perspective on the PPP's mission and objectives. Trust and related relationship issues generally occur during the start-up phase of the PPP, particularly during the first year.[43] The negotiation process preceding the project start, the decisions made, and the behavior of the different participants, will play a determining role in the PPP's success.[44] Trust is translated in the confidence of partners to share information and know-how regardless of the risk that other partners might benefit from such sharing. If these issues are not addressed carefully during the start-up phase of the project, an "us versus them" mindset might cause a potential failure of the PPP.[45] Lessons learned should be communicated to other initiatives via best practices or expert fora.[46] (See Box 6.2.)

Notwithstanding the abundance of precompetitive PPPs, their impact and performance can be at stake when there is a lack of trust among the stakeholders. This lack of trust may find its origin in the IP hurdles, especially with regard to access to background IPRs and information sharing.[47] Through their hybrid structures, PPPs are subject to

[37] Stevens et al., *Perspectives*, *supra* note *, at 138.
[38] Stevens et al., *Perspectives*, *supra* note *, at 138.
[39] Bart Van Looy et al., *Entrepreneurial Effectiveness of European Universities: An Empirical Assessment of Antecedents and Trade-Offs*, 40 Res. Pol'y 553, 560 (2011).
[40] Rudolf Strohmeier et al., *IMI Moves Forward*, 29 Nature Biotechnology 689, 689 (2011).
[41] Stevens et al., *Perspectives*, *supra* note *, at 138.
[42] Micheal J. Kelly et al., *Managing Alliance Relationships: Key Challenges in the Early Stages of Collaboration*, 32 R&D Mgmt. 11, 13 (2002); Maria Bengtsson and Soren Kock, *"Coopetition" in Business Networks – To Cooperate and Compete Simultaneously*, 29 Indus. Mktg. Mgmt. 411, 411–13 (2000).
[43] Kelly et al., *supra* note 43, at 12.
[44] *Id.*, at 12.
[45] *Id.*, at 13.
[46] Stevens and Huys, *Case Study Analysis*, *supra* note *, at 25–27. In the IMI Case Study, the interview participants clearly expressed the need to communicate, besides the scientific results, also, and equally important, the consortium experiences and best practices, such as how to best create trust between different stakeholder groups or contract templates to share information IP between different parties. These best practices or guidelines developed in expert fora could help other consortia to speed up the development process and save precious time.
[47] Stevens et al., *Perspectives*, *supra* note *, at 137.

Box 6.2. Recommendations for sustainable and successful (early-research) PPPs

1. Maximize trust building and communication between the different stakeholders
2. Consider precompetitive PPPs as a scouting platform for future collaborations
3. Foster IP as a tool for collaboration in PPPs, not as the centerpiece of the partnership
4. Provide clear and transparent guidelines for managing IP
5. Consider a stage-gate process
6. Optimize sharing through a flexible IP policy
7. Implement the honest broker model
8. Appoint a neutral IP manager
9. Share (non)confidential data in a data warehouse to increase the stakeholders' level of openness
10. Anticipate a sustainability plan
11. Assure wide dissemination of best practices via, e.g., expert fora
12. Conduct more research in PPP performance evaluation
13. Include sufficient Key Performance Indicators based on qualitative measures
14. Provide an overview of the PPP landscape to avoid duplication
15. Exchange information on the legal framework to ease global research demand
16. Investigate how PPPs with varying objectives (e.g., PPPs focusing on noncommunicable diseases (NDCs) vs. PPPs focusing on poverty-related and neglected (tropical) diseases (PRNDs)) can share best practices and lessons learned

unbalanced power relations between academia, biotech SMEs, and industry.[48] For academia and biotech SMEs, background IPRs are often seen as a barrier to participation in precompetitive PPPs. The reach-through access rights to background IP can cause tensions and suspicion.[49] For example, by participating in PPPs, biotech SMEs, whose business model may be based upon offering drug toxicity testing services on their mouse models to large pharma companies, might fear that they are expected to offer these models to the participating companies for free or unfavorable terms.

The level of trust among stakeholders will determine the capability of precompetitive PPPs to become effective networking platforms. For the PPPs to be information-sharing platforms, flexibility in the IP policy is of key importance.[50] Flexible arrangements, whereby room to renegotiate well-defined issues when predefined milestones have been reached or certain deliverables have been accomplished is provided, can anticipate uncertainties in the negotiation process. This stepwise approach, also sometimes referred to as the stage-gate process,[51] could facilitate trust building. (See Box 6.2.)

Such milestone-driven research also allows for redirecting resources. Contributions could be kept modular in order to reduce the risk if a specific module fails.[52] Precompetitive PPP project results should form the base of an open platform for further drug

[48] Danna Karen Ciccone, *Arguing for a Centralized Coordination Solution to the Public–Private Partnership Explosion in Global Health*, 17 Glob. Health Promotion 48, 49 (2010).

[49] Stevens et al., *Perspectives*, *supra* note *, at 137; *see also* Natasha Gilbert, *Universities Shun Europe's Drug Initiative*, 466 Nature 306, 306–07 (2010).

[50] Intellectual Property Watch, *Partnership To Share Research, Keep IP Rights, On Neglected Diseases*, ¶ 2, IP-watch.org (Jan. 6, 2011), www.ip-watch.org/2011/06/01/partnership-to-share-research-keep-ip-rights-on-neglected-diseases/.

[51] Stevens et al., *Perspectives*, *supra* note *, at 138.

[52] David Southwood, Comment, *Research Collaboration: When International Partnerships Go Wrong*, 488 Nature 451, 453 (2012).

development. Whether a partnership-focused, an open-collaboration, or a hybrid strategy is applied, in each of the early-phase research PPPs or PPP projects, the partners engage to share information with each other. Even in partnership-focused PPPs that apply restrictive access rights rules, the partners are convinced that openness toward different stakeholders within the partnership during the project, and beyond the partnership after project termination, as well as sharing of non-confidential information, is pivotal to advancing the projects towards achieving the project objectives. Within the partnership-focus strategy as applied by IMI, for example, partners are able to contractually decide on applying a more open-collaboration strategy. This approach is taken in the U-BIOPRED consortium, where the results from biomarker research are immediately made publicly available in scientific publications. The decision to openly share the results of the U-BIOPRED's biomarker research followed the debate about the Myriad breast cancer gene patent, which was perceived by stakeholders as hindering innovation.

However, the open-ended nature of precompetitive PPPs introduces complexities on the level of IPRs as well as on the sustainability of such platform. More specifically, to accommodate the requisite degree of openness, a maximum amount of information should be shared,[53] while guaranteeing partners IP and other data protection aspects.

IP policies can entail a certain degree of flexibility, incorporating boundaries wherein partners can operate. The IMI IP Policy,[54] for example, allows for a certain degree of flexibility to negotiate IP ownership, the modalities of the access rights to IP, and the management of IP. (See Box 6.3.) However, the IMI IP Policy does not define the roles and responsibilities specific for the different stakeholders. Together with the specific IP clauses with respect to terms and conditions, these roles and responsibilities of the different partners are negotiated prior to the approval of the project agreement and the final description of work.[55]

IV IP Ownership and Access Rights

The ownership of the background IP typically remains with the respective party and poses no particular difficulties.[56] By contrast, the access rights to the background IP might pose difficulties.[57] Here, aspects pertinent to background IP are considered briefly.

A *General Considerations*

The valuation of background IP before the project start is a very difficult and delicate process, especially with respect to the valuation of patents covering basic research inventions.[58] Due to its unique nature, IP should be valued on a case-by-case

[53] Stevens et al., *Perspectives*, *supra* note *, at 138.
[54] IMI, *IMI Intellectual Property [IP] Policy*(Jul. 1, 2007), https://ec.europa.eu/research/participants/portal/doc/call/fp7/imi-ju-03–2010/30831-imi-ipr-policy01august2007_en.pdf.
[55] Stevens, The Role of Intellectual Property, *supra* note *, at 137.
[56] Stevens et al., *Intellectual Property Policies*, *supra* note *, at 505.
[57] Stevens et al., *Perspectives*, *supra* note *, at 138.
[58] Thomas L. Bereuter et al., *IPR-Codes and Guidelines in Europe Facilitating Collaboration of Publicly Funded Research Organizations (PROs) with Businesses*, 46 les Nouvelles 226, 226, 229, (2011); Jon F. Merz, WHO, *Intellectual Property and Product Development Public/Private Partnerships*, 7 (May 16, 2005), www.who.int/intellectualproperty/studies/Merz%20WHO%20report.pdf?ua=1.

Box 6.3. The IMI IP Policy[59]

The IMI IP Policy was issued at the start of IMI in 2007. Several guidance documents have been published to address the issues of clarity and the lack of clear definitions such as the IMI IP Guidance Note,[60] the IMI Explanatory Note,[61] and the IMI Clarification Note[62] to the IMI IP Policy.

The IMI 2 JU Model Grant Agreement[63] was released on January 12, 2015, and includes the new provisions regarding the IMI IP Policy applied in IMI 2. In addition, the guidance documents have been implemented in the new IMI 2 JU Model Grant Agreement.[64] An overview of the main elements of the IMI IP Policy is provided, and the major changes with the IMI IP Policy as issued in 2007, are highlighted in Table 6.2.

Table 6.2. Summary of the IMI 2 IP Policy, based on previous experiences from IMI 1.[65]

IMI 2 IP Policy – based on previous experience		
	BACKGROUND (necessary and identified)	FOREGROUND
OWNERSHIP	Remains with owner (1)	Results belong to the beneficiary who generated it (1,2)
ACCESS RIGHTS GRANTED BY A BENEFIARY TO/ON (3)		
Beneficiaries **for completion of the project**	**Royalty-free**	**Royalty-free**
Beneficiaries and affiliates **for research use (4)**	**Fair & reasonable terms (5)** for background needed for using the results	**Fair & reasonable terms (5)**
Third parties **for research use (4)** after the project (6)	**Fair & reasonable terms (5)** for background needed for using the results	**Fair & reasonable terms (5)**
Beneficiaries and affiliates or third parties **for direct exploitation (7)**	To be negotiated	To be negotiated
IP MANAGEMENT		Mandatory for beneficiaries receiving funding (NEW!)/ Common practice: * lies with the owner(s) in adequate and effective manner → relevant (national) legal provisions, action peculiarities, legitimate interests * if valuable results left unprotected → to be discussed within the consortium

[59] *IMI IP Policy*, *supra* note 55.

[60] IMI, *IMI Guidance Note for IMI Applicants and Participants* (Nov. 2010), www.imi.europa.eu/sites/default/files/uploads/documents/apply-for-funding/intellectual-property/GuidanceNote_Draft3-1_10Nov2010.pdf (last visited Nov. 23, 2017).

[61] IMI, *IMI Explanatory Note* (Jul. 2008), www.imi.europa.eu/sites/default/files/uploads/documents/apply-for-funding/intellectual-property/ipr-helpdesk-doc-on-imi-ipr-policy_en.pdf (last visited Nov. 23, 2017).

[62] IMI, *Clarification Note to the IMI IP Policy* (on file with authors).

[63] IMI, IMI 2 Joint Undertaking [IMI 2 JU] Model Grant Agreement, art. 23(a)-31 (Jan. 12, 2015), www.imi.europa.eu/sites/default/files/uploads/documents/apply-for-funding/call-documents/imi2/h2020-mga-imi_en.pdf (last visited Nov. 23, 2017).

[64] *Id.*

[65] Stevens, The Role of Intellectual Property, *supra* note *, at 82–83.

(1) Possible transfer of ownership: (a) within the consortium to affiliates and purchasers without prior notification, and (b) on a case-by-case basis.
(2) Joint ownership of results: Individual use of jointly owned results, provided prior notice and fair and reasonable compensation to the other joint owners (based on previous experiences).
(3) Granting modalities: Access rights are granted on written request unless otherwise agreed. Almost all on-going IMI projects agreed that access rights to background IP are granted without any additional administrative step. Time-limits for requesting access rights: To be agreed in the Project Agreement.
(4) Research use: Use of results or background necessary to use the results for all purposes other than for completing the project or for direct exploitation (based on previous experiences).
(5) The terms to grant access rights to beneficiaries and affiliates for research use have changed. In the IMI 1 IP Policy, it was stated to be granted on *royalty-free* OR fair and reasonable terms.
(6) Access rights to results for third parties: (a) only after the end of the project, (b) possibility to exclude specific elements of background (based on previous experiences), and (c) time-limits to be agreed.
(7) Direct exploitation: to develop for commercialization or to commercialize the results.

Disseminating modalities: Each beneficiary has the obligation to disseminate its own results: a) as soon as reasonably possible, and b) for publications open access is mandatory. Additionally, it is mandatory to mention the IMI support & Partners in-kind contribution in patent applications / all communications.

Source: Stevens, Hilde, The Role of Intellectual Property in (Precompetitive) Public–Private Partnerships in the Biomedical Sector 82–83 (2015).

basis.[66] If it concerns an invention, the best approach is to identify the development stage; if it concerns a database, then to identify the completeness and type of data, and the investment needed to translate it to a marketable product or therapy.[67] Highly innovative technologies or products require higher investments and more risks to be taken. Other factors that should be taken into account are the type of product or therapy, the manufacturing process, and the intended market.[68] Furthermore, it is important to include disincentives such as regulatory and liability concerns carried by the pharmaceutical industry once the product goes on the market.[69]

Proper compensation for background IP included in the PPP project is essential to create trust between the different stakeholders. Lack of trust between the parties or competitors might hinder the inclusion of relevant background IP, especially patents, under the preagreed (for free or fair and reasonable) conditions in the PPP's project agreement. Proper compensation for the inclusion of background IP is also essential for the creation of foreground IP.[70]

The stage-gate approach, whereby the general conditions and terms regarding access rights to background IP are discussed during the initial IP negotiations, and more specific

66 European Commission, *Final Report from the Expert Group on Intellectual Property Valuation*, 5, 13 (Nov. 29, 2013), https://ec.europa.eu/research/innovation-union/pdf/Expert_Group_Report_on_Intellectual_Property_Valuation_IP_web_2.pdf.

67 Jennifer Giordano-Coltart and Charles W. Calkins, *Best Practices in Patent License Negotiations*, 25 Nature Biotechnology 1347, 1348 (2007).

68 Steve Brooke and Janet G. Vail, *Public- and Private-Sector Partnerships in Contraceptive Research and Development: Guiding Principles*, 67 Int'l J. of Gynecology and Obstetrics S125, S134 (1999).

69 *Id.*, at S131.

70 Michael R. Boyd, *The Position of Intellectual Property Rights in Drug Discovery and Development From Natural Products*, 51 J. Ethnopharmacology 17, 18 (1996).

conditions are discussed when the opportunity presents itself, could further facilitate the negotiation process.[71] This is discussed in more detail below in the section addressing the importance of clear and transparent IP policies.

Valuation of early-stage research requires the partners to conduct the due diligence exercise for themselves as well as for their future partners.[72] This is a major challenge in precompetitive PPP negotiations.[73] The PPP managing body, responsible for the day-to-day management of the PPP, can help overcome IP hurdles by operating as a neutral mediating party.[74]

An IP policy analysis of thirty precompetitive PPPs revealed that access rights to background IP are granted on royalty-free conditions or on "fair and reasonable" terms.[75] For example, in the IMI IP Policy,[76] it is stated that access to background IP should be granted on a royalty-free basis during the project. After the project ends, access rights to background IP should be granted on royalty-free *or* fair and reasonable conditions, as predefined in the consortium agreement. Fair and reasonable means that the preferential price to compensate a partner for its input is set as low as possible to provide access to the unprotected IP while guaranteeing that partner a reasonable rate of return.[77]

PPPs focusing on PRNDs explicitly state a preference that research results be placed in the public domain (open-collaboration strategy); however, when necessary to meet a project's objectives, patenting is possible, private ownership will be assigned, and a conditional licensing structure will be negotiated (hybrid strategy).

A clear view on the IP ownership strengthens the collaboration. Pursuing IP ownership *an sich* should not be an end in itself. Ownership structures should be concluded to serve the PPP's objective.[78]

B *Foreground IP: Patents and Other Knowledge Assets*

Typically, the ownership of foreground IPRs is assigned to the party who generated the knowledge. The life cycle to develop drugs is relatively long, and IP protection is pivotal to guarantee a return on investment (ROI) to the investor(s). IPRs legally underpin the potential ROI of the innovation process. However, although the value of businesses is greatly defined by the creation of intangible assets, the understanding of the scope of IP differs widely amongst the various stakeholders.[79]

The different stakeholders often specifically address the role of patents in PPPs, but fail to consider other significant forms of IP, such as database rights, as well as other intangible resources prevalent in such collaborations, such as the creation of know-how and

[71] Stevens et al., *Perspectives*, *supra* note *, at 138.
[72] Melese et al., *supra* note 17, at 504.
[73] Stevens et al., *Perspectives*, *supra* note *, at 138.
[74] Strohmeier et al., *supra* note 41, at 689.
[75] Stevens, The Role of Intellectual Property, *supra* note *, at 146.
[76] *IMI IP Policy*, *supra* note 55.
[77] *Clarification Note to the IMI IP Policy*, *supra* note 60, at 7.
[78] Antony Taubman, Council on Health Research for Development [COHRED], *Public–Private Management of Intellectual Property for Public Health Outcomes in the Developing World: The Lessons of Access Conditions in Research and Development Agreements*, 17 (2004), http://announcementsfiles.cohred.org/gfhr_pub/assoc/s14831e/s14831e.pdf.
[79] European Commission, *supra* note 67, at 5.

knowledge sharing mechanisms.[80] In the case of IMI, by contrast, reference to background IP was primarily directed towards types of IP such as know-how of the participating research groups and databases. In the eTOX consortium, pharmaceutical companies shared their nonconfidential and, more importantly, confidential data, which was new to the sector, with the consortium partners. The honest broker model, whereby one neutral trusted party supplies a data warehouse, is a model that convinced the companies to increase their level of openness with respect to confidential data sharing. (See Box 6.2.) The inclusion of patents as background IP is thus not always the major driving force behind the scientific excellence of precompetitive PPPs.[81]

One lesson is that partners should carefully consider whether scientific results yielded by precompetitive research need to be protected by patents to advance sciences in general, and to improve the collaborative activities between the stakeholders in particular.[82] (See Box 6.2.) For industry, the main objective is not necessarily IP ownership per se but, rather, the capacity to gain access rights to the IP (both foreground and background IP) in order to be able to further develop or even commercialize the knowledge generated within the consortium.[83] By participating in precompetitive PPPs, industry stakeholders desire to build long-term relationships with highly trained experts present in other stakeholder groups. This could lead them to a preferred position in negotiating access on know-how and IPRs beyond that developed within the precompetitive PPPs. It also offers them the possibility to assess the partners' negotiating strength in accessing third party's technologies. With this additional insight, we argue – again – that precompetitive PPPs are a scouting forum for future partnerships.[84] (See Box 6.2).

The idea that industry is best placed to bring products and therapies to the market is justifiable in several cases. In general, IP ownership should be assigned to the party that generated the IP. In cases where more than one party generated the IP, joint ownership should be the rule. The fact that industry brings new drugs or therapies to the market is thus not an argument *contra* joint ownership, as license agreements exist to solve this issue. An argument to avoid joint ownership, however, is the lack of clear legal provisions about joint ownership. Joint ownership issues might be raised when different parties are entitled to multiple rights in different national patent laws.[85] Current national, European, and international patent legislation has not yet adapted to the trend of collaborative creation and national laws differ in the scope of the exploitation rights accompanying a jointly owned patent.[86] The same holds true for the protection of trade secrets, although the recently approved European trade secrets directive intends to create more harmonization.[87] Internationally harmonized legal provisions concerning joint ownership or trade secret protection

[80] Stevens et al., *Perspectives*, *supra* note *, at 131; Stevens, The Role of Intellectual Property, *supra* note *, at 158, 161.
[81] Stevens, The Role of Intellectual Property, *supra* note *, at 156–57.
[82] *Id.*, at 156.
[83] Stevens et al., *Perspectives*, *supra* note *, at 132, 136.
[84] *Id.*, at 138–39.
[85] Arina Gorbatyuk et al., *Intellectual Property Ownership in Coupled Open Innovation Processes*, 47 Int'l Rev. of Intell. Prop. and Competition L. 262, 265, 281 (2016).
[86] *Id.*, at 281, 285.
[87] The Council adopted a directive setting our rules for protection of trade secrets and confidential information of European companies. The different member states will have a maximum of two years to incorporate the new provisions into domestic law. European Commission, Trade Secrets, https://ec.europa.eu/growth/industry/intellectual-property/trade-secrets_en (last visited Nov. 18, 2017).

are currently lacking.[88] (See Box 6.2.) Due to the uncertainty accompanying the lack of clear legal provisions on joint ownership of patents at this point in time, joint ownership should not be considered as a default solution, and especially not as the easy option.[89]

General rules about joint ownership of patents tends to be avoided in most of the IP policies of precompetitive PPPs.[90] Alternatives to joint ownership of patents, such as agreeing on sole ownership for one party, with a license back to the other party who has helped to generate the foreground IP, can circumvent potential issues arising with joint ownership of patents. However, this solution, whereby the owner has the rights to exploit the coinvented technology, while the non-owner licensee is compensated, raises the question whether this agreement reflects the shared efforts of the different parties in the collaboration.[91] This solution resembles more a service contract-relationship between the different parties.

C *Data and Other Knowledge Outputs*

There is increased reliance on "big data," that is, the bits and bytes recording the huge volumes of chemical, metabolic, genomic, phenotypic, and other types of data, generated by multidisciplinary research groups. This supports the recent trend towards more open, and in specific cases, even free sharing of scientific information.[92] Different stakeholders realize that patenting research results might not be a *conditio sine qua non* for protection of scientific achievements anymore.[93] Due to the growing number of collaborative research projects, wherein sharing of techniques and ideas is needed, and the rise of open innovation,[94] the eagerness to seek patent protection for every scientific achievement has changed.[95]

88 Gorbatyuk et al., *supra* note 86, at 262, 281.

89 European IPR Helpdesk, Case Study: Allocation of Shares of Jointly Developed Results, 3 (Feb. 2014), www.iprhelpdesk.eu/sites/default/files/newsdocuments/CS_Allocation_of_shares_of_jointly_developed_results.pdf.

90 Stevens et al., *Intellectual Property Policies, supra* note *, at 507.

91 Robert J. Paradiso and Elizabeth Pietrowski, *Dilemmas of Joint Patent Ownership: Provide a Clear Understanding of the Parties' Expectations*, 197 N.J. L. J. 912, 913 (2009).

92 Maja Larson and Margaret Chon, *The Greatest Generational Impact: The Open Neuroscience Movement as an Emerging Knowledge Commons, in* GOVERNING MEDICAL KNOWLEDGE COMMONS (Katherine Strandburg, Brett M. Frischmann, & Michael J. Madison eds. 2017)

93 Colin Macilwain, *Sharing Information Is Preferable to Patenting*, 498 NATURE 273 (2013).

94 The partnership-focused strategy can be considered most in line with Chesbrough's "Open Innovation" principles. Henry Chesbrough, OPEN BUSINESS MODELS: HOW TO THRIVE IN THE NEW INNOVATION LANDSCAPE (2006) (describing firm-centered innovation and the sharing of knowledge with other, specifically selected actors). This system is dominated by the for-profit sector, based on IP, with subsequent license contracts creating restricted openness. *See generally* GEERTRUI VAN OVERWALLE G, *Inventing Inclusive Patents. From Old to New Open Innovation, in* KRITIKA-ESSAYS ON INTELLECTUAL PROPERTY, VOL. 1, 206 (Peter Drahos et al. eds., Edward Elgar 2015).

We prefer to use the term "partnership-focused" rather than "Open Innovation" to dissociate from the firm-centered perspective, as these PPPs are partnerships wherein all partners are equal, and the "firm-centered" connotation does not reflect the presence of a more balanced network. The open-collaboration strategy, on the other hand, can be compared with the nonprofit motivated user- and community-centered innovation, wherein universal access is aimed for by refraining from focusing too much on (private) ownership of IP, and/or semi-openness (where IP access and use is restricted to a specific group of users) and universal openness (where nobody can be excluded from IP access and use) is targeted. The most extreme form of the open-collaboration strategy is the dedication of foreground IP to the public domain (see Table 6.1), Stevens et al., *Intellectual Property Policies supra* note *, at 504.

95 Macilwain, *supra* note 94.

Early-phase research PPPs will not produce ready-to-market drugs or therapies. Instead, tools and technologies that enable the development of downstream products and therapies will be developed. Biomarkers, for example, are research tools aimed at predicting the response of the human body to drugs in terms of toxicity and efficacy. The various case law decisions with respect to the patenting of genes have significantly changed the patent landscape for the biomarker discovery projects focusing on personalized medicine, as a result of which patenting genetic sequences as well as genetic diagnostic methods has become very difficult.[96] In basic science research consortia, some representatives realize that patenting prognostic or diagnostic applications might hinder the steps towards further clinical validation, and therefore they instead focus on the opportunity offered by the PPP to progress such findings towards the step of clinical validation. In the IMI consortia analyzed, whether or not biomarker research is publicly disseminated or kept as trade secrets, patents are considered an option for the biomarker-based companion diagnostics under development and codeveloped therapeutics, or biomarker-based diagnostics developed to guide drug use after drug approval.

The aggregation of and access to datasets of several companies is a major asset of collaborative projects. For example, one of the objectives of precompetitive R&D PPPs could be the setup of toxicology prediction models to screen drug compounds or other types of technology platforms. Open access to parts of the company's database allows for participants to expand the compound libraries used for screening and identification of lead compounds. Access to a company's library might be granted case-by-case; this allows for the company to select nonproprietary restricted structures and structures that are at that moment not subject to the company's internal proprietary research. The confidential data of companies can be masked; sensitive data is firewalled for nonauthorized project participants, for example, whereby the full molecular structure information is kept proprietary. The research potential of the collaborative database is related to the number of participants; with each additional party granting restricted access to its database, the number of screening possibilities increases exponentially. The expanded chemical diversity offers routes for innovative exploration of new entries for medicinal chemistry.[97]

In the case of databases covering clinical trial information, the discussion of collaborative parameters is even more sensitive. On the one hand, there is a need for openness and sharing of clinical trial data among PPP consortia members allowing research to be reanalyzed or to conduct new analysis with existing data. The Clinical Trials Regulation (CTR) (EC) No 536/2014[98] and some other policies at the European Medicines Agency cover principles to disclose results and clinical study reports. On the other hand, confidentiality needs to be guaranteed, for instance, in order to respect and protect the trial participants' privacy, or to prevent the conflict of interest of the sponsor.[99]

[96] Aaron Kesselheim et al., *The Evolving Role of Biomarker Patents in Personalized Medicine*, 95 CLINICAL PHARMACOLOGY THERAPEUTICS 127, 127 (2014).

[97] Peter B. Simpson and Melvin Reichman, Comment, *Opening the Lead Generation Toolbox*, 13 NATURE REVS. DRUG DISCOVERY 3, 3–4 (2014).

[98] Regulation 536/2014 of the European Parliament and of the Council of Apr. 16, 2014, on Clinical Trials on Medical Products for Human Use and Repealing Directive 2001/20/EC, 2014 O.J. (L 158).

[99] With regard to potential conflicts of interest of the sponsor, the US Food and Drug Administration, for example, notes: "We recognize that the potential conflicts of interest faced by government sponsors can be different from those of industry sponsors, so that the implications for the approach to monitoring, particularly with regard to confidentiality and independence issues (*see* Section 4.2 and Section 6), may also differ to some extent." FOOD AND DRUG ADMIN. [FDA], GUIDANCE FOR CLINICAL TRIAL

In the IMI Case Study, it was revealed that aggregated databases with enormous potential were created.[100] These databases allowed researchers to explore new routes by grabbing information from combined datasets of an unprecedented size and increasing accompanying research potential. The inclusion of datasets in the Project Agreement clearly specified the difference between nonconfidential and confidential datasets included by the partners.

The IMI IP Policy reflects restricted openness.[101] However, the flexibility incorporated in the IMI IP Policy allows for the PPP projects to decide on the permission constraints (or the level of openness) on a case-by-case base. During the project, only partners within the project are allowed to access the background IP (in case the aggregated database is built upon background IP of one or more consortium partners) or the foreground IP (in case the aggregated database is built upon the efforts performed during the project), and only if needed to complete certain tasks and to develop foreground IP[102]. The preferred access granted to consortium partners is a major incentive for the partners to participate in IMI.[103]

Due to the innovative character and the size of the shared databases, the sustainability thereof requires serious reflection. During the project, the databases created allow researchers to explore combined datasets with different access and security levels. The financial sustainability of such model, and especially the idea of opening up parts of the databases to the wider research community, is still unclear. The EC has stressed the need to explore options to support the datasets' sustainability.[104] Some IMI consortia have reflected on models for sustainability, for instance hosting the databases in a separate foundation.

D *Knowledge Sharing Mechanisms and Models*

A key prerequisite to enhance sharing capabilities is the development of knowledge sharing mechanisms. For example, the creation of an honest broker mediated data warehouse in IMI's eTOX consortium, represents a scientific endeavor of high excellence that allows advancement towards POC-oriented research. It highlights the importance of creating such sharing mechanisms for knowledge exchange, especially of different types of IPRs and knowledge assets, including nonpatented knowledge, in precompetitive PPP settings.[105]

The development of standards and templates for material, data, and information transfer and access such as Material Transfer Agreements (MTAs), Data Transfer Agreements (DTAs), and Confidentiality Disclosure Agreements (CDAs) might be a precompetitive PPP's highest added value for further collaboration. These tools and technologies facilitate the sharing of data, materials, and information. Sharing of nonconfidential data,

Sponsors: Establishment and Operation of Clinical Trial Data Monitoring Committees (2006), www.fda.gov/OHRMS/DOCKETS/98fr/01d-0489-gdl0003.pdf.

100 Stevens, The Role of Intellectual Property, *supra* note *, at 155.

101 IMI IP Policy, *supra* note 55.

102 *Id.* at 6.

103 Stevens et al., *Perspectives, supra* note *, at 136; Stevens et al., *Intellectual Property Policies, supra* note *, at 505–506.

104 IMI Governing Board Meeting, Chaired by Dr. Rudolf Strohmeier, Deputy-Director General of Directorate General for Research and Innovation (DG RTD) at the European Council, (Oct. 29, 2013).

105 *Id.*, at 164.

but more importantly, confidential data, enables the development and validation of data standards, research tools, and criteria for new clinical trial design.[106]

A substantial number of the IP policies lack basic clarity and definitions, such as definitions of background and foreground IP, not to mention rules on IP ownership, access, and use. This leaves too much room for ambiguity. Transparency is of utmost importance, not only for the partners in a consortium but also for the general public. Transparency and standardization of definitions could ease the exchange of data and materials between PPPs and avert legal interoperability issues, resulting in reduced coordination costs.[107]

It is essential to establish clear rules regarding IP ownership of potential IP and access rights thereto, in order to provide insight and an understanding of the parties' expectations.[108] Different ideas about protection via IPRs, IP ownership, and access to IP can seriously hinder the negotiations.[109] The IP policy should include rules on IP ownership, the terms and conditions on which parties apportion the ownership shares, as well as definitions of the ownership shares, the conditions to grant access rights to different partners and third parties, the compensation for this access, and the exploitation rights and obligations of the knowledge accessed.[110] Contractual flexibility allows the potential partners to agree upon the rules. This agreement should be established at a very early stage, before the start of the project.[111] A clear, transparent, and unambiguous IP framework, concluded in the PPP's IP policy, provides insight in the objectives of the PPP and the IP framework designed to enable the accomplishment of those objectives. In this way, the different stakeholders are able to align their expectations and their institutions' objectives with the objectives defined in the PPP. The problem, however, is that persons participating in the PPP do not always have the expertise for the development of a solid IP and data management plan. Especially when innovative data results will be created, partners may be confronted with lack of experience in drafting appropriate rules that may govern their future activities.

Different views on stakeholders' objectives, especially the different objectives of the nonprofit and the for-profit partners, might result in lengthy and difficult negotiations, and difficulties in the partnership in general.[112] A lack of a long-term plan for the PPP could impede collaborations. Further, a certain degree of flexibility is deemed to be necessary as not all possible contingencies can be foreseen at the initial phase of the project.[113] The majority of the precompetitive PPPs provide flexibility to negotiate and contractually agree on the terms and conditions with respect to IP within the boundaries of the PPP's IP policy.[114]

106 *Id.*, at 158; Mark D. Lim, *Consortium Sandbox: Building and Sharing Resources*, 6 Sci. Translational Med. 242, 1, 5, 6 (2014).

107 Stevens et al., *Perspectives*, *supra* note *, at 136; Stevens et al., *Intellectual Property Policies*, *supra* note *, at 504, 509; Tania Bubela et al., *Recalibrating Intellectual Property Rights to Enhance Translational Research Collaborations*, 4 Sci. Translational Med 122, at 4 (2012).

108 IPR Helpdesk, *supra* note 90, at 2; Paradiso, *supra* note 92, at 1, 2.

109 Taubman, *supra* note 79, at 28.

110 Stevens et al., *Intellectual Property Policies*, *supra* note *, at 507.

111 European IPR Helpdesk, *supra* note 90, at 3.

112 Brooke et al., *supra* note 69, at S130.

113 Seungwoo Son, Legal Analysis on Public–Private Partnerships Regarding Model PPP Rules, presented at International Colloquium on Public–Private Partnerships (PPPs) in Vienna, 15 (June 2012), www.uncitral.org/pdf/english/colloquia/public-private-partnerships-2013/20120704_Report_on_PPP_legal_Issues Son_Seungwoover.11.pdf.

114 Stevens et al., *Intellectual Property Policies*, *supra* note *, at 507.

Although trust – important as it is – is usually created at the negotiation stage, too much time is lost during this initial phase of the projects.[115] Clear and transparent IP policies should be made publicly available in order to inform potential partners from the beginning. Precompetitive PPPs should be viewed as a scouting forum to investigate the possibility to collaborate with some of the partners in a more advanced setting. Hence, the IP should be framed accordingly.[116]

As alluded to above, a stage-gate approach could be considered, whereby the flexibility of the partners to negotiate the IP framework applied within the PPP project is discussed and renegotiated at predefined milestones. In this approach, the general rules and contract clauses are negotiated before the project starts, and potentially renegotiated at a later point in time. It offers the partners the opportunity to agree upon a general IP framework at the start. Then when certain opportunities arise or unexpected developments occur (and more trust has been created between the partners), partners may renegotiate the specific terms and conditions needed to optimize the opportunities or tackle the challenges that partners face during the project progress.[117] This stage-gate approach could also be applied for other PPPs such as PDPs, whereby new contracts are negotiated based on milestones reached in the product development phase. For each new phase, new rules and clauses are agreed between the PPP and its respective partners.

The importance of patents in precompetitive PPPs should be balanced with the importance of the creation of scientific databases and the exchange of information based on trade secrets, which is currently underemphasized in importance. Only a few precompetitive PPPs include some information with regard to non-patent IP in their IP policy,[118] while it is clear that the inclusion of such background IP and the development of such foreground IP is highly significant in early-phase research PPPs.[119] Because there is a clear lack of harmonized legislation, especially with regard to the protection of trade secrets, the IP policy issued by the precompetitive PPP could offer an additional basis to create trust. Literature suggests that the success of a PPP depends partly on the implementation and use of an IP framework,[120] which might be related to the trust creation when the partners agree upon clear rules.

V Knowledge-Sharing Strategies in Early-Phase Research PPPs

Early-phase research PPPs apply a variety of IP frameworks or knowledge-sharing strategies to structure IP ownership, access, and use. By linking elements such as the nature of the research (project focus), the objectives of the PPP (envisioned project deliverables), the PPP business model and its feasibility (funding), three types of IP strategies can

[115] Stevens, The Role of Intellectual Property, *supra* note *, at 157.
[116] Stevens et al., *Perspectives, supra* note *, at 138.
[117] *Id.*
[118] Stevens, The Role of Intellectual Property, *supra* note *, at 157–158.
[119] *Id.*, at 151–152.
[120] Richard T. Mahoney et al., *The Introduction of New Vaccines into Developing Countries: IV: Global Access Strategies*, 25 Vaccine 4003, 4007 (2007); Bart Leten et al., *IP Models to Orchestrate Innovation Ecosystems; IMEC, a Public Research Institute in Nano-Electronics*, 55 Cal. Mgmt. Rev. 51, 51, 52, 61 (2013).

be discerned, as mentioned in an earlier section. These are: (i) partnership-focused, (ii) open-collaboration, and (iii) hybrid strategies (See Table 6.1).[121]

The partnership-focused strategy is dominated by the for-profit sector and builds on the presence of IP, with subsequent license contracts creating restricted openness.[122] The open-collaboration strategy, on the other hand, can be compared with nonprofit user- and community-centered innovation, wherein the main goal is universal access. The most extreme form of the open-collaboration strategy is the dedication of foreground IP to the public domain.[123]

PPPs applying a partnership-focused strategy tend to provide IP policies that facilitate information and knowledge exchange. Owing to information negotiated before the project initiation – such as the establishment of clear definitions, templates and guidelines, as well as information on IP ownership, use, and licensing structure – trust is more easily created. The partners, who might be potential competitors in a later stage of drug development, know exactly what to expect and how to optimally share information according to their respective business strategies and with respect to downstream development. Nevertheless, the IP information is not frequently available to the public. This could be explained by PPPs preferring not to share such details with non-participants.[124]

The partnership-focused PPPs allow for the partners to build a unique IP portfolio at lower cost and in less time than if they were working in isolation.[125] Patenting marketable research results is common, and alternative protection is considered when results are not patentable. Such PPPs generally use a private ownership structure (i.e., background IP remains with the owner, and foreground IP belongs to the idea generator) and a private access structure (i.e., consortium members acquire preferred and conditional access to background and/or foreground IP – see Table 6.1).[126] In exceptional circumstances, the ownership of the foreground IP can be assigned partly to the PPP, whereby the PPP becomes one of the legal owners, together with one or more partners. Ownership or co-ownership of foreground IP allows the PPP to build the strong technological base instrumental for its sustainability.[127]

Partnership-focused PPPs apply IP policies that clearly set out certain constraints, creating a restricted openness. Only project partners are allowed access to background IP and then only to complete certain tasks and to develop foreground IP. The partnership-focused PPP is an investment-friendly model, as preferred access is a major incentive for industrial partners. Contracts – that is, project agreements – are the main legal tools to define the parameters of partners' activities. The PPPs applying this IP framework focus most of their research on drug-development tools, drugs, therapies, or diagnostic tests (or a mix of those deliverables) for NCDs (see Table 6.1). Funding for the majority of these PPPs is provided by both for-profit and nonprofit institutions.[128]

On the other end of the contingency spectrum are open-collaboration PPPs, wherein the main target is to share the foreground IP resulting from the project with a broad

[121] Stevens et al., *Intellectual Property Policies, supra* note *, at 504, 509.
[122] Van Overwalle, *supra* note 95, at 9.
[123] Stevens et al., *Intellectual Property Policies, supra* note *, at 508.
[124] *Id.*, at 504, 509.
[125] Leten et al., *supra* note 121, at 51–52.
[126] Stevens et al., *Intellectual Property Policies, supra* note *, at 504, 509.
[127] Leten et al., *supra* note 121, at 51, 61.
[128] Stevens et al., *Intellectual Property Policies, supra* note *, at 505–507.

research community or the general public (see Table 6.1).[129] Forms of collaboration such as open source, open access, and open transfer were developed as a response to the proprietary approach to DNA sequencing[130] and to mitigate the effect of patent thickets.[131] Several collaborative projects are aimed at resolving patent thickets for key biotechnology tools to ensure that they are available to scientists and for addressing problems in underserved communities.[132]

Sharing with a broader community entails a specific license signed by a user, whereas dedicating research results to the public domain ensures that anyone may gain access to or use the information. This type of IP framework includes different forms of open models, such as open source PPPs (for example, the Open Source Drug Discovery), open access PPPs (for example, the Structural Genomics Consortium), and PPPs applying the commons principles (for example, Sage Bionetworks). The open-collaboration IP framework applies a private ownership–public access logic. Although the PPPs provide users with open access to research results, the use is limited by predefined boundaries. In the majority of PPPs, sharing is organized by means of an open entry license model that specifies the community's level of access and freedom to operate. Users can easily obtain an open entry license. Often, research results can be improved, modified, and used for commercial or noncommercial purposes, but such results must be provided to the PPP or, if patent applications are filed, blocking of the PPP's activities is not allowed. "Open" does not necessarily mean that patents (or other forms of legally protected IP) are never involved. Patenting research results is accepted in specific cases.[133]

Commercial entities may be less likely to invest in open-collaboration PPPs, given the requirement to share foreground IP and the limits placed on patents for results arising from PPP information. Nevertheless, this IP framework is applied by PPPs focusing on NCDs, when the project deliverables are research tools, platform technologies, shared databases, and predictive models – all upstream results leading to precompetitive biotechnology tools aimed at speeding up drug development. Common to all these PPPs is that commercialization of drugs is not yet the primary objective. In the field of NCDs, the competition to develop research tools such as models, probes, or assays is high. And the cost implications of patenting can be a hurdle, as it is not always clear which tool might trigger the winning pathway to a solution for the disease.

Research in the field of PRNDs is characterized by unpredictability, uncertainty, and risk. The distribution of probability is unknown, and the time horizon for ROI is considerable. Owing to unpredictability in terms of business strategy, private ownership might not work. The result is a market failure to which PPPs can offer a potential solution. Innovative business models and government incentives will need to convince the pharmaceutical industry and will provide building blocks to develop a model to provide

[129] *Id.*, at 506.

[130] Geertrui Van Overwalle, *Of Thickets, Blocks, and Gaps. Designing Tools to Resolve Obstacles in the Gene Patents Landscape*, *in* Gene Patents and Collaborative Licensing Models, 383 (2009); *supra* note 24; *see generally* Geertrui Van Overwalle, *Exclusive Ownership Versus Open Commons: The Case of Gene Patents*, 4 The WIPO J. 139 (2013).

[131] Bubela et al., *supra* note 108, at 3; Robin Feldman & Kristopher A. Nelson, *Open Source, Open Access, and Open Transfer: Market Approaches to Research Bottlenecks*, 1–2, 7 (May 2, 2008), http://ssrn.com/abstract=1127571.

[132] Robin Feldman, *The Open Source Biotechnology Movement: Is It Patent Misuse?*, 6 Minn. J. L., Sci. & Tech. 117, 118, 132 (2004).

[133] Stevens et al., *Intellectual Property Policies*, *supra* note *, at 508.

more equitable access to medical care to patients in LMICs. IP frameworks applied in PPPs that encourage further investment thus seem not only appropriate but preferable. It remains to be awaited whether early-phase PPPs focusing on NCDs for commercially attractive markets might inspire and provide enough incentive for the pharma industry to invest in diseases affecting people in LMICs.[134]

Between the partnership-focused and open-collaboration strategies is a hybrid strategy, in which the IP framework applied is negotiated on a case-by-case basis. PPPs applying a hybrid strategy provide a limited IP policy with respect to ownership, use, and transfer of knowledge and materials (see Table 6.1). The PPPs explicitly state a preference that research results be placed in the public domain; however, when necessary to meet a project's objectives, patenting is possible, private ownership will be assigned, and a conditional licensing structure will be negotiated (see Table 6.1). Access to research results outside the consortium, however, is strongly preferred, and freedom to operate is restricted through licensing. This hybrid strategy is an interesting IP framework for development of downstream diagnostic tests and drugs for PRNDs, as it allows for negotiation of project agreements, including IP clauses, with industrial partners to create more commercially interesting incentives compared to an open-collaboration strategy. Hybrid PPPs typically are nonprofit funded.[135]

VI The Evaluation of IP in the Performance of Early-Phase PPPs: Suggested Approaches

Current empirical studies are lacking in which the effectiveness of these partnerships is assessed. Very little research has been performed to identify the key components of successful early-phase research PPPs.[136] However, in the IMI Case Study, the short-term outputs, the long-term outcomes, the added value, and the (so far unexplored) opportunities of the consortia under the umbrella of IMI have been investigated.[137] Some of the conclusions drawn from this case study are discussed here.

The knowledge gathered in the different IMI projects exceeds pure scientific results. An enormous number of templates, harmonized protocols, and standardization endeavors for information exchange has been developed within and between consortia. It took the consortium members considerable efforts and time to come to these harmonized and standardized templates and protocols. Therefore, any assessment of effectiveness should valorize these knowledge assets. One valuable way to leverage these assets could be through the creation of a forum to exchange best practices and disseminate existing knowledge on the legal and regulatory landscape, including topics such as governance, IP, and dissemination of results,[138] to prove the impact and added value of collaboration within PPPs for the society, in addition to scientific excellence.[139]

134 *Id.*, at 508.
135 *Id.*, at 508.
136 Bubela et al., *supra* note 108, at 4; Magdalini Papadaki and Gigi Hirsch, *Curing Consortium Fatigue*. 5 SCI. TRANSLATIONAL MED. 200sf35, 1 (2013).
137 STEVENS, THE ROLE OF INTELLECTUAL PROPERTY, *supra* note *, at 99–100.
138 *Id.*, at 119.
139 IMI, *Report of the Independent Expert Panel Accompanying the Commission Report: Assessment of European Innovative Medicines Initiative 2, A Joint Technology Initiative Under Horizon 2020*, at 6–7 (Dec. 23, 2012), https://ec.europa.eu/research/health/pdf/imi-ppp-expert-panel-report_en.pdf.

Performance of scientific research, and in particular the evaluation of IP in PPPs, is quantitatively demonstrated by key performance indicators (KPIs), often tangible deliverables such as number and impact of publications, number of citations, or number of patents.[140] However, a patent application is far from being the only value-critical step in drug R&D.[141] As such, an over-focus on patent filings as a KPI to evaluate the performance of the precompetitive PPP might distort the evaluation of the project progress and success of the precompetitive PPP. The precompetitive research phase is situated too early in the drug development cycle to rely on solely quantitative metrics such as number of patents filed to evaluate the performance of precompetitive PPPs.[142] In addition, not all PPPs cover patentable research results, which might give a misleading picture of the progress or successes of such often valuable projects. Defining a framework for KPIs is highly intertwined with capturing the different project objectives or strategic interests, as well as the different scientific and nonscientific deliverables and milestones defined by the parties at defined moments (delivery on objectives at different stages). KPIs should also capture the development of, and access to technologies, capability, and talent, as well as the provision of improved rules for decision making or to reduce costs (impact on R&D productivity).[143]

In research-oriented precompetitive PPPs, it should be carefully considered when and if scientific results need to be protected by patents. Expressing a precompetitive PPP's performance solely by means of quantitative KPIs neglects to measure other key missions of PPPs, such as networking or sharing and development of know-how. The balance between quantitatively and qualitatively measuring the tangible and the intangible assets should be considered carefully.[144] Important KPIs to measure the success of IMI are the (1) funding, (2) acquirement of highly performing employees, (3) stimulation of qualitative collaboration between the different parties, (4) development of important changes in R&D, (5) guarantee of quality of reports, and (6) generalization of efficient and continuous sharing of knowledge.[145]

Further, the KPIs measured should reflect both the current value of the PPP and the perceived future value of the PPP, especially in precompetitive PPPs since the time to deliver maximum value is often underestimated in such PPPs. The evaluation of performance also depends on the maturity of the PPP.[146]

[140] David A. Pardoe et al., *Assessing the Value of R&D Partnerships*, 12 Drug Discovery World 9, ¶ 3 (2010).

[141] J. P. Hughes et al., *Principles of Drug Discovery*, 162 British J. Pharmacology 1239, 1240, 1243 (2011).

[142] Stevens, The Role of Intellectual Property, *supra* note *, at 149; IMI, *Bibliometric Analysis of Ongoing Projects: Innovative Medicines Initiative Joint Undertaking (IMI) Third Report*, 9 (Oct. 2013), www.imi.europa.eu/sites/default/files/uploads/documents/reference-documents/IMI_BibliometricReport_3.pdf (last visited Nov. 23, 2017); IMI, *Bibliometric Analysis of Ongoing Projects: Innovative Medicines Initiative Joint Undertaking (IMI) Fourth Report*, 9–10 (Apr. 2014), www.imi.europa.eu/sites/default/files/uploads/documents/reference-documents/BibliometricReport4_Final.pdf (last visited Nov. 23, 2017).

[143] Pardoe et al., *supra* note 141, at ¶ 10.

[144] Stevens, The Role of Intellectual Property, *supra* note *, at 161.

[145] Michel Goldman, The Innovative Medicines Initiative: A European Response to the Innovation Challenge, 91 Clinical Pharmacology 418, 423 (2012).

[146] Stevens, The Role of Intellectual Property, *supra* note *, at 162; Tom Denee et al., *Measuring the Value of Public–Private Partnerships in the Pharmaceutical Sciences*, 11 Nature Revs. Drug Discovery 419 (2012).

It is important to value the PPPs' performance to justify the investments of public and private stakeholders in the partnership. By evaluating the PPP, success scenarios as well as pitfalls can be identified and be used to set up guidelines and best practices.[147] As stated earlier, there is a lack of adequate KPIs to measure the performance of (precompetitive) PPPs.[148] Some researchers have identified seven domains to monitor different types of organizations' progress: (a) funding, (b) talent, (c) dissemination, (d) collaboration, (e) output, (f) validation, and (g) external uptake.[149] Dependent on the type of organization, the influence of certain domains, as well as the KPIs that define the progress in these domains, will differ.

The added value of the PPP needs to be measured at different stages: at the start of the project (input), during the project (process), at the time of project termination (outputs), and in the long term (outcomes).[150] For example, the societal impact of PPPs in general, and of IMI in particular, can be measured by the generation of more and better quality research, in addition to the contribution they will make to healthcare via the production of new drugs. The dissemination and sharing of results are critical complements to the R&D itself, and might be the *raison d'être* of IMI. A lack of proper dissemination of research results will diminish the innovative value of carrying out research. On the other hand, dissemination of research results might lead to progressive collaboration and attract new investors. This, in turn, might lead to additional research, job creation, and spin-out companies, whereby the biopharmaceutical industrial level is improved and expanded. Maximizing the social return is one of the key justifications of public expenditure on IMI.[151]

The importance of the creation of knowledge sharing agreements between partners and/or project consortia requires a significant investment and should be valued accordingly. As for the domain of know-how, the sharing of knowledge can be evaluated, by means of measuring the background IP in the broadest sense. This includes knowledge shared by the different stakeholders at the start of the project (input), the amount of foreground IP developed during the project (process), and the IP exploited after the project has ended (short-term output). This also includes both license agreements involving the foreground IP and those involving long-term (outcome) products and/or therapies in development.[152]

The foreground IP developed in PPPs can be used as background IP in other PPPs. Sharing foreground IP with other PPPs might already occur in the process stage. The rules for sharing nonconfidential and confidential know-how within a PPP and also between PPPs can be captured in knowledge sharing models, such as a Memorandum of Understanding (MoU), and knowledge sharing tools, such as MTAs, DTAs, or CDAs to contractually define the exchange of material, data, or information. The practice thereof

[147] *Id.*, at 419.

[148] *Id.*, at 419; Bubela et al., *supra* note 108, at 4; Papadaki, *supra* note 137, at 1.

[149] Robert Pozen & Heather Kline, *Defining Success for Translational Research Organizations*, 3 Sci. Translational Med. 94cm20, 3–4 (2011).

[150] Denee et al., *supra* note 147, at 419.

[151] European Commission, *Commission Staff Working Document: Accompanying Document to the Proposal for the Council Decision on the Setting Up the Innovative Medicines Initiative Joint Undertaking*, SEC (2007) 568 (2007) 28, https://ec.europa.eu/research/jti/pdf/imi_com_sec(2007)0568_en.pdf.

[152] Stevens, The Role of Intellectual Property, *supra* note *, at 164–65.

should also be taken into account when evaluating PPPs, e.g., through a content analysis of MoUs, with accompanying CDAs, DTAs, or MTAs concluded between projects.[153] IMI fosters collaboration between consortia, and even requests that future projects start from results and knowledge gained from previous IMI PPPs.[154]

It is essential to gain additional expertise in the development of KPIs for PPP valuation,[155] as these indicators could support investors in decision making with respect to future investments to sustain the PPPs' progress, to improve its performance or, in case value is not being realized, to redirect investments to PPPs of higher value.[156] The valuation process needs to be done at regular and up-front well-defined moments in order to proactively steer the PPPs in delivering maximum value. For that reason, we argue that a flexible, stage-gate approach is important.[157]

The generation and dissemination of best practices and guidelines could also be taken into account when evaluating PPPs' performance. The dissemination should occur within the PPP's different consortia, and by extension, between different PPPs globally. Further, the time invested in the creation of such data sharing mechanisms should be acknowledged by the PPP, and by extension by the entire scientific research community by rewarding the publication of these best practices in peer-reviewed scientific literature, especially by academic research community. The reward mechanism for (academic) researchers should indeed not primarily consist of the number of scientific publications in high level journals, or the number of patent applications filed. An alternative KPI could be included, whereby the network built by the researcher is taken into account (e.g., quantitatively measured by the number of co-citations, and qualitatively measured by the degree of participation in national and international collaborations, and the number of follow-on partnerships established in the research field).[158]

Conclusion

Medical innovations have improved lives of millions of people, and science and technology create the potential for further advances in medicine and healthcare in the near future. At the same time, we witness the painful reality that many people around the world remain in need of effective life-saving treatments and preventive therapies. R&D efforts do not always seem to be directed to the health needs of all people. In September 2016, the United Nations High-Level Panel on Innovation and Access to Health Technologies (UN High Level Panel) issued a report depicting hard figures about urgent worldwide health needs.[159] To address this enormous gap, the 2030 Agenda for Sustainable Development, as adopted by a total of 193 member states of the United Nations (UN) in September 2015, includes Sustainable Development Goal (SDG) 3, which aims

[153] *Id.*, at 165.
[154] Stevens & Huys, *Case Study Analysis*, *supra* note *, at 26, 30, 37, 40–41.
[155] Lim, *supra* note 107, at 6.
[156] Pardoe et al., *supra* note 141, at ¶ 23.
[157] Stevens et al., *Perspectives*, *supra* note *, at 138.
[158] Stevens, The Role of Intellectual Property, *supra* note *, at 166.
[159] U.N. Secretary-General, *High-Level Panel on Access to Medicines*, 13–15 (Sep. 2016), https://static1.squarespace.com/static/562094dee4b0d00c1a3ef761/t/57d9c6ebf5e231b2f02cd3d4/1473890031320/UNSG+HLP+Report+FINAL+12+Sept+2016.pdf.

"to ensure healthy lives and promote the well-being of all people of all ages."[160] SDG 3 has as one of its targets to "provide access to affordable essential medicines and vaccines, in accordance with the Doha Declaration on the TRIPS Agreement and Public Health, which affirms the right of developing countries to use to the full the provisions in the TRIPS Agreement regarding flexibilities to protect public health."

Aside from IPRs as embedded in TRIPS and national frameworks, other incentives prove to be imperative for health care advances to become reality. This pluralistic approach is also recommended by the UN High Level Panel.[161] Different stakeholders in the domain of medical innovation face complex biomedical questions, risks of failure, and high costs of R&D. This is why PPPs aimed at sharing risks and costs are proposed as a model to make medical advancements and bring science closer to those in need. According to the UN SDG 17, a successful sustainable development agenda requires partnerships between governments, the private sector, and civil society,[162] echoing the UN Millennium Development Goal 8, namely, "to provide access to affordable essential drugs in developing countries in cooperation with pharmaceutical companies."[163]

Other than from PRNDs, new types of PPPs focusing on diseases of affluence have entered the scene in the last decades. Since those research domains are highly competitive, collaborations at the precompetitive level (precompetitive or early-phase research PPPs) have proven to be successful in the developed world, with the IMI as world's largest PPP operating in the precompetitive and even the POC phase in the health-care sector. Lessons drawn from the IMI experience, albeit in the realm of diseases of affluence, suggest possible mechanisms for IP management, sharing, and negotiations in the context of PPPs directed to PRNDs. The first is the stepwise approach for negotiations,[164] starting from the creation of an open platform as a basis for further drug development, with the necessary flexibilities for sharing ideas about IP ownership and expectations among partners, rather than viewing IP ownership as an aim in itself. Second are transparent, clear, flexible, and unambiguous IP policies covering short but also long-term expectations of partners.[165] Third is the creation of fora or educational workshops for sharing experiences and best practices about conducting PPPs, negotiating IPRs. This can form a first step in creating awareness about the importance of having clear IP arrangements up front of the PPP start. An honest-broker model might support such arrangements and may offer a basis for trust among partners. And finally trust is vitally important. Trust building among stakeholders of the various precompetitive PPPs that developed a virtual business model, especially the open-collaboration PPPs, is less exposed.[166]

[160] *Sustainable Development Goal* 3, U.N. SUSTAINABLE DEVELOPMENT, https://sustainabledevelopment.un.org/sdg3.

[161] U.N. Secretary-General, *supra* note 160, at 29–32.

[162] *Sustainable Development Goal 17*, U.N. Sustainable Development, www.un.org/sustainabledevelopment/globalpartnerships/.

[163] Goal 8: Develop a Global Partnership for Development, Target 8.E, U.N. MILLENNIUM DEVELOPMENT GOALS AND BEYOND 2015, www.un.org/millenniumgoals/global.shtml.

[164] Stevens et al., *Perspectives*, *supra* note *, at 138.

[165] Stevens et al., *Intellectual Property Policies*, *supra* note *, at 504, 509.

[166] Munos, *supra* note 3, at 6–7.

The many conceptual building blocks for successful partnerships depicted in this chapter need to be further explored and aligned. Only with the knowledge and expertise from civil society, industry, academia, and multilateral organizations such as the UN, can the major sustainable development challenges be addressed to the benefit for all patients, suffering from PRNDs as well as from NCDs, in both developed and developing countries.

References

Bengtsson, Maria and Soren Kock, *"Coopetition" in Business Networks – To Cooperate and Compete Simultaneously*, 29 Indus. Mktg. Mgmt. (2000).

Bereuter, Thomas L. et al., *IPR-Codes and Guidelines in Europe Facilitating Collaboration of Publicly Funded Research Organizations (PROs) with Businesses*, 46 les Nouvelles (2011).

Börzel, Tanja A. and Thomas Risse, *Public–Private Partnerships: Effective and Legitimate Tools of International Governance?*, *in* Complex Sovereignty: On the Reconstitution of Political Authority in the 21st Century (Edgar Grande & Louis W. Pauly eds., 2002).

Boyd, Michael R., *The Position of Intellectual Property Rights in Drug Discovery and Development From Natural Products*, 51 J. Ethnopharmacology (1996).

Brinkerhoff, Jennifer M., *Government-Nonprofit Partnership: A Defining Framework*, 22 Public Admin. Dev. (2002).

Brooke, Steve and Janet G. Vail., *Public- and Private-Sector Partnerships in Contraceptive Research and Development: Guiding Principles*, 67 Int'l J. of Gynecology and Obstetrics (1999).

Bubela, Tania et al., *Recalibrating Intellectual Property Rights to Enhance Translational Research Collaborations*, 4 Sci. Translational Med 122, at (2012).

Buse, Kent Buse and Gill Walt, *Global Public–Private Partnerships: Part I - A New Development in Health?*, 78 Bull. of the World Health Org. (2000).

Centre for Drug Design & Discovery, *What is CD3?*, www.cd3.eu/about-cd3/about-cd3what-is-cd3 (last visited Nov. 18, 2017).

Ciccone, Danna Karen, *Arguing for a Centralized Coordination Solution to the Public–private Partnership Explosion in Global Health*, 17 Glob. Health Promotion (2010).

Chesbrough, Henry, Open Business Models: How to Thrive in the New Innovation Landscape (2006).

Cressey, Daniel, *Comment, Animal Research: Battle Scars*, 470 Nature (2011).

Denee, Tom et al., *Measuring the Value of Public–Private Partnerships in the Pharmaceutical Sciences*, 11 Nature Revs. Drug Discovery (2012).

Editorial, *Expanding Precompetitive Space*, 10 Nature Rev. Drug Discovery (2011).

Editorial, *With Strings – Researchers Should Shrug Off Their Fears and Welcome the Concept of Venture Philantrophy*, 475 Nature (2011).

Elkins, Sean, Maggie A. Z. Hupcey, and Antony J. Williams (eds.), Collaborative Computational Technologies for Biomedical Research (John Wiley & Sons, Inc. 2011).

European Commission, *Commission Staff Working Document: Accompanying Document to the Proposal for the Council Decision on the Setting Up the Innovative Medicines Initiative Joint Undertaking*, SEC(2007) 568 (2007) 28, https://ec.europa.eu/research/jti/pdf/imi_com_sec(2007)0568_en.pdf (last visited Nov. 18, 2017).

European Commission, *Commission Staff Working Document: Joint Technology Initiatives: Background, State-of-Play and Main Features*, SEC(2007) 692 (2007) 3, 12, https://ec.europa.eu/research/jti/pdf/background_jtis_en.pdf (last visited Nov. 18, 2017).

European Commission, *Final Report from the Expert Group on Intellectual Property Valuation*, 5, 13 (Nov. 29, 2013), https://ec.europa.eu/research/innovation-union/pdf/Expert_Group_Report_on_Intellectual_Property_Valuation_IP_web_2.pdf (last visited Nov. 18, 2017).

European Commission, Trade Secrets, https://ec.europa.eu/growth/industry/intellectual-property/trade-secrets_en (last visited Nov. 18, 2017).

European IPR Helpdesk, Case Study: Allocation of Shares of Jointly Developed Results, 3 (Feb. 2014), www.iprhelpdesk.eu/sites/default/files/newsdocuments/CS_Allocation_of_shares_of_jointly_developed_results.pdf (last visited Nov. 18, 2017).

European Parliament, Regulation 536/2014 of the European Parliament and of the Council of Apr. 16, 2014, on Clinical Trials on Medical Products for Human Use and Repealing Directive 2001/20/EC, 2014 O.J. (L 158).

Feldman, Robin, *The Open Source Biotechnology Movement: Is It Patent Misuse?*, 6 Minn. J. L., Sci. & Tech. (2004).

Feldman, Robin and Kristopher A. Nelson, *Open Source, Open Access, and Open Transfer: Market Approaches to Research Bottlenecks*, 1–2, 7 (May 2, 2008), http://ssrn.com/abstract=1127571.

Food and Drug Admin., Guidance for Clinical Trial Sponsors: Establishment and Operation of Clinial Trial Data Monitoring Committees, (2006), www.fda.gov/OHRMS/DOCKETS/98fr/01d-0489-gdl0003.pdf (last visited Nov. 18, 2017).

Gilbert, Natasha, *Universities Shun Europe's Drug Initiative*, 466 Nature (2010).

Giordano-Coltart, Jennifer and Charles W. Calkins, *Best Practices in Patent License Negotiations*, 25 Nature Biotechnology (2007).

Goldman, Michel, *Comment, Reflections on the Innovative Medicines Initiative*, 10 Nature Rev. Drug Discovery (2011).

Goldman, Michel, *The Innovative Medicines Initiative: A European Response to the Innovation Challenge*, 91 Clinical Pharmacology (2012).

Goldman, Michel, et al., *The Innovative Medicines Initiative: An Engine for Regulatory Science*, 14 Nature Rev. Drug Discovery (2014).

Gorbatyuk, Arina et al., *Intellectual Property Ownership in Coupled Open Innovation Processes*, 47 Int'l Rev. of Intell. Prop. and Competition L. (2016).

Hughes, J. P., S. Rees, S. B. Kalindjian and K. L. Philpott, *Principles of Drug Discovery*, 162 British J. Pharmacology (2011).

Innovative Medicines Initiative, *Bibliometric Analysis of Ongoing Projects: Innovative Medicines Initiative Joint Undertaking (IMI) Third Report*, 9 (Oct. 2013), www.imi.europa.eu/sites/default/files/uploads/documents/reference-documents/IMI_BibliometricReport_3.pdf (last visited Nov. 23, 2017).

Innovative Medicines Initiative, *Bibliometric Analysis of Ongoing Projects: Innovative Medicines Initiative Joint Undertaking (IMI) Fourth Report*, 9–10 (Apr. 2014), www.imi.europa.eu/sites/default/files/uploads/documents/reference-documents/BibliometricReport4_Final.pdf (last visited Nov. 23, 2017).

Innovative Medicines Initiative, *Clarification Note to the IMI IP Policy* (on file with authors).

Innovative Medicines Initiative, IMI 2 Joint Undertaking, Model Grant Agreement, art. 23(a)–31 (Jan. 12, 2015), www.imi.europa.eu/sites/default/files/uploads/documents/apply-for-funding/call-documents/imi2/h2020-mga-imi_en.pdf (last visited Nov. 23, 2017).

Innovative Medicines Initiative, *IMI Explanatory Note* (Jul. 2008), www.imi.europa.eu/sites/default/files/uploads/documents/apply-for-funding/intellectual-property/ipr-helpdesk-doc-on-imi-ipr-policy_en.pdf (last visited Nov. 23, 2017).

Innovative Medicines Initiative, Governing Board Meeting, Chaired by Dr. Rudolf Strohmeier, Deputy-Director General of Directorate General for Research and Innovation (DG RTD) at the European Council, (Oct. 29, 2013) (notes on file with authors).

INNOVATIVE MEDICINES INITIATIVE, *IMI Guidance Note for IMI Applicants and Participants* (Nov. 2010), www.imi.europa.eu/sites/default/files/uploads/documents/apply-for-funding/intel lectual-property/GuidanceNote_Draft3-1_10Nov2010.pdf (last visited Nov. 23, 2017).

INNOVATIVE MEDICINES INITIATIVE, *The Innovative Medicines Initiative (IMI) Strategic Research Agenda: Revision 2011*, 3, 10, 25 (June, 16, 2011), www.imi.europa.eu/sites/default/ files/uploads/documents/reference-documents/SRArevised2011.pdf (last visited Nov. 23, 2017).

INNOVATIVE MEDICINES INITIATIVE, *IMI Intellectual Property Policy*, (Jul. 1, 2007), https://ec .europa.eu/research/participants/portal/doc/call/fp7/imi-ju-03–2010/30831-imi-ipr-policy01august 2007_en.pdf (last visited Nov. 18, 2017).

INNOVATIVE MEDICINES INITIATIVE, *Report of the Independent Expert Panel Accompanying the Commission Report: Assessment of European Innovative Medicines Initiative 2, A Joint Technology Initiative Under Horizon 2020*, at 6–7 (Dec. 23, 2012), https://ec.europa.eu/ research/health/pdf/imi-ppp-expert-panel-report_en.pdf (last visited Nov. 18, 2017).

INNOVATIVE MEDICINES INITIATIVE, *The Innovative Medicines Initiative (IMI) Research Agenda: Creating Biomedical R&D Leadership for Europe to Benefit the Patients and Society*, 3, 7 (Feb. 15, 2008), http://rp7.ffg.at/upload/medialibrary/IMI-GB-research-agenda-006v2–15022008.pdf (last visited Nov. 18, 2017).

INTELLECTUAL PROPERTY WATCH, *Partnership To Share Research, Keep IP Rights, On Neglected Diseases*, ¶ 2, IP-WATCH.ORG (Jan. 6, 2011), www.ip-watch.org/2011/06/01/partnership-to-share-research-keep-ip-rights-on-neglected-diseases/ (last visited Nov. 18, 2017).

Kaplan, Warren, Veronika Wirtz, Aukje Mantel, Pieter Stolk, Béatrice Duthy, and Richard Laing, WORLD HEALTH ORGANIZATION, *Priority Medicines for Europe and the World 2013 Update*, 186–87 (May 6, 2013), http://www.who.int/medicines/areas/priority_medicines/MasterDoc June28_FINAL_Web.pdf (last visited Nov. 18, 2017).

Kelly, Micheál J., Jean-Louis Schaan and Helene Joncas, *Managing Alliance Relationships: Key Challenges in the Early Stages of Collaboration*, 32 R&D MGMT. (2002).

Kesselheim, Aaron and N. Shiu, *The Evolving Role of Biomarker Patents in Personalized Medicine*, 95 CLINICAL PHARMACOLOGY THERAPEUTICS (2014).

Jim Kling, *Biotechs Follow Big Pharma Lead Back into Academia*, 29 NATURE BIOTECHNOLOGY (2011).

Larson, Maja and Margaret Chon, *The Greatest Generational Impact: The Open Neuroscience Movement as an Emerging Knowledge Commons, in* GOVERNING MEDICAL KNOWLEDGE COMMONS (Katherine J. Strandburg, Brett M. Frischmann, & Michael J. Madison eds., 2017).

Leten, Bart, et al., *IP Models to Orchestrate Innovation Ecosystems; IMEC, a Public Research Institute in Nano-Electronics*, 55 *Cal. Mgmt. Rev.* (2013).

Lim, Mark D., *Consortium Sandbox: Building and Sharing Resources*, 6 SCI. TRANSLATIONAL MED. (2014).

Macilwain, Colin, *Sharing Information Is Preferable to Patenting*, 498 NATURE (2013).

Mahoney, Richard T., et al., *The Introduction of New Vaccines into Developing Countries: IV: Global Access Strategies*, 25 VACCINE (2007).

MECTIZAN DONATION PROGRAM, www.mectizan.org/ (last visited Sep. 22, 2017).

Melese, Teri, Salima M. Lin, Julia L. Chang and Neal H. Cohen, *Open Innovation Networks Between Academia and Industry: An Imperative for Breakthrough Therapies*, 15 NATURE MED. (2009).

Merz, Jon F., WHO, *Intellectual Property and Product Development Public/Private Partnerships*, 7 (May 16, 2005), www.who.int/intellectualproperty/studies/Merz%20WHO%20report.pdf?ua=1 (last visited Nov. 18, 2017).

Mullard, Asher, *Could Pharma Open its Drug Freezers*, 10 NATURE REV. DRUG DISCOVERY (2011).

Munos, Bernard H., *Can Open-Source R&D Reinvigorate Drug Research?*, 5 NATURE REV. DRUG DISCOVERY (2006).

Napa, Jagadeesh, Editorial, *Open Source Drug Discovery*, PHARMA FOCUS ASIA, https://www.pharmafocusasia.com/strategy/open-source-drug-discovery (last visited Nov. 18, 2017).

Passi, Jaakko, Katri Valkokari, Tuija Rantala, Soili Nystén-Haarala, Nari Lee and Laura Huhtilainen. BAZAAR OF OPPORTUNITIES FOR NEW BUSINESS DEVELOPMENT – BRIDGING NETWORKED INNOVATION, INTELLECTUAL PROPERTY AND BUSINESS (2013).

Papadaki, Magdalini and Hirsch, Gigi, *Curing Consortium Fatigue*. 5 SCI. TRANSLATIONAL MED. (2013).

Paradiso, Robert J. and Elizabeth Pietrowski, *Dilemmas of Joint Patent Ownership: Provide a Clear Understanding of the Parties' Expectations*, 197 N. J. L. J. (2009).

Pardoe, David A. et al., *Assessing the Value of R&D Partnerships*, 12 DRUG DISCOVERY WORLD 9, ¶ 3 (2010).

Pozen, Robert and Heather Kline, *Defining Success for Translational Research Organizations*, 3 SCI. TRANSLATIONAL MED. (2011).

Rai, Arti K., Reichman, Jerome H. Reichmann, Paul F. Uhlir, and Colin R. Crossman, *Pathways Across the Valley of Death: Novel Intellectual Property Strategies for Accelerated Drug Discovery in* GENE PATENTS AND COLLABORATIVE LICENSING MODELS. PATENT POOLS, CLEARINGHOUSES, OPEN SOURCE MODELS AND LIABILITY REGIMES (Geertrui Van Overwalle Ed., 2009).

Ridley, Robert G., *Putting the Partnership into Public–private Partnerships*, 79 BULL. OF THE WORLD HEALTH ORG. (2001).

Simpson, Peter B. and Melvin, Reichman, *Comment, Opening the Lead Generation Toolbox*, 13 NATURE REVS. DRUG DISCOVERY (2014).

Son, Seungwoo, Legal Analysis on Public–Private Partnerships Regarding Model PPP Rules, presented at International Colloquium on Public–Private Partnerships (PPPs) in Vienna, 15 (June 2012), www.uncitral.org/pdf/english/colloquia/public-private-partnerships-2013/20120704_Report_on_PPP_legal_IssuesSon_Seungwoover.11.pdf (last visited Nov. 18, 2017).

Southwood, David, *Comment, Research Collaboration: When International Partnerships Go Wrong*, 488 NATURE (2012).

Stevens, Hilde et al., *Intellectual Property Policies in Early-Phase Research in Public–Private Partnerships*, 34 NATURE BIOTECHNOLOGY (2016).

Stevens, Hilde et al., *Perspectives and Opportunities for Precompetitive Public–Private Partnerships in the Biomedical Sector*, 32 BIOTECHNOLOGY L. REP. (2013).

Stevens, Hilde, THE ROLE OF INTELLECTUAL PROPERTY IN (PRECOMPETITIVE) PUBLIC–PRIVATE PARTNERSHIPS IN THE BIOMEDICAL SECTOR (2015).

Stevens, Hilde, Isabelle Huys, Koenraad Debackere, Michel Goldman, Philip Stevens, and Richard T. Mahoney, *Vaccines: Accelerating Innovation and Access*, WIPO Global Challenges Report (2017).

Stevens, Hilde and Isabelle Huys, *Case study analysis on behalf of IMI JU Executive Office under a service contract procedure: SUMMIT – IMIDIA – Open PHACTS NEWMEDS – eTOX – U-BIOPRED Innovative Medicines Initiative Joint Undertaking (IMI), summary in* IMI, *Annual Activity Report 2013*, 25–27 (Feb. 14, 2014), www.europarl.europa.eu/document/activities/cont/201408/20140818ATT87695/20140818ATT87695EN.pdf.

Stevens, Hilde, Geertrui Van Overwall, Bart Van Looy, and Isabelle Huys, *Innovative Medicines Initiative (IMI) Case Study Analysis Reveals the True Added Value of Early-Phase Public–Private Partnerships (PPPs)*, 34 BIOTECHNOLOGY L. REP. (2015).

Stolk, Pieter, *Background Paper 8.1 Public Private Partnerships*, 5, 12, 13 (May 1, 2013), www.who.int/medicines/areas/priority_medicines/BP8_1PPPs.pdf (last visited Nov. 18, 2017).

Strohmeier, Rudolf, et al., *IMI Moves Forward*, 29 NATURE BIOTECHNOLOGY (2011).

Taubman, Antony, Council on Health Research for Development, *Public–Private Management of Intellectual Property for Public Health Outcomes in the Developing World: The Lessons of Access Conditions in Research and Development Agreements*, 17 (2004), http://announcementsfiles.cohred.org/gfhr_pub/assoc/s14831e/s14831e.pdf (last visited Nov. 18, 2017).

Treaty on European Union, art. 129, Feb. 7, 1992, 1992 O.J. (C 191), 31 I. L. M. 253.

U.N. MILLENNIUM DEVELOPMENT GOALS AND BEYOND, Goal 8: Develop a Global Partnership for Development, Target 8.E, 2015, www.un.org/millenniumgoals/global.shtml (last visited Nov. 18, 2017).

U.N. Secretary-General, *High-Level Panel on Access to Medicines*, 13–15, (Sep. 2016), https://static1.squarespace.com/static/562094dee4b0d00c1a3ef761/t/57d9c6ebf5e231b2f02cd3d4/1473890031320/UNSG+HLP+Report+FINAL+12+Sept+2016.pdf (last visited Nov. 18, 2017).

U.N. SUSTAINABLE DEVELOPMENT, *Sustainable Development Goal 3*, https://sustainabledevelopment.un.org/sdg3 (last visited Nov. 18, 2017).

U.N. SUSTAINABLE DEVELOPMENT, *Sustainable Development Goal 17*, www.un.org/sustainabledevelopment/globalpartnerships/ (last visited Nov. 18, 2017).

Van Overwalle, Geertrui, *Exclusive Ownership Versus Open Commons: The Case of Gene Patents*, 4 THE WIPO J. (2013).

VAN OVERWALLE, GEERTRUI, *Inventing Inclusive Patents. From Old to New Open Innovation*, *in* KRITIKA-ESSAYS ON INTELLECTUAL PROPERTY, VOL. 1 (Peter Drahos et al. eds., Edward Elgar 2015).

Van Overwalle, Geertrui, *Of Thickets, Blocks, and Gaps. Designing Tools to Resolve Obstacles in the Gene Patents Landscape*, *in* GENE PATENTS AND COLLABORATIVE LICENSING MODELS: PATENT POOLS, CLEARINGHOUSES, OPEN SOURCE MODELS AND LIABILITY REGIMES (Geertrui Van Overwalle ed. 2009).

Van Looy, Bart, Paolo Landoni, Julie Callaert, Brunovan Pottelsberghe, Eleftherios Sapsalis, and Koenraad Debackere, *Entrepreneurial Effectiveness of European Universities: An Empirical Assessment of Antecedents and Trade-Offs*, 40 RES. POL'Y (2011).

Vargas, Gabriel, B. Boutouyrie, S. Ostrowitzki, and L. Santarelli, *Arguments Against Precompetitive Collaboration*, 87 CLINICAL PHARMACOLOGY & THERAPEAUTICS (2010).

Wagner, Janet A., M. Prince, E.C. Wright, M. M. Ennis, J. Kochan, D. J. R., Nunez, B. Schneider, M.-D. Wang, Y. Chen, S. Ghosh, B. J. Musser, and M. T. Vassileva, *The Biomarkers Consortium: Practice and Pitfalls of Open-Source Precompetitive Collaboration*, 87 CLINICAL PHARMACOLOGY & THERAPEUTICS (2010).

Widdus, Roy, *Public–Private Partnership*, 99 TRANSACTIONS OF THE ROYAL SOC'Y TROPICAL MED. & HYGIENE (Supp.1 2005).

Widdus, Roy, *Public–Private Partnerships for Health: Their Main Targets, Their Diversity, and Their Future Directions*, 79 BULL. OF THE WORLD HEALTH ORG. (2001).

Williams, R. Sanders and Susan Desmond-Hellman, *Making Translation Work*, 332 SCIENCE (2011)

Woodcock, Janet, *Precompetitive Research: A New Prescription for Drug Development?*, 87 CLINICAL PHARMACOLOGY & THERAPEUTICS (2010).

WORLD HEALTH ORGANIZATION, *Health in 2015: from MDGs, Millennium Development Goals to SDGs, Sustainable Development Goals*, 28 (2015), www.who.int/gho/publications/mdgs-sdgs/en/ (last visited Nov. 23, 2017).

Part II

Education, ICT, and Libraries

7 A Publisher Perspective on a Public–Private Partnership for Access to Biomedical Information

Jens Bammel

"The knowledge gap between rich and poor must be overcome if we are to reduce poverty."[1]

Introduction

Must copyright's inherent scarcity lead to a knowledge gap for the poor?

A market-based economy requires scarcity. Copyright protection is designed to create scarcity of the works it protects. It is therefore the basis of many creative industries. Yet in the digital environment, there is almost no obstacle to instant global availability and distribution. This makes copyright the logical target for many civil society organisations fighting to increase access to knowledge for users more broadly, including in particular economically disadvantaged populations. It is also why some advocates see the weakening of copyright as a primary route towards improved access to information for all.

From this perspective, increased access can be achieved by limiting the extent of copyright protection, strengthening the public domain, expanding copyright exceptions, and, overall, taking the "economy" out of the knowledge economy. What could be the knowledge economy then becomes a service industry, which does not allow the work that is embodied in creative manifestations to become an economic asset. This dynamic is playing out in many developing countries where film and music producers cannot use their copyright as assets to secure credit or economic returns.

Under such circumstances, creativity can then only be leveraged where it results in a physical monopoly or dominant market position, protected by high investment barriers, critical mass requirements, or superior technical infrastructure. All of these factors favour technology-savvy start-ups whose business model often implicitly ignores the interests of those who rely on copyright to leverage their own creative, technological, or financial investment. Ultimately this is, in macro-economic terms, a form of either free riding or rent seeking. Rent seeking appears to be the appropriate term because as one scholar put it: "it usually takes the form of restrictions on competition or on the use of property rights, [and] the desire to gain rents through political power distorts the operation of the market process."[2]

[1] Gro Harlem Brundland, *Forty New Countries Given Low Cost Access To Health Journals*, World Health Organisation (WHO), (Jan. 27, 2003) www.who.int/mediacentre/news/releases/2003/pr3/en/.

[2] Sanford Ikeda, *Rent-Seeking: A Primer*, Ideas on Liberty 26 (Nov. 2003), https://fee.org/media/4553/ikeda1103.pdf.

But is it inevitable that copyright's inherent scarcity must lead to a knowledge gap for the poor? Or do alternative policy choices exist?

Public–private partnerships (PPPs) managing intellectual property (IP) could be such an alternative. By making use of private assets, in this case copyright protected works, through licences that are negotiated with rightsholders, access can be expanded without substantially limiting the commercial value of the copyright assets.

This chapter looks at such IP-based PPPs from a rightsholder perspective, specifically from a publisher perspective, in partnerships where the private contribution lies primarily in copyright licensing. It seeks to help readers understand what motivates copyright holders to join and engage in such partnerships, as well as what obstacles exist to increasing access through such partnerships, and how to overcome them. The chapter will also demonstrate that it is possible to vastly improve access through licensing, which is better than many approaches and policy initiatives that are ideologically and theoretically more "open" but do not in practice lead to better access and use of information.

The chapter's examination of the potential of PPPs centers around a case study of the Health InterNetwork Access to Research Information (HINARI), which is the World Health Organisation's (WHO) PPP for providing access to scientific information. The HINARI PPP demonstrates how access to scientific information can at times be achieved within the constraints of copyright, by taking advantage of the role that publishers play in knowledge distribution and harnessing their added value and expertise. Collaborative partnerships based on licensing are not a complete panacea to the challenge of unequal access to information, but the success of this partnership (and its sister partnerships in the "Research for Life" family[3]) demonstrates that there is value in exploring partnerships that make use of the publishing industry's skills rather than to fight them. HINARI is one demonstration that creating a win-win partnership for the production of public goods in the areas of health, agriculture, and the environment can achieve remarkable success.

Part I of this chapter provides the background to the current policy debate by summarizing some long-standing issues around scholarly communication and copyright. The next section is an in-depth look at the origins of HINARI. Following this, Part III examines some of HINARI's structural characteristics, including qualifying countries and institutions, organisational and technical setup, and legal agreements. Parts IV and V delve into the success factors, in particular those that were required to enable publishers to engage fully, as well as solutions to key obstacles, including the challenge of the transition from aid to trade, that is, for countries leaving the qualifying brackets. Finally, the chapter concludes with an assessment of HINARI's impact, both past and future.

I Background: Scholarly Communication and Copyright

Nowhere has the issue of copyright and open access been discussed more passionately and in a more polarised way than in the area of scholarly communication. The fundamental ethical principle of the universality of science includes the notion that science and research are performed for the advancement of knowledge and for the benefit of

[3] *See* RESEARCH4LIFE, www.research4life.org/.

all mankind.[4] As the publication of research findings is an integral part of research, this principle must include the publication of research findings itself, the dissemination of this publication, and access to it.

This ethos conflicts with traditional business models that underpin the dissemination of scholarly research articles, that is, journal subscriptions by libraries and research-intensive businesses. Unsurprisingly, the academic open access movement arose as soon as the Internet materialised and appeared to promise global availability at seemingly near-zero costs. Early initiatives to disintermediate journal publishers either brought sobering outcomes or demonstrated the true cost of quality publishing.[5] Since then, open access initiatives have become more diverse. This is also true on the publishing side: As a business model, open access has appeared in various "gold" or "green" permutations,[6] as an alternative to the traditional subscription model. And the business models of publishers are gradually evolving: Subscriptions to individual journals have expanded to become subscriptions to comprehensive journal collections and databases, and all major publishers now include open access journals or allow articles individually to be reused by their authors, in broader albeit concisely delineated ways.

In the almost three decades since scientists invented the World Wide Web in order to improve information sharing, we are still not close to universal access to the published scientific record free at the point of access. Compared to the dramatic disruptions in the music or audio-visual industries, the actual pace of change in the business model of scholarly publishing remains rather slow. There are commercial reasons for this, including the reluctance of university as well as learned and professional society publishers to relinquish subscription or royalty income, and the recognition of the true costs of online publishing.

The slow speed of change is also a reflection of the caution that is built into a five-hundred-year-old communication tradition. Real and perceived risks are associated with the change of a business model that has now turned to authors, and their funders, for sustaining it. For example, if poor researchers have free access, but now cannot afford the publishing fees for open access, then one obstacle to the participation in scholarly communication (access to publications) would have been replaced by a new obstacle (the need to finance publication). This change has also worsened the problem of predatory open access journals, which publish works under important sounding, but internationally unrecognised, journal names. These can be created with little regard for the author's interests, yet they are all too eager to get their hands on the author's publication fee.

Nowhere is the challenge of providing open access more apparent than in the area of biomedical information. And therefore nowhere was there a stronger case for a PPP.

4 *See The Annual Report for the Year 2016 Sums up our Key Achievements in the Year*, International Council for Science (ICFS), www.icsu.org/publications/annual-report-2016/universality-of-science.

5 *See, e.g.*, PEER Publishing and the Ecology of European Research, www.peerproject.eu/.

6 For definitions, *see* House of Commons Innovation and Skills Committee, *Open Access: Fifth Report of Session 2013–14*, at 3, House of Commons Doc. HC 99-I (2013), www.publications.parliament.uk/pa/cm201314/cmselect/cmbis/99/99.pdf.

II The History of HINARI

While the issue of access to medicines has been at the forefront of the international debate on global health and IP, access to the latest biomedical research and information has played a similarly important role in the research community.

A WHO survey from 2002 found that biomedical researchers and academics in developing countries saw access to journals as one of their most pressing problems: "In the lowest-income countries, 56 per cent of the institutions had no current subscriptions to international journals and 21 per cent had an average of only two journal subscriptions. In the tier with the next-lowest incomes, 34 per cent of institutions had no current subscriptions, and 34 per cent had two to five journal subscriptions."[7] Could PPPs help solve this problem?

PPPs are a relatively recent addition to the tool sets used in the UN system. Throughout the second half of the twentieth century, UN agencies typically saw private sector companies as suppliers, not partners.[8] The perspective began to change in the late 1990s when a number of US philanthropists such as Ted Turner and Bill and Melinda Gates, and so on, began making large financial contributions available to UN agencies. Since then PPPs have become an established tool for development.[9]

In the area of scholarly communication, credit must be given to former UN Secretary General Kofi Annan who appeared to believe that the only way to bridge the digital divide in health information was through PPPs. In preparing the Millennium Development Goals (MDGs) the Secretary General proposed, in what appears to be a personal initiative, a health information network based upon PPPs. He was perhaps influenced in his thinking by some early "dotcom" start-ups that were created around that time.[10] For these young companies, PPPs with the UN were a simple way to rapidly and massively increase "eyeballs", the colloquial term used for the number of users. This was the prevailing metric that led to often astonishing company valuations before the first "dotcom" bubble burst. It can only be speculated, but the choice at the very top of the UN to take the initiative, and to present the WHO more or less with a fait accompli, is more likely to have been a deliberate choice than a procedural error or diplomatic oversight.

The MDGs provided the perfect opportunity. On 6 September 2000 UN Secretary General Kofi Annan presented his report: "We the Peoples: The Role of the United Nations in the 21st Century"[11] to the United Nations Millennium Summit. In it he announced the WHO's flagship project, the "Health InterNetwork", to the public.

[7] Barbara Aronson, *Improving Online Access to Medical Information for Low-Income Countries*, 350(10) N. Eng. J. Med. 966–968 (2004).

[8] U.N. Foundation, Understanding Public-Private Partnerships, at 2 (2003), www.globalproblems-globalsolutions-files.org/unf_website/PDF/understand_public_private_partner.pdf.

[9] *See e.g.*, Public-Private Partnerships Sustainable Territories 2030 Platform, http://platform.un-ppp.org/content/background-documents.

[10] For these young companies, PPPs with the UN were a simple way to rapidly and massively increase "eyeballs", the colloquial term used for the number of users, which were the metric that led to often astonishing company valuations before the first "dotcom" bubble burst.

[11] U.N. Secretary-General Kofi Annan, We the Peoples: The Role of the United Nations in the 21st Century, U.N. (2000), www.un.org/en/events/pastevents/pdfs/We_The_Peoples.pdf.

> This network will establish and operate 10,000 on-line sites in hospitals, clinics and public health facilities throughout the developing world. It aims to provide access to relevant up-to-date health and medical information, tailored for specific countries or groups of countries.[12]

The WHO immediately began a number of pilot schemes, including one led by Barbara Aronson, former Collection Development Librarian at WHO, who was appointed HINARI Programme Manager. Dr. Tikki Pang, the Director of the WHO Research Policy & Cooperation Department, reached out to the publishing industry, initially seeking to pilot an inclusion of a selected number of developing country research institutions in an expanded WHO library subscription. The publishing industry reacted swiftly and positively, and it soon became clear to all concerned that there was a willingness on all sides to make an even bolder move.

On 9 July 2001, led by the British Medical Journal, six leading international biomedical publishers[13] made a public commitment to provide access to researchers in the developing world. Intended to benefit research, academic, and other organisations in developing countries working for the public good, they stated that "the partners in the Initiative acknowledge that access to primary biomedical journals is a critical issue in developing countries ... and are willing to work with committed governments, international organisations and others to find ways to open up access to this information."[14]

While other HealthInterNetwork pilots soon faded, the partnership with publishers did not even go through a pilot phase. The momentum on all sides allowed for it to be readily formalised and was soon named "HINARI" (acronym for Health InterNetwork Access to Research Information). It was launched in 2002 by the then-Director General of the WHO, Gro Harlem Brundland, with the words: "It is perhaps the biggest step ever taken towards reducing the health information gap between rich and poor countries."[15]

Her words have proven prescient. As of 1 June 2016, HINARI provides access to some 14,000 journals and 47,000 other digital information resources from more than 180 publishers that have volunteered and signed up to the programme. The number of users is equally impressive: more than 5,800 eligible institutions in 105 eligible countries have registered for access to HINARI.

The success of HINARI for biomedical information has spawned three other PPPs on scholarly communication with different topical focal points, including both public and private partners, but following the same technical and IP policy approach and with great success. These include AGORA, which provides access to agricultural research through the Food and Agriculture Organisation (FAO) since 2003; OARE, which provides environmental research through the United Nations Environment Programme (UNEP) since 2006; and ARDI, which provides information on IP, and specifically patents, through the World Intellectual Property Organization (WIPO) since 2011.

[12] *Id.* at 35.

[13] Blackwell, Elsevier Science, Harcourt Worldwide STM Group, Springer Verlag, John Wiley, and Wolters Kluwer International Health & Science.

[14] *Publishers' Statement of Intent*, HINARI RESEARCH FOR HEALTH, www.who.int/hinari/statementofintent/en/.

[15] WHO, *Top Publishers to Help Scientists in Developing Nations Access Information*, U.N. NEWS CENTRE, (July 9, 2001), www.un.org/apps/news/story.asp?NewsID=811&Cr=&Cr1=#.V01QtJN97eQ.

In total, as of June 2016, more than 69,000 peer-reviewed international scientific journals, books, and databases from more than 185 participating (and many more co-opted) publishers are being accessed by more than 8,000 institutions and organisations in more than 105 countries[16]. They now share an organisational framework, called "Research4Life,"[17] which has a light shared governance structure to facilitate information sharing and coordination. This chapter focuses, by means of example, on HINARI, because it is the longest standing partnership, has the greatest wealth of experience, and has the largest reach – both on the publisher side and on the user side.

III HINARI's Structural Attributes

A *Qualifying Countries and Institutions*

Institutions in 120 countries and territories qualify for privileged access to HINARI. In 73 "Group A" countries and territories, no licence fee is charged to qualifying institutions. In 47 "Group B" countries institutions must pay US$1,500 per year for access. This fee was increased from US$1,000 in 2015. It is paid to WHO and ring-fenced for use within HINARI. WHO makes no administrative deductions. No money flows back to publishers.

The eligibility criteria for countries is determined by a set of World Bank provided criteria, in particular the Human Development Index and Gross National Income. There are some notably absent countries among the 120 poorest countries, including the most populous ones including China, India and Pakistan, Indonesia, Philippines, and South Africa, and their absence can be equally explained with publisher commercial reasons rather than metrics, as we shall see later on. The exclusion of India and China is based on a rule that all countries with a Gross National Income exceeding US$1 trillion are excluded.

In eligible countries, a range of different types of institutions can obtain access to HINARI. Qualifying institutions include national libraries and documentation centres, any government office, universities, colleges, vocational colleges, and research institutions, and any national not-for-profit NGO, hospitals, teaching hospitals, and health centres. The range of qualified users is intended to be broad, all the while excluding multinational entities and for-profit companies and organisations. The humanitarian effort is not intended to subsidize businesses.

B *Organisational and Technical Setup*

Despite providing more than 5,700 institutions access to publications numbering in excess of 60,000 (comprising books and journals from more than 180 actively participating publishers), the sharing of responsibilities and the technical infrastructure are remarkably simple. The WHO is responsible for registering qualified organisations. A top tier academic library, the Yale University Library, manages the online catalogue of available resources. Software companies, including Microsoft and ProQuest, have donated and maintain the necessary customer relationship management and discovery software. Once an institution has been formally recognised by WHO's dedicated HINARI Staff as

[16] *HINARI Eligibility*, HINARI RESEARCH FOR HEALTH, www.who.int/hinari/eligibility/en/.
[17] RESEARCH4LIFE, *supra* note 3.

eligible, requests from qualified institutions go via WHO servers to the participating publishers. Publishers treat these requests as they would any other requests from an authorised user and deliver the requested content to the user. While the technical side of the delivery process has somewhat changed over time, the essence remains: publishers hold on to their content and can monitor its use; WHO and the libraries manage all downstream aspects through a simple, transparent, and relatively easily managed infrastructure.

The expense is shared among the participants. Once the initial setup has been organised, publishers can absorb some of the operational costs in their on-going operations. The largest single expense is the collective governance and oversight of the partnership. The WHO must set aside personnel, IT infrastructure, and bandwidth. Overall, all four projects under the "Research 4 Life" Umbrella cost US$2.8m per year to maintain. More than half of these costs, approximately US$1,050,000 is borne by WHO. The publishers and their associations spend in excess of US$850,000 per year.

For an organisation and structure with such reach and impact, the legal basis is surprisingly sparse. HINARI has no legal persona; it is a partnership administered by WHO. Furthermore, no formal licensing agreement exists between individual publishers and WHO. Instead, publishers are asked to sign the initial letter of intent.[18] Downstream, eligible customers are required to sign a licence agreement, in which WHO acts on behalf of the publishers that have signed the letter of intent. The wording of this licence is the same for Group A and Group B countries, with the exception of the fee provision. The wording has not materially changed since 2002.[19] Legally, this is a copyright licence by the eligible organization with each and all the publishers that participate in HINARI.

The original statement of intent of 9 September 2001 is probably not sufficiently specific to qualify as a licence without extensive interpretation. The letter itself speaks of the "broad terms and principles on which this initiative is based," without ever specifying them, and expressly retains the right of publishers "to provide specific agreements."[20] The terms of the authorisation of WHO to act on behalf of existing and newly joining publishers are not clearly spelled out.

The licence that participating organisations sign and return to WHO, who appears to be acting on behalf of the publishers annexed to the agreement, is a very simple library licence. Employees and affiliates of the licensed institution may access all content, download within certain limits, and include works in course packs.

There are certain restrictions to the licence. For example, walk-in users have full access, but may not be from for-profit corporations. Remote access, particularly from foreign countries, is not allowed. Document delivery may not be provided to third parties. The logic behind these restrictions is twofold. To the extent that persons from for-profit organisations are excluded, this is because commercial licences are available to them and therefore they are not covered by the humanitarian goal of this agreement. Persons coming from other eligible institutions should obtain their access through their own institutions, which can provide access to them. The exclusion of remote access,

[18] *See* HINARI, *supra* note 14.

[19] *Institution User Licence For Hinari Group* A, HINARI, www.who.int/entity/hinari/about/HINARI_licence_Group_A_2016.doc?ua=1.

[20] *See* HINARI, *supra* note 14.

specifically when travelling abroad, has been included to prevent unauthorized use by persons who do not live and work in qualifying countries.

These clauses make sense in the logic of this project. And there has been little controversy, if any, around the licence terms and restrictions. While some clauses would most likely be controversial in licensing negotiations in developed countries, they appear to be common sense in this particular context. If copyright exceptions were to override such licensing terms, as has been suggested *de lege ferenda*, this would destabilize the licensing approach. Charitable donation of content could then eat away at existing commercial markets. It is therefore important to maintain the ability to use licences to regulate not-for-profit partnerships such as HINARI.

Rather than being a weakness of this arrangement, the lack of a detailed licensing arrangement between publishers and WHO is arguably one of its strengths. Indeed, this lack of a detailed licensing basis was one of the reasons for the initial speed of delivery of HINARI. In the past, a number of collective creative industry partnerships in other creative industry sectors failed to get off the ground, because the negotiations around the details of the underlying licences proved divisive. One reason for this is that legal counsel tend to reduce risk for each possible case, positing a panoply of imaginable harmful events (some realistic, others fanciful). Risk is mitigated through strong legal positions, guarantees, or indemnities. Not surprisingly, this risk-averse approach will often complicate discussions of a partnership arrangement.

In order to start quickly with HINARI, its stakeholders chose a different path. Maurice Long was seconded by the BMJ Group (the British Medical Journal's publisher) to HINARI to develop its publisher relationships. He understood that detailed licensing terms are not necessary, as long as publishers have a sense of ownership and feel that they can leave the arrangement should any unmanageable problems arise. This arrangement also gave HINARI space to develop flexibly, as the project had to follow the spirit of the shared objective, rather than the letter of a licence.

Probably the most important reason for success of this partnership is a shared interest by all stakeholders, including publishers, to expand access to published works. The genuine mission and interest of scholarly publishers to reach the ideal of non-discriminatory, universal access to science is often overlooked. This is self-evidently true for the many scholarly publishing houses that are owned by universities, are scientific unions, and who share the mission of their universities, societies and researchers. Here the institutional pressure for open access, however, needs to be balanced by the importance of publishing income to the survival of the societies themselves or the surplus income that goes back to the universities. The same is also obviously true for the commercial publishers who publish such journals on behalf of scientific unions. On closer inspection, it is also true for the purely commercial publishers, who carefully nurture their relationship with the best scholarly authors and will make every effort to be their publisher of first choice, by serving their stated or implicit needs, including broad availability.

This publisher desire to increase access for scientific progress is evidenced in unequivocal declarations of intent, such as the Scientific, Technical and Medical (STM) Publishers Association's Brussels Declaration.[21] It is also demonstrated by changes in

[21] *Brussels Declaration*, STM, www.stm-assoc.org/public-affairs/resources/brussels-declaration/.

copyright assignment policies, partnerships with the library community on digital archiving, and ground-breaking work on universal metadata for articles, data, and authors. These all have shown that all publishers wish to increase access to research articles they publish, albeit always with an eye on its sustainability.

IV Addressing Publisher Concerns

The 2002 statement by the initial publishers allows us to infer some conditions that were important for the willingness of publishers to join this project. In essence, the following areas of concern to publishers needed to be addressed:

1. Clear limitations in time and scope
2. No interference with commercial markets
3. Limited resource implications
4. Voluntary participation and easy withdrawal
5. Limited risk of massive unauthorised use
6. A clear exit path for countries whose initial qualification expires

Each of these is discussed briefly in this section.

A *Limitations in Time and Scope*

The original 2002 letter of intent spoke of an engagement for three years. This original term has regularly been extended and participants are now committed until 2020. The review of this time frame is a serious exercise and there remains a consensus on all sides that this programme is intended to last only as long as there is a humanitarian case for this kind of access. Still, HINARI deliberately avoids the word "project" to describe itself, but instead uses the word "programme", which highlights its ongoing nature. HINARI is also limited to a very specific research area. The focus on biomedical information (with the later Research4Life initiatives focusing on food, nutrition and environment, and patent information) shows that this is a targeted humanitarian project. It is not intended to cover all areas of scholarly communication. The restriction was important to signal to all stakeholders that this is a humanitarian effort, rather than a model for scholarly communication overall. Its implications and significance for scholarly communications in developed countries are therefore limited.

B *No Interference with Commercial Markets*

Secondly, the initiative is limited to "most" lower and middle income countries as determined by a number of set criteria, mainly based on World Bank data. This shows that publishers are willing to be accommodating and generous, provided that existing commercial arrangements are not at stake. The initiative is intended to reach countries that the commercial services and subscriptions offered by publishers are unable to reach, and only these countries. In other words, this PPP operates to address a certain type of market failure. This explains why a methodology was found to keep large publishing industry customers, such as China, India, the Philippines, and Indonesia off this list. The humanitarian purpose of HINARI also does not require to cover these countries as these countries are targeted by the commercial offerings of publishers. Still, it is not easy for publishers to exclude markets. Publishers who in 2011 attempted to pull 2,500 journals from HINARI for Bangladesh quickly encountered a public outcry[22] and angry articles in the Lancet[23] and the British Medical Journal[24].

C *Limited Resource Implications*

Third, publisher participation would have been difficult for publishers if it had involved many resources, whether financial, technological, or managerial. Opportunity costs begin to weigh in very heavily rather quickly. For the participating publishers, HINARI is operationally simply an additional, albeit rather large, customer. The relationship with registered institutions is managed through WHO. Responsibilities for governance, transparency, and oversight are largely provided through staff from the STM publishers association. Major publishers add this responsibility to staffers whose responsibility it is to expand access to their journals in a way that does not interfere with their commercial interests. Such efforts are well received by the authors, whose interest and concerns remain the prime focus of their publishers.

D *Voluntary Participation and Easy Withdrawal*

Publishers join by signing the letter of intent. The letter states that publishers "... will offer access in the broad terms of the principles on which this Initiative is based, and will be free to provide specific arrangements according to its own business model."[25] Even though the vast majority of publishers will have been selective regarding the content they include in this arrangement, by only including journal titles related to its biomedical focus, no publishers have created specific licensing terms to date. Withdrawal is technically possible at an instant: publishers can simply de-list HINARI as a customer and stop responding to their article requests. This ability to control access at any time has paradoxically led to a situation where no publishers that have joined have so far withdrawn from the project.[26]

E *Limited Risk of Massive Unauthorised Use*

Fifth, where there is little impact on the commercial market and little cost of participation, the issue of risk of potential leakage still remains. The concern was whether this project would facilitate unauthorised use. The ease of withdrawal by publishing partners has allowed this risk to be put to the test. As it turns out, the download patterns from HINARI and the number of unauthorized uses or suspicious download patterns are not markedly different from those of other subscribers. When unusual spikes in download or download patterns occur, the subscriber is cut off, and WHO is notified. They will then

[22] *GLOBAL: HINARI and the Dream of Free Journal Access*, UNIVERSITY WORLD NEWS, (Feb. 20,2011) www.universityworldnews.com/article.php?story=20110218224836123.

[23] Bad Decisions for Global Health, THE LANCET, Jan. 20, 2011, www.thelancet.com/journals/lancet/article/PIIS0140-6736%2811%2960066-4/fulltext.

[24] Zosia Kmietowicz, *Publishers Withdraw 2500 Journals From Free Access Scheme in Bangladesh*, THE BMJ, January 11, 2011, www.bmj.com/content/342/bmj.d196.

[25] *See* HINARI, *supra* note 14.

[26] This information is accurate as of 1 September 2016.

contact the relevant organization and jointly explore what has been happening. As with other customers, many suspicious behaviours turn out to be misunderstandings, technical errors, or reasonable in the light of specific research – and these cases are resolved. No particular risk has emerged, and publishers are satisfied with the now established mechanisms, developed over time, to resolve any issues.

F *A Clear Path for Countries to Grow Out of the Ambit of this Programme*

Finally, and perhaps controversially, HINARI has hard qualification criteria for countries, and consequently their institutions. A number of countries have therefore exited the programme, some repeatedly as their economies went through dramatic cycles. Over the past ten years, the following countries progressed in their national development to rise above the thresholds: Azerbaijan, Belarus, Bulgaria, Costa Rica, Cuba, Dominican Republic, Panama, Peru, and Serbia. Furthermore Egypt, Indonesia, Iran, Lebanon, Pakistan, Philippines, South Africa, and Thailand have never been part of the HINARI core eligible countries, but because of their development metrics they became part of the transitional path when it was created (even though they were not transitioning out of previous eligibility). From 2017, eligibility criteria will be changing. Egypt and Pakistan will then become eligible for core HINARI access for the first time while Serbia will return to eligibility.

At first glance, the process of moving countries out of HINARI may appear harsh: how can institutions move from access to a large selection of content for a flat sum to the free market of scholarly communications? In practice, HINARI was given time to develop a way to help their clients manage such change. Exiting countries are offered a "path of transition,"[27] which is softened by a number of factors: some content remains available to them for free. Furthermore there are other access provision programmes that such institutions now qualify for, many of which offer steep discounts, such as INASP,[28] EIFL,[29] or some of the other initiatives listed by Liblicence.[30]

Not all is bad for institutions stepping out of HINARI. Rather than having to contend with the fixed menu offered by HINARI, they can now identify and focus on the journals that match their organisations' research requirements more closely. This is particularly beneficial for universities that are active in areas that are not within Research4Life's scope. Scholarly resources from a broader range of disciplines can benefit from such programmes.

Overall, this transition path reinforces a fundamental understanding by the publishers involved in HINARI. HINARI remains a finite programme: nobody is locked in perpetually, and it shall itself come to an end should its objectives be met. HINARI reviews its own usefulness periodically and its self-critical attitude, as exemplified by the 2016 Strategic Plan[31] shows that this review is more than a pro forma exercise.

27 Transitional Path Offer, Hinari Research for Health, www.who.int/hinari/eligibility/transitional_path_offer/en/.

28 INASP Strategy 2016–2020, INASP, www.inasp.info/.

29 EIFL, www.eifl.net/.

30 LIBLICENSE, http://liblicense.crl.edu/licensing-information/developing-nations-initiatives/.

31 *Our Vision for 2020 and Beyond: Research4Life's Strategic Plan*, research4life, www.research4life.org/wp-content/uploads/2016/09/R4L_strategy_report_web_v2.pdf.

V Obstacles in Implementation

HINARI did not become a success overnight. Once the service was made available, a number of other obstacles to access needed to be overcome. The first of these was making the service known to potential user organisations. While the most astute and internationally connected universities were quick to join, they represented only a small percentage of the potential beneficiaries. HINARI benefited from the existing international network of WHO, but further efforts were needed to reach the librarians who could assume responsibility on the user end.

Additionally, the lack of bandwidth in developing countries was an obvious concern. This issue, and the related issue of lack of appropriate hardware, has since improved. Nonetheless the physical tools required for access to the Internet can still be a concern. The problem has moved from being an insurmountable to a gradual one, and one that will continue to improve over time.

But even where HINARI was successfully made available, actual use could be slow. It required significant resources to be invested, not just in promoting awareness for the service, but also in training users. Once a service is made available, researchers needed to be trained on how to log in and use the interface. The technical aspects were the smaller part of that education. Training also includes a modern researcher's tools to conduct discovery and ensure a complete understanding of the relevant scientific record. In fact, the training portal on Research for life's web site[32] now covers the full range of training topics from information literacy, to scholarly authorship, to reference management tools building, to training on how to promote the use of these databases to students and researchers.

External training has proven useful to empower users to make use of the existing research findings. From the outset, researchers in developing countries were more ambitious. They identified as one of the key problems as the absence of their own voices in the international published discourse. This is why the publishers' letter of intent also included a clause about "encouraging research publishing programmes in developing nations."[33]

The step from becoming research consumers to research contributors is logical but substantial. It requires a change of mindset and a confidence in one's own capacities and abilities. It has therefore taken some time before the number of contributors from organisations that are participants in HINARI has been noticeable. Today, anecdotal evidence from individual publishers indicates that the group of researchers from HINARI beneficiaries is the fastest growing author category. All stakeholders take particular pride in this development because it shows that this programme has created a virtuous circle. Science as a whole benefits from such a programme that allows more great minds to contribute to scientific advancement through their publications.

Conclusion: HINARI's Outlook

HINARI has achieved remarkable success, but it is still expanding its reach to more qualified institutions and organisations. Publishers are continuing to join the effort, but

[32] *Training Portal*, RESEARCH4LIFE, www.research4life.org/training/.

[33] HINARI, *supra* note 14.

subject coverage has reached near saturation and most publishers joining today are part of the very "long tail". On the beneficiary side, numbers continue to grow and a plateau does not yet appear to have been reached.

This success was not without setbacks. The outcry over the brief withdrawal of certain journals from Bangladesh, as well as the need to develop training and to actively reach out to institutions in developing countries, exemplify the challenges this project has faced. They are also a result of the almost improvised way this project was allowed to develop and to try out different options or solutions.

While publisher commitment to HINARI was originally limited for three years to 2004, this has been reexamined periodically and consistently extended. The current formal consensus of all stakeholders is to continue HINARI at least until 2020. Given the past history, this PPP is likely to continue beyond that time, for as long as universal open access at the point of consumption has not been achieved, or for as long as there are countries at low levels of economic development.

Publishers have come to trust HINARI. Trust among the partners in this PPP has developed because publishers were involved, their concerns were taken seriously, and the practical issues raised (such as occasional unauthorised use) were handled transparently and in accordance with agreed upon procedures. Constant dialogue has given HINARI the space to find its way, occasionally through trial and error. This trust has had manifest positive effects: Some publishers have already made all their scholarly journal content, and not just biomedical information, available through HINARI. The role of WHO as a trusted intermediary is worth particular praise. Both publishers and developing country institutions understood and continue to rely on WHO to provide not only the technical infrastructure, but also the institutional and social framework in which the necessary trust and good faith could be developed.

References

Aronson, Barbara, *Improving Online Access to Medical Information for Low-Income Countries*, 350(10) N. Eng. J. Med. (2004).

Brundland, Gro Harlem, *Forty New Countries Given Low Cost Access To Health Journals*, World Health Organisation (WHO), (Jan. 17, 2003), www.who.int/mediacentre/news/releases/2003/pr3/en/ (last visited Nov. 18, 2017).

EIFL, www.eifl.net/ (last visited Nov. 18, 2017).

European Union, PEER Publishing and the Ecology of European Research, www.peerproject.eu/ (last visited Nov. 18, 2017).

Hinari Research for Health, *HINARI Eligibility*, www.who.int/hinari/eligibility/en/ (last visited Nov. 18, 2017).

Hinari Research for Health, *Institution User Licence For Hinari Group A*, www.who.int/entity/hinari/about/HINARI_licence_Group_A_2016.doc?ua=1 (last visited Nov. 18, 2017).

Hinari Research for Health, *Publishers' Statement of Intent*, www.who.int/hinari/statementofintent/en/ (last visited Nov. 18, 2017).

Hinari Research for Health, *Transitional Path Offer*, www.who.int/hinari/eligibility/transitional_path_offer/en/ (last visited Nov. 18, 2017).

INASP Strategy 2016–2020, INASP, www.inasp.info/ (last visited Nov. 18, 2017).

International Council for Science, *The Annual Report for the Year 2016 Sums up our Key Achievements in the Year*, www.icsu.org/publications/annual-report-2016/universality-of-science (last visited Nov. 18, 2017).

Ikeda, Sanford, *Rent-Seeking: A Primer*, IDEAS ON LIBERTY 26 (Nov. 2003), https://fee.org/media/4553/ikeda1103.pdf (last visited Nov. 18, 2017).

Kmietowicz, Zosia, *Publishers Withdraw 2500 Journals From Free Access Scheme in Bangladesh*, THE BMJ, January 11, 2011, www.bmj.com/content/342/bmj.d196 (last visited Nov. 18, 2017).

THE LANCET, Bad Decisions for Global Health, Jan. 20, 2011 www.thelancet.com/journals/lancet/article/PIIS0140-6736%2811%2960066-4/fulltext (last visited Nov. 18, 2017).

LIBLICENSE, http://liblicense.crl.edu/licensing-information/developing-nations-initiatives/ (last visited Nov. 18, 2017).

PUBLIC-PRIVATE PARTNERSHIPS SUSTAINABLE TERRITORIES 2030 PLATFORM, http://platform.un-ppp.org/content/background-documents (last visited Nov. 18, 2017).

RESEARCH4LIFE, www.research4life.org (last visited Nov. 18, 2017).

RESEARCH4LIFE, *Our Vision for 2020 and Beyond: Research4Life's Strategic Plan*, www.research4life.org/wp-content/uploads/2016/09/R4L_strategy_report_web_v2.pdf (last visited Nov. 18, 2017).

RESEARCH4LIFE. *Training Portal*, www.research4life.org/training/ (last visited Nov. 18, 2017).

Sharma, Yojama, *GLOBAL: HINARI and the Dream of Free Journal Access*, UNIVERSITY WORLD NEWS, February 20, 2011, www.universityworldnews.com/article.php?story=20110218224836123 (last visited Nov. 18, 2017).

STM, *Brussels Declaration*, www.stm-assoc.org/public-affairs/resources/brussels-declaration/ (last visited Nov. 18, 2017).

[U.K.] House of Commons Innovation and Skills Committee, *Open Access: Fifth Report of Session 2013–14*, at 3, House of Commons Doc. HC 99-I (2013), www.publications.parliament.uk/pa/cm201314/cmselect/cmbis/99/99.pdf (last visited Nov. 18, 2017).

U.N. Foundation, UNDERSTANDING PUBLIC-PRIVATE PARTNERSHIPS (2003), www.globalproblems-globalsolutions-files.org/unf_website/PDF/understand_public_private_partner.pdf (last visited Nov. 18, 2017).

U.N. NEWS CENTRE, *World Health Organization, Top Publishers to Help Scientists in Developing Nations Access Information* (July 9, 2011), www.un.org/apps/news/story.asp?NewsID=811&Cr=&Cr1=#.V01QtJN97eQ (last visited Nov. 18, 2017).

U.N. Secretary-General Kofi Annan, WE THE PEOPLES: THE ROLE OF THE UNITED NATIONS IN THE 21ST CENTURY, U.N. (2000), www.un.org/en/events/pastevents/pdfs/We_The_Peoples.pdf (last visited Nov. 18, 2017).

8 A Sustainable Development Agenda for the World Intellectual Property Organization: Networked Governance and Public–Private Partnerships

Sara Bannerman*

Introduction

The adoption of the United Nation (UN)'s sustainable development goals (SDGs) in 2015, intended to carry forward the UN's development agenda past the 2015 target set for the completion of the Millennium Development Goals (MDGs), signals a way forward not only for the UN more broadly, but also for the World Intellectual Property Organization (WIPO), a UN agency. The SDGs offer a revised vision of development for the UN, and they also suggest that partnerships, including public–private partnerships (PPPs), will play a key role in meeting the SDG targets.[1]

This chapter considers WIPO's use of PPPs through the lens of networked governance, and links it to current and ongoing deliberations and initiatives on intellectual property (IP) and development efforts at the organization. The concept of networked governance, sometimes also referred to as "nodal governance," recognizes that governance (the regulation of behavior) is often undertaken not solely by the state and multilateral organizations, but by a plurality of networked actors (states, corporations, and technologies) through a plurality of mechanisms (legal, market, and social).[2] PPPs are an important form of networked governance.

A development agenda for WIPO was first proposed in 2004 by the governments of Argentina and Brazil, which saw WIPO as falling short in its contributions to international development and to the overall goals of the UN system. The WIPO Development Agenda was formally established in 2007 following negotiations sparked by the 2004 proposal. It connected only loosely to the UN's MDGs, stating simply, "WIPO's norm-setting activities should be supportive of the development goals agreed within the United Nations system, including those contained in the Millennium Declaration."[3]

This chapter claims that the future of WIPO's Development Agenda should entail a new sustainable development agenda, connecting more fully and broadly to the new SDGs. This would involve two shifts. First, a more comprehensive adoption of the SDGs

* The author would like to thank her Research Assistant Sheena Jary. This work was supported by the Canada Research Chairs Program and McMaster University.

1 *Sustainable Development Knowledge Platform*, U.N. Dep't of Econ. and Soc. Affairs, https://sustainabledevelopment.un.org/ (last visited Nov. 19, 2017).

2 Scott Burris, Peter Drahos, and Clifford Shearing, *Nodal Governance*, 30 Austl. J. Leg. Phil. 30–58 (2005).

3 *Development Agenda for WIPO*, WIPO, www.wipo.int/ip-development/en/agenda/ (last visited Nov. 19, 2017).

by WIPO would entail WIPO's adoption of the broader understanding of "development" signaled by the SDGs. To date, the implementation of the WIPO Development Agenda has focused, to a large extent, on economic and institutional visions of development: that is, encouraging economic growth and building national and regional IP institutions. However, the SDGs call for a broader understanding of the various roles – both positive and negative – that IP can play in the full range of SDGs, such as those relating to poverty, hunger, health, education, and gender equality. The SDGs are a call to action for *all* UN member states to meet sustainable development goals. They call for *all* WIPO member states, not only developing countries, to ensure that WIPO is aligned and supportive of SDG implementation.

Second, a sustainable development agenda for WIPO would involve both public and private actors, therefore requiring a greater focus on the democratic qualities of networked governance arrangements. The framework of networked governance recognizes that networked forms of governance, including partnerships such as PPPs, can support, or can circumvent, democratic processes. This framework thus provides several tools for the evaluation of PPPs by asking: Who has access to nodes of governance, defined as a site of governance where "knowledge, capacity and resources are mobilized to manage a course of events? . . . And [h]ow is governing power distributed as between 'public' and 'private' governing nodes? How are powerful nodes made accountable, if at all – ie, how if at all do the less powerful have the means to regulate the more powerful?"[4]

The first part of this chapter reviews the history of networked governance and PPPs at WIPO and asks more broadly whether, and how, public–private partnerships at WIPO can best be structured to work for sustainable development. Part II of this chapter then evaluates the WIPO Development Agenda project entitled *Specialized Databases' Access and Support* (Phase I and II) as a case study of PPPs, as they currently operate in WIPO. Under this project, WIPO and private partners provide access to scholarly literature and patent data. This part of the chapter examines the extent to which the "Access to Research for Development and Innovation" (ARDI) program – a part of the *Specialized Databases* project contributes first to policy participation by the users most affected by the program, and second to equity and access. In the third part, the chapter examines the concept of development embedded in the ARDI program.

The chapter concludes that WIPO partnerships, to date, are not recognized as the forms of governance they are. Nor do they conform to participatory nor egalitarian ideals of networked governance. It argues that, if WIPO is to adopt a sustainable development agenda in which partnerships play a major role, consistent with the intent of the SDGs, it must adopt higher standards for public–private partnership governance.

I WIPO and Public–private Partnerships

International IP norms have developed, historically, through networks of governance. They have been developed not by states alone, but by transnational networks of state, civil society, and private actors.[5] NGOs, such as *the Association littéraire et artistique*

[4] Scott Burris et al., *supra* note 2, at 37, 54.
[5] Margaret Chon, *PPPs in Global IP (Public-Private Partnerships in Global Intellectual Property)* in Methods and Perspectives in Intellectual Property 262–64, 261–98 (Graeme B. Dinwoodie ed., 2013).

internationale (ALAI), and private industry actors, such as the Intellectual Property Committee, have played prominent roles in the construction of IP norms.[6]

The balance between state, civil society, and private actors engaged in the networked governance of IP has changed dramatically over time.[7] Throughout the twentieth century, as international regulation and international civil society expanded, a growing number of mainly private-interest-groups became influential in international IP governance.[8] For many international organizations, the term "NGO" applies to nonprofit organizations that seek to advance the public interest. However, at WIPO, the term "NGO" applies to any organization that is independent from government, including private sector organizations. There is no requirement that the NGO be nonprofit or that it be associated with public interest. WIPO differs from other international institutions such as the World Bank, which defines NGOs as "private organizations that pursue activities to relieve suffering, promote the interests of the poor, protect the environment, provide basic social services, or undertake community development."[9] This expansive definition of NGO contributed to coalitions of private corporations wielding tremendous influence and control over international IP norm-setting by the 1990s, dwarfing the voices of civil society representatives at WIPO.[10]

Public–private partnerships are defined as "institutionalized transboundary interactions between public and private actors, which aim at the provision of public goods," where private actors may include for-profit entities, or nonprofit or civil society organizations.[11] By the turn of the millennium, the popularity of PPPs in the UN system gave private corporations additional prominence in international governance and development. At present, PPPs have made only limited inroads at WIPO, but these inroads promise to grow, altering once again the balance of networked IP governance.

The original 2004 proposal for a development agenda for WIPO placed little emphasis on partnerships.[12] However, partnerships became increasingly important in the design and implementation of the WIPO Development Agenda as established in 2007; it incorporated several PPPs. Of the thirty-three Development Agenda implementation

6 *See generally* Susan Sell, Public Power, Private Law: The Globalization of Intellectual Property Rights (2003).

7 *See generally* Sara Bannerman, Intellectual Copyright And Access To Knowledge (2016).

8 *Id.*, at 166–67.

9 Center for International Environmental Law, A *Citizen's Guide to WIPO* 5 (2007) (citing to World Bank, *Nongovernmental Organizations in World Bank-Supported Projects*, ix, (1999)). This means that at WIPO, unlike at other international institutions, business groups and private sector organizations are considered to be NGOs.

10 Susan Sell, *supra* note 6, at 97–100.

11 Marco Schäferhoff, Sabine Campe, and Christopher Kaan, *Transnational Public-Private Partnerships in International Relations: Making Sense of Concepts, Research Frameworks and Results*, 11 International Studies Review 451, 455 (2007).

12 The original proposal made no mention of partnerships. *See Proposal by Argentina and Brazil for the Establishment of a Development Agenda for WIPO*, WO/GA/31/11 (2004). An elaborated proposal made mention of research partnerships with developing country researchers and an information-sharing program that would provide information to developing countries about past successful partnerships between agencies and domestic firms. *See Elaboration on Proposal to Establish Development Agenda for WIPO*, IIM/1/4, 27–28, (2005).

projects, a few are based on a PPP model,[13] and several more seek to identify and/or showcase PPPs in IP.[14]

Indeed, WIPO's Director General, Francis Gurry, has recently publicly recognized the potential role of PPPs in WIPO's work beyond the WIPO Development Agenda stating that:

> Public-private partnerships can deliver on the objectives set by member states. They provide access both to intellectual resources and to financial capital that do not exist in the public sector.[15]

Gurry also has recognized the importance of careful management of WIPO's PPPs:

> Public private partnership initiatives at WIPO are carefully managed in line with the Organizations [*sic*] principles of good governance. They feature in our Program and Budget proposals, which are reviewed and adopted by member states, and like any other program activity, they are subject to rigorous oversight, audit and reporting requirements.

They must also have a practical mechanism, a committee or a board made up of stakeholder representatives, to guide the operations of the partnership.[16]

A 2011 evaluation of WIPO's technical assistance activities recommended that "WIPO should pursue more cost-sharing partnerships, collaborations, and in-kind arrangements," and that WIPO should "draft an organization-wide policy and strategy on outreach, engagement and partnerships with IGOs and non-government stakeholders, including NGOs, industry, academia and IP practitioners, for approval by Member States."[17] To date, a WIPO policy and strategy on PPPs has not been adopted.

A *Partnerships: What For?*

In a world of networked governance, concepts of representative democracy may not always apply. However, theories of cosmopolitan democracy require consultation with those most affected by a decision; similarly, theories of participatory democracy require broad participation in collective decision-making. And theories of liberal institutionalist democracy (where governance is undertaken by international institutions) measure

[13] WIPO, Specialized Databases' Access and Support; Specialized Databases' Access and Support – Phase II; Project on Capacity Building in the Use of Appropriate Technology-Specific Technical and Scientific Information as a Solution for Identified Development Challenges.

[14] These include: *Conference on "Mobilizing Resources for Development*; *IP Development Matchmaking Database (IP-DMD)*; *IP Advantage Database (ex E-SPEED)*, which showcases case studies in the use of IP, numerous of which involve e public–private partnerships); *IP and Technology Transfer: Common Challenges – Building Solutions* (this project includes a study of "Policies Fostering the Participation of Businesses in Technology Transfer"); and *Open Collaborative Projects and IP-Based Models* (which discusses the partnerships involved in some Open Collaborative Projects). WIPO, *Projects for Implementation of Development Agenda Recommendations* (2016), www.wipo.int/ip-development/en/agenda/projects.html (last visited Nov. 19, 2017).

[15] *Harnessing the Power of the Private Sector – An Interview with Francis Gurry*. WIPO MAGAZINE September 2015, www.wipo.int/wipo_magazine/en/2015/05/article_0001.html (last visited Nov. 19, 2017).

[16] *Id.*

[17] Carolyn Deere Birkbeck and Santiago Roca, *An External Review of WIPO Technical Assistance in the Area of Cooperation for Development*, WIPO Doc. CDIP/8/INF1, xxiii, xviii, (2011).

legitimacy of these governance efforts by the degree of representation and participation.[18] Analyses of networked governance frameworks, or multi-stakeholder governance, must therefore ask how governing power is distributed as between "public" and "private" governing nodes, how powerful nodes are made accountable, and how the less powerful have the means to regulate the more powerful.[19] Participation in policy making by those most affected, and by those who hold the least power, is critical to the legitimacy of networked governance structures.

In theory, PPPs combine the strengths of multiple sectors: the openness to public scrutiny, stability, and social responsibility of the public sector; the financial resources, efficiency, and entrepreneurialism of the private sector; and the ethics and commitment of nonprofits or civil society sector.[20] Drawing on these combined strengths, partnerships ideally can be used to serve goals of equity, access, and participation, drawing on the strengths of the private sector to provide innovative or competitive goods or services, while also drawing on the strengths of public and civil society sectors in ensuring that such provision is equitable and accessible to all, including vulnerable populations. As state or international organization-driven initiatives, partnerships should encourage policy participation, accountability, and citizen input, thus incorporating democratic principles. On a transnational level, partnerships are seen as a way of addressing governance gaps through participatory multilateralism and multi-stakeholder dialogue.[21]

Critics of PPPs suggest that, in practice, partnerships often do not involve close collaboration between partners, and may even border on privatization.[22] They often do not "conform to normative principles of democracy nor contribute to the democratization of global governance."[23] Thus, though partnerships may derive legitimacy from their effectiveness (so-called output legitimacy), they may nevertheless fail to conform to normative democratic principles.[24]

The implementation of the WIPO Development Agenda, and potentially its work towards the SDGs, relies to some extent on partnerships, including PPPs. We must ask, then, not only whether these partnerships are effective but also whether they serve the goals of equity, access, and democracy and, furthermore, whether they encourage policy participation and citizen input. We must also ask whether they are tools that will help WIPO to contribute ultimately towards advancing the overall goals of sustainable development.

The changing shape of governance at WIPO, and the place of partnerships within the organization, must be seen in the context of broader trends in the history of international and state governance. There are two major competing perspectives in this regard. First, critics of neoliberalism note that WIPO emerged as part of an American-led postcolonial agenda that saw privatization as one of developments' main tools and opportunities.

[18] Karin Bäckstrand, *Are Partnerships for Sustainable Development Democratic and Legitimate? in* Public Private Partnerships for Sustainable Development, 167, 165–82, (Philipp Pattberg, Frank Biermann, Sander Chan, and Ayşem Mert eds., 2012).

[19] Burris et al., *supra* note 2, at 54.

[20] Pauline Vaillancourt Rosenau, *The Strengths and Weaknesses of Public-Private Policy Partnerships*, 43 Am. Behav. Scientist, 10–34, 11 (1999).

[21] Bäckstrand, *supra* note 18, at 166–67, 165–82.

[22] Rosenau, *supra* note 20, at 12.

[23] Bäckstrand, *supra* note 18, at 167, 165–82.

[24] Bäckstrand, *supra* note 18, at 167–68, 165–82.

WIPO, in this perspective, has acted as one among a series of international neoliberal institutions enrolled in privatizing state enterprises and extending the privatization of knowledge in ways that have undermined state institutions and public access to knowledge.[25] In fact, the role of the private sector is more prominent in WIPO, which receives a majority of its income from private users of its services.[26]

A second view is somewhat more optimistic. Some argue that the period since the 1980s never gave rise to true neoliberalism, but rather to regulatory capitalism: growth in state spending on regulation, a proliferation of regulatory agencies, and an expansion of experimental forms of governance.[27] Seen in this context, WIPO has played a role, along with the World Trade Organization (WTO), in facilitating the growth of multilevel regulatory capitalism in which states regulate, and are regulated by, international organizations. WIPO, in regulating its member states' own regulatory structures, facilitated the expansion of IP along with a series of mechanisms and institutions for regulating – encouraging, measuring, collecting, and distributing – IP and the royalties it generates.

Whereas the first perspective, or the critique of neoliberalism, would dismiss PPPs as a form of privatization or hollowing out of governance and state institutions, the second perspective is more agnostic as to the effects of the rise of regulatory capitalism.[28] PPPs might, as critics of neoliberalism suggest, reduce democracy, transparency, and legitimacy. But they may also be implemented in ways that incorporate and facilitate forms of regulation that encourage equality, access to goods and services, accountability transparency, deliberation, and policy participation.[29] A key question, then, is whether the partnerships generated under the WIPO Development Agenda have, to date, succeeded in promoting equality, access, and accountability. And moving forward, how might WIPO partnerships ensure these important democratic governance objectives are met?

B *Moving to Sustainable Development*

The WIPO Development Agenda has brought a greater focus on development to WIPO, building on a discourse of international development, which began in the 1960s. A sustainable development agenda for WIPO would encompass a broader definition and understanding of development, as signaled by the SDGs.

Development had begun to move from a peripheral to a central position in the Geneva-based IP system in the 1960s and 1970s. As a result of decolonization and the rising concern of international organizations with postwar reconstruction and development, concern with development became more central in international institutions. However, WIPO was originally (in 1967) established as a more narrowly and technically

[25] *See generally* Ha-Joon Chang, Kicking Away the Ladder: Development in Historical Perspective (2002); Chidi Oguamanam, Intellectual Property in Global Governance: A Development Question (2012).

[26] Carolyn Deere Birkbeck, The Governance of the World Intellectual Property Organization: A Reference Guide 57 (2015).

[27] *See generally* John Braithwaite, Regulatory Capitalism (2008).

[28] Philipp Pattberg, Frank Biermann, Sander Chan, and Ayşem Mert, *Introduction: Partnerships for Sustainable Development, in* Public-Private Partnerships for Sustainable Development: Emergence, Influence and Legitimacy, 1, 1–18 (Philipp Pattberg, Frank Biermann, Sander Chan, and Ayşem Mert eds.); *See also* Bäckstrand, *supra* note 18, at 169, 165–82.

[29] Pattberg et al., *supra* note 28, at 1–2, 1–18; *See also* Bäckstrand, *supra* note 18, at 170, 165–82.

focused agency with the mandate "to promote the protection of IP throughout the world through cooperation among States."[30] It was not until 1974 that WIPO became a specialized agency of the UN.[31]

For WIPO, joining the UN system would mean grafting concepts of development from the UN system onto WIPO. The agreement to join the UN mentions several development priorities, including the promotion of technology transfer "to accelerate economic, social and cultural development."[32] However, the grafting of the UN discourse of development onto the IP system was accompanied by a shift to a near-unitary emphasis on economic development, and by the relative erasure of concepts of development that had previously competed in the discursive ecosystem of international IP.[33]

Prior to the 1960s and 1970s, the term "development" had been used in international IP discourse, though in more diverse and often different senses from the "development agenda" associated with the mission of the UN today. In the late nineteenth century, when the international copyright system was established, "development" meant the creation and perfection of IP rights in and of themselves. Second, "development" meant the generation of international law and institutions, as well as national IP laws and institutions. Third, in the case of copyright, "development" involved fostering literature, the arts, and culture. Only in the 1960s did economic development come to dominate the development discourse of the Geneva-based IP system.[34]

The dominance of economic measures of development, when used to the exclusion of broader concepts of development and social welfare, can "have brutal consequences."[35] An exclusive focus on economic development can shift the focus of policymaking away from the distributional consequences of policies in ways that, on a global scale, can be catastrophic, restricting access to medicine and patented technologies.[36] The original proposal by Argentina and Brazil for a development agenda at WIPO, to some extent, contested the view that IP protection contributed unequivocally to economic development. It noted that:

> IP protection is a policy instrument the operation of which may, in actual practice, produce benefits as well as costs, which may vary in accordance with a country's level of development. Action is therefore needed to ensure, in all countries, that the costs do not outweigh the benefits of IP protection.[37]

The original proposal noted, in particular, that international IP protection could also "run counter" to public objectives and that "while access to information and knowledge

[30] Convention Establishing the World Intellectual Property Organization, July 14, 1967, as amended on September 28, 1979, 21 U.S.T. 1749, 828 U.N.T.S. 3.

[31] WIPO, Agreement between the United Nations and the World Intellectual Property Organization, WIPO Doc. TRT/UN-WIPO/001 (1974); Arpad Bogsch, THE FIRST TWENTY-FIVE YEARS OF THE WORLD INTELLECTUAL PROPERTY ORGANIZATION FROM 1967 TO 1992 (1992).

[32] WIPO, Agreement between the United Nations and the World Intellectual Property Organization, *supra* note 31, at Preamble.

[33] Arturo Escobar, ENCOUNTERING DEVELOPMENT: THE MAKING AND UNMAKING OF THE THIRD WORLD (1995).

[34] Bannerman, *supra* note 7.

[35] Margaret Chon, *Intellectual Property and the Development Divide*, 27 CARDOZO L. REV. 2823–24, 2813–2904 (2006).

[36] *Id.*

[37] *Proposal by Argentina*, *supra* note 12.

sharing are regarded as essential elements in fostering innovation and creativity in the information economy, [...] new layers of intellectual property protection [...] would obstruct the free flow of information."[38]

The establishment of the UN's SDGs in 2015 as part of the 2030 Agenda for Sustainable Development[39] is, in some respects, an effort to further broaden the discourse and mandate of development beyond purely economic measures, like the prior MDGs. Only three of the seventeen SDGs deal directly with economic or industrial development;[40] others focus on education (4), gender equality (5), inequality (11), and peace and justice (16), among others.

Yet WIPO's discourse of and approach to development has not, to date, similarly broadened. The prioritization of economic over other aspects of development still dominates WIPO's approach to IP and development. Despite joining the UN system in 1974, WIPO has in many respects remained distant from the UN. This distance may be due to WIPO's financial independence, or to its pre-UN heritage, which originally had little in common with the UN mandate or development objectives.[41] The WIPO Director General has typically not attended the UN General Assembly, and WIPO has considered closing its New York liaison office.[42]

This distance has continued upon the UN's adoption of its SDGs. In September 2015, WIPO, in a Question and Answer document, minimized its own role, and that of IP, in the SDGs:

> In recent years, the dominant area of work by the UN in New York is the political processes related to the post 2015 Development Agenda, including the Sustainable Development Goals and Financing for Development. While important, IP is only a small element of these broader processes.[43]

A preliminary analysis conducted by WIPO of the ways in which its work supported SDGs viewed most of WIPO's work as contributing to goal 9, the building of infrastructure and industrialization, as well as goal 8, that of economic growth. Surprisingly few of WIPO's activities were viewed as contributing to the SDGs of education, hunger, protecting biodiversity, combatting climate change, or ensuring human health.[44]

38 *Id.* at 1, 3.

39 Sustainable Development Knowledge Platform, *Transforming Our World: The 2030 Agenda for Sustainable Development*, U.N. Dep't of Econ. And Soc. Affairs, https://sustainabledevelopment.un.org/post2015/transformingourworld (last visited Nov. 19, 2017).

40 Goal 8 deals with economic growth, 1 with poverty, and 9 with infrastructure and industrialization.

41 Bannerman, *supra* note 7.

42 William New, *Are the UN And WIPO Drifting Apart?* INTELLECTUAL PROPERTY WATCH (Sep. 23, 2015), www.ip-watch.org/2015/09/23/are-the-un-and-wipo-drifting-apart/ (last visited Nov. 19, 2017).

43 *Q&A: Proposed Program and Budget 2016/17 (and other PBC Documents)*, WIPO Doc. WO/PBC/24/Q & A, 24, (2015).

44 This analysis may change as WIPO continues to develop its conceptualization of its contribution to the SDGs. It has asked member states to "provide written submissions to the Secretariat as regards the SDGs they deem relevant to WIPO's work, together with an explanation / justification of their views." *See Committee on Development and Intellectual Property (CDIP), Seventeenth Session: Summary by the Chair*, WIPO 2 (2016); *Mapping of WIPO Activities Related to the Sustainable Development Goals (SDGs) Implementation*, WIPO Doc. CDIP/17/8 (2016). WIPO is also not singled out in a UN consultant's report on the functions and capacities of the UN development system. U.N., System-Wide Outline of the Functions and Capacities of the U.N. Development System Consultant's Report (Jun. 2017), iwww.un.org/ecosoc/sites/www.un.org.ecosoc/files/files/en/qcpr/sg-report-dalberg_unds-outline-of-functions-and-capacities-june-2017.pdf (last visited Nov. 19, 2017).

It is clear that IP plays an important role in relation to many SDGs, including those related to food and agriculture, health, innovation, climate change, biodiversity, and technology transfer.[45] As the original proponents of a development agenda for WIPO noted, the IP system as currently constituted may sometimes work counterproductively to achievement of the SDGs, by locking up agricultural innovation, inflating drug prices, stalling follow-on innovation, rewarding the invention and sale of polluting technologies, reducing biodiversity, and preventing technology transfer. There is no shortage of proposals for reform that would help to address these problems,[46] yet these are not mainstreamed into WIPO's development approaches.

Problems such as inflated drug prices are problems that affect all countries, not just developing countries. A sustainable development agenda for WIPO must therefore involve a shift away from developing countries or least developed countries as the sole focus. In fact, the SDGs call on all countries to meet sustainable development goals. The shift from the goal of development to the goal of sustainable development involves the recognition that all countries are developing; countries that formerly considered themselves as so-called developed countries, or sitting at the end state of development, must now transform to adopt sustainable development practices. As Henrietta Moore writes:

> Unlike their predecessors, the millennium development goals (MDGs), which only applied to those countries deemed to be "developing," the SDGs will require all nations to work towards them. So, in a sense, we are all developing nations from now on.[47]

In this new view, some traditional forms of development may be neither sustainable, nor contributors to a higher quality of life, much less to flourishing communities and individuals. These include the production of some polluting forms of energy through patents, the prioritization of industrial forms of knowledge over traditional knowledge in the patent, copyright, and trademark systems, and the concentration of wealth in the hands of a few IP owners. The effective implementation of the SDGs requires all countries, through WIPO and at national levels, to examine and rethink the international IP system fundamentally.

WIPO must acknowledge and embrace a broader view of development, and must broaden its own work in an effort to envision and institute an international intellectual property system that better serves all SDGs. WIPO's hesitant approach to the incorporation of the UN's SDGs may be reflective of some member states' hesitance, but it is difficult to understand given that WIPO has adopted a Development Agenda and as part of the UN system should actively contribute to the realization of the SDGs.

A sustainable development agenda for WIPO should not only embrace a broader vision of its role in implementing the SDGs, but also place importance on the *democratic qualities* of the partnerships and forms of networked governance, noting that partnerships can embrace, but can also fail to implement, democratic values.[48]

[45] New, *supra* note 42.

[46] Ahmed Abdel-Latif, *Intellectual Property Rights and the Transfer of Climate Change Technologies: Issues, Challenges, and Way Forward*, 15 CLIMATE POLICY 103 (2015); *See generally* Michael Blakeney, INTELLECTUAL PROPERTY RIGHTS AND FOOD SECURITY (2009); Susan Sell, *supra* note 6.

[47] Henrietta Moore, *The Sustainable Development Goals: We're All Developing Countries Now: Inequality in the UK and US is a Stark Reminder that the Patronising Relationship between the Global North and South Is Misplaced*, THE GUARDIAN, Sept. 25, 2015.

[48] Pattberg et al., *supra* note 28, at 1–2, 1–18; Bäckstrand, *supra* note 18, at 170, 165–82.

This is particularly important when partnerships take place between so-called developed and developing country actors, and the potential for power imbalance is acute, and can work counter to the construction of partnerships in the true sense as involving relatively equal actors. However, adequately designed PPPs have the potential to encourage equality, access to goods and services, accountability, transparency, deliberation, and policy participation.

II From Partnerships to Democratic Partnerships

Given the rising emphasis on partnerships in the UN system and in the discourse of sustainable development, this section examines the current practice of partnership at WIPO, taking as a case study the "Access to Research for Development and Innovation" (ARDI) program, a public–private partnership under WIPO's Specialized Databases' Access and Support project. ARDI is one of four or five prominent PPPs at WIPO.[49] This section examines how ARDI contributes, first, to policy participation, and second, to equity and access. Third, it examines the concept of development embedded in the ARDI program.

A *ARDI: Partnerships for Equity and Access, and Policy Participation*

WIPO's Specialized Databases' Access and Support project (Phase I and II) involves two programs: the ARDI program and the "Access to Specialized Patent Information" (ASPI) program. These programs were designed to implement Recommendation 8 of the WIPO Development Agenda, that WIPO "develop agreements with research institutions and with private enterprises with a view to facilitating the national offices of developing countries, especially LDCs, as well as their regional and subregional IP organizations to access specialized databases for the purposes of patent searches."[50] This section of the chapter focuses on ARDI as an exemplar PPP within WIPO.

Recognizing that, alongside specialized patent search data, "access to scholarly literature is critical to the innovation process," the ARDI program launched in 2009. Coordinated by WIPO, provides access to approximately 20,000 journals, books, and reference works.[51] WIPO's private partners in the project include Cambridge University Press, Elsevier, John Wiley & Sons, Oxford University Press, Sage, Taylor & Francis, and other major academic and scientific publishers.[52] ARDI now falls under a broader publishers' initiative called *Research4Life*, which is a collaborative effort between ARDI and three

[49] Others include Re: Search, the Accessible Books Consortium (ABC), and WIPO GREEN. *See Harnessing the Power, supra* note 15; see also Susan Isiko Štrba, chapter 9, *infra*; Ahmed Abdel-Latif, chapter 11, *infra*.

[50] *Development Agenda, supra* note 3.

[51] WIPO, *Access to Research for Development and Innovation* 2 (n.d.); World Intellectual Property Organization, *ARDI – Research for Innovation*, WIPO, www.wipo.int/ardi/en/ (last visited Nov. 19, 2017); World Intellectual Property Organization, *Frequently Asked Questions (FAQs) About ARDI*, www.wipo.int/ardi/en/faq/ (last visited Nov. 19, 2017).

[52] WIPO, *Access to Research for Development and Innovation* 5 (n.d.). *See also* Jens Bammel, chapter 7, *supra*.

other programs, all of which are focused on "providing affordable access to critical scientific research."[53]

ARDI must be viewed in part as an element of for-profit publishers' defensive response to the threat of the open access and access to knowledge movements.[54] Such movements have called for greater access to scientific publishing through open access licenses, and through broader limitations and exceptions to copyright. Thus, when measuring its success as a partnership in terms of providing access to goods and services, as well as enhancing equity, and encouraging policy participation, ARDI must be viewed alongside other open access solutions.

B *Policy Participation*

The original proponents of a Development Agenda for WIPO emphasized the importance of policy participation in the development of IP laws and institutions. In their proposal for the establishment of a Development Agenda for WIPO, proponents noted that WIPO technical assistance programs and activities should ensure that IP laws "are fully responsive to the specific needs and problems of individual societies. The assistance should correspond to the needs of various stakeholders in developing and least developed countries, and not just the intellectual property offices and rightholders."[55]

The ARDI program was developed based on a needs assessment, in its effort to ensure that it responded to the needs and problems of individual societies. The needs assessment analysis examined statistics pertaining to national patenting activity, so as to assess the fields of technology in which developing countries had the most patenting activity. In addition to the statistical analysis, a needs self-assessment questionnaire was circulated to developing country IP offices.[56] Publishers, in collaboration with WIPO and developing country IP offices, are the nodes of governance that had the most influence on the design of the *Specialized Databases* project. A broader range of stakeholders does not appear to have been involved in the needs assessment.

While the notion of needs assessment appears to be an appropriate step towards distributed influence on the development of the ARDI program, this is arguably illusory. IP offices in developing countries have been knit over time into a global system of patent administration that is built by, and serves, global IP owners:

53 ARDI joined *Research4Life* in 2011; *About*, Research4Life, www.research4life.org/about/ (last visited Nov. 19, 2017); *Evaluation Report on the Project on Specialized Databases' Access and Support – Phase II*, WIPO Doc. CDIP/14/5, 9, (2014).

54 Open access means "free availability on the public internet, permitting any users to read, download, copy, distribute, print, search, or link to the full texts of these articles, crawl them for indexing, pass them as data to software, or use them for any other lawful purpose, without financial, legal, or technical barriers other than those inseparable from gaining access to the internet itself." *See* Budapest Open Access Initiative, www.budapestopenaccessinitiative.org/read (last visited Nov. 19, 2017). The Access to Knowledge movement was initiated by a diverse set of NGOs and developing countries with a diverse set of aims that all hope to realize technological and human potential by making knowledge more accessible. *See also* Bannerman, *supra* note 7.

55 WIPO, *Elaboration on Proposal to Establish Development Agenda for WIPO*, WIPO Doc. IIM/1/4, 22 item 66 (2005).

56 WIPO, *Study Paper Regarding Recommendation* 8, WIPO Doc. CDIP/3/INF/2/Study/III/INF/1, 45 (2010).

> The Trilateral Offices [the United States Patent and Trademark Office, the European Patent Office, and the Japanese Patent Office] have [. . .] integrated developing country patent offices into an emerging global system of patent administration.[57]

In many cases, rather than being integrated into national development strategies, instead, as Peter Drahos notes, "developing country patent offices have been integrated into a system of international patent administration."[58] Consultation of private publishers with developing country IP offices cannot replace broader consultation with developing country governments, nor can it stand in for policy participation by a range of civil society actors or the public interest.

The ARDI program provides few mechanisms for policy participation by the less powerful or those working outside its beneficiary institutions and states. It is controlled primarily by participating publishers. These participants have the authority to review, from time to time, the list of countries eligible for access, and to arrange, according to their own business models, the range of access to be provided.[59] Participating publishers can and do reduce the selection of publications made available through the program; such reductions have been noted by program evaluators as a key risk and a "global trend" facing the future of the program.[60]

At the same time, the broader program, *Research4Life*, of which ARDI is a part, does provide, to a limited extent, broader civil society input. *Research4Life* has an advisory council staffed with a range of representatives, drawn from university, library, and research bodies in developing countries.[61] However, the advisory council does not have a policy-making role, but is characterized as "a forum for direct engagement between the Research4Life user community and the partnership."[62] The highest-level body in *Research4Life* is a body of its partners – publishers and international organizations – which meets annually along with user representatives of its services.[63] An Executive Council, made up of the major contributing partners – again, publishers and international organizations – makes ongoing operational decisions between General Partners Meetings.[64]

By contrast, the original proponents of a Development Agenda for WIPO emphasized the importance of participation of public interest NGOs in WIPO activities:

> WIPO should foster the active participation of public interest non-governmental organizations in its subsidiary bodies to ensure that in IP norm-setting a proper balance is struck between the producers and users of technological knowledge, in a manner that fully services the public interest.[65]

[57] Peter Drahos, *"Trust Me": Patent Offices in Developing Countries*, 34 Am. J. L. Med. 173 (2008).

[58] *Id.* at 153.

[59] WIPO, *Partners' Statement of Intent*, www.wipo.int/ardi/en/statement.html (last visited Nov. 19, 2017).

[60] *Evaluation Report*, *supra* note 53, at 10.

[61] *Advisory Council*, Research4Life, www.research4life.org/about/advisory-council/ (last visited Nov. 19, 2017).

[62] *Id.*

[63] *Strategic Plan: Beyond the 2015 Horizon*, Research4Life 6, www.research4life.org/about/strategic-plan/ (last visited Nov. 19, 2017).

[64] *Id.*

[65] WIPO, *supra* note 37, at 6.

III ARDI and Development

Viewing ARDI through the lens of networked governance reveals that it keeps copyright holders and an international network of IP offices in the drivers' seat of knowledge governance. PPPs such as ARDI, Hinari, or WIPO's Re:Search partnership (explored in separate chapters in this book) do improve access to copyright works or patented medicines for developing countries, but they do so in a way that is selective, controlled by IP holders, and contingent on the good will of IP holders. Thus, ARDI falls prey to a common fault of PPPs: affected actors and countries of the South tend to be underrepresented, such that partnerships tend to replicate the imbalances of representation found in multilateral and other institutions.[66] Rather than enhancing policy participation by networking a diversity of nodes of governance, more powerful stakeholders dominate.

A *Democratic Legitimacy*

Other initiatives show that PPPs can be structured in ways that are more inclusive of the less powerful and the most affected. The Global Fund to Fight AIDS, Tuberculosis and Malaria (GFATM), for example, has ensured, to a greater extent, broad formal governance participation by developing countries and NGOs.[67] While the GFATM's mechanisms of civil society participation are not flawless, they are more robust than those of ARDI.[68]

The core problem may be that PPPs are not envisaged as a vehicle for enhancing policy participation at WIPO. Director General Francis Gurry emphasized this in a 2015 interview:

> I want to underline that that public-private partnerships are not a vehicle for establishing intellectual property (IP) laws or policies. WIPO's normative program remains the prerogative of member states, and member states alone. It is a purely public function.[69]

While it may be proper for states to play primary roles in intellectual property treaty-making, Gurry's view fails to acknowledge the roles that program partnerships also play in IP governance, or the role that PPPs such as ARDI play in providing forms of access to goods and services. Through the lens of networked governance, the provision of access to copyright works by private publishers is as much a form of governance as is the public provision of services. Moreover, the policies that govern such access, whether set through program parameters or private licensing contracts, are key tools of governance. WIPO PPPs must ensure that affected groups are represented within PPP governance structures.

ARDI can be compared not only to other PPPs but also to other knowledge governance mechanisms, such as open access licensing. Both ARDI and open access licensors, such as Creative Commons and those who use Creative Commons licenses, engage in forms of knowledge governance undertaken, to a significant extent, by private actors and private licensing arrangements. Open access licenses are nodes of governance that any copyright holder, including the publishers involved in the ARDI initiative, can utilize.

[66] Schäferhoff, *supra* note 11, at 465–67.
[67] *Id.* at 6.
[68] Wolfgang Hein, Scott Burris and Clifford Shearing, *Conceptual Models for Global Health Governance, in* Making Sense of Global Health Governance: A Policy Perspective 87, 72–98 (2009).
[69] *Harnessing the Power, supra* note 15.

Any user, in any country, who has access to open access publications, may use them according to the liberal terms of open access licenses.[70]

In 2002, a relatively small civil society coalition developed and signed on to the Budapest Open Access Initiative. Since then, thousands of organizations and individuals worldwide have signed on to the initiative, which indicates the widespread adoption in state, civil society, and private sectors, of open access principles of knowledge governance.[71] This broad network thereby legitimates open access as a form of networked knowledge governance, not only due to its efficacy in making works available, but also according to principles of participatory democracy, (emphasizing broad participation and uptake), and cosmopolitan democracy, where decision-making rests with those actors most affected.

In examining PPPs through the lens of networked governance, we must ask whether the less powerful have the means to regulate the more powerful. In the case of ARDI, few if any real mechanisms exist for the less powerful to regulate access to copyright works. Many groups are excluded as users of the service, and many have neither a seat at the table nor the mechanisms to influence the governance of the project. In contrast, other transnational PPPs do include affected users on formal governance bodies. Open access systems, such as Creative Commons licenses, permit anyone – rather than a select few – both to benefit from the access provided, and to take up open access licensing as a tool of governance.

PPPs can expand, or restrict, policy participation by affected actors. The legitimacy of PPPs thus hinges, to a large extent, on their institutional design.[72] Examples exist of networked governance through PPPs, and through licensing models, which approach standards of participatory and cosmopolitan governance. The ARDI program fails to meet such standards.

B *Access and Equity*

Even if they are not justified on the grounds of governance through democratic means, Karin Bäckstrand suggests that PPPs might find legitimacy on the grounds that they are effective, and that they achieve "output legitimacy," or demonstrate problem-solving capacity.[73] It is therefore imperative to ask also whether ARDI is effective at providing access to copyright works, and whether it does so equitably.

According to the WIPO evaluation of ARDI, there is high demand for the program among stakeholders consulted, and a majority of the stakeholders consulted have had a positive experience with the program.[74] The number of institutions using ARDI had grown to 349 by 2014, though approximately only 60 percent of the institutions registered with ARDI are active users of the program.[75] The following table gives the regional distribution of the 349 institutions making use of the ARDI database:

[70] *Licensing Types*, Creative Commons, https://creativecommons.org/share-your-work/licensing-types-examples/ (last visited Nov. 19, 2017).

[71] *Read the Budapest Open Access Initiative*, Budapest Open Access Initiative, www.budapestopenaccessinitiative.org/read (last visited Nov. 19, 2017); *View Signatures*, Budapest Open Access Initiative, www.budapestopenaccessinitiative.org/list_signatures (last visited Nov. 19, 2017).

[72] Schäferhoff, *supra* note 11, at 469.

[73] Bäckstrand, *supra* note 18, at 165, 165–182.

[74] *Evaluation Report on the Project, supra* note 53, at 7.

[75] *Id.* at 13.

Table 8.1. Regional distribution of the 349 institutions making use of the ARDI database.[76]

Region	*ARDI Users (registered/active)*
Africa	167/101
Arab countries	34/14
Central/Eastern European	47/26
Asia and Pacific	67/47
Latin American and Caribbean	34/19
Total	349/207

Source: Evaluation Report on the Project on Specialized Databases' Access and Support – Phase II, WIPO Doc. CDIP/14/5, 9, (2014).

There is little doubt that ARDI is successful in providing access to open access content and non–open access content to the academic, research, and IP institutions registered with the program. As of this writing, 4,272 open access journals and 4,110 non–open access journals, 19,893 non–open access books, and 12 non–open access reference works were being made available to user institutions through the program.[77]

However, the access that ARDI provides user institutions in low-income countries is limited in a variety of ways. Publishers making material available through ARDI provide access to only some of their non–open access publications, and access is limited to very specific site locations and users. The "target beneficiaries" of the ARDI project are intended to be "among others IPOs, individual inventors, small and medium enterprises (SMEs), industry, researchers in technology centers and universities, academia, IP professionals, and government policy-makers."[78] This excludes independent researchers, professionals working in noncovered institutions, and the general public from access. Furthermore, access is limited to only certain countries, and even this access is time-bound; once a country is removed from the list of countries approved for free access by Research4Life, fees will commence and, if unpaid, a country might be removed from the list of beneficiary countries altogether. As Chan, Kirsop, and Arunachalam note, programs like ARDI "may be serving as a marketing device to prepare the ground for national site licenses in the countries with rising GDP or growing research needs."[79]

Alongside the limitations on potential beneficiaries of the ARDI program, there are also functional limitations. For those works provided through ARDI that are not open access licensed, full freedom to exchange ARDI works, to collaborate by drawing on ARDI works, and/or to do particular forms of research, is not provided. As Chan, Kirsop, and Arunachalam note, open access licensing provides broader freedom than does ARDI and other Research4Life programs:

[76] Adapted from *Evaluation Report on the Project*, *supra* note 53, at 13.

[77] ARDI, http://ardi.wipo.int/ (last visited Nov. 19, 2017).

[78] WIPO, *Study Paper*, *supra* note 56.

[79] Leslie Chan, Barbara Kirsop, and Subbiah Arunachalam, *Towards Open and Equitable Access to Research and Knowledge for Development*, 8 PLoS MEDICINE 1, 1–4 (2011).

> [Open Access] resources provides [*sic*] a far greater degree of freedom for researchers to exchange and collaborate, for knowledge to be translated into useable forms by frontline health workers, and for emerging technologies such as text mining and semantic tagging for faster knowledge discovery to be used. It must be underscored that such usages and redistribution are not permitted by donated content included in the Research4Life programs.[80]

The establishment of ARDI and related programs follows a strategy set out previously by other IP owners – in this case, pharmaceutical companies – who, when confronted by the Access to Medicine movement, established a PPP referred to earlier (the GFATM). Hein, Burris, and Shearing argue that this was "an attempt to alleviate pressure towards compromises in the IPR field" in the face of criticism that the global IP system was responsible for millions of deaths from AIDs and tuberculosis.[81] ARDI can equally be seen as alleviating pressure by critics who argue that the international copyright system is responsible for causing a so-called book or information famine in countries of the South. Thus, although it could be viewed as a humanitarian effort, arguably one of its purposes is heading off both the incursion of open access licensing and pressures for broader changes in the international copyright system.[82]

While ARDI has some level of success in providing access to copyright works, this success is highly circumscribed when compared to other potential options, including open access licensing or other potential norm-setting measures that may better provide broader levels of access, while still permitting a broader degree of freedom to use works and conduct follow-on research. Open access provides greater equity to developing country researchers than does the ARDI program, ensuring not only access to research of the North by researchers of the South, but also ensuring access to researchers of the Souths' work by researchers of the North. This is a key element of access to knowledge. The level of equity in access and freedom provided by ARDI falls far short of other alternatives.

The ARDI program, and WIPO's analysis of its contributions to the SDGs, is symptomatic of WIPO's narrowly defined definition of development. Narrowly focused on infrastructure and economic development, the ARDI program fails to address the importance of access to copyright works to ensure educational opportunities, reduce inequality, promote inclusive societies, and ensure inclusive institutions at all levels. As Chan, Kirsop, and Arunachalam note, "information philanthropy [. . .] is not a long-term sustainable solution" to ensure access to knowledge, nor to development in general.[83]

Conclusion

A new sustainable development agenda for WIPO is urgently needed. However, the opportunity such an agenda could offer may be lost if a true commitment to finding ways for the IP system to contribute to the full range of SDGs is not made. Unless WIPO and its member states commit to a broad vision of development, and to building and retooling

[80] *Id.*
[81] Hein et al., *supra* note 68, at 87, 72–98.
[82] Chan, *supra* note 79.
[83] *Id.*, at 1–4.

IP institutions for sustainable development, they may instead legitimate IP norms that do not contribute fully to sustainable development.

WIPO should thus overcome its reluctance to acknowledging its own role in contributing to the UN's SDGs and take an active role in their realization.

In this context, can public–private partnerships contribute to WIPO's efforts in meeting the UN's SDGs? The answer to this question hinges on how such partnerships are constructed. WIPO should adopt a sustainable development agenda that would broaden the organization's conceptualization of development while working to ensure that all its partnerships, including PPPs, involve full policy participation and empower those most affected. Moreover, this chapter also argues that WIPO should articulate and adopt a policy on PPPs, requiring that WIPO PPPs encourage policy participation and equitable access in all of its PPPs. It suggests that this policy on PPPs should be adopted in the context of an overall sustainable development agenda for WIPO.

A WIPO agenda on sustainable development and partnerships requires commitment to enabling partnerships on the basis of equal contributions by the powerful and the least powerful as well as the empowerment of those most affected. This is true not only in traditional governance, but also in networked forms of governance such as partnerships. To the extent that PPPs are increasingly a part of WIPO's sustainable development work, they must be recognized as vehicles of knowledge governance; policy participation, equity, and access must be written into their institutional governance arrangements. Models of PPPs that incorporate these values exist, but to date, ARDI does not meet the standard of affording control to the least powerful and those most affected, including user communities more broadly.

As part of a sustainable development agenda, it is critical that WIPO adopt higher standards for public–private partnership governance. Affirmative efforts must be taken by WIPO to "open up governance to the poor" in its partnership structures, and in its own governance.[84] The world's most impoverished must be the main beneficiaries – and guiders – of these sustainable development efforts.

References

Abdel-Latif, Ahmed, *Intellectual Property Rights and the Transfer of Climate Change Technologies: Issues, Challenges, and Way Forward*, 15 Climate Policy 103 (2015).

Bäckstrand, Karin, *Are Partnerships for Sustainable Development Democratic and Legitimate? in* Public Private Partnerships for Sustainable Development (Philipp Pattberg, Frank Biermann, Sander Chan, and Ayşem Mert eds., 2012).

Bannerman, Sara, International Copyright And Access To Knowledge (2016).

Birkbeck, Carolyn D., The Governance of the World Intellectual Property Organization: A Reference Guide (2015).

Birkbeck, Carolyn D. and Santiago Roca, *An External Review of WIPO Technical Assistance in the Area of Cooperation for Development*, WIPO Doc. CDIP/8/INF1 (2011).

Blakeney, Michael, Intellectual Property Rights And Food Security (2009).

Bogsch, Arpad, The First Twenty-Five Years Of The World Intellectual Property Organization From 1967 To 1992 (1992).

Braithwaite, John, Regulatory Capitalism (2008).

[84] Hein et al., *supra* note 68, at 93, 72–98.

Budapest Open Access Initiative, www.budapestopenaccessinitiative.org/read (last visited Nov. 19, 2017).

Budapest Open Access Initiative, *Read the Budapest Open Access Initiative*, www.budapestopenaccessinitiative.org/read (last visited Nov. 19, 2017).

Budapest Open Access Initiative, *View Signatures*, www.budapestopenaccessinitiative.org/list_signatures (last visited Nov. 19, 2017).

Burris, Scott, Peter Drahos, and Clifford Shearing, *Nodal Governance*, 30 Austl. J. Leg. Phil. (2005).

Center for International Environmental Law, A *Citizen's Guide to WIPO* (2007).

Chan, Leslie, Barbara Kirsop, and Subbiah Arunachalam, *Towards Open and Equitable Access to Research and Knowledge for Development*, 8 PLoS Medicine 1 (2011).

Chang, Ha-Joon, Kicking Away the Ladder: Development in Historical Perspective (2002).

Chon, Margaret, *Intellectual Property and the Development Divide*, 27 Cardozo L. Rev. 2823 (2006).

Chon, Margaret, *PPPs in Global IP (Public-Private Partnerships in Global Intellectual Property) in* Methods and Perspectives in Intellectual Property (Graeme B. Dinwoodie ed., 2013).

Convention Establishing the World Intellectual Property Organization, July 14, 1967, as amended on September 28, 1979, 21 U.S.T. 1749, 828 U.N.T.S. 3.

Creative Commons, *Licensing Types*, https://creativecommons.org/share-your-work/licensing-types-examples/ (last visited Nov. 19, 2017).

Drahos, Peter, *"Trust Me": Patent Offices in Developing Countries*, 34 Am. J. L. Med. 173 (2008).

Escobar, Arturo, Encountering Development: The Making And Unmaking Of The Third World (1995).

Hein, Wolfgang, Scott Burris, and Clifford Shearing, *Conceptual Models for Global Health Governance, in* Making Sense of Global Health Governance: A Policy Perspective (2009).

Moore, Henrietta, *The Sustainable Development Goals: We're All Developing Countries Now: Inequality in the UK and US Is a Stark Reminder that the Patronising Relationship between the Global North and South Is Misplaced*, The Guardian, Sep. 25, 2015.

New, William, *Are The UN And WIPO Drifting Apart?* Intellectual Property Watch (Sep. 23, 2015), www.ip-watch.org/2015/09/23/are-the-un-and-wipo-drifting-apart/ (last visited Nov. 19, 2017).

Oguamanam, Chidi, Intellectual Property in Global Governance: A Development Question (2012).

Pattberg, Philipp, Frank Biermann, Sander Chan, and Ayşem Mert, *Introduction: Partnerships for Sustainable Development, in* Public-Private Partnerships for Sustainable Development: Emergence, Influence and Legitimacy (Philipp Pattberg, Frank Biermann, Sander Chan, and Ayşem Mert eds.).

Research4Life, *About*, www.research4life.org/about/ (last visited Nov. 19, 2017).

Research4Life, *Advisory Council*, www.research4life.org/about/advisory-council/ (last visited Nov. 19, 2017).

Research4Life 6, *Strategic Plan: Beyond the 2015 Horizon*, www.research4life.org/about/strategic-plan/ (last visited Nov. 19, 2017).

Rosenau, Pauline V., *The Strengths and Weaknesses of Public-Private Policy Partnerships*, 43 Am. Behav. Scientist, 10–34, 11 (1999).

Schäferhoff, Marco, Sabine Campe, and Christopher Kaan, *Transnational Public-Private Partnerships in International Relations: Making Sense of Concepts, Research Frameworks and Results*, 11 International Studies Review 451–474 (2007).

Sell, Susan, Public Power, Private Law: The Globalization of Intellectual Property Rights (2003).

U.N., System-Wide Outline of the Functions and Capacities of the U.N. Development System Consultant's Report (Jun. 2017), www.un.org/ecosoc/sites/www.un.org.ecosoc/files/files/en/qcpr/sg-report-dalberg_unds-outline-of-functions-and-capacities-june-2017.pdf (last visited Nov. 19, 2017).

U.N. Dep't of Econ. and Soc. Affairs, *Sustainable Development Knowledge Platform*, https://sustainabledevelopment.un.org/ (last visited Nov. 19, 2017).

U.N. Dep't of Econ. And Soc. Affairs, Sustainable Development Knowledge Platform, *Transforming Our World: The 2030 Agenda for Sustainable Development*, https://sustainabledevelopment.un.org/post2015/transformingourworld (last visited Nov. 19, 2017).

World Intellectual Property Organization, *Access to Research for Development and Innovation*, WIPO 2 (n.d.).

World Intellectual Property Organization, *Access to Research for Development and Innovation*, WIPO (Geneva: WIPO, n.d.), 2.

World Intellectual Property Organization, *Access to Research for Development and Innovation*, WIPO 5 (n.d.).

World Intellectual Property Organization, Agreement between the United Nations and the World Intellectual Property Organization, WIPO Doc. TRT/UN-WIPO/001 (1974).

World Intellectual Property Organization, *ARDI – Research for Innovation*, WIPO, www.wipo.int/ardi/en/ (last visited Nov. 19, 2017).

World Intellectual Property Organization, *Committee on Development and Intellectual Property (CDIP), Seventeenth Session: Summary by the Chair*, WIPO 2 (2016).

World Intellectual Property Organization. *Development Agenda for WIPO*, WIPO, www.wipo.int/ip-development/en/agenda/ (last visited Nov. 19, 2017).

World Intellectual Property Organization. *Elaboration on Proposal to Establish Development Agenda for WIPO*, IIM/1/4 (2005).

World Intellectual Property Organization, *Elaboration on Proposal to Establish Development Agenda for WIPO*, WIPO Doc. IIM/1/4, 22 item 66 (2005).

World Intellectual Property Organization, *Evaluation Report on the Project on Specialized Databases' Access and Support – Phase II*, WIPO Doc. CDIP/14/5 (2014).

World Intellectual Property Organization, *Frequently Asked Questions (FAQs) About ARDI*, WIPO www.wipo.int/ardi/en/faq/ (last visited Nov. 19, 2017).

World Intellectual Property Organization, *Harnessing the Power of the Private Sector – An Interview with Francis Gurry. WIPO MAGAZINE* September 2015, www.wipo.int/wipo_magazine/en/2015/05/article_0001.html (last visited Nov. 19, 2017).

World Intellectual Property Organization, *Mapping of WIPO Activities Related to the Sustainable Development Goals (SDGs) Implementation*, WIPO Doc. CDIP/17/8 (2016).

World Intellectual Property Organization, *Partners' Statement of Intent*, WIPO, www.wipo.int/ardi/en/statement.html (last visited Nov. 19, 2017).

World Intellectual Property Organization, *Projects for Implementation of Development Agenda Recommendations*, WIPO (2016), www.wipo.int/ip-development/en/agenda/projects.html (last visited Nov. 19, 2017).

World Intellectual Property Organization, *Proposal by Argentina and Brazil for the Establishment of a Development Agenda for WIPO*, WO/GA/31/11 (2004).

World Intellectual Property Organization, *Q&A: Proposed Program and Budget 2016/17 (and other PBC Documents)*, WIPO Doc. WO/PBC/24/Q & A (2015).

9 The Marrakesh Treaty, Public–Private Partnerships, and Access to Copyrighted Works by Visually Impaired Persons

Susan Isiko Štrba*

Introduction

Under the 2030 Agenda for Sustainable Development, the international community has prescribed partnerships as a mechanism for the implementation of the United Nation's Sustainable Development Goals (SDGs).[1] In particular, Goal 17 is about strengthening the means of implementation and revitalizing the global partnership for sustainable development.[2] Addressing systemic institutional issues, it spells out, in what seem precise terms, partnerships and their purpose. The global partnership for sustainable development is complemented by multi-stakeholder partnerships the purpose of which is to mobilize and share knowledge, expertise, technology, and financial resources, in order to support the achievement of the sustainable development goals in all countries, in particular developing countries.[3] In addition, this Goal aims to encourage and promote effective public, public–private, and civil society partnerships, by building on the experience and resourcing strategies of existing partnerships.[4] Thus the SDGs envisage public–private-partnerships (PPPs) to include public, private, and civil society stakeholders.

The World Intellectual Property Organization's (WIPO) Accessible Books Consortium (ABC or Consortium) is a partnership platform for mobilizing and sharing financial resources, knowledge, technology, and expertise. As will be discussed in more detail in this chapter, the ABC consists of public, private, and civil society partners, such as the Canadian National Institute for the Blind, International Authors Forum, and Sightsavers. The ABC's stated objective is to complement the entry into force of the Marrakesh Treaty to Facilitate Access to Published Works for Persons Who Are Blind, Visually Impaired, or Otherwise Print Disabled (Marrakesh Treaty or VIP Treaty).[5] Although created before the SDGs came into effect, the ABC corresponds to the broad description of partnership

* The author is grateful to the various people who availed themselves for interviews or responded to email enquiries and takes responsibility for any mistakes in this chapter.

1 G.A. A/Res/70/1, Transforming Our World: 2030 Agenda for Sustainable Development, ¶39 (Oct. 21, 2015).

2 *Goal 17: Revitalize the Global Partnership for Sustainable Development*, United Nations, www.un.org/sustainabledevelopment/globalpartnerships/ (last visited Aug. 9, 2016).

3 *Id.* (emphasis added).

4 *Id.*

5 Marrakesh Treaty to Facilitate Access to Published Works for Persons Who Are Blind, Visually Impaired, or Otherwise Print Disabled, June 27, 2013, VIP/DC/8 (entered into force Sept. 30, 2016) www.wipo.int/edocs/mdocs/diplconf/en/vip_dc/vip_dc_8_rev.pdf.

envisaged by the SDGs, and illustrates some of the potential benefits as well as challenges of partnerships to achieve development goals within global intellectual property (IP) regimes.

This chapter compares different approaches to realizing the SDGs through access to information and learning, especially by persons who are blind, visually impaired, or otherwise print disabled (VIPs). The Marrakesh Treaty by itself cannot solve the so-called[6] book famine,[7] but it does remove some legal obstacles, which then paves the way to establish necessary global infrastructures.[8] The parties to the VIP Treaty are committed to increasing the availability of published works for the VIPs community as quickly as possible, and this expected cooperation between these parties will be an important step toward achieving that goal. Thus, the VIP Treaty itself anticipates partnership amongst contracting states, authorized entities (which can be either public or nonprofit private entities), and the WIPO International Bureau. And as this chapter will make clear, the Consortium constitutes one possible initiative, amongst others, to implement the objectives of the Marrakesh VIP Treaty at a practical level. Equal access to copyrighted works in formats designed to be accessible to those with sight loss and print disabilities (accessible formats) will not be solved by limitations and exceptions to copyright (copyright L&Es) alone, as provided in the Marrakesh Treaty, but rather via multipronged approaches involving both public and private law and policy initiatives. In this sense, the ABC complements the Marrakesh Treaty by demonstrating methods to increase both inclusive publishing as well as capacity building to use accessible formats by all readers, including VIPs.

Understanding both the ABC and the Marrakesh Treaty therefore allows fuller appreciation of the extent to which the ABC complements the entry into force of the Treaty. It also provides a basis for evaluating how well either of these approaches alone, or both working together, contribute toward the SDGs. The Marrakesh Treaty aims to increase the number of published books in accessible formats designed for use by VIPs through copyright L&Es enacted into public legal frameworks. By contrast, the ABC's objective is to increase the number of books world-wide that are available for use by print-disabled people through licensing agreements between private parties. The approaches of the Marrakesh Treaty and the ABC may differ, but their aims remain similar. And arguably, both the Marrakesh Treaty and the ABC indirectly contribute toward Goal 4 of the SDGs, in which the international community aspires to "[e]nsure inclusive and equitable quality education and promote lifelong learning opportunities for all."[9] This Goal can be realized in part by access to information and learning. Indeed, during the first discussion at WIPO on the needs of VIPs, the World Blind Union (WBU), speaking on

[6] Book famine refers to the lack of books accessible to print-disabled people in which "only 5% of books are made available in accessible formats such as large print, audio or braille." *See On Track For A Book Without Borders*, World Blind Union, www.worldblindunion.org/English/our-work/our-priorities/Pages/On-Track-For-A-Book-Without-Borders.aspx (last visited July 14, 2017).

[7] Harpur, Paul and Nicolar Suzor, *Copyright Protections and Disability Rights: Turning the Page to a New International Paradigm*, 36 University of New South Wales Law Journal 745–747 (2013); Shaver, Lea, *The Right to Read*, 54 Columbia Journal of Transnational Law 1, 36 (2015).

[8] This idea was developed during an email exchange with Teresa Hackett, Copyright and Libraries Programme Manager, Electronic Information for Libraries (July 30, 2016).

[9] *Goal 4: Ensure Inclusive and Quality Education for all and Promote Lifelong Learning*, United Nations, www.un.org/sustainabledevelopment/education/ (last visited Mar. 17, 2017). Target 3 under this Goal is to "ensure equal access for all women and men to affordable and quality technical, vocational and tertiary education, including university" by 2030. *Id.*

behalf of VIPs, highlighted "the balance that should be struck between copyright and rights of access to information and learning."[10]

This chapter explores the contribution of the ABC as a type of partnership (multi-stakeholder and/or PPP) to the implementation of the SDGs, especially Goal 4. Based on interviews conducted in 2016 with participating stakeholders in the ABC (including WIPO, representatives of libraries, VIP communities, and publishers), the chapter first maps the challenge of access to information by VIPs, highlighting the role of copyright. It then provides a background to the Marrakesh Treaty and summarizes its main provisions. The next section describes in detail the ABC – what it is and how it works. Following this description is a detailed evaluation of the ABC as a partnership. The chapter concludes by discussing the achievements, shortcomings, and challenges of the ABC, highlighting lessons for implementing the Marrakesh Treaty, and suggesting how the IP goals of innovation and access to information may be realized through partnerships implementing the SDGs.

I Copyright and Access to Information for VIPs

International copyright law recognizes the need to balance the rights of authors of creative works with the public interest, by allowing some uses of copyrighted material without having to seek authorization from the rightsholder or to pay royalties. The legal foundation of international copyright law, the Berne Convention for the Protection of Literary and Artistic Works of 1886 (Berne Convention),[11] and its subsequent revisions, all contain provisions for L&Es to copyright. The Berne Convention provides specific exemptions, for example, for short quotations, news reporting, and illustrative use for teaching purposes.[12] Otherwise, national governments have the freedom to define what limitations and exceptions are permitted "in certain special cases, provided that such reproduction does not conflict with a normal exploitation of the work and does not unreasonably prejudice the legitimate interests of the author" – the so-called three-step test.[13] Subsequent IP treaties like the Agreement on Trade-related Aspects of Intellectual Property Rights (TRIPS)[14] and the WIPO Copyright Treaty (WCT)[15] also contain

[10] World Blind Union, Presentation at the Standing Committee on Copyright and Related Rights, Information Meeting on Digital Content for the Visually Impaired (Nov. 3, 2003).

[11] Berne Convention for the Protection of Literary and Artistic Works (9 Sept. 1886), TRT/BERNE/001, (as revised by the Act of Stockholm (1967), and by the Paris Act (1971) and amended in 1979), Publication of the World Intellectual Property Organization no. 287(E) (hereinafter Berne Convention).

[12] The Berne Convention, *supra* note 11, article 10(2).

[13] The Berne Convention, *supra* note 11, art 9(2). This is often referred to as the three-step test. *See* Martin Senftleben, Copyright, Limitations and the Three-Step Test: An Analysis of the Three-Step Test in International and EC Copyright Law, 52 (2004).

[14] Agreement on Trade-Related Aspects of Intellectual Property Rights, Annex 1C to the Marrakesh Agreement Establishing the World Trade Organization, 15 April 1994, *in* World Trade Organization, The Results of the Uruguay Round of Multilateral Negotiations, The Legal Texts. Geneva: WTO (1995) (hereinafter TRIPS Agreement).

[15] WIPO Copyright Treaty, adopted in Geneva on December 20, 1996 (entered into force on Mar. 6, 2002), WIPO Publication no. 226(E) (*hereinafter* WCT).

various formulations on L&Es, including the three-step test, in responding to developments in the technological environment.[16]

Various studies show that L&Es contained in national copyright laws vary widely.[17] In this context it is relevant to note that the WCT provides for Technological Protection Measures (TPM) and Rights Management Information (RMI).[18] In the digital environment, legally permitted L&Es can be rendered impossible to use by TPMs. In addition, in many countries, copying for private use is free, yet only a few countries make exceptions for distance learning.[19] Moreover, any national exemptions apply only in the country concerned and do not apply across national borders. The general lack of explicit national laws on permitted uses, combined with lack of international harmonization on copyright L&Es, creates legal uncertainty, especially in the digital environment in which copies of copyrighted works can be made and transmitted across borders with a few mouse clicks.[20] Against this background, WIPO's Standing Committee on Copyright and Related Rights (SCCR), a committee charged with norm setting in the field of copyright and related rights[21] has been considering international harmonization of certain L&Es since 2004.[22]

A *Background to the Marrakesh Treaty*

According to the World Health Organization, there are more than 285 million visually impaired persons in the world, 90 per cent of whom live in developing countries.[23] The World Blind Union estimates that less than 10 per cent of published books can be read by blind or low vision people in developed countries.[24] In developing countries, the situation is even worse, as less than 1 per cent of books are ever made into accessible formats such as braille, DAISY, audio, large print, e-books, or other formats.[25] For example, while the library of the Organización Nacional de Ciegos Españoles

[16] Ruth L. Okediji, *International Copyright Limitations and Exceptions as Development Policy*, *in* REFRAMING COPYRIGHT LAW IN THE AGE OF LIMITATIONS AND EXCEPTIONS, 429, 444 (Ruth L. Okediji ed., 2017).

[17] Lucie Guibault, *The Nature and Scope of Limitations and Exceptions to Copyright and Neighbouring Rights with Regard to General Interest Missions for the Transmission of Knowledge: Prospects for Their Adaptation to the Digital Environment*, E-COPYRIGHT BULL., 1, 40 (2003); Judith Sullivan, *Study on Copyright Limitations and Exceptions for Visually Impaired Persons*, Standing Committee on Copyright and Related Rights, Fifteenth Session, Sept. 11–13, 2006, WIPO Doc. SCCR/15/7 (Feb. 20, 2007); Susan Isiko Štrba, "*A Model for Access to Educational Resources and Innovation in Developing Countries,*" *in* INTELLECTUAL PROPERTY, TRADE AND DEVELOPMENT: STRATGIES TO OPTIMISE DEVELOPMENT IN A TRIPS-PLUS ERA 286, 294 (Daniel Gervais ed., 2015).

[18] WCT, *supra* note 15, articles 11–12.

[19] Štrba, *supra* note 17, at 294.

[20] ACCESSIBLE BOOKS CONSORTIUM, www.accessiblebooksconsortium.org (last visited June 10, 2016).

[21] STANDING COMMITTEE ON COPYRIGHT AND RELATED RIGHTS, www.wipo.int/policy/en/sccr/ (last visited 28 July 2017).

[22] Proposal by Chile on the Subject "Limitations and Exceptions to Copyright and Related Rights," Standing Committee on Copyright and Related Rights, Twelfth Session, Nov. 17 – 19, 2004, WIPO Doc. SCCR/12/3 (Nov. 2, 2004).

[23] *Visual Impairment and Blindness*, fact Sheet No. 282, WORLD HEALTH ORGANIZATION, www.who.int/mediacentre/factsheets/fs282/en/ (last visited June 15, 2016).

[24] *Millions of People are Denied Access to Books and Printed Materials - WBU Press Release for World Book and Copyright Day*, WORLD BLIND UNION, www.worldblindunion.org/English/news/Pages/Millions-of-People-are-Denied-Access-to-.aspx (last visited Mar. 15, 2017).

[25] *Id.*

(National Organization of Spanish Blind People) in Spain has more than one hundred thousand titles in accessible formats and Argentina has over fifty thousand such titles, these cannot be shared with the nineteen Spanish-speaking countries across Latin America. Similarly, some years ago, charities working in five English-speaking countries, including the Royal National Institute for the Blind in the United Kindom and Vision Australia, were obliged to produce five identical braille master files for the same Harry Potter book, costing them valuable time and money for this duplication.[26]

A WIPO survey in 2006 found that fewer than sixty countries have copyright L&Es clauses in their copyright laws that make special provision for VIPs, for example, by permitting braille, large print, or digitized audio versions of copyrighted texts.[27] Furthermore, due to the territorial nature of copyright law, national copyright L&Es usually do not cover the import or export of works converted into accessible formats, even between countries with similar legal rules. Organizations serving VIPs in each country must negotiate licenses with the rightsholders to either exchange special formats across borders, or produce their own materials. Both of these are costly undertakings that severely limit access by the beneficiaries to printed works of all kinds.

Member States of WIPO have sought to harmonize copyright L&Es more generally. Outside of the specific context of access to copyrighted works by VIPs, the first attempt at harmonization of copyright L&Es at WIPO was a 2005 proposal by Chile to the SCCR to establish an agreement on L&Es for purposes of public interest. This proposal envisaged a minimum standard of L&Es in all national copyright legislation for the benefit of the community, "especially to give access to the most vulnerable or socially prioritized sectors."[28] Proposals for discussions on L&E harmonization ran parallel to calls for inclusion of a development dimension in WIPO's work. In 2004, a year prior to the Chilean proposal, Argentina and Brazil launched a proposal for a development agenda for WIPO.[29] The push for L&Es gained momentum after the adoption of the WIPO Development Agenda in 2007.[30] At its Sixteenth Session in 2008, the SCCR for the first time formally included the topic of L&Es on its agenda. The delegations of Brazil, Chile, Nicaragua, and Uruguay had submitted a proposal for further discussions on copyright L&Es. They proposed that SCCR create a work plan for mandatory minimum L&Es, especially with regard to educational activities, people with disabilities, libraries, and archives. Furthermore, they proposed copyright exceptions to foster technological innovation, as well as formal recognition and commitment to creating mandatory minimum L&Es by appropriate means, such as by amendments to existing treaties and/or national legislation.[31] In making their case for L&Es, some delegations charged that "discussions

[26] *Limitations and Exceptions: Access to Books for the Visually Impaired – Background Brief*, WIPO Press, www.wipo.int/pressroom/en/briefs/limitations.html#note (last visited June 15, 2016).

[27] Sullivan, *supra* note 17, at 70.

[28] *See supra* note 22.

[29] Proposal by Argentina and Brazil for the Establishment of a Development Agenda for WIPO, WIPO General Assembly, Thirty-first (15th Ordinary) Session, Mar. 10–12, 2008, WIPO Doc. WO/GA/31/11 (Sept. 27, 2004).

[30] Assemblies of the Member States of WIPO, Forty-Third Series of meetings, Sept. 24–3 Oct. 2007, WIPO Doc. A/43/6 E, Annex (Nov. 12, 2007).

[31] *Proposal by Brazil, Chile, Nicaragua and Uruguay for Work Related to L&Es*, Standing Committee on Copyright and Related Rights, Sixteenth Session, Mar. 10–12, 2008, WIPO Doc. SCCR/16/2 (E) (July 17, 2008).

on limitations and exceptions should be deliberated in the light of the implementation of the WIPO Development Agenda which was approved by the General Assembly."[32]

At the Seventeenth Session of the SCCR in 2009,[33] delegations and NGOs made their case that copyright L&Es were directly related to the WIPO Development Agenda, with the objective of promoting access to knowledge.[34] Subsequently, the SCCR acknowledged the special needs of visually impaired persons and stressed the importance of dealing with the needs of VIPs, without undue delay. The Committee agreed to a two-pronged work program, which was to include both analysis of L&Es on the one hand, and the possible establishment of a Stakeholders' Platform at WIPO, through which technological, contractual, and other arrangements could be facilitated to secure access for the disabled persons to protected works, on the other.[35] Eventually, this Platform was established and evolved in the Consortium described in detail in this chapter. The ABC is a multi-stakeholder partnership of fifteen institutions including WIPO, organizations that serve or represent VIPs, as well as authorized entities, rightsholders,[36] and any other organization that has an active interest in the objectives of the ABC.

Member States of WIPO began discussion of exemptions to international copyright law with a view to boosting the global availability of works in accessible formats. Hundreds of negotiators from nations around the world convened in Morocco in 2013 to finalize an international treaty designed to ease access to published material for VIPs, through L&Es to copyright.[37] The meeting in Marrakesh, hosted by the Kingdom of Morocco and WIPO, was the culmination of over a decade of discussions on how to bring more accessible works in formats like braille, large print, and audio books to the beneficiaries, many of whom live in lower-income countries.[38] The preceding decade of discussions reflected the sensitivity of issues and difficulty in coming to a mutually agreed solution, but the final negotiations were surprisingly rapid. They resulted in the June 2013 adoption by WIPO Member States of the Marrakesh Treaty to Facilitate Access to Published Works for Persons Who Are Blind, Visually Impaired, or Otherwise Print Disabled.[39] The Marrakesh Treaty was to enter into force three months after 20 WIPO Members ratified or acceded to it.[40] On 30 June 2016, Canada deposited its instrument of

[32] WIPO, *supra* note 30, at ¶ 69.

[33] Standing Committee on Copyright and Related Rights, Seventeenth Session, Geneva, November 3 to 7, 2008.

[34] Report, Standing Committee on Copyright and Related Rights, Seventeenth Session, Nov. 3–7, 2008, WIPO Doc. SCCR/17/5 (Mar. 25, 2009), *see, e.g.*, ¶ 20, 28, 54, 122.

[35] *Id.* at Annex I.

[36] According to the Governance Document Establishing the ABC, "Rightsholders" means authors and publishers of books. *See* Accessible Books Consortium (Mar. 16, 2016) www.accessiblebooksconsortium.org/export/sites/visionip/portal/en/doc/abc_governance.doc (last visited June 10, 2016).

[37] Diplomatic Conference to Conclude a Treaty to Facilitate Access to Published Works by Visually Impaired Persons and Persons with Print Disabilities, June 17–28, 2013 WIPO Doc. VIP/DC/INF (2013).

[38] The first discussion on the subject within the WIPO framework took place in the form of an Information meeting on the sidelines of the SCCR. WIPO, Information Meeting on Digital Content for the Visually Impaired, WIPO Doc. DIGVI/IM/03 (Nov. 3, 2003).

[39] *Historic Treaty Adopted, Boosts Access to Books for Visually Impaired Persons Worldwide*, WIPO, www.wipo.int/pressroom/en/articles/2013/article_0017.html (last visited June 6, 2016).

[40] Marrakesh Treaty, *supra* note 5, article 18.

accession, bringing the number of ratifications to 20.[41] Accordingly the Treaty entered into force on 30 September 2016.

The Marrakesh Treaty is the latest addition to the international copyright treaties administered by WIPO. It has a clear humanitarian and social development dimension; its main goal is to create a set of mandatory L&Es, so as to increase the number of books in accessible formats for the benefit of VIPs. It addresses what is commonly referred to as a book famine by requiring the member states who have joined the treaty (contracting parties) to introduce a standard set of L&Es to copyright rules in order to permit reproduction, distribution, and the making available of published works in accessible formats.[42] The treaty also provides for the exchange of these accessible format works, made under copyright L&Es or otherwise pursuant to the operation of law, by organizations that serve VIPs.[43] Thus it is intended to facilitate the harmonization of copyright L&Es so that these organizations can operate across borders. Significantly, an authorized entity is permitted to distribute or make available accessible copies to another authorized entity or beneficiary person in another contracting party, without authorization of the rightsholder.[44] As defined in the treaty, an "authorized entity" is "an entity that is authorized or recognized by the government to provide education, instructional training, adaptive reading or information access to beneficiary persons on a nonprofit basis. It also includes a government institution or nonprofit organization that provides the same services to beneficiary persons as one of its primary activities or institutional obligations."[45]

The Marrakesh Treaty is also designed to provide assurances to authors and publishers that the system will not expose their published works either to misuse or to distribute to anyone other than the intended beneficiaries. Therefore, the treaty reiterates the requirement that the cross-border sharing of works that are created based on copyright L&Es must be limited by a three-step test, that is, to certain special cases that do not conflict with the normal exploitation of the work and do not unreasonably prejudice the legitimate interests of the author or rightsholder.[46]

Of importance for this chapter's focus, the VIP Treaty calls for international cooperation amongst its contracting parties in order to foster the anticipated cross-border exchanges.[47] As stated earlier, the VIP Treaty thus creates a type of partnership amongst contracting states, authorized entities (which can be either public or nonprofit private entities), and the WIPO International Bureau. It encourages voluntary sharing of information amongst authorized entities and designates WIPO as the information access

[41] *Canada's Accession to Marrakesh Treaty Brings Treaty into Force*, WIPO Press Room, www.wipo.int/pressroom/en/articles/2016/article_0007.html (last visited June 30, 2016). *See also* Information on contracting parties to Marrakesh Treaty, WIPO, www.wipo.int/treaties/en/ShowResults.jsp?lang=en&treaty_id=843 (last visited Aug. 6, 2016).

[42] The Marrakesh Treaty defines "accessible format copy" as a copy of a work in an alternative manner or form which gives a beneficiary person access to the work, including to permit the person to have access as feasibly and comfortably as a person without visual impairment or other print disability. Marrakesh Treaty, *supra* note 5, article 2(b).

[43] *Id.* article 5.

[44] *Id.* article 5(a) and (b).

[45] *Id.* article 2(c).

[46] *Id.* article 11. This article duplicates the language of the three-step test in the TRIPS Agreement, which refers to legitimate interests of the rightsholder, and that of the Berne Convention and the WIPO Copyright Treaty which refer to the legitimate interests of the author.

[47] *Id.* article 9(4).

point. At the same time, contracting parties to the treaty are required to endeavour to foster cross-border exchanges of accessible formats by encouraging the voluntary sharing of information to assist authorized entities to identify each other, as well as to assist their authorized entities to make information available.[48]

Through the implementation of the Marrakesh Treaty provisions, it is anticipated that sharing of works in accessible formats should increase the overall number of works available, by eliminating duplication and therefore increasing efficiency. For example, instead of five countries producing accessible versions of the same work, any one of the five countries will be able to produce a single accessible version of a single work, which can then be shared with each of the other countries in need of that accessible format.[49]

II The Accessible Books Consortium

In parallel to the negotiation of the Marrakesh Treaty, WIPO invited key stakeholders to form a Stakeholders' Platform to work on a number of practical pilot projects, and to report regularly to the SCCR on their activities. It may be recalled that the Stakeholder's Platform was initially envisioned within the SCCR discussions as a forum through which technological, contractual, and other arrangements could be facilitated to secure access for VIPs to protected works.[50] In May 2014, the Stakeholder's Platform recommended to WIPO's Member States that it be moved from an initial phase to a permanent institutional structure.[51] The result was the ABC, which was launched in June 2014.

The ABC is a multi-stakeholder partnership of fifteen institutions including WIPO, organizations that serve or represent VIPs, as well as authorized entities, rightsholders, and any other organization that has an active interest in the objectives of the ABC.[52] Although the establishment of the ABC predates the SDGs, the ABC exemplifies the definitions provided in SDG 17 of multi-stakeholder and public–private partnerships. And although the ABC was established before the adoption of the Marrakesh Treaty in June 2013, it uses the same definition of "authorized entity" found in the Marrakesh Treaty, a negotiated definition acceptable to both publishers and intended beneficiaries of the Marrakesh Treaty.[53]

48 *Id.* article 9.

49 Laurence R. Helfer et al., The World Blind Union Guide to the Marrakesh Treaty, 51–59 (2017).

50 WIPO, *supra* note 37.

51 Eight Interim Report of the Stakeholders Platform, Standing Committee on Copyright and Related Rights, Twenty-seventh Session, Apr. 28–May 2, 2014, WIPO Doc. SCCR/27/4, www.wipo.int/meetings/en/doc_details.jsp?doc_id=272272 (last visited June 6. 2016).

52 At the time of writing, (March 2017), the following 15 institutions were partners to the ABC: Canadian National Institute for the Blind, DAISY Consortium, Dorina Nowill Foundation for the Blind, Elsevier, International Authors' Forum (IAF), International Council for Education of People with Visual Impairment, International Federation of Library Associations and Institutions (IFLA), International Federation of Reproduction Rights Organizations (IFRRO), Perkins School for the Blind, International Publishers' Association (IPA), Publishers' Association of South Africa (PASA), Sightsavers, South African Library for the Blind, World Blind Union (WBU), and WIPO. Information available at www.accessiblebooksconsortium.org/about/en/ (last visited Mar. 15, 2017). According to the Governance Document Establishing the ABC, "Rightsholders" means authors and publishers of books. *See* Accessible Books Consortium, Mar. 16, 2016, www.accessiblebooksconsortium.org/export/sites/visionip/portal/en/doc/abc_governance.doc (last visited June 10, 2016).

53 Marrakesh Treaty, *supra* note 5, article 2(c).

The objective of the ABC, as stated in its governance document, is to complement the entry into force of the Marrakesh Treaty. The aim of the Consortium is to contribute meaningfully to ending the book famine by increasing the number of books worldwide in accessible formats – such as braille, audio, and large print – and to make them available to VIPs.[54] It is hoped that this will be accomplished in accordance with the Marrakesh VIP Treaty and other applicable WIPO treaties. The ABC constitutes one possible initiative, amongst others, to implement the objectives of the Marrakesh Treaty at a practical level.[55]

In terms of governance, the ABC secretariat is located at WIPO's headquarters in Geneva, Switzerland, and is audited by the WIPO Auditor.[56] The ABC is governed by a Board comprised of a maximum of nineteen members,[57] and is chaired by the WIPO Director General or his representative. The purpose of the Board is to provide technical expertise to the Consortium and to ensure transparency and efficient communication with the stakeholder community. The Board includes members from organizations representing people with print disabilities, libraries serving the print disabled, organizations representing publishers and authors, and major donors.

An appreciation of the role of the ABC as a PPP in implementing the SDGs calls for a clear understanding of how the ABC works and evaluation of its achievements. The activities of the ABC include: (a) development and implementation of appropriate tools, systems and business processes, such as the Trusted Intermediary Global Accessible Resources ("TIGAR") service; (b) capacity building to improve relevant skills and knowledge in order to increase the number of accessible books for VIPs in developing and least developed countries; (c) promotion and training of publishers in the use of accessible format technologies; and (d) encouraging cooperation and fostering relationships amongst VIPs, authorized entities, rightsholders, and technology companies.[58] These activities are carried out through three main projects; the TIGAR project, the Capacity Building project, and the Inclusive Publishing project, which are described in detail later in this chapter.

A *Trusted Intermediary Global Accessible Resources*

The TIGAR service is a global library of books in accessible formats that supports institutions serving the needs of the VIPs community.[59] Hosted by WIPO, the TIGAR is a joint collection of seventeen international catalogues, representing more than 315,000 fully produced titles in fifty-five different languages. It allows libraries to share items in their collections rather than duplicating the costs of converting them to accessible formats. Participating libraries[60] contribute their catalogues of searchable titles

[54] Accessible Books Consortium, Governance Document Establishing the Consortium, article 2, www.accessiblebooksconsortium.org/export/sites/visionip/portal/en/doc/abc_governance.doc.

[55] *Id.*

[56] *Id.*

[57] As of August 2, 2016, the Board was composed of fifteen entities who were also the multi-stakeholders.

[58] Accessible Books Consortium, *supra* note 54, article 3.

[59] The ABC refers only to print disabled which is a narrower group than "blind, visually impaired, or otherwise print disabled" addressed by the Marrakesh Treaty.

[60] As of July 31, 2016, there were nineteen institutions participating in the TIGAR, as follows: Visability (Australia), Vision Australia (Australia), Dovina Nowill Foundation for the Blind (Brazil), Canadian

to the TIGAR service to make accessible format books available to VIPs as well as to enable secure and transparent file exchange amongst institutions for use by institutions serving the needs of those within the VIPs community. The TIGAR makes it easier for participating institutions to search internationally for books in accessible formats, and to exchange them across national borders.

Thus far, over seventy-nine thousand people with print disabilities have borrowed accessible books through the nineteen participating libraries in the TIGAR,[61] with the South African Library for the Blind (SALB) alone borrowing over six hundred titles within a period of six months in 2016.[62] Participation in the TIGAR is free of charge, meaning there is no membership fee or financial contribution required from a participating institution or end-user. In theory, a participating institution lacking the capacity to contribute material to the catalogue can still download books. However, for an institution to use the material, it must be designated an authorized entity as defined in the Marrakesh Treaty. There is no mechanism to scrutinise and admit such entities to the TIGAR, but the tendency is to pick from those already established institutions accepted by rightsholders or publishers as qualifying authorized entities. The risk with this approach is that entities not acknowledged as authorized entities before TIGAR was established may never be admitted.

The type of material in the TIGAR is mostly for leisure reading. The explanation for this is that the major clients of most institutions involved in the TIGAR project are elderly who have aged into blindness.[63] An example of this kind of participating library is the Canadian National Institute for the Blind, which was founded just after the First World War. Thus, the material primarily available through TIGAR does not address all the needs of VIPs, including their access to educational materials.

In terms of copyright, the TIGAR service sets out conditions for participants for the exchange of copyrighted materials, based on individual licensing arrangements. The TIGAR currently requires that permission be granted by copyright holders in order to allow the cross-border exchange of electronic files of accessible books that have already been produced legitimately by an institution. WIPO negotiates the licences on behalf of institutions interested in using any book listed in the catalogue, as there is some concern that most institutions will not be granted the permission if they negotiated on their own.[64] By contrast, once the Marrakesh Treaty is implemented via national legislation by

National Institute for the Blind (Canada), Danish National Library for Persons with Print Disabilities (Nota) (Denmark), Association Valentin Haüy (France), Celia Library (Finland), Icelandic Talking Books Library (HBS) (Iceland), National Council for the Blind of Ireland (Ireland), Dedicon (Netherlands), Royal New Zealand Foundation of the Blind (New Zealand), South African Library for the Blind (South Africa), Swedish Agency for Accessible Media (MTM) (Sweden), Association pour le Bien des Aveugles et Malvayants (Switzerland), Swiss Library for the Blind, Visually Impaired and Print Disabled (Switzerland), Bibliothèque Sonore Romande (Switzerland), National Library Service for the Blind and Physically Handicapped (United States), information available at www.accessiblebooksconsortium.org/tigar/en/ (last visited 2 Aug. 2016).

61 Accessible Books Consortium, www.accessiblebooksconsortium.org/portal/en/ (last visited June 2016).

62 SALB reported that its members had downloaded 180 titles during the period January to March 2016 (South African Library for the Blind, Nakwenzeke Newsletter, 1 (March 2016) and 224 titles in the period April to June 2016. South African Library for the Blind, Nakwenzeke Newsletter, 3 (June 2016).

63 Interview with Monica Hallil Lövblad, Coordinator of ABC, WIPO Secretariat (June 14, 2016).

64 Interview with Michael Jung, WIPO Secretariat (May 26, 2016).

the countries that have ratified the Treaty, permission clearance should no longer be required in cross-border exchanges involving the contracting states.

Additionally, an institution that participates in the TIGAR service must confirm that it has adequate security mechanisms in place to prevent unauthorized access to electronic files of accessible books that it has received and also that it does not make a profit through the distribution of electronic files of those books.[65] The TIGAR catalogue includes only collections agreed to by the publisher. Of the nineteen institutions participating in the TIGAR, only three are from developing countries: Bangladesh, Brazil, and South Africa. This might be explained by lack of capacity of developing country-based authorized entities to provide assurances of adequate security mechanisms to prevent unauthorised access.[66] As will become clearer later, the Capacity Building and Inclusive Publishing projects aim at addressing this problem. The books produced by Bangladesh under capacity building are supplied to TIGAR.[67]

To mark the entry into force of the Marrakesh Treaty on 30 September 2016, WIPO organized a symbolic transfer of accessible books in audio format from Canada to Australia through the book service of the ABC. For the first time, this transfer occurred without the legal obligation to request permission from the copyright owners. The transfer from the Canadian National Institute for the Blind to Vision Australia via the ABC Book Service means that Vision Australia does not need to reproduce the books themselves, thereby incurring savings of approximately US$2,000 per book.[68] It should be noted that both Canada and Australia are parties to the Marrakesh Treaty and at the same time users of the TIGAR catalogue. There is no guarantee that the transfer of books, symbolic or otherwise, would be possible between countries that are not parties to the Treaty. This is because under ABC, the exchange of books is subject to individual licensing arrangements. No standard licence exists, which makes it necessary for WIPO to negotiate individually with the TIGAR participating entity whose books have been requested to be borrowed.

B *Capacity Building Project*

A second way through which the ABC conducts it activities is capacity building. Through its Capacity Building Project, the ABC seeks public and private sector partners to collaborate on diverse projects to help build the technical skills in developing and least developed countries to produce and distribute books in accessible formats. A key objective of the project is to share technical skills so organizations that support VIPs – including the publishing industry and national government services – can build their capacity to

[65] Accessible Books Consortium, www.accessiblebooksconsortium.org/tigar/en/ (Mar. 15, 2017).

[66] In principle only publishing entities can be part of the TIGAR. However, following criticisms that the ABC was for the "elite" and not representative of VIPs' needs, efforts were made to work out a criterion to include nonpublishing entities while at the same time catering for the concerns of publishers. Semi-structured confidential telephone interview with the ABC representative of the International Council of Educators for the Visually Impaired on May 27, 2016.

[67] Jung, *supra* note 64.

[68] *First Cross-Border Book Transfer by ABC Following Entry Into Force of Marrakesh Treaty*, ACCESSIBLE BOOKS CONSORTIUM, www.accessiblebooksconsortium.org/news/en/2016/news_0010.html, (last visited Oct. 3, 2016).

produce, convert, and distribute accessible format versions of books. In partnership with the DAISY Consortium,[69] the ABC provides technical training in developing countries to local NGOs, education ministries, and commercial publishers to facilitate the production and distribution of books in accessible formats. Various activities fall under capacity building, including:

- training and assisting organizations that serve people with print disabilities to produce and distribute educational materials in accessible formats in national languages;
- training organizations how to use the TIGAR service to obtain books in accessible formats that are available internationally;
- organizing training workshops on accessible publishing techniques for publishers and government services producing educational materials for schools;
- training in developing countries for local NGOs, government departments, and commercial publishers who want to produce and distribute their books in accessible formats;
- training people with print disabilities on the use of reading devices;
- helping establish local libraries for people with print disabilities, including a "loaning system" for reading devices;
- providing funding to institutions to produce accessible materials in local languages; and
- building links amongst government agencies, organizations serving people with print disabilities, IT developers, and publishers to ensure enhanced awareness amongst all stakeholders about the production of materials in accessible formats, as well as the availability of reading devices.[70]

Action is required at many levels in developing and least developed countries to help produce school books in national languages or languages of instruction in accessible formats. Through partnerships, the ABC has tried to respond to the accessibility needs of local communities by boosting the availability of books in accessible formats in local languages. For example, a project in Bangladesh is training a local organization to produce accessible educational materials in Bengali, and teaching blind students to use reading devices. Through funding received from the Government of Australia, the project in Bangladesh enabled workers from an NGO in Bangladesh to go to India, and to receive training in the latest technologies including training in producing audio books. Back in Bangladesh, these trainees are now using their new skills to convert into audio those books that are most needed by students at the University of Chittagong.[71]

Apart from India and Bangladesh, other capacity building activities are being conducted in Sri Lanka and Nepal. The activities include training of NGOs, Ministry of Education, and Commercial Publishers, to produce so-called born accessible books – meaning the books are already in accessible formats when produced (discussed in more

[69] Daisy Consortium, www.daisy.org/ (last visited July 28, 2017).

[70] Accessible Books Consortium, www.accessiblebooksconsortium.org/portal/en/index.html (last visited June 6, 2016).

[71] Accessible Books Consortium, www.accessiblebooksconsortium.org/export/abc/abc_brochure.pdf (last visited June 6, 2016).

detail in the next section). It is reported that the ABC, through the capacity building projects, financed an NGO to produce born accessible formats within just a year.[72]

ABC is also expanding its capacity building projects to other parts of the world. As a result of discussions held at the Africa Forum on the unavailability of accessible educational materials, the Consortium invited project proposals from organizations in Africa working on the problem of accessibility.[73] This is one way of increasing production of accessible format books in developing countries.

C *Inclusive or Born Accessible Publishing*

Inclusive publishing is the promotion within the commercial publishing industry of accessible book production techniques so that published books are usable from the outset by both sighted people and those with print disabilities. The idea of inclusive publishing was first floated by the International Federation of Library Associations and Institutions (IFLA) during the very first WIPO meeting on VIPs in November 2003.[74] The Libraries for the Blind section of IFLA suggested cooperation and consultations between libraries for the blind, WIPO, and IP institutions in "publishing for all."[75]

The WIPO ABC Inclusive Publishing project (formally the "Enabling Technologies Framework") aims to promote publishing processes through which publishers deliver born accessible publications. It is believed that properly engineered publishing processes should be able to yield digital products that can be used effectively by every member of society. The target is for the same product to be usable by print disabled at the same time they are published for sighted people.[76]

This project includes various activities to promote accessible book production techniques within the commercial publishing industry. The ABC is a sponsor of the Charter for Accessible Publishing,[77] to which publishers of all kinds are invited to sign, and the Accessibility Guidelines (ABC Charter). The ABC Charter contains fundamental principles that publishers are required to adhere to with the aim of making their ebooks and other digital publications accessible to persons with print disabilities. As of 30 June 2016, six major publishers' associations had endorsed the ABC Charter.[78] In addition, the ABC provides three types of Accessibility Guidelines for inclusive publishers on publishing in accessible formats.[79] The Accessibility Guidelines highlight some of the potential

[72] Interview with Monica Hallil Lövblad, Coordinator of ABC, WIPO Secretariat (June 14, 2016).

[73] *ABC at the African Forum: Support Available for Educational Accessibility Projects*, Accessible Books Consortium, www.accessiblebooksconsortium.org/news/en/2015/news_0007.html (last visited Oct. 11, 2016.)

[74] Information Meeting on Digital Content for the Visually Impaired, Standing Committee on Copyright and Related Rights, Presentation by IFLA/Libraries for the Blind, ¶ 7 (Nov. 3, 2003).

[75] *Id.*

[76] Accessible Books Consortium, Inclusive Publishing, www.accessiblebooksconsortium.org/publishing/en/ (last visited June 6, 2016).

[77] Accessible Books Consortium, Charter for Accessible Publishing, www.accessiblebooksconsortium.org/export/sites/visionip/publishing/en/pdf/accessible_best_practice_guidelines_for_publishers.pdf (last visited June 6, 2016).

[78] *ABC Snapshot: News from Accessible Books Consortium*, Accessible Books Consortium, http://accessiblebooksconsortium.org/news/en/2016/news_0006.html (June 30, 2016) (last visited July 10, 2016).

[79] These are the Books for all Starter Kit for Accessible Publishing in Developing and Least Developed Countries; the Accessible eBook Guidelines for Self-Publishing Authors, which was launched recently by the ABC; and the Accessible Publishing Best Practice Guidelines for Publishers.

challenges and outline steps to help publishers make their works more accessible to people with print disabilities.

A few points relevant to understanding of the nature of the ABC partnership and its contribution to implementing the SDGs are described briefly here. The ABC Books for All Starter Kit for Accessible Publishing in Developing and Least Developed Countries (Kit)[80] provides stakeholders in these countries with information on how they can work together to significantly increase the number of books in accessible formats at the national level. The writing of the Kit was a partnership between the DAISY Consortium and the Centre for Internet and Society (India), with funding from the Government of Australia. The involvement of the Centre for Internet and Society, which was very active in negotiating the Marrakesh Treaty, arguably renders credibility to the Kit as one of the means to increase the number of works in accessible formats.

The Kit draws on the experience of the ABC's training and technical assistance projects established in Bangladesh, India, Nepal, and Sri Lanka. These four pilot projects resulted in the production of 1,588 educational books in national languages in accessible formats, which benefited 23,500 students with sight loss and print disabilities. The Kit highlights the importance of a multi-stakeholder approach to inclusive publishing, which is necessary for producing and making available accessible formats. A range of organizations is required to contribute to the many different components of a national "Books for All" strategy, which include:

- production of books in accessible formats;
- producing and making available reading devices and assistive technologies;
- distributing accessible books through local library services;
- training in distribution of accessible format books;
- implementation of, or improvements to, limitations and exceptions in national copyright legislation;
- collaboration, prioritization, and planning amongst stakeholder organizations;
- promotion and communication of solutions and services available; and
- funding.

Reinforcing the need for partnerships, the Consortium therefore encourages a multi-stakeholder approach. This approach, however, requires changes throughout the publishing and accessibility ecosystem. Because partnerships are key to the success of inclusive publishing, local champions need to advocate on behalf of VIPs and act as a catalyst to get the different stakeholders to work together. A case study on Bangladesh demonstrates how a multi-stakeholder approach to inclusive publishing can lead to more availability of accessible format books. In 2014, the Consortium sponsored a training workshop on inclusive publishing in Bangladesh. A total of eighteen participants, consisting of representatives from commercial publishers, governmental publishers, NGOs, and organizations of people with disabilities, participated in this three day intensive hands on training program.[81]

It is beyond the scope of this chapter to describe the Bangladesh case study in detail, but it will suffice to highlight some lessons. First is the importance of government taking

[80] Accessible Books Consortium, Books for All Starter Kit for Accessible Publishing in Developing and Least Developed Countries, www.accessiblebooksconsortium.org/export/abc/abc_starter-kit_300616.pdf (last visited July 28, 2017).

[81] Information for this case study is taken from the Accessible Books Consortium, *id.*, Annex 3.

an active, if not leading role, in any partnership initiative. The Bangladesh Ministry of Education participated in the training workshop. Consequently, the Ministry adopted a policy to provide books in accessible format to students with blindness. With the help of the Young Power in Social Action, a nonprofit social development organization in Bangladesh, school textbooks were produced in a full-text full-audio DAISY format. Thus, with the help of the government of Bangladesh, the project is now undertaking braille production for students, as well as expanding its work to make available texts for students at the university level.

Second, the Starter Kit highlights the importance of access to reading devices and assistive technologies. This access is key to any effort to provide accessible format for print disabled persons, including meaningful implementation of the Marrakesh Treaty. In order to be able to use accessible digital books, people with sight loss and print disabilities need reading devices with assistive technology software that meets their specific requirements. Affordability issues are inevitable regarding the purchase of such devices by individuals; therefore, funding will be needed to make them available and policies will be required about which devices to make available. Where devices are being provided to pupils in a school, for example, additional assistance to provide network access will be required so that accessible books can be downloaded. Text to speech software may not be yet available in one or more national languages and there may be a need to work with specialist organizations to develop such software.[82]

Related to this point, publishers determine the extent to which accessible format devices serve VIPs. They can greatly assist users if they provide files in formats that are compliant with the end user devices, by delivering accessible formats that are free of digital locks. For example, the EPUB 3 file format, which is also used by the ABC, has been hailed as a way to both ease publishing and make it possible to produce books that are usable by both abled and disabled readers.[83] Yet, convenient as it is to use, EPUBcan be layered by TPMs. The challenge therefore is not one of copyright or technology as such but rather industry will and trust.

A third lesson that can be drawn from the Bangladesh case study is the need for library services for access to and distribution of accessible books. People with sight loss and print disabilities need to be able to discover which accessible digital books are available, search and browse for the books they want or need, and then obtain them either by download or delivery on a storage device such as, for example, a DVD or CD. This needs to be done in a controlled manner and usually requires a library management and distribution system as well as the resources to manage and support it.[84]

III Evaluation of the ABC: Achievements, Challenges, and Lessons for Implementation of the SDGs

Has the ABC realized its objectives to act as a complement to the promotion of the entry into force of the Marrakesh Treaty and to increase the number of books in accessible

[82] Accessible Books Consortium, *supra* note 80, ¶ 3.2.
[83] Book Industry Study Group, *BISG Quick Start Guide to Accessible Publishing* 10 (2016), http://bisg.org/news/297929/The-BISG-Quick-Start-Guide-to-Accessible-Publishing-Moving-Inclusion-Forward.htm.
[84] Accessible Books Consortium, *supra* note 80, ¶ 3.3.

formats? What are the challenges for the ABC and lessons to be drawn for the implementation of the SDGs, innovation, and access to information?

There is no doubt that the ABC has increased the number of books in accessible formats. It has also facilitated access to and exchange of such books through the TIGAR service. Libraries have downloaded forty-six hundred books, saving US$9.2 million in duplicating production of accessible formats.[85] In addition, inclusive publishing and capacity building projects such as the ones described in this chapter are clear ways to increase availability of books in accessible formats.

However, many books in accessible formats are likely to be in English. Yet inclusive publishing is important in many developing and least developed countries where English may not be the first language, necessitating development of accessible formats in local languages. In addition, digitisation of books is expensive and slow, which renders additional support to the concept of inclusive publishing.[86] The ABC is the "practical arm of the Marrakesh Treaty,"[87] to the extent that it provides practical ways of producing, distributing and using accessible format books. Through its multiple projects, ABC specifically addresses the challenge of building capacity in developing and least developed countries, not only to produce but also to distribute and use accessible formats. The Starter Kit, although designed for commercial publishers, provides useful information and guidelines for any aspiring accessible format publishers. The Kit is also a useful tool for policy makers, government, NGOs, libraries, or any institution intending to engage in or support accessible publishing as well as users of accessible works. Nonetheless these activities, however laudable, are not exhaustive and cannot be said to be the only way to provide accessible formats.

Like any partnership, the ABC is not free from challenges and shortcomings. Producing accessible formats remains expensive and slow. WIPO is the main funder of the ABC. Since the ABC is housed at WIPO and the governing Board is chaired by the WIPO's Director General, some concerns have been expressed that the Consortium serves only rightsholders' interest.[88] While representatives of the VIPs community on the Board do not seem to share this view,[89] this worry may point to the need for transparency in sharing of information amongst partners and their outside constituencies.

The size of the collection and conditions of access to content in the TIGAR may raise questions about the effectiveness or popularity of the licencing system under the ABC. After more than two years of existence, there are 315,000 titles in the TIGAR international catalogue. These books must be exchanged under individual licensing arrangements. Licensing clearance under the TIGAR is a long and time-consuming process, and the results uncertain since the rightsholders can refuse to licence.[90] By comparison, the

[85] Monica Hallil Lövblad, Presentation on ABC/WIPO – Bringing Books to Persons with Print Disability, Made at Take Part – Human Perspectives on Inclusive Publishing, Stockholm, May 16–18, 2016. www.youtube.com/watch?v=fF9h5y6CFIM.

[86] Interview with Jens Bammel, Former Secretary General of the International Publishers Association (May 23, 2016).

[87] Lövblad, *supra* note 85.

[88] Email exchange with Markus Low, Former Head of Policy at Treatment Action Campaign (May 11, 2016).

[89] Semi-structured confidential telephone interview with the ABC Representative of the International Council of Educators for the Visually Impaired (May 27, 2016).

[90] Jung, *supra* note 64.

Sugamya Pustakalaya, India's largest online library for blind and print disabled, launched recently at the end of August 2016, contains 233,095 books available for free download.[91] The library was created in partnership with international agencies like Bookshare, DAISY Forum of India, and ABC. Just like the ABC, Sugamya Pustakalaya is a collaborative effort of several organizations to end the book famine faced by people with print disabilities. It is a facilitating partnership platform for producers of accessible content to work jointly on producing and providing accessible books to VIPs. However, unlike the TIGAR where books are accessed on an individual licensing basis and with most material in the collections existing basically in English,[92] books in Sugamya Pustakalaya exist in diverse languages from various libraries across India and are accessible for free.

The TIGAR remains a licensing system, open only to participating institutions. While this model might arguably encourage publishers to contribute their books to the catalogue, associated risks and disadvantages exist. For example, there is lack of transparency as to acceptable rates for licencing, making accessible formats a privilege of those who can afford to pay any price. Thus, the ABC approach cannot replace the use of the Marrakesh mechanism to allow sharing of books in already accessible formats through copyright L&Es and cross-border exchange of books.

Finally, individual countries and organizations fund specific activities. This model is not sustainable. There is need to diversify the sources of funding, for the sake of sustainability but also to minimize risks such as lack of transparency, the funding of only activities that accord direct benefit to the funder, or the abandoning of the projects before completion.

IV General Lessons for Implementing the SDGs

The ABC illustrates the importance of partnerships in implementing the SDGs. In the case of innovation and access to information for education, a global movement (comprised of policy makers, institutions dealing with VIPs, NGOs, publishers, libraries, and authors) has been a critical force in advocating for the rights of people with sight loss and print disabilities. The ABC has demonstrated that is it possible to have all these stakeholders work together for the common goal of increasing books in accessible formats, albeit through a private licensing model.

It also highlights the need for public and private policies on appropriate technology to facilitate effective use of accessible formats, whether provided via the Marrakesh Treaty or through private licensing. The assistive technology needed by a user on a device will depend on the individual's specific requirements, the device itself, and the format of the accessible book. Many devices have built in accessibility features that may provide text to speech access to different formats and allow changes to the presentation of text. However, some formats may require additional software or apps to be added (for example, to be able to access DAISY, EPUB 3, or PDF files). In an important number of developing countries, there may be a need to develop text to speech software for national languages if such software is not already available. For example, in an ABC project for the production and distribution of accessible books in Sri Lanka in 2015, software was developed to produce an effective text to speech tool in Sinhalese. Such assistive technologies are also

[91] Sugamya Pustakalaya, https://library.daisyindia.org/NALP/welcomeLink.action (last visited Oct. 3, 2016).

[92] The catalogue contains collections in fifty-five languages, but they are mainly in English.

crucial for the effective implementation of the Marrakesh Treaty, especially in developing and least developed countries, which are likely to be the major beneficiaries of imported accessible format books. The ABC, through the Starter Kit, helps highlight the need for capacity building in creating as well as using assistive technology.

The transition from traditional to fully accessible practices and/or inclusive publishing in a country is a long-term process that requires commitment, financing, other kinds of support, and collaboration from many stakeholders. Many developing countries do not yet have an established e-book market and accessible reading devices are not widely available. The ABC Kit encourages stakeholders in developing and least developed countries to work together to embrace the opportunities that digital technologies now provide to significantly increase the number of accessible books.[93] In addition the ABC Accessibility Guidelines help and encourage collaboration and pooling of resources.

Clearly, the "Books for All" strategy exemplified by the ABC Kit presents advantages for the implementation of the SDGs, at least for those within the VIPs community. People with sight loss and print disabilities are able to make a fuller contribution to society as well as lead more fulfilled and independent lives. In particular, children can attain higher levels of education and qualifications by accessing the curriculum through digital books. Adults are more easily able to gain employment. The strategy can be seen as a means of integrating everyone in society and thus leading to sustainable development.

A common understanding of accessible publishing and collaboration amongst stakeholders will also assist the implementation of the Marrakesh Treaty.[94] The Marrakesh Treaty by itself cannot solve the book famine, and it does not address the needs of the majority of readers, who are outside the VIPs community. But it does remove some of the legal obstacles, which in turn paves the way to establish global infrastructures that are needed.[95] As clearly stated in the Governing Document of the ABC, the Consortium constitutes one possible initiative, amongst others, to implement the objectives of the Marrakesh VIP Treaty at a practical level. In this sense, the ABC is complementary to the Marrakesh Treaty, to the extent that it demonstrates some practical ways and challenges to inclusive publishing, to increase both accessible works and capacity building to use accessible formats.

However, only a small percentage of persons with print disability are blind, while the vast majority of print disabled people have low vision or are dyslexic. A good e-book reader can allow manipulations that can help many people within that spectrum of disabilities, for example, by increasing the font size or colour or text to speech.[96] Accessibility can be realized by different initiatives by publishers and also by technology providers; for example, the Apple iPad and iPhone can deliver text to speech in a variety

[93] Accessible Books Consortium, *supra* note 80, at 6.

[94] Through the "born accessible" projects, the ABC partnership in a way extends beyond the registered participants in the Consortium. From the initial fifteen partners, the ABC has added many contributors, making the ABC a unique public–private partnership.

[95] This idea was developed during an email exchange with Teresa Hackett, Copyright and Libraries Programme Manager, Electronic Information for Libraries (July 30, 2016).

[96] Jens Bammel, the former Secretary General of the International Publishers' Association in Parallel WIPO Initiative On Access For Visually Impaired Steps Up, IP Watch, www.ip-watch.org/2014/03/04/parallel-wipo-initiative-on-access-for-visually-impaired-community-steps-up/ (last visited Aug. 1, 2016).

of languages, out of the box. The ABC demonstrates in detail, for example, through the Starter Kit and capacity building projects in Bangladesh, how some of these technologies can work for developing countries, helping both publishers and authors understand the needs of users of accessible formats. But it remains for publishers to incorporate features in their e-books to make them easier to navigate and use for people with print disability. This is pertinent for the realization of the objectives of both the Marrakesh Treaty and the SDGs. It is not a question of legislation but of motivation, for example, by providing assurances to publishers that there will be no abuse of their published works.

The efforts by publishers to engage in inclusive publishing projects are an attempt at providing long-term solutions to production of accessible books in developing and least developed countries. However, besides being expensive, inclusive publishing is not a practical avenue where access is needed urgently. In addition, there is a risk of duplication of effort by producing books that already exist in accessible formats and only need to be exchanged. Availability of the accessible formats hinges on the interests of the inclusive publisher and not the specific needs of people who need those works. To avoid wastage of resources and becoming an obstacle to implementation of the Marrakesh Treaty, it would make economic sense if the ABC encourages production of only books that are not available in accessible formats. At the same time, WIPO could encourage ratification of the Marrakesh Treaty by WIPO member states who are still not contracting parties to it.

Inclusive publishing may even negatively impact the Marrakesh Treaty in that "inclusive" making of formats by publishers discourages conversion of books by authorized entities. This may work against the goals of the Marrakesh Treaty, which grants a right to these entities to convert a work "to an accessible format copy, which may include any means needed to navigate information in the accessible format, but does not introduce changes other than those needed to make the work accessible to the beneficiary person."[97] Indeed the Marrakesh Treaty envisages that a "limitation or exception provided in national law should permit changes needed to make the work accessible in the alternative format."[98] Authorized entities, rather than publishers, know best the access needs of their patrons. There are several risks associated with private ordering in making and distribution[99] of accessible formats available. The most obvious risk is that publishers will invest primarily or exclusively where there is high profit and supply to communities that can pay the most.

Conclusion

The Accessible Books Consortium is a public–private partnership that promotes innovation in creation, distribution, and use of accessible books formats. It has increased the available number of books through its TIGAR. As a PPP, the ABC's main features are collaboration amongst governments, publishers, authors, organizations representing VIPs, and NGOs. It contributes to the implementation of SDG 4, which is to "ensure

97 Marrakesh Treaty, *supra* note 5, Article 4(2)(iii).
98 *Id.* Article 4(1)(a).
99 Through the TIGAR or similar arrangements.

inclusive and equitable quality education and promote lifelong learning opportunities for all" via a partnership model set forth by SDG 17, which calls for "[s]trengthening the means of implementation and revitalize the global partnership for sustainable development." It does so by increasing the number of books available in accessible formats, albeit under a private licensing model, the TIGAR. The inclusive publishing approach promotes publishing techniques that enable publishers to produce born accessible books, while the capacity building projects provide technical skills to various organizations supporting VIPs, governments, publishers, and NGOs to produce, convert and distribute accessible formats. All of these facilitate access to information and learning by VIPs.

The ABC partnership provides some models for technical assistance and capacity building both in publishing and use of accessible formats. Concerning the latter, through its Starter Kit, the ABC draws attention to some of the challenges to the use of these accessible formats, which will not be solved by the legal platform of the Marrakesh Treaty or other legal means, but rather by policy initiatives and the intentional collaboration of publishers of accessible formats with other stakeholders. However, the TIGAR model of individual licensing contracts limits the availability of those books to the very few institutions participating in the TIGAR, without transparency as to pricing. This is a significant institutional limitation to wide dissemination of information and learning material.

As this chapter illustrates, the relationship of partners to each other and to actual control of the PPP is critical to its ability to promote public interest, in this case access to knowledge still under copyright.[100] Because the ABC is based on a private licensing model, the publishers' interests may drive the direction of the PPP. Public law frameworks, in this case the Marrakesh Treaty, are important in terms of providing clear public policy goals for the various stakeholders operating within PPPs.

References

ACCESSIBLE BOOKS CONSORTIUM, *ABC at the African Forum: Support Available for Educational Accessibility Projects*, www.accessiblebooksconsortium.org/news/en/2015/news_0007.html (last visited Oct. 11, 2016.)

ACCESSIBLE BOOKS CONSORTIUM, *ABC Snapshot: News from Accessible Books Consortium*, (June 30, 2016) (last visited July 10, 2016).

ACCESSIBLE BOOKS CONSORTIUM, [UNTITLED DOCUMENT] (Mar. 16, 2016) www.accessiblebooksconsortium.org/export/sites/visionip/portal/en/doc/abc_governance.doc (last visited June 10, 2016).

ACCESSIBLE BOOKS CONSORTIUM, Books for All Starter Kit for Accessible Publishing in Developing and Least Developed Countries, www.accessiblebooksconsortium.org/export/abc/abc_starter-kit_300616.pdf. (last visited July 28, 2017).

ACCESSIBLE BOOKS CONSORTIUM, Charter for Accessible Publishing, www.accessiblebooksconsortium.org/export/sites/visionip/publishing/en/pdf/accessible_best_practice_guidelines_for_publishers.pdf. (last visited June 6, 2016).

ACCESSIBLE BOOKS CONSORTIUM, *First Cross-Border Book Transfer by ABC Following Entry into Force of Marrakesh Treaty*, www.accessiblebooksconsortium.org/news/en/2016/news_0010.html, (last visited Oct. 3, 2016).

[100] Margaret Chon, *PPPs in Global IP (public-private partnerships in global intellectual property), in* METHODS AND PERSPECTIVES IN INTELLECTUAL PROPERTY 296 (Graeme B. Dinwoodie ed., 2013).

Accessible Books Consortium, Governance Document Establishing the Consortium, article 2, www.accessiblebooksconsortium.org/export/sites/visionip/portal/en/doc/abc_governance.doc.

Accessible Books Consortium, www.accessiblebooksconsortium.org (last visited June 10, 2016).

Accessible Books Consortium, www.accessiblebooksconsortium.org/tigar/en/ (Mar. 15, 2017).

Accessible Books Consortium, www.accessiblebooksconsortium.org/portal/en/index.html (last visited June 6, 2016).

Bammel, Jens, in *Parallel WIPO Initiative on Access for Visually Impaired Steps Up*, IP Watch, www.ip-watch.org/2014/03/04/parallel-wipo-initiative-on-access-for-visually-impaired-community-steps-up/ (last visited Aug. 1, 2016)

Book Industry Study Group, *BISG Quick Start Guide to Accessible Publishing* 10 (2016), http://bisg.org/news/297929/The-BISG-Quick-Start-Guide-to-Accessible-Publishing-Moving-Inclusion-Forward.htm.

Chon, Margaret, *PPPs in Global IP (public–private partnerships in global intellectual property), in* Methods and Perspectives in Intellectual Property 296 (Graeme B. Dinwoodie ed., 2013).

Daisy Consortium, www.daisy.org/ (last visited July 28, 2017).

Email exchange with Markus Low, Former Head of Policy at Treatment Action Campaign (May 11, 2016).

Guibault, Lucie, *The Nature and Scope of Limitations and Exceptions to Copyright and Neighbouring Rights with Regard to General Interest Missions for the Transmission of Knowledge: Prospects for their Adaptation to the Digital Environment*, e-Copyright Bull., 1, 40 (Oct.–Dec. 2003).

Harpur, Paul & Nicolas Suzor, *Copyright Protections and Disability Rights: Turning the Page to a New International Paradigm*, 36 University of New South Wales Law Journal 745 (2013).

Helfer, Laurence R., Molly K. Land, Ruth L. Okediji & Jerome H. Reichman, The World Blind Union Guide to the Marrakesh Treaty, 51–59 (2017).

Interview with Jens Bammel, Former Secretary General of the International Publishers Association (May 23, 2016).

Interview with Michael Jung, WIPO Secretariat (May 26, 2016).

Interview with Monica Hallil Lövblad, Coordinator of ABC, WIPO Secretariat (June 14, 2016).

Isiko Štrba, Susan, *A Model for Access to Educational Resources and Innovation in Developing Countries, in* Intellectual Property, Trade and Development: Strategies to Optimise Development in a TRIPS-Plus Era 286, 294 (Daniel Gervais ed., 2015).

Lövblad, Monica Hallil, Presentation on ABC/WIPO – Bringing Books to Persons with Print Disability, Made at Take Part – Human Perspectives on Inclusive Publishing, Stockholm, May 16 – 18, 2016. www.youtube.com/watch?v=fF9h5y6CFIM.

Okediji, Ruth L., *International Copyright Limitations and Exceptions as Development Policy, in* Reframing Copyright Law in the Age of Limitations and Exceptions, 429, 444 (Ruth L. Okediji ed., 2017).

Pustakalaya, Sugamya, https://library.daisyindia.org/NALP/welcomeLink.action (last visited Oct. 3, 2016).

Semi-structured confidential telephone interview with the ABC Representative of the International Council of Educators for the Visually Impaired (27 May 2016).

Senftleben, Martin, Copyright, limitations and the Three-Step Test: An Analysis of the Three-Step Test in International and EC Copyright Law 52 (2004).

Shaver, Lea, *The Right to Read*, 54 Columbia Journal of Transnational Law 1 (2015).

South African Library for the Blind, Nakwenzeke Newsletter (June 2016).

Sullivan, Judith, *Study on Copyright Limitations and Exceptions for Visually Impaired Persons*, Standing Committee on Copyright and Related Rights, Fifteenth Session, Sept. 11–13, 2006, WIPO Doc. SCCR/15/7 (Feb. 20, 2007).

United Nations, *Goal 17: Revitalize the Global Partnership for Sustainable Development*, www.un.org/sustainabledevelopment/globalpartnerships/ (last visited Aug. 9, 2016).

United Nations, *Goal 4: Ensure Inclusive and Quality Education for all and Promote Lifelong Learning*, www.un.org/sustainabledevelopment/education/ (last visited Mar. 17, 2017).

United Nations General Assembly A/Res/70/1, Transforming Our World: 2030 Agenda for Sustainable Development, ¶ 39 (Oct. 21, 2015).

World Blind Union, *Millions of People are Denied Access to Books and Printed Materials - WBU Press Release for World Book and Copyright Day*, www.worldblindunion.org/English/news/Pages/Millions-of-People-are-Denied-Access-to-.aspx (last visited Mar. 15, 2017).

World Blind Union, *On Track for a Book Without Borders*, www.worldblindunion.org/English/our-work/our-priorities/Pages/On-Track-For-A-Book-Without-Borders.aspx (last visited July 14, 2017).

World Blind Union, Presentation at the Standing Committee on Copyright and Related Rights, Information Meeting on Digital Content for the Visually Impaired (3 Nov. 2003).

World Health Organization, *Visual Impairment and Blindness*, fact Sheet No. 282, www.who.int/mediacentre/factsheets/fs282/en/ (last visited June 15, 2016).

World Intellectual Property Organization, Assemblies of the Member States of WIPO, Forty-Third Series of meetings, Sept. 24–3 Oct. 2007, WIPO Doc. A/43/6 E, Annex, (12 Nov. 2007).

World Intellectual Property Organization, Berne Convention for the Protection of Literary and Artistic Works (9 Sept. 1886), TRT/BERNE/001 (as revised by the Act of Stockholm (1967), and by the Paris Act (1971) and amended in 1979), Publication of the World Intellectual Property Organization no. 287(E).

World Intellectual Property Organization, Canada's Accession to Marrakesh Treaty Brings Treaty into Force, WIPO Press Room, www.wipo.int/pressroom/en/articles/2016/article_0007.html (last visited June 30, 2016).

World Intellectual Property Organization, Diplomatic Conference to Conclude a Treaty to Facilitate Access to Published Works by Visually Impaired Persons and Persons with Print Disabilities, June 17–28, 2013 WIPO Doc. VIP/DC/INF (2013).

World Intellectual Property Organization, Eight Interim Report of the Stakeholders Platform, Standing Committee on Copyright and Related Rights, Twenty-seventh Session, Apr. 28–May 2, 2014, WIPO Doc. SCCR/27/4, www.wipo.int/meetings/en/doc_details.jsp?doc_id=272272 (last visited June 6, 2016).

World Intellectual Property Organization, *Historic Treaty Adopted, Boosts Access to Books for Visually Impaired Persons Worldwide*, www.wipo.int/pressroom/en/articles/2013/article_0017.html (last visited June 6, 2016).

World Intellectual Property Organization, Information Meeting on Digital Content for the Visually Impaired, Standing Committee on Copyright and Related Rights, Presentation by IFLA/Libraries for the Blind, ¶ 7 (3 Nov. 2003).

World Intellectual Property Organization, Information on contracting parties to Marrakesh Treaty, WIPO, www.wipo.int/treaties/en/ShowResults.jsp?lang=en&treaty_id=843 (last visited Aug. 6, 2016).

World Intellectual Property Organization, *Limitations and Exceptions: Access to Books for the Visually Impaired – Background Brief*, WIPO Press, www.wipo.int/pressroom/en/briefs/limitations.html#note (last visited June 15, 2016).

World Intellectual Property Organization, Marrakesh Treaty to Facilitate Access to Published Works for Persons Who Are Blind, Visually Impaired, or Otherwise Print Disabled,

27 June 2013, VIP/DC/8 (entered into force 30 Sept. 2016) www.wipo.int/edocs/mdocs/diplconf/en/vip_dc/vip_dc_8_rev.pdf.

World Intellectual Property Organization, *Marrakesh Treaty Brings Treaty into Force*, WIPO Press Room, www.wipo.int/pressroom/en/articles/2016/article_0007.html (last visited June 30, 2016).

World Intellectual Property Organization, Proposal by Argentina and Brazil for the Establishment of a Development Agenda for WIPO, WIPO General Assembly, Thirty-first (15th Ordinary) Session, Mar. 10–12, 2008, WIPO Doc. WO/GA/31/11 (27 Sept. 2004).

World Intellectual Property Organization, Proposal by Brazil, Chile, Nicaragua, and Uruguay for Work Related to L&Es, Standing Committee on Copyright and Related Rights, Sixteenth Session, Mar. 10–12, 2008, WIPO Doc. SCCR/16/2 (E) (17 July 2008).

World Intellectual Property Organization, Proposal by Chile on the Subject "Limitations and Exceptions to Copyright and Related Rights," Standing Committee on Copyright and Related Rights, Twelfth Session, Nov. 17–19, 2004, WIPO Doc. SCCR/12/3 (2 Nov. 2004).

World Intellectual Property Organization, Report, Standing Committee on Copyright and Related Rights, Seventeenth Session, Nov. 3–7, 2008, WIPO Doc. SCCR/17/5 (Mar. 25, 2009), *see, e.g.*, ¶¶ 20, 28, 54, 122.

World Intellectual Property Organization, Standing Committee on Copyright and Related Rights, www.wipo.int/policy/en/sccr/ (last visited July 28, 2017).

World Intellectual Property Organization, Standing Committee on Copyright and Related Rights, Seventeenth Session, Geneva, Nov. 3–7, 2008.

World Intellectual Property Organization, WIPO Copyright Treaty, adopted in Geneva on 20 December 1996 (entered into force on Mar. 6, 2002), WIPO Publication no. 226(E) (*hereinafter* WCT).

World Trade Organization, Agreement on Trade-Related Aspects of Intellectual Property Rights, Annex 1C to the Marrakesh Agreement Establishing the World Trade Organization, 15 April 1994, *in* World Trade Organization, The Results of the Uruguay Round of Multilateral Negotiations, The Legal Texts. Geneva: WTO (1995).

10 Intellectual Property and Public–Private Partner Motivations: Lessons from a Digital Library

Melissa Levine

Introduction

Cultural institutions such as libraries and museums are characteristically associated with public interests, broadly considered here as encompassing both the public good *and* public goods.[1] These institutions often engage in collaborative relationships with for-profit firms or enterprises to better further a public educational, scholarly, or other publicly oriented mission. Thus, the public–private partnership model (PPP) is not new for memory institutions like museums, libraries, and archives, whether governmental actors like the Smithsonian Institution or private ones like the J. Paul Getty Museum. These relationships typically leverage mutual interests and recognize the distinct motivations of the respective parties. They often embody a symbiotic exchange of corporate expertise and financial resources, on the one hand – and on the other hand, subject matter expertise and collections associated the cultural institution, whether a museum, library, or archive. This is especially the case where the partnership facilitates the ability of a cultural institution to improve access to reproductions of collection images, books, films, and educational materials.

This chapter considers a partnership formed between the University of Michigan Library (UML or the Library) and Google Inc. (Google), leading up to the creation of the HathiTrust Digital Library (HathiTrust). It reflects on the key motivations for this collaborative relationship between the Library as a cultural institution housed within a public research university serving multiple stakeholders and Google as a private corporation with a duty to its shareholders. This PPP leveraged common interests *and* recognized the distinct goals of each partner. As each partner entered the relationship, it remained true to its core responsibilities and missions. The genesis of and ongoing collaboration exemplified by HathiTrust thus provides a case study of a unique and

[1] Many kinds of corporate entities address public or cultural purposes in each country. In this chapter, "cultural institutions" refers to organizational mission rather than the particular formal legal status as, for example, government agency, for-profit, tax exempt, or other corporate form. This chapter considers high-level common features of public–private partnerships in the cultural and educational arenas – regardless of the specific kind of entity. That said, there is an overarching recognition of the difference between an entity that has a public purpose for its stakeholders and a corporation with a primary duty to its shareholders. Further, the use of the terms "partner" and "partnership" throughout this chapter refer generically to the formalized collaborative relationships discussed and are explicitly not partnerships in the corporate legal sense.

successful PPP with broader implications for global intellectual property (IP) governance and the U.N. Sustainable Development Goals (SDGs).

As explored in this chapter, PPPs such as HathiTrust may help support the SDGs in the global context. But the inconsistency of library exceptions to copyright across nations as well as the lack of harmonization of such exceptions globally makes it difficult to apply such exceptions across borders. These IP concerns place high risk on partners and pose a huge disincentive for cooperation that otherwise might benefit research and education through libraries in support of addressing SDGs. Thus, the multilateral public law framework, in this case, the global copyright regime, is an essential aspect of understanding the work that PPPs can do to foster global development.

Arguably, the United States was a particularly fitting jurisdiction for the HathiTrust project, given the solid foundation of the fair use exception to copyright as an established part of the US Copyright Act,[2] and its robust interpretation in US case law. US copyright law specifically limits the copyright holder's rights by authorizing special uses for libraries and archives in Section 108 of the 1976 Copyright Act.[3] In addition to special reproduction rights for libraries under prescribed circumstances, US copyright law additionally features fair use as stated in Section 107 of the 1976 Act.[4] Indeed, Section 108 (which addresses exceptions and limitations to copyright, for libraries and archives) explicitly refers to the section 107 fair use as a right: "Nothing in this section in any way affects the *right* of fair use as provided by section 107 . . ."[5]

Despite these clearly available exceptions, the legal complexity of the Google scanning project and scale of resulting litigation against Google and UML and other libraries by authors and publishers over the better part of a decade was groundbreaking. That Google and HathiTrust prevailed in this costly litigation raises questions about lessons learned, specifically, whether this arguably unique approach is replicable in other jurisdictions – or whether instead the multilateral copyright framework requires recalibration in order to promote and support similar PPP collaborations elsewhere.

This chapter begins in Part I with a brief history of HathiTrust, including the motivations on the part of UML as well as Google to form this PPP. In Part II, it describes the background of general concerns, including those of research librarians with book preservation as well as those of librarians in general regarding access to information by persons with visual disabilities. The chapter then turns in Part III to the importance of copyright exceptions and limitations as a prerequisite for the partnership formed as a result of the mutual interests of UML and Google. Part IV then details the partnership itself, by discussing some key provisions in the partnership contract that allow the project to be of both private and public benefit. This section also touches upon significant social relationships that allowed the partnership to move forward constructively, as well as the benefits expected and realized by participating partners. The chapter concludes in Part V with an exploration of the role of IP as a distinct challenge to the partnership goals,

[2] U.S. Copyright Act, 17 U.S.C §§ 101–1332 (2012). Fair use is a unique feature of US copyright law, although Israel, Poland, and South Korea have similar provisions. Fair use and the related (but distinct) concept of fair dealing find their origins in England and have been translated in former UK spheres of influence. *See* Jonathan Band & Jonathan Gerafi, Fair use/Fair Dealing Handbook (2015), http://infojustice.org/wp-content/uploads/2015/03/fair-use-handbook-march-2015.pdf.

[3] 17 U.S.C. § 108.

[4] 17 U.S.C. §§ 107–108.

[5] Limitations on Exclusive Rights: Reproduction by Libraries and Archives, 17 U.S.C. § 108(f)(4).

beginning with difficulties associated in locating the boundaries of the public domain. It also provides some suggestions for adjusting both international and national copyright practice as well as the existing legal and policy framework to better serve both public and private interests of PPPs with similar goals.

Overall, the case study explored here demonstrates how PPPs can propel nonprofit mission, thus helping libraries to better meet the informational needs implicit in the SDGs, by improving global access to knowledge and information with more clarity for both copyright holders and cultural institutions. The potential beneficiaries of the suggestions made here are not directly the cultural institutions per se. Rather, the ultimate beneficiaries are the individuals served by these institutions, including those who generate research and scholarship, encourage education, and engage in creative endeavor. Librarians among others are trying to address the critical need for access to information, knowledge, and exposure to the diversity of culture and opinion, for purposes of advancing any and all of the SDGs.[6] PPPs can be effective ways to address the SDGs, yet successful partnerships can be challenging to form and maintain. This chapter attempts to provide some insights into why this particular PPP works.

I What Is HathiTrust?

At the core of the PPP between UML and Google was the decision to scan the collection of the UML. To understand the UML's reasons for this decision, one needs to know something about HathiTrust and its genesis. Research libraries contain centuries of collections in book format, in addition to other text and nontextual materials. Digital surrogates of participating research library collections form most of the corpus of HathiTrust. HathiTrust is a collaborative partnership of libraries engaged in shared solutions to preserve research library collections.

> HathiTrust began in 2008 as a collaboration of the universities of the Committee on Institutional Cooperation and the University of California system to establish a repository to archive and share their digitized collections. HathiTrust has quickly expanded to include additional partners and to provide those partners with an easy means to archive their digital content.
>
> The initial focus of the partnership has been on preserving and providing access to digitized book and journal content from the partner library collections. This includes both in copyright and public domain materials digitized by Google, the Internet Archive, and Microsoft, as well as through in-house initiatives. The partners aim to build a comprehensive archive of published literature from around the world and develop shared strategies for managing and developing their digital and print holdings in a collaborative way.
>
> The primary community that HathiTrust serves are the members (faculty, students, and users) of its partners [*sic*] libraries, but the materials in HathiTrust are available to all to the extent permitted by law and contracts, providing the published record as a public good to users around the world.[7]

6 *Development and Access to Information 2017*, Int'l Fed'n of Libr. Ass'ns Insts. [IFLA] (2017).

7 *See Our Partnership*, HathiTrust, www.hathitrust.org/partnership. See also *infra* note 23 for a description of the Committee on Institutional Cooperation.

Several key motivations for the scanning collections and creating HathiTrust from the perspective of research libraries include: general access to works in the public domain, general access to works for which permissions are secured, improved search and discovery, long-standing preservation concerns regarding brittle books, and the opportunity to provide meaningful accessibility to library collections for people with print disabilities.[8] Preservation of and access to cultural collections were both significant priorities for the UML as well as other participating libraries. These two aims were addressed by the opportunity presented in the form of the mutually beneficial PPP between Google, the Library, and other libraries that participated in the Google Library Project ("Project").[9] They provide context for the formation of the PPP, the intersection of IP interests in the partnership relationship, and how the PPP advances the SDGs.

II The Preservation Problem: Books Fall Apart

In the late twentieth century, research libraries shared a serious concern about the survival of books in paper format in library collections. Libraries also increasingly recognized the need to develop new book preservation strategies beyond paper facsimiles and microfilm.[10] In total, the scale of actual and likely loss was potentially staggering in terms of the physical media of paper on which memory, knowledge, and expression were significantly retained. The preservation concerns extended even more urgently to sound recordings and moving images, given the fragility of the media and even flammability in the case of films notorious for their physical instability and flammable qualities. As stated in a 2004 report by the Association of Research Libraries, "[d]igitization can address the conversion needs of other types of media beyond paper based printed materials (e.g., audio, film, video) and can allow collections containing a wide variety of formats to be presented

[8] Regarding some of the issues associated with identifying whether a work is in the public domain, *see* discussion of the Copyright Review Management System *infra* note 52. Regarding permissions, copyright holders may give HathiTrust permission to "open" works that are in copyright. Copyright holders may designate a Creative Commons license. *See HathiTrust Permission Agreements*, HathiTrust, www.hathi trust.org/permissions_agreement (last visited Jul. 23, 2017).

These issues are also discussed by the trial court in *Authors Guild v. HathiTrust*, with particularly relevant commentary on the proposition of making books available for blind people ("Although I recognize the facts here may on some levels be without precedent, I am convinced that they fall safely within the protection of fair use such that there is not genuine issue of material fact. I cannot imagine a definition of fair use that would not encompass the transformative uses made by [the HDL] and would require that I terminate this invaluable contribution to the progress of science and the cultivation of the arts that at the same time effectuates the ideals espoused by the [Americans With Disabilities Act of 1990, Pub. L. No. 101–336, 104 Stat 327 (codified as amended at 42 U.S.C. §§ 12101, et seq.)]."). Authors Guild, Inc. v. HathiTrust, 902 F. Supp. 2d 445, 460–64, (S.D.N.Y. 2012) [hereinafter *HathiTrust* district court opinion].

[9] Another benefit: once in digital formats, these initiatives improved access by making it easier to locate works through aggregators, especially those tailored to the interests of education and culture like the Digital Public Library of America (DPLA) *available at* https://dp.la/, and Europeana *available at* www.europeana .eu/portal/en.

[10] There was similar concern about the need to develop collection and preservation strategies for digital content – both digital copies of analog materials and "born digital" materials. For example, *LC21: A Digital Strategy for the Library of Congress* published nearly twenty years ago by the National Academy of Sciences identified well-known and still relevant preservation challenges for digital collections specifically listing fragile storage media, technology obsolescence, and "legal questions surrounding copying and access." LC21: A Digital Strategy for the Library of Congress, Nat'l Res. Council (2000), www.nap.edu/read/9940/chapter/1#ii.

and seamlessly accessed from a single interface."[11] Regarding the preservation concern for books in particular, Shannon Zachary of the University of Michigan observes that "people were aware of the problem of deteriorating modern paper even as early as the first quarter of the 19th century and certainly by the last quarter. Many papers turned brittle, but not all paper. The big push about the 'brittle book crisis' came in the 1980s."[12]

The brittle book problem refers to paper produced from the mid-nineteenth century using materials like wood pulp and alum-rosin sizing that has a high level of acid. Over time, the acid in the paper causes the paper to become brittle. Such paper often becomes yellow or brown in color and crumbles easily even with careful handling. Before the mid-nineteenth century, paper was typically made from mildly acidic or alkaline materials like cotton or linen rag. These older papers can last for centuries without becoming brittle, especially if stored and handled with care. Ironically, it is the relatively newer materials of the late nineteenth through the twentieth century that are at greatest preservation risk. As these books held in library collections age, they represent an urgent preservation concern. Research libraries have a critical stewardship role, first in preserving books and then in providing meaningful access to them for research and learning.

Libraries preserve and care for brittle books (and all kinds of media) and they reformat – or replace such books when possible to ensure continued access to these works. According to Zachary, "[t]he brittle books crisis has also been mitigated since the early 1990s, when significant numbers of paper mills converted to an alkaline process (for economic reasons, not for preservation). Most paper made today – even wood pulp paper – is naturally alkaline." That said that, "there are still a lot of brittle books out there on the shelves published between around 1870–1990."[13]

In the early 2000s, many research libraries were contemplating the implications and possibilities of digitizing all the books in library holdings. By 2000, there was growing experience with digitization in the field, in the form of initiatives like the Library of Congress' American Memory, a seminal digitization initiative through the 1990s that aspired to (and exceeded in) the goal of digitizing five million objects about American history in a variety of media.[14] By the early 2000s, research libraries had an overarching preservation concern and a foundational belief that digital preservation deeply supports and enhances research and scholarship.[15] But they had no means to take on the

[11] Kathleen Arthur et al., RECOGNIZING DIGITALIZATION AS A PRESERVATION REFORMATTING METHOD, ASS'N OF RES. LIBRS. (2004), www.arl.org/storage/documents/publications/digitization-preservation-reformatting-2004.pdf.

[12] Email from Shannon Zachary, Head of Preservation, University of Michigan Library, to author (February 15, 2017).

[13] For more on library concerns with the brittle book problem, *see* Deanna Marcum, DUE DILIGENCE AND STEWARDSHIP IN A TIME OF CHANGE AND UNCERTAINTY, ITHAKA (2016), www.sr.ithaka.org/publications/due-diligence-and-stewardship-in-a-time-of-change-and-uncertainty/ (discussing a recent historical look at preservation). *See also* Mary Lynn Ritzenthaler, PRESERVING ARCHIVES AND MANUSCRIPTS ch. 3 (2nd ed., 2010) (providing a good introductory description on the nature of paper and how it deteriorates). The 1993 edition is available full text. *See* HATHITRUST, https://babel.hathitrust.org/cgi/pt?id=mdp.39015032925144;view=1up;seq=1; Abby Smith, THE FUTURE OF THE PAST (1999), www.clir.org/pubs/reports/reports/pub82/pub82text.html (provides another excellent overview of the brittle book problem).

[14] Note: the author served as Legal Advisor to American Memory and the National Digital Library Project at the Library of Congress from 1996 to 2001.

[15] *See, e.g.*, Abby Smith, THE EVIDENCE IN HAND: REPORT ON THE TASK FORCE ON THE ARTIFACT IN LIBRARY COLLECTIONS (Council on Libr. and Info. Res. 2001), www.clir.org/pubs/reports/pub103/pub103.pdf (discussing the preservation challenges for collections including analog (physical) materials, digital

Box 10.1. Alignment of Public and Private Goals

Mary Sue Coleman, then president of the University of Michigan, articulated compelling urgency and opportunity in a pivotal 2006 speech to the American Association of Publishers (AAP). Her speech described the opportunity presented by the university's partnership with Google, the urgency of the problem it addressed, and the opportunity it envisioned to preserve books for scholarship. It also summarized the university's motivation in the context of library professionals' concerns and thinking circa 1990s about digitization as preservation. Additionally, it framed how the parties were poised for even greater opportunities to serve the public good in line with their respective missions:

> The University of Michigan's partnership with Google offers three overarching qualities that help fulfill our mission: the preservation of books; worldwide access to information; and, most importantly, the public good of the diffusion of knowledge ... We are the repository for the whole of human knowledge, and we must safeguard it for future generations. It is ours to protect and to preserve.[16]

Herculean and costly digitization task of this ambition despite the urgency. Thus, the need and idea were already in place, and were ignited by the resources presented by Google.

When Google approached the Library, it presented an opportunity that aligned the right resource with the right need at the right time to help stem the exposure presented by the brittle book problem. (See Box 10.1.) The ensuing relationship created a path forward to address an impending preservation issue that would have had a dramatically negative effect on libraries and, in turn, memory, knowledge, and scholarship available for current and future scholars.[17]

III The Access Problem: Books for People with Print Disabilities

In addition to preservation, libraries recognized the tremendous opportunities digital formats offered to advance access for people with print disabilities, by enabling archival search generally, and therefore facilitating a profound range of new scholarship and

reformatting, and born digital). "If libraries, archives, or historical societies do not collect instances of recorded information, then the chance of their survival is slim. Loss is inevitable." *Id.* at 3. Smith notes that humanities scholars already valued then-new databases that made it feasible to search collections more thoroughly than before. "The observation that use is "obligatory" means that these scholars are now able to avail themselves of otherwise-scarce texts." *Id.* at 26. The report also acknowledges the challenges to preservation presented by copyright. *Id.* at 54.

16 Kevin Bergquist, *Google Project About the Public Good*, Univ. Rec. (Feb. 8, 2006) www.ur.umich.edu/0506/Feb06_06/22.shtml (quoting Mary Sue Coleman, President, Ass'n of Am. Univs., *The Khmer Rouge and the Public Good*, at the annual meeting of the Professional/Scholarly Publishing Division. The title of her talk references destruction of Cambodia's national library: "Nature, politics and war have always been the mortal enemies of written works ... In the 1970s, the Khmer Rouge regime in Cambodia took over the national library, throwing books into the street and burning them, while using the empty stacks as a pigsty. Less than 20 percent of the library survived.").

17 As it happened, the Library did not scan the most fragile items with Google, choosing to handle those more individually. In the end, it chose to scan the multitude of items that were at risk of becoming subject to the inevitable short-term deterioration concerns of brittle books. Once brittle, the scanning process is necessarily more bespoke to the item and cannot easily be handled efficiently or at scale.

research possibilities. HathiTrust also recognized that "[o]ne key facet of the access services that HathiTrust provides is to users who have disabilities – for example, blindness, dyslexia, physical or cognitive impairments – that prevent them from being able to easily read printed material ("print disabilities")."[18] The Chafee Amendment to the 1976 Copyright Act[19] approved this important possibility for improved means of access for people who have print disabilities.[20]

For people with print disabilities as well as other readers, digital formats offer greater access (as well as greater enablement of archival search generally) and therefore facilitate a profound range of new scholarship and research possibilities. Important exceptions and limitations to copyright undergird the HathiTrust model and are discussed later in this chapter. Arguably, the existence of a strong and evolving fair use right in US copyright was a fundamental requirement for the creation of the Google Library Project and HathiTrust more generally. The Project involved scanning entire library collections by Google, typically in exchange for a set of scans those respective libraries could use for their own purposes as permitted by law. These secure digital copies were key to addressing the preservation issue presented by the brittle books problem. The partnership relied on several provisions of US copyright law such as sections 107 and 108, which limit the otherwise exclusive rights of authors. This also presented the opportunity to provide access to people with print disabilities because the digital formats can be marked up for use with readers and other devices that support reading by the blind and others for whom books are inaccessible.

Roughly concurrently with the formative years of HathiTrust, the World Intellectual Property Organization (WIPO) facilitated the negotiation of the Marrakesh Treaty to Facilitate Access to Published Works for Persons Who Are Blind, Visually Impaired or Otherwise Print Disabled (the Marrakesh Treaty or the Treaty). The Treaty was adopted on June 27, 2013, and went into effect on September 30, 2016.[21] As of April 2018, thirty-five countries were signatories.[22] (To date, the United States is not a signatory.) The importance of this Treaty cannot be overstated in terms of its potential impact on millions of lives. According to the World Blind Union, less than 10 percent of all published materials are accessible to blind and low vision people. This has enormous impact on human development.[23] The World Health Organization (WHO) statistics as of 2010 estimated that more than 285 million people worldwide live with visual impairments,

[18] Angelina Zaytsev, *HathiTrust and a Mission for Accessibility*, 18 J. Elec. Publ'g (2015), http://quod.lib.umich.edu/j/jep/3336451.0018.304?view=text;rgn=main. Zaytsev is HathiTrust Collection Services Librarian.

[19] 17 U.S.C. § 121. According to the Chafee Amendment, when authorized entities reproduce and distribute copies or phono records of previously published works in specialized formats exclusively for the blind or print disabled, such reproduction and distribution does not constitute infringement.

[20] *HathiTrust* district court opinion, *supra* note 8; Authors Guild, Inc. v. HathiTrust, 755 F.3d 87 (2d Cir. 2014); Author's Guild, Inc. v. Google Inc., 804 F. 3d 202 (2d Cir. 2015).

[21] *Marrakesh Treaty to Facilitate Access to Published Works for Persons Who Are Blind, Visually Impaired, or Otherwise Print Disabled*, World Intell. Prop. Org. [WIPO] (Jun. 27, 2013), www.wipo.int/treaties/en/ip/marrakesh/.

[22] *WIPO-Administered Treaties: Contracting Parties>Marrakesh VIP Treaty (Total Contracting Parties: 35)*, WIPO, www.wipo.int/treaties/en/ShowResults.jsp?treaty_id=843 (last visited Apr. 18, 2018).

[23] "In developed regions like North America & Europe, employment of blind people is only about 25% and in developing areas of the globe like Africa, Asia & Latin America, the number of blind people employed falls below 10%." In addition, ". . . over 90% of all published materials cannot be read by blind or low vision people." *WBU Priorities and Goals*, World Blind Union [WBU], www.worldblindunion.org/English/our-work/our-priorities/Pages/default.aspx (last visited Jul. 30, 2016).

thirty-nine million of whom are blind.[24] This is a profound area of concern and suggests opportunity in significantly addressing the SDGs.

We are starting to see the fruit of HathiTrust's commitment to provide meaningful access to the visually impaired globally. Access at HathiTrust partner University of Australia is already having impact.[25] The primary impediment to making greater access possible for the millions of people affected by visual impairment is existing copyright laws that fail to have clear, appropriately calibrated limitations to address this urgent need. HathiTrust can be part of addressing this challenge. Obvious and compelling reasons exist to assist this huge population. The technical issues can be efficiently addressed. The challenge is one of our own making, one that can be addressed in a cost-effective manner and without negative impact on copyright holders. This is possible with better implementation of appropriately calibrated, well-managed copyright exceptions as discussed later in this chapter.[26]

IV The Partnership

A *The Partnership Contract*[27]

In 2004, the University of Michigan entered a cooperative agreement with Google that formed the basis of the PPP contemplated in this chapter. This was a public document from the outset.[28] This public transparency provides a rare opportunity to describe and analyze the promises and pitfalls of this hybrid public–private institutional framework.[29]

[24] *Global Data on Visual Impairments 2010*, World Health Org. [WHO] (2012), www.who.int/blindness/publications/globaldata/en/.

[25] *See* Paul Harpur, *My Experience and the Experience of Millions*, HathiTrust: Perspectives from HathiTrust (May 24, 2017), www.hathitrust.org/blogs/perspectives-from-hathitrust/my-experience-and-experience-of-millions (discussing the 'book famine for the print disabled' and the transformative power of HathiTrust's work in this area: "A decade ago I was very print disabled. Now, with help from the HathiTrust and others, I am far less print disabled. In fact, when it comes to accessing many academic and cultural works, I am more print inconvenienced now. My parents, supporters and I used to spend hours scanning books for my studies and work. Now I ignore books I cannot access in an E-Book format that is not available in an E-Book that is accessible to persons with print disabilities. While it would be ideal to have reading equality; to go from difficult, time consuming and expensive access to a few books, to easy, cheap and rapid access to millions of books in a matter of a few years is an amazing, liberating and joyous experience. I would like the HathiTrust to be aware of the substantial personal and professional impact they are having upon the world's print disabled."). *See also* Paul Harpur, Discrimination, Copyright and Equality: Opening the E-Book for the Print Disabled (2017).

[26] *See also* Susan Isiko Štrba, chapter 9, *infra*.

[27] The words contract, partnership, and cooperative agreement are used interchangeably in this chapter. Formally, the document was called a memorandum of understanding (MOU).

[28] "We knew that the agreement would get a lot of attention and thought that rather than putting people to a lot of trouble and inundating the FOIA [Michigan Freedom of Information Act] office with requests that it would facilitate both ease of access and our proclivity toward transparency to put it up." Email from Jack Bernard, Assistant General Counsel, Office of the VP & Gen. Counsel, Univ. of Mich., to author (May 24, 2017). *See* Michigan Freedom of Information Act, M.C.L. 15.231.

[29] Google entered subsequent, similar agreements with other libraries. For example, in 2006 the Committee on Institutional Cooperation (CIC) entered a similar relationship with Google. The CIC "is a consortium of the Big Ten member universities plus the University of Chicago. For more than half a century, these world-class research institutions have advanced their academic missions, generated unique opportunities for students and faculty, and served the common good by sharing expertise, leveraging campus resources, and collaborating on innovative programs." *About*, Big Ten Acad. All. [BIG], www.btaa.org/about. Other

Box 10.2. Access Provisions in the Google-UML Partnership Contracts

4.4.2 Use of U of M Digital Copy in Cooperative Web Services. Subject to the restrictions set forth in this section, U of M shall have the right to use the U of M Digital Copy, in whole or in part at the U of M's sole discretion, as part of services offered in cooperation with partner research libraries such as the institutions in the Digital Library Federation. Before making any such distribution, U of M shall enter into a written agreement with the partner research library and shall provide a copy of such agreement to Google, which agreement shall: (a) contain limitations on the partner research library's use of the materials that correspond to and are at least as restrictive as the limitations placed on U of M's use of the U of M Digital Copy in section 4.4.1; and (b) shall expressly name Google as a third party beneficiary of that agreement, including the ability for Google to enforce the restrictions against the partner research library. [added emphasis.]

Contracts between Google and its other library partners are not in all cases publicly disclosed, and the precise terms of partnership agreements vary by library; however, at least some of these other partner libraries were presumably entitled to a copy of the digital copies made from its respective collections, in the same way that UML is.

At its most basic level, the Google-UML agreement provided that Google would be permitted to borrow books in order to scan the UML's collection to produce a set of digital facsimiles; in exchange, the library would receive access to a full set of those scans.[30] In negotiating the agreement, the university included a clause regarding the right and ability of the Library to share its library copy with members of the Digital Library Federation (DLF) and other similar consortia.[31]

This clause provides the foundation for the subsequent creation of HathiTrust by explicitly permitting the UML to use its digital copies at its discretion in cooperation with other research institutions. (See Box 10.2.)

The UML's agreement with Google is ongoing. There are dates in the agreement for trigger events, as well as obligations in contract regarding quality of scans, security, and uses of the scans. These terms are critical for ensuring that the both parties maintain their commitments. The agreement reflects mutual interdependencies and business goals.

early participants included the New York Public Library, Harvard, Stanford, and Oxford University. The overarching collaboration was referred to as the "Google Print Project" and later as the "Google Book Search Project."

30 U. Mich., Cooperative Agreement (2004), www.lib.umich.edu/files/services/mdp/um-google-cooperative-agreement.pdf.

31 The DLF was founded in 1995 with the vision of creating a distributed, open, digital library. It was initially composed of twelve academic libraries along with the Library of Congress, New York Public Library, the U.S. National Archives, and the Commission on Preservation and Access (now the Council on Library and Information Resources). Digital Library Federation [DLF], www.diglib.org/aboutdlf/ (last visited Aug. 1, 2017). Note that the Library of Congress and the U.S. National Archives are agencies of the US federal government. Today, the DLF has grown to 162 members today and, "is a robust and ever more diverse and inclusive community of practitioners who advance research, learning, social justice, and the public good through the creative design and wise application of digital library technologies." For a list of the current membership, *see Our Members*, DLF, www.diglib.org/members/. For more about the founding of the DLF, *see* Robert L. Jacobson, *Librarians Agree on Coordination of Digital Plans*, The Chron. of Higher Educ., May 12, 1995, www.chronicle.com/article/Librarians-Agree-on/84554/.

By contrast, many if not most purely charitable relationships can typically be rescinded at any time. Successful PPPs are likely to share meaningful obligations, enforceable through explicit contractual provisions.

B *Partnerships Shaped by People, Relationships, and Common Interests*

The contract between Google and the University of Michigan is an important artifact for understanding the motivations of the partners and the long-standing personal relationships that girded the Project. Google was quite candid in its interest in this partnership. The contract is a pragmatic business expression of Google's audacious investment in the PPP. Publicly available annual reports include letters from Google founders Sergey Brin and Larry Page to shareholders that mention the Project and where it fit in the overarching aspirations of the company relative to short-term profit.[32]

Additionally, one of the interesting aspects of this story is how it underscores personal connections as opportunities for common understanding and partnership building. (See Box 10.3.) Personal relationships engender trust and constructive risk taking. Universities have a central role in this story as platforms for relationship building. These connections between people and the sharing of ideas among them shaped a sense of what might be possible and demonstrate a series of social networks. In the absence of these social networks, it is unlikely that this project would have occurred at all.

Libraries engaged in these partnerships with Google began to think about what they could do to advance their collective mission as the result of this initiative. For example, there was a long-standing, recognized need for a shared digital repository.[33] Research

[32] The 2004 Founders' IPO letter starts with the defining statement that, "Google is not a conventional company." The letter continues affirm its commitment to "making the world a better place" along with a global perspective:

> We have also emphasized an atmosphere of creativity and challenge, which has helped us provide unbiased, accurate and free access to information for those who rely on us around the world ...
>
> We will not shy away from high-risk, high-reward projects because of short term earnings pressure. Some of our past bets have gone extraordinarily well, and others have not. Because we recognize the pursuit of such projects as the key to our long term success, we will continue to seek them out. For example, we would fund projects that have a 10% chance of earning a billion dollars over the long term. Do not be surprised if we place smaller bets in areas that seem very speculative or even strange when compared to our current businesses. Although we cannot quantify the specific level of risk we will undertake, as the ratio of reward to risk increases, we will accept projects further outside our current businesses, especially when the initial investment is small relative to the level of investment in our current businesses.

Larry Page and Sergey Brin, *IPO Letter: An Owner's Manual for Google Shareholders* (2004), *available at* https://abc.xyz/investor/founders-letters/2004/ipo-letter.html.

[33] "Digital Repositories offer a convenient infrastructure through which to store, manage, reuse, and curate digital materials. They are used by a variety of communities, may carry out many different functions, and can take many forms. The meaning of the term 'digital repository' is widely debated. Contemporary understanding has broadened from an initial focus on software systems to a wider and overall commitment to the stewardship of digital materials; this requires not just software and hardware, but also policies, processes, services, and people, as well as content and metadata. Repositories must be sustainable, trusted, well-supported and well-managed in order to function properly. Digital Repositories are also commonly referred to as 'institutional repositories' or 'digital archives.'" Nadja Semple, *Digital Repositories*, DCC Briefing Papers: Introduction to Curation. Edinburgh: Digital Curation Centre. Handle: 1842/3372. Available online: www.dcc.ac.uk/resources/briefing-papers/introduction-curation.

Box 10.3. Personal Relationships Leading to the Partnership

The significance of individual participants can be surmised in some of the relationships. For example, Google's Manager of Library Partnerships, Ben Bunnell, received a master's degree from the University of Michigan School of Information in 1998 and later graduated from the University of Michigan's Ross School of Business with a Master's in Business Administration in 2002. Bunnell is Google's Manager of Library Partnerships having joined Google AdWords in 2002 and the Book Search Project in 2004. In another University of Michigan connection, Google founder Larry Page earned his undergraduate degree at the University of Michigan in 1995, majoring in engineering and concentration in computer engineering."[34]

Jeremy York was one of the early HathiTrust staff members, serving first as Project Librarian from 2008 to 2013 and then as Assistant Director from 2013 to 2015. York began working for HathiTrust in 2008, the same year he finished his Master of Science in Information degree at the University of Michigan School of Information. At that time, there were 2.2 million scans of books in MBooks, the Library's digital book repository. MBooks was expanded and rebranded to become HathiTrust in October 2008. York recalled that in the fall of 2006, Paul Courant (then provost and later Dean of Libraries at the University of Michigan) and Bunnell (an alum) visited one of his classes to talk about the Google Library Project. The discussion focused in particular on the relationships Bunnell had with both Google and the University, which were instrumental to the partnership's formation.[35]

libraries have a long history of working cooperatively to address common challenges. Consistent with this cooperative culture, the formation of HathiTrust was:

> a bold move by leading research libraries to move their collections and traditional values into a new digital era. The governance and repository structures ... have been engineered to create a library that never forgets ... HathiTrust can be the universal library, but it is something we will all need to be a part of, and something it will take all of our institutions to create.[36]

C *Partnership Motivations: Private and Public Benefits*

Google's motivations are stated on the Google Books web page regarding the Library Project:

> The [Google] Library Project's aim is simple: make it easier for people to find relevant books – specifically, books they wouldn't find any other way such as those that are out of print – while carefully respecting authors' and publishers' copyrights. Our ultimate goal

[34] *Growth Strategies: Larry Page and Sergey Brin*, ENTREPRENEUR (Oct. 6, 2008), www.entrepreneur.com/article/197848; Nicole Casal Moore, *Google Co-Founder, U-M Alum Larry Page to Present Commencement Address*, MICH. NEWS (May 3, 2009), http://ns.umich.edu/new/releases/6934-google-co-founder-u-m-alum-larry-page-to-present-commencement-address (referencing date of graduation).

[35] Email from Jeremy York, PhD student at the University of Michigan School of Information, to author (Feb. 17, 2017). *See* Tom Tigani, *University-Google digitization effort turns page toward future book access*, THE UNIV. REC. ONLINE (Dec. 4, 2006), www.ur.umich.edu/0607/Dec04_06/09.shtml (for other comments from Bunnell).

[36] Jeremy York, *This Library Never Forgets: Preservation, Cooperation, and the Making of the HathiTrust Digital Library*, ARCHIVING 2009 FINAL PROGRAM AND PROCS. 5, 9 (2009).

> is to work with publishers and libraries to create a comprehensive, searchable, virtual card catalog of all books in all languages that helps users discover new books and publishers discover new readers.[37]

This language states Google's plain aspiration in partnering with libraries to create universal access to the world's knowledge and to develop improved search tools. The digital corpus resulting from electronic facsimiles of analog library collections would facilitate research and development for Google's products and services, such as its translation capacities. At the same time, its stated shared goals with the libraries and publishers included increasing access to information and expanding markets for books, respectively.

For participating libraries, the various goals of preservation, accessibility for people with print disabilities, access to public domain works, access to in-copyright works where permission was granted by a copyright holder were – and are – all aligned with Google's business proposition regarding HathiTrust. There was widespread recognition of the enormous investment by and risk to Google, in order to achieve this undertaking. As one knowledgeable observer noted,

> The library project is breathtaking in its scope and cost, and revolutionary in its implications ... While a handful of governments and corporations had the money and ... the interest to undertake this project, none had stepped up to the plate. Google was willing to spend big to make this happen, and it was willing before anyone else. If there are financial risks, copyright thickets, and logistical problems, and there undoubtedly are, Google had the courage and vision to see that risks were worth taking and the problems worth solving. (This doesn't detract from earlier digitization projects from others, some of them very large; none is this large.)[38]

For libraries, the scanning meant that there would be an enormous advance in a collective solution to the brittle book concern for a huge number of books, which would also have the collateral effect of increasing access for reading where legally feasible (for example, works in the public domain, works subject to rights like fair use or library exceptions, or with permission of a copyright holder). Libraries did not have the resources to address these concerns and opportunities at the scale Google was able to invest. Further, until that time, libraries had tended to focus on materials in the public domain. Works still in copyright were copied for preservation and access once they began falling apart – which made the timing and resource decisions an ongoing conundrum for libraries as stewards of memory.[39] Libraries were not willing to be challenged in court and actively avoided conflict around IP.

[37] *Google Library Project*, GOOGLE BOOKS, https://books.google.com/googlebooks/library/ (last visited Jul. 7, 2017).

[38] Peter Suber, *Google's Gigantic Library Project*, SPARC OPEN ACCESS NEWSL. (Jan. 2, 2005), https://dash.harvard.edu/bitstream/handle/1/4552061/suber_googlelibraryintro.htm?sequence=1.

[39] For example, the groundbreaking Making of America digitization project (MOA) began in 1995 as a joint effort of Cornell University and University of Michigan. The project focused on materials dating into the 1930s. After MOA, Michigan shifted to digitizing materials that met preservation requirements, regardless of copyright status with the belief that Section 108 supported that activity. Access to the preservation copies might be limited due to possible copyrights. Email from John P. Wilkin, Juanita J. and Robert E. Simpson Dean of Libraries, Univ. of Ill. at Urbana-Champaign, to author (May 30, 2017). "Making of America (MoA) is a digital library of primary sources in American social history from the antebellum period through reconstruction. The collection is particularly strong in the subject areas of education, psychology,

That said, in the larger legal context, new uses of digital technology were being litigated, thus giving early reassuring guidance for legally responsible strategies. For example, the 2003 case of *Kelly v. Arriba* held that making thumbnail copies of in copyright works for search purposes was a fair use under US law.[40]

There were and are many vocal critics of Google who were concerned that this scanning Project would result in a monopoly on world knowledge.[41] In the case of the Library's contract with Google, this fear was ultimately unfounded because provisions were made for the Library to retain its own set of scans for its own purposes. The Library would ultimately be able to use the scans however it saw fit within the confines of its responsibility as a steward of the copyrights embodied in the works.[42]

The partnership contracts between Google and its respective library partners such as UML functionally served as an escrow to the copyrighted works. Thus, Google could not proverbially hold the knowledge of the world hostage. Key contractual provisions in the UML partnership agreements prevented that risk and facilitated significant advance toward a leap in research and access to knowledge without fear of information lock-up. (See Box 10.2.) The formation of HathiTrust and retention of preservation scans by libraries with a distinct public mission, rather than a corporate commercial responsibility, reduced the risk of intellectual monopoly. The partnership relationship as expressed in the contracts reflected the different roles and responsibilities of the parties and the commitment to their respective stakeholders and shareholders.

The contracts provided for long-term independence from each other. This mutual independence may be an important aspect of a successful PPP because the incentives were functional, aligned to each partner's distinct mission. Google's stated interests were idealistic but also consciously aligned with their responsibilities to their stockholders as a publicly traded company. The Library, in obtaining its own set of scans, acted consistently with its centuries' old mission to its stakeholders as custodian of information for the public.[43]

American history, sociology, religion, and science and technology. The collection currently contains approximately 10,000 books and 50,000 journal articles with 19th century imprints." For more details about the project, see *About MoA*, MAKING OF AM. [MoA], http://quod.lib.umich.edu/m/moagrp/about.html. Making of America was supported by a grant from the Andrew W. Mellon Foundation. MOA website at http://quod.lib.umich.edu/m/moagrp/about.html

[40] Kelly v. Arriba Soft Corporation, 280 F.3d 934 (9th Cir. 2002) *withdrawn*, re-filed at 336 F.3d 811 (9th Cir. 2003); Pamela Samuelson, *Mass Digitization as Fair Use*, 57 COMM. ACM 20 (2014), http://scholarship.law.berkeley.edu/cgi/viewcontent.cgi?article=3353&context=facpubs; *See Authors Guild v. HathiTrust, supra* note 20.

[41] The 2013 documentary, *Google and the World Brain*, presented this anxiety. While the film included interviews with supporters of the Project, many interviewees expressed the fear that Google would monopolize the world's knowledge as contained in the worlds' great libraries. GOOGLE AND THE WORLD BRAIN (Polar Star Films 2013).

[42] *Id.* The title references H. G. Wells's essays in book of speeches he gave at the Royal Institution of Great Britain in which he expressed his sense of urgency and possibility of a utopian collective intelligence. H. G. WELLS, WORLD BRAIN (Methuen Publishing, Ltd.1938).

[43] Academic research utilizing the corpus as data (rather than as books for reading) is possible through the HathiTrust Research Center (HTRC), jointly launched by Indiana University and the University of Illinois at Urbana-Champaign. "Leveraging data storage and computational infrastructure at Indiana University and the University of Illinois at Urbana-Champaign, the HTRC will provision a secure computational and data environment for scholars to perform research using the HathiTrust Digital Library. The center will break new ground in the areas of text mining and nonconsumptive research, allowing scholars to fully

Some of Google's purposes coincided with library purposes; search and discovery were critical to the early discussions for all parties, in addition to preservation and access for those with print disabilities. For Google, possession of these scans – even if not used as books for individual reading purposes – provided a rich opportunity for research and product development in semantics, linguistics, machine intelligence, and improved search engine functions to name a few examples. As documented by the University of Michigan,

> Bunnell said [the] company and University officials also would like to expand access to texts in different languages. Bunnell said a system that would answer queries in one language by searching library data in all languages is a sort of "holy grail" that company officials and librarians everywhere would like to see one day, "but we're not there yet."[44]

These product development goals obviously impacted the overall market in digital information. Google had developed the Google Publisher Partner program that facilitated sales for and by publisher copyright holders of books embodied in the digital copies held by Google.[45] Thus the Project also arguably gave Google a competitive advantage that was hotly contested in litigation by other corporate behemoths in the digital technology industries.[46]

Some research indicates that, "the typical half-life of a publicly traded company is about a decade."[47] In contrast, the University of Michigan observed its bicentennial in 2017. Research library collections like UML are developed over centuries with a consciousness in each generation of the importance of collection and preserving for the very long term. The continuing mission of these research libraries differs radically from the drive of publicly traded companies to deliver near-term positive earnings in quarterly reports and financial value over time. The partnership was structured in a way that took into account the legitimate and distinct responsibilities of the respective parties: for the libraries, to their stakeholders, and for Google, to its shareholders. Pragmatism would seem to improve the likelihood of success of facilitating the differences between parties with such different goals.

utilize content of the HathiTrust Library while preventing intellectual property misuse within the confines of current U.S. copyright law." *See Our Research Center*, HATHITRUST, www.hathitrust.org/htrc.

44 *See* Tigani *supra* note 34. UML was also motivated by these opportunities. "I believe that these were also library purposes, from the beginning. Search and discovery were critical to the early discussion, along with preservation and access for those who have print disabilities." Email from Paul Courant, Arthur F. Thurnau Professor, Harold T. Shapiro Collegiate Professor of Public Policy, Professor of Economics, Professor of Information, and Faculty Associate in the Institute for Social Research, Univ. of Mich. to author (Jun. 4, 2017).

45 *See* Corinna Baksik, *Fair Use or Exploitation? The Google Book Search Controversy*, 6 PORTAL: LIBRS. AND THE ACAD. 399, 401 (2006), www.press.jhu.edu/sites/default/files/PLA-6.4-baksik.pdf (discussing Google's publisher program and its opt out policy implemented in the summer of 2005). "The policy allows copyright holders to upload a list of titles that they do not want scanned as part of the library project. When Google encounters these titles in a library, they will not scan them." The Authors Guild and the Association for American Publishers still filed suit against Google in September and October 2005, respectively.

46 *See, e.g., Author's Guild, Inc. v. Google, supra* note 20.

47 Madeleine I. G. Daepp et al., *The Mortality of Companies*, 12 J. ROYAL INTERFACE 1 (Apr. 1, 2015) *discussed in* Bourree Lam, *Where Do Firms Go When They Die?*, THE ATLANTIC, Apr. 12, 2015, http://rsif.royalsocietypublishing.org/content/12/106/20150120.

Box 10.4. The Litigation[48]

The Authors Guild, Inc. (Authors Guild), a collective of individuals and associational organizations, first brought action against HathiTrust, Inc. (HathiTrust), a public–private partnership of universities and university officials, in the Southern District of New York. The Authors Guild alleged that the HathiTrust Digital Library (HDL), a mass digitization of copyrighted books owned by universities, was a violation of the Copyright Act. The US District Court found that HathiTrust's use of copyrighted works constituted fair use and therefore not an infringement of copyright. Upon appeal, the US Court of Appeals for the Second Circuit affirmed this decision. The Second Circuit's fair use analysis included examining the purpose and character of the new work. HathiTrust's provision allowing print-disabled individuals to read the books contained in the HDL was, according to the court, a valid purpose under fair use. The Chafee Amendment within the Copyright Act as well as the Americans with Disabilities Act also supported HathiTrust's purpose in copying books to increase access to print-disabled individuals. In addition, the Court observed the amount of copying was reasonably necessary in relation to the purpose because full-text and image copies were necessary to fulfill their purpose of facilitation of searches and access for print-disabled individuals.

The Authors Guild also brought action against Google, Inc. (Google) who partnered with HathiTrust through the Google Books project. The US District Court found transformative use because the original texts were turned into "a comprehensive word index that helps readers, scholars, researchers, and others find books" by allowing users to see snippets of the original. The Second Circuit agreed that Google's search function is highly transformative. It also found that the snippet view provides the user with just enough context on the page to make sense of the results from the search function. Though Google made entire copies of books, this was found to be a reasonably necessary amount, much like in the aforementioned *HathiTrust* case because Google's snippet view function indicates only what is necessary and therefore does not usurp the original in the marketplace.

V Intellectual Property at the Core of the Partnership Equation

This narrative presents a kind of success, but with great cost and challenge even where the parties are aligned. The Google/UML partnership is one kind of relationship where practical interests were aligned in the face of considerable copyright questions for all parties that are the subject of now familiar litigation. (See Box 10.4.)

A *Copyright and Access to Knowledge*

In this new arena, there is an opportunity to change the deeply embedded assumptions about copyright and its relationship to access to knowledge and core development interests. Is it an overly broad truism that strong IP rights inevitably incentivize creation, innovation, and investment? Can the mutual incentives and motivations in this particular PPP demonstrate elements that could be modeled in other kinds of partnerships? Is the larger opportunity to advance the SDGs more effectively and predictably with

[48] *Author's Guild v. HathiTrust* and *Author's Guild, Inc. v. Google Inc.*, *supra* note 20.

more robust, internationally coherent copyright exceptions and limitations in support of the work of libraries and archives? These are key questions that global and national copyright policy must face in order to maximize access to knowledge consistent with the SDGs. While PPPs can facilitate work on the SDGs, in the domain of copyright and libraries, the most cost effective and least time intensive path is to update and align existing exceptions and limitations to copyright already provided to libraries.

There are some ways to generalize about lessons from this particular partnership. That said, for libraries to provide meaningful access to information in a shared way, the greater urgency is in consequential exceptions and limitations to copyright, which are tailored to meeting the mission of libraries while respecting the interests of copyright holders – a subject on ongoing multilateral consideration under WIPO.[49] Meaningful copyright exceptions and limitations at a global scale may be more effective at making broader progress on the SDGs in terms of knowledge sharing. Greater clarity for library-type uses would be likely to discourage infringement and create more fertile ground for respect for IP law, because the balance between the interests of rights holders and users would be better calibrated across different geographic regions.

Cultural trade statistics published by the United Nations indicate that the vast majority of import and/or export of cultural material is between the United States and Europe, and between Asia and southeast Asia, with a growing dominance of China. Other countries represent only small overall percentages.[50] Are these markets then neglected because they are not economically worth providing services for information provision? Are there other factors? What partnerships would be commercially valid for companies *and* support the SDGs in most of the countries located in the developing world? There is an obvious need for broader library use rights and multiple ways for qualified libraries to work together, but we are just beginning to explore these possibilities through settings like WIPO.

There is an analogous challenge in determining whether a work is in the public domain, as a legal matter. This legal issue is addressed next.

B *The Difficulty of the Public Domain*

One practical response to the question of the copyright status of books in HathiTrust was the Copyright Review Management System (CRMS) project, which emphasized the identification of books in the public domain within the HathiTrust collection. This

[49] Library issues were addressed as recently as May 1–5, 2017, at the meeting of the World Intellectual Property Organization's (WIPO) Standing Committee on Copyright and Related Rights (SCR/34) regarding limitations for libraries and archives. Among them, the Committee will update Kenneth D. Crews' study on these limitations (first published in 2008, updated in 2014 and 2015) and to continue collection of data relating to limitations and exceptions for museums. WIPO, *Standing Committee on Copyright and Related Rights: Summary by the Chair*, WIPO Doc. SCCR 34 (May 1–5, 2017), www.wipo.int/edocs/mdocs/copyright/en/sccr_34/sccr_34_ref_summary_by_the_chair.pdf; *see also* Teresa Hackett, *Three Outcomes for Libraries at WIPO*, Elec. Info. for Librs. [EIFL] blog, (May 22, 2017), www.eifl.net/blogs/three-outcomes-libraries-wipo.

[50] *See* U.N. Educ., Sci., and Cultural Org. [UNESCO]: Inst. of Stat., *The Globalisation of Cultural Trade: A Shift in Consumption, International flows of cultural goods and services 2004–2013*, 16–19 figs.4, 5, & 6 (2016).

CRMS project was only possible because of the existence of the scans produced by the Google/Library PPP. CRMS was the brainchild of John Wilkin as the founding director of HathiTrust.[51]

In negotiating the contract with Google and forming HathiTrust, Wilkin recognized the urgency of identifying public domain works in HathiTrust and making them as widely available as possible. CRMS identified public domain books that were: (1) published in the United States between 1923 and 1963 ("CRMS US"); and (2) published in the United Kingdom, Canada, and Australia ("CRMS World"). The CRMS US reviews focus on the existence or absence of formalities once required for works published in the United States under US law; the CRMS World reviews focus on identifying author death dates.

This copyright determination initiative was achievable through an interface that made possible secured access to scans to designated reviewers. The biggest challenge and cost of copyright research is the difficulty of obtaining legally relevant information in a cost-efficient way. To this point, the CRMS project reflected a significant investment. The initiative continued formally for nine years supported by three critical grants from the Institute for Museum and Library Services (a federal agency of the US government) totaling US$2,016,192 in grant funding, over sixty reviewers, and seventeen libraries.[52]

It should be a relatively simple and straightforward task to determine whether a given book is or is not in the public domain in a given jurisdiction. It is not. In fact, it is a complex task with often-indeterminate results that can vary by jurisdiction. This makes international solutions both critical and challenging. Identifying works in the public domain is a significant piece of the overall access picture, in addition to aligned library exceptions. Access to works in the public domain is critical to the overall bargain of copyright.

One suggestion based upon this extensive CRMS experience is that perhaps library exceptions could consider the application of the rule of the shorter term *in the context of libraries* so that works in the public domain in their country of origin could also be made available in an appropriately prescribed way for the balance of the term in the context of a qualified library (which would have to be defined). This might at least allow access for the difference in the term, whether or not the country overall adheres to the rule of the shorter term, especially for works that are not commercially available.[53]

[51] John P. Wilkin served as the associate university librarian for publishing and technology at the University of Michigan Library and as executive director of HathiTrust. He conceived and was the initial principal investigator for the first grant supporting the CRMS project. I served as the principal investigator for the two subsequent grants.

[52] Grant numbers LG-05–08-0141–08, LG-05–11-0150–11, and LG-05–14-0042–14.

For a detailed discussion of CRMS, see FINDING THE PUBLIC DOMAIN: COPYRIGHT REVIEW MANAGEMENT SYSTEM TOOLKIT (Levine, Melissa et al. eds., 2016), http://quod.lib.umich.edu/cgi/t/text/idx/c/crmstoolkit?page=home. *See also*, Melissa Levine, *Finding the Public Domain: The Copyright Review Management System*, ITHAKA, (Oct. 26, 2016), https://doi.org/10.18665/sr.289081.

[53] WIPO, *Berne Convention for the Protection of Literary and Artistic Arts*, Article 7 §8 (1979) ("In any case, the term shall be governed by the legislation of the country where protection is claimed; however, unless the legislation of that country otherwise provides, the term shall not exceed the term fixed in the country of origin of the work").

C *Meaningful Policy, Effective Law*

As a public policy matter, library use rights are well established and ubiquitous in national and international law – although they vary in form and consistency. Key limitations to the otherwise exclusive rights of a copyright holder such as fair use are explicitly included in US copyright law to further legal and public policy, as described earlier. This illustrates that strong copyright needs to be balanced with strong, properly calibrated rights for the public, including those for libraries to support initiatives like the HathiTrust that fill a need not met by the private sector alone. These rights of the public and, in tandem, the various copyright exceptions and limitations in support of public uses, are as important as the rights of copyright holders in maintaining the system. That said, an intrinsic tension plays out in the international copyright background regarding the activity of a PPP such as HathiTrust. Library exceptions at the WIPO level require that limitations on an author's otherwise exclusive IP right are subject to the three-step test; that is, these exceptions may be allowed only to the extent that they "do not conflict with a normal exploitation of the work" and "do not unreasonably prejudice the legitimate interests of the author."[54] Arguably, there are also practical tensions between right to education and authorship in the various international human rights instruments that cover the area of knowledge and education.[55]

In US research libraries, there is growing confidence regarding the application of fair use in recent years as the result of the litigation arising from the Google Books Project (see box 3) as well as other cases like *Kelly v. Arriba Soft*. However, at the time the UML and Google entered their formal relationship, there was considerably more legal uncertainty than exists today. The partners had to commit resources and accept the risk of mounting a legal defense, which posed a significant cost even anticipating that they would prevail. In the absence of appropriate, administrable exceptions to copyright tailored to libraries, the potential legal risk and litigation costs make this kind of partnership prohibitive for most, thus reducing the possibility of otherwise valuable PPPs that would respect copyright and simultaneously support the SDGs.

[54] *Berne Convention, supra* note 53, at Article 9 §2. Right of Reproduction. This is often referred to as the three-step test. Article 11 of the Marrakesh Treaty duplicates the language of the three-step test in the TRIPS Agreement, which refers to legitimate interests of the rights holder, and that of the Berne Convention and the WIPO Copyright Treaty, which refer to the legitimate interests of the author. *WIPO Copyright Treaty*, WIPO (Dec. 20, 1996), www.wipo.int/treaties/en/ip/wct/; TRIPS: Agreement on Trade-Related Aspects of Intellectual Property Rights, Marrakesh Agreement Establishing the World Trade Organization, Annex 1C, 1869 U.N.T.S 299 (Apr. 15, 1994). *See* Laurence R. Helfer et al., The World Blind Union Guide to the Marrakesh Treaty 51–59 (2017); Martin Senftleben, Copyright, Limitations and the Three-Step Test: An Analysis of the Three-Step Test in International and EC Copyright Law 52 (2004).

[55] *United Nations Universal Declaration of Human Rights of 1948*, which explicitly addresses a right to education in Article 26 while the latter part of Article 27 recognizes authors' intellectual property rights, each expressing core humanist values written in the wake of the Second World War's devastation. Section 1 of Article 26 of the *United Nations Universal Declaration of Human Rights of 1948* states in part that, "Everyone has the right to education." Section 1 of Article 27 states that, "Everyone has the right freely to participate in the cultural life of the community, to enjoy the arts and to share in scientific advancement and its benefits. Section 2 states that, "Everyone has the right to the protection of the moral and material interests resulting from any scientific, literary or artistic production of which he is the author." G. A. Res. 217 (III) A, Universal Declaration of Human Rights, U.N. Doc. A/810, at Article 27 (1948), www.un.org/en/universal-declaration-human-rights/.

Productive results such as this could be obtained through more collaborative partnerships, fewer hardline positions on copyright matters in the library context, and more nuanced understanding in WIPO and similar international fora. Private sector support for library-type exceptions to copyright would facilitate preservation and some level of access by institutions with publicly oriented missions. Carefully tailored library-type exceptions to copyright in public laws, including treaty law, would facilitate preservation, encourage legally appropriate access, and reduce concerns about the complexity of navigating varied legal regimes in a cost-effective manner. They may also reduce copyright infringement and increase respect for rule of law that will, over time, improve the security of works relying on copyright for investment.

These partnership relationships did not explicitly assume any formal development agenda in the context of the SDGs (which were formulated roughly concurrently with the establishment of Google). Yet, the SDGs are implicitly served through increased access to information and broader participation in the knowledge ecosystem, because each SDG requires access to information and knowledge for reliable research and to inspire new ideas and connections.[56] The issues and opportunities raised by this particular library–corporate relationship have bearing upon the successful implementation of all of the SDGs to the extent that greater access to knowledge, expression, and information are foundational to informed decision making, research, education, and innovation. Access to knowledge and information is assumed as an underpinning to all the SDGs. Libraries have a significant and unique but not exclusive role in this endeavor.

Conclusion

What are the ingredients for a sustainable partnership commitment? This is an essential question to ask in any relationship and is not unique to PPPs. This chapter demonstrates some best practices that optimize the success of one particular partnership that promotes preservation of and access to knowledge.

As a practical matter, it is possible for anyone, anywhere to have access to cultural collections in electronic form. The romantic promise of a global digital Library of Alexandria is tantalizingly possible. With sufficient private investment, cultural institutions could provide unprecedented access to research, scholarship, and memory collections. In turn, more universalized access to such collections would contribute to new knowledge generation that is foundational to achieving any and all of the SDGs. Strategic partnerships between cultural institutions, like public libraries and private sector partners reflect mutual incentives. Private actors can be incentivized to work with cultural institutions for reasons that go beyond producing reproductions (search engine, natural language research, access to collections, or reputation enhancement by association). The relationship benefits each entity and their respective constituents. The PPP between UML and Google – among others – amply demonstrate the power of such partnerships to support knowledge preservation and facilitate access to knowledge by people with print disabilities.

56 IFLA, *supra* note 6.

References

Americans With Disabilities Act of 1990, Pub. L. No. 101–336, 104 Stat 327 (codified as amended at 42 U.S.C. §§ 12101, et seq.).

Arthur, Kathleen, Sherry Byrne, Elisabeth Long, Carla Q. Montori, and Judith Nadler, RECOGNIZING DIGITALIZATION AS A PRESERVATION REFORMATTING METHOD, ASS'N OF RES. LIBRS. (2004), www.arl.org/storage/documents/publications/digitization-preservation-reformatting-2004.pdf (last visited Nov. 23, 2017).

Author's Guild, Inc. v. Google Inc., 804 F. 3d 202 (2d Cir. 2015).

Authors Guild, Inc. v. HathiTrust, 755 F.3d 87 (2d Cir. 2014).

Authors Guild, Inc. v. HathiTrust, 902 F. Supp. 2d 445, 460–64, (S.D.N.Y. 2012).

Baksik, Corinna, *Fair Use or Exploitation? The Google Book Search Controversy*, 6 PORTAL: LIBRS. AND THE ACAD. 399, 401 (2006), www.press.jhu.edu/sites/default/files/PLA-6.4-baksik.pdf (last visited Nov. 23, 2017).

Band, Jonathan and Jonathan Gerafi, FAIR USE/FAIR DEALING HANDBOOK (2015), http://infojustice.org/wp-content/uploads/2015/03/fair-use-handbook-march-2015.pdf (last visited Nov. 23, 2017).

Bergquist, Kevin, *Google Project About the Public Good*, UNIV. REC., (Feb. 8, 2006) www.ur.umich.edu/0506/Feb06_06/22.shtml (last visited Nov. 23, 2017).

Big Ten Academic Alliance, *About* www.btaa.org/about (last visited Nov. 23, 2017).

Daepp, Madeleine I. G. et al., *The Mortality of Companies*, 12 J. ROYAL INTERFACE 1, (Apr. 1, 2015) http://rsif.royalsocietypublishing.org/content/12/106/20150120 (last visited Nov. 23, 2017).

Digital Library Federation, www.diglib.org/aboutdlf/(last visited Nov. 23, 2017).

Digital Library Federation, *Our Members*, www.diglib.org/members/ (last visited Nov. 23, 2017).

Digital Public Library of America, https://dp.la/ (last visited Nov. 23, 2017).

Europeana, www.europeana.eu/portal/en (last visited Nov. 23, 2017).

G. A. RES. 217 (III) A, Universal Declaration of Human Rights, U.N. Doc. A/810, at Article 27 (1948), www.un.org/en/universal-declaration-human-rights/ (last visited Nov. 23, 2017).

G. A. RES. 217 (III) A, Universal Declaration of Human Rights, U.N. Doc. A/810, at Article 27 (1948), www.un.org/en/universal-declaration-human-rights/ (last visited Nov. 23, 2017).

GOOGLE AND THE WORLD BRAIN (Polar Star Films 2013).

Google Books, *Google Library Project*, https://books.google.com/googlebooks/library/ (last visited Nov. 23, 2017).

Growth Strategies: Larry Page and Sergey Brin, ENTREPRENEUR (Oct. 6, 2008), www.entrepreneur.com/article/197848 (last visited Nov. 23, 2017).

Hackett, Teresa, *Three Outcomes for Libraries at WIPO*, ELEC. INFO. FOR LIBRS. [EIFL] BLOG, (May 22, 2017), www.eifl.net/blogs/three-outcomes-libraries-wipo (last visited Nov. 23, 2017).

Harpur, Paul, DISCRIMINATION, COPYRIGHT AND EQUALITY: OPENING THE E-BOOK FOR THE PRINT DISABLED (2017).

Harpur, Paul, *My Experience and the Experience of Millions*, HATHITRUST: PERSPECTIVES FROM HATHITRUST (May 24, 2017), www.hathitrust.org/blogs/perspectives-from-hathitrust/my-experience-and-experience-of-millions (last visited Nov. 23, 2017).

HATHITRUST, *Our Partnership*, https://www.hathitrust.org/partnership. (last visited Nov. 23, 2017).

HATHITRUST, *Our Research Center*, www.hathitrust.org/htrc (last visited Nov. 23, 2017).

HATHITRUST, *HathiTrust Permissions Agreements*, www.hathitrust.org/permissions_agreement.

Helfer, Laurence R., Molly K. Land, Ruth L. Okediji, and Jerome H. Reichman, THE WORLD BLIND UNION GUIDE TO THE MARRAKESH TREATY (2017).

International Federation of Library Associations and Institutions, *Development and Access to Information 2017* (2017).

Jacobson, Robert L., *Librarians Agree on Coordination of Digital Plans*, THE CHRON. OF HIGHER EDUC., May 12, 1995, www.chronicle.com/article/Librarians-Agree-on/84554/ (last visited Nov. 23, 2017).

Kelly v. Arriba Soft Corporation, 280 F.3d 934 (9th Cir. 2002) *withdrawn*, re-filed at 336 F.3d 811 (9th Cir. 2003).

Lam, Bourree, *Where Do Firms Go When They Die?*, THE ATLANTIC, Apr. 12, 2015.

MAKING OF AMERICA, *About MoA*, http://quod.lib.umich.edu/m/moagrp/about.html.

NATIONAL RESEARCH COUNCIL, LC21: A DIGITAL STRATEGY FOR THE LIBRARY OF CONGRESS (2000), www.nap.edu/read/9940/chapter/1#ii.

Levine, Melissa, Richard C. Adler, Justin Bonfiglio, Kristina Eden, and Brian S. Hall, FINDING THE PUBLIC DOMAIN: COPYRIGHT REVIEW MANAGEMENT SYSTEM TOOLKIT (2016), http://quod.lib.umich.edu/cgi/t/text/idx/c/crmstoolkit?page=home (last visited Nov. 23, 2017).

Levine, Melissa, *Finding the Public Domain: The Copyright Review Management System*, ITHAKA, (Oct. 26, 2016), https://doi.org/10.18665/sr.289081 (last visited Nov. 23, 2017).

Marcum, Deanna, DUE DILIGENCE AND STEWARDSHIP IN A TIME OF CHANGE AND UNCERTAINTY, ITHAKA (2016), www.sr.ithaka.org/wp-content/uploads/2016/04/SR_Issue_Brief_Due-Diligence_Stewardship042616.pdf (last visited Nov. 23, 2017).

Michigan Freedom of Information Act, M.C.L. 15.231.

Moore, Nicole Casal, *Google Co-Founder, U-M Alum Larry Page to Present Commencement Address*, MICH. NEWS (May 3, 2009), http://ns.umich.edu/new/releases/6934-google-co-founder-u-m-alum-larry-page-to-present-commencement-address (last visited Nov. 23, 2017).

Page, Larry and Sergey Brin, *IPO Letter: An Owner's Manual for Google Shareholders* (2004), *available at* https://abc.xyz/investor/founders-letters/2004/ipo-letter.html (last visited Nov. 23, 2017).

Ritzenthaler, Mary Lynn, PRESERVING ARCHIVES AND MANUSCRIPTS (2nd ed., 2010).

Samuelson, Pamela, *Mass Digitization as Fair Use*, 57 COMM. ACM 20 (2014), http://scholarship.law.berkeley.edu/cgi/viewcontent.cgi?article=3353&context=facpubs (last visited Nov. 23, 2017).

Semple, Nalja, *Digital Repositories*, DCC Briefing Papers: Introduction to Curation. Edinburgh: Digital Curation Centre. Handle: 1842/3372. Available online: www.dcc.ac.uk/resources/briefing-papers/introduction-curation (last visited Nov. 23, 2017).

Senftleben, Martin, COPYRIGHT, LIMITATIONS AND THE THREE-STEP TEST: AN ANALYSIS OF THE THREE-STEP TEST IN INTERNATIONAL AND EC COPYRIGHT LAW (2004).

Suber, Peter, *Google's Gigantic Library Project*, SPARC OPEN ACCESS NEWSL. (Jan. 2, 2005), https://dash.harvard.edu/bitstream/handle/1/4552061/suber_googlelibraryintro.htm?sequence=1 (last visited Nov. 23, 2017).

Smith, Abby, THE EVIDENCE IN HAND: REPORT ON THE TASK FORCE ON THE ARTIFACT IN LIBRARY COLLECTIONS (Council on Libr. and Info. Res. 2001), www.clir.org/pubs/reports/pub103/pub103.pdf (last visited Nov. 23, 2017).

Smith, Abby, THE FUTURE OF THE PAST: PRESERVATION IN AMERICAN RESEARCH LIBRARIES (1999), www.clir.org/pubs/reports/reports/pub82/pub82text.html (last visited Nov. 23, 2017).

Tigani, Tom, *University-Google digitization effort turns page toward future book access*, THE UNIV. REC. ONLINE (Dec. 4, 2006), www.ur.umich.edu/0607/Dec04_06/09.shtml (last visited Nov. 23, 2017).

University of Michigan, COOPERATIVE AGREEMENT (2004), www.lib.umich.edu/files/services/mdp/um-google-cooperative-agreement.pdf (last visited Nov. 23, 2017).

U.N. EDUCATIONAL, SCIENTIFIC, AND CULTURAL ORGANIZATION, INST. OF STAT., *The Globalisation of Cultural Trade: A Shift in Consumption, International flows of cultural goods and services 2004–2013*, 16–19 figs. 4, 5 & 6 (2016).

U.S. Copyright Act, 17 U.S.C §§ 101–1332 (2012).

WBU Priorities and Goals, World Blind Union, www.worldblindunion.org/English/our-work/our-priorities/Pages/default.aspx (last visited Nov. 23, 2017).

Wells, H. G., World brain (Methuen Publishing, Ltd. 1938).

World Health Org. *Global Data on Visual Impairments 2010* (2012), www.who.int/blindness/publications/globaldata/en/ (last visited Nov. 23, 2017).

World Intellectual Property Organization [WIPO], *Marrakesh Treaty to Facilitate Access to Published Works for Persons Who Are Blind, Visually Impaired, or Otherwise Print Disabled* (Jun. 27, 2013), www.wipo.int/treaties/en/ip/marrakesh/(last visited Nov. 23, 2017).

WIPO, *WIPO Copyright Treaty* (Dec. 20, 1996), WIPO, www.wipo.int/treaties/en/ip/wct/ (last visited Nov. 23, 2017).

WIPO, *WIPO-Administered Treaties: Contracting Parties>Marrakesh VIP Treaty (Total Contracting Parties: 30)*, WIPO, www.wipo.int/treaties/en/ShowResults.jsp?treaty_id=843 (last visited Nov. 23, 2017).

WIPO, *Berne Convention for the Protection of Literary and Artistic Arts*, Article 7 §8 (1979).

WIPO, *Standing Committee on Copyright and Related Rights: Summary by the Chair*, WIPO Doc. SCCR 34 (May 1–5, 2017), www.wipo.int/edocs/mdocs/copyright/en/sccr_34/sccr_34_ref_summary_by_the_chair.pdf (last visited Nov. 23, 2017).

World Trade Organization, Agreement on Trade-Related Aspects of Intellectual Property Rights, Marrakesh Agreement Establishing the World Trade Organization, Annex 1C, 1869 U.N.T.S 299 (Apr. 15, 1994).

York, Jeremy, *This Library Never Forgets: Preservation, Cooperation, and the Making of the HathiTrust Digital Lib*rary, Archiving 2009 Final Program and Procs. 5, 9 (2009).

Zaytsev, Angelina, *HathiTrust and a Mission for Accessibility*, 18 J. Elec. Publ'g (2015), http://quod.lib.umich.edu/j/jep/3336451.0018.304?view=text;rgn=main (last visited Nov. 23, 2017).

Part III

Environmental Issues: Green Technologies and Agriculture

11 The Rise of Public–Private Partnerships in Green Technologies and the Role of Intellectual Property Rights

Ahmed Abdel-Latif*

Introduction

Innovation and the large-scale diffusion of green technologies are widely recognised as key elements both to implement the Sustainable Development Goals (SDGs) and to address climate change. At the same time, there is also broad agreement that boosting innovation and accelerating the diffusion of these technologies requires increased public and private investments as well as more collaborative efforts. As a result, in recent years, we have witnessed a proliferation of public–private partnerships (PPPs) in green technologies.[1]

While PPPs have acquired greater importance in addressing global challenges in general, and particularly in public health, they have received relatively little attention in relation to green technologies. Against this background, this chapter will outline how the multilateral regimes governing climate change and sustainable development not only recognises the role of PPPs, but also, increasingly, seeks to enhance their contribution to global efforts to accelerate technology diffusion and innovation in green technologies. These efforts by PPPs connect the multilateral mechanisms for encouraging the production and dissemination of green technologies within the specific space of climate change mitigation and adaption to the more comprehensive and holistic SDGs of the 2030 Agenda for Sustainable Development (2030 Agenda).[2] The chapter first provides an overview of the evolution of technology and innovation in the context of global climate change and sustainable development discussions. The next section examines how these discussions have addressed intellectual property (IP) issues to date. Following this is an account of how PPPs in green technologies have sought to approach IP matters in a pragmatic manner that stands in contrast to the general stalemate which has characterised in recent years the related debates on intellectual property rights (IPRs) at the multilateral level. The chapter concludes with examples of PPPs at the multilateral level (WIPO GREEN) as well as at the bilateral level (the US–China Clean Energy Research Center and the US–India Partnership to Advance Clean Energy).

* This chapter is written in a personal capacity. The views expressed are those of the author and do not necessarily reflect the views of any institution with which he is affiliated.

[1] The term 'green technologies' is used in the broad sense of 'environmentally sound technologies' including climate change, clean energy and renewable energy technologies.

[2] G. A. Res. A/70/1,*Transforming Our World: The 2030 Agenda for Sustainable Development*, A/RES/70/1 (Sep. 25, 2015), *available at*: www.un.org/ga/search/view_doc.asp?symbol=A/RES/70/1&Lang=E [hereinafter 2030 *Agenda*].

I Technology, Innovation and PPPs in the Global Climate and Sustainable Development Regimes

The international community has long recognised the importance of technology and innovation for the realization of sustainable development and for global efforts to tackle climate change. This section provides a brief overview of pertinent multilateral agreements and developments in this area.

Agenda 21, adopted by the Rio Earth summit (1992), emphasized the central role of the transfer of "environmentally sound"[3] technologies. Following suit, most of the multilateral environmental agreements (MEAs), adopted at the Rio Summit and thereafter, included provisions on technology transfer. This is the case, for instance, of the [1992] United Nations Framework Convention on Climate Change (UNFCCC or Convention). Article 4.5 of the Convention states:

> The developed countries (. . .) shall take all practicable steps to promote, facilitate and finance, as appropriate, the transfer of or access to environmentally sound technologies and know how to other Parties, particularly developing country Parties, to enable them to implement the provisions of the Convention (. . .).[4]

Furthermore, Article 4.7 of the Convention makes the extent to which developing countries will implement their commitments under the Convention conditional on the effective implementation by developed countries of their commitments related to financial resources and transfer of technology.

However, for many years and often along a North–South divide, countries wrangled over how such provisions should be implemented. On the one hand, developed countries argued that market forces and the private sector were the main vehicles for technology diffusion and thus the focus should be on fostering an enabling environment in developing countries for attracting investments and on strengthening local capacities to absorb technologies. On the other hand, developing countries contended that industrialised countries had considerable leeway to orient technology flows through a broad range of public policy and financial instruments and pointed to the fact that public research institutions played an important role in technology development in these countries. They pressed on the need for concrete mechanisms at the international level to promote technology transfer.

As this North–South debate continued, agreement was nevertheless reached in 2001 at the Marrakesh Conference of the Parties (COP) of the UNFCCC on a framework to implement these technology transfer provisions. This framework consisted of the identification of the technology needs of developing countries, information exchange, capacity building, enabling environments, and the creation of an expert group on technology transfer.[5] Subsequently, the platform TTClear was established as an information clearing

[3] U.N. Conference on Environment and Development (UNCED), *Earth Summit Agenda 21: Programme of Action for Sustainable Development*, ¶¶34.1 – 34.29 (Dec. 1994), *available at:* www.dataplan.info/img_upload/7bdb1584e3b8a53d337518d988763f8d/agenda21-earth-summit-the-united-nations-programme-of-action-from-rio_1.pdf [hereinafter *Agenda 21*].

[4] United Nations Framework Convention on Climate Change [UNFCCC], art. 4.5 (Jun. 4, 1992), *available at:* https://unfccc.int/resource/docs/convkp/conveng.pdf.

[5] UNFCC, *Report of the Conference of the Parties on Its Seventh Session, Held at Marrakesh From 29 October to 20 November 2001*, Decision 4/CP.7, FCCC/CP/2001/13/Add.1 (Jan. 21, 2002).

house on climate technologies and the Expert Group on Technology Transfer (EGTT) was created. Technology needs assessments (TNAs) were carried out to identify the barriers to technology transfer facing developing countries. Yet, this overall framework did not meet sufficiently the expectations of many developing countries aspiring for more ambitious measures.

In 2007, at the Bali COP, a new process of negotiations was launched and technology transfer was identified as one of the key priorities and building blocks of the future international climate regime. In 2010, at the Cancun COP, the parties agreed on the creation of a new institutional arrangement under the Convention, the so-called Technology Mechanism (TM), to accelerate the development and diffusion of climate change technologies. The TM is composed of two bodies: a policy body known as the Technology Executive Body (TEC), as well as an operational arm, which is called the Climate Technology Centre and Network (CTCN). The TEC and the CTCN have been in operation, respectively, since 2011 and 2014. The United Nations Environment Programme (UNEP) hosts the CTCN in collaboration with the United Nations Industrial Development Organization (UNIDO) and with the support of a consortium of partners. The Paris Agreement endorsed the TM and the 2015 decision adopting the Agreement calls for strengthening it.[6]

The TM is an important milestone in efforts to operationalise the technology transfer provisions of the UNFCCC. Its mandate embodies a more novel and dynamic approach to technology transfer reflecting many of the changes at work in the past two decades. This approach includes a greater focus on innovation as an overarching concept and priority, a stronger recognition of the role of the private sector, and an acknowledgement of the growing technological capabilities of some developing countries, particularly emerging economies. It broadly marks a shift away from the North–South divide and the top-down approach that characterised the original debates on technology transfer towards a more collaborative, decentralized, and dynamic one.[7]

The emphasis on public–private collaboration and partnerships in the mandates of the TM and of its two bodies, the TEC and the CTCN, is one of the novel features emblematic of this new approach. For instance, one of the functions of the TEC is to

> [p]romote and facilitate collaboration on the development and transfer of technology for mitigation and adaptation between governments, the private sector, non-profit organizations and academic and research communities.[8]

The CTCN's mandate also underlines the importance of such collaboration as one of its functions is to be

[6] The Paris Agreement, Apr. 22, 2016, *available at:* http://unfccc.int/files/essential_background/convention/application/pdf/english_paris_agreement.pdf. Article 10 (3) of the Agreement states that the TM 'shall serve this Agreement.' For an overview of Article 10 of the Paris Agreement on Technology, *see* Heleen de Coninck and Ambuj Sagar, *Technology Development and Transfer (Article 10), in* THE PARIS AGREEMENT ON CLIMATE CHANGE: ANALYSIS AND COMMENTARY (Daniel Klein, María Pía Carazo, Meinhard Doelle, Jane Bulmer, and Andrew Higham eds., 2017).

[7] Ahmed Abdel-Latif, *The Climate Technology Mechanism: Issues and Challenges*, International Centre for Trade and Sustainable Development [ICTSD] (Mar. 2011), www.ictsd.org/downloads/2011/04/technologymechanism.pdf.

[8] UNFCCC, *The Cancun Agreements: Outcome of the Work of the Ad Hoc Working Group on Long-term Cooperative Action Under the Convention*, ¶121(d), Decision 1/CP.16, FCCC/CP/2010/7/Add.1 (Mar. 15, 2011) [hereinafter *The Cancun Agreements*].

> [s]timulating and encouraging, through collaboration with the private sector, public institutions, academia and research institutions, the development and transfer of existing and emerging environmentally sound technologies, as well as opportunities for North/ South, South/South and triangular technology cooperation.[9]

More importantly, the CTCN's mandate makes specific reference to international PPPs in terms of it

> facilitating a Network of national, regional, sectoral and international technology centres, networks, organizations and initiatives with a view to: (ii) Facilitating international partnerships among public and private stakeholders to accelerate the innovation and diffusion of environmentally sound technologies to developing country Parties.[10]

The TEC has touched upon PPPs in the context of its work on innovation. For instance, in its key messages to COP 23, the TEC recommended that Parties are encouraged "to enhance public and private partnership in the RD&D of climate technologies by increasing expenditure for it and providing a clear policy signal of a long-term commitment to act on climate change."[11] On its part, the CTCN has developed a large Network of Members (Network) comprised of academic, finance, non-government, private sector, public sector, and research entities, as well as over 150 National Designated Entities (NDEs) which are national focal points selected by their countries. The Network engages in technical services, information exchange, and capacity building activities, particularly in the context of responding to the technical assistance requests from developing countries, which is the CTCN's core activity. This Network could be broadly considered in itself a PPP to accelerate the diffusion of green technologies.[12] At the same, much potential remains to further develop and flesh out the implementation of the CTCN's mandate regarding the facilitation of international PPPs, through specific initiatives for certain technologies and sectors, particularly given that the CTCN is still at an early stage of its work.

Beyond the TM, it is also important to note that the emphasis on the collaboration and complementarity between public and private actors is a central aspect of the overall philosophy underpinning the approach which led to the adoption of the Paris Agreement. Two initiatives, *Mission Innovation* and the *Breakthrough Coalition*, both launched at the Paris Climate Conference in 2015, are prime examples in clean energy innovation. *Mission Innovation* (MI) is a global initiative of twenty-two countries and the European Union which have committed to seek to double their clean energy research and development (R&D) investments over five years with the objective of dramatically accelerating global clean energy innovation. MI's launch statement states that participating countries may also pursue joint research efforts through PPPs as well as joint research among participating countries.[13] The *Breakthrough Energy Coalition* is a partnership of

[9] *The Cancun Agreements*, *supra* note 8, at ¶123(b).

[10] *The Cancun Agreements*, *supra* note 8, at ¶123(b)(ii).

[11] UNFCCC, *Joint Annual Report of the Technology Executive Committee and the Climate Technology Centre and Network for 2017*, FCCC/SB/2017/3, ¶62(b), at: http://unfccc.int/resource/docs/2017/sb/eng/03.pdf [hereinafter *Joint Annual Report*].

[12] As of September 2017, the Network consisted of 377 members with the private sector representing 42 per cent of the total network membership, followed by academic and research organizations (24%). *Joint Annual Report*, *supra* note 11, at ¶77.

[13] Press Release, Mission Innovation, Joint Launch Statement (Nov. 30, 2015), *available at:* www.mission-innovation.net/wp-content/uploads/2015/11/Mission-Innovation-Joint-Launch-Statement.pdf.

leading investors committed to broad investment in new energy technologies in over twenty countries. The Coalition committed to invest capital in early-stage technology development coming out of MI countries, so as to catalyse broad business participation in the commercialization and deployment of clean energy technologies worldwide.[14]

The simultaneous and coordinated launch of these two initiatives at the Paris COP signalled that the scale and magnitude of the challenge to foster clean energy innovation requires an active involvement of both the public actors represented by governments and the private sector.

These efforts are also linked to Agenda 2030's sustainable development focus. Although Sustainable Development Goal (SDG) 9 specifically calls for "fostering innovation,"[15] technology and innovation play a critical role in the implementation of most of the Sustainable Development Goals (SDGs). SDG 17's emphasis on 'revitalising the global partnership for development' puts partnerships at the heart of global efforts to implement all the SDGs. In 2015, a Technology Facilitation Mechanism (TFM) was launched to support the implementation for the SDGs. The TFM was first envisaged in the RIO+20 Declaration (2012) and was inspired from the example of the climate TM.[16] The TFM is tasked with facilitating multi-stakeholder collaboration and partnerships through the sharing of information, experiences, best practices, and policy advice among Member States, civil society, the private sector, the scientific community, and United Nations entities.[17] It has three components: a United Nations Interagency Task Team on Science, Technology and Innovation for the SDGs (IATT), including a ten-member group of representatives from civil society, the private sector, and the scientific community; a collaborative Multi-stakeholder Forum on Science, Technology and Innovation for the SDGs (STI Forum); and an online platform as a gateway for information on existing STI initiatives, mechanisms, and programs.

The important point to highlight about initiatives such as the climate TM, the TFM, and others is that partnerships and collaboration involving public and private sector actors in the field of technology and innovation are now solidly anchored in the overall international frameworks for climate and sustainable development cooperation whether it is the Paris Agreement or the 2030 Agenda.

II The Debate on Intellectual Property and Green Technologies[18]

Although the 1992 Agenda 21 document includes extensive and bold mentions to intellectual property rights in relation to the transfer of environmentally sound technologies,[19] it has proven challenging to address IPRs in subsequent global sustainable development

[14] *See Breakthrough Energy Coalition*, Breakthrough Energy, www.b-t.energy/coalition/.

[15] Sustainable Development Knowledge Platform, *Sustainable Development Goal* 9, U.N. Dep't of Econ. and Soc. Affairs, https://sustainabledevelopment.un.org/sdg9.

[16] U.N. Conference on Sustainable Development, *The Future We Want: Outcome Document of the United Nations Conference on Sustainable Development*, ¶273 (2012), *available at:* https://sustainabledevelopment.un.org/content/documents/733FutureWeWant.pdf [hereinafter *Future We Want*].

[17] *2030 Agenda*, *supra* note 2, at ¶70.

[18] For an in-depth overview of this issue, see Ahmed Abdel-Latif, *Intellectual Property Rights and the Transfer of Climate Change Technologies: Issues, Challenges, and Way Forward*, 15 Climate Policy 103, (Dec. 24, 2014) [hereinafter Abdel-Latif, *Transfer of Climate Change*]. *See also* Matthew Rimmer, Intellectual Property and Climate Change: Inventing Clean Technologies (2011).

[19] *Agenda 21*, *supra* note 3, at ¶34.18(e)(iv) (Chapter 34 of Agenda 21 includes, for instance, a reference to the use of compulsory licensing).

and climate discussions.[20] There is no mention of IPRs in the UNFCCC itself, or in the Paris Agreement. There is a reference to IPRs in the Rio+20 Outcome document, *The Future We Want* (2012), but simply to "recall the provisions on technology transfer, finance, access to information and intellectual property rights as agreed in the Johannesburg Plan of Implementation" of 2002 but without further elaboration.[21]

The reason for such a stalemate stems from widely diverging views on the role of IP rights in the development and diffusion of green technologies. Many developing countries have advanced that IPRs can be a barrier to the large-scale diffusion of these technologies and the affordable access to them. They have thus made proposals in recent years both at the UNFCCC and at the World Trade Organisation (WTO) that seek possible changes to global IP rules to address this situation.

In March 2013, Ecuador made a submission to the WTO TRIPS Council requesting it to reaffirm "the existing flexibilities in the TRIPS Agreement so that Members use them in connection with Environmentally Sound Technologies (ESTs), for example through a declaration addressing flexibilities in the TRIPS Agreement, climate change and access to ESTs."[22] This proposal draws on the model of the 2001 Doha Declaration on TRIPS and Public Health.[23] Other proposals in the submission include: a review of Article 31 of the TRIPS Agreement on compulsory licensing to determine which of its provisions may excessively restrict access to and dissemination of ESTs; and an evaluation of Article 33 to establish a special reduction in the term of protection for a patent of [X] years in order to facilitate free access to specific patented ESTs for adaptation and/or mitigation of the effects of climate change because of urgent need in the public interest.

Industrialised countries and the private sector have vehemently opposed such proposals as they view IPRs as an essential incentive for innovation and technology development, without which no transfer or diffusion can take place. At the UNFCCC, the proposals of developing countries have narrowed down over the years from initial demands to change IP rules to more general language about the need to address IPRs in a pragmatic manner and to use financial mechanisms, such as the Green Climate Fund (GCF), to fund "IPR costs."[24]

In any case, the empirical evidence in this area remains inconclusive. Categorical generalisations about IP rights are difficult to make, especially given the great diversity of green technologies. These technologies encompass a broad range sectors, and the effects of IPRs tend to be sector-sensitive, with greater monopolistic effects in sectors such as pharmaceuticals, chemicals, and agro-chemical products. In addition, geographic

[20] Ahmed Abdel-Latif, *Intellectual Property Rights and Green Technologies from Rio to Rio: An Impossible Dialogue*, ICTSD (Jul. 2012), www.ictsd.org/sites/default/files/research/2012/07/intellectual-property-rights-and-green-technologies-from-rio-to-rio-an-impossible-dialogue.pdf.

[21] *Future We Want*, *supra* note 16, at ¶269. It should be noted that para.142 addresses the use of TRIPS flexibilities to protect public health and to promote access to medicines.

[22] Communication by Ecuador to the TRIPS Council of the WTO, *Contribution of IP to Facilitating the Transfer of Environmentally Rational Technology*, IP/C/W/585 (March 5, 2013). The *Agreement on Trade-Related Aspects of Intellectual Property Rights (TRIPS)* was concluded on April 15, 1994, and entered into force on January 1, 1995.

[23] World Trade Organization [WTO], Ministerial Declaration of 14 November 2001, WT/MIN (01)/DEC/2, (2002) [hereinafter Doha Declaration].

[24] Abdel-Latif, *Transfer of Climate Change*, *supra* note 18.

differences are salient. Several studies have shown relatively few patents on clean energy technologies, for instance, in Africa[25] and Latin America.[26]

At the same time, the impact of IP rights on technology innovation and diffusion needs continuous monitoring. Patenting clean energy technologies is certainly on the rise, including in a number of emerging economies.[27] More research and analysis is needed on a sector and country level, as well as for specific technologies, including cutting edge technologies, to identify where IPR-related challenges might arise.[28] For the moment, changes to global IP rules, such as those of the WTO TRIPS agreement,[29] to foster greater diffusion of green technologies do not seem a realistic prospect.

Pending further analysis and empirical evidence, addressing the interface of IPRs and green technologies could start by focusing on more practical and concrete solutions.[30] This includes several initiatives such as fast-tracking green patent applications,[31] making information on patents in clean energy technologies more accessible through new search tools and classifications such as the Y02 classification scheme of the European Patent Office (EPO) covering climate-change mitigation and smart grid technologies[32] and the INSPIRE platform of the International Renewable Energy Agency (IRENA) for patents in renewable energy technologies.[33]

Some private sector led initiatives have sought to approach IPRs and innovation in the green space in an unconventional manner. Such initiatives include the *ECO-Patent*

[25] United Nations Environment Programme [UNEP] and European Patent Office [EPO], *Patents and Clean Energy Technologies in Africa* (2013), http://documents.epo.org/projects/babylon/eponet.nsf/0/f87537c7cbb85344c1257b24005e7119/$FILE/patents_clean_energy_technologies_in_Africa_en.pdf.

[26] UNEP and EPO, *Patents and Climate Change Mitigation Technologies in Latin America and the Caribbean* (2014), http://documents.epo.org/projects/babylon/eponet.nsf/0/2841b369787d5e72c1257da800335111/$FILE/patents_Latin_America_report_en.pdf.

[27] UNEP, EPO, and ICTSD, *Patents and Clean Energy, Bridging the Gap Between Policy and Evidence* (2010), www.ictsd.org/sites/default/files/research/2010/09/summarypatentscleanenergyspanish2.pdf [hereinafter UNEPP, EPO, and ICTSD (2010)].

[28] Dean Baker, Arjun Jayadev, and Joseph Stiglitz, *Innovation, Intellectual Property and Development, A Better Set of Approaches for The 21st Century*, 52–53 (Jul. 2017).

[29] *Agreement on Trade-Related Aspects of Intellectual Property Rights*. The TRIPS Agreement was concluded on April 15, 1994, and entered into force on January 1, 1995.

[30] Ahmed Abdel-Latif, Keith E. Maskus, Ruth Okediji, Jerome H. Reichman, & Pedro Roffe, *Overcoming the Impasse on Intellectual Property and Climate Change at the UNFCCC: A Way Forward* (2011), www.ictsd.org/sites/default/files/research/2012/02/overcoming-the-impasse-on-intellectual-property-and-climate-change-at-the-unfccc-a-way-forward.pdf.

[31] Measures to fast-track "green" patent applications can reduce the time needed to obtain a patent from several years to just a few months. *See* Antoine Dechezleprêtre, *Fast-tracking green patent applications: An empirical analysis*, ICTSD (2013), http://ictsd.org/downloads/2013/02/fast-tracking-green-patent-applications-anempirical-analysis.pdf.

[32] The EPO established the Y02 classification scheme for technical attributes of technologies that can be loosely referred to as climate change mitigation. This makes it easier to retrieve patent document that cover these technologies. *See* UNEP, EPO, and ICTSD (2010), *supra* note 27.

[33] INSPIRE is an online platform designed to provide up-to-date information on standards and patents for renewable energy. The platform helps users search through, locate and analyse more than two million patents and around four hundred international standards for renewable energy technology. INSPIRE was developed by the International Renewable Energy Agency (IRENA) in collaboration with the European Patent Office (EPO) and the International Electrotechnical Commission (IEC). *See* International Standards and Patents in Renewable Energy [IRENA], *INSPIRE – International Standards and Patents in Renewable Energy*, INFOCUS (Nov. 2016), http://remember.irena.org/sites/Documents/Shared%20Documents/In%20Focus%20def/INSPIRE.pdf.

Commons and the *Greenxchange* platform. The *Eco-Patent Commons* is an online collection of environmentally beneficial patents pledged by the member companies for free use by anyone. Since its launch in 2008, about one hundred patents have been pledged by eleven companies, representing a variety of industries worldwide: Bosch, Dow, Fuji-Xerox, HP, IBM, Nokia, Pitney Bowes, Ricoh, Sony, Taisei and Xerox.[34] The *Greenxchange* platform, launched in 2010 by Nike along with nine other organisations, is a web-based marketplace where companies can collaborate and share IP using the Creative Commons' licensing approach with the aim to foster new sustainability business models and innovation. However, the uptake of both initiatives appears to be limited.[35]

III The Rise of PPPs in Green Technologies

Against this background, PPPs have emerged as important hybrid institutions in global efforts seeking to facilitate the diffusion of green technologies in a practical manner. Examples of such PPPs examined in this section include WIPO GREEN and bilateral clean energy research partnerships.

Several observers have contended for some time that PPPs should be pursued more pro-actively to facilitate access to green technologies. In 2005, Smith argued that PPPs constitute "a more potent technology transfer strategy" as they can be "more rapidly implemented on a broad scale than can IPR solutions" and "comprehensively address non-IPR barriers to technology transfer."[36] He also considered that "PPPs have the potential to aid ongoing multilateral negotiations aimed at producing a comprehensive global climate regime, while IPR solutions are likely to hinder such efforts."[37] Similarly, looking at waste management and waste-to-energy projects in Thailand and the Philippines, Forsyth pointed to how partnerships between the private sector and host communities can contribute to technology diffusion by reducing the costs of technology transfer, and making technology more appropriate to developing countries. He concluded that successful PPPs between investors and communities depend on minimizing transaction costs, strengthening assurance mechanisms, and maximizing public trust and accountability of partnerships.[38]

More recently, PPPs in green technologies have naturally found favour with the private sector which see them as an alternative to proposals seeking to facilitate access to green technologies through changes to IP rules. Santamauro, for instance, pointing to the growing number of PPPs in public health, stresses that "while the pharmaceutical and climate change context are quite different, there are similar opportunities for creative

[34] *See* Wayne Balta, *Welcome to the Eco-Patent Commons*, Corporate Eco Forum [CEF]: EcoInnovator Blog (Sep. 7, 2015), www.corporateecoforum.com/welcome-to-the-eco-patent-commons/.

[35] Bassem Awad, *Global Patent Pledges: A Collaborative Mechanism for Climate Change Technology*, Centre for International Governance Innovation [CIGI], (Nov. 2015), www.cigionline.org/sites/default/files/no.81.pdf. The website of Greenxchange is no longer active.

[36] Van Smith, *Enabling Environments Or Enabling Discord: Intellectual Property Rights, Public–private Partnerships, And The Quest For Green Technology Transfer*, 42 Georgetown Journal of International Law 817 (2011).

[37] *Id.*

[38] Tim Forsyth, *Enhancing Climate Technology Transfer through Greater Public–Private Cooperation: Lessons from Thailand and the Philippines*, 29 Natural Resource Forum 165 (2005).

partnerships." He pleads for "creatively adapting existing incentives through the use of licensing and partnerships arrangements to create technology collaboration based on 'win-win' contracts intended to spread climate technologies."[39] As an example, he makes reference to the partnership between the Syngenta Foundation, the University of Berne, and the Ethiopian Institute for Agricultural Research – a PPP aiming to develop drought resistant cultivars of teff, an important seed variety in Ethiopia.

Some developing country voices have also advocated greater reliance on PPPs, even asserting that "technology collaboration may be the new technology transfer."[40] Such views also stress the need to address IP-related matters in these partnerships based on the premise "that flexibility in intellectual property provisions helps to protect private innovators, but also allows for partnerships to evolve and respond to changing technological needs over time.[41]

Some observers have made suggestions on the design of PPPs in green technologies, detailing how they could be better integrated into the work of the UNFCCC TM. A piece by Morgera and Kulovesi suggests drawing lessons from the experience of Multilateral Environmental Agreements (MEAs), specifically *the Basel Convention on the Transboundary Movement of Hazardous Wastes and Their Disposal,* where PPPs – although not focused on technology transfer – are embedded in the institutional framework of the Convention. They describe how such PPPs, like the Mobile Phone Partnership, have spurred cooperation between the Secretariat, Parties, and the private sector in the collaborative development of standards directly applying to the private sector.[42]

While proposing to draw on this approach in the climate change area, these authors also point to some of the challenges facing these PPPs as well as some risks. Among the challenges they describe are the "lack of uniform practice, difficulty in moving from the development of partnership to its implementation stage, and lack of systematic monitoring or assessment of these initiatives."[43] Risks include "partnering with companies that may be economically and politically more powerful than certain states parties or have a vested interest in the use of certain environmental resources (...)", "alienating partner NGOs, indigenous peoples and other stakeholders" and "undermining the independence of the MEA because of funding provided by the private sector."[44]

Furthermore, Morgera and Kulovesi suggest a number of important structural aspects of PPPs to ensure that they are well designed and managed for success. They emphasize that "a fair, transparent and effective MEA-private sector partnership needs to build a

[39] Jon P. Santamauro, *Failure Is Not an Option: Enhancing the Use of Intellectual Property Tools to Secure Wider and More Equitable Access to Climate Change Technologies,* 93–94, *in* Environmental Technologies, Intellectual Property and Climate Change 84 (Abbe E. L. Brown ed., 2013).

[40] Rajeev Palakshappa, *Is Technology Collaboration the New Technology Transfer? But How To Do It?,* Council on Energy, Environment, and Water: Official Blog (Jul. 6, 2011) at: http://ceew.in/blog/?p=19.

[41] Arunabha Ghosh, Anupama Vijayakumar & Sudatta Ray, *Climate Technology Partnerships: Form, Function and Impact,* CIGI (Oct. 27, 2015), www.cigionline.org/publications/climate-technology-partnerships-form-function-and-impact.

[42] Elisa Morgera & Kati Kulovesi, *Public–Private Partnerships for Wider and Equitable Access to Climate Technologies, in* Environmental Technologies, Intellectual Property and Climate Change 128, 140–42 (Abbe E. L. Brown ed., 2013) [hereinafter Morgera & Kulovesi].

[43] Morgera & Kulovesi, *supra* note 42, at 139–140.

[44] Morgera & Kulovesi, *supra* note 42, at 140.

clear framework composed of time-defined targets, minimum standards of conduct [,] and transparency guarantees for joining the partnerships and for decision-making in its framework. The adoption of guidelines on conflict of interest may also be needed."[45] They also stress that partnerships can be useful for increased access to and transfer of climate technologies as long as their risks and shortcomings are actively managed."[46]

Some of these challenges and risks are not unique to PPPs in green technologies and arise in different sectors, as several chapters of this book have shown. At the same time, they are useful to bear in mind when looking at specific examples of PPPs in this area. An important point to retain from this analysis is that PPPs in the Basel Convention were not the result of an *ad hoc* initiative but of a multi-stakeholder process involving the Secretariat, Parties, the private sector, and NGOs, as part of the programmatic activities and institutional framework of the Convention.

Morgera and Kulovesi suggest this partnership process could be replicated in other forums such as the UNFCCC. They propose that "PPPs [be] formalized through an agreement with the MEA Secretariat and/or TORs" with "work plans to be endorsed by the COP so as to be embedded in the governance structure of MEAs as a multi-stakeholder endeavour."[47] In this framework, "Secretariats can play the role of facilitator and neutral broker. MEA parties through the COP, subsidiary bodies and as active participants in the partnership meetings and activities will be able to oversee the process. NGOs would also be able to provide inputs on an equal footing with business representatives."[48]

It is useful to reflect on this model of multi-stakeholder discussions and engagement to develop PPPs when examining examples of PPPs in green technologies at the multilateral level (WIPO GREEN) as well as at the bilateral level, described in more detail below.

A *Multilateral PPPs: WIPO GREEN*

WIPO GREEN is a specialised platform administered by the World Intellectual Property Organisation (WIPO) formally launched in 2013 as an "interactive marketplace that promotes innovation and diffusion of green technologies by connecting technology and service providers with those seeking innovative solutions."[49] This PPP consists primarily of a freely accessible online database and a network. The Database offers a broad listing of green technology products, services and IP assets, and also allows individuals and companies to list green technology needs.

WIPO GREEN "traces its origins to WIPO's discussions with the Japan Intellectual Property Association (JIPA) and other industry partners, who were keen to establish a mechanism that would inject transparency into green technology markets, particularly for developing countries."[50] It has an Advisory Board and is governed by a Charter.[51] The Board, which comprises the partners and the WIPO Secretariat, provides guidance to the

[45] Morgera & Kulovesi, *supra* note 42, at 140.
[46] Morgera & Kulovesi, *supra* note 42, at 143.
[47] Morgera and Kulovesi, *supra* note 42, at 143.
[48] *Id.*
[49] *Multi-stakeholder Platforms*, World Intellectual Property Organization [WIPO], www.wipo.int/cooperation/en/multi_stakeholder_platforms/.
[50] *About WIPO GREEN*, WIPO GREEN, www3.wipo.int/wipogreen/en/aboutus/.
[51] *The Charter*, WIPO GREEN, www3.wipo.int/wipogreen/docs/en/charter.pdf.

platform's activities. For example, the Board advises on strategy, amendments to the Charter, and the classification of green technologies on the WIPO GREEN database, as well as undertaking outreach to other networks and institutions.

The WIPO GREEN Charter is a short document that makes reference to a number of principles such as transparency,[52] partnerships,[53] and needs.[54] It stipulates that WIPO GREEN's mission is to contribute to the accelerated adaptation, adoption, and deployment of green technology solutions, in both developing and developed countries. Partners must endorse in writing the WIPO GREEN Charter and abide by its principles. WIPO GREEN partners include IGOs, trade associations, companies, public institutions, financing institutions, SMEs and SME networks, universities, and consultancy firms.[55]

With regard to IPRs, the Charter states that they "are an important policy tool to encourage innovation" and "they provide economic incentives to develop new technology and help diffuse innovation, and structure relationships that underpin commercial transactions."[56] It further states that:

> The sustained deployment and uptake of technologies occurs when parties freely enter into a contract on mutually agreed terms. Agreements that originate through the use of the WIPO GREEN are the responsibility of the contracting parties.[57]

It is thus interesting to note that WIPO GREEN has no specific prescriptive licensing arrangements or terms in place (though it offers a Licensing Checklist; see below). The technologies uploaded to the WIPO GREEN database remain the property of the rights holder. It is then up to them and the collaborating parties to structure agreements in the manner they feel is most appropriate and effective. This feature has shielded it from some of the issues and challenges raised by the licensing arrangements of other multi-stakeholder partnerships, including those in which WIPO is involved, and examined elsewhere in this book.[58]

In terms of its activities, WIPO GREEN has over eighty partners and five thousand network members (Partners, Users, Experts, and subscribers) in more than seventy countries. By end 2017, the number of registered users in the database reached over one thousand and the number and type of technologies available for license, sale or collaboration reached twenty-five hundred. There were 150 needs registered on the database mostly from developing countries. WIPO GREEN has facilitated more than three

[52] "Transparency in the marketplace leads to greater efficiency. WIPO GREEN, as a global repository of technologies, best practices and analyses, contributes to a more open market." *Id.*, at 1.

[53] "Partnerships are critical to achieving synergies and fostering the transfer of technologies, and, as appropriate, associated know how." *Id.*

[54] "A comprehensive understanding of needs is essential for effective deployment of green technology. WIPO GREEN offers a space for publicizing needs, allowing interested parties to respond to and offer solutions." *Id.*

[55] Amongst these partners are The Asian Development Bank, UNEP, The Danish Patent and Trademark Office (DKPTO), the Brazilian Institute of Industrial Property (INPI), InfoDev World Bank, the Kenya Climate Innovation Centre (CIC), the International Centre for Trade and Sustainable Development (ICTSD), and private firms such as General Electric and Siemens. *See About WIPO GREEN*, *supra* note 50.

[56] *The Charter*, *supra* note 51, at 1.

[57] *The Charter*, *supra* note 51, at 1.

[58] *See* Anatole Krattiger et al., chapter 3, *supra*; Katy M. Graef et al., chapter 4, *supra*; Jens Bammel, chapter 7, *supra*.

hundred connections, "putting those in need of resources, information, training, expertise, and green tech solutions in touch with those who can provide answers."[59]

There are no fees to register with WIPO GREEN.[60] The platform also offers its users access to WIPO services such as capacity building in areas related to IP management as well as patent filing via the Patent Cooperation Treaty (PCT) System and WIPO Arbitration and Mediation services at a reduced rate.

WIPO GREEN adopts a broad definition of green technologies which follows the definition of environmentally sound technologies in Chapter 34 of Agenda 21.[61] By the end of 2017, technologies from the Association of University Technology Managers (AUTM) represented 67 per cent of all technologies on the database (down from 90% in 2014). The distribution of the technologies on the database by sector is as follows: energy (51%), pollution and waste (18%), water (9%), farming and forestry (7%), green products (6%), chemicals and advanced materials (5%), buildings and construction (1%), transportation (2%), and others (< 1%). Not all technologies and products listed in the WIPO GREEN online database are patent protected. Technology transfer of those not protected by patents likely centers around the transfer of know-how or trade secrets. Several thousand inventions from the Federal Laboratory Consortium for Technology Transfer are being uploaded, a process that will be completed in 2018.

WIPO GREEN organises matchmaking events[62] and technology exhibitions[63] as well as capacity-building and outreach activities. In 2016, it made available a Licensing Checklist, which provides a list of key issues that should be considered when negotiating and concluding licensing agreements, on the WIPO GREEN website.[64] In 2017, a WIPO GREEN Experts Database was launched and features green technology specialists willing to provide their services and expertise.[65]

Two projects illustrate proactive engagement by WIPO GREEN to facilitate technology transfer: one on wastewater technologies in South East Asia and the other on

[59] As of December 2016. *See* WIPO GREEN, *Year in Review* 2016, www.wipo.int/edocs/pubdocs/en/wipo_pub_greenreport_2016.pdf [hereinafter WIPO GREEN *2016*].

[60] However, it is mentioned in the website that: "fees for technology providers might be reconsidered in future, "though no fee will be introduced without first offering existing users an opportunity to withdraw their membership. SMEs and academic institutions would be offered a substantial discount as would institutions from developing countries." WIPO GREEN, *Frequently Asked Questions*, www3.wipo.int/wipogreen/en/faqs.html.

[61] Green technologies "protect the environment, are less polluting, use all resources in a more sustainable manner, recycle more of their wastes and products, and handle residual waste in a more acceptable manner than the technologies for which they were substitutes."

[62] *See, for example*, WIPO GREEN, *Facilitating the Transfer and Diffusion of Clean Technology: Opportunities on Wastewater Treatment in South East Asia. Report of a Pilot Project.* Global Challenges Program (Geneva 2016), www.wipo.int/edocs/mdocs/mdocs/en/wipo_ip_mnl_15/wipo_ip_mnl_15_report.pdf; WIPO GREEN, *Facilitating the Transfer of Clean Technologies in East Africa: Opportunities in Agriculture and Water Technologies*, Global Challenges Program (Geneva 2017), www3.wipo.int/wipogreen/docs/en/wipo green_eastafrica_matchmaking_report2016.pdf; and WIPO GREEN, *Innovate 4 Water: A Matchmaking Forum for Sustainable Development* (Geneva, 2017), www3.wipo.int/wipogreen/en/events/2017/news_0001.html.

[63] WIPO GREEN, *Showcasing Innovative Climate Solutions for Africa: Exhibition and Roundtables: WIPO GREEN at COP 22 in Marrakech* (Nov. 17, 2016), www3.wipo.int/wipogreen/en/news/2016/news_0007.html.

[64] WIPO GREEN, *WIPO GREEN Network*, www3.wipo.int/wipogreen/en/network/.

[65] WIPO GREEN, *Search the WIPO GREEN Experts Database*, www3.wipo.int/wipogreen-expertsdatabase/searchResult.

agriculture and water technologies in East Africa. These two projects both sought to identify technology needs in these areas by local stakeholders and technology seekers and then connected them at matchmaking events held respectively in Manila (2015) and in Nairobi (2016). In the case of the South-East Asia project, "a total of 16 letters of intent were signed between technology providers and seekers aimed at exploring business transactions."[66] For the East Africa project, "nine letters of intent were signed, as well as one memorandum of understanding." In addition, eight additional connections were made between seekers and organisations such as the Climate Technology Initiative/The Private Financing Advisory Network (CTI-PFAN), GIZ, and the African Development Bank."[67] In cooperation with the Climate Technology Centre & Network (CTCN) and others, WIPO GREEN and InvenTrust launched two Open Challenge contests related to energy efficient water desalination and the elimination of leakage in water distribution.[68] Finally, a matchmaking project on clean energy, air, water, and agriculture in the Asia-Pacific region is being planned for early 2018 with the support of the Government of Australia.

WIPO GREEN is a PPP administered by an international intergovernmental organisation (WIPO) to serve a public policy objective of accelerating the diffusion of green technologies.[69] In practice, it operates as a match-making platform for these technologies and promotes collaborative efforts between public and private entities which provide an important share of the technologies listed in the database.

WIPO GREEN has found a favourable reception with a number of companies and technology suppliers Most recently, the Japanese firm Fujitsu announced, in September 2017, that it will be adding over two hundred IP assets to WIPO GREEN's database by the end of March 2018 and that it "intends to license the technologies listed to interested individuals, companies and organizations under reasonable terms, and it will also provide technological support as necessary."[70] Through membership in WIPO GREEN, Fujitsu states that it "seeks to support efforts to advance Sustainable Development Goals."[71]

International professional IP associations such as the International Association for the Protection of Intellectual Property (AIPPI) have also been supportive of WIPO GREEN. At its 2016 Congress, AIPPI adopted a resolution that mentioned WIPO GREEN among

[66] Nine of these letters were signed between Korean companies and various technology seekers from Indonesia and Viet Nam; five were between a company from Malaysia and Indonesian technology seekers; and two were between a company from Malaysia and technology seekers from the Philippines. *Facilitating the Transfer and Diffusion of Clean Technology: Opportunities on Wastewater Treatment in South East Asia, Report of a Pilot Project*. Global Challenges Program (Geneva 2017), www.wipo.int/edocs/mdocs/mdocs/en/wipo_ip_mnl_15/wipo_ip_mnl_15_report.pdf.

[67] WIPO GREEN, *Facilitating the Transfer of Clean Technologies in East Africa: Opportunities in Agriculture and Water Technologies* (2017), www3.wipo.int/wipogreen/docs/en/wipogreen_eastafrica_matchmaking_report2016.pdf.

[68] WIPO GREEN, *InvenTrust and WIPO GREEN Launch "Open Challenges Contest"* (Aug. 23, 2017), www3.wipo.int/wipogreen/en/news/2017/news_0007.html [hereinafter *InvenTrust*].

[69] WIPO GREEN is listed under Public Private Partnerships in the Report of the Director General to the 2016 Assemblies, along with WIPO Re:Search, described above in this volume (Anatole Krattiger et al., chapter 3, *supra*; and Katy M. Graef et al., chapter 4, *supra*). *See* WIPO, *Report of the Director General to the 2016 WIPO Assemblies* (2016), www.wipo.int/edocs/pubdocs/en/wipo_pub_1050_2016.pdf [hereinafter *Director General Report 2016*].

[70] Press Release, Fujitsu, Fujitsu Partners with WIPO GREEN to Achieve SDGs (Sep. 19, 2017), www.fujitsu.com/global/about/resources/news/press-releases/2017/0919-02.html.

[71] *Id.*

"initiatives that have demonstrated that IP laws can be implemented in such a way as to promote the development, dissemination and implementation of green technologies" and that should therefore be supported.[72] Along similar lines, a 2014 report by the AIPPI Standing Committee on Intellectual Property and Green Technology stated that WIPO GREEN should be supported and "evaluated over time to determine to what extent it is effective in promoting green technology transfer."[73] In addition, the Public Interest Intellectual Property Advisors (PIIPA) has pledged 300 hours of pro bono services for selected WIPO GREEN users from developing country SMEs and public sector institutes who may apply directly via its website.[74]

The need for an evaluation of WIPO GREEN over time, as mentioned in the AIPPI report, could contribute to a better understanding of its impact. For instance, the extent to which matchmaking activities, connections, and letters of intent translate into real transactions and deals contributing to technology diffusion requires further examination and deepening. These kinds of metrics are important for many PPPs, but especially because WIPO GREEN, as a PPP promoted by an IGO, can contribute towards setting a standard for best practices with regard to PPP activities and goals-setting.[75]

Overall, WIPO GREEN seems to be an attempt by WIPO to address the need and demands for a greater diffusion of green technologies that have emerged in sustainable development and climate discussions. Its voluntary nature and its light governance structure and arrangements are features found in other PPPs examined in this book.[76] At the same time, the absence of specific licensing arrangements and terms, which are left for agreement between technology providers and seekers, differentiates it from other PPPs such as WIPO Re:Search.[77] WIPO GREEN is still at a relatively early stage of its development. Further evaluation over time would be useful in assessing the extent of its effectiveness in achieving its mission and in better informing how it could be improved.

B *Bilateral PPPs: The US-China Clean Energy Research Centre and the US-India Partnership to Advance Clean Energy*

At the bilateral level, a growing number of cooperation frameworks in clean energy are being established between industrialised countries, such as the United States (US) and the European Union (EU) and emerging economies such as China, Brazil, and India. Examples include: the US–China Clean Research Energy Center (CERC) and the US–India Clean Energy Partnership (PACE). This section examines these two examples as

[72] International Association for the Protection of Intellectual Property [AIPPI], *Resolution on Patent Rights and Green Technology / Climate Change*, AIPPI Congress Milan (Sep. 20, 2016), http://aippi.org/wp-content/uploads/2016/10/Resolution-on-Patent-Rights-and-Green-Technology-Climate-Change-English.pdf.

[73] AIPPI, *Climate Change and Environmental Technologies – the Role of Intellectual Property, esp. Patents* (Sep. 2014), http://aippi.org/wpcontent/uploads/committees/198/Report198Report+Climate+Change+and+Environmental+Technologies+-+The+Role+of+IP+esp.+PatentsEnglish.pdf.

[74] WIPO GREEN, *Pro Bono IP Advice for WIPO GREEN Users* (Jun. 30, 2015), www3.wipo.int/wipogreen/en/news/2015/news_0006.html.

[75] Again, this is analogous to some issues facing WIPO Re:Search, which is also in its early stages. *See InvenTrust, supra* note 68.

[76] *See, e.g.*, Jens Bammel, chapter 7, *supra*; Susan Isiko Štrba, chapter 9, *supra*.

[77] *See Director General Report 2016, supra* note 69.

they prominently feature collaborative arrangements between private and public sector entities, and also seek to address IP-related matters.

Launched in 2009, the US–China Clean Energy Research Center (CERC) is a R&D partnership between the United States and China to accelerate research, development, and deployment of clean energy technologies to transition to an efficient and low-carbon economy while delivering economic and environmental benefits to both countries.[78] It facilitates collaborative research and development, engaging scientists and engineers from universities, research institutions, and industry leaders.

CERC focuses its R&D activities in five consortia: advanced coal technologies, including carbon capture and storage; building energy efficiency; clean vehicles; water and energy technologies; and medium- and heavy-duty trucks. Members of CERC includes businesses, governments, and nongovernmental entities.[79]

In its first phase (2011–2015), CERC had a budget of US$150 million. For its current phase (2016–2020), CERC is supported by public and private funding of at least US$250 million over five years, split evenly between the two countries. All US government resources flow to US-based partners and all Chinese government resources flow to Chinese-based partners.

One of the interesting features of the CERC is its approach to intellectual property rights. The Protocol establishing the Centre mentions "effective protection of intellectual property rights" as one of the five principles underpinning the agreement.[80] It further states that "the allocation of intellectual property rights shall be determined on a case-by-case basis, as appropriate" pursuant to an Annex on this matter.[81]

According to the Annex on IP, the United States and China "shall ensure adequate and effective protection of intellectual property created or furnished under this Protocol and relevant implementing Project Annexes."[82] At the same time, both countries, and subject to the Annex, "shall support the widest dissemination of scientific information they generate in the execution of this Protocol."[83] The Annex envisages the elaboration of a joint Technology Management Plan (TMP) to further flesh out the IP arrangements in each area.[84] If parties cannot agree on a joint TMP for a particular research project, work under that research project cannot commence.[85]

Overall, CERC's IP framework enables research partners to share information and to retain rights for new technologies they create. It defines how IP may be shared or licensed in each country and how IP terms and conditions may be negotiated. It also envisages

[78] *Overview*, US-China Clean Energy Research Center [CERC], www.us-china-cerc.org/overview/.

[79] For instance, the CERC Water and Energy Technologies Consortium is led on the US side by the University of California, Berkeley and on the Chinese side by the Research Institute of Petroleum Exploration & Development (RIPED). Public and private partners in the Consortium on the US and Chinese side are listed at: *Water and Energy Technologies*, CERC, www.us-china-cerc.org/water-and-energy-technologies/.

[80] Protocol Between the Department of Energy of the United States (USDOE) and the Ministry of Science and Technology (MOST) and the National Energy Administration (NEA) of the People's Republic of China For Cooperation On an Energy Research Center, art. III (Nov. 17, 2009) [hereinafter Protocol].

[81] *Id.*, at art. VII.

[82] *Id.*, at Preamble, Annex on IP.

[83] *Id.*

[84] The TMPs for each consortium can be found at: *Intellectual Property*, CERC, www.us-china-cerc.org/intellectual-property/.

[85] *See* Protocol, *supra* note 80, at art. II Provision B, 2 (d) and (e).

joint ownership of IP resulting from collaborative research activities and invented jointly by signatories to the CERC protocol from the United States and China. Where IP is created in a jointly funded research project, the project's participants in both countries have the right to obtain a non-exclusive license to the IP.[86] There are also provisions in the TMP that encourage the sharing of data and information with the public, except when there is a need to preserve confidentiality associated with a given project and it also stipulates the protection of confidential information.[87]

This framework also delineates how IP disputes should be handled first by mutually agreeable resolution and, if not, then by an arbitration tribunal for binding arbitration in accordance with the applicable rules of international law. Unless parties agree otherwise, the arbitration rules of the United Nations Commission on International Trade Law (UNCITRAL) shall apply.[88] This is rare in collaborative research efforts, which tend to leave any disputes to the individual laws of the relevant countries to resolve.[89]

Overall, CERC has engaged 254 US researchers and 840 Chinese researchers. As of June 2016, 82 US partners and 123 Chinese partners were participating in it. Phase 1 (2011–2015) resulted in 44 significant research outcomes, 39 invention disclosures and patent applications filed, and, as reported, 275 million tons of CO2 avoided by 2025.[90] In addition, over 400 scientific papers were published.

As highlighted by one observer, CERC merits examination not just as a "platform for cooperation that engages both public and private sectors to advance the development of technologies, but also as the test bed for a novel arrangement to manage IP rights.[91] Under CERC, it is intended that research projects are undertaken together under joint research work plans enhancing the prospect of joint development of clean energy-related IP. Yet, the CERC's activities seem so far not to be fully meeting this objective as many of the inventions are indeed being developed by national CERC consortia members from academia, research institutes, and industry "but not necessarily jointly."[92] There have been efforts to address this recently. In February 2017, it was announced that the US–China Clean Energy Research Center Building Energy Efficiency (CERC-BEE) researchers drafted CERC's first US–China joint intellectual property (IP) agreement for the development of an open-source, online, building energy efficiency audit tool. This was hailed as a first of its kind 'precedent' for future US–China joint IP agreements under CERC.[93]

The US–India Partnership to Advance Clean Energy (PACE) is similar to CERC in its mission of accelerating innovation in clean energy technologies. Launched in 2009, PACE includes a research component funded by US Department of Energy (DOE) and the Indian Ministry of Science and Technology, the US–India Joint Clean Energy R&D

[86] *See generally supra*, note 80, Article II on Allocation of Rights.
[87] *Id.*, See Article III, on Business-confidential information.
[88] *Id.*, *See* Paragraph D in Article I, Scope.
[89] Joanna Lewis, *A Better Approach to Intellectual Property?: Lessons from the US-China Clean Energy Research Center*, 9 (Jun. 2015), www.paulsoninstitute.org/wp-content/uploads/2015/06/PPEE_US-China-Coop-in-Cleantech-IP_English.pdf [hereinafter Lewis, *Lessons*].
[90] CERC, *Annual Report 2014–2015 and Review of CERC Phase 1*, www.us-china-cerc.org/pdfs/CERC-AR-508-compliant-spreads_FINAL_Onscreen.pdf.
[91] Lewis, *Lessons*, *supra* note 89 at 7.
[92] *Id.*, at 9.
[93] CERC, *CERC BEE Drafts Groundbreaking Joint IP Agreement* (Feb. 2017), www.us-china-cerc.org/2017/02/20/cerc-bee-drafts-groundbreaking-joint-ip-agreement/.

Center (JCERDC, also referred to as PACE-R).[94] In 2012, the US and Indian governments awarded funding to three PACE-R consortia in the areas of solar energy, energy efficiency of buildings, and second generation biofuels. In January 2015, the US President and India's Prime Minister renewed their commitment to the JCERDC under PACE and announced several new activities including a US$125 million program jointly funded by the two governments and the private sector. The renewal included extending funding for three existing research tracks of solar energy, building energy efficiency, and advanced biofuels for five years and launching a new track on smart grid and grid storage technology.[95]

PACE-R so far lacks the IP framework which is found in CERC. Intellectual property rights in the context of PACE-R are subject to the IPR Annex of the Agreement on Science and Technology Cooperation between the US and India of 2005.[96] Lewis is of the view that the lack of a specific IP framework, with a TMP-like agreement found in CERC, may be one of the reasons for the modest progress PACE-R has achieved compared to CERC.[97] Another possible reason she points out is the fact that most of the its activities focus on capacity building, which is also likely due to the overall gap in technical capacity in the clean energy space between India and China.[98]

According to Lewis, "a model for IP management may be emerging from the CERC and could ultimately be applied to a broader range of IP-focused collaborative ventures, including but not limited to China."[99] Lewis has also argued that the TMP model of CERC could be potentially integrated into the Paris Agreement TM to facilitate bilateral and multilateral low carbon technology transfer and cooperation.[100]

Conclusion

There seems to be ample scope for enhancing the contribution of PPPs to global efforts to accelerate innovation and the diffusion of green technologies in the pursuit of sustainable development and a climate safe world.

This could be pursued, for example, by strengthening the role of PPPs for climate change technologies in the implementation of the Paris Agreement which calls for greater public and private collaboration. The TM could give greater attention to PPPs. The CTCN could further enhance the role of PPPs in its activities through its Network and the TEC could provide guidance on their design and implementation through

[94] Agreement Between the Department of Energy of the United States of America (USDOE) and the Planning Commission of the Republic of India Cooperation Agreement on a Joint Clean Energy Research and Development Centre (2010), www.state.gov/documents/organization/159460.pdf.

[95] *See* Press Release, The White House Office of the Press Secretary, US-India Joint Statement – "Shared Effort; Progress for All" (Jan. 25, 2015), https://obamawhitehouse.archives.gov/the-press-office/2015/01/25/us-india-joint-statement-shared-effort-progress-all.

[96] Joint Energy Research and Development Center [JCERDC], *Indo-US Joint Clean Energy Research and Development Center*, www.iusstf.org/story/53-61-Joint-Clean-Energy-Research-and-Development-Center (JCERDC).html.

[97] Lewis, *Lessons*, *supra* note 89 at 11

[98] *Id.*, at 12

[99] Lewis, *Lessons*, *supra* note 89 at 13; *see also* Arunabha Ghosh, *Effective Climate Technology Partnerships*, Business Standard (Oct. 15, 2015), www.business-standard.com/article/opinion/arunabha-ghosh-effective-climate-tech-partnerships-115101501416_1.html.

[100] *Id.*, at, at 12–13.

indicative guidelines[101] At the same, it is important to avoid an excessively top-down approach with unwarranted formalism and bureaucratisation in dealing with PPPs.

Multilateral PPPs such as WIPO GREEN and bilateral partnerships such as the US-China Clean Energy Research Centre (CERC) and the US-India Partnership to Advance Clean Energy (PACE) bring a more pragmatic approach to international IP cooperation, and stand in contrast to the stalemate in international discussions on the role of IP in green technologies. The breadth and sophistication of the IP framework developed under CERC, in particular, merits further examination in terms of its relevance for the development of the international IP regime and for facilitating international technology and R&D collaboration in the green technology space. It has also helped foster a collaborative relationship between two countries which often experience tensions on IP matters at the bilateral level, as we have witnessed even recently. To which extent such a framework could be impacted by these tensions in the future would be a matter worthwhile observing. At the same time, it is also interesting to note that several of the bilateral partnerships mentioned above are focusing on emerging economies and fewer focus on low-income countries. Having such partnerships also encompass least-developed countries (LDCs) would be important, particularly in terms of contributing to the implementation of the Paris Agreement.[102]

Ultimately, the extraordinary diversity of green technologies and the pace of innovation makes the design and implementation of PPPs particularly challenging in this area. Arguably, they also make PPPs a promising vehicle for generating green innovation, by virtue of their potentially less formal structures and more rapid responses. While recognizing the promise of carefully designed PPPs, the chapter also underlines the need for constant adaptation and evaluation of the extent to which they are realising their stated objectives and are being responsive to the needs of recipients and stakeholders, particularly from developing countries.

Finally, it is also important to highlight that the fast pace of innovation in green technologies might foster novel strategies by entrepreneurs and the private sector which challenge traditional IP management approaches. In 2014, Elon Musk, the CEO of Tesla announced that Tesla would apply the open source philosophy to its patents and would not initiate patent lawsuits against anyone who, in good faith, wants to use its technology, on the premise that "other companies making electric cars, and the world would all benefit from a common, rapidly evolving technology platform."[103] Such initiatives might have far-reaching effects for the innovation and diffusion of green technologies. Therefore, it is also important to put in perspective that PPPs are part of a broader and dynamic landscape and only one among other options that can be pursued in this context.

[101] This has been suggested by Morgera and Kulovesi among other ideas.

[102] Particularly in light of the fact that Article 10 of the Paris Agreement which addresses technology puts emphasis on accelerating innovation and strengthening collaborative efforts on research and development.

[103] Elon Musk, *Our Patents Belong to You*, TESLA (Jun. 12, 2014), www.tesla.com/blog/all-our-patent-are-belong-you.

References

Abdel-Latif, Ahmed, *The Climate Technology Mechanism: Issues and Challenges*, International Centre for Trade and Sustainable Development [ICTSD] (Mar. 2011), www.ictsd.org/downloads/2011/04/technologymechanism.pdf.

Abdel-Latif, Ahmed, *Intellectual Property Rights and Green Technologies from Rio to Rio: An Impossible Dialogue*, ICTSD (Jul. 2012), www.ictsd.org/sites/default/files/research/2012/07/intellectual-property-rights-and-green-technologies-from-rio-to-rio-an-impossible-dialogue.pdf.

Abdel-Latif, Ahmed, *Intellectual Property Rights and the Transfer of Climate Change Technologies: Issues, Challenges, and Way Forward*, 15 Climate Policy 103, (Dec. 24, 2014).

Abdel-Latif, Ahmed, Keith E. Maskus, Ruth Okediji, Jerome H. Reichman, and Pedro Roffe, *Overcoming the Impasse on Intellectual Property and Climate Change at the UNFCCC: A Way Forward* (2011), www.ictsd.org/sites/default/files/research/2012/02/overcoming-the-impasse-on-intellectual-property-and-climate-change-at-the-unfccc-a-way-forward.pdf

Agreement Between the Department of Energy of the United States of America (USDOE) and the Planning Commission of the Republic of India Cooperation Agreement on a Joint Clean Energy Research and Development Centre (2010), www.state.gov/documents/organization/159460.pdf.

Awad, Bassem, *Global Patent Pledges: A Collaborative Mechanism for Climate Change Technology*, Centre for International Governance Innovation [CIGI], (Nov. 2015), www.cigionline.org/sites/default/files/no.81.pdf.

Baker, Dean, Arjun Jayadev, and Joseph Stiglitz, *Innovation, Intellectual Property and Development, A Better Set of Approaches for The 21st Century*, 52–53 (Jul. 2017).

Balta, Wayne, *Welcome to the Eco-Patent Commons*, Corporate Eco Forum [CEF]: Eco-Innovator Blog (Sep. 7, 2015), www.corporateecoforum.com/welcome-to-the-eco-patent-commons/.

Breakthrough Energy Coalition, Breakthrough Energy, www.b-t.energy/coalition/.

CERC, *CERC BEE Drafts Groundbreaking Joint IP Agreement* (Feb. 2017), www.us-china-cerc.org/2017/02/20/cerc-bee-drafts-groundbreaking-joint-ip-agreement/.

CERC, *Intellectual Property*, CERC, www.us-china-cerc.org/intellectual-property/.

CERC, *Overview*, CERC, www.us-china-cerc.org/overview/.

CERC, *Water and Energy Technologies*, CERC, www.us-china-cerc.org/water-and-energy-technologies/

de Coninck, Heleen and Ambuj Sagar, *Technology Development and Transfer (Article 10)*, *in* The Paris Agreement on Climate Change: Analysis and Commentary (Daniel Klein, María Pía Carazo, Meinhard Doelle, Jane Bulmer, & Andrew Higham eds., 2017).

Dechezleprêtre, Antoine, *Fast-tracking green patent applications: An empirical analysis*, ICTSD (2013), http://ictsd.org/downloads/2013/02/fast-tracking-green-patent-applications-anempirical-analysis.pdf.

Forsyth, Tim, *Enhancing Climate Technology Transfer through Greater Public–Private Cooperation: Lessons from Thailand and the Philippines*, 29 Natural Resource Forum 165 (2005).

Fujitsu, Fujitsu Partners with WIPO GREEN to Achieve SDGs (Sep. 19, 2017), www.fujitsu.com/global/about/resources/news/press-releases/2017/0919-02.html.

Ghosh, Arunabha, *Effective Climate Technology Partnerships*, Business Standard (Oct. 15, 2015), www.business-standard.com/article/opinion/arunabha-ghosh-effective-climate-tech-partnerships-115101501416_1.html.

Ghosh, Arunabha, Anupama Vijayakumar, and Sudatta Ray, *Climate Technology Partnerships: Form, Function and Impact*, Centre for International Governance Innovation (Oct. 27, 2015), www.cigionline.org/publications/climate-technology-partnerships-form-function-and-impact.

International Association for the Protection of Intellectual Property, *Climate Change and Environmental Technologies – The Role of Intellectual Property, esp. Patents* (Sep. 2014), http://aippi.org/

wpcontent/uploads/committees/198/Report198Report+Climate+Change+and+Environmental +Technologies+-+The+Role+of+IP+esp.+PatentsEnglish.pdf.

International Association for the Protection of Intellectual Property, *Resolution on Patent Rights and Green Technology/Climate Change*, AIPPI Congress Milan (Sep. 20, 2016), http://aippi.org/wp-content/uploads/2016/10/Resolution-on-Patent-Rights-and-Green-Technology-Climate-Change-English.pdf.

International Standards and Patents in Renewable Energy [IRENA], *INSPIRE – International Standards and Patents in Renewable Energy*, INFOCUS (Nov. 2016), http://remember.irena.org/sites/Documents/Shared%20Documents/In%20Focus%20def/INSPIRE.pdf

Joint Energy Research and Development Center [JCERDC], *Indo-US Joint Clean Energy Research and Development Center*, www.iusstf.org/story/53-61-Joint-Clean-Energy-Research-and-Development-Center(JCERDC).html.

Lewis, Joanna, *A Better Approach to Intellectual Property? Lessons from the US-China Clean Energy Research Center*, (Jun. 2015), www.paulsoninstitute.org/wp-content/uploads/2015/06/PPEE_US-China-Coop-in-Cleantech-IP_English.pdf.

Mission Innovation, Joint Launch Statement (Nov. 30, 2015), *available at:* www.mission-innovation.net/wp-content/uploads/2015/11/Mission-Innovation-Joint-Launch-Statement.pdf.

Morgera, Elisa and Kati Kulovesi, *Public–private Partnerships for Wider and Equitable Access to Climate Technologies, in* ENVIRONMENTAL TECHNOLOGIES, INTELLECTUAL PROPERTY AND CLIMATE CHANGE 128 (Abbe E. L. Brown ed., 2013).

Musk, Elon, *Our Patents Belong to You*, TESLA (Jun. 12, 2014), www.tesla.com/blog/all-our-patent-are-belong-you.

Palakshappa, Rajeev, *Is Technology Collaboration the New Technology Transfer? But How To Do It?*, COUNCIL ON ENERGY, ENVIRONMENT, AND WATER: OFFICIAL BLOG (Jul. 6, 2011) at: http://ceew.in/blog/?p=19.

The Paris Agreement, Apr. 22, 2016, *available at:* http://unfccc.int/files/essential_background/convention/application/pdf/english_paris_agreement.pdf.

Protocol Between the Department of Energy of the United States (USDOE) and the Ministry of Science and Technology (MOST) and the National Energy Administration (NEA) of the People's Republic of China For Cooperation On an Energy Research Center, art. III (Nov. 17, 2009) www.us-china-cerc.org/pdfs/US/US_China_CERC_Protocol_and_IP_Annex_English_17_Nov_2009.pdf.

Rimmer, Matthew, INTELLECTUAL PROPERTY AND CLIMATE CHANGE: INVENTING CLEAN TECHNOLOGIES (2011).

Santamauro, Jon. P, *Failure Is Not an Option: Enhancing the Use of Intellectual Property Tools to Secure Wider and More Equitable Access to Climate Change Technologies, in* ENVIRONMENTAL TECHNOLOGIES, INTELLECTUAL PROPERTY AND CLIMATE CHANGE 84 (Abbe E. L. Brown ed., 2013).

Smith, Van, *Enabling Environments or Enabling Discord: Intellectual Property Rights, Public–Private Partnerships, and the Quest for Green Technology Transfer*, 42 GEORGETOWN JOURNAL OF INTERNATIONAL LAW 817 (2011).

United Nations (U.N.) G. A. RES. A/70/1, *Transforming Our World: The 2030 Agenda for Sustainable Development*, A/RES/70/1 (Sep. 25, 2015), *available at*: www.un.org/ga/search/view_doc.asp?symbol=A/RES/70/1&Lang=E.

U.N. Conference on Environment and Development (UNCED), *Earth Summit Agenda 21: Programme of Action for Sustainable Development*, ¶¶34.1 – 34.29 (Dec. 1994), *available at:* www.dataplan.info/img_upload/7bdb1584e3b8a53d337518d988763f8d/agenda21-earth-summit-the-united-nations-programme-of-action-from-rio_1.pdf.

U.N. Conference on Sustainable Development, *The Future We Want: Outcome Document of the United Nations Conference on Sustainable Development*, ¶273 (2012), *available at:* https://sustainabledevelopment.un.org/content/documents/733FutureWeWant.pdf.

U.N. Environment Programme [UNEP] & European Patent Office [EPO], *Patents and Clean Energy Technologies in Africa* (2013), http://documents.epo.org/projects/babylon/eponet.nsf/0/f87537c7cbb85344c1257b24005e7119/$FILE/patents_clean_energy_technologies_in_Africa_en.pdf.

UNEP & EPO, *Patents and Climate Change Mitigation Technologies in Latin America and the Caribbean* (2014), http://documents.epo.org/projects/babylon/eponet.nsf/0/2841b369787d5e72c1257da80033511l/$FILE/patents_Latin_America_report_en.pdf.

UNEP, EPO, & ICTSD, *Patents and Clean Energy, Bridging the Gap Between Policy and Evidence*, (2010), www.ictsd.org/sites/default/files/research/2010/09/summarypatentscleanenergyspanish2.pdf.

U.N. Framework Convention on Climate Change [UNFCCC], art. 4.5 (Jun. 4, 1992), *available at:* https://unfccc.int/resource/docs/convkp/conveng.pdf.

UNFCCC, *The Cancun Agreements: Outcome of the Work of the Ad Hoc Working Group on Long-term Cooperative Action Under the Convention*, ¶121(d), Decision 1/CP.16, FCCC/CP/2010/7/Add.1 (Mar. 15, 2011).

UNFCCC, *Joint Annual Report of the Technology Executive Committee and the Climate Technology Centre and Network for 2017*, FCCC/SB/2017/3, ¶62(b), at: http://unfccc.int/resource/docs/2017/sb/eng/03.pdf.

UNFCC, *Report of the Conference of the Parties on Its Seventh Session, Held at Marrakesh From 29 October to 20 November 2001*, Decision 4/CP.7, FCCC/CP/2001/13/Add.1 (Jan. 21, 2002).

US-China Clean Energy Research Center [CERC], *Annual Report 2014–2015 and Review of CERC Phase 1*, www.us-china-cerc.org/pdfs/CERC-AR-508-compliant-spreads_FINAL_Onscreen.pdf.

U.N. Sustainable Development Knowledge Platform, *Sustainable Development Goal 9*, U.N. DEP'T OF ECON. AND SOC. AFFAIRS, https://sustainabledevelopment.un.org/sdg9.

The White House Office of the Press Secretary, US-India Joint Statement – "Shared Effort; Progress for All" (Jan. 25, 2015), https://obamawhitehouse.archives.gov/the-press-office/2015/01/25/us-india-joint-statement-shared-effort-progress-all.

WORLD INTELLECTUAL PROPERTY ORGANIZATION [WIPO], *Multi-stakeholder Platforms*, www.wipo.int/cooperation/en/multi_stakeholder_platforms/.

WIPO, *Report of the Director General to the 2016 WIPO Assemblies* (2016) www.wipo.int/edocs/pubdocs/en/wipo_pub_1050_2016.pdf.

WIPO, *About WIPO GREEN*, WIPO GREEN, www3.wipo.int/wipogreen/en/aboutus/.

WIPO, *The Charter*, WIPO GREEN, www3.wipo.int/wipogreen/docs/en/charter.pdf.

WIPO GREEN, *Facilitating the Transfer and Diffusion of Clean Technology: Opportunities on Wastewater Treatment in South East Asia*. Report of a Pilot Project. Global Challenges Program (2016), www.wipo.int/edocs/mdocs/mdocs/en/wipo_ip_mnl_15/wipo_ip_mnl_15_report.pdf.

WIPO GREEN, *Facilitating the Transfer of Clean Technologies in East Africa: Opportunities in Agriculture and Water Technologies* (2017), www3.wipo.int/wipogreen/docs/en/wipogreen_eastafrica_matchmaking_report2016.pdf.

WIPO GREEN, *Facilitating the Transfer and Diffusion of Clean Technology: Opportunities on Wastewater Treatment in South East Asia*. Report of a Pilot Project. Global Challenges Program (2016), www.wipo.int/edocs/mdocs/mdocs/en/wipo_ip_mnl_15/wipo_ip_mnl_15_report.pdf.

WIPO GREEN, *Frequently Asked Questions*, www3.wipo.int/wipogreen/en/faqs.html.

WIPO GREEN, *InvenTrust and WIPO GREEN Launch "Open Challenges Contest"* (Aug. 23, 2017), www3.wipo.int/wipogreen/en/news/2017/news_0007.html.

WIPO GREEN, *Pro Bono IP Advice for WIPO GREEN Users* (Jun. 30, 2015), www3.wipo.int/wipogreen/en/news/2015/news_0006.html.

WIPO GREEN, *Showcasing Innovative Climate Solutions for Africa: Exhibition and Roundtables: WIPO GREEN at COP 22 in Marrakech* (Nov. 17, 2016), www3.wipo.int/wipogreen/en/news/2016/news_0007.html.

WIPO GREEN Network, WIPO GREEN, www3.wipo.int/wipogreen/en/network/.

WIPO GREEN, *Year in Review 2016*, www.wipo.int/edocs/pubdocs/en/wipo_pub_greenreport_2016.pdf.

World Trade Organization [WTO], Ministerial Declaration of 14 November 2001, WT/MIN (01)/DEC/2, (2002).

WTO, Communication by Ecuador to the TRIPS Council of the WTO, *Contribution of IP to Facilitating the Transfer of Environmentally Rational Technology*, IP/C/W/585 (March 5, 2013).

12 Innovation Law and Policy Choices for Climate Change-Related Public–Private Partnerships

Joshua D. Sarnoff* and Margaret Chon

Introduction

The impacts and costs of climate change will depend substantially upon the rapid development and widespread dissemination of a wide variety of new climate change mitigation and adaptation technologies. A staggering range of technologies emit greenhouse gases (GHGs) or otherwise have climate effects or, on the other hand, can be used to accomplish mitigation or adaption goals. For example, one US study identified hundreds of technologies in various categories, such as "end-use/infrastructure (e.g. transportation), energy supply (e.g. hydrogen), carbon capture-storage (e.g. geologic storage), non-CO2 [carbon dioxide] GHGs (e.g. methane from landfills), [and] measuring & monitoring capabilities (e.g. oceanic CO2 sequestration)."[1] A European study identified fifty-one categories of technology, organized by industry sector, or by conservation or pollution reduction goals.[2] Many other studies have noted that the need for patents or other intellectual property (IP) rights – to induce investment and technology and economic development – may differ dramatically in regard to different kinds of technologies, industry sectors, users, and innovators.[3] Accordingly, the research and

* Some portions of this chapter are drawn from and build upon Joshua D. Sarnoff, *The Patent System and Climate Change*, 16 VA. J. L. & TECH. 301 (2011) [hereinafter Sarnoff, *Patent System*]; Joshua D. Sarnoff, *Government Choices in Innovation Funding (with Reference to Climate Change)*, 62 EMORY L. J. 1087 (2013) [hereinafter Sarnoff, *Government Choices*]; Joshua D. Sarnoff, *The Likely Mismatch Between Federal R&D Funding and Desired Innovation*, 18 VANDERBILT J. ENTER. & TECH. L. 363 (2016) [hereinafter Sarnoff, *Mismatch*]; RESEARCH HANDBOOK ON INTELLECTUAL PROPERTY AND CLIMATE CHANGE 200–33, 334–51 (Joshua D. Sarnoff ed., 2016) [hereinafter Sarnoff, RESEARCH HANDBOOK]; Joshua D. Sarnoff, *Intellectual Property and Climate Change, with an Emphasis on Patents and Technology Transfer*, *in* THE OXFORD HANDBOOK OF INTERNATIONAL CLIMATE CHANGE LAW 391–416 (Gray, Kevin R., Richard Tarasofsky, & Cinnamon P. Carlarne eds., 2016); Jesse L. Reynolds, Jorge L. Contreras & Joshua D. Sarnoff, *Solar Climate Engineering and Intellectual Property: Toward a Research Commons*, 18 MINN. J. L., SCI. & TECH. 1 (2017); Joshua D. Sarnoff, *Patent Eligible Inventions after Bilski: History and Theory*, 63 HASTINGS L. J. 53 (2011); Henrik Holzapfel & Joshua D. Sarnoff, *A Cross-Atlantic Dialog on Experimental Use and Research Tools*, 48 IDEA 123 (2008); Joshua D. Sarnoff & Christopher Holman, *Recent Developments Affecting the Enforcement, Procurement, and Licensing of Research Tool Patents*, 23 BERKELEY TECH. L. J. 1299, 1357 (2008).

1 *See, e.g.*, Thomas L. Brewer, *Technology Transfer and Climate Change: International Flows, Barriers, and Frameworks*, in CLIMATE CHANGE, TRADE AND COMPETITIVENESS (Lael Brainerd and Isaac Sorkin eds.) (citing the US Climate Change Technology Program).

2 *Id.* (citing the European Commission Environmental Technologies Action Plan).

3 *See generally, e.g.*, Keith E. Maskus & Ruth L. Okediji, *Legal and Economic Perspectives on International Technology Transfer in Environmentally Sound Technologies*, *in* INTELLECTUAL PROPERTY RIGHTS: LEGAL

development (R&D) and IP landscapes for technology transfer regarding climate change technologies is highly heterogenous.

The Paris Agreement (Paris Agreement)[4] of the UN Framework Convention on Climate Change (UNFCCC)[5] obligated significant funding for mitigation and adaptation, which will combine with large potential private markets for mitigation, adaptation, and infrastructure measures. These funds will attract new technological development. The Paris Agreement follows the approach to technology R&D[6] financing and dissemination[7] through various methods – which may include private market flows – adopted by the UNFCCC in Cancún in 2010.[8]

This chapter addresses the choices that government policy-makers and private actors must and will make within the innovation policy system to fund and develop climate change-related mitigation and adaptation technologies (whether or not subject to IP rights) as well as to transfer those technologies around the world to address climate change-related needs. In this chapter, the term "technology transfer" refers to the many methods of disseminating climate-change mitigation and adaptation technologies,[9] even though technology transfer in the UNFCCC and in the Paris Agreement, as well as in some other contexts, may sometimes have a narrower meaning.[10]

The Paris Agreement placed substantial emphasis on R&D and technology transfer through private markets, contrary to competing recommendations to rely more on public funding[11] and despite the many government alternatives that exist for funding technology development and transfer.[12] In particular, governments can play an important role in

AND ECONOMIC CHALLENGES FOR DEVELOPMENT 392 (2014) [hereinafter Maskus & Okediji, *Legal and Economic Perspectives*]; Keith Maskus & William Ridley, *Intellectual Property-Related Preferential Trade Agreements and the Composition of Trade* (draft of Mar. 17, 2017) (on file with the author); David Autor et al., *Foreign Competition and Domestic Innovation: Evidence from U.S. Patents* (NBER Working Paper No. 22879, Nov. 2016); Wesley M. Cohen et al., *Protecting Their Intellectual Assets: Appropriability Conditions and Why U.S. Manufacturing Firms Patent (Or Not)* (Nat'l Bureau of Econ. Research, Working Paper No. W7552, 2000) (empirical analysis of differences between products and processes and across industries); Korhan Arun & Durmus C. Yildirim, *Effects of Foreign Direct Investment on Intellectual Property, Patents and R&D*, 7 QUEEN MARY J. INTELL. PROP. 226 (2017); Richard C. Levin et al., *Appropriating the Returns from Industrial Research and Development*, 18 BROOKINGS PAPERS ON ECON. ACTIVITY 783 (1987); Katherine J. Strandburg, *Users as Innovators: Implications for Patent Doctrine*, 79 U. COLO. L. REV. 467, 478 (2008); Michael W. Carroll, *The Problem of Uniformity Cost in Intellectual Property Law*, 55 AM. U. L. REV. 55, 848 (2008).

4 UNFCCC, *Paris Agreement*, FCCC/CP/2015/L.9/Rev.1, Draft Decision –/CP.21 Annex (2015), [hereinafter Paris Agreement].

5 1771 U.N.T.S. 107, *signed* Jun. 1992, *entered into force* Mar. 21, 1994 [hereafter UNFCCC].

6 R&D is often combined with the term 'demonstration' and referred to collectively as 'RD&D.' Demonstration is often necessary after development in order to assure fitness of the technology for desired purposes.

7 'Dissemination' and 'RD&D' collectively are sometimes referred to as 'RDD&D,' although the term 'deployment' is more frequently used in this context than the broader term 'dissemination.'

8 *See* UNFCCC (2010), Draft Decision CP.16, Outcome of the work of the Ad Hoc Working Group on Long-term Cooperative Action under the Convention, ¶¶ IV.A.98–99 [hereinafter UNFCCC, Cancún Agreement].

9 See the discussion of the meaning of technology transfer in Part I.A.

10 *Paris Agreement*, *supra* note 4 at Annex, Preamble ¶ 3.

11 *See, e.g.*, Gwyn Prins et al., *The Hartwell Paper: A New Direction for Climate Policy After the Crash of 2009*, 5 (2010). *Cf.* Jomo Kwame Sundaram, Anis Chowdhury, Krishnan Sharma, & Daniel Platz, *Public-Private Partnerships and the 2030 Agenda for Sustainable Development: Fit for Purpose?* 6 (U.N. Dept. of Econ. & Soc. Affairs, DESA Working Paper No. 148, ST/ESA/2016/DWP/148, Feb. 2016) (critically evaluating "blended finance" in public–private partnerships).

12 *See generally* Sarnoff, *Government Choices*, *supra* note *.

stimulating innovation and technology transfer. Mechanisms that are available for governments to fund, develop, and transfer innovations include public provision of necessary infrastructure, subsidized research, and prioritized public procurement. All of these options can substitute for, supplement, or support market-driven intellectual property (IP) rights. But there are limits to government resources (particularly at local levels), and the public sector "does not always have the resources required to push through new projects independent of the IP-related costs involved."[13] Given the political difficulties of committing to massive expenditures as public obligations, the choice to rely primarily on private markets and consequent IP rights to generate the bulk of the committed funding for climate change-related mitigation and adaptation technologies hardly comes as a surprise.

Reliance on private sector development and transfer thus will encourage the acquisition of IP rights (of differing kinds, to differing degrees, and in various industries) in the hopes of appropriating greater economic returns. In turn, the costs of climate change mitigation and adaptation measures will depend in part on whether specific climate change technologies are subject to IP rights, on how those rights are licensed, and on what technological substitutes are affordably available.[14] For example, widely cited assessments have assumed there would be price constraints on patented climate change technologies because of the availability of ready substitutes for existing technologies, or because of development of incremental rather than breakthrough technologies. But these assumptions may not always hold,[15] as climate technologies are very diverse. These assumptions are particularly unlikely to be true if we move to novel geoengineering solutions that have not previously been deployed in markets, such as carbon capture and sequestration technologies or solar climate engineering methods (which include the use of aerosols or marine cloud brightening to increase the Earth's albedo, i.e., reflectivity).[16]

[13] Chatham House Workshop Report, *IPRs and the Innovation and Diffusion of Climate Technologies*, 3 (2007).

[14] *See* John H. Barton, *Intellectual Property And Access To Clean Energy Technologies In Developing Countries: An Analysis Of Solar Photovoltaic, Biofuel, And Wind Technologies* (2007), International Center for Trade and Sustainable Development Issue Paper No. 2, x–xii; John H. Barton, *Mitigating Climate Change Through Technology Transfer: Addressing the Needs of Developing Countries*, Chatham House, Energy, Environment and Development Programme: Programme Paper 08/02, 9–10 (2008); *see also* Copenhagen Economics, *Are IPRs a Barrier to the Transfer of Climate Change Technologies?*, 4 (2009). *Cf.* Bronwyn Hall & C. Helmers, *The Role of Patent Protection In (Clean/Green) Technologies* 7 (National Bureau of Economic Research, Working Paper 16323 (2010).

[15] Maskus & Okediji, *Legal and Economic Perspectives*, *supra* note 3; *See, e.g.*, Maria J. Oliva et al., *Climate Change, Technology Transfer and Intellectual Property Rights*, International Centre for Trade and Sustainable Development 67 (2008); Keith E. Maskus & Ruth Okediji, *Intellectual Property Rights and International Technology Transfer to Address Climate Change: Risks, Opportunities and Policy Options*, International Centre for Trade and Sustainable Development 10 (2010) [hereinafter Maskus & Okediji, *Intellectual Property Rights*].

[16] *See generally* World Energy Council, *World Energy Resources: Carbon Capture and Storage 2016*; Jesse L. Reynolds, *Solar Climate Engineering, Law, and Regulation*, *in* The Oxford Handbook on the Law and Regulation of Technology 799–822 (Roger Brownsword, Eloise Scotford, & Karen Yeung eds., 2016); Edward A. Parson, *Starting the Dialog on Climate Engineering Governance: A World Commission*, Centre for International Governance Innovation. *But cf.* Jeffrey Rismann & Robbie Orvis, *Carbon Capture and Storage: An Expensive Option for Reducing U.S. CO2 Emissions*, Forbes (May 3, 2017). Note that some cost-effective and efficient geoengineering techniques are very old, and geoengineering approaches could simply promote natural processes. *See, e.g.*, R.D. Schuiling & Oliver Tickel, *Olivine Against Climate Change and Ocean Acidification*, Innovation Concepts (n.d.), available at: http://www.innovationconcepts.eu/res/literatuurSchuiling/olivineagainstclimatechange23.pdf (last visited June 12, 2018).

All of these factors take on renewed significance and urgency when considered in light of the UN Sustainable Development Goals (SDGs), adopted in September 2015 as part of the 2030 Agenda for Sustainable Development (2030 Agenda).[17] SDG 9 commits member states to "promote inclusive and sustainable industrialization and foster innovation,"[18] while SDG 13 commits them to "[t]ake urgent action to combat climate change and its impacts."[19] And as SDG 17 indicates, all of the SDGs are to be implemented through partnerships comprised of heterogenous institutions – including private sector partners (whether for profit or nonprofit) that may not be primarily oriented toward sustainable development.[20] The overall global landscape of climate change and of energy technology innovation and transfer already is populated by public–private partnerships (PPPs),[21] reflecting various forms of ownership of and control over those technologies.[22] Many more such partnerships are anticipated to form. In light of this reality, it is interesting how few extant analyses are available of the likely impact of the increased private sector involvement in development-oriented efforts addressing climate change through R&D and technology transfer.[23]

The emphasis on PPPs to achieve the SDGs, including use of PPPs to address climate and energy SDGs, requires careful calibration of the many different law and policy choices.[24] This chapter refers to policies underlying climate change-related innovation laws as "innovation policies." It refers to governmental and private choices made to effectuate the laws as well as related administrative or private policies as "innovation choices." Both public sector and private sector innovation policies can permit, encourage, and/or generate innovation choices, which choices in turn can be exercised by either or both public sector and private sector partners within particular technology environments. Critical among the many possible laws and policies shaping innovation are those that relate to innovation funding choices.

17 U.N. Dep't of Econ. and Soc. Affairs, Sustainable Development Knowledge Platform, *Transforming Our World: The 2030 Agenda for Sustainable Development*, https://sustainabledevelopment.un.org/post2015/transformingourworld (last visited June 12, 2018).

18 *Id.*, *Sustainable Development Goal 9*, https://sustainabledevelopment.un.org/sdg9.

19 *Id.*, *Sustainable Development Goal 13*, https://sustainabledevelopment.un.org/sdg13.

20 *Id.*, *Sustainable Development Goal 17*, https://sustainabledevelopment.un.org/sdg17.

21 Some of these PPPs are analyzed in other chapters in this volume. *See* Ahmed Abdel-Latif, chapter 11, *supra*; Ayşem Mert & Philipp Pattberg, chapter 13, *infra*.

22 *See generally* Geertrui Van Overwalle, *Individualism, Collectivism and Openness in Patent Law: Promoting Access Through Exclusion*, in INDIVIDUALISM AND COLLECTIVENESS IN INTELLECTUAL PROPERTY LAW (Jan Rósen, ed., 2011) (discussing various forms of multiple ownership and various licensing approaches available for use by those forms).

23 Cf. Carolyn Deere-Birkbeck, *Global Governance in the Context of Climate Change: The Challenges of Increasingly Complex Risk Parameters*, 85 INT'L AFFAIRS 1173, 1191–92 (2009).

24 Some have used the term "eco-innovation" to address innovation management within the climate change technology arena. *See, e.g.*, Cristina Díaz-García, Ángela González-Moreno & Francisco J. Sáez-Martínez, *Eco-Innovation: Insights From a Literature Review*, 17 INNOVATION: ORGANIZATION & MANAGEMENT 6 (2015), (defining "eco-innovation" as the "production, assimilation or exploitation of a product, production process, service or management or business method that is novel to the organisation [developing or adopting it] and which results, throughout its life cycle, in a reduction of environmental risk, pollution and other negative impacts of resources use [including energy use] compared to relevant alternatives"; also performing literature review and identifying areas of further research in eco-innovation studies).

While the objects of "law" and "policy" often result from public sector choices, the hybrid nature of PPPs[25] requires adoption of both public sector and private sector policies and choices in a wider range of contexts, including in the public or private production of public goods. For simplicity of exposition, we refer below interchangeably to "innovation policy choices," "innovation policies," and "innovation choices," although we may mean in context: (1) choices by government entities to adopt particular laws or policies; (2) choices by PPPs or private sector entities to adopt particular requirements or policies; (3) choices made by the relevant public sector, hybrid, or private sector entities pursuant to those laws, requirements, or policies (e.g., decisions regarding what price to charge, whether to license exclusively or nonexclusively, and whether to develop technology or to allow others to do so); or (4) a combination of these choices.

Innovation policy choices, including government funding choices, are embedded in the structure and decisions of institutions, including PPPs. Made by the people that comprise those institutions, such choices are shaped by the networks in which these institutions are located and by the power arrangements that the institutions reflect.[26] Partners within collaborative networks may sometimes seek to achieve different and/or possibly conflicting innovation goals, rendering particular innovation policy choices suboptimal or ineffective. Conversely, the institutions may align in ways that cause particular forms of innovation policy choices, including funding, to be better choices than alternatives that – all things being equal – otherwise might be considered preferable.[27] For all these reasons, collaborative networked institutions, such as development-oriented PPPs, should coordinate with the overall global governance and policy-making framework led by decisions of national, state, and local governments, as well as of intergovernmental organizations (INGOs). Steering by these various public sector partners are more likely to maximize the public goods outputs of PPPs and to better achieve the SDGs.

Unfortunately, far too little is yet known about the mechanisms by which hybrid institutions such as PPPs might optimally be structured so as to best encourage the development and transfer of climate change-related technologies.[28] To begin to address

[25] Tanja A. Börzel & Thomas Risse, *Public-Private Partnerships: Effective and Legitimate Tools of Transnational Governance?*, *in* COMPLEX SOVEREIGNTY: RECONSTITUTING POLITICAL AUTHORITY IN THE TWENTY-FIRST CENTURY 195, 196 (Edgar Grande & Louis W. Pauly eds., 2005) ("Transnational PPPs ... [are] institutionalized cooperative relationships between public actors (both governments and international organizations) and private actors beyond the nation-state for governance purposes. By governance purposes, we mean the making and implementation of norms and rules for the provision of goods and services that are considered to be binding by members.").

[26] See, e.g., Walter W. Powell, Jason Owen-Smith, & Laurel Smith-Doerr, *Sociology and the Science of Science Policy*, in THE SCIENCE OF SCIENCE POLICY: A HANDBOOK 56–57 (Kaye H. Fealing et al. eds., 2011) (defining "institutions" as "the formal and informal rules and conventions that guide a great deal of social life," "networks" as "patterned relationships that connect both individual and organizational participants in a field," and "power relations" as "particular, asymmetric forms of network ties"). *See generally* Sarnoff, *Mismatch*, *supra* note *.

[27] *See, e.g.*, Amy Kapczynski, *The Cost of Price: Why and How to Get Beyond Intellectual Property Internalism*, 59 UCLA L. REV. 970, 996–97 (2012) (noting that intellectual property rations access according to price, whereas "the background allocation of resources may be unjust" and arguing that it is debatable that efficiency goals should be prioritized over distributive justice, but in any event it has not been shown that intellectual property approaches and reliance on price is a more efficient innovation strategy).

[28] *See, e.g.*, Angela Triguero, Lourdes Moreno-Mondéjar, & Maria A. Davia, *Eco-Innovation By Small And Medium-Sized Firms In Europe: From End-Of-Pipe To Cleaner Technologies*, 17 INNOVATION: ORG. &

this knowledge gap, Part I of this chapter first briefly discusses some of the global inequalities that likely will result from existing unequal patterns of creation and distribution of climate change technologies and associated ownership of IP rights. This section also discusses how the costs of accessing climate change technologies protected by IP rights may further exacerbate the current unequal impacts and differential climate change obligations of countries. Without concerted efforts to change existing innovation laws and policies, including funding choices, the corresponding costs of these impacts and obligations may impose significant stresses on the IP system, as they have with other serious global problems such as with access to essential medicines.[29]

Part II then explains how PPPs pose significant challenges for specific policy choices regarding innovation funding of climate change technologies and associated IP. To do so, it first presents a typology of public sector choices in innovation funding, including decisions to rely on the private sector for funding. This section then explains how these basic national policies may affect the nature, direction, and roles of PPPs in the climate change and energy development domains. The policy choices for innovation funding proposed in this Part are relevant both to increasing domestic innovation capacity for climate change R&D as well as to technology transfer across jurisdictions.

Part III explains why the geographical imbalances of wealth and innovation capacity discussed in Part I may pose serious problems for technology transfer, particularly when attempting to leverage PPP efforts across jurisdictional borders. It then proposes three sets of approaches to overcoming innovation, access, and price constraints that may result from public sector policies that rely primarily on PPPs, on private markets, and on IP rights to fund the development and transfer of climate change-related technologies. These approaches include public sector innovation laws and policies as well as innovation choices made within the private sector (or by governments or PPPs acting as proprietors).[30] Similarly, greater involvement of local actors in adapting technologies to local conditions will normally be needed for effective and efficient

Mgt. 24 (2015) (finding, for example, that "[n]etwork involvement measured by cooperation with universities and research agencies is essential in … eco-innovation in small firms, but not for mid-sized firms. With regard to environmental regulation, subsidies are important only for small firms, especially for the adoption of cleaner technologies. On the contrary side, existing environmental regulation is a key factor to explain the adoption of cleaner technologies for medium firms but not for smaller ones."); Chulhyun Kim and Moon-Soo Kim, *Identifying Core Environmental Technologies Through Patent Analysis*, 17 Innovation: Org. & Mgt. 139–158 (2015).

29 *See* Ahmed Abdel-Latif et al., *Overcoming the Impasse on Intellectual Property and Climate Change at the UNFCCC: A Way Forward*, International Centre for Trade and Sustainable Development Policy Brief No. 11 (November 2011).

30 Although some of the proposals are best addressed to developed countries like the United States, others may be better addressed to developing countries or private sector actors (such as universities), or may depend on the particular laws and policies in place in those countries. And although these recommendations are made by two academics located in the United States, we believe they have broader application, even if they may require tailoring to the conditions and needs of different countries or of particular PPPs or private sector entities. For example, as discussed in Part III, some countries have legal regimes where private entities are entitled to take title to patented inventions generated with governmental innovation funds; other countries may not. Similarly, the 'international exhaustion' requirements adopted by various countries (or regions) may differ. Accordingly, careful thought should be given to modifying these proposals as appropriate to the context of particular countries and private-sector practices.

technology transfer, particularly for determining which technologies should be transferred, modified, or developed.[31]

The chapter concludes with a renewed call for greater public funding[32] and for more careful management of the innovation policies and innovation choices made in establishing and operating climate change-related PPPs.

I Climate Change Technology Transfer and Intellectual Property Inequality

A *Climate Change Technology Transfer under the UNFCCC*

The amount of greenhouse gases that have been emitted over time and the extent of climate change impacts they will cause are unequally distributed by country and by levels of economic development.[33] The United States and the European Union alone account for over 50 percent of the cumulative emissions of carbon dioxide (CO_2) that has occurred from 1850 to 2011.[34] China was the third largest cumulative emitter from 1850 to 2011, and has become the largest worldwide emitter of CO_2.[35]

In 1992 (and earlier), the United Nations (UN) recognized both these inequalities and the unequal abilities of countries to address climate change and to finance responses while simultaneously addressing other social needs. The UNFCCC thus explicitly adopted the principle of "common but differentiated responsibilities and respective capabilities" for addressing climate change.[36] The UNFCCC imposed obligations for the countries principally responsible for climate change to transfer funds and technology to the developing world, and made compliance with UNFCCC mitigation and adaptation goals by developing countries contingent on the fulfillment of those developed country obligations.

[31] Padmashree Gehl Sampath & Pedro Roffe, *Unpacking the International Technology Transfer Debate: Fifty Years and Beyond Research*, ICTSD Issue Paper No. 36, 17, 19 (Nov. 2012). ("[T]echnological learning is domestically induced through a range of proactive policy choices, which are critical to explain the technological underpinnings of export success stories ... National capabilities are not simply built on the basis of R&D and science capacity, but are fostered through linkages of economic and non-economic agents within the economy. Such a policy framework therefore involves purposive sets of actions by national governments to promote innovation capacity. These policy actions are aimed at strengthening linkages and collaborative bonds between a variety of actors and networks in the economy.")

[32] Recent economic scholarship emphasizes the substantial returns to government funding of the innovation system, not only through direct government funding of both basic and applied research but also through tax credits for private investments in research and development. *See Returns to Federal Investments in the Innovation System: Proceedings of a Workshop – in Brief*, National Academies of Science, Engineering & Medicine (Oct. 2017).

[33] *See, e.g., Fifth Assessment Synthesis Report, Summary for Policymakers*, Intergovernmental Panel on Climate Change (IPCC) at 14 (2014) ("Regional Key Risks and Potential for Risk Reduction").

[34] *See, e.g.*, Mengpin Ge et al., *6 Graphs Explain the World's Top 10 Emitters* (Cumulative CO_2 Emissions 1850–2011), World Resources Institute (2014).

[35] *See, e.g., id.; see also Global Greenhouse Gas Emission Data*, US Environmental Protection Agency (EPA) (2016).

[36] UNFCCC, *supra* note 5, Preamble ¶ 6 ("*Acknowledging* that the global nature of climate change calls for the widest possible cooperation by all countries and their participation in an effective and appropriate international response, in accordance with their common but differentiated responsibilities and respective capabilities and their social and economic conditions"). *See, e.g., id.* Art. 3.1.

Article 4.5 of the UNFCCC obligated developed countries to "promote, facilitate, and finance, as appropriate, the transfer of, or access to, environmentally sound technologies and know-how to other Parties, particularly developing country Parties, to enable them to implement the provisions of the Convention" designed to mitigate and adapt to climate change.[37] These environmentally sound technologies (ESTs)[38] are therefore central to the obligations under the UNFCCC. Similarly, Article 4.7 of the UNFCCC provided that:

> [t]he extent to which developing country Parties will effectively implement their commitments under the Convention will depend on the effective implementation by developed country Parties of their commitments under the Convention related to financial resources and transfer of technology and will take fully into account that economic and social development and poverty eradication are the first and overriding priorities of the developing country Parties.[39]

The 2015 Paris Agreement of the UNFCCC reiterated the Framework Convention's recognition of the inequality of causes, impacts, and obligations regarding climate change.[40] It also reinforced the obligation of developed countries to "provide financial resources to assist developing country Parties with respect to both mitigation and adaptation in continuation of their existing obligations under the [UNFCCC]."[41] The parties to the Paris Agreement agreed to meet voluntarily pledged mitigation goals,[42] and for developed country parties to transfer at least US$100 billion per year until 2025, as well as to transfer technologies to developing country parties for their mitigation and adaptation activities.[43]

Notably for purposes of this chapter, the funds committed by countries under the Paris Agreement will include a mix of private and public sources, and will go to both products and services in the form of technology transfers. Vast amounts of money, mobilized in part by the prospect of large commercial markets and prompted in part by governmental development funding, thus will be spent in the energy, transport, agriculture, forestry, and other industrial and social sectors. Some of that funding will go toward infrastructure development.[44] Nevertheless, the promised funds under the UNFCCC are substantially

[37] UNFCCC, *supra* note 5, Art. 4.5.

[38] The transfer and adaptation of effective technologies to developing countries on a sustainable basis is necessary to address the adverse affects of climate change. As noted in Article 4.5 of the UNFCCC, developed countries are required to promote and help finance international technology transfer and access to environmentlally sound technologies and know-how to enable developing countries to implement the provisions of the Convention. *See* Maskus & Okediji, *Legal and Economic Perspectives*, *supra* note 3, at 392.

[39] UNFCCC, *supra* note 5, Art. 4.7.

[40] *See Paris Agreement*, *supra* note 4, Preamble ¶ 3 ("*In pursuit* of the objective of the Convention, and being guided by its principles, including the principle of equity and common but differentiated responsibilities and respective capabilities, in the light of different national circumstances.").

[41] *Id.*, at Art. 9.1.

[42] *See Paris Agreement*, *supra* note 4, Art. 3, Art. 4, ¶¶ 2, 3, 8, 11–14, Art. 6, ¶ 1.

[43] *See Paris Agreement*, *supra* note 4, Arts. 9, 10; Draft Decision –/CP.21, ¶¶ 54, 67–68.

[44] *Cf.* Manuel F. Montes, *Industrialization, Inequality and Sustainability: What Kinds of Industry Policy Do We Need?*, South Center Policy Brief (Aug. 2017) (discussing postcolonial-era challenges to the SDG 9 commitment to "build resilient infrastructure, promote inclusive and sustainable industrialization, and foster innovation," in light of the current structure of United Nations' development assistance, international legal structure, and institutions).

less than the amounts that were thought needed by World Bank estimates in 2009,[45] and by the substantially higher estimates that have been developed since,[46] particularly in light of new information on the rapidly accelerating changes to the climate.[47]

Technology transfer occurs in many different forms. As a working group of the Intergovernmental Panel on Climate Change (IPCC) defined it, technology transfer is:

> a broad set of processes covering the flows of know-how, experience and equipment for mitigating and adapting to climate change amongst different stakeholders such as governments, private sector entities, financial institutions, non-governmental organizations (NGOs) and research/ education institutions ... the broad and inclusive term 'transfer' encompasses diffusion of technologies and technology cooperation across and within countries. It covers technology transfer processes between developed countries, developing countries, and countries with economies in transition. It comprises the process of learning to understand, utilize and replicate the technology, including the capacity to choose and adapt to local conditions and integrate it with indigenous technologies.[48]

Since the 2010 Conference of the Parties in Cancún, the UNFCCC has focused its technology transfer efforts through new subsidiary institutions: the Technology Executive Committee (TEC) and the Climate Technology Center and Network (CTCN), and the Green Climate Fund (GCF).[49] The Paris Agreement continues to employ and to rely on these organs formed under the UNFCCC.[50] Some of their mechanisms for facilitating technology transfer are described in Box 12.1.

45 *See World Development Report 2010: Development and Climate Change*, WORLD BANK 6–7 (2009) [hereinafter World Development Report 2010].

46 *See* United Nations Environment Programme (UNEP), *The Adaptation Gap Finance Report 2016*, at 3 (May 2016) (needs 2–3 times higher than World Bank estimates of $70–100 billion/year by 2030; 4–5 times higher by 2050).

47 *See, e.g.*, Christiana Figueres et al., *Comment: Three Years to Safeguard Our Climate*, 546 NATURE 593 (Jun. 29, 2017); *Earth's Oceans are Warming 13% Faster Than Thought, and Accelerating*, THE GUARDIAN (Mar. 10, 2017).

48 Stephen O. Andersen et al., *Technical Summary*, *in* METHODOLOGICAL AND TECHNOLOGICAL ISSUES IN TECHNOLOGY TRANSFER: A SPECIAL REPORT OF IPCC WORKING GROUP III 15–16 (2000).

49 "The TEC consists of 20 technology experts representing both developed and developing countries ... The CTCN is hosted by the United Nations Environment Programme in collaboration with the United Nations Industrial Development Organization, and is supported by 11 partner institutions. The Centre facilitates a network of national, regional, sectoral and international technology centres, networks, organizations and private sector entities." UNFCCC, *Support for Implementing Climate Technology Activities*, TT:CLEAR, http://unfccc.int/ttclear/support/technology-mechanism.html. The partners include universities and private foundations. *See, e.g.*, *Consortium Partners*, CTCN, www.ctc-n.org/about-ctcn/consortium-partners (last visited Oct. 10, 2017). The GFC's role continues to grow as the largest international climate fund helping developing countries respond to climate change. *See GFC in Numbers*, GREEN CLIMATE FUND, 2017.

50 *See Paris Agreement*, *supra* note 4, Art. 10, ¶ 3; *id.* Draft Decision –/CP.21, ¶¶ 55, 59, 64. The TEC and the CTCN form the Technology Mechanism serving the Paris Agreement; the TEC plays a key role in supporting countries to identify climate technology policies that help them to achieve the Agreement's objectives. The CTCN promotes the accelerated transfer of environmentally sound technologies for low carbon and climate resilient development at the request of developing countries. *See TT:CLEAR*, http://unfccc.int/ttclear/support/technology-mechanism.html.

Box 12.1. UNFCCC Mechanisms for Facilitating Technology Transfer

The TEC has adopted six principal 'modalities' for technology development and transfer[51] and has prioritized efforts to perform 'technology needs assessments' and to understand better the barriers to technology transfer.[52] Similarly, the CTCN, which is currently being hosted by the United Nations Environment Programme (UNEP),[53] has adopted modalities and procedures in six areas, including facilitating the financing of the activities.[54] The GCF, in turn, has focused so far on developing the mechanisms of funding for mitigation and adaptation (including technology transfers), and on encouraging a balance of funding for mitigation and adaptation needs. The GCF established its Secretariat with the UNFCCC and the Global Environment Facility (GEF),[55] created a Financial Intermediary Fund with the World Bank as interim trustee, and authorized the Republic of Korea to be the more permanent host for the GCF.[56]

The UNFCCC as a whole has called for developed countries to expedite their short-term ('fast-track') funding and to scale up their commitments to long-term funding to developing countries (earlier to US$100 billion by 2020, and in Paris to treat that amount as a 'floor' and continue it at least through 2025).[57] These funds (even if ultimately provided) are likely to be much too low to achieve the Paris Agreement's stated goal of limiting temperature increases to no more than two-degrees Celsius above pre-industrial levels, much less to achieve the more ambitious one-and-one-half degree Celsius goal in light of recent acceleration of warming effects.[58] The UNFCCC has also called for a "significant share" of the new multilateral funding for adaptation activities to "flow through" the GCF, and for developed countries to "channel a substantial share of public funds" to

[51] These are "(a) Analysis and synthesis; (b) Policy recommendations; (c) Facilitation and catalysing; (d) Linkage with other institutional arrangements; (e) Engagement of stakeholders; [and] (f) Information and knowledge sharing." *Report of the Conference of the Parties on its Seventeenth Session, Held in Durban from 28 November to 11 December 2011: Decision 4/CP.17 Technology Executive Committee – Modalities and Procedures*, UNFCCC, Report No. FCCC/CP/2011/9/Add.1 ¶ 4 (a)-(f) (2011) [hereinafter UNFCCC, "COP17 Report"].

[52] *See Report of the Conference of the Parties on its Eighteenth Session, Held in Doha from 26 November to 8 December 2012*, UNFCCC, Report No. FCCC/CP/2012/8/Add.2. ¶ 10, (2012) [hereinafter UNFCCC, "COP18 Report"].

[53] *Id.*, at Decision 14/CP.18, *Arrangements to make the Climate Technology Centre and Network Fully Operational.*

[54] The other five are: "(a) identifying currently available climate-friendly technologies for mitigation and adaptation that meet development needs; (b) facilitating the preparation of project proposals for existing technologies for mitigation and adaptation; (c) facilitating adaptation and deployment of currently available technologies to meet local needs and circumstances; (d) facilitating research, development and demonstration of new climate-friendly technologies for mitigation and adaptation; (e) enhancing human and institutional capacity to manage the technology cycle . . ." *See* UNFCCC, COP17 Report, *supra* note 51, at Decision 2/CP.17, *Outcome of the work of the Ad Hoc Working Group on, Long-term Cooperative Action under the Convention*, ¶ 135(a)-(f).

[55] The GEF structure is more complex than the TEC; it includes scientific and technical advisory panels of "internationally recognized experts in the GEF's key areas of work . . . [which are] are supported by a global network of experts and institutions." *Organization*, GEF, www.thegef.org/about/organization.

[56] *See* UNFCCC, COP18 Report, *supra* note 52 at Decision 6/CP.18, *Report of the Green Climate Fund to the Conference of the Parties and Guidance to the Green Climate Fund*, preamble and ¶¶ 3, 7(b).

[57] *See Paris Agreement*, *supra* note 4, at Draft Decision –/CP.21, ¶ 54.

[58] *See id.*, at Art. 2.1(a); US Global Climate Change Research Program, *Climate Science Special Report* (CSSR) (Jun. 28, 2017), www.nytimes.com/packages/pdf/climate/2017/climate-report-final-draft-clean.pdf.

such activities.[59] The Paris Agreement recognizes the need for developed countries to "provide financial resources to assist developing country Parties with respect to both mitigation and adaptation" and to "take the lead in mobilizing climate finance from a wide variety of sources, instruments, and channels, noting the significant role of public funds."[60] Significantly, as noted by the TEC in its 2012 Report, "[i]ntellectual property rights were identified as an area for which more clarity would be needed on their role in the development and transfer of climate technologies based upon evidence on a case by case basis."[61] However, the Paris Agreement does not itself mention IP rights.

B *Unequal Climate Technology R&D and Patent Ownership*

Most new, patented mitigation and adaptation technologies are being invented in a small group of developed countries (collectively referred to as the "North") and a few emerging economy countries – particularly Brazil, Russia, India, China, South Korea, and Mexico (referred to as the "BRICs-plus" countries), rather than in the developing world (collectively referred to along with emerging economy countries as the "South").[62] More specifically, the first tier of climate change technology development includes principally Japan, Germany, and the United States (the "Big Three") for a very wide range of technologies, and the United Kingdom and France for particular sectors such as energy generation. Through self-conscious planning and large amounts of government funding, China soon may reach the point of creating "Big Four" status.[63] The second tier includes the BRICS-plus countries, which are preeminent in specific sectors such as cement or renewable energy technologies.[64]

59 *See* UNFCCC, COP18 Report, *supra*, note 52, at Decision 1/CP.18, *Agreed outcome pursuant to the Bali Action Plan*, ¶¶ 63–68. *See also Report of the Conference of the Parties on its Nineteenth Session, Held in Warsaw from 11 to 23 November 2013: Decision 3/CP19, Long-term Climate Finance*, UNFCCC, Report No. FCCC/CP/2013/10/Add.1 ¶¶ 7–9 (2013); *Paris Agreement*, *supra* note 4, at Draft Decision –/CP.21, ¶ 55, 59.

60 *Paris Agreement*, *supra* note 4, at Art. 9, ¶¶ 1, 3.

61 *Report on Activities and Performance of the Technology Executive Committee for 2012*, UNFCCC, Report No. FCCC/SB/2012/2 ¶ 35(g) (2012).

62 *See, e.g.*, Antoine Dechezleprêtre et al., *Invention and Transfer of Climate Change Mitigation Technologies on a Global Scale: A Study Drawing on Patent Data* 4 (CERNA, Mines Paris Tech, Agence Française de Dévelopment, Working Paper, 2008) [hereinafter Dechezleprêtre 2008a], https://sallan.org/pdf-docs/Dechezlepretre.pdf; Bernice Lee, Ilian Iliev & Felix Preston, *A Chatham House Report: Who Owns Our Low Carbon Future?: Intellectual Property and Energy Technologies*, Royal Institute of International Affairs, viii (2009); UNEP, European Patent Office, (EPO) and International Centre for Trade and Sustainable Development (ICTSD), *Patents and Clean Energy: Bridging the Gap Between Evidence and Policy: Final report*, 9, 30–36 (2010) [hereinafter UNEP/EPO/ICTSD Study]. A recent patent study confirmed these continuing disparaties between the North and South, as well as found an emphasis on pollution control rather than energy efficiency technologies. *See generally* Gemma Durán-Romero & Ana Urraca-Ruiz, *Climate Change and Eco-Innovation. A Patent Data Assessment of Environmentally Sound Technologies*, 17 Innovation: Org. & Mgmt. 115 (2015).

63 *See generally*, Cheung, Tai Ming, et al. (Univ. of Cal. Institute on Global Conflict and Cooperation), *Planning for Innovation: Understanding China's Plans for Technological, Energy, Industrial, and Defense Development* (2016).

64 *See* Dechezleprêtre 2008a, *supra* note 62, at 3–4; Lee, Iliev & Preston, *supra* note 62, at viii; UNEP/EPO/ICTSD Study, *supra* note 62, at 30–36.

Between 1978 and 2003, most of the climate change mitigation technologies developed and patented in thirteen categories – as measured by data from the EP/OECD World Patent Statistical Database – came from the Big Three, although in two categories the BRICS-plus countries were increasingly developing patented technologies.[65] In particular, China has been spending extensively on R&D and consequently has been patenting more.[66] From 1998 to 2003, patenting of climate change technologies grew on average by 9 percent per year overall and 18 percent for emerging economies.[67] The Big Three accounted for roughly 60 to 85 percent of all patented inventions in all categories measured.[68] Japan alone accounted for over 50 percent in three categories.[69]

These unequally distributed technology developments reflect gains from specialization that are likely to continue or to heighten existing imbalances of technological sophistication and wealth accumulation through "clustering" effects.[70] "Specialization gains are seemingly important in climate change innovation,"[71] and various countries (particularly Japan) have a substantial, existing competitive advantage in regard to green technology development.[72] These imbalances in local patenting also may reflect differences in R&D budgets[73] and in the head start that many developed countries already possess in scientific and technological development.

Although it is widely recognized that greater public financing for R&D (particularly for low-carbon R&D) is needed, it may be difficult to generate the political will to achieve the needed consistent levels of funding or to raise prices sufficiently on carbon emissions to induce private R&D.[74] This could change quickly, however, with growing recognition of the rapidly increasing harms and costs of climate change. It is to be hoped

65 *See* Dechezleprêtre 2008a, *supra* note 62, at 26.

66 *See, e.g.*, Yahong Li, Imitation to Innovation in China: The Role of Patents in Biotechnology and Pharmaceutical Industries 70 (2010).

67 *See* Dechezleprêtre 2008a, *supra* note 62, at 3–4.

68 *See ibid.* at 18 & Table 3. *See also* Antoine Dechezleprêtre et al., *Invention and Transfer of Climate Change-Mitigation Technologies: A Global Analysis*, 5 Rev. Envt'l. Econ. Pol'y 109, 115–16 (2011) (Big Three accounted for 59% of patented worldwide climate mitigation inventions from 2000–2005, and 53% of high-value inventions).

69 *See* Dechezleprêtre 2008a, *supra* note 62, at 16.

70 *See, e.g.*, Michael E. Porter, *Clusters of Innovation: Regional Foundations of U.S. Competitiveness*, Council on Competitiveness (2001); Jonathan Sallet et al., *The Geography of Innovation: The Federal Government and the Growth of Regional Innovation Clusters*, Science Progress 1 (2009).

71 Antoine Dechezleprêtre et al., *Invention and Transfer of Climate Change Mitigation Technologies on a Global Scale: A Study Drawing on Patent Data* 4 (CERNA, Mines Paris Tech, Agence Française de Dévelopment, Working Paper, November 2008).

72 *See, e.g.*, Sam Fankauser et al., *Who Will Win the Green Race? In Search of Environmental Competitiveness and Innovation*, 23 Global Envtl. Change 902, 906 (2013).

73 *See, e.g.*, Carlos M. Correa, *Review of the TRIPS Agreement: Fostering the Transfer of Technology to Developing Countries*, 2 J. World Intel. Prop. 939, 944 (1999).

74 *See, e.g.* Antoine Dechezleprêtre & D. Popp, *Fiscal and Regulatory Instruments for Clean Technology Development in the European Union*, London Sch. of Econ. & Pol. Sci., Policy Paper, at 10, 18–20 (Jul. 2015) (discussing the "double externality" problem that results in underfunding environmental R&D, noting that carbon pricing may be too low to induce desired levels of R&D, and that positive spillovers from clean technologies are sufficiently large to justify greater R&D subsidies); Antoine Dechezleprêtre et al., *Climate Change Policy, Innovation, and Growth*, London Sch. of Econ. & Pol. Sci., (2016) at 9–19 (discussing competitiveness advantages and R&D funding for clean technology spillovers).

that Paris Agreement efforts through the TEC and GCF will more rapidly generate greater and more widespread international support for increased public R&D financing.

The principal emphasis on private markets and patent rights to develop needed climate change technologies will likely generate substantial trade tensions. These will arise as IP protected goods flow from the North to the South, while revenues from the sale of those technologies may flow in the opposite direction.[75] The costs of such technology transfers thus will result in significant wealth transfers that will run against the flow of the UNFCCC's technology transfer and financing obligations based on "common but differentiated responsibilities and respective capabilities." As in areas outside of climate change technologies, the geographic imbalances in patenting behaviors are likely to further exacerbate existing IP, trade, and scientific differences, as well as to generate political tensions along the North–South divide. Further, the reliance principally by the North on private funding, private markets, and the patent system, and the varying benefits of the patent system for the wide range of technologies and markets in the South,[76] may pose additional challenges to technology transfer.[77] These patterns in the transfer of climate change technology are a familiar, if more recent, example of a long history regarding technology transfer between the North and South more generally.[78]

This is the background against which PPPs have been proposed as a principal means of implementation for the SDGs, which specifically include combatting climate change under SDG 13. The next section explores a particularly important subset of public and private innovation policy choices, i.e., innovation funding mechanisms, that will be used to address climate change-related technology development and transfer.[79]

II Innovation Funding Policies and Choices for Climate Change-Technology Development and Transfer

A *Sustainable Development via PPPs Raises New Questions about the Funding Structure of Climate Change-Related Technology Development and Transfer*

The Paris Agreement supplements the UN Framework Convention on Climate Change to make even clearer the link between sustainable development and environmental protection in regard to climate change. Specifically, the Agreement's objectives for mitigation, adaptation, and financing efforts (and, implicitly, for technology transfer) make this link explicit. It is worth repeating the language here:

[75] *See generally* David A. Gantz & Padideh Ala'i, *Climate Change Innovation, Products and Services Under the GATT/WTO System, in* Sarnoff, Research Handbook, *supra* n. * at 271; WTO & United Nations Environment Programme (UNEP), *Trade and Climate Change WTO-UNEP Report* (2009).

[76] *See, e.g.*, Ricardo Cavazos & Douglas Lippoldt, *The Strengthening of IPR Protection: Policy Complements*, 2 W.I.P.O. J. 99, 101–2, 110–12 (2010).

[77] *See, e.g.*, Brewer, *supra* note 1, at 3–5.

[78] Sampath & Roffe, *supra* note 31.

[79] The following section is largely taken from International Council on Human Rights Policy, *Beyond Technology Transfer: Protecting Human Rights in a Climate-Constrained World*, in Sarnoff, Research Handbook, *supra* note *, at 126.

> This Agreement, in enhancing the implementation of the Convention, including its objective, aims to strengthen the global response to the threat of climate change, *in the context of sustainable development and efforts to eradicate poverty*, including by:
>
> (a) Holding the increase in the global average temperature to well below 2 °C above pre-industrial levels and to pursue efforts to limit the temperature increase to 1.5 °C above pre-industrial levels, recognizing that this would *significantly reduce the risks and impacts of climate change*;
>
> (b) Increasing *the ability to adapt to the adverse impacts of climate change and foster climate resilience and low greenhouse gas emissions development, in a manner that does not threaten food production*;
>
> (c) Making finance flows consistent with a pathway towards *low greenhouse gas emissions and climate-resilient development.*[80]

As stated earlier, many different climate change and energy technologies potentially fall within the scope of achieving such sustainable development efforts for climate change mitigation and adaptation. Article 4.5 of the UNFCCC and Paragraph 68(d) of the Paris Agreement encourage such technologies for adaptation to be "environmentally sound."[81] This concern is necessarily of a different kind than same requirement for "environmentally sound" technologies (ESTs) with regard to mitigation technologies. Whereas mitigation technologies must necessarily aim at an ideal horizon of carbon neutrality, ESTs for adaptation must aim at global benchmarks recognizing local variations of development and of need. Adaptation technologies must reflect best available environmental standards in current use, given costs, resources, and the urgency of adaptation. Thus, it is critically important to examine how government funding traditionally has operated in technology transfer generally, and how different funding and coordination approaches might impact the direction of PPPs engaged in climate change and energy innovation and technology transfer.

B *Taxonomy of Government Innovation Funding Mechanisms and Their Relationship to PPPs*

PPPs by definition involve some degree of public sector involvement, including possible funding, policy-making, steering and operational control, and oversight.[82] But very little analytic work has been done to elucidate the various specific mechanisms of government involvement in and governance of PPPs.[83] This is especially true of innovation policy

[80] *Paris Agreement*, *supra* note 4, Art. 2.1(a) (emphasis added).

[81] UNFCCC, *supra* note 5, Art. 4.5 ("The developed country Parties and other developed Parties included in Annex II shall take all practicable steps to promote, facilitate and finance, as appropriate, the transfer of, or access to, environmentally sound technologies and know-how to other Parties, particularly developing country Parties, to enable them to implement the provisions of the Convention."); *Paris Agreement*, *supra* note 4, at ¶68(d) ("The enhancement of enabling environments for and the addressing of barriers to the development and transfer of socially and environmentally sound technologies").

[82] This section is substantially condensed from the Joshua D. Sarnoff, *Government Choices*, *supra* note *. For a more detailed analysis, please refer to that discussion.

[83] A notable exception is the historic and developing literature on "commons" institutions that are PPPs. *See, e.g.*, Elinor Ostrom, Governing the Commons: The Evolution of Institutions for Collective Action (Political Economy of Institutions and Decisions, 1990); Governing Knowledge Commons (Brett M. Frischmann, Michael J. Madison, & Katherine J. Strandburg eds., 2014) [hereinafter Governing Knowledge Commons].

choices involving funding choices for technology innovation funding and transfer. Using a broad brush for classification, government choices to fund innovation can be grouped into five categories: (1) subsidization; (2) procurement; (3) direct development; (4) constructed commons; and (5) product, process, and market regulation (which affect the flows of private funding to and within markets).[84] There is no magic to this proposed classification; different categories are reasonable to employ, particularly as some of the contents of the categories may overlap.[85] The five categories listed above reflect five fundamentally different approaches to funding innovation. Some of these categories may have more obvious impact than others on technology innovation and transfer within PPPs. But all are discussed briefly below.

1 Subsidies

Subsidization is a very broad class that has different comparative effects on innovation.[86] The most basic form of subsidy to R&D and innovation is (1) direct and targeted subsidization of R&D and innovation efforts, such as government agency funding of university, corporate, or small business R&D, and government support for education more broadly.[87] Other subsidies include: (2) prizes, rewards, and other *ex post* development funding; (3) consumption or production subsidies; (4) tax subsidies; (5) administrative subsidies; and (6) foreign aid.

The choices that government can make among the various kinds of subsidies should depend on the degree to which the innovation outputs can reliably be predicted; the commercial nature of the research; and the comparative effectiveness of government administrators and firm actors in making predictions, directing the R&D and generating innovation outputs.[88] It will also depend in part on World Trade Organization (WTO) R&D subsidy disciplines.[89] Targeted R&D tax subsidies (and the *ex ante* incentives they generate) are useful principally for profit-making ventures, and they will leave control of

[84] *See* Michael Madison, Brett M. Frischmann, & Katherine Strandburg, *Constructing Commons in the Cultural Environment*, 95 Cornell L. Rev. 657, 667 (2010); Tuomas Takalo, *Rationales and Instruments for Public Innovation Policies*, Bank of Finland Research Discussion Papers, Paper No. 1, 10–19 (2013), http://papers.ssrn.com/sol3/papers.cfm?abstract_id=2217502; Michael W. Carroll, *One Size Does Not Fit All: A Framework for Tailoring Intellectual Property Rights*, 70 Ohio St. L.J. 1361, 1368 (2009); Brett Frischmann, *Innovation and Institutions: Rethinking the Economics of U.S. Science and Technology Policy*, 24 Vt. L. Rev. 347, 354, 374 n.102, 387 (2000) [hereinafter Frischmann, *Innovation*]; William Fisher, *Intellectual Property and Innovation: Theoretical, Empirical, and Historical Perspectives*, 37 Industrial Property, Innovation, and the Knowledge-based Economy, Beleidsstudies Technologie Economie, 2–3 (on-line version 2001), cyber.law.harvard.edu/people/tfisher/Innovation.pdf.

[85] *See* Joseph E. Stiglitz, *Lecture, Economic Foundations of Intellectual Property Rights*, 57 Duke L. J. 1693, 1722 (2008) (employing a different, three-part classification – patents, prizes, and government-funded research – and focusing on six attributes of these choices: selection of research targets; financing methods; dissemination incentives; nature of the risks; innovation incentives; and transaction costs).

[86] *See* Organization for Economic Cooperation and Development, *National Systems for Financing Innovation*, 11–12 (1995).

[87] *See* Frischmann, *Innovation*, *supra* note 84, at 387.

[88] *See id.* at 352–3; Henrik Kristensen et al., *Adopting Eco-Innovation in Danish Polymer Industry Working with Nanotechnology: Drivers, Barriers and Future Strategies*, 6 Nanotech. L. & Bus. 416, 433 (2009). *See also* Frischmann, *Innovation*, *supra* note 84, at 392.

[89] Keith Maskus, *Research and Development Subsidies: A Need for WTO Disciplines?* E15 Initiative, International Centre for Trade and Sustainable Development (ICTSD) and World Economic Forum (2015), http://e15initiative.org/wp-content/uploads/2015/01/E15_Subsidies_Maskus_final.pdf.

innovation development to such firms, which often is (debatably) argued to be better than having the government direct which innovations to target.[90]

But such simple insights do not get us very far because other forms of subsidies are available that could potentially induce more effective and efficient R&D and innovation development in the private sector. Such alternative subsidies include funds provided to universities and nonprofit research centers, or development through resources provided by private foundations. There are simply too many potentially effective alternative subsidy mechanisms to choose from[91] with too little analysis of the relative institutional competencies of the various actors, including government bureaucrats and the decision-making processes that they follow.[92] Different kinds of subsidies are illustrated by many of the other chapters in this book discussing the operation of PPPs in the global health sector.[93]

2 Procurement

Procurement resembles R&D innovation subsidies, but it typically provides incentives by conditioning funding on achieving innovation outputs that are commercial or non-commercial products. Although there is no theoretically necessary relationship between government procurement and the creation of IP rights, the US Bayh-Dole Act (under which private recipients of government funding may acquire patent title to inventions developed with that funding) applies to US Government procurement contracts 'for the performance of experimental, developmental, or research work funded in whole or in part by the Federal Government' as well as to grants.[94]

The effects of procurement on innovation depend partly on whether the contracts take the form of 'push' or 'pull' mechanisms with regard to existing or future markets. Push mechanisms (*ex ante* market procurement) provide a demonstration of technology and a stimulus to market development so that industry may subsequently be more willing to risk market entry.[95] Push mechanisms raise questions as to the size of the government sector and its adequacy to demonstrate commercial viability in a broader market without government subsidies to production or consumption. Regulation of market prices for innovation outputs (or rate-based returns to regulated industries, as in the electric utility sector) further complicates the evaluation of the inducement effectiveness and adequacy of innovation returns to procurement funding.[96]

Pull mechanisms (*ex post* market procurement) provide *ex ante* innovation incentives based on assurances of *ex post* (relative to the time of creating innovations) procurement

[90] *See* Frischmann, *Innovation*, *supra* note 84, at 352–53.
[91] *Id.* at 392–95.
[92] *See* Tomain at 404–16; Mark Radka, *Some Perspectives About the Climate Technology Centre/Climate Technology Network*, U.N. Environment Programme 101 (2012), http://unfccc.int/files/meetings/ad_hoc_working_groups/lca/application/pdf/some_perspectives_about_the_ctc_ctn.pdf.
[93] See chapters in this book by Frederick M. Abbott, chapter 2, *supra*; Anatole Krattiger et al., chapter 3, *supra*; Katy M. Graef et al., chapter 4, *supra*; Esteban Burrone, chapter 5, *supra*; Hilde Stevens et al., chapter 6, *supra*.
[94] Patent Rights in Inventions Made With Federal Assistance: Definitions, 35 U.S.C. §201(b) (2006).
[95] *See, e.g.*, Vernon W. Ruttan, IS WAR NECESSARY FOR ECONOMIC GROWTH? MILITARY PROCUREMENT AND TECHNOLOGY DEVELOPMENT 108–09 (2006).
[96] *See, e.g.*, Paul L. Joskow & Nancy L. Rose, *The Effects of Economic Regulation*, *in* HANDBOOK OF INDUSTRIAL ORGANIZATION 1464–77 (1989); C.O. Ruggles, *Problems of Public-Utility Rate Regulation and Fair Return*, 32 J. POL. ECON. 543, 543–58 (1924).

funding and adequacy of scale for commercialization, which again reduces market entry risks. These *ex post* assurances of procurement (such as advanced purchase commitment contracts) are, effectively, *ex post* innovation consumption subsidies, where the government acts as a consumer on behalf of itself or of the general public. However, the price terms of these *ex post* innovation contracts may be highly uncertain. They also may be subject to statutory and 'march-in' rights regarding patented innovation outputs and to other contractually retained rights of the government or PPP procuring entity. Often in PPPs, the scope of the market purchase guarantees, conditions on market behavior, pricing terms and treatment of developed (foreground) IP, and retained ownership rights are negotiated in advance.[97]

Examples of procurement strategies by PPPs abound in the global health area, for example, the GAVI and other PPPs that work with advance commitments.[98]

3 Direct Development

Governments directly engage in all sorts of R&D and innovation development, funded through general or specific taxes and other sources of revenue. This reflects that government employees are user-innovators, that government agencies engage in R&D to generate different kinds of innovation outputs in the course of conducting their statutory mandates, and that government sometimes creates specialized bureaucracies to perform R&D and to generate innovation in particular sectors. The most well-known of these specialized R&D bureaucracies are the national laboratories.

US government policy permits cooperative R&D agreements (CRADAs) with private entities.[99] This allows for greater leveraging of federal funding for particular forms of innovation conducted within the government. Further, private entities may manage government research bureaucracies, such as the National Renewable Energy Laboratory (NREL) of the US Department of Energy – originally, the Solar Energy Research Institute – thereby blurring the line between the public and private sectors.[100] Additionally, government can collaborate among its own agencies,[101] with subsidiary or foreign governments, or with INGOs through interpersonnel agreements[102] and other collaborative efforts and personnel exchanges.[103] Government also can engage in collaborative R&D efforts, thereby pooling funds, technology, and other resources like in joint-venturing.

97 *See* Ron Bouchard, *Qualifying Intellectual Property II: A New Innovation Index for Pharmaceutical Patents & Products*, 28 Santa Clara Comp. & High Tech. L.J. 287, 382 (2011).

98 *See* Frederick M. Abbott, chapter 2, *supra*.

99 *See* Federal Technology Transfer Act, 15 U.S.C. 3710 §12(d)(1) (1986); Matthew Rimmer, Intellectual Property and Climate Change: Inventing Clean Technologies 276–77 (2001).

100 *See, e.g.*, National Renewable Energy Laboratory, Batelle, www.battelle.org/our-work/laboratory-management/national-renewable-energy-laboratory.

101 *See, e.g.*, OMB 2013 Budget Report, at 369 (Apr. 29, 2013).

102 *See, e.g.*, Intergovernmental Personnel Act of 1970, Pub. L. No. 91–648, 84 Stat. 1909 (1971) (codified as amended at 42 U.S.C. §4701 et seq. (2006)).

103 *See, e.g.*, US Department of State, Memorandum of Understanding to Enhance Cooperation on Climate Change, Energy and Environment Between the Government of the United States of America and the Government of the People's Republic of China (Jul. 2009), https://2009–2017.state.gov/r/pa/prs/ps/2009/july/126592.htm; US Department of State, Memorandum of Understanding Signed Between the Government of India and the Government of the United States, (Nov. 30, 2009), https://2009–2017.state.gov/p/sca/rls/press/2009/132776.htm.

Government direct development thus may lead to the generation of government-owned IP rights. For example, NREL possesses a significant portfolio of patents on wind turbines, generators, power systems, cooling towers, biofuels, and geothermal technologies and building construction. NREL has also developed an online database – the Energy Efficiency and Renewable Energy Technology Portal – to license its rights.[104] Depending on how they are exercised, these government-owned IP rights may have further effects on domestic and foreign markets and trade flows.[105] Whether and how the government chooses to license its IP rights for further R&D or innovation then becomes an important issue, as the government may choose to compete with the private sector in the market (although it rarely does). Even if the government does not directly compete with the private sector and supplies only to the government sector, government development and supply can lead to price reductions in the commercial market through competitive development. Furthermore, government direct development may impact private market shares that would be smaller without the inclusion of the government sector, allowing private entities to better recoup their innovation investments.

4 Constructed Commons

Yet another form of government innovation funding relates to the creation of various kinds of commons for managing physical or information resources to induce innovation.[106] The most obvious form of commons is government-created or government-subsidized physical infrastructure, such as the highway system or the Internet.[107] But commons in information also may be constructed, subsidized, or regulated by government. For example, the World Meteorological Organization – a United Nations specialized agency – and others sponsor and make available data on polar climate conditions that are generated and submitted by both governments and private sector scientists.[108] Another example, the Conservation Commons, is a cooperative effort of INGOs, non-governmental organizations, governments, academic institutions, and entities from the private sector. The Conservation Commons supports open access to data and sharing (with attribution) of information regarding biodiversity.[109] The US Government's Global Positioning Satellite (GPS) signals are freely available from the military and NASA, following an international incident after which NASA concluded that the public

[104] Rimmer, *supra* note 99, at 290–91.

[105] *Id.* at 266 (citing Daniel Roth, *The Radical Pragmatist*, WIRED, 104, 108 (2010)).

[106] *See* Michael W. Carroll, *Copyright, Fair Use, and Creative Commons Licenses, in Risk and Entrepreneurship in* LIBRARIES: SEIZING OPPORTUNITIES FOR CHANGE 18 (Pamela Bluh & Cindy Hepfer eds., 2009); Madison, Frischmann, & Strandburg, *supra* note 84, at 681–82.

[107] *See* Brett M. Frischmann, INFRASTUCTURE: THE SOCIAL VALUE OF SHARED RESOURCES 5–6 (2012); Brett M. Frischmann, *An Economic Theory of Infrastructure and Commons Management*, 89 MINN. L. REV. 917, 923–24, 956 (2005) [hereinafter cited as Frischmann, *An Economic Theory*]; Gregory N. Mandel, *When to Open Infrastructure Access*, 35 ECOLOGY L. Q. 205, 208–10 (2008); Konstantinos Styianou, *An Innovation-Centric Approach of Telecommunications Infrastructure Regulation*, 16 VA. J.L. & TECH. 221, 231–40 (2011).

[108] *See* Welcome to the Polar Information Commons (PIC), POLAR INFORMATION COMMONS, www.polarcommons.org/.

[109] *See, e.g.*, *Conservation Commons*, CONSERVEONLINE, http://conserveonline.org/workspaces/commons/.

benefits of new, nonmilitary, and nonaviation uses of the data justified continuing to provide it free of cost.[110]

Governments also may subsidize and regulate private sector commons institutions regarding prices of inputs and outputs, access and other terms of interaction, and may choose to limit the application of competition law and policy to facilitate commons development.[111] Similar to government direct development, government-commons approaches may supplement or compete with the private sector with regard to innovation promotion. For example, governments may affect commons-based activities by requiring or encouraging the pooling of technology or IP rights;[112] providing or supporting free or low-cost access to information outputs that are R&D or innovation inputs;[113] and engaging in or encouraging interpersonal exchanges.[114] If technology- or patent-pooling occurs, significant competition regulation issues will arise.

Similarly, public-sourced or public-sponsored commons may compete with private efforts to create commons, whether through the creation of technology or IP pools or databases, or through the encouragement of liberal licensing policies.[115] However, government-constructed and government-managed commons do not normally or purposefully compete with private R&D or innovation activity in research or production markets, even if they generate information outputs that are inputs to further R&D or innovation. Rather, such public commons typically seek to facilitate public or private R&D and innovation by lowering investment costs through creating infrastructure or other forms of commons resources, and by pooling expertise and information that otherwise might not as readily be compiled. Such public commons thus typically supplement other forms of government sponsorship of public and private R&D and innovation, rather than substitute for them. Longtime expert observers have recently proposed such a data commons and an IP pledging community for solar climate engineering research and technological developments.[116]

110 *See* James Love & Tim Hubbard, *Paying for Public Goods*, *in* CODE: COLLABORATIVE OWNERSHIP AND THE DIGITAL ECONOMY 207, 208–09 (James Love, Tim Hubbard, & Rishab Aiyer Ghosh eds., 2005).

111 *See, e.g.*, C. Scott Hemphill, *Network Neutrality and the False Promise of Zero-Price Regulation*, 25 YALE J. REG. 135, 164–75 (2008); Michael Madison, Brett M. Frischmann, & Katherine Strandburg, *The University as Constructed Cultural Commons*, 30 WASH. U. J. L. & POL'Y 365, 375–76 (2009). *See generally* Lawrence Lessig, CODE: VERSION 2.0 (2006).

112 *See* Dustin Szakalski, *Progress in the Aircraft Industry and the Role of Patent Pools and Cross-Licensing Agreements*, 15 UCLA J. L. & TECH. 1 (2011); Harry Dykman, *Patent Licensing Within the Manufacturer's Aircraft Association (MAA)*, 46 J. PAT. & TRADEMARK OFF. SOC'Y 646 (1964); Robert P. Merges & Richard R. Nelson, *On the Complex Economics of Patent Scope*, 90 COLUM. L. REV. 839, 888–90 (1990).

113 *See, e.g.*, US Department Energy Off. Sci., Human Genome Project Information (2011), www.ornl.gov/sci/techresources/Human_Genome/home.shtml; International HapMap Project (2011), http://hapmap.ncbi.nlm.nih.gov; Technology Mechanism, UNFCCC (2013), http://unfccc.int/ttclear/templates/render_cms_page?TEM_home.

114 *See, e.g.*, US Dept. of Energy, DOE/NNSA Overseas Presence Advisory Board's Overseas Corps Training Program Agreement, http://energy.gov/sites/prod/files/DOE-Overseas-Corps-Training-Program.pdf.

115 *See* GREEN EXCHANGE (2012), http://www.greenexchange.com; Wayne Balta, *Welcome to the Eco-Patent Commons*, CEF ECOINNOVATOR BLOG, www.corporateecoforum.com/welcome-to-the-eco-patent-commons/; *Welcome to PLOS*, PUBLIC LIBRARY OF SCIENCE, www.plos.org; *Creative Commons*, SCIENCE, https://creativecommons.org/about/program-areas/open-science; R. Kunstadt & I. Maggioni, *A Proposed "U.S. Public Patent Pool,"* LES NOUVELLES, 10–13 (2011).

116 Reynolds, Contreras, & Sarnoff, *supra* note *.

5 Market Regulation

The fifth and final mechanism of government innovation funding is market regulation, which is also a very broad category. Regulation covers: (a) direct product and process regulation; (b) information reporting and government disclosures, which may also lead to (or induce private action to avoid) direct product and process regulation;[117] (c) recognition and certification programs,[118] the premises of which are to provide incentives to direct private actions and to convey a market advantage that induces directed consumption patterns and thus greater innovation;[119] and (d) a wide variety of market-structure and market-operation regulations, including market-entry, price, competition, and IP rights regulations. All of these may affect innovation incentives by governing market-based returns of PPPs. Of these various forms of market regulation, this section focuses on IP and antitrust (competition) laws. It contextualizes the innovation policy choices within larger debates about the global IP legal regime and related global governance of climate change technologies.

In considering direct regulation by governments of market structures and operations, both IP and competition laws are the most obvious places to look (although price controls, crown use, statutory and compulsory licensing, and other forms of regulation of private market returns relating to technological products and services also may be used).[120] IP rights may be viewed as a form of market regulation, although they also provide a government subsidy (a property right), given that the exclusive right regulates market behaviors through government regulatory clearances and litigation mechanisms (which can include actions brought by the government).[121] Further, even when viewed as subsidies, IP rights are subject to IP and competition law doctrines that regulate how such rights relate to and are used in markets, whether such rights are considered to be property rights or to be regulatory rights, or a combination of both.[122]

The optimal strength, scope, and duration of IP rights that governments may grant depend on multiple, competing considerations. These include the following eight concerns: (a) private reliance on IP rights as a means of recouping investments in innovation, combined with government market regulation of the returns on such investments;[123]

[117] *See* Wesley A. Magat & W. Kip Viscusi, Informational Approaches to Regulation 4–5 (1992).

[118] *See, e.g.*, U.S. EPA, Climate Leadership Awards, www.epa.gov/climateleadership/awards/index.html; Margaret Chon, *Trademark Goodwill as a Public Good: Brands and Innovations in Corporate Social Responsibility*, 21 Lewis & Clark L. Rev. 277 (2017).

[119] *See, e.g.*, U.S. EPA, Energy Star® – The Power to Protect the Environment Through Energy Efficiency, EPA 430-R-03–008, 2–3 (2003).

[120] *See, e.g.*, Lionel Nesta, Francesco Vona, & Francesco Nicolli, *Environmental Policies, Product Market Regulation and Innovation in Renewable Energy* (2012) (unpublished manuscript), http://papers.ssrn.com/sol3/papers.cfm?abstract_id=2192441. *See generally*, B. Zorina Khan, *Antitrust and Innovation Before the Sherman Act*, 77 Antitrust L.J. 757, 759–60, 784–5 (2011).

[121] *See, e.g.*, Criminal Offenses, 17 U.S.C. §506(a) (2006); Criminal Infringement of a Copyright, 18 U.S.C. §2319(a) (2006).

[122] *See, e.g.*, Oil States Energy Servs., LLC v. Greene's Energy Group, LLC, 138 S.Ct. 1365 (2018) (holding that patents are "public franchises" even if they are private property, and thus fall under the "public rights" doctrine).

[123] *See generally* Cohen et al., *supra* note 3, at 2; Wesley M. Cohen & Richard C. Levin, *Empirical Studies of Innovation and Market Structure*, in 2 Handbook of Industrial Organization 1059 (Richard Schmalensee & Robert Willig eds., 1989); Wesley M. Cohen et al., *Firm Size & R&D Intensity: A Re-Examination*, 35 J. Industrial Econ. 543, 548–49 (1987).

(b) public funding of inputs to private research and development; (c) values of private researchers (or their firms) regarding the public's interests; (d) the pioneering or cumulative nature of the research; (e) the degree of centralization of firm structures; (f) dependence on IP for funding of R&D or firm ventures; (g) documentation and publication practices that make it harder to build on others' work or to avoid infringement or clear rights; and (h) various types of network externalities.[124] Unfortunately, economic and theoretical analyses of direct measures to restrict static social welfare losses of granting property rights in intellectual productions, and of efforts to balance those losses against dynamic innovation-incentive losses – such as price controls or compulsory licensing – have proven theoretically intractable.[125] As remains true more than a decade after it was said, '[e]fforts to identify an optimal balance of these various effects continue, but no solution is yet in sight'.[126]

Antitrust analyses reflect similar theoretical and empirical limitations. Much has been written about differences of innovation and product markets and the need to differentiate antitrust and IP doctrines as a result of different market structures and dynamics for different products and timeframes.[127] Innovation market concerns reflect the insight 'that a merger between the only two, or two of a few, firms in R&D might increase the incentive to suppress at least one of the research paths.'[128] As a recent criticism of even a limited discussion of innovation markets has stated, the 'fundamental flaws in the innovation market concept are ... [that we] don't know about the relationship between market structure and effect, that error costs are high, and that competition is multidimensional. In other words, we don't know a lot and acting on our ignorance ... is costly.'[129]

As stated earlier, many people and institutions have recognized the unequal technology transfer framework for climate change and energy innovation. To address these concerns, numerous changes, some highly controversial, have been proposed to the global patent regime.[130] These include: broad, categorical exclusions of environmentally sound or climate friendly technologies from the patent system; and regulation of licensing and market behaviors, including compulsory licensing, antitrust scrutiny, and price controls.[131] These direct means of regulating prices and competition will remain legally

[124] *See* Fisher, *supra* note 84, at 17–18, 24–25.

[125] *See, e.g.*, Suzanne Scotchmer, *Standing on the Shoulders of Giants: Cumulative Research and the Patent Law*, Winter 1991 J. ECON. PERSP. 33–35 (2009); Rudolph J. R. Peritz, *Competition Within Intellectual Property Regimes: The Instance of Patent Rights, in* INTELLECTUAL PROPERTY AND COMPETITION LAW: NEW FRONTIERS 27 (Steven Anderman & Ariel Ezrachi eds., 2011).

[126] Fisher, *supra* note 124, at 9.

[127] *See, e.g.*, Janusz A. Ordover, *Economic Foundations and Considerations in Protecting Industrial and Intellectual Property*, 53 ANTITRUST L. J. 503, 514–18 (1984); J. Thomas Rosch, *Antitrust Regulation of Innovation Markets: Remarks at the ABA Antitrust Intellectual Property Conference*, (2009). *See generally* Jonathan Barnett, *Property as Process: How Innovation Markets Select Innovation Regimes*, 119 YALE L. J. 384 (2009); Mark Lemley, *Industry-Specific Antitrust Policy for Innovation*, 2011 COLUM. BUS. L. REV. 637 (2011).

[128] Michael A. Carrier, INNOVATION FOR THE 21ST CENTURY: HARNESSING THE POWER OF INTELLECTUAL PROPERTY AND ANTITRUST LAW 297 (2009).

[129] Geoffrey Manne, *Assuming More Than We Know About Innovation Markets: A Review of Michael Carrier's Innovation in the 21st Century*, 61 ALA. L. REV. 553, 555 (2010). *But cf.* Michael Carrier, *Innovation for the 21st Century: A Response to Seven Critics*, 61 ALA. L. REV. 597, 601–3 (2010).

[130] Abdel-Latif, et al., *supra* note 29.

[131] *See, e.g.*, K. Ravi Srinivas, *Climate Change, Technology Transfer and Intellectual Property Rights, Research and Information System for Developing Countries*, Discussion Paper No. 153, 26–7 (2009),

available to governments that hope to induce – but may be forced to compel – more favorable licensing and pricing practices than would voluntarily occur.[132]

Although further amendment of the WTO Agreement on Trade Related Aspects of Intellectual Property (TRIPS Agreement) – as has been discussed by the United Nations Secretariat[133] – is a theoretical possibility, consensus for adopting amendments in the short term is highly unlikely. Without such treaty amendments, countries (particularly those in the developing South) may seek to make greater use of existing TRIPS Agreement flexibilities to tailor their patent doctrines to assure access and to lower costs. They may adopt exclusions from patent eligibility, exceptions to patent rights, and alternatives to private licensing (such as a global technology pool). They also may expand access to publicly funded technologies to better promote technology development, transfer, and use.[134] These options may provide greater *ex ante* predictability "in accessing technologies and [may] further enable much-needed research and development for local adaptation and dissemination, which would further reduce the cost of the technologies."[135]

Governments addressing private refusals to license patented technologies or high prices for access to those technologies may regulate such conduct directly, by adopting compulsory licenses or by imposing price control regulations.[136] Alternatively, they may regulate such conduct indirectly, by treating restrictive or costly licensing as a competition violation (for example, as an abuse of dominant position) or by treating the patents themselves as essential facilities (that is, as products or services that are considered competitive necessities and for which access also can be required by compulsory licenses).[137]

http://papers.ssrn.com/sol3/papers.cfm?abstract_id=1440742; Jerome H. Reichman, *Intellectual Property in International Perspective: Institute for Intellectual Property & Information Law Symposium*, 48 Hous. L. Rev. 1137–8 (2009) [hereinafter Reichman, *International Perspectives*]; Peter Lee, *Toward a Distributive Commons in Patent Law*, 2009 Wis. L. Rev. 974–6 (2009); Estelle Derclaye, *Not Only Innovation But Also Collaboration, Funding, Goodwill and Commitment: Which Role for Patent Laws in Post-Copenhagen Climate Change Action*, 9 J. Marshall Rev. Intell. Prop. L. 663 (2010).

132 Concerns over IP rights and climate change technologies have already caused significant political tensions. At an earlier stage of international negotiations, the UNFCCC Ad Hoc Working Group on Long-term Cooperative Action (WG-LCA) considered various proposals that had been suggested by some countries in the South. These measures would have placed significant restrictions on the traditional operation of the patent system. The measures ranged from requiring patent pooling and royalty free compulsory licensing to excluding green technologies entirely from patenting – even retroactively revoking existing patent rights. *See, e.g., Ad Hoc Working Group on Long-Term Cooperative Action Under the Convention, Ideas and proposals on the elements contained in paragraph 1 of the Bali Action Plan*, 23 UNFCCC (2009); Ad Hoc Working Group on Long-Term Cooperative Action Under the Convention, Report of the Ad Hoc Working Group on Long-Term Cooperative Action under the Convention on its Seventh Session, UNFCCC Doc. No. FCCC/AWGLCA/2009/14, 156 (2009).

133 Agreement on Trade-Related Aspects of Intellectual Property Rights (April 15, 1994), Marrakesh Agreement Establishing the World Trade Organization, Annex 1C, Legal Instruments – Result of the Uruguay Rounds 33 I.L.M. 81 (1994) [hereinafter TRIPS Agreement]. *See, e.g., World Economic and Social Survey 2009*, U. N. Dept. of Econ. and Soc. Affairs 133–34 (2009).

134 *See World Economic and Social Survey 2010*, U. N. Dept. of Econ. and Soc. Affairs 97 (2010).

135 *Id.*

136 *See, e.g.*, Keith E. Maskus, *The Curious Economics of Parallel Imports*, 2 W.I.P.O. J. 123–4 (2010) [hereinafter Maskus, *Parallel Imports*].

137 *See, e.g.*, Jay P. Choi, *Compulsory Licensing as an Antitrust Remedy*, 2 W.I.P.O. J. 74, 74–77 (2010). European Commission Dec. of 13 May 2009, COMP/37.990 (Intel) ¶¶ 1749–53, http://ec.europa.eu/competition/antitrust/cases/dec_docs/37990/37990_3581_11.pdf. *But see Verizon v. Trinko*, 540 U.S. 398, 407–08 (2004).

Such direct or indirect regulation, moreover, may be largely ineffective in regard to assuring transfers of tacit knowledge.[138]

Both direct and indirect approaches to regulating access and prices will be highly controversial, and may threaten substantial trade retaliation or may prompt withholding by businesses of technology and foreign investment. Compulsory licensing, price regulation, and antitrust treatment have been repeatedly resisted by the United States and (somewhat less so) by other developed countries, particularly in foreign markets where the countries do not bear the costs but reap the benefits of technology exports.[139] The developing South may be unwilling to resist such trade pressures, even if the threats and trade sanctions would be found illegal under WTO rules.[140] These legal and political constraints bring us to proposals discussed in the next Part of this chapter, which emphasize private sector, voluntary initiatives to increase access and technology transfer, within a context of public sector laws and policies that promote innovation and access.

III Key Innovation Policy Choices in Climate Change Technology Transfer

In contrast to the comparative advantages that would lead to further extending the developed North's innovation and patenting head start, international action on climate change may help to narrow the gap either through cooperative trade measures like trade-tariff exemptions or through cooperative technology development efforts, such as multinational joint ventures or joint manufacturing for particular climate change technologies.[141] Similarly, international efforts may transfer technology directly to developing countries, through foreign-funded, in-country R&D, through joint ventures, and through foreign direct investment in R&D.[142] However, many obstacles exist to such foreign-funded or participatory R&D efforts that rely principally on market-based approaches – including significant fears of loss of control over technologies protected by patents and trade secrets, given the perceived lack of adequate enforcement of patent and trade secret rights in developing countries.[143] This Part first discusses some of the challenges to technology transfer given the global imbalances discussed in Part I and additional concerns specific to climate change technology transfer, then proposes six innovation policy choices that could help to mobilize R&D and to transfer technology more effectively.

[138] *See, e.g.*, Jerome H. Reichman, *Comment: Compulsory Licensing of Patented Pharmaceutical Inventions: Evaluating the Options*, 37 J.L. MED. & ETHICS 253–57 (2009).

[139] *Cf. id.* at 255.

[140] *See, e.g.*, *id.* at 258–59.

[141] *See, e.g.*, Lee, Iliev, & Preston, *supra* note 62, at xi; UNEP/EPO/ICTSD Study, *supra* note 62, at 21–23; Robert Fair, *Does Climate Change Justify Compulsory Licensing of Green Technology*, 6 B.Y.U. INT'L L. & MGMT. REV. 21, 40–41 (2009).

[142] *See, e.g.*, Lee, Iliev, & Preston, *supra* note 62, at ix-x, 58; Elizabeth Burleson, *Energy Policy, Intellecutal Property, and Technology Transfer to Address Climate Change*, 18 TRANSNAT'L L. & CONTEMP. PROBS. 69, 86 (2009).

[143] *See, e.g.*, Lee, Iliev & Preston, *supra* note 62, at 8; Daniel Johnson & Kristina Lybecker, *Challenges to Technology Transfer: A Literature Review of the Constraints on Environmental Technology Dissemination* (2009). *See generally* Peter K. Yu, *Enforcement, Economics and Estimates*, 2 W.I.P.O. J. 1 (2010).

A *Geographic Imbalances in Technology Transfer to, and Costs of Access in, the Developing South*

Technology transfer typically occurs through trade, foreign direct investment (FDI), joint venturing, or licensing.[144] Although some studies suggest that licensing and FDI (and consequently technology transfers) are positively correlated with stronger IP rights,[145] other studies specific to climate change technologies demonstrate that so far these technologies have not been widely licensed to developing countries (even to those having competitive markets). This may be due to IP ownership over those technologies in the developed North or to other factors, such as the lack of scientific capability, adverse market conditions, and poor investment climates in the developing South.[146] Although some studies have concluded that North–South licensing for climate change-related technologies are no lower than for other technologies (while desires to transfer climate change-related technologies are higher),[147] other studies have concluded that climate change mitigation technologies "are less likely to cross country borders than the average technology," are principally transferred among developed countries, and "seem to crowd out local innovations."[148]

Technology flows thus occur principally among developed countries (about seventy-five percent of exported inventions) and are "almost non-existent" between emerging countries.[149] The general pattern of low levels of technology transfer from the developed to the developing world is likely to remain stable for climate change technologies. Given reliance on private markets and IP rights, these general patterns may skew even more strongly against flows to and among developing countries, notwithstanding funding from international agreements that could potentially change these patterns.

Moreover, the development and/or patenting of climate change technologies within developing countries remains low. For example, one study finds that "less than 1% of the world's clean energy technology related patent applications from 1980 to 2009 have been filed in Africa."[150] As noted in another study, the surveyed data "all suggest that companies from developing countries are facing some difficulties in obtaining technologies, whether it is the high cost of licensing or having to obtain technologies from second-tier technology holders," that is, from companies other than leading manufacturers (who are reluctant to license potential competitors).[151] To enhance the dissemination of

144 *See* Hall & Helmers, *supra* note 14, at 7.

145 *See, e.g.*, *id.* at 11; Lee Branstetter et al., *Has the Shift to Stronger Intellectual Property Rights Promoted Technology Transfer, FDI, and Industrial Development?*, 2 W.I.P.O. J. 93, 96–98 (2010).

146 *See, e.g.*, UNEP/EPO/ICTSD Study, *supra* note 62, at 58; Kaitlin Mara, *New Climate Technologies Rarely Reaching Developing Countries, Panel Says*, IP Watch (Jul. 13, 2010).

147 *See, e.g.*, UNEP/EPO/ICTSD Study, *supra* note 62, at 9, 58–59.

148 Dechezleprêtre 2008a, *supra* note 62, at 25.

149 *See id.* at 4.

150 EPO-UNEP, *Patents and Clean Energy Technologies in Africa*, Eur. Pat. Off., www.epo.org/news-issues/technology/sustainable-technologies/clean-energy/patents-africa.html. The EPO has also a study on Latin America reaching relatively similar conclusions. *See Overview of the Latin American and Caribbean Clean Energy Potential and Exploitation Levels*, Eur. Pat. Off., http://documents.epo.org/projects/babylon/eponet.nsf/0/2841b369787d5e72c1257da800335111/$FILE/patents_Latin_America_summary_en.pdf.

151 UNEP/EPO/ICTSD Study, *supra* note 62, at 22–23.

climate change-related technologies, developing nations are under pressure to reduce tariffs. But such countries also may have been pressured to patent new technologies. This may impose a "double penalty" of foreign competition on local technology development (by lower import tariffs and domestic patenting of foreign technologies) that might otherwise proceed at lower costs through (unpatented) imitation.[152] In contrast, local imitation may sometimes be difficult or may require significant adaptation to local conditions.[153]

Developing countries, as well as developed countries and international agencies funding such technology deployment and dissemination, may therefore be more likely to challenge patent rights that prevent lower-cost production and acquisition of such technologies. In turn, this raises the possibility of disputes under the TRIPS Agreement[154] and under international investment protection agreements.[155] Alternatively, climate change technology-rich countries may adopt explicit or implicit export subsidies to facilitate technology transfers, which may generate additional trade disputes.[156]

The global imbalances in patenting noted earlier thus are also reflected in global imbalances in licensing and technology transfers from the developed North to the developing South. Even without regard to the dramatic geographical imbalances in patenting and licensing behaviors, patented climate change technologies so far have taken very long times to reach the mass market and to achieve widespread dissemination.[157] As the recent effort to achieve a worldwide cell-phone standard has also demonstrated, patent rights may delay or interfere with coordinated approaches to achieve worldwide technology development and deployment.[158] When technology has been developed through R&D subsidies and transferred at low cost to developing countries, its use still may require additional subsidies to overcome the sunk costs of existing infrastructure or equipment, and local adaptation (or invention) may be needed to provide sufficient comparative benefits to actual users, given that the technology needs in developing countries may differ from those in developed countries.[159] Thus, relying on private markets and patents to distribute the needed technologies to the South may prove both costly and less than optimally effective.

152 Keith E. Maskus, *Intellectual Property and the Transfer of Green Technologies: An Essay on Economic Perspectives*, 1 W.I.P.O. J. 133, 137 (2009).

153 *See* Eur. Pat. Off., *supra* note 150, at 17.

154 TRIPS Agreement, *supra* note 133.

155 *See, e.g.*, Canada NAFTA Decision, Case No. UNCT/14/2, final award, (Mar. 16, 2017), www.ippractice.ca/blog/wp-content/uploads/2017/03/Lilly-v-Canada-NAFTA-Arb-Award.pdf. *See generally* Hall & Helmers, *supra* note 14; Ad Hoc Working Group on Long-Term Cooperative Action Under the Convention Report of the Ad Hoc Working Group on Long-term Cooperative Action under the Convention on its Seventh Session, U.N. Doc. FCCC/AWGLCA/2009/14, at 156 (Nov. 20, 2009). *See generally* Lahra Liberti, *Intellectual Property Rights in International Investment Agreements* (OECD, Working Paper No. 2010/01, 2010); Bertram Boie, *The Protection of Intellectual Property Rights through Bilateral Investment Treaties: Is there a TRIPS-plus Dimension?* (NCRR Trade Regulation, Working Paper No. 2010/19, Nov. 2010).

156 *See, e.g.*, Thomas L. Brewer, *The Trade Regime and the Climate Regime: Institutional Evolution and Adaptation*, 3 Climate Pol'y 329, 338 (2003).

157 *See* Lee, Iliev, & Preston, *supra* note 62, at vii; World Development Report 2010, *supra* note 45, at 293.

158 *See, e.g.*, Branislav Hazucha, International Standards and Essential Patents: From International Harmonization to Competition of Technologies, 27, 30 (2010).

159 *See* Hall & Helmers, *supra* note 14, at 4–6.

B *Innovation Policy Choices to Enhance Access and to Reduce Costs of Intellectual Property Rights in Climate Change Technologies*

Some of the proposed innovation policy choices discussed in this section are public sector-based, some are private sector-based ownership controls,[160] and some are a combination of both. The first set of approaches focus on public sector laws and policies, seeking to expand freedom-to-innovate and to develop local innovation capacity and indigenous R&D within particular jurisdictions. They would do so by restricting the definition of what can be patented and by authorizing certain experimental and other uses of climate change-related technologies, so as to promote greater sequential innovation and to assure functionality and development or regulatory information. The second set of approaches focus on the private sector policies and choices (although they are applicable to the public sector and PPP choices when acting as proprietors rather than as regulators). They seek to leverage ownership powers to require licensing innovation choices that better assure access to climate change-related technologies at reasonable costs. The final set of approaches again focus principally on the public sector, and seek to clarify when it will regulate private licensing of inventions deriving from government subsidies and to better assure that climate change-related technology can be transferred within the private sector from one jurisdiction to another.

These alternatives focus on achieving the greatest benefits for climate change innovation, in both the developed and developing world, in ways generally recognized as consistent with existing international IP treaty laws. They thus promise a greater likelihood of being employed to develop the needed technologies, compared to more politically intractable treaty revisions, while controlling the costs of access and better assuring transfer of the needed technologies.[161]

1 Protecting Basic Research and Sequential Innovation

The first set of innovation policy choices focuses on protecting basic research and sequential innovation and use of technologies through governmental patent laws and policies. The first measure would assure that significant additional creativity beyond basic scientific discovery is needed for patent eligibility.[162] This approach is based on adopting

[160] *See, e.g.*, Colleen V. Chien, *Opening Up The Patent System: Exclusionary And Diffusionary Levers In Patent Law*, 89 So. Calif. L. Rev. 793, 801, 820 (2016) (defining "Defensive patenting – holding patents in order to facilitate freedom to operate – is practiced by an estimated half or more of patent holders" and stating further that "[w]hile it often seems that there are only two approaches for supporting innovation with patents – to opt-in and exclude, or to opt-out and share, intellectual property, a widely-used approach between them is to acquire patents in order to share, or "defensive patenting. . . . It is widely recognized that different industries use patents differently, and that patents support a diversity of business models. Allowing innovators to individually tailor patent rights, and in some cases, to change these options over the lifetime of the patent, would provide precise controls to those in the best position to know the optimal balance between exclusion and diffusion with respect to a particular invention."). *See generally* van Overwalle, *supra* note 22.

[161] Dominique Foray, *Technology Transfer in the TRIPS Age: The Need for New Types of Partnerships between the Least Developed and Most Advanced Economies*, 38 (2009); Oliva, et al., *supra* note 15, at 5–7; Maskus & Okediji, *Intellectual Property Rights*, *supra* note 15, at vii–viii, 26–7.

[162] *See* Joshua D. Sarnoff, *Patent Eligible Inventions after Bilski: History and Theory*, *supra* note *; Peter Lee, *Inverting the Logic of Scientific Discovery: Applying Common Law Patentable Subject Matter Doctrine to Constrain Patents on Biotechnology Research Tools*, 19 Harv. J.L. & Tech, 84 (2005).

a restrictive interpretation of the meaning of "invention" as used in Article 27.1 of the TRIPS Agreement.[163] The second measure assumes that relevant climate change technologies exist under patent in a jurisdiction, and would encourage and (where needed) expand robust legal exceptions to infringement liability for experimental uses, reverse engineering, development of information for pre-market approval, and inter-operability. This would permit scientific research and continued access to important technologies to proceed unfettered by patent rights.[164] These proposed measures remain consistent with the permissive language for mandatory coverage of patents under Article 27.1 of the TRIPS Agreement, as well as for exceptions and limitations to rights under Article 30 of the TRIPS Agreement.[165] They also would help to allow scientific knowledge to flow to the developing South, and to permit downstream development and use of the creative technologies that result, just as dependent patent licenses and "government use compulsory licenses"[166] may sometimes be needed to assure the ability to operate, market access and reasonable-cost technology transfer.

2 Expanding Ownership Controls over Downstream Licensing Mechanisms

The next two sets of innovation policy choices are particularly salient to PPPs because they would originate principally from the private sector, although similar actions could be taken by governments or PPPs when acting as proprietary owners of the relevant IP. The purpose of these proposals would be to seek to assure that upstream owners of patented climate change technologies retain various rights when licensing for commercial development, so as to assure the potential for continued R&D and for widespread and low-cost access. As Keith Maskus and Ruth Okediji have noted, contractual arrangements "govern the majority of inter-firm and intra-firm transfers of knowledge and technology in both domestic and international markets."[167] Thus these approaches exert management-based (or private, market-driven) policy choices of innovation via ownership controls.[168]

[163] *See* TRIPS Agreement, *supra* note 133, Art. 27.1.

[164] *See, e.g.*, 35 U.S.C. § 271(e); *Merck KGAA v. Integra LifeSciences I Ltd.*, 545 U.S. 193, 202–08 (2005); Agreement Relating to Community Patents, Dec. 15, 1989, art. 27; European Parliament and European Council Directive 2004/27, art. 1.8(6), [2004] OJ L136/34 (EC) (amending Council Directive 2001/83 art. 10 (EC)); Carlos M. Correa, *Multilateral Agreements and Policy Opportunities*, POLICY DIALOGUE 11 (2008); Frischmann, *An Economic Theory*, *supra* note107, at 995–97; Peter Lee, *Patents, Paradigm-Shifts, and Progress in Biomedical Science*, 114 YALE L.J. 692–93 (2004); *cf.* Rochelle Cooper Dreyfuss, *Reconsidering Experimental Use*, AKRON L. REV. (forthcoming 2017). *See generally* Holzapfel & Sarnoff, *supra* note *.

[165] *See* TRIPS Agreement, *supra* note 133, Art. 30; Panel Report, Canada – Patent Protection of Pharmaceutical Products, WTO Doc. WT/DS114/R, ¶¶ 7.54–7.57, 7.69 (adopted Apr. 7, 2000): *Competition & Tax Law, Declaration on the Three-Step Test*, Max Planck Institute for Intellectual Property (2009), www.ip.mpg.de; Holzapfel & Sarnoff, *supra* note *, at 175–79; Maskus & Okediji, *Intellectual Property Rights*, *supra* note 15, at 32; Pamela Samuelson, *Reverse Engineering Under Siege*, Berkeley School of Information 1–3.

[166] *Cf.* Reichman, *International Perspectives*, *supra* note 131, at 139, 1140–41; Abdel-Latif, et al. *supra* note 29, at 30–31.

[167] Maskus & Okediji, *supra* note 15, at 8.

[168] Aseem Prakash, GREENING THE FIRM: THE POLITICS OF CORPORATE ENVIRONMENTALISM 152 (2000) (claiming that "firms adopt beyond-compliance [policy] initiatives primarily to preempt even more stringent regulations or to shape future regulations."); Overwalle, *supra* note 22; Chien, *supra* note 160.

One set of ownership measures would be for upstream owners to retain the power to authorize experimental uses (to the extent that any jurisdiction lacks such restrictions on patent rights) and to permit "humanitarian" uses (at low or no cost) for climate mitigation and adaptation needs.[169] A second ownership measure would change the default resort from exclusive to nonexclusive licensing (unless the former has been demonstrated to be needed).[170] Such measures would be adopted voluntarily by patent owners in the first instance, and thus should encounter no legal concerns and should not trigger inter-governmental retaliation. In contrast, new legal requirements (or at least regulatory policy-based choices) may be needed for government agencies to *condition* private ownership of government-funded inventions on the preservation of such retained rights and default licensing policies.

Rather than for owners to start at the most restrictive level and for governments through regulation to have to override such choices, the retained rights approach can start at the most permissive level and ratchet up or differentiate restrictions if there are insufficient grantees or licensees to accept the initially offered conditions. Nonexclusive licensing of government-funded inventions thus could be required by law or regulatory policy as a default, and appropriately differentiated in response to market conditions or unforeseen circumstances. Such changes can be made much more quickly and more readily in response to market conditions than trying to reverse the effects of broad initial grants of rights for full patent terms through *ex post* regulatory measures and more formal adjudications.

Related to this approach (and therefore it is not treated as a separate measure) would be the greater use of patent holder and other IP rights-holder pledges, which could include nonexclusive and reasonable cost licensing, as described in detail by Jorge Contreras.[171] Pledges are:

> [public] commitments voluntarily made by patent holders to limit the enforcement or other exploitation of their patents. These pledges encompass a wide range of technologies and firms: from promises by multinational corporations like IBM and Google not to assert patents against open-source software users; to commitments by developers of industry standards to grant licenses on terms that are fair, reasonable, and non-discriminatory (FRAND); to the recent announcement by Tesla Motors that it will

169 *See, e.g.*, Peter Lee, *Contracting to Preserve Open Science: Consideration-Based Regulation in Patent Law*, 58 Emory L.J. 920–38 (2009); National Research Council, *Managing University Intellectual Property in the Public Interest*, National Academies Press 7 (2010) (discussing (Mar. 6, 2007) *In the Public Interest: Nine Points to Consider in Licensing University Technology*), https://otl.stanford.edu/documents/whitepaper-10.pdf); Paul A. David, *Mitigating "Anticommons" Harms to Research, in Science and Technology: New Moves in "Legal Jujitsu" against Unintended Adverse Consequences of the Exploitation of Intellectual Property Rights on Results of Publicly and Privately Funded Research*, 2 W.I.P.O. J. 59, 69 (2010); *see* About Science Commons, Science Commons, http://sciencecommons.org/about; Alan B. Bennett, *Reservation of Rights for Humanitarian Uses, in* Intellectual Property Management in Health and Agriculture Innovation: A Handbook of Best Practices 41 (Anatole Krattiger et al. eds., 2007); Carol Mimura, *Technology Licensing for the Benefit of the Developing World: UC Berkeley's Socially Responsible Licensing Program*, 21 J. Assoc. Univ. Tech. Managers, 15, 17–24 (2007).

170 *See, e.g.*, Reichman, *International Perspectives*, *supra* note 131, at 1137; Anthony D. So et al., *Is Bayh-Dole Good for Developing Countries? Lessons from the US Experience*, 6 PLoS Biol. 2080–81; *see, e.g.*, Abdel-Latif, et al., *supra* note 29, at 15.

171 Jorge L. Contreras, *Patent Pledges: Between the Public Domain and Market Exclusivity*, 2015 Mich. St. L. Rev. 787.

not enforce its substantial patent portfolio against any company making electric vehicles in "good faith."[172]

3 Leveraging Private Licensing and Technology Transfer Choices through Government-Funding Regulatory Policies and International Exhaustion Laws

The final two sets of innovation policy choices cut across public regulatory policies and private sector ownership initiatives. The first set of measures would clarify "march in" criteria under the US Bayh-Dole Act (or equivalent legislation in other jurisdictions), where the government retains rights to assure the working of patents or the accessibility of inventions created with government funds.[173] The second set of measures would clarify international "exhaustion" requirements to adopt permissive transfers without triggering patent rights, at least within certain geographical regions or among countries having similar levels of wealth or development.

March-in rights seek to facilitate access, but typically do so through cumbersome and controversial administrative processes (subject to judicial review).[174] *Ex ante* clarification of the conditions on which march-in should occur would allow governments more readily to march in when owners of patents funded with government money (or their licensees) fail to make the technology sufficiently accessible at affordable costs. As with conditions on licensees imposed through (private or government proprietary) ownership powers or that are imposed by law (such as the earlier proposals for research and interoperability exceptions to infringement), government-imposed presumptions of march-in conditions may have important signaling and demonstration effects, inducing private commercial entities to adopt similar conditional, nonexclusive, and reasonable-cost licensing policies.

Clarifying conditions for march-in *ex ante* should further reduce any concerns that might arise from use of such governmental power. If march-in does occur, the government's exercise of *agreed-to* conditions of the private party's "title" should pose much less concern for foreign direct investment or for other technology transfer mechanisms. Certainly, march-in should then pose much less concern than *ex post* compulsory licensing, price controls, or other *ex post* regulatory measures that governments inherently retain.[175] Governments, moreover, may retain "crown" rights or may otherwise authorize governmental conduct that would be infringing, in order to perform research or to produce patented products or provide patented services for public purposes.[176] Further, march-in rights are not needed if nonexclusive, reasonable-cost licensing is

[172] *Id.*

[173] *See, e.g.*, March-In Rights, 35 U.S.C. § 203(a).

[174] *See* March-In Rights, 35 U.S.C. § 203(b); Arti K. Rai & Rebecca S. Eisenberg, *Bayh-Dole Reform and the Progress of Biomedicine*, 66 LAW & CONTEMP. PROBS. 294 (2003).

[175] *Cf.* Fair, *supra* note 141, at 37 (posing concerns over loss of foreign direct investment from compulsory licensing).

[176] *See, e.g.*, Disposition of Rights, 35 U.S.C. § 202(c)(4); Domestic and Foreign Proteciton of Federally Owned Inventions, 35 U.S.C. § 207(a)(2); Sarnoff & Holman, *supra* note * (citing "Report of the National Institutes of Health (NIH), *Working Group on Research Tools, App. D*). The extent to which the government can rely on private parties to assist in exercising such retained powers without triggering infringement and required compensation – that may then be compensated under a "statutory takings" provision such as provided in the United States at 18 U.S.C. § 1498 – may be uncertain.

made a default condition for private parties to acquire title to rights in government-funded, private inventions in the first instance.

The final proposed measure would make greater use of the so-called "exhaustion" principle of patent law. Exhaustion permits parallel importation – importation of products produced and sold in other jurisdictions – and mandates unrestricted downsream (from initial sale) use and resale of patented technologies. It is a rapidly developing area of IP law and policy of increasing importance, and thus is treated at some length here.[177]

In theory, exhaustion should occur whenever patent owners or their licensees voluntarily supply a market, and thus obtain their "reward" through the first sale, even if the product is sold at low cost. Given the patent-holder's decision to itself make or otherwise authorize such low-cost sales, parallel importation of such sold products can achieve wider dissemination of climate change technologies that patent owners (or their licensees) voluntarily bring to the market. Thus, the public sector policy may have a dramatic effect on the private choices to transfer technologies across jurisdictions.

Given the global nature of the technologies and problems to be addressed, disputes over patent exhaustion are very likely to arise in the climate change context.[178] This regulatory policy choice has taken on even more significance in light of the US Supreme Court's recent decision in *Impression Products v. Lexmark*, which announced a policy of international exhaustion and automatic domestic exhaustion upon sale of patented technologies (including patented components of products).[179] The principle of "automatic" exhaustion of patent rights and the inability to constrain reuse or resale of patented products (and components) will dramatically affect the ability to engage in restrictive licensing for particular markets and for price arbitrage across jurisdictions with regard to mitigation and adaptation technologies (as well as for all other patented goods). Accordingly, international exhaustion runs the risk of encouraging patent holders not to sell to, or at prices that can be afforded by, some low-income jurisdictions.

Although the *Impression Products* opinion discussed preserving contract remedies to enforce such contractual restrictions following sales (in dicta),[180] it is possible that such contract remedies may (in jurisdictions that recognize such principles) be considered

177 *See generally* Research Handbook On Intellectual Property Exhaustion and Parallel Imports (Irene Calboli & Edward Lee eds., 2017).

178 *See, e.g., Get Ready for the Clean Tech IP Boom*, 182 Managing Intell. Prop., 44 (2008).

179 Impression Products, Inc. v. Lexmark Int'l, Inc., 137 S.Ct. 1523 (2017). *See, e.g., id.* at 1534–35 ("The misstep in this logic is that the exhaustion doctrine is not a presumption about the authority that comes along with a sale; it is instead a limit on "the scope of the *patentee's rights*.' . . . In sum, patent exhaustion is uniform and automatic. Once a patentee decides to sell – whether on its own or through a licensee – that sale exhausts its patent rights, regardless of any postsale restrictions the patentee purports to impose, either directly or through a license."); *id.* at 1536 ("Applying patent exhaustion to foreign sales is just as straightforward. Patent exhaustion, too, has its roots in the antipathy toward restraints on alienation . . . and nothing in the text or history of the Patent Act shows that Congress intended to confine that borderless common law principle to domestic sales. In fact, Congress has not altered patent exhaustion at all; it remains an unwritten limit on the scope of the patentee's monopoly.").

180 *See id.* at 1535, 1538 ("Once sold, the [patented products] passed outside of the patent monopoly, and whatever rights Lexmark retained are a matter of the contracts with its purchasers, not the patent law. . . . The purchasers might not comply with the restriction, but the only recourse for the licensee is through contract law, just as if the patentee itself sold the item with a restriction. . . . Exhaustion does not arise because of the parties' expectations about how sales transfer patent rights. More is at stake when it comes to patents than simply the dealings between the parties, which can be addressed through contract law.").

"preempted" by patent law. After all, it is only because of the "automatic" application of the principle of "exhaustion" that there is no meaning or effect to be given (as a matter of patent law and policy) to the contractual language that purports to restrict the transfer of such "authority" upon the first "sale" (so as to prohibit downstream uses or resales). And if this is so, it is hard to understand how enforcing such contractual provisions would not conflict with the legislated (national) policy of exhaustion; those contractual provisions would then permit the very same restrictions to be effectuated as a matter of (often subsidiary jurisdiction) *contract* law remedies. The questions of exhaustion and preemption will take many years to resolve. Similarly, questions also will arise and take years to resolve about whether such contractual restrictions on use and resale legally can be imposed by "licensing" rather than by "selling" patented products to the public (likely by combining such contract restrictions with mechanisms for "leasing" rather than "selling" the products).[181]

These matters necessarily will be decided under national laws of particular jurisdictions, raising potential conflicts of approach. This is because Article 6 of the TRIPS Agreement precludes international regulation by the WTO of national policies to address the exhaustion of patent rights and other IP rights, such as copyright.[182] Thus, national jurisdictions can adopt whatever approach they choose regarding the placing of goods on (first) sale or in use, so long as national treatment and most-favored-nation treatment principles are respected.[183]

Accordingly, nations will remain free to provide either or both international and domestic exhaustion effect to patented goods sold in foreign and domestic markets. This will permit low-cost resale and transfers from markets (or market segments) where patent holders have voluntarily placed goods on sale.[184] Correspondingly, to the extent that national law limits international or domestic exhaustion, firms can implement contractual policies that explicitly permit (as opposed to questionably prohibit) the same. Parallel importation measures to promote access thus can cut across both public law frameworks and private sector contractual arrangements.

In summary, these six sets of innovation policy choices collectively could help to mitigate concerns that IP rights will adversely affect innovation and access, as well as mitigate concerns for reducing *ex ante* investment and innovation incentives that inherently attend *ex post* government regulation by compulsory licensing, price regulation, or otherwise. Thus, these measures may help to accomplish the goals of promoting climate change technology R&D and assuring widespread access to such technologies at reasonable costs. Investors and inventors will know the limits of the patent rights, and can decide in advance whether the rewards warrant the limitations and risks. These proposals

[181] *See generally* Sean O'Connor, *Origins of Patent Exhaustion: Jacksonian Politics, 'Patent Farming,' and the Basis of the Bargain*, University of Washington School of Law Research Paper No. 2017–05 (Mar. 8, 2017), https://papers.ssrn.com/sol3/papers.cfm?abstract_id=2920738.

[182] *See, e.g.*, Kirtsaeng v. John Wiley & Sons, 568 U.S. 519 (2013) (international exhaustion of copyrighted works); Impression Prods., Inc. v. Lexmark Int'l., Inc., 137 S.Ct. 1523 (2017) (international exhaustion of patented works).

[183] TRIPS Agreement, *supra* note 133, Art. 6. ("For the purposes of dispute settlement under this Agreement, subject to the provisions of Articles 3 and 4 nothing in this Agreement shall be used to address the issue of the exhaustion of IP rights.").

[184] *See, e.g.*, Maskus, *Parallel Imports*, *supra* note 136, at 123–32.

also would encourage investors and inventors to make extensive use of private mechanisms in order to facilitate access and technology transfer.[185] Finally, greater use of these measures could help to avoid national resort to some of the more controversial measures that national governments retain under international IP and regulatory laws to assure greater access to and to regulate prices of patented climate-change-related goods and services.[186] They may thereby reduce international and trade tensions, and simultaneously reduce pressures to alter the international IP regime.

Conclusion

Climate change not only imposes unequal impacts and obligations, but also will lead to further unequal technology development and transfers, thereby imposing unequal costs on those who must suffer the impacts or shoulder the obligations. These inequalities will substantially impact the international regimes governing climate change, IP, and the implementation of the SDGs. PPPs raise particular concerns regarding the distribution of the benefits of the innovation policy choices that must be made when responding to climate change.[187] Institutional, network, and power effects may exacerbate existing disparities of innovative activity, wealth, and power globally in ways that generate additional global or domestic political tensions.

The turn to multi-stakeholder partnerships such as PPPs to implement international development policy, including the SDGs, is based on the recognition that globalization has already strained not only government efforts to develop human capital, but also the managerial competencies of both government bureaucrats and firm decision makers.[188] Whether in the public sector, the private sector, or PPPs, effective management of complex inputs and networks requires information that is rarely available, predictive judgments that are fallible, and skill sets that are in short supply.

In combatting climate change, greater reliance on PPPs must involve better evaluation of the spectrum of possible innovation policy choices, to avoid wasting massive resources and missing opportunities in the generation of desperately needed innovation outputs. At a minimum, public sector involvement in PPPs should provide more innovation funding, policy-making, steering and operational control, and oversight, in order to induce the market to supply additional funding.

185 *See generally* Chien, *supra* note 160.

186 *See* Sarnoff, *Patent System, supra* note *, at 333–60.

187 Powell, *supra* note 26, at 57–58 ("[S]cience policy is an effort to alter the trajectory, workings, and content of the social system of science with the relatively weak lever of control over some, largely formal, aspects of institutions. . . . [T]he institutional, network, and power mechanisms at work . . . have wider implications for legitimacy claims, labor market processes, industrial clustering, and race/gender inequalities that span many fields of science.").

188 Rising to the Challenge: U.S. Innovation Policy for the Global Economy 53, 118–21 (Charles W. Wessner & Alan W. Wolff eds., 2012) (discussing the need for human capital); Phillip Brown, Hugh Lauder & David Ashton, *Education, Globalization and the Future of the Knowledge Economy*, 7 Eur. Educ. Res. J. 131, 140 (2008) ("[V]irtually all [managers] we spoke to in China, Korea, India and Singapore, as well as the United States, Germany and Britain, believed that they were in a war for talent, which was increasingly global."); *see generally* Deborah Agostino et al., *Developing a Performance Measurement System for Public Research Centers*, 7 Int. J. of Bus. Sci. & Applied Mgmt. 43, 44–45 (2012) (discussing development of key performance indicators for performance management systems that balance the information needs of different stakeholders).

A more intentional approach to innovation management of PPPs also will require better understanding and tracking of innovation funding and other resource inputs and outputs, so as to better deploy the available innovation policies described here. In that way, PPPs will be better able to maximize the benefits of technology transfer generated through collaborative networks.

As stated in a recent summary of the conclusions of a World Bank Report, which addressed historic failures to achieve SDGs in regard to water supply, sanitation, and hygiene, achieving the SDGs will require changing innovation funding and technology development practices.

> [The report] suggests making three broad shifts to hasten implementation of the SDGs. They include: [1] coordinating investments and interventions across sectors to improve human development outcomes; [2] better targeting and efficiently allocating future investments, given the limited fiscal space of most countries; and [3] gaining a better understanding of the broader governance context within which [these] services are delivered, to bridge gaps between policy and implementation.[189]

These recommendations are equally applicable to climate change. But we would add two more recommendations (although the first is implicit in the World Bank's recommendations): [4] encouraging greater creativity and risk-taking in making innovation policy choices that overcome historic and political inertia; and [5] placing a greater emphasis on empathy and altruism, by rejecting the belief that climate change mitigation and adaptation are "someone else's problem."

References

Abdel-Latif, Ahmed, et al., *Overcoming the Impasse on Intellectual Property and Climate Change at the UNFCCC: A Way Forward*, ICTSD Policy Brief No. 11, November 2011 (December 2011).

Agostino, Deborah, Marika Arena, Giovanni Azzone, Martina Dal Molin, & Cristina Masella, *Developing a Performance Measurement System for Public Research Centers*, 7 Int. J. of Bus. Sci. & Applied Mgmt. 43 (2012).

Agreement Relating to Community Patents, Dec. 15, 1989, art. 27.

Anderson, Lauren, *World Bank calls for Broad Shift in Thinking to hasten* WASH, SDG Implementation (Aug. 29, 2017), http://sdg.iisd.org/news/world-bank-calls-for-broad-shift-in-thinking-to-hasten-wash-sdg-implementation/?utm_medium=email&utm_campaign=2017–08–29%20-%20SDG%20Update%20AE&utm_content=2017–08–29%20-%20SDG%20Update%20AE+CID_1ef3d184061a4a424444fd3f204597a4&utm_source=cm&utm_term=World%20Bank%20Calls%20for%20Broad%20Shift%20in%20Thinking%20to%20Hasten%20WASH%20SDG%20Implementation (last visited Nov. 19, 2017).

Andersen, Stephen O. et al., *Technical Summary, in* Methodological and Technological Issues in Technology Transfer: A Special Report of IPCC Working Group III 15–16 (2000), www.ipcc.ch/pdf/special-reports/spm/srtt-en.pdf (last visited Oct. 10, 2017).

Arun, Korhan & Durmus C. Yildirim, *Effects of Foreign Direct Investment on Intellectual Property, Patents and R&D*, 7 Queen Mary J. Intell. Prop. 226 (2017).

[189] Lauren Anderson, *World Bank calls for Broad Shift in Thinking to hasten* WASH, SDG Implementation (Aug. 29, 2017) (quoting World Bank Group, Reducing Inequalities in Water Supply, Sanitation, and Hygiene in the Era of the Sustainable Development Goals Synthesis Report of the Water Supply, Sanitation, and Hygiene (WASH) Poverty Diagnostic Initiative (2017)).

Autor, David, David Dorn, Gordon H. Hanson, Gary Pisano, & Pian Shu, *Foreign Competition and Domestic Innovation: Evidence from U.S. Patents* (NBER Working Paper No. 22879, Nov. 2016), www.nber.org/papers/w22879 (last visited Nov. 19, 2017).

Balta, Wayne, *Welcome to the Eco-Patent Commons*, CEF ECOINNOVATOR BLOG, www.corporate ecoforum.com/welcome-to-the-eco-patent-commons/ (last visited Nov. 19, 2017).

Barnett, Jonathan, *Property as Process: How Innovation Markets Select Innovation Regimes*, 119 YALE L. J. 384 (2009).

Barton, John H., *Intellectual Property and Access to Clean Energy Technologies in Developing Countries: An Analysis of Solar Photovoltaic, Biofuel, and Wind Technologies*, International Center for Trade and Sustainable Development Issue Paper No. 2, http://ictsd.net/downloads/2008/11/intellectual-property-and-access-to-clean-energy-technologies-in-developing-countries_barton_ictsd-2007.pdf (last visited Nov. 23, 2015).

Barton, John H., *Mitigating Climate Change Through Technology Transfer: Addressing the Needs of Developing Countries*, Chatham House, Energy, Environment and Development Programme: Programme Paper 08/02 (2008).

Bennett, Alan B., *Reservation of Rights for Humanitarian Uses*, *in* INTELLECTUAL PROPERTY MANAGEMENT IN HEALTH AND AGRICULTURE INNOVATION: A HANDBOOK OF BEST PRACTICES 41 (Anatole Krattiger et al. eds., 2007).

Boie, Bertram, *The Protection of Intellectual Property Rights through Bilateral Investment Treaties: Is there a TRIPS-plus Dimension?* (NCRR Trade Regulation, Working Paper No. 2010/19, Nov. 2010), www.wti.org/media/filer_public/c5/47/c5475d4a-f97c-4a8b-a12a-4ae491c6abb3/the_protection_of_iprs_through_bits.pdf (last visited Jun. 17, 2016).

Börzel, Tanja A. & Thomas Risse, *Public-Private Partnerships: Effective and Legitimate Tools of Transnational Governance?*, *in* COMPLEX SOVEREIGNTY: RECONSTITUTING POLITICAL AUTHORITY IN THE TWENTY-FIRST CENTURY 195, 196 (Edgar Grande & Louis W. Pauly eds., 2005).

Bouchard, Ron, *Qualifying Intellectual Property II: A New Innovation Index for Pharmaceutical Patents & Products*, 28 SANTA CLARA COMP. & HIGH TECH. L.J. 287 (2011).

Branstetter, Lee, C. Fritz Foley, & Kamal Saggi, *Has the Shift to Stronger Intellectual Property Rights Promoted Technology Transfer, FDI, and Industrial Development?*, 2 W.I.P.O. J. 93 (2010).

Brewer, Thomas L., *Technology Transfer and Climate Change: International Flows, Barriers, and Frameworks*, in CLIMATE CHANGE, TRADE AND COMPETITIVENESS (Lael Brainerd and Isaac Sorkin eds.).

Brewer, Thomas L., *The Trade Regime and the Climate Regime: Institutional Evolution and Adaptation*, 3 CLIMATE POL'Y 329 (2003).

Brown, Phillip, Hugh Lauder & David Ashton, *Education, Globalization and the Future of the Knowledge Economy*, 7 EUR. EDUC. RES. J. 131 (2008), http://orca.cf.ac.uk/19085/1/Brown%20Lauder.pdf (last visited Nov. 19, 2017).

Burleson, Elizabeth, *Energy Policy, Intellecutal Property, and Technology Transfer to Address Climate Change*, 18 TRANSNAT'L L. & CONTEMP. PROBS. 69 (2009).

Calboli, Irene & Edward Lee eds., RESEARCH HANDBOOK ON INTELLECTUAL PROPERTY EXHAUSTION AND PARALLEL IMPORTS (2017).

Canada NAFTA Decision, Case No. UNCT/14/2, final award, (Mar. 16, 2017), www.ippractice.ca/blog/wp-content/uploads/2017/03/Lilly-v-Canada-NAFTA-Arb-Award.pdf (last visited Nov. 19, 2017).

Carrier, Michael A., INNOVATION FOR THE 21ST CENTURY: HARNESSING THE POWER OF INTELLECTUAL PROPERTY AND ANTITRUST LAW (2009).

Carrier, Michael, *Innovation for the 21st Century: A Response to Seven Critics*, 61 ALA. L. REV. 597 (2010).

Carroll, Michael W., *Copyright, Fair Use, and Creative Commons Licenses, in* RISK AND ENTREPRENEURSHIP IN LIBRARIES: SEIZING OPPORTUNITIES FOR CHANGE 18 (Pamela Bluh & Cindy Hepfer eds., 2009).
Carroll, Michael W., *One Size Does Not Fit All: A Framework for Tailoring Intellectual Property Rights*, 70 OHIO ST. L.J. 1361 (2009).
Carroll. Michael W., *The Problem of Uniformity Cost in Intellectual Property Law*, 55 AM. U. L. REV. 55 (2008).
Cavazos, Ricardo & Douglas Lippoldt, *The Strengthening of IPR Protection: Policy Complements*, 2 W.I.P.O. J. 99 (2010).
Cheung, Tai Ming, Thomas Mahnken, Deborah Seligsohn, Kevin Pollpeter, Eric Anderson, & Fan Yang (University of California Institute on Global Conflict and Cooperation), *Planning for Innovation: Understanding China's Plans for Technological, Energy, Industrial, and Defense Development* (2016), www.uscc.gov/Research/planning-innovation-understanding-china's-plans-technological-energy-industrial-and-defense (last visited Nov. 19, 2017).
Chien, Colleen V., *Opening up the Patent System: Exclusionary and Diffusionary Levers in Patent Law*, 89 SO. CALIF. L. REV. 793, 801 (2016).
Chatham House Workshop Report, *IPRs and the Innovation and Diffusion of Climate Technologies* (2007).
Choi, Jay P., *Compulsory Licensing as an Antitrust Remedy*, 2 W.I.P.O. J. 74 (2010).
Chon, Margaret, *Trademark Goodwill as a Public Good: Brands and Innovations in Corporate Social Responsibility*, 21 Lewis & Clark L. Rev. 277 (2017).
Cohen, Wesley M., Richard R. Nelson, & John P. Walsh, *Protecting Their Intellectual Assets: Appropriability Conditions and Why U.S. Manufacturing Firms Patent (Or Not)* (Nat'l Bureau of Econ. Research, Working Paper No. W7552, 2000), www.nber.org/papers/w7552 (last visited Jun. 16, 2016).
Cohen, Wesley M. & Richard C. Levin, *Empirical Studies of Innovation and Market Structure*, in 2 HANDBOOK OF INDUSTRIAL ORGANIZATION 1059 (Richard Schmalensee & Robert Willig eds., 1989).
Cohen, Wesley M. et al., *Firm Size & R&D Intensity: A Re-Examination*, 35 J. INDUSTRIAL ECON. 543 (1987).
Competition & Tax Law, Declaration on the Three-Step Test, Max Planck Institute for Intellectual Property (2009), www.ip.mpg.de (last visited Nov. 19, 2017).
Conservation Commons, CONSERVEONLINE, http://conserveonline.org/workspaces/commons/ (last visited Nov. 19, 2017).
Consortium Partners, CTCN, www.ctc-n.org/about-ctcn/consortium-partners (last visited Oct. 10, 2017).
Copenhagen Economics, *Are IPRs a Barrier to the Transfer of Climate Change Technologies?*, 4 (2009), http://trade.ec.europa.eu/doclib/docs/2009/february/tradoc_142371.pdf (last visited Jul. 23, 2013).
Correa, Carlos M., *Multilateral Agreements and Policy Opportunities*, POLICY DIALOGUE 11 (2008), http://policydialogue.org/files/events/Correa_Multilateral_Agreements_and_Policy_Opportunities.pdf (last visited Nov. 23, 2015).
Correa, Carlos M., *Review of the TRIPS Agreement: Fostering the Transfer of Technology to Developing Countries*, 2 J. World Intel. Prop. 939 (1999).
Contreras, Jorge L., *Patent Pledges: Between the Public Domain and Market Exclusivity*, 2015 MICH. ST. L. REV. 787.
CREATIVE COMMONS, Open Science, https://creativecommons.org/about/program-areas/open-science (last visited Nov. 19, 2017).
David, Paul A., *Mitigating "Anticommons" Harms to Research, in Science and Technology: New Moves in "Legal Jujitsu" against Unintended Adverse Consequences of the Exploitation*

of Intellectual Property Rights on Results of Publicly and Privately Funded Research, 2 W.I.P.O. J. 59 (2010).

Dechezleprêtre, Antoine, Ralf Martin, & Samuela Bassi, *Climate Change Policy, Innovation, and Growth*, London Sch. of Econ. & Pol. Sci., at 9–19, www.lse.ac.uk/GranthamInstitute/wp-content/uploads/2016/01/Dechezlepretre-et-al-policy-brief-Jan-2016.pdf (last visited Jun. 16, 2016).

Dechezleprêtre, Antoine, Matthieu Glachant, Ivan Haščič, Nick Johnstone, & Yann Ménière, *Invention and Transfer of Climate Change-Mitigation Technologies: A Global Analysis*, 5 Rev. Envt'l. Econ. Pol'y 109 (2011).

Dechezleprêtre, Antoine, Matthieu Glachant, Ivan Hascic, Nick Johnstone, & Yann Ménière, *Invention and Transfer of Climate Change Mitigation Technologies on a Global Scale: A Study Drawing on Patent Data* 4 (CERNA, Mines Paris Tech, Agence Française de Développement, Working Paper, 2008), https://sallan.org/pdf-docs/Dechezlepretre.pdf (last visited Nov. 19, 2017).

Dechezleprêtre, Antoine, *Invention and Transfer of Climate Change Mitigation Technologies on a Global Scale: A Study Drawing on Patent Data* 4 (CERNA, Mines Paris Tech, Agence Française de Développement, Working Paper, November 2008), http://citeseerx.ist.psu.edu/viewdoc/download?doi=10.1.1.153.3100&rep=rep1&type=pdf (last visited Jul. 15, 2012).

Dechezleprêtre, Antoine & D. Popp, *Fiscal and Regulatory Instruments for Clean Technology Development in the European Union*, London Sch. of Econ. & Pol. Sci., Policy Paper, at 10, 18–20 (Jul. 2015), www.lse.ac.uk/GranthamInstitute/publication/fiscal-and-regulatory-instruments-for-clean-technology-development-in-the-european-union/ (last visited Jun. 18, 2016) (last visited Nov. 19, 2017).

Deere-Birkbeck, Carolyn, *Global Governance in the Context of Climate Change: The Challenges of Increasingly Complex Risk Parameters*, 85 Int'l Affairs 1173 (2009).

Derclaye, Estelle, *Not Only Innovation But Also Collaboration, Funding, Goodwill and Commitment: Which Role for Patent Laws in Post-Copenhagen Climate Change Action*, 9 J. Marshall Rev. Intell. Prop. L. 663 (2010).

Díaz-García, Cristina, Ángela González-Moreno, & Francisco J. Sáez-Martínez, *Eco-Innovation: Insights from a Literature Review*, 17 Innovation: Organization & Management 6 (2015).

Dreyfuss, Rochelle Cooper, *Reconsidering Experimental Use*, Akron L. Rev. (Forthcoming Jun. 2017) https://ssrn.com/abstract=3010401 (last visited Nov. 19, 2017).

Durán-Romero, Gemma & Ana Urraca-Ruiz, *Climate Change and Eco-Innovation. A Patent Data Assessment of Environmentally Sound Technologies*, 17 Innovation: Org. & Mgmt. 115 (2015).

Dykman Harry, *Patent Licensing Within the Manufacturer's Aircraft Association (MAA)*, 46 J. Pat. & Trademark Off. Soc'y 646 (1964).

European Commission Decision of 13 May 2009, COMP/37.990 (Intel) ¶¶ 1749–53, http://ec.europa.eu/competition/antitrust/cases/dec_docs/37990/37990_3581_11.pdf (last visited Nov. 19, 2017).

European Parliament and European Council Directive 2004/27, art. 1.8(6), [2004] OJ L136/34 (EC), https://ec.europa.eu/health/sites/health/files/files/eudralex/vol-1/dir_2004_27/dir_2004_27_en.pdf (last visited Nov. 19, 2017).

European Patent Office [EPO], *Overview of the Latin American and Caribbean Clean Energy Potential and Exploitation Levels*, http://documents.epo.org/projects/babylon/eponet.nsf/0/2841b369787d5e72c1257da800335111/$FILE/patents_Latin_America_summary_en.pdf.

EPO-United Nations Environmental Programme [UNEP], *Patents and Clean Energy Technologies in Africa*, http://www.epo.org/news-issues/technology/sustainable-technologies/clean-energy/patents-africa.html (last visited Nov. 19, 2017).

Fair, Robert, *Does Climate Change Justify Compulsory Licensing of Green Technology*, 6 B.Y.U. INT'L L. & MGMT. REV. 21 (2009).

Fankauser, Sam, Alex Bowen, Raphael Calel, Antoine Dechezleprêtre, David Grover, James Rydge, & Misato Sato, *Who Will Win the Green Race? In Search of Environmental Competitiveness and Innovation*, 23 GLOBAL ENVTL. CHANGE 902 (2013).

Fifth Assessment Synthesis Report, Summary for Policymakers, Intergovernmental Panel on Climate Change (IPCC) at 14 (2014), ("Regional Key Risks and Potential for Risk Reduction"), www.ipcc.ch/pdf/assessment-report/ar5/syr/AR5_SYR_FINAL_SPM.pdf (last visited Jun. 16, 2016).

Figueres, Christiana, Hans Joachim Schellnhuber, Gail Whiteman, Johan Rockström, Anthony Hobley, & Stefan Rahmstorf, *Comment: Three Years to Safeguard Our Climate*, 546 NATURE 593 (Jun. 29, 2017).

Fisher, William, *Intellectual Property and Innovation: Theoretical, Empirical, and Historical Perspectives*, 37 Industrial Property, Innovation, and the Knowledge-Based Economy, Beleidsstudies Technologie Economie (2001), cyber.law.harvard.edu/people/tfisher/Innovation.pdf (last visited Nov. 19, 2017).

Foray, Dominique, *Technology Transfer in the TRIPS Age: The Need for New Types of Partnerships between the Least Developed and Most Advanced Economies* (2009), www.ictsd.org/downloads/2012/02/technology-transfer-in-the-trips-age.pdf (last visited Nov. 19, 2017).

Frischmann, Brett M., *An Economic Theory of Infrastructure and Commons Management*, 89 MINN. L. REV. 917 (2005).

Frischmann, Brett M., INFRASTUCTURE: THE SOCIAL VALUE OF SHARED RESOURCES (2012).

Frischmann, Brett, *Innovation and Institutions: Rethinking the Economics of U.S. Science and Technology Policy*, 24 VT. L. REV. 347 (2000).

Gantz, David A. & Padideh Ala'i, *Climate Change Innovation, Products and Services Under the GATT/WTO System*, *in* RESEARCH HANDBOOK ON INTELLECTUAL PROPERTY AND CLIMATE CHANGE 271 (Joshua D. Sarnoff, ed., 2016).

Ge, Mengpin, Johannes Friedrich, & Thomas Damassa, *6 Graphs Explain the World's Top 10 Emitters* (Cumulative CO_2 Emissions 1850–2011), World Resources Institute (2014), www.wri.org/blog/2014/11/6-graphs-explain-world%E2%80%99s-top-10-emitters (last visited Jun. 16, 2016).

Global Environmental Facility, *Organization*, www.thegef.org/about/organization (last visited Nov. 19, 2017).

GOVERNING KNOWLEDGE COMMONS (Brett M. Frischmann, Michael J. Madison, & Katherine J. Strandburg eds., 2014).

GREEN CLIMATE FUND, *GFC in Numbers*, 2017, www.greenclimate.fund/documents/20182/24871/GCF_in_Numbers.pdf/226fc825-3c56-4d71-9a4c-60fd83e5fb03 (last visited Nov. 19, 2017).

GREEN EXCHANGE (2012), www.greenexchange.com (last visited Nov. 19, 2017).

THE GUARDIAN, *Earth's Oceans are Warming 13% Faster Than Thought, and Accelerating* (Mar. 10, 2017), www.theguardian.com/environment/climate-consensus-97-per-cent/2017/mar/10/earths-oceans-are-warming-13-faster-than-thought-and-accelerating, (last visited Oct. 10, 2017).

Hall, Bronwyn & C. Helmers, *The Role of Patent Protection in (Clean/Green) Technologies* 7 (National Bureau of Economic Research, Working Paper 16323, 2010), www.nber.org/papers/w16323 (last visited Nov. 23, 2015).

Hazucha, Branislav, INTERNATIONAL STANDARDS AND ESSENTIAL PATENTS: FROM INTERNATIONAL HARMONIZATION TO COMPETITION OF TECHNOLOGIES (2010).

Hemphill, C. Scott, *Network Neutrality and the False Promise of Zero-Price Regulation*, 25 YALE J. REG. 135 (2008).

Holzapfel, Henrik & Joshua D. Sarnoff, *A Cross-Atlantic Dialog on Experimental Use and Research Tools*, 48 IDEA 123 (2008).

International Council on Human Rights Policy, *Beyond Technology Transfer: Protecting Human Rights in a Climate-Constrained World*, in Sarnoff, Joshua D., RESEARCH HANDBOOK ON INTELLECTUAL PROPERTY AND CLIMATE CHANGE (2016).

Impression Products, Inc. v. Lexmark Int'l., Inc., 137 S.Ct. 1523 (2017).

International HapMap Project (2011), http://hapmap.ncbi.nlm.nih.gov (last visited Nov. 19, 2017).

Johnson, Daniel & Kristina Lybecker, *Challenges to Technology Transfer: A Literature Review of the Constraints on Environmental Technology Dissemination* (2009) http://ssrn.com/abstract=1456222 (last visited Jul. 15, 2012).

Joskow, Paul L. & Nancy L. Rose, *The Effects of Economic Regulation*, *in* HANDBOOK OF INDUSTRIAL ORGANIZATION 1464 (1989).

Kapczynski, Amy, *The Cost of Price: Why and How to Get Beyond Intellectual Property Internalism*, 59 UCLA L. REV. 970 (2012).

Khan, B. Zorina, *Antitrust and Innovation Before the Sherman* Act, 77 ANTITRUST L.J. 757 (2011).

Kim, Chulhyun & Moon-Soo Kim, *Identifying Core Environmental Technologies Through Patent Analysis*, 17 INNOVATION: ORG. & MGT. 139 (2015).

Kristensen, Henrik, K. F. Vinding, K. Grieger, & S. F. Hansen, *Adopting Eco-Innovation in Danish Polymer Industry Working with Nanotechnology: Drivers, Barriers and Future Strategies*, 6 NANOTECH. L. & BUS. 416 (2009).

Kirtsaeng v. John Wiley & Sons, 568 U.S. 519 (2013).

Kunstadt, R. & I. Maggioni, *A Proposed "U.S. Public Patent Pool,"* LES NOUVELLES, 10 (2011).

Lee, Bernice, Ilian Iliev, & Felix Preston, *A Chatham House Report: Who Owns Our Low Carbon Future? Intellectual Property and Energy Technologies*, Royal Institute of International Affairs, (2009).

Lee, Peter, *Inverting the Logic of Scientific Discovery: Applying Common Law Patentable Subject Matter Doctrine to Constrain Patents on Biotechnology Research Tools*, 19 HARV. J.L. & TECH 84 (2005).

Lee, Peter, *Patents, Paradigm-Shifts, and Progress in Biomedical Science*, 114 YALE L.J. 69 (2004).

Lee, Peter, *Toward a Distributive Commons in Patent Law*, 2009 WIS. L. REV. 974 (2009).

Lemley, Mark, *Industry-Specific Antitrust Policy for Innovation*, 2011 COLUM. BUS. L. REV. 637 (2011).

Lessig, Lawrence, CODE: VERSION 2.0 (2006).

Levin, Richard C., Alvin K. Klevorick, Richard R. Nelson, & Sidney G. Winter, *Appropriating the Returns from Industrial Research and Development*, 18 BROOKINGS PAPERS ON ECON. ACTIVITY 783 (1987).

Li, Yahong, IMITATION TO INNOVATION IN CHINA: THE ROLE OF PATENTS IN BIOTECHNOLOGY AND PHARMACEUTICAL INDUSTRIES 70 (2010).

Liberti, Lahra, *Intellectual Property Rights in International Investment Agreements* (OECD, Working Paper No. 2010/01, 2010), www.oecd.org/daf/inv/investment-policy/WP-2010_1.pdf (last visited Jun. 17, 2016).

Love, James & Tim Hubbard, *Paying for Public Goods*, *in* CODE: COLLABORATIVE OWNERSHIP AND THE DIGITAL ECONOMY 207 (James Love, Tim Hubbard, & Rishab Aiyer Ghosh eds., 2005).

Madison, Michael, Brett M. Frischmann, & Katherine Strandburg, *The University as Constructed Cultural Commons*, 30 WASH. U. J. L. & POL'Y 365 (2009).

Magat, Wesley A. & W. Kip Viscusi, INFORMATIONAL APPROACHES TO REGULATION (1992).

Mandel, Gregory N., *When to Open Infrastructure Access*, 35 ECOLOGY L. Q. 205 (2008).

Manne, Geoffrey, *Assuming More Than We Know About Innovation Markets: A Review of Michael Carrier's Innovation in the 21st Century*, 61 Ala. L. Rev. 553 (2010).

Mara, Kaitlin, *New Climate Technologies Rarely Reaching Developing Countries, Panel Says*, IP Watch (Jul. 13, 2010), www.ip-watch.org/weblog/2010/07/13/new-climate-technologies-rarely-reaching-developing-countries-panel-says (last visited Nov. 23, 2015).

Maskus, Keith, *Research and Development Subsidies: A Need for WTO Disciplines?* E15 Initiative, International Centre for Trade and Sustainable Development [ICTSD] and World Economic Forum (2015), http://e15initiative.org/wp-content/uploads/2015/01/E15_Subsidies_Maskus_final.pdf (last visited Nov. 19, 2017).

Maskus, Keith E., *The Curious Economics of Parallel Imports*, 2 W.I.P.O. J. 123 (2010).

Maskus, Keith E. & Ruth Okediji, *Intellectual Property Rights and International Technology Transfer to Address Climate Change: Risks, Opportunities and Policy Options*, International Centre for Trade and Sustainable Development 10 (2010), http://ictsd.org/i/publications/97782/ (last visited Nov. 23, 2015).

Maskus, Keith E. & Ruth L. Okediji, *Legal and Economic Perspectives on International Technology Transfer in Environmentally Sound Technologies, in* Intellectual Property Rights: Legal and Economic Challenges for Development 392 (2014).

Maskus, Keith & William Ridley, *Intellectual Property-Related Preferential Trade Agreements and the Composition of Trade* (draft of Mar. 17, 2017) (on file with the author).

Merck KGAA v. Integra LifeSciences I Ltd., 545 U.S. 193 (2005).

Merges, Robert P. & Richard R. Nelson, *On the Complex Economics of Patent Scope*, 90 Colum. L. Rev. 839 (1990).

Mimura, Carol, *Technology Licensing for the Benefit of the Developing World: UC Berkeley's Socially Responsible Licensing Program*, 21 J. Assoc. Univ. Tech. Managers 15 (2007).

Montes, Manuel F., *Industrialization, Inequality and Sustainability: What Kinds of Industry Policy Do We Need?*, South Center Policy Brief (Aug. 2017), www.southcentre.int/policy-brief-44-august-2017/ (last visited Nov. 19, 2017).

National Academies of Science, Engineering & Medicine, *Returns to Federal Investments in the Innovation System: Proceedings of a Workshop – in Brief*, (Oct. 2017), https://doi.org/10.17226/24905 (last visited Oct. 12, 2017).

National Renewable Energy Laboratory, Batelle, www.battelle.org/our-work/laboratory-management/national-renewable-energy-laboratory (last visited Nov. 19, 2017).

National Research Council, *Managing University Intellectual Property in the Public Interest*, National Academies Press 7 (2010).

O'Connor, Sean, *Origins of Patent Exhaustion: Jacksonian Politics, 'Patent Farming,' and the Basis of the Bargain* (Mar. 8, 2017), https://papers.ssrn.com/sol3/papers.cfm?abstract_id=2920738 (last visited Nov. 19, 2017).

Organization for Economic Cooperation and Development, *National Systems for Financing Innovation* (1995).

Nesta, Lionel, Francesco Vona, & Francesco Nicolli, *Environmental Policies, Product Market Regulation and Innovation in Renewable Energy* (2012) (unpublished manuscript), http://papers.ssrn.com/sol3/papers.cfm?abstract_id=2192441 (last visited Nov. 19, 2017).

Oil States Energy Servs., LLC v. Greene's Energy Group, LLC, 639 Fed. App'x 639 (Fed. Cir. 2016), *cert. granted*, 137 S.Ct. 2239 (U.S. Nov. 23, 2016).

Oliva, Maria J. et al., *Climate Change, Technology Transfer and Intellectual Property Rights*, International Centre for Trade and Sustainable Development (2008), http://ictsd.org/i/publications/31159 (last visited Nov. 23, 2015).

OMB 2013 Budget Report (Apr. 29, 2013).

Ordover, Janusz A., *Economic Foundations and Considerations in Protecting Industrial and Intellectual Property*, 53 Antitrust L. J. 503 (1984).

Ostrom, Elinor, GOVERNING THE COMMONS: THE EVOLUTION OF INSTITUTIONS FOR COLLECTIVE ACTION (POLITICAL ECONOMY OF INSTITUTIONS AND DECISIONS (1990).

Panel Report, Canada – Patent Protection of Pharmaceutical Products, WTO Doc. WT/DS114/R, ¶¶ 7.54–7.57, 7.69 (adopted Apr. 7, 2000), www.wto.org/english/tratop_e/dispu_e/7428d.pdf (last visited Nov. 19, 2017).

Parson, Edward A., *Starting the Dialog on Climate Engineering Governance: A World Commission*, Centre for International Governance Innovation, www.cigionline.org/sites/default/files/documents/Fixing%20Climate%20Governance%20PB%20no8_0.pdf (last visited Nov. 19, 2017).

Peritz, Rudolph J. R., *Competition Within Intellectual Property Regimes: The Instance of Patent Rights, in* INTELLECTUAL PROPERTY AND COMPETITION LAW: NEW FRONTIERS 27 (Steven Anderman & Ariel Ezrachi eds., 2011).

POLAR INFORMATION COMMONS, Welcome to the Polar Information Commons (PIC), www.polarcommons.org/ (last visited Nov. 19, 2017).

Porter, Michael E., *Clusters of Innovation: Regional Foundations of U.S. Competitiveness*, Council on Competitiveness (2001).

Powell, Walter W., Jason Owen-Smith, & Laurel Smith-Doerr, THE SCIENCE OF SCIENCE POLICY: A HANDBOOK (Kaye H. Fealing et al. eds., 2011).

Prakash, Aseem, GREENING THE FIRM: THE POLITICS OF CORPORATE ENVIRONMENTALISM (2000).

Prins, Gwyn et al., *The Hartwell Paper: A New Direction for Climate Policy After the Crash of 2009*, 5 (2010), http://eprints.lse.ac.uk/27939/ (last visited Nov. 23, 2015).

PUBLIC LIBRARY OF SCIENCE, *Welcome to PLOS*, www.plos.org (last visited Nov. 18, 2017).

Radka, Mark, *Some Perspectives About the Climate Technology Centre/Climate Technology Network*, U.N. Environment Programme (2012), http://unfccc.int/files/meetings/ad_hoc_working_groups/lca/application/pdf/some_perspectives_about_the_ctc_ctn.pdf (last visited Nov. 19, 2017).

Rai, Arti K. & Rebecca S. Eisenberg, *Bayh-Dole Reform and the Progress of Biomedicine*, 66 LAW & CONTEMP. PROBS. 294 (2003).

Reichman, Jerome H., *Comment: Compulsory Licensing of Patented Pharmaceutical Inventions: Evaluating the Options*, 37 J.L. MED. & ETHICS 253 (2009).

Reichman, Jerome H., *Intellectual Property in International Perspective: Institute for Intellectual Property & Information Law Symposium*, 48 HOUS. L. REV. 1137 (2009).

Reynolds, Jesse L., *Solar Climate Engineering, Law, and Regulation, in* THE OXFORD HANDBOOK ON THE LAW AND REGULATION OF TECHNOLOGY 799 (Roger Brownsword, Eloise Scotford & Karen Yeung eds., 2016), https://ssrn.com/abstract=2862471 (last visited Nov. 19, 2017).

Reynolds, Jesse L., Jorge L. Contreras, & Joshua D. Sarnoff, *Solar Climate Engineering and Intellectual Property: Toward a Research Commons*, 18 MINN. J. L., SCI. & TECH. 1 (2017).

Rimmer, Matthew, INTELLECTUAL PROPERTY AND CLIMATE CHANGE: INVENTING CLEAN TECHNOLOGIES (2001).

Rismann, Jeffrey & Robbie Orvis, *Carbon Capture and Storage: An Expensive Option for Reducing U.S. CO2 Emissions*, FORBES (May 3, 2017), www.forbes.com/sites/energyinnovation/2017/05/03/carbon-capture-and-storage-an-expensive-option-for-reducing-u-s-co2-emissions/#420d40956482 (last visited Nov. 19, 2017).

Rosch, J. Thomas, *Antitrust Regulation of Innovation Markets: Remarks at the ABA Antitrust Intellectual Property Conference* (2009), www.ftc.gov/speeches/rosch/090205innovationspeech.pdf (last visited Nov. 19, 2017).

Ruggles, C.O., *Problems of Public-Utility Rate Regulation and Fair Return*, 32 J. POL. ECON. 543 (1924).

Ruttan, Vernon W., IS WAR NECESSARY FOR ECONOMIC GROWTH? MILITARY PROCUREMENT AND TECHNOLOGY DEVELOPMENT (2006).

Sallet, Jonathan, Ed Paisley & Justin Masterman, *The Geography of Innovation: The Federal Government and the Growth of Regional Innovation Clusters*, Science Progress 1 (2009), www.scienceprogress.org/wp-content/uploads/2009/09/eda_paper.pdf (last visited Jul. 15, 2012).

Sampath, Padmashree Gehl & Pedro Roffe, *Unpacking the International Technology Transfer Debate: Fifty Years and Beyond Research*, ICTSD Issue Paper No. 36, 17, 19 (Nov. 2012), www.ictsd.org/sites/default/files/research/2012/11/unpacking-the-international-technology-transfer-debate-fifty-years-and-beyond.pdf (last visited Nov. 19, 2017).

Samuelson, Pamela, *Reverse Engineering Under Siege*, Berkeley School of Information 1–3, http://people.ischool.berkeley.edu/~pam/papers/CACM%20on%20Bunner.pdf (last visited Nov. 19, 2017).

Sarnoff, Joshua D., *Government Choices in Innovation Funding (with Reference to Climate Change)*, 62 EMORY L. J. 1087 (2013).

Sarnoff, Joshua D., *Intellectual Property and Climate Change, with an Emphasis on Patents and Technology Transfer, in* THE OXFORD HANDBOOK OF INTERNATIONAL CLIMATE CHANGE LAW 391 (Gray, Kevin R., Richard Tarasofsky, & Cinnamon P. Carlarne eds., 2016).

Sarnoff, Joshua D., *Patent Eligible Inventions after Bilski: History and Theory*, 63 HASTINGS L. J. 53 (2011).

Sarnoff, Joshua D., *The Likely Mismatch Between Federal R&D Funding and Desired Innovation*, 18 VANDERBILT J. ENTER. & TECH. L. 363 (2016).

Sarnoff, Joshua D., *The Patent System and Climate Change*, 16 VA. J. L. & TECH. 301 (2011).

Sarnoff, Joshua D. & Christopher Holman, *Recent Developments Affecting the Enforcement, Procurement, and Licensing of Research Tool Patents*, 23 BERKELEY TECH. L. J. 1299 (2008).

Sarnoff, Joshua D. (ed.), RESEARCH HANDBOOK ON INTELLECTUAL PROPERTY AND CLIMATE CHANGE (2016).

Schuiling, R. D. & Oliver Tickel, *Olivine Against Climate Change and Ocean Acidification*, Innovation Concepts, www.innovationconcepts.eu/res/literatuurSchuiling/olivineagainstclimatechange23.pdf (last visited Nov. 19, 2017).

SCIENCE COMMONS, About Science Commons, http://sciencecommons.org/about (last visited Nov. 19, 2017) (last visited Nov. 19, 2017).

Scotchmer, Suzanne, *Standing on the Shoulders of Giants: Cumulative Research and the Patent Law*, Winter 1991 J. ECON. PERSP. 33 (2009).

So, Anthony D., Bhaven N Sampat, Arti K Rai, Robert Cook-Deegan, Jerome H Reichman, Robert Weissman, & Amy Kapczynski, *Is Bayh-Dole good for developing countries? Lessons from the US experience*, 6 PLOS BIOL. (2008) http://journals.plos.org/plosbiology/article?id=10.1371/journal.pbio.0060262 (last visited Nov. 19, 2017).

Srinivas, K. Ravi, *Climate Change, Technology Transfer and Intellectual Property Rights, Research and Information System for Developing Countries*, Discussion Paper No. 153, 26 (2009), http://papers.ssrn.com/sol3/papers.cfm?abstract_id=1440742 (last visited Nov. 19, 2017).

Stiglitz, Joseph E., *Lecture, Economic Foundations of Intellectual Property Rights*, 57 DUKE L. J. 1693 (2008).

Strandburg, Katherine J., *Users as Innovators: Implications for Patent Doctrine*, 79 U. COLO. L. REV. 467 (2008).

Styianou, Konstantinos, *An Innovation-Centric Approach of Telecommunications Infrastructure Regulation*, 16 VA. J.L. & TECH. 221 (2011).

Sundaram, Jomo Kwame, Anis Chowdhury, Krishnan Sharma, & Daniel Platz, *Public-Private Partnerships and the 2030 Agenda for Sustainable Development: Fit for Purpose?* 6 (U.N. Dept. of Econ. & Soc. Affairs, DESA Working Paper No. 148, ST/ESA/2016/DWP/148, Feb. 2016).

Szakalski, Dustin, *Progress in the Aircraft Industry and the Role of Patent Pools and Cross-Licensing Agreements*, 15 UCLA J. L. & Tech. 1 (2011).

Takalo, Tuomas, *Rationales and Instruments for Public Innovation Policies*, Bank of Finland Research Discussion Papers, Paper No. 1 (2013), http://papers.ssrn.com/sol3/papers.cfm?abstract_id=2217502 (last visited Nov. 19, 2017).

United Nations [U.N.] Ad Hoc Working Group on Long-Term Cooperative Action Under the Convention Report of the Ad Hoc Working Group on Long-term Cooperative Action under the Convention on its Seventh Session, U.N. Doc. FCCC/AWGLCA/2009/14, at 156 (Nov. 20, 2009).

U.N. Department of Economic and Social Affairs [UNDESA], Sustainable Development Knowledge Platform, *Transforming Our World: The 2030 Agenda for Sustainable Development*, https://sustainabledevelopment.un.org/post2015/transformingourworld (last visited Nov. 19, 2017).

UNDESA, *World Economic and Social Survey 2009* (2009).

UNDESA, *World Economic and Social Survey 2010* (2010).

United Nations Environment Programme [UNEP], *The Adaptation Gap Finance Report 2016*, at 3 (May 2016), http://web.unep.org/adaptationgapreport/2016 (last visited Jun. 16, 2016).

UNEP, EPO and ICTSD, *Patents and Clean Energy: Bridging the Gap Between Evidence and Policy: Final Report* (2010), http://documents.epo.org/projects/babylon/eponet.nsf/0/cc5da4b168363477c12577ad00547289/$FILE/patents_clean_energy_study_en.pdf (last visited Nov. 23, 2015).

U.N. Framework Convention on Climate Change [UNFCCC], 1771 U.N.T.S. 107, *signed* Jun. 1992, *entered into force* Mar. 21, 1994.

UNFCCC, *Paris Agreement*, FCCC/CP/2015/L.9/Rev.1, Draft Decision –/CP.21 Annex (2015), http://unfccc.int/resource/docs/2015/cop21/eng/l09r01.pdf (last visited Dec. 21, 2015).

UNFCCC, *Report of the Conference of the Parties on its Seventeenth Session, Held in Durban from 28 November to 11 December 2011: Decision 4/CP.17 Technology Executive Committee – Modalities and Procedures*, UNFCCC, Report No. FCCC/CP/2011/9/Add.1 ¶ 4 (a)-(f) (2011).

UNFCCC, *Report of the Conference of the Parties on its Eighteenth Session, Held in Doha from 26 November to 8 December 2012*, UNFCCC, Report No. FCCC/CP/2012/8/Add.2. ¶ 10, (2012).

UNFCCC, *Report of the Conference of the Parties on its Nineteenth Session, Held in Warsaw from 11 to 23 November 2013: Decision 3/CP19, Long-term Climate Finance*, UNFCCC, Report No. FCCC/CP/2013/10/Add.1 ¶¶ 7–9 (2013).

UNFCCC, *Report on Activities and Performance of the Technology Executive Committee for 2012*, UNFCCC, Report No. FCCC/SB/2012/2 ¶ 35(g) (2012).

UNFCCC, *Support for Implementing Climate Technology Activities*, TT:CLEAR, http://unfccc.int/ttclear/support/technology-mechanism.html (last visited Oct. 10, 2017).

UNFCCC, Technology Mechanism (2013), http://unfccc.int/ttclear/templates/render_cms_page?TEM_home (last visited Nov. 19, 2017).

UNFCCC, *TT:CLEAR*, http://unfccc.int/ttclear/support/technology-mechanism.html (last visited Nov. 19, 2017).

UNFCCC Ad Hoc Working Group on Long-Term Cooperative Action Under the Convention, *Ideas and proposals on the elements contained in paragraph 1 of the Bali Action Plan*, 23 UNFCCC (2009), http://unfccc.int/resource/docs/2009/awglca5/eng/misc01.pdf.

UNFCCC Ad Hoc Working Group on Long-Term Cooperative Action Under the Convention, Report of the Ad Hoc Working Group on Long-term Cooperative Action under the Convention on its Seventh Session, UNFCCC Doc. No. FCCC/AWGLCA/2009/14, 156 (2009), http://unfccc.int/resource/docs/2009/awglca7/eng/14.pdf.UNFCCC, Draft Decision CP.16,

Outcome of the work of the Ad Hoc Working Group on long-term Cooperative Action under the Convention (2010), ¶¶ IV.A.98–99, http://unfccc.int/files/meetings/cop_16/application/pdf/cop16_lca.pdf (last visited Nov. 23, 2015).
[U.N.] Sustainable Development Knowledge Platform, *Sustainable Development Goal 9*, U.N. Dep't of Econ. and Soc. Affairs, https://sustainabledevelopment.un.org/sdg9 (last visited Nov. 19, 2017).
[U.N.] Sustainable Development Knowledge Platform, *Sustainable Development Goal 13*, U.N. Dep't of Econ. and Soc. Affairs, https://sustainabledevelopment.un.org/sdg13 (last visited Nov. 19, 2017).
[U.N.] Sustainable Development Knowledge Platform, *Sustainable Development Goal 17*, U.N. Dep't of Econ. and Soc. Affairs, https://sustainabledevelopment.un.org/sdg17 (last visited Nov. 19, 2017).
U.S. Code 15 U.S.C. 3710 §12(d)(1) (1986) ([Commerce and trade] Cooperative research and development agreements).
17 U.S.C. §506(a) (2006) ([Copyrights] Criminal offenses).
18 U.S.C. §2319(a) (2006) (Criminal infringement of a copyright).
35 U.S.C. §201(b) (2006) ([Patents] Definitions).
35 U.S.C. § 202(c)(4) (2006) ([Patents] Disposition of rights).
35 U.S.C. § 203(a) (2006) ([Patents] March-in rights).
35 U.S.C. § 207(a)(2) (2006) ([Patents] Domestic and foreign protection of federally owned inventions).
35 U.S.C. § 271(e) (2006) ([Patents] Infringement of Patent).
42 U.S.C. §4701 et seq. (2006) ([The Public Health and Welfare] Congressional findings and declaration of policy).
U.S. Department Energy Off. Sci., Human Genome Project Information (2011), www.ornl.gov/sci/techresources/Human_Genome/home.shtml (last visited Nov. 19, 2017).
U.S. Department of Energy, DOE/NNSA Overseas Presence Advisory Board's Overseas Corps Training Program Agreement, http://energy.gov/sites/prod/files/DOE-Overseas-Corps-Training-Program.pdf (last visited Nov. 19, 2017).
U.S. Department of State, Memorandum of Understanding Signed Between the Government of India and the Government of the United States, (Nov. 30, 2009), https://2009–2017.state.gov/p/sca/rls/press/2009/132776.htm (last visited Nov. 19, 2017).
U.S. Department of State, Memorandum of Understanding to Enhance Cooperation on Climate Change, Energy and Environment Between the Government of the United States of America and the Government of the People's Republic of China (Jul. 2009), https://2009–2017.state.gov/r/pa/prs/ps/2009/july/126592.htm (last visited Nov. 19, 2017).
U.S. Environmental Protection Agency [U.S. EPA], Climate Leadership Awards, http://www.epa.gov/climateleadership/awards/index.html (last visited Nov. 19, 2017).
U.S. EPA, Energy Star® – The Power to Protect the Environment Through Energy Efficiency, EPA 430-R-03–008, 2–3 (2003).
U.S. EPA, *Global Greenhouse Gas Emission Data*, (2016), www3.epa.gov/climatechange/ghgemissions/global.html (last visited Jun. 15, 2016).
U.S. Global Climate Change Research Program, *Climate Science Special Report* (CSSR) (Jun. 28, 2017), www.nytimes.com/packages/pdf/climate/2017/climate-report-final-draft-clean.pdf (last visited Nov. 19, 2017).
Van Overwalle, Geertrui, *Individualism, Collectivism and Openness in Patent Law: Promoting Access Through Exclusion*, Individualism and Collectiveness in Intellectual Property Law (Jan Rósen, ed., 2011), https://papers.ssrn.com/sol3/papers.cfm?abstract_id=1718687 (last visited Nov. 19, 2017).

Verizon v. Trinko, 540 U.S. 398 (2004).
Wessner, Charles W. & Alan W. Wolff eds., RISING TO THE CHALLENGE: U.S. INNOVATION POLICY FOR THE GLOBAL ECONOMY 53 (2012).
World Development Report 2010: Development and Climate Change, WORLD BANK (2009).
World Energy Council, *World Energy Resources: Carbon Capture and Storage 2016*, www.worldenergy.org/wp-content/uploads/2017/03/WEResources_CCS_2016.pdf (last visited Nov. 19, 2017).
World Trade Organization [WTO], Agreement on Trade-Related Aspects of Intellectual Property Rights (April 15, 1994), Marrakesh Agreement Establishing the World Trade Organization, Annex 1C, LEGAL INSTRUMENTS – RESULT OF THE URUGUAY ROUNDS 33 I.L.M. 81 (1994).
WTO & UNEP, *Trade and Climate Change WTO-UNEP Report* (2009).
Yu, Peter K., *Enforcement, Economics and Estimates*, 2 W.I.P.O. J. 1 (2010).

13 How Do Climate Change and Energy-Related Partnerships Impact Innovation and Technology Transfer?: Some Lessons for the Implementation of the UN Sustainable Development Goals

Ayşem Mert and Philipp Pattberg

Introduction

Public–private partnerships (PPPs) – that is, networks among different societal actors, including governments, international organizations, companies, research institutions, and civil society organizations – have been widely endorsed and applied across a number of global public policy arenas, from health to climate change. For example, in 2000, former United Nations Secretary-General Kofi Annan launched the Global Compact, a voluntary partnership between corporations and the United Nations (UN). More recently, PPPs have been discussed as a major implementation mechanism for the UN's ambitious 2030 Agenda for Sustainable Development (2030 Agenda) and its related Sustainable Development Goals (SDGs).[1] Furthermore, partnerships now also form an integral part of the non-state action agenda on climate change.[2] In the words of former UN Secretary-General Ban Ki-Moon, "[a]ddressing global challenges requires a collective and concerted effort, involving all actors. Through partnerships and alliances, and by pooling comparative advantages, we increase our chances of success."[3]

Partnerships for sustainable development emerged as voluntary cooperative arrangements between governments and non-state actors to address specific sustainability goals. They were promoted, particularly at the 2002 Johannesburg World Summit on Sustainable Development (WSSD), where PPPs clearly emerged as an alternative governance mechanism to the traditional intergovernmental agreements and diplomatic processes, which the Summit failed to produce. Since then, PPPs have become widespread, if not the dominant mode of governance in various issue areas, particularly in the transnational climate, energy, and sustainability policies.[4] For example, the United Nations

[1] Sustainable Development Knowledge Platform, *Transforming our World: the 2030 Agenda for Sustainable Development*, U.N. Dep't of Econ. and Soc. Affairs, https://sustainabledevelopment.un.org/post2015/transformingourworld. In particular, SDG 9 exhorts member states to "[b]uild resilient infrastructure, promote inclusive and sustainable industrialization and foster innovation" and SDG 13 specifically urges them to "[t]ake urgent action to combat climate change and its impacts."

[2] Sander Chan et al., *Reinvigorating International Climate Policy: A Comprehensive Framework for Effective Nonstate Action*, 6 Global Pol'y 466–473 (2015).

[3] United Nations Office for Partnerships, nonwww.un.org/partnerships/.

[4] We understand the transnational level as involving at least one non-state actor involved in cross-border governance, whereas the global level involves nation-states and/or non-state actors engaging in activities that focus on worldwide governance. Thus, global can refer to either transnational governance and/or to more traditional initiatives via public sector and inter-governmental regulatory regimes.

Commission on Sustainable Development (UNCSD) has over 330 registered initiatives (largely overlapping with the sample discussed later in this chapter). In the 2012 Rio+20 Summit, over seven hundred voluntary arrangements were added to the list of similar voluntary arrangements. Launched in early 2016, UN's Partnerships for SDGs database has 2,088 registered initiatives, and the international cooperative initiatives (so-called ICIs) that are emerging in the aftermath of the 2015 Paris Agreement are also growing rapidly. These operate beyond the auspices of the UNFCCC and are driven by smaller groups of like-minded countries, often including companies, NGOs, academia, international organizations and sub-national public actors such as cities.

Despite their memetic success, the role and relevance of these partnerships remain contested. Some observers view the new emphasis on PPPs as problematic, since voluntary public–private governance arrangements might privilege more powerful actors[5] in particular those located in the so-called global North, comprised almost entirely of industrialized countries. In addition, these arrangements arguably consolidate the privatization of governance and dominant neo-liberal modes of globalization,[6] wherein institutions are installed but neither governance deficits are addressed nor public goods procured.[7] Some also argue that partnerships lack accountability and democratic legitimacy.[8] By contrast, others see PPPs as a governance innovation that addresses various deficits of inter-state politics by bringing together key actors across the public, private, and nonprofit sectors.[9] While some scholars regard governance deficits as a generic phenomenon in international relations,[10] others focus on a particular governance deficit such as the democratic deficit and problems of legitimacy,[11] the implementation deficit, or the regulatory deficit impacting global regimes such as global climate change regulation.

Despite these critiques and observations, PPPs are relevant for the governance of climate change and energy, and the related challenge of technology transfer for the following reasons. As a descriptive matter, in the follow-up to the 2015 Paris Agreement, transnational non-governmental actors have become a main provider of public goods and policies. Since then, the economic and discursive transformations in climate politics have consistently been focused around the steering and orchestrating powers of the states and inter-state system, which enable collaborations of non-state actors with sub-state

[5] Verena Bitzer et al., *Intersectoral Partnerships for a Sustainable Coffee Chain: Really Addressing Sustainability or Just Picking (Coffee) Cherries?*, 18 Global Envtl. Change 271–284 (2008); Karlijn Morsink et al., *Multi-stakeholder Partnerships for Transfer of Environmentally Sound Technologies*, 39 Energy Pol'y 1–5 (2011).

[6] Marina Ottaway, *Corporation Goes Global: International Organizations, Nongovernmental Organization Networks, and Transnational Business*, 7 Global Governance 265–292 (2001).

[7] Ayşem Mert, *The Privatisation of Environmental Governance: On Myths, Forces of Nature, and other Inevitabilities*, 21 Envtl. Values 475–498 (2012).

[8] James Meadowcroft, *Who is in Charge Here? Governance for Sustainable Development in a Complex World*, 9 J. Envtl. Pol'y & Plan. 299–314 (2007); Ayşem Mert, Environmental Governance Through Partnerships: A Discourse Theoretical Study 230–249 (2015).

[9] *See generally* Wolfgang H. Reinicke, Global Public Policy: Governing Without Government? (1998); Charlotte Streck, *New Partnerships in Global Environmental Policy: The Clean Development Mechanism*, 13 J. Env't & Dev. 295–322 (2004).

[10] Peter Haas, *When Does Power Listen to Truth? A Constructive Approach to the Policy Process*, 11 J. Eur. Pub. Pol'y 569–592 (2004).

[11] Karin Bäckstrand, *Democratizing Global Environmental Governance? Stakeholder Democracy after the World Summit on Sustainable Development*, 12 Eur. J. Int'l Rel. 467–498 (2006).

agents and communities. Secondly, PPPs are intended to facilitate the provision of global *public* goods.[12] Relatedly, individual partners may lack full global, regional, or regulatory authority to reach their aims; therefore, the provision of goods or services depends on a coalition of social forces. Consequently, by involving various stakeholders, the promise of partnerships is to produce public goods with more consensus and participation. In this context, the supervision, oversight, and liability emerge as critical issues for PPP researchers to investigate further.

In the context of this chapter, we understand the relationship between partnerships and intellectual property rights (IPRs) as part of a broader inquiry relating to technology transfer and institutional innovation. First, we examine whether climate and energy-related partnerships focus on technical implementation of existing technologies, technology transfer, knowledge dissemination, and/or innovation. Then we analyse their success in tackling the problems they were set up to tackle. To achieve this end, the chapter draws on a multi-year research project on the emergence and effectiveness of PPPs for sustainable development that utilizes a large database, the Global Sustainability Partnerships Database (GSPD), to understand better the role and relevance of PPPs in contemporary global environmental governance.[13] The empirical focus in this chapter is on partnerships focusing on climate change and/or energy.

The chapter first defines partnerships as a case of network governance and briefly discusses the origins of partnerships for sustainable development. We then provide an overview of the status of technology innovation and technology transfer in multilateral environmental governance. This provides important context for the next section, an empirical analysis of the performance of PPPs in the climate and energy sub-field. Three findings from our study are particularly noteworthy. First, neither technological nor social innovation is a dominant function of climate and energy partnerships, despite the transformative potential of such innovations for sustainability. Second, even accepting any stakeholder from a developing country as representative of the poor countries, significant issues pertain to the democratic legitimacy of individual partnerships, the technologies transferred, the resulting innovation regimes, and their overall orchestration by the UNCSD. Third, the climate and energy partnerships surveyed here show alarmingly low levels of potential effectiveness. After these findings are presented and supported, the chapter concludes with lessons learned and suggestions for improving partnerships as an instrument of change as envisioned by the 2030 Agenda.

I PPPs and the Transformation of World Politics: Context and Definitions

A *Partnerships as Networks*

Environmental policy, both domestic and international, traditionally falls under the authority of the government. However, in recent years, this state-centric conception of environmental governance is increasingly contested. Scholars have highlighted the

[12] Joseph E. Stiglitz, *Knowledge as a Global Public Good, in* GLOBAL PUBLIC GOODS: INTERNATIONAL COOPERATION IN THE 21ST CENTURY 308 (Inge Kaul et al. eds., 1999).

[13] *See generally* PUBLIC–PRIVATE PARTNERSHIPS FOR SUSTAINABLE DEVELOPMENT: EMERGENCE, INFLUENCE AND LEGITIMACY (Philip Pattberg et al. eds., 2012).

transformation of a territorial-based global order to one of multiple spheres of authority in flexible and issue-specific arrangements.[14] Mirroring debates about the organizational transformation of the modern nation state, theorists of international relations have begun to reflect on the changing nature of the state system itself.[15] One central empirical observation is the emergence of networked forms of organization that operate under a different logic compared to other ideal types of social organization, such as markets and hierarchies.[16] Whereas in the domestic context network governance has been discussed as a complementary and gradual innovation of older forms of policy making (for example, corporatism), networks at the transnational and global level have been largely conceptualized as new forms of governance that would overcome the limitations of traditional top-down intergovernmental policy making.[17]

Within the field of political science, broadly speaking, networks are understood as interactions of organizational actors. Consequently, the concept of policy networks refers to the production of public policies through a relatively stable and defined interaction of actors within a policy field. Policy networks are analysed as polycentric governance arrangements that integrate the competing interests of actors within a horizontal structure. This conceptualization stands in contrast to older conceptions, according to which the formulation and implementation of public policies are the sole responsibility of governments (in their attempt to transform the preferences of voters into adequate political programs) and the organized interests of non-state actors are recognized only insofar as they address the public decision-making process.

The policy network approach reflects the transformation of policy making in modern societies. It analyses the emergence of network governance as a reaction to a number of interconnected trends, including neo-liberal globalization and the resulting narratives that identify public and private interests, the increase in sub-systemic autonomy within the formerly monolithic nation state, the increasingly versatile demands from the state resulting in more state functions and its accompanying bureaucracies, as well as the growth and further differentiation of civil society.

Public–private partnerships as a form of network governance are by no means a novel phenomenon. Before taking centre stage in scholarship on global governance and international relations in the early 2000s, PPPs enjoyed sustained attention in the domestic policy context, in particular in health and infrastructure. PPPs were actively promoted as an instrument to increase governance effectiveness as part of the "New Public Management" paradigm of the early 1980s. Since the 1990s, PPPs have also been promoted at the international level as instruments for good governance and deliberative democracy,

[14] James N. Rosenau, Along the Domestic-Foreign Frontier: Exploring Governance in a Turbulent World 467 (1997); Philipp Pattberg & Johannes Stripple, *Beyond the Public and Private Divide: Remapping Transnational Climate Governance in the 21st Century*, 8 Int'l Envtl. Agreements: Pol., L. & Econ. 367–388 (2008).

[15] Alexander Wendt, *Anarchy is What States Make of it: The Social Construction of Power Politics*, 46 Int'l Org. 391–425 (1992); Mark W. Zacher, *The Decaying Pillars of the Westphalian Temple: Implications for International Order and Governance*, *in* Governance Without Government: Order and Change in World Politics 58 (James N. Rosenau & Ernst-Otto Czempiel eds., 1992).

[16] Gráinne de Búrca, *New Governance and Experimentalism*, 2010 Wisc. L. Rev. 227, 232 (2010).

[17] Tanja A. Börzel, *Organizing Babylon – On the Different Conceptions of Policy Networks*, 76 Pub. Admin. 253–273 (1998); *see also* Margaret Chon, *PPPs in Global IP (public–private partnerships in global intellectual property)*, *in* Methods and Perspectives in Intellectual Property 296 (Graeme B. Dinwoodie ed., 2013).

with the additional aim to increase the legitimacy and effectiveness of multilateral policies. Mirroring many aspects of the debate about new public management at the domestic level, the concept of network governance has been recently transferred to the global level. The appropriateness of the network approach in this context is frequently justified by referring to the changing capacity of states to govern effectively under the constraints of de-nationalization and accelerating globalization.[18] However, the growing literature on PPPs suffers from conceptual confusion, rival definitions, disparate research traditions, and oftentimes an implicit normative and value-laden agenda of promoting partnerships. This state of conceptual vagueness has led some scholars to question the usefulness of the concept and to dismiss the term PPP as empty and misleading[19]. While the conceptual broadness of this key term, with its multiple uses, has hampered knowledge accumulation on the subject, it has not prevented a diverse literature on PPPs as novel global governance instruments. Partnerships, both national and transnational, have been analysed as hybrid governance arrangements for the provision of collective goods that contribute to the transformation of political authority from government and public actors towards non-state actors, such as business and non-governmental organizations (NGOs)[20].

In this chapter, we build upon a scholarly tradition that understands public–private, multi-stakeholder partnerships for sustainable development as a form of global governance beyond traditional forms of international cooperation. Most scholars agree on several features that constitute PPPs.[21] Important characteristics include:

- transnationality (involving cross-border interactions and non-state relations);
- public policy objectives (as opposed to public bads or exclusively private goods); and
- a network structure (coordination by participating actors rather than coordination by a central hierarchy).

While this common understanding is quite narrow, it still covers a wide range of phenomena. For example, the functions of partnerships are varied and include agenda setting, rule-making and standard setting, advocacy, implementation, and service provision.[22] Furthermore, PPPs appear in different sectors such as sustainable development, health, human rights development, security, and finance. They vary in degree of institutionalization and permanence. In the public health sector, as described by several chapters in this volume, partnerships have enabled greater accessibility of treatments at lower prices. Finally, partnerships have different geographical scopes from the local, national, and regional, to the global level.

[18] Michael Zürn, REGIEREN JENSEITS DES NATIONALSTAATES (1998); THE EMERGENCE OF PRIVATE AUTHORITY IN GLOBAL GOVERNANCE 1–248 (Rodney B. Hall & Thomas Biersteker eds., 2002).

[19] Derick W. Brinkerhoff & Jennifer M. Brinkerhoff, *Public–Private Partnerships: Perspectives on Purposes, Publicness, and Good Governance*, 31 PUB. ADMIN. AND DEV. 2–14 (2011).

[20] Marco Schäferhoff et al., *Transnational Public–Private Partnerships in International Relations: Making Sense of Concepts, Research Frameworks, and Results*, 11 INT'L STUD. REV. 451–474, 455 (2009); Pattberg & Stripple, *supra* note 14.

[21] Schäferhoff, *supra* note 20, at 455.

[22] Jens Marten, *Multi-stakeholder Partnerships-Future Models of Multilateralism?*, FRIEDRICH-EBERT-STIFTUNG: OCCASIONAL PAPERS BERLIN (January 2007), http://library.fes.de/pdf-files/iez/04244.pdf; *See generally* Benedicte Bull & Desmond McNeill, DEVELOPMENT ISSUES IN GLOBAL GOVERNANCE: PUBLIC-PRIVATE PARTNERSHIPS AND MARKET MULTILATERALISM (2007).

B *The Origins of WSSD Partnerships in Environmental Governance*

Partnerships for sustainable development were defined as "voluntary multi-stakeholder initiatives, which contribute to the implementation of inter-governmental commitments" in Agenda 21, as well as in the Programme for the Further Implementation of Agenda 21 and in the Johannesburg Plan of Implementation. A set of guidelines (the Bali Guiding Principles) were developed, defining partnerships within the UN system.[23] The definitions of partnerships as voluntary implementation instruments as well as the Bali Guidelines were both agreed upon in the preparatory process to the 2002 WSSD.[24] These negotiations involved not only delegates and UN representatives, but also non-state actors. The resulting conceptualization was a compromise; the guidelines were non-binding criteria that lacked screening, monitoring, or reporting procedures. No central body was designated to oversee the evolving partnerships regime. Nonetheless, partnerships became an official part of the UN environmental governance system once they were accepted as an official outcome of the WSSD, despite opposition from several major groups (particularly environmental NGOs and trade unions) and country delegations (particularly those from poor countries).

Although the term partnership can be found in UN documents at least since 1992, partnerships were only considered as an official outcome of an intergovernmental process in the preparatory phase of the WSSD, because pressure to produce a concrete deliverable at the WSSD in Johannesburg was mounting.[25] Shortly after the United Nations Department for Economic and Social Affairs (UNDESA) proposed non-binding outcomes in the form of partnerships as a possible outcome, "the US expressed appreciation for [them] and called for "space" at the WSSD to allow for related dialogues."[26] The concept had earlier been developed by UNDESA to increase NGO involvement and reflect on a past decade of environmental governance. But most importantly, partnerships were meant to break through existing donor fatigue: as reported by one UNDESA representative, "[e]very responsibility was being put at the feet of the governments. There was a strong push that this [responsibility to implement] should be shared."[27]

During the run-up to the WSSD conference, the United States and business and industry representatives explicitly supported a vaguely defined partnership process, which raised suspicions with NGO and other country representatives. The issues were numerous: for instance, European Union delegations and environmental NGOs were worried that partnerships could become an instrument to repudiate international environmental agreements. Another concern of the NGO community was the increasing business involvement in the UN and the expected green-/blue-washing of corporate activities. Some delegations had started to perceive partnerships as a threat to their sovereignty.

[23] United Nations Brochure, *Partnerships for Sustainable Development*, U.N. Doc. DPI/2323 — 03-46703 (August 2003), www.un.org/esa/sustdev/partnerships/publications/brochure_E.pdf. The Bali Guiding Principles are criteria that guide the formation of the UNCSD partnerships agreed at the Fourth Preparatory Committee Meeting to the WSSD, in Bali (27 May–7 June 2002).

[24] The World Summit on Sustainable Development (WSSD or Earth Summit 2002) took place in Johannesburg, South Africa, from 26 August to 4 September 2002.

[25] The final decision of PrepCom IV mentions partnerships as "events" to take place before the summit.

[26] *Earth Negotiations Bulletin- Summary of the Second Session of the Preparatory Committee for the World Summit on Sustainable Development*, International Institute for Substantial Development (Feb 11, 2002) www.iisd.ca/vol22/enb2219e.html.

[27] Interview with a UNDESA representative at the time of the WSSD in New York (May 2007).

Developing country delegations (particularly China, Indonesia, and Malaysia) had become increasingly worried about the possibility that developmental projects within their national borders would pick and choose which international or national NGOs to work with. As a result, some delegations raised questions about non-state actor participation.

The framework that was ultimately negotiated was meant to address various governmental concerns in order to make partnerships an agreeable outcome to all parties involved. The resulting Bali Guidelines establish the framework that guides the arrangement and registration of partnerships with the UNCSD. These guidelines consisted of conflicting visions regarding the role, function, and nature of partnerships; while warning about potential negative effects, they failed to address and avoid them[28]. For instance, PPPs were to complement inter-governmental agreements, but the Summit failed to produce any binding agreements, even on the most pressing issues such as climate change, or biodiversity governance. It was not clear whether their main goal was to address the implementation deficit, or to create more participatory processes. By listing various expectations in their framing, the guidelines depicted sustainability partnerships in an ideal form, almost impossible to reach with their actual capacity. Most importantly, the partnerships process remained non-binding. Because they were not accompanied by a strong screening process or a monitoring mechanism, effective implementation of sustainability principles was unlikely.

Thus in the various preparatory meetings for the WSSD, partnerships were defined, negotiated, and re-constructed such that they would be acceptable to all parties involved. In this process, conflicts about who the relevant stakeholders are (inclusive or not of businesses and NGOs), what the aim of partnerships should be (implementation versus participation), and how they should be screened and monitored were not addressed head-on. Nonetheless, with the Bali Guidelines, partnerships have been defined as voluntary multi-stakeholder initiatives to achieve the sustainability goals agreed upon through the inter-governmental system. One of the main expectations from these new governance mechanisms was to create win-win situations wherein the interests of all actors would be served. This has already made partnerships desirable for most parties, because staying outside of these networks meant 'not to win.'

Social innovation is at the heart of global environmental governance and it is also intricately related to sustainability partnerships. Various academic disciplines have recently studied this relationship[29] revealing how the UN's focus on partnership and technology transfer as major sustainability goals prioritizes a particular type of partnership and innovation over others. For instance, partnerships have been regarded as a social and legal innovation of transnational governance since Agenda 21, as they allow for stakeholder involvement, and address the participation deficit. However, there are various complications in the implementation of this principle: The participation principle is only nominally operative in partnerships. Having a local partner from a recipient country is

[28] Ayşem Mert, *Hybrid Governance Mechanisms as Political Instruments: The Case of Sustainability, Partnerships*, 14 Int'l Envtl. Agreements 225–244 (2013).

[29] John D. Wolpert, *Breaking Out of the Innovation Box*, 80 Harv. Bus. Rev. 76–83 (2002);
John Adeoti et al., *Biotechnology R&D Partnership for Industrial Innovation in Nigeria*, 25 Technovation 349–365 (2005); Dominique Kleyn, et al., *Partnership and Innovation in the Life Sciences*, 11 Int'l J. Innovation Mgmt. 323–330 (2007).

regarded as sufficient condition to deem the partnership democratic, even though this does not ensure the social acceptability of the technologies transferred. Furthermore, any stakeholder from a developing country can represent recipient countries, even if this partner has no connection to the communities in question. The UN narratives on innovation and partnerships do not ensure legitimate participation practices, and in extreme cases they assume a false singularity of opinion among all stakeholders in a community, all communities in a country, or across countries. In sum, technology transfer in sustainable development potentially results in partnerships that reflect the already existing power inequalities, making innovation work for those who have something to offer: "If you don't have some money on the table, some time, and expertise, you are not a partner."[30]

II Technology Transfer in Multilateral Environmental Governance

One of the earliest references to the role of IPRs in environmental governance is made in Agenda 21, a non-binding, voluntarily implemented action plan for sustainable development, adopted by more than 178 governments at the United Nations Conference on Environment and Development held in Rio de Janerio, in 1992 (the Rio Summit).[31] These references can be found in a chapter devoted to *Transfer of Environmentally Sound Technology, Cooperation and Capacity-building.*[32] In this context, the transfer of technology and access to state-of-the-art technologies is regarded as a significant goal for sustainable development, for all countries. This foundational text foreshadows the dominant framing of IPRs in environmental governance. Technology transfer is central to this framing, which can be summarised as follows:

- It is recognised that "international business is an important vehicle for technology transfer," and advised that the power of such knowledge should be combined with "local innovations to generate alternative technologies."[33]
- The underlying necessity for technology transfer is explained as to enable developing countries "to make more rational technology choices," which can be achieved by providing access to technologies selected by the global North.[34]
- IPRs are regarded as rights that need protecting from abuse (mentioned three times).[35]

[30] Kent Buse, *Governing Public–Private Infectious Disease Partnerships*, 10 Brown J. World Aff. 232, 225–242 (2004).

[31] The United Nations Conference on Environment and Development (UNCED, also known as the Rio Summit, Rio Conference, and Earth Summit) was a major United Nations conference held in Rio de Janeiro from 3 to 14 June 1992.

[32] *U.N. Documents: Gathering a Body of Global Agreements*, U.N. Agenda 21 Chapter 34 ¶ 11, www.un-documents.net/agenda21.htm [hereinafter UN Documents]. IPRs are also mentioned elsewhere, for instance in the decisions following the Montreal Protocol of 1987 in a generic fashion, but are not decided upon in these contexts. *See* United Nations Environment Programme – Ozone Secretariat, Handbook for the Montreal Protocol on Substances that Deplete the Ozone Layer, UNEP/ Earthprint (2006).

[33] UN Documents, *supra* note 32, at ¶ 11.

[34] UN Documents, *supra* note 32, at ¶ 12.

[35] UN Documents, *supra* note 32, at ¶ 18. The document does not determine, however, what the threat is or from where it originates.

- In order to promote and support "access to transfer of technology" to developing countries, Agenda 21 sets the goal of facilitating and financing "environmentally sound technologies and corresponding know-how, [...] on favourable terms, including on concessional and preferential terms [...] for the implementation of Agenda 21," and "to promote long-term technological partnerships between holders of environmentally sound technologies and potential users."[36]
- In terms of policy measures, the suggested action is the Northern countries to purchase the necessary patents and licences "on commercial terms for their transfer to developing countries on non-commercial terms as part of development cooperation" or even to promote acquisition through compulsory licensing to prevent their abuse.[37]
- Finally, regarding the management of technology transfer, it is emphasised that "the possibility of assigning this activity to already existing regional organizations should be fully explored before creating entirely new institutions, and funding of this activity through public–private partnerships should also be explored, as appropriate."[38]

The main aim of the various texts produced at the 1992 Rio Summit was to consolidate the ideological premises of sustainable development across the globe. The political function of Agenda 21, in particular, was to translate the global goals agreed upon at the Rio Summit into blueprints for local and national policy. To do this, it was critical to assure the private sector that the devices through which corporations exerted power (e.g., patents, liberal trade regimes, and commitment to growth) would not be threatened by the newly emerging sustainability regimes. Framing the roles of IPRs and technology transfer in this fashion allowed for a harmonious resolution of the contradictory goals of infinite economic growth with ecological limits. On the one hand, the technological know-how would be shared with the so-called developing countries through mechanisms such as compulsory licensing, which is an arguably bold and unprecedented reference in an international environmental text. On the other hand, various agencies and organizations in the international system were to be mobilised so that the property regimes would not be challenged by this action.

Following the Rio Summit, the role of IPRs in technology transfer was framed accordingly in both trade and environmental negotiations. The general framing of IPRs was fixed to the logic of IPRs' "dual role" in (i) fostering sustainability-focused technological innovation and (ii) its transfer.[39] Furthermore, the 1995 agreement on Trade-Related Aspects of Intellectual Property Rights (TRIPS) sets the objective that "the protection and enforcement of intellectual property rights should contribute to the promotion of technological innovation and to the transfer and dissemination of technology, to the mutual advantage of producers and users of technological knowledge and in a manner conducive to social and economic welfare, and to a balance of rights and obligations."[40]

[36] UN Documents, *supra* note 32, at ¶ 14.
[37] UN Documents, *supra* note 32, at ¶ 18.
[38] UN Documents, *supra* note 32, at ¶ 26.
[39] Ahmed Abdel-Latif et al., Overcoming the Impasse on Intellectual Property and Climate Change at the UNFCCC: A Way Forward (*International Centre for Trade and Sustainable Development*, Policy Brief No. 11, 2011), http://scholarship.law.duke.edu/faculty_scholarship/2480.
[40] Agreement on Trade-Related Aspects of Intellectual Property Rights (April 15, 1994), Marrakesh Agreement Establishing the World Trade Organization, Annex 1C, Legal Instruments – Result of the Uruguay Rounds 33 I.L.M. 81 (1994), www.wto.org/english/docs_e/legal_e/27-trips_01_e.htm.

Agenda 21 itself does not provide an explicit blueprint to achieve this ambitious mixture of policy goals with regard to technological innovation and transfer, but rather suggests the prioritisation of the existing inter-governmental institutions and the exploration of PPPs as another means of policy implementation. Thus, the link between partnerships and IPRs was established at the same time as the founding of United Nations Framework Convention on Climate Change (UNFCCC) and as sustainable development was becoming the dominant discourse in global environmental governance. This point is important in understanding how partnerships have become a highly visible and highly discussed element of global sustainability governance.

As noted in the previous section, transnational PPPs have multiplied, especially since the 2002 Johannesburg Summit. And recently they have become an official action point for the UN in the context of Sustainable Development Goals (SDG), with SDG #17 aiming to "revitalize the global partnership for sustainable development."[41] In policy and academic debates alike, partnerships are promoted as solutions to deadlocked intergovernmental negotiations, ineffective treaties, overly bureaucratic international organizations, and many other real or perceived problems of regulatory coordination among states. Since their conception, partnerships have become a political process wherein opposing rationales are simultaneously upheld, whether the political rationales of the left and right, or the economic rationales of public and private[42]. However, systematic evidence of the impacts of transnational PPPs is scarce and the broader consequences of outsourcing and privatizing global and transnational environmental governance are not well understood. Most importantly, the strategy of introducing partnerships as a policy solution to conflicting interests and goals has not been assessed in a systematic fashion.

To summarize, there are two problems emerging from the particular way partnerships emerged around technology transfer issues: First, it reinforced the highly selective and partial relationship between innovation and international mandates, which has been observed also in TRIPS and the CBD[43]: Already in 1993, the Bellagio Declaration noted that those "who do not fit this model –custodians of tribal culture and medical knowledge, collectives practicing traditional artistic and musical forms, or peasant cultivators of valuable seed varieties, for example–are denied intellectual property protection."[44] Secondly, the win-win narrative, often used to legitimate PPPs, can have questionable and undesirable consequences.[45] Specifically, it prioritizes two issues on the UN's development agenda: The first one was institutional mainstreaming across the globe, a "one size fits all" solution regardless of historical differences. This was neatly named *institutional capacity building*, suggesting a lack in some places *vis-à-vis* others. The second issue was technology development and transfer. In a globalizing world, where capital and

[41] Sustainable Development Goals, *Goal 17: Revitalize the Global Partnership for Sustainable Development*, U.N. Dep't of Econ. and Soc. Affairs (Sept.29, 2017), www.un.org/sustainabledevelopment/globalpartnerships/.

[42] *See generally* Niels Åkerstrøm Andersen, Partnerships: Machines of Possibilities (2008).

[43] Eric Deibel & Ayşem Mert, *Partnerships and Miracle Crops: On Open Access and the Commodification of Plant Varieties*, 16 Asian Biotechnology and Dev. Rev., 1–33 (2014).

[44] *Statement of the Bellagio Conference on Cultural Agency/Cultural Authority: Politics and Poetics of Intellectual Property in the Post-Colonial Era*, IPCA (March 11, 1993) http://case.edu/affil/sce/BellagioDec.html [hereinafter Bellagio Statement].

[45] Ayşem Mert, Environmental Governance Through Partnerships: A Discourse Theoretical Study 230–249 (2015).

resources were regarded as flexible and transferable across markets, the sphere of environmental conservation provided a puzzling impediment: the most accessible 'resources' for energy production for the historically impoverished countries were the fossil fuels. Their governments now argued for their sovereign rights on these resources, which resulted in a fragmented climate/energy governance and difficult climate negotiations. With their win-win strategies, partnerships (in principle) would reduce the poverty levels in these areas by providing them with certain specific technologies. In return, the so-called developing countries would become testing grounds or resource providers or perhaps simply open their markets to some new products or technologies of the North.

This is not to suggest that the win-win solutions always work against the recipients. Many partnerships do introduce technologies that are necessary and needed by the communities that are on the receiving side of the transfer. Particularly when diverse sets of local stakeholders are involved, partnerships seem to find the most appropriate technologies that give communities more autonomy in its use and maintenance.[46] Examples of such technology transfer projects include the re-/introduction of indigenous technologies or water harvesting techniques to increase the resilience of communities at risk.

The point remains, however, that corporate involvement often assumes a neutral, if not benevolent, role to achieve the SDGs (and their predecessor Millennium Development Goals). Technology transfer is a central part of this image but it should not be taken for granted. For instance, many partnerships operate as platforms for controversial technologies allowing for a rebranding of nuclear energy, PVC, water purification chemicals, and so on.[47] Some instances of such involvement include Dow Chemical's sponsoring the Blue Planet Run to "bring safe drinking water to 1.2 billion people" (UNOP 2010), Coca Cola Foundation and Procter and Gamble both promoting not only a water disinfectant but also behavioural techniques directed towards improved hygiene in water deprived poor countries, or Royal Dutch Shell's membership in the Clean Air Initiative to enhance air quality in Asian cities.[48]

With this important background and context, the next section turns to our empirical findings.

III Empirical Analysis of WSSD Partnerships

In this section, we utilize a multi-year research project on the emergence and effectiveness of PPPs for sustainable development and the corresponding large database, the Global Sustainability Partnerships Database (GSPD) to understand the role and relevance of public–private partnerships in contemporary global environmental governance. The empirical analysis focuses on two sets of questions. First, we ask whether partnerships working on climate change and energy address issues of innovation and technology transfer in developing countries. For this to be the case, climate and energy partnerships would likely (i) implement on-the-ground projects that aim to transfer technology or

[46] Ayşem Mert & Eleni Dellas, *Assessing the Legitimacy of Technology Transfer Through Partnerships for Sustainable Development in the Water Sector*, *in* Public–Private Partnerships for Sustainable Development: Emergence, Influence and Legitimacy 209 (Philip Pattberg et al. eds., 2012).

[47] Mert, *supra* note 28; Mert and Dellas, *supra* note 46.

[48] CAI-Asia, Clean Air Initiative for Asian Cities (2010).

produce/disseminate knowledge; (ii) in poorer countries; (iii) with stakeholders from both rich and poor countries; (iv) and have legally binding contracts between partners.

Second, we scrutinize the overall effectiveness of climate change and energy partnerships. To do this, we use the GSPD, which was developed between 2006 and 2009 at the Institute for Environmental Studies, VU University Amsterdam. Based on data provided by the UNCSD, extensive desk studies, and numerous expert interviews, the GSPD provides information on descriptive categories such as partnership name, existence of website, number of countries in which partnerships implement their activities, number of and type of partners, type of lead partners, area of policy implementation and functions performed, geographical scope, duration, date of establishment, and resources reported to be required for each of the 330 partnerships registered with the UNCSD at the time the coding was completed in 2009. In addition, the GSPD also contains information about individual partnership output, that is, the concrete activities and programmes of partnerships for sustainable development. All data was coded by a team of researchers for whom an inter-rater reliability check has been performed. This chapter focuses on the general sample and the selection of partnerships that focus on climate and energy related goals of global sustainability governance.

The GSPD thus focuses on two effectiveness-related dependent variables: *global governance deficits* and *function-output fit*. We briefly explain these two concepts: The assessment of the overall effectiveness and influence of the partnership regime is based on three hypothetical *global governance deficits*[49] that partnerships are supposed to address: the regulatory deficit, the implementation deficit, and participatory deficit. First, partnerships are expected to confront the regulatory deficit in current sustainability governance by providing avenues for cooperation and joint problem-solving in areas where intergovernmental regulation is largely non-existent. A second deficit that partnerships are believed to fill is an implementation deficit in sustainability governance. That is, partnerships could help implement intergovernmental regulations that do exist but that are only poorly implemented, if at all. Third, partnerships are often expected to assist in solving a participation deficit in global governance. In this view, intergovernmental negotiations are seen as dominated by powerful governments and international organizations, while partnerships, by contrast, might ensure higher participation of less privileged actors, including voices from youth, the poor, women, indigenous people, and civil society at large. Increased participation from such groups is viewed as needed to improve the implementation of international agreements and to strengthen the overall legitimacy, accountability, and democratic quality of current governance systems.

After assessing whether PPPs contribute to addressing existing governance deficits, the GSPD was also constructed to evaluate *function-output fit*, i.e., the fit between a concrete function performed by a partnership and the output it creates (i.e., measurable results such as organizing training programs, publishing reports, developing curricula, and/or building infrastructure). While a more direct assessment of impacts would be preferable, no such assessments currently exist due to the methodological challenges involved. However, by comparing what the partnerships claim as their goal and function with their actual activities and products (output), the function-output fit reveals the accuracy and consistency of these declarations. The underlying assumption is that partnerships

[49] Haas, *supra* note 10.

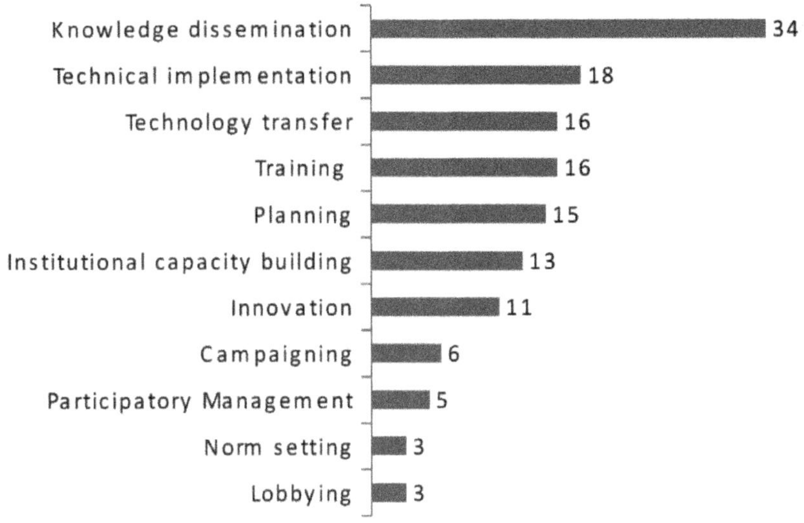

Figure 13.1. Goals and functions of climate and energy partnerships.

that have a good fit between function and output will be better equipped to have a positive effect on environmental indicators in the end.

To illustrate this reasoning, a partnership that claims to be first and foremost about implementation (e.g., through building new infrastructure) would be expected to have measurable output in this area, for example concrete infrastructure programs. A partnership that aims at knowledge transfer would in contrast be expected to have output in the field of research/publications, communications, or training. If the function and observed output are not aligned, conclusions about reaching the explicit goals can be drawn.

A *Innovation and Technology Transfer*

Among the 330 partnerships in GSPD, sixty partnerships focus on energy and climate issues. Approximately 56 per cent of partnerships focus on innovation, technology transfer, technical implementation, and knowledge dissemination.

The distribution of these functions reveals a concerning picture. On the one hand, the focus of climate and energy partnerships is more often on transforming infrastructure and disseminating knowledge. On the other hand, this transformation does not necessarily prioritize innovation or producing new knowledge. In fact, only eleven partnerships in this group aim at innovation, whereas others have the goal of disseminating already existing ideas, knowledge systems, and technologies.

In this context, it is necessary to ask if this apparent dependency for rights, technologies, and episteme is further exacerbated with the inclusion of business and industry in the partnerships. We have argued elsewhere[50] that the decision-making power of non-state actors as partners is rather limited, although their practices transform global governance in indirect ways. These indirect influences are important and at times they reveal intentions of the actors.

[50] Pattberg et al. 2012, *supra* note 13; Mert 2015, *supra* note 7.

For instance, voluntary and flexible governance mechanisms and commitments via partnerships can be organized on various issues by various actor constellations adhering to a number of internationally accepted norms. Equally telling are the omissions: At what level partnerships are not formed, what actors do not get involved, and which issues they do not address. The fact that partnerships do *not* emerge on indigenous and non-technological/low-tech ways of producing energy and generating a low-carbon future can therefore be contrasted to their more obvious technology transfer and knowledge dissemination focus.

Furthermore, the UNCSD is not the only platform in which climate and energy innovation would be transnationally governed. It is therefore of critical importance to study some of these cases in a more in-depth fashion in qualitative case studies. Although this qualitative assessment is beyond the purview of this chapter, some of our findings regarding the prominence of the business partners in the UNCSD climate and energy sample are set forth in greater detail in the next section.

B *Effectiveness*

In terms of partnership effectiveness, our findings are mixed. Forty per cent of climate and energy partnerships are not active or have produced no measurable output at all. Among the thirty-six partnerships that produce output, 42 per cent have a complete fit between their promised function and produced output, and 25 per cent have partial fit.

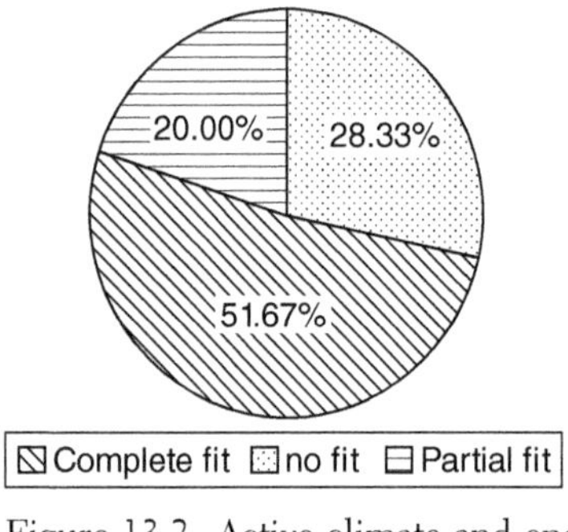

Figure 13.2. Active climate and energy partnership registered with CSD.

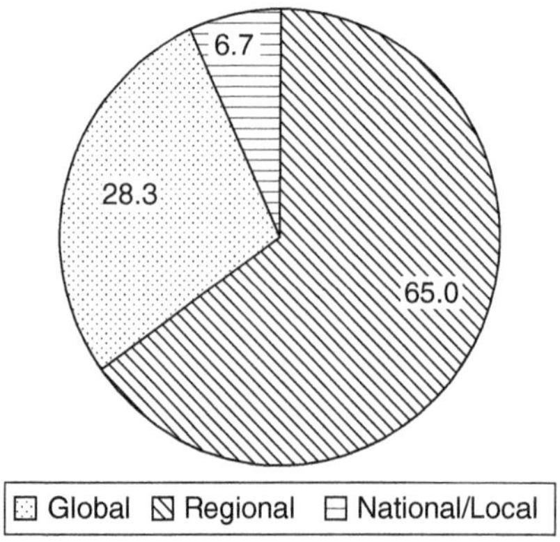

Figure 13.3. General characteristics of sample.

More specifically, sixteen of these partnerships focus on technology transfer. Ten of these sixteen partnerships have a partial or complete fit between the output they produced and their indicated goals of technology transfer.

The participatory/democratic deficit refers to the problem that those who are affected by decisions are rarely and very selectively included in the making of these decisions. Two indicators are used here to investigate the contribution of climate partnerships to closing the participatory/democratic deficit in global environmental governance. For partnerships to play a role in this area, we would expect at least

(1) a balanced distribution of *lead partners* (i.e., partners with a specific role to manage, organize and implement the partnership) from industrialised and developing countries; and from state and non-state actors;
(2) the presence of partners from developing countries and from among underrepresented groups.

This would show that the goal of addressing the participatory deficit is achieved at least to some degree through the inclusion of those who are often excluded. In the overall sample, neither of these expectations was found to be the case. Lead actors are often governments from the industrialized countries, or actors from the public sector at large (e.g., intergovernmental organizations), whereas the underrepresented groups remain excluded. Among partnerships focusing only on climate and energy policies, a similar picture emerges with regard to the participatory deficit. The first aspect that falls under the heading of participation is the concrete distribution of lead partners among state and non-state actors (see Figure 13.5). In short, climate partnerships are predominantly led by state actors, UN organizations, or other intergovernmental agencies, accounting for 60.2 per cent of all partnerships in the sample. While state involvement might be considered a positive sign in other issue areas, the climate change governance arena now critically depends on the involvement of non-state actors to implement the Paris Agreement. We therefore would expect a broader representation of these actors in the actual implementation stages.

This observation is comparable to the overall WSSD sample.

What is noteworthy in this context, however, is the level of business involvement: Climate and energy partnerships have a much larger number of business actors as lead

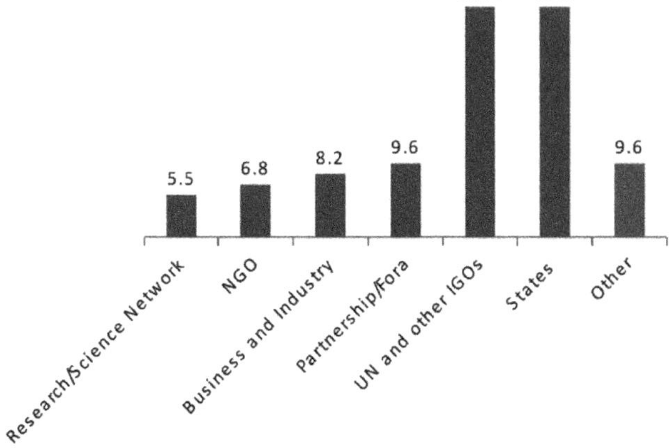

Figure 13.4. Lead partners among state and non-state actors.

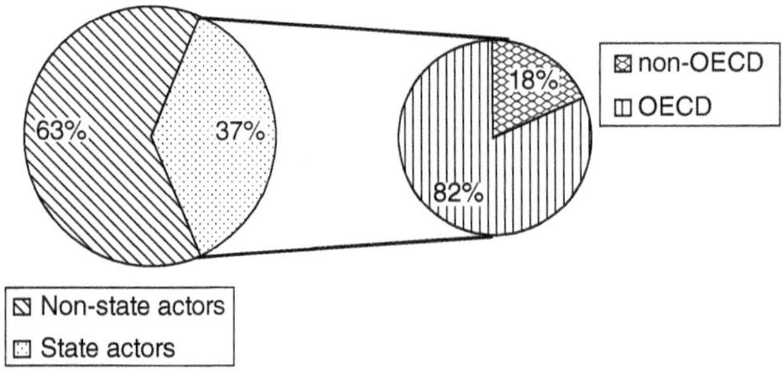

Figure 13.5. Lead partners in climate and energy partnerships.

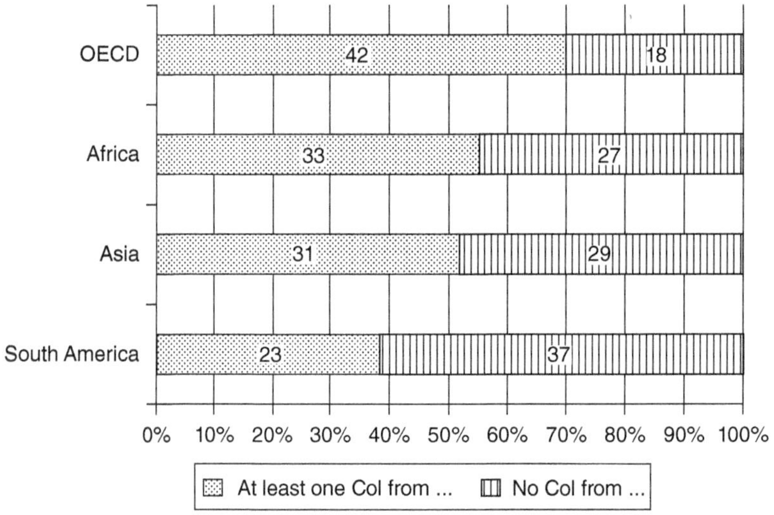

Figure 13.6. Countries of implementation.

partners (8.2 per cent) compared to the overall sample (3.2 per cent). Furthermore, analyzing the geographical origin of lead partners in climate and energy partnerships (see Figure 13.6), we observe that a majority of state-led partnerships have an OECD country (state agency or government) as a lead partner. Inversely, if the lead partner is a government, 82 per cent of the time it is an OECD country, demonstrating the dominance of Northern state actors.

Finally, among climate and energy partnerships, the group of countries that make up most of the implementation area is the OECD. This observation calls into question a number of assumptions frequently encountered in the literature. Far from being operative in those regions with the most pressing needs, partnerships seem to favor implementation contexts that are characterized by institutional stability and the rule-of-law.

Conclusions

Sustainability partnerships take on an essential role within the context of managing the many different kinds of resources that have become market-based, including access to technological knowledge integral to sustainable development. The governance of climate change and energy is being shaped and re-oriented to refer to very different sets of activities, which is highly dependent on forms of hybrid governance in the context of the UN mandates on climate and energy, intellectual property, and environmental issues.

In this chapter, we have examined whether public–private partnerships focus on technical implementation of existing technologies, technology transfer, knowledge dissemination, and innovation. We ask whether such partnerships are effective in tackling the problems they were set up to tackle. To this end, the chapter utilized a multi-year research project on the emergence and effectiveness of PPPs for sustainable development and the corresponding large-N database (GSPD) to understand the role and relevance of PPPs in contemporary global environmental governance. The empirical focus of this chapter was on partnerships working in the climate change and/or energy field.

As stated in the chapter's introduction, three issues are of particular relevance. First, despite the transformative potential of technological and social innovations for sustainability, neither type of innovation is a dominant function (at least so far) of climate and energy partnerships. Second, significant issues pertain to the democratic legitimacy of individual partnerships, the technologies transferred, the resulting innovation regimes, and their overall orchestration by the UNCSD. Third and finally, the climate and energy partnerships surveyed here show alarmingly low levels of potential effectiveness to date.

Recent and renewed attention to the partnership model in the climate governance arena can be found in the non-state actor zone of climate action to the UNFCCC, which is crowded with PPPs.[51] Thus it is important to suggest some institutional safeguards for minimum effectiveness and accountability.[52] We want to stress in particular the necessity for a critical screening mechanism that could ensure transparency, accountability, co-benefits, and fit with the 2030 Agenda, as well as ensuring adequate levels of participation for marginalized actors in this multi-stakeholder institutional framework. Finally, while perhaps politically challenging in the current situation, the possibility of deregistering failed and underperforming partnerships from the UN registries should be considered. These measures would ensure that the full potential of PPPs for sustainable development could still be reached in the 2030 Agenda process, which is still at its early stages of implementation.

References

Abdel-Latif, Ahmed, et al., *Overcoming the Impasse on Intellectual Property and Climate Change at the UNFCCC: A Way Forward (International Centre for Trade and Sustainable Development*, Policy Brief No. 11, 2011), http://scholarship.law.duke.edu/faculty_scholarship/2480.

Adeoti, John, et al., *Biotechnology R&D partnership for industrial innovation in Nigeria*, 25 TECHNOVATION 349–365 (2005).

Andersen, Niels Åkerstrøm, PARTNERSHIPS: MACHINES OF POSSIBILITIES (2008).

Bäckstrand, Karin, *Democratizing Global Environmental Governance? Stakeholder Democracy after the World Summit on Sustainable Development*, 12 EUROPEAN J. OF INT'L RELATIONS 467–498 (2006).

[51] Oscar Widerberg & Philipp Pattberg, *International Cooperative Initiatives in Global Climate Governance: Raising the Ambition Level or Delegitimizing the UNFCCC?*, 6 GLOBAL POL'Y 45–56 (2015).

[52] Oscar Widerberg & Johannes Stripple, *The Expanding Field of Corporate Initiatives for Decarbonization: A Review of Five Databases*, 7 WILEY INTERDISCIPLINARY REV.: CLIMATE CHANGE 486–500 (2016).

Benner, Thorsten et al., *Progress or Peril? Networks and Partnerships in Global Environmental Governance*, The Post-Johannesburg Agenda (2003).

Bitzer, Verena, et al., *Intersectoral Partnerships for a Sustainable Coffee Chain: Really Addressing Sustainability or Just Picking (Coffee) Cherries?*, 18 GLOBAL ENVTL. CHANGE 271–284 (2008).

Börzel, Tanja A., *Organizing Babylon—On the Different Conceptions of Policy Networks*, 76 PUB. ADMIN 253–273 (1998).

Brinkerhoff, Derick W. & Jennifer M. Brinkerhoff, *Public–Private Partnerships: Perspectives on Purposes, Publicness, and Good Governance*, 31 PUB. ADMIN. & DEVELOP. 2–14 (2011).

Bull, Benedict & Desmond McNeill, DEVELOPMENT ISSUES IN GLOBAL GOVERNANCE: PUBLIC–PRIVATE PARTNERSHIPS AND MARKET MULTILATERALISM (2007).

Buse, Kent, *Governing Public–Private Infectious Disease Partnerships*, 10 THE BROWN J. WORLD AFFAIRS 232 (2004).

CAI-Asia, Clean Air Initiative for Asian Cities (2010).

Chan, Sander, et al., *Reinvigorating International Climate Policy: A Comprehensive Framework for Effective Nonstate Action*, 6 GLOBAL POL'Y, 466–473 (2015).

Chon, Margaret, *PPPs in Global IP (public–private partnerships in global intellectual property), in* METHODS AND PERSPECTIVES IN INTELLECTUAL PROPERTY 296 (Graeme B. Dinwoodie ed., 2013).

Deibel, Eric & Ayşem Mert, *Partnerships and Miracle Crops: On Open Access and the Commodification of Plant Varieties*, 16 ASIAN BIOTECHNOLOGY AND DEVELOP REV. 1–33 (2014).

de Búrca, Gráinne, *New Governance and Experimentalism*, 2010 WISC. L. REV. 227 (2010).

Haas, Peter, *When Does Power Listen to Truth? A Constructive Approach to the Policy Process*, 11 J. EUROPEAN PUB. POL'Y, 569–592 (2004).

THE EMERGENCE OF PRIVATE AUTHORITY IN GLOBAL GOVERNANCE (Rodney B. Hall & Thomas Biersteker eds., 2002).

Earth Negotiations Bulletin – Summary of the Second Session of the Preparatory Committee for the World Summit on Sustainable Development, International Institute for Substantial Development www.iisd.ca/vol22/enb2219e.html (last visited Sept. 28, 2017).

Kleyn, Dominique, et al., *Partnership and Innovation in the Life Sciences*, 11 INT'L J. INNOVATION MGMT., 323–330 (2007).

Marten, Jens, *Multi-stakeholder Partnerships – Future Models of Multilateralism?*, Friedrich-Ebert-Stiftung, Occasional Papers Berlin, January 2007.

Meadowcroft, James, *Who Is in Charge Here? Governance for Sustainable Development in a Complex World*, 9 J. ENVTL. POL'Y & PLANNING, 299–314 (2007).

Mert, Ayşem, ENVIRONMENTAL GOVERNANCE THROUGH PARTNERSHIPS: A DISCOURSE THEORETICAL STUDY (2015).

Mert, Ayşem, *Hybrid Governance Mechanisms as Political Instruments: The Case of Sustainability, Partnerships*, 14 INT'L ENVTL. AGREEMENTS, 225–244 (2013).

Mert, Ayşem, *The Privatisation of Environmental Governance: On Myths, Forces of Nature, and Other Inevitabilities*, 21 ENVTL. VALUES, 475–498 (2012).

Mert, Ayşem & Eleni Dellas, *Assessing the Legitimacy of Technology Transfer Through Partnerships for Sustainable Development in the Water Sector, in* PUBLIC–PRIVATE PARTNERSHIPS FOR SUSTAINABLE DEVELOPMENT: EMERGENCE, INFLUENCE AND LEGITIMACY 209 (Philip Pattberg et al. eds., 2012).

Morsink, Karlijn et al., *Multi-Stakeholder Partnerships for Transfer of Environmentally Sound Technologies*, 39 ENERGY POL'Y 1–5 (2011).

Ottaway, Marina, *Corporation Goes Global: International Organizations, Nongovernmental Organization Networks, and Transnational Business*, 7 GLOBAL GOVERNANCE 265–292 (2001).

Pattberg, Philipp & Johannes Stripple, *Beyond the Public and Private Divide: Remapping Transnational Climate Governance in the 21st Century*, 8 INT'L ENVTL. AGREEMENTS: POLITICS, LAW AND ECONOMICS 367–388 (2008).

PUBLIC–PRIVATE PARTNERSHIPS FOR SUSTAINABLE DEVELOPMENT: EMERGENCE, INFLUENCE AND LEGITIMACY (Philip Pattberg et al. eds., 2012).

Reinicke, Wolfgang H., Global Public Policy: Governing Without Government? (1998).

Rosenau, James N., ALONG THE DOMESTIC-FOREIGN FRONTIER: EXPLORING GOVERNANCE IN A TURBULENT WORLD (1997).

Marco Schaferhoff et al., *Transnational Public–Private Partnerships in International Relations: Making Sense of Concepts, Research Frameworks, and Results*, 11 INT'L STUDIES REV., 451–474 (2009).

Statement of the Bellagio Conference on Cultural Agency/Cultural Authority: Politics and Poetics of Intellectual Property in the Post-Colonial Era, March 11, 1993, http://case.edu/affil/sce/BellagioDec.html.

Streck, Charlotte, *New Partnerships in Global Environmental Policy: The Clean Development Mechanism*, 13 J. ENVTL. & DEVELOP, 295–322 (2004).

United Nations [UN] Brochure, *Partnerships for Sustainable Development*, U.N. Doc. DPI/2323 – 03–46703 (August 2003), www.un.org/esa/sustdev/partnerships/publications/brochure_E.pdf.

UN Documents Cooperation Circles, Gathering a Body of Global Agreements, *Agenda 21 Chapter*, www.un-documents.net/agenda21.htm.

UN Environment Programme – Ozone Secretariat, Handbook for the Montreal Protocol on Substances that Deplete the Ozone Layer, UNEP/Earthprint (2006).

Wendt, Alexander, *Anarchy Is What States Make of It: The Social Construction of Power Politics*, 46 INT'L ORG. 391–425 (1992).

Widerberg, Oscar & Johannes Stripple, *The Expanding Field of Corporate Initiatives for Decarbonization: A Review of Five Databases*, 7 WILEY INTERDISCIPLINARY REVIEWS: CLIMATE CHANGE 486–500 (2016).

Widerberg, Oscar & Philipp Pattberg, *International Cooperative Initiatives in Global Climate Governance: Raising the Ambition Level or Delegitimizing the UNFCCC?*, 6 GLOBAL POL'Y, 45–56 (2015).

Wolpert, John D., *Breaking Out of the Innovation Box*, 80 HARV. BUS. REV., 76–83 (2002).

World Trade Organization, TRIPS: Agreement on Trade-Related Aspects of Intellectual Property Rights. Part I – General provisions and basic principles, WTO (Jan. 21, 2017), www.wto.org/english/tratop_e/trips_e/t_agm2_e.htm.

Zacher, Mark W., *The Decaying Pillars of the Westphalian Temple: Implications for International Order and Governance, in* GOVERNANCE WITHOUT GOVERNMENT: ORDER AND CHANGE IN WORLD POLITICS 58 (James N. Rosenau & Ernst-Otto Czempiel eds., 1992).

Zürn, Michael, REGIEREN JENSEITS DES NATIONALSTAATES (1998).

14 One Size Does Not Fit All: The Roles of the State and the Private Sector in the Governing Framework of Geographical Indications*

Irene Calboli and Delphine Marie-Vivien

Introduction

The book in which this chapter is published maps the contours of a variety of partnerships between public and private stakeholders – often referred to as public–private-partnerships (PPPs) – in several contexts, including education, health care and access to medicines, as well as agriculture clean energy and food security. In particular, the book's objective is to study the growing importance of shared governance between public and private entities as a suitable model through which a variety of stakeholders can collaborate more efficiently and achieve (more) successful outcomes. As a contribution to this effort, this chapter focuses on the role that the state, the private sector, and the relationship between them in building an optimal framework for governing geographical indications of origin (GIs). As this chapter describes, GIs are signs that are used to identify products that have a specific geographical origin and possess particular qualities or a reputation that are essentially attributable to that origin. Traditionally, GI protection has been justified both on the consumer information function of GIs as well as on the role of GIs as tools to incentivize local and rural development, most commonly in agriculture intensive countries.

Generally, national frameworks of governing GIs consists of the state and the private sector assuming different roles with respect to the stages of GI application, GI registration, and ensuring quality control and marketing of GI products. However, the level of involvement of the state and the private sector varies considerably across jurisdictions.[1] In some countries, like France and members of the European Union (EU), the GI protection scheme is primarily a producer-driven, bottom-up process. Under this approach, the state guarantees due process, that is, ensuring that producers and stakeholders follow the correct procedures and legal requirements, first in the application and registration phases, and later in the quality control and product standard conformity phases.[2]

* This chapter builds on our previous publications in this area. We are grateful to Nicole Ann Lim Jia Ying for editorial assistance.

[1] For a detailed review of the various states' involvement in GI governance, see Estelle Biénabe & Delphine Marie-Vivien, *The Multifaceted Role of the State in the Protection of Geographical Indications: A Worldwide Review*, 98 World Dev. 1 (2017) [hereinafter Biénabe & Marie-Vivien, *The Multifaceted Role of the State*].

[2] *See, e.g.*, Delphine Marie-Vivien, Laurence Bérard, Jean-Pierre Boutonnet, & Francois Casabianca, *Are French Geographical Indications Losing Their Soul? Analyzing Recent Developments in the Governance of the Link to the Origin in France*, 98 World Dev. 24 (Oct. 2015) [hereinafter Marie-Vivien et al., *Are French Geographical Indications Losing Their Soul?*]. *See also* the discussion *infra* Section IV.

In other countries, the GI protection scheme is instead a state-driven, top-down process, in which the state initiates and supervises GI registration, and is often involved in selecting producers.[3] Moreover, in some countries, the state can even be the applicant for GI registrations.[4] Finally, in states without GI-intensive industries, GI protection systems are generally enacted simply to fulfil an obligation under international law. Accordingly, the GI governance systems in those countries are developed only to a minimum.[5]

In this chapter we attempt to survey these different approaches in order to answer the following questions: Which is the best GI governance model for achieving the public policy objectives of GI protection? Specifically, would this model be based primarily on state-driven action, or rather on the actions by the private sector? Or would the most suitable model be a system in which the state and the private sector share responsibility for the various stages of GI governance? Ultimately, we conclude that a system in which the state or the private sector has exclusive, or majoritarian, control may not be the optimal system for GI governance. Instead, coordination between both the state and private stakeholders work is a requirement – but not necessarily to the same degree, or even at the same time, given that national circumstances and needs may require different approaches.

The chapter proceeds as follows. In Section I, we offer a brief overview of GIs and their international protection. In Section II, we detail the characteristics of *sui generis* protection and briefly contrast it to alternative systems of GI protection under trademark law. This comparison highlights the specific features of both systems, specifically the role of the state *vis-à-vis* the private sector in the GI governance process. We explore the *sui generis* system, in particular, where the state is involved both *ex ante*, in the process leading up to the GI registration, and *ex poste* in the management and quality control of the products. In Section III, we analyze the various roles that the state and the private sector can assume in the lifecycle of GIs with particular attention to three *sui generis* jurisdictions, namely, France, India, and Singapore. In France, the country from which GIs originate, the role of the state has been dwindling, especially in the past two decades and is evolving toward a different kind of coordination between public and private sectors. France's system of GI governance is then juxtaposed with India, a country where GI governance is run primarily by the state or through government agencies. Finally, we analyze Singapore, a country without national GI-intensive industries that has implemented *sui generis* GI protection only as a result of international obligations and international trade agreements. In Section IV, we conclude that it is neither possible nor advisable to pinpoint *the* perfect system of GI governance. Instead, the optimal system remains one that is based on a collaboration between the state and the private sector, each playing different roles to varying degrees depending on the needs of each jurisdiction.

[3] For several examples of countries where the top-down process is used, see the contributions in GEOGRAPHICAL INDICATIONS AT THE CROSSROADS OF TRADE, DEVELOPMENT, AND CULTURE: FOCUS ON ASIA-PACIFIC (Irene Calboli & Ng-Loy Wee Loon eds., 2017) [hereinafter Calboli & Ng-Loy, *Geographical Indications*].

[4] *See infra* Section IV.

[5] *Id.*

I A Brief Primer on Geographical Indications: International Aspects and Public Policy Objectives

As not all readers are familiar with GIs, we provide a brief overview of the topic in this Section. GIs remain one of the most controversial areas of intellectual property law.[6] However, despite the never-ending disagreements over the nature, scope of protection, and rights granted by GIs, it is generally accepted that GIs originated in Europe, specifically in France, in the late 1800s.

The genesis of GI protection can be traced back to a 1905 French law against frauds. At that point in time, a pandemic of philloxera led to a reduction in wine production. The limited supply of wine in the market consequently saw a raise in adulterated wine. In response, the French government enacted the 1905 law in order to stop the growing misuse of false indications of the origin of goods in the agro-food sector, especially in the wine sector.[7] Later, in 1919, a law on the protection of appellation of origin (AO), the first legal nomenclature given to geographical indicators) was introduced. The 1919 law provided that only producers from a specific area could designate their products with the AO, and in turn file complaints against uses that were considered prejudicial to their rights.[8] Under this law, the courts were responsible for determining production areas and/or production methods, which had to be "local, fair and constant."[9] In 1935, a subsequent law[10] conferred the task of defining and governing AOs upon a special committee composed of both public and private stakeholders. The French laws of 1905, 1919, and 1935 also codified the principle that geographical names should be used only by authorized parties because of the linkage between the products identified by those names, and the place where the products are grown and processed. This linkage became known as the *terroir* – the connection between the products and the land, which includes both natural elements, such as the soil, the air, and the climate, as well as the human skills and knowledge to grow or process the products.

[6] For recent discussions outlining the arguments in favour of or against the protection of geographical indications [hereinafter GIs], see the contributions in Dev Gangjee (ed.), RESEARCH HANDBOOK ON INTELLECTUAL PROPERTY AND GEOGRAPHICAL INDICATIONS, 2016 and in 46 *International Review of Intellectual Property and Competition Law* (2005). *See also* Irene Calboli, *Of Markets, Culture, and* Terroir: *The Unique Economic and Culture-Related Benefits of Geographical Indications of Origin, in* INTERNATIONAL INTELLECTUAL PROPERTY: A HANDBOOK OF CONTEMPORARY RESEARCH 433 (Daniel J. Gervais ed., 2015) [hereinafter Calboli, *Markets, Culture, and* Terroir]; DEV GANGJEE, RELOCATING THE LAW OF GEOGRAPHICAL INDICATIONS (2012) [hereinafter GANGJEE, RELOCATING GIs]; DANIELE GIOVANNUCCI ET AL., GUIDE TO GEOGRAPHICAL INDICATIONS: LINKING PRODUCTS AND THEIR ORIGINS (2009); Justin Hughes, *Champagne, Feta, and Bourbon: The Spirited Debate About Geographical Indications*, 58 HASTINGS L. J. 299 (2006); BERNARD O'CONNOR, THE LAW OF GEOGRAPHICAL INDICATIONS (2004).

[7] Loi du 1er Août 1905 sur les Fraudes et Falsífications en Matière des Produits ou de Services, JOURNAL OFFICIEL DE LA RÉPUBLIQUE FRANÇAISE [J.O.] [Official Gazete of France], Aug. 5, 1905, p. 4813. *See* GANGJEE, RELOCATING GIs, *supra* note 6, at 98–101.

[8] Loi du 6 Mai 1919 Relative à la Protection des Appelations d'Origine, JOURNAL OFFICIEL DE LA RÉPUBLIQUE FRANÇAISE [J.O.] [Official Gazette of France], May 8, 1919, at 4726. *See* Marie-Vivien et al., *Are French Geographical Indications Losing Their Soul?*, *supra* note 2, at 24–26.

[9] *See* Marie-Vivien et al., *Are French Geographical Indications Losing Their Soul?*, *supra* note 2, at 26.

[10] Décret-loi du 30 Juillet 1935 Relatif à la Défense du Marché du Vins et au Régime Economique de l'alcool, JOURNAL OFFICIEL DE LA RÉPUBLIQUE FRANÇAISE [J.O.] [Official Gazete of France], Jul. 31, 1935, p. 8314 (creating a system based on controlled appellations of origin). *See* Marie-Vivien et al., *Are French Geographical Indications Losing Their Soul?*, *supra* note 2, at 26.

The concept of *terroir* was later embedded in the 1958 Lisbon Agreement for the Protection of Appellations of Origin and their International Registration (Lisbon Agreement),[11] which entered into force in France in 1966.[12] The Lisbon Agreement was the first comprehensive international agreement that offered protection against both confusing and misleading uses of AOs and their "imitation or usurpation." The protection also extends to unauthorized uses of AOs that are accompanied by terms such as "like, type, or style." The Lisbon Agreement also created an international registry, which is currently administered by the World Intellectual Property Organization (WIPO). Countries who are members of the Lisbon Agreement are responsible for registering AOs at the international level. Yet, despite the strong level of protection, the impact of the Lisbon Agreement is considerably limited by the small number of signatories. In the 1990s, drawing largely on the French tradition, the EU later harmonized the protection of geographical indicators across Europe in 1992 with specific EU regulations, this time referring to them as GIs, the same term that would be used a few years later in the 1994 Agreement on Trade Related Aspects to Intellectual Property Rights (TRIPS).[13] Under EU law, the public policy objectives and justification for GI protection are based on the notion of *terroir*, even though the link between the product and the land became less stringent than under the original French laws and the 1958 Lisbon Agreement.[14]

Underlying the GI protection regime are several public policy objectives, the first of which is to reduce information asymmetry between consumers and producers.[15] By providing consumers with information related to the products' geographical (physical) location, and the characteristics and reputation associated with this location, GIs reduce the information asymmetries between consumers and producers about the GI-denominated products.[16] A second policy justification is that GIs represent important economic incentives for regional, local, and rural development.[17] In particular, it has been argued that GIs can incentivize local producers to invest in the region and adopt long-term strategies to

[11] The Lisbon Agreement for the Protection of Appellations of Origin and their International Registration, 923 U.N.T.S. 205 (Oct. 31, 1958) [hereinafter "Lisbon Agreement"].

[12] The Lisbon Agreement was introduced in France with the Law No. 66–48 of 6 July 1966. Both regulations amended the Law of 1919.

[13] *See* AGREEMENT ON TRADE-RELATED ASPECTS OF INTELLECTUAL PROPERTY RIGHTS arts. 22–24 (April 15, 1994), Marrakesh Agreement Establishing the World Trade Organization, Annex 1C, LEGAL INSTRUMENTS – RESULT OF THE URUGUAY ROUNDS vol. 31, 33 I.L.M. 81 (1994) [hereinafter TRIPS].

[14] In particular, EU law distinguishes between "Protected Denominations of Origin" (PDOs) and "Protected Geographical Indications" (PGIs). PDOs and PGIs enjoy the same protection, However, the link between the *terroir* and the products is stronger for PDOs than PGIs. For details and a critique of the expansion of the link of origin under EU law, see Irene Calboli, *In Territorio Veritas? Bringing Geographical Coherence into the Ambiguous Definition of Geographical Indications of Origin*, 6 WIPO J. 57 (2014) [hereinafter Calboli, In Territorio Veritas].

[15] For a summary of the public policy objectives of GIs, see EUROPEAN COMMISSION, TRADE, GEOGRAPHICAL INDICATIONS, http://ec.europa.eu/trade/policy/accessing-markets/intellectual-property/geographical-indications/. *See also* the literature cited in note 6.

[16] *See, e.g.*, Luisa Menapace & Gian Carlo Moschini, *Quality Certification by Geographical Indications, Trademarks, and Firm Reputation*, 39(4) EUROPEAN REVIEW OF AGRICULTURAL ECONOMICS 544 (2012); Luisa Menapace et al., *Consumers' Preference for Geographical Origin Labels: Evidence from the Canadian Olive Oil Market*, 38 EUR. REV. AGRIC. ECON. 193, 209–10 (2011); Michelle Agdomar, *Removing the Greek From Feta and Adding Korbel to Champagne: The Paradox of Geographical Indications in International Law*, 18 FORDHAM INTELL. PROP. MEDIA & ENT. L.J. 541, 586–8 (2008).

[17] *See, e.g.*, Sarah Bowen, *Embedding Local Places in Global Spaces: Geographical Indications as a Territorial Development Strategy*, 75(2) RURAL SOCIOLOGY 209 (2010); Margaret Ritzert, *Champagne is from*

safeguard their well-being and productivity. Finally, GI supporters have also pointed out that GIs can promote culture-related interests. This is because GIs embody elements related to the cultural identity and heritage of a place, in terms of both the place's natural elements and traditional skills necessary to grow and/or process the products. Accordingly, GIs could assist in achieving a third public policy objective of safeguarding and promoting cultural diversity.[18] In this respect, it could be supported that GI protection, and in turn GI-specific policies, could potentially support various of the UN Sustainable Development Goals (SDG), including SDG 2 ("Zero Hunger"), SDG 9 ("Industry, Innovation and Infrastructure"), SDG 12 ("Responsible Consumption and Production") and SDG 15 ("Life on Land"), among others,[19] even though this statement could meet with criticism by GI skeptics.[20]

At the international level, GI protection only reached the international stage in the 1990s after the TRIPS[21] negotiations and the creation of the World Trade Organization (WTO). During TRIPS negotiations, GIs were supported by the EU (and within it by agriculture intensive countries such as France and Italy), and equally opposed by the United States, Australia, New Zealand, and other "New World" countries. Because of the divergence of opinions, both sides had to compromise. Accordingly, TRIPS offered a twofold system of protection: first, a general protection for all GIs against uses that could mislead "the public as to the geographical origin of the goods,"[22] or that could "constitute an act of unfair competition;"[23] and second, a higher level of protection for GIs identifying wines and spirits (products relevant for the economies of both "Old" and "New World" countries). Like the Lisbon Agreement, TRIPS prohibits the unauthorized use of these GIs, or similar terms, including situations when "the true origin of the goods is indicated" on the products, or when these GIs are used "in translation or accompanied by expression such as 'kind,' 'type,' 'style,' 'imitation,' or the like."[24]

Champagne: An Economic Justification for Extending Trademark-Level Protection to Wine-Related Geographical Indicators, 37 AIPLA Q.J. 191, 212–20 (2009); Sarah Bowen & Ana Valenzuela Zapata, *Geographical Indications,* Terroir, *and Socioeconomic and Ecological Sustainability: The Case of Tequila*, 25(1) J. Rural Studies 108 (2009); Dwijen Rangnekar, *Indications of Geographical Origin in Asia: Legal and Policy Issues to Resolve*, *in* Intellectual Property and Sustainable Development: Development Agendas in a Changing World 273 (Ricardo Meléndez-Ortiz & Pedro Roffe eds., 2009) [hereinafter Rangnekar, *Indications of Geographical Origin*]. *But see* Rosemary J. Coombe et al., *Geographical Indications: The Promise, Perils and Politics of Protecting Place-Based Products*, *in* The Sage Handbook of Intellectual Property 207 (Matthew David & Deborah Halbert eds. 2014).

18 *See, e.g.*, Dev Gangjee, *Geographical Indications and Cultural Heritage*, 4 WIPO J. 92, 98 (2012). *But see* Tomer Broude, *Taking "Trade and Culture" Seriously: Geographical Indications and Cultural Protection in the WTO*, 26 U. Pa. J. Int'l Econ. L. 623 (2005).

19 Sustainable Development Knowledge Platform, *Sustainable Development Goals*, U.N. Dep't of Econ. and Soc. Affairs, https://sustainabledevelopment.un.org/sdgs.

20 Criticisms have been expressed in this respect, noticing that GIs incentive standardization, and thus can promote monocultures leading to increased erosion of biodiversity and bringing little benefits to poor farmers. The case of Tequila and Mezcal in Mexico are often pointed out to as examples in this context. *See* Pablo Perez Akaki, *Mexican Agrifood Geographical Indications: Between Productivity and Sustainability*, *in* AC&SD, Agri-Chain and Sustainable Development, 52, 52–4 (2016), https://acsd2016.cirad.fr/content/download/4317/32688/version/1/file/Book+of+abstracts.pdf.

21 TRIPS, *supra* note 13.

22 *Id.* at Art. 22.

23 *Id.* at Art. 22(2).

24 *Id.*

Nevertheless, TRIPS included several situations which would be exempted from the GI protection regime. In particular, TRIPS included provisions that: (a) grandfather validly registered national trademarks;[25] (b) safeguard the protection of homonymous names in different countries;[26] and (c) guarantee the use of terms that are deemed to be generic within the territory of national jurisdictions.[27] TRIPS members also agreed to engage in further negotiations – notably, to consider: (a) establishing a multilateral registry for GIs for wines and spirits;[28] and (b) extending higher standards of protection beyond misleading uses and consumer confusion to all GIs.[29] Yet, no progress was made in these respects for several years and, in 2001, GIs were included in the agenda for discussion in the Doha "Development" Round of WTO negotiations.[30] Here again, the positions on GIs continued to diverge sharply and TRIPS members could not find an agreement to advance the negotiations on GIs as mandated under TRIPS.[31] The disagreements on the issue similarly arose recently, when a revised text of the Lisbon Agreement was adopted after a diplomatic conference held in Geneva in May 2015. Supporters of the Geneva Act of the Lisbon Agreement hoped that the new agreement, which is largely modelled after TRIPS, could facilitate a membership increase. However, as controversy continues to plague the debate over GIs and GI protection, the number of signatories to the Geneva Act remains limited.[32]

The impasse at the multilateral level eventually led to the relocation of the GI discussion to the bilateral and regional free trade agreements (FTAs) front. This strategy has thus far been a success for GI supporters. In particular, the EU succeeded in obtaining protection for a long list of EU GIs and "clawing back" several terms that are protected as GIs in the EU[33] in FTAs concluded with Canada, South Korea, Singapore, Vietnam, several South American countries, and other countries.[34] As of now, the EU is set to continue ongoing negotiations, including with Japan, Malaysia, New Zealand,

[25] *Id.* at Art. 24(5).

[26] *Id.* at Art. 24(4).

[27] TRIPS, *supra* note 13, at Art. 24(6). Ongoing disputes over the use of words like Budweiser, Champagne, Parmesan, Feta, Gouda, Darjeeling, between selected Members of the WTO (including New and Old World countries) are examples of the national (still controversial) application of some of these exceptions.

[28] TRIPS, *supra* note 13, at Art. 23(4).

[29] *Id.* at Art. 24(1).

[30] *See* The Ministerial Declaration, WTO Doc. WT/MIN(01)/DEC/1 (adopted in Doha, Qatar, Nov. 14, 2001).

[31] Interestingly, in 2008, pro-GI countries and pro-biodiversity countries tabled a joint proposal/package called "Draft modalities" that broke the traditional "old" and "new" world divide on the topic. For details, see *North-South Coalition Sets Out "Draft Modalities" on TRIPS*, International Centre for Trade and Sustainable Development [ICTSD], www.ictsd.org/north-south-coalition-sets-out-%E2%80%98draft-modalities%E2%80%99-on-trips.

[32] *See* WIPO, *Diplomatic Conference for the Adoption of a New Act of the Lisbon Agreement – The Geneva Act of the Lisbon Agreement on Appellations of Origin and Geographical Indications* (2015), www.wipo.int/meetings/diplomatic_conferences/2015/en/; The Geneva Act of the Lisbon Agreement on Appellations of Origin and Geographical Indications, WIPO Lex. No. TRT/LISBON/009 (May 20, 2015), *available at* www.wipo.int/wipolex/en/details.jsp?id=15625.

[33] For a detailed discussion on the EU's success in obtaining GI protection for EU GIs, see Irene Calboli, *Time to Say Local Cheese and Smile at Geographical Indications? International Trade and Local Development in the United States*, 53 Hous. L. Rev. 373, 408–18 (2015), which discusses the EU's strategy as part of CETA and suggests a solution that is an acceptable compromise between GI supporters and opponents for the TTP negotiations.

[34] On this point, see the contributions in Calboli & Ng-Loy, *Geographical Indications*, *supra* note 3.

Australia, and the United States.[35] On their side, GI-skeptic countries such as the United States, Australia, and New Zealand have also used FTAs as fora to negotiate provisions defending their marks against EU GIs, or to restate the generic status of controversial terms used by their producers, particularly with respect to dairy products. For example, the Trans-Pacific Partnership (TPP) includes a long list of provisions related to GIs and their relationship with trademarks.[36] Several TPP members such as Mexico, Japan, Chile, Vietnam, and Malaysia have national interests in GI protection – as opposed to Canada, Australia, and New Zealand who continue to oppose GIs. Thus, the final draft of the TPP leaves signatories free to partially "negotiate around" TPP provisions should any of the signatories enter into an FTA with a non-TPP member.[37] It is worth noting, however, that the U.S. withdrew from the TPP in February 2017.[38] As the United States is one of the primary opponents of GI protection, its withdrawal may possibly offer additional momentum for the EU and other GI supporting countries to further promote the GI agenda during FTA negotiations across the globe.

II The Role of the State *vis-à-vis* the Private Sector in the Governing Framework of Geographical Indications

Even though TRIPS brought GIs to the forefront of the international intellectual property agenda, TRIPS also left members free to implement GI protection however they wished so long as the threshold of protection mandated in TRIPS was met.[39] Many scholars (including ourselves and our co-authors) have compared the two main alternative instruments to implement the TRIPS' obligation, that is, either a *sui generis* system of protection specifically modeled and dedicated to protecting GIs, or a system based on existing trademark laws. Supporters of *sui generis* protection have stated that trademarks cannot effectively protect GIs, while supporters of trademark protection have criticized *sui generis* protection as unnecessary, too bureaucratic, and excessive.[40] National approaches with respect to the principle of "first in time, first in right" – that attempts to regulate the relationship between *sui generis* protection of GIs and preexisting trademark

[35] For details on the FTAs concluded by the EU and other countries, or are currently under negotiation, see *European Commission's Trade Policy Portal*, EUROPEAN COMMISSION, http://ec.europa.eu/trade/policy/accessing-markets/intellectual-property/geographical-indications/ (last visited Jul. 20, 2017).

[36] *See* TPP Agreement, Chapter 18: Intellectual Property, *available at* https://ustr.gov/sites/default/files/TPP-Final-Text-Intellectual-Property.pdf (last visited Jul. 20, 2017).

[37] *Id.* at Art. 18.36. Several TPP members – Vietnam, Malaysia, and Singapore – have concluded, or are discussing, Free Trade Agreements with the EU. *See* The EU-Vietnam Free Trade Agreement, EU-Viet. (Aug. 5, 2015), http://trade.ec.europa.eu/doclib/docs/2015/august/tradoc_153674.pdf (last visited Jul. 20, 2017); EU-Singapore Free Trade Agreement, EU-Sing., Sept. 20, 2013, http://ec.europa.eu/trade/policy/countries-and-regions/countries/singapore/ (last visited Jul. 20, 2017).

[38] *See The United States Officially Withdraws from the Transpacific-Partnership*, OFFICE OF THE UNITED STATES TRADE REPRESENTATIVE (USTR), https://ustr.gov/about-us/policy-offices/press-office/press-releases/2017/january/US-Withdraws-From-TPP (last visited Jul. 20, 2017).

[39] TRIPS, *supra* note 13, at Arts. 22–24.

[40] *See, generally,* Dev Gangjee, *Quibbling Siblings: Conflicts Between Trademarks and Geographic Indications*, 82 CHI. KENT L. REV. 1253, 1256–9 (2007) [herein after Gangjee, *Quibbling Siblings*] (offering a very detailed overview of the scholarly discussion on the possibility of protecting GIs under trademark law).

rights – also vary. Such variation has led, unsurprisingly, to more international conflicts as countries desire to safeguard their respective national interests in the global arena.[41]

In this section, we focus on the *sui generis* system of GI governance, a system that we believe is more comprehensive and better suited for GI protection in light of the public policy role that GIs should play as instruments for economic and rural development, and consumer protection. As will be elaborated on in this section, one of the main characteristics of this system is the complex relationship between the state and private stakeholders, involving coordination between public and private sectors, and, more importantly, the role of the state as guarantor of due process in GI governance.[42] The main difference between a system of GI protection based on *sui generis* rights versus one premised on trademark rights lies in a larger state involvement in the former, as compared to the latter. Consequently, it does not come as a surprise that, to a large extent, a large number of common law countries have supported, and in several instances strongly preferred trademark protection (i.e., oppose *sui generis* rights). This position is intrinsically linked to the traditional skepticism towards government interference in market activities,[43] even though some common law countries – such as India and South Africa – recently implemented *sui generis* protection (due to their relevant interests in agriculture and other traditional products). Still, civil law countries have conventionally been more prone to accept higher degrees of state intervention in trade-related affairs. Thus, this has translated also in the fact that the creation of *sui generis* system of GI protection originated in a civil law country, France, and that sui generis protection has later expanded with little or no resistance across many civil law countries.[44]

In particular, the preference for the trademark system reflects the utilitarian approach that is generally adopted in common law countries not only with respect to GIs but to intellectual property rights in general.[45] Under this approach, intellectual property protection is necessary to encourage innovation; however, government intervention should be kept to a minimum. Thus, under the trademark approach, geographical names are protected through certification marks, collective marks, or simply trademarks, and are governed by rules of use, which are generally determined by the trademark owners, and focus primarily on unfair competition. Moreover, GIs can become generic terms and can be used descriptively as long as there is no confusion among consumers. As noted by Delphine Marie-Vivien and others recently, under this system "[t]hreats to the collective reputation do not justify external restrictions on producer and company behaviors, which [to the contrary] in *sui generis* systems condition the access to the protection, i.e. restrictions in the GI product specifications on the production area and methods."[46] In this

[41] Article 22(3) of TRIPS requires that WTO Members "shall … refuse or invalidate the registration of a trademark which contains or consists of a geographical indication with respect to goods not originating in the territory" when the use of the GI can "mislead the public as to the true place of origin." TRIPS, *supra* note 13, at Art. 22(3). *But see id.* at Arts. 24(6) and 25(5) (providing exceptions to this requirement).

[42] *See, generally,* Delphine Marie-Vivien, *The Role of the State in the Protection of Geographical Indications: from Disengagement in France/Europe to Significant Involvement in India*, 13(2) J. of World Intell. 121 (2010) (analysing the role of the state in the governance of GIs, with particular attention on France and India) [hereinafter Marie-Vivien, *The Role of the State in the Protection of Geographical Indications*].

[43] *See* Biénabe & Marie-Vivien, *The Multifaceted Role of the State*, *supra* note 1, at 3.

[44] *Id.*

[45] *Id.*

[46] *Id.*

respect, the influence of the trademark system is evident in the floor protection provided for in TRIPS, which states that GIs are protected only against uses that can mislead or confuse consumers.[47]

In direct contrast with the utilitarian foundation and the trademark approach is the notion of "natural rights," and to a certain extent "moral rights" of the producers under the *sui generis* system of GI protection.[48] Additionally, the *sui generis* system is also based on the concept that GIs are collective assets, which belong to the community of producers, and to the community living in a region at large.[49] This (collective-based) approach is strikingly different from the (private-based) trademark approach. As collective assets, GIs embody the reputations that are embedded in the essential nature and characteristics of the various products originating from the local community. Accordingly, GIs and their reputation have to be protected against any use, including their mere unauthorized evocation, even when this evocation may not cause any consumer confusion, to safeguard the interests of the local community.

The two pillars of a *sui generis* system are a product specification demonstrating the link with origin, and efficient control procedures. The higher level of protection granted to GIs under a *sui generis* system versus a trademark system directly relies on the wording in the specification to define the scope of protection against any unauthorized uses of GIs.[50] More specifically, the state is directly involved in the assessing, the drafting, the maintenance, and possibly the alteration of the GI's specification. However, as we elaborate in Section IV, there are still variations among countries that have *sui generis* systems in various aspects, for example, the nature of the applicant and the possibility of the state filing an application. The lack of a uniform stance in turn has major implications for the definition of GI specifications.[51]

In any event, as a general rule, while a GI application may be initiated by private stakeholders or the state, the establishment, inspection and enforcement of a GI application/registration necessarily requires the involvement of the state via the public administration or the judiciary. Moreover, regardless of whether the state or the private sector are driving the product specification initiative, the motivation for a new GI application is generally related to the advancement of specific public policies concerning national or regional rural development strategies. As such, the role of the state remains crucial in this process, since a coherent public policy cannot be designed and carried out in its absence.

Under the *sui generis* system, the definition of the GI specification remains the most important element of reference for governing GIs, in terms of ensuring compliance with the requirements for registration, post-registration quality control, and enforcement

[47] TRIPS, *supra* note 13, at Art. 22.

[48] *See* Biénabe & Marie-Vivien, *The Multifaceted Role of the State*, *supra* note 1, at 3.

[49] *Id.*; *see also* Rosemary J. Coombe & Nicole Aylwin, *Bordering Diversity and Desire: Using Intellectual Property to a Mark Place-Based Products*, 43 ENV'T AND PLANNING 2027, 2027–29 (2011) (coining the definition "marks indicating conditions of origin" (MICOs), which encompasses GIs, appellations and denomination of origin, as well as collective and certification marks indicating products' geographical origin).

[50] Biénabe & Marie-Vivien, *The Multifaceted Role of the State*, *supra* note 1, at 3.

[51] *See infra* Section IV for the discussion on the importance of GI specifications for GI governance.

against possible infringements.[52] Generally, a product specification should include, in addition to the applicant's details, the following: the name and description of the product, a definition of the geographical area, the proof of the product's origin (traceability), a description of the method of production, the linkage between the product and the area, the nomination of an inspection body, and labeling information. In addition, the specification should indicate details relating to the products' packaging, or forms of sales, such as whether the product should be sold as a whole or can be sold in other forms, e.g., sliced or grated.[53] As we explain in Section IV, the actual level of control exercised by control bodies still vary in practice, with developing countries lagging behind in the implementation and execution of such control.[54]

Generally, in many of the countries that implement a *sui generis* regime, the responsibility for GIs lie with the respective country's minister in charge of agriculture or intellectual property. In countries that have both state and federal authorities, these competences are shared and divided between institutions at both the local and federal levels. While the definition of GI specification is always within the purview of public authorities, private independent organizations may have the authority to control and certify the quality of GI products in several instances.[55] The reason for this division of tasks lies in the fact that private independent inspection bodies are often considered to be better suited and equipped to control the quality of the products. Moreover, when private organizations are in charge of quality control, the costs of these controls are born by producers, which makes the system less costly for the public at large.[56] Besides these external controls, producer groups frequently conduct internal checks on their members. Such inspections assist in monitoring and certifying the quality of the products. As we elaborate in Section V, this partnership between the state and private entities, both at the national, regional, and local level, are essential for creating effective and comprehensive GI governance frameworks.

III Comparing Diverse Experiences: The Governing Framework of Geographical Indications in France, India, and Singapore

In this section, we elaborate on specific examples of *sui generis* GI protection and compare three jurisdictions – France, India, and Singapore. In particular, we focus on the variation in the level of engagement of the state versus private stakeholders in the governance of GIs. We thus note that: (a) in France, the state's hitherto dominant role in GI governance has diminished in recent times while the role of the private sector has grown; (b) in India, the state always has and continues to play a driving role in the

[52] *See supra* Section II for the discussion on the policy objectives of GIs. For further discussion, *see* Calboli, *Markets, Culture, and* Terroir, *supra* note 6; Marie-Vivien, *The Role of the State in the Protection of Geographical Indications*, *supra* note 42, at 123.

[53] *See* Case C-108/01, Consorzio del Prosciutto di Parma en Salumificio S. Rita SpA v. Asda Stores Ltd. and Hygrade Foods Ltd., 2003 E.C.R. I-5163. (The Court of Justice of the European Union held that GI protection can extend to operations such as the grating, slicing, and packaging of the product if these conditions were adequately publicised in Community legislations such that they are brought to the attention of economic operators).

[54] *See infra* Section IV.

[55] *Id.*

[56] *Id.*

governance of GIs, so as to achieve public policy and national development objectives; and (c) in Singapore, attention has been focused mainly on creating a system of protection for foreign GIs; however, the role of the state and the private sector under the Singapore system remains unclear. In Section V, we will refer to these three different experiences in order to draw some observations on the importance of the partnership between the state and public sector in the governance of GIs.

A *France*

As mentioned in Section II, the protection of GIs in France is based on the tradition of AOs, and predates the European Regulations protecting GIs as well as relevant international agreements.[57] Since the very beginning, AOs were used by the French government, especially the National Institute of Appellation of Origin (INAO, now known as the National Institute of Origin and Quality) as tools to shape public policy.[58] The INAO was created in 1947 to replace the National Committee for Wines and Spirits; the latter initially comprised of producers responsible for defining product standards and maintaining quality control of wine but later became a specialized public sector organization which oversaw all agricultural products in 1990.[59] In 1992, the protection of GIs was harmonized at the EU level with EU Regulation 2081/92.[60] In turn, this affected the French legal system as the competence for registering GIs was split into two levels, one national level and one EU level.[61] Regulation 2081/92 was later amended and replaced by Regulation 516/2006 in order to ensure compliance with a 2005 WTO Dispute Settlement Body decision, which found that Regulation 2081/92 violated the principle of national treatment.[62] At the same time, the French legal framework was also substantively amended in order to reduce public spending. Consequently, more responsibilities were given to the private sector. This in turn reinforced the role of the producers in the building of GI specifications and provided for the disengagement of INAO from inspection and control activities.

One of the main purposes of the 2006 review of the French law was to strengthen the postregistration control of GI products.[63] Notably, the review established a new division of responsibilities between the state and industry professionals, for example, farmers, processors, and distributors. More specifically, the 2006 French Regulation provided for the creation of an Organization for the Defence and the Management for each GI. This organization is the only body entitled to manage the GI in question. In addition,

[57] *See* discussion *supra* Section II.

[58] *See* Marie-Vivien et al., *Are French Geographical Indications Losing Their Soul?*, *supra* note 2 at 25–26.

[59] *Id.*

[60] Council Regulation 2081/92 of 14 Jul. 1992 on the Protection of Geographical Indications and Designations of Origin for Agricultural Products and Foodstuffs, 1992 O.J. (L 208) 1.

[61] Marie-Vivien et al., *Are French Geographical Indications Losing Their Soul?*, *supra* note 2, at 25–26; Marie-Vivien, *The Role of the State in the Protection of Geographical Indications*, *supra* note 42, at 125–28.

[62] *See* Complaint by the United States, *EC - Trademarks and Geographical Indications for Agricultural Products and Foodstuffs*, WTO Doc. WT/DS174/R (adopted Apr. 20, 2005); Complaint by Australia, *EC - Protections of Trademarks and Geographical Indications for Agricultural Products and Foodstuffs*, WTO Doc. WT/DS290/R (adopted Apr., 20, 2005); *see also* Lothar Ehring, *National Treatment Under the GATT 1994*, *in* The Principle of National Treatment in International Economic Law – Trade, Investment and Intellectual Property 34 (Anselm Kamperman Sanders ed., 2014).

[63] Marie-Vivien, *The Role of the State in the Protection of Geographical Indications*, *supra* note 42, at 125–28.

membership is mandatory before a producer is entitled to the specific GI protection. This new system replaces the old practice of several producer groups managing each GI, and where membership for these group was not mandatory.[64] The purpose of the centralization was to strengthen the GI value chain through a unique organization, which would ensure all stakeholders (operators) were equally involved in the GI governance process. Specifically, the Organization is responsible for drafting the specification of each respective GI, ensuring its proper use by the operators through the implementation of certification and inspection schemes, updating the register of operators, and appearing before the courts in respect of any GI-related actions. Accordingly, starting in 2006, specifications are primarily drafted by the Organization and examined by the INAO, which is also in charge of forwarding them to the EU Commission once the national opposition term has passed. This is in contrast to the early days where the INAO would work together with the producers to decide the content of a GI's specification.[65] Similarly, starting in 2006, operators would register directly with the respective Organization, whereas pre-2006 they would register with the INAO.[66]

Another major change brought about by the 2006 French Regulation was the organization of controls. Previously, the control of a GI's specification and production conditions was carried out by the INAO. Since 2006, it has been conducted by independent, impartial, and competent certification and inspection bodies.[67] These inspection bodies are chosen by the GI Organization, accredited according to the European standard 17065, and approved by INAO. The certification and inspection bodies must also be able to guarantee their independence, impartiality, and competence. The certification schemes set up by the certification or the inspection bodies must be approved by INAO.[68] These schemes include the controls undertaken by the operator itself (self-control), the controls undertaken by the Organization (internal control), and the controls undertaken by the certification body (external control). The cost of the certification is borne by the operators. This system is a radical shift from the past, as pre-2006, the control function was performed by the state through the INAO. Although the French Regulation 2006 was introduced to ensure compliance with EU law, France's deliberate choice to vest the responsibilities of control in the control bodies and not the competent authority, which is only in charge of the control at the second level, confirms the state's evolution from a body that issued regulations and took charge of specification and control tasks to a body that oversees the actions of the various Organizations in a partnership coordinator role.[69]

B *India*

In contrast to the French regime, the Indian legal framework for GI protection is based on post-TRIPS and WTO obligations and simultaneously influenced by its history and

[64] *Id.*
[65] *Id.*
[66] *Id.*
[67] *Id.*
[68] Marie-Vivien, *The Role of the State in the Protection of Geographical Indications*, *supra* note 42, at 128.
[69] *Id.*

cultural heritage.[70] In India, GI protection is available through a *sui generis* system operationalized through the Geographical Indications of Goods (Registration & Protection) Act of 1999 (GI Act) and the Geographical Indications of Goods (Registration and Protection) Rules of 2002.[71] Under this system, the Intellectual Property Office in Chennai is in charge of the GI Registry for India. To date, the Registry has successfully registered almost 300 Indian GIs, including agricultural products, handicrafts, and manufactured products.[72] The application for GI protection contains the technical standards comprising an in-depth description of the characteristics of the product, its methods of production, and the geographical area of production. The Indian GI Act distinguishes between the applicant of the GI, who will be the registered proprietor, and the authorized user, who is any person claiming to be the producer of the goods in respect of which a GI has been registered.[73] In addition, since GIs are conceptually conceived as a collective right, the GI Act provides that the applicant shall be any association of persons or producers or any organization or authority representing the interests of the producers of the concerned goods.[74]

Since the implementation of the GI Act, the Indian government has been consistently involved in GI governance either by initiating registration of GIs on behalf of producers, or as the applicant itself via its various entities.[75] Moreover, even though the final applicant may be a society or an association, the initiative to register a specific GI can still come from the state, be it directly or indirectly. The role of the state in the Indian GI registration process also allows for the situation where the applicant is a board or a statutory body, which is not producing the products, but which will become the GI registrant and later supervises the production of the GI products. For example, the Indian Ministry of Commerce encourages several Indian statutory bodies, for example, the Coffee Board, the Agriculture & Processed Food Products Export Board, the Development Authority, the Tea Board, and the Spices Board to actively register GIs.[76] Consequently, the Spices Board registered Coorg green cardamom and Malabar pepper as GIs.[77] Similarly, the Tea Board registered Darjeeling, the most famous GI in India, as a GI.[78] Apart from statutory bodies, GI applicants can also be government controlled companies for the promotion and marketing of products, or agencies specialized in intellectual property, like the Patent Information Center, or institutes operating under

[70] *See* Yogesh Pai & Tania Singla, *"Vanity GIs:" India's Legislation on Geographical Indications and the Missing Regulatory Framework*, in GEOGRAPHICAL INDICATIONS AT THE CROSSROADS OF TRADE, DEVELOPMENT, AND CULTURE: FOCUS ON ASIA-PACIFIC 333 (Irene Calboli & Ng-Loy Wee Loon eds., 2017); Estelle Biénabe & Delphine Marie-Vivien, *Institutionalizing Geographical Indications in Southern Countries: Lessons Learned from Basmati and Rooibos*, 98 WORLD DEV. 58 (Oct. 2017); Marie-Vivien, *The Role of the State in the Protection of Geographical Indications*, *supra* note 42, at 128–42.

[71] The Geographical Indications of Goods (Registration & Protection) Act, No. 48 of 1999; Geographical Indications of Goods (Registration and Protection) Rules, 2002.

[72] Geographical Indication Registry, *State Wise Registration Details of G.I. Applications*, www.ipindia.nic.in/newsdetail.htm?283/State+wise+registration+details+of+GI+applications+15th+September+2003+Till+Date (last visited Aug. 18, 2017).

[73] Marie-Vivien, *The Role of the State in the Protection of Geographical Indications*, *supra* note 42, at 128.

[74] *Id.*

[75] *Id.*

[76] *Id.* at 131.

[77] *Id.*

[78] *Id.* at 132.

the government's supervision, such as the Craft Development Institute.[79] In several cases, GI applicants are also government controlled companies or cooperatives that produce the products.[80]

In general, the described level of state intervention in India has been justified as a means to defend the interest of underprivileged producers; as a mean to guarantee the quality of the product; and as a mean to protect national identity.[81] Nevertheless, this state intervention also raises several questions. For example, is the state qualified to be a GI applicant and later the holder of GI rights? Even if the state can legally be a GI applicant under the definition provided in the Indian GI Act, can the state equally represent all the relevant producers or would it favour the producers closely linked with government agencies or the like? Above all, to what extent does the role played by the India government enter into conflict with its other important roles, such as its role as guarantor of due process during the registration of GIs and of quality control and product conformity with the product specification? As GIs grant private intellectual property rights to their owners, these rights should be granted through an impartial examination conducted by an independent authority. Yet, the role of the state as applicant of the GIs brings the impartiality of the GI Registry in conducting the examination into question. Notably, the GI Registry is under the umbrella of the Ministry of Commerce, which itself encourages the registration of GIs. It might thus be difficult for the GI Registry to conduct a substantive and independent examination of GI applications when the applicant is the government or one of its boards, agencies, company, or cooperative, even when there are consultative groups.

C *Singapore*

Singapore's GI protection system was enacted to fulfil its obligation under TRIPS. This initially resulted in the enactment of the Geographical Indications Act of 1999 (1999 Act).[82] In 2013, Singapore subsequently concluded the negotiations of the European Union (EU) and Singapore Free Trade Agreement (EU-Singapore FTA)[83] and passed a new Geographical Indications Act (2014) on 14 April 2014,[84] to comply with the obligation of the FTA. Although the 2014 Act is intended to replace the 1999 Act, there have been no indications as to when the 2014 Act will be brought into force. As such, the regime under the 1999 Act remains in place.

Under the 1999 Act, a producer, or trader of goods identified by GIs can institute civil proceedings under its terms of protection, which mirrors TRIPS's two levels of protection. The two levels of protection consists of a general protection for GIs based on uses that constitute misrepresentation or unfair competition, and an enhanced level of

[79] *Id.* at 132–33.
[80] *Id.* at 133.
[81] *Id.* at 141–42.
[82] Geographical Indications Act (Cap 117B, 1999 Rev. Ed.) (Sing.) [hereinafter GI Act 1999]. For a detailed discussion on GI protection in Singapore, *see* Susanna H. S. Leong, *European Union-Singapore Free Trade Agreement: A New Chapter for Geographical Indications in Singapore*, in GEOGRAPHICAL INDICATIONS AT THE CROSSROADS OF TRADE, DEVELOPMENT, AND CULTURE: FOCUS ON ASIA-PACIFIC 33 (Irene Calboli & Ng-Loy Wee Loon eds., 2017).
[83] *See* EU-Singapore Free Trade Agreement, *supra* note 37.
[84] Geographical Indications Act (No. 19 of 2014) (Sing.) [hereinafter GI Act 2014].

protection to GIs identifying wines and spirits.[85] Importantly, under the 1999 Act, GI owners are first required to obtain a court declaration to prove that they are entitled to GI protection in Singapore.[86] It is only thereafter are they then able to file a claim for the infringement of a GI.

In the light of Singapore's strategic role as an international trade hub, and one of the major destinations of GI exports from the EU, the lack of a GI registration system is not an ideal solution, especially for foreign GI products sold in Singapore. This system will change under the 2014 Act, which, once it is implemented, will bring about the following significant changes: (a) it will establish a GI registry;[87] (b) it will increase the protection for all GIs in Singapore;[88] and (c) it will strengthen border enforcement measures for GIs.[89] The new GI registry will be housed within the Intellectual Property Office of Singapore (IPOS). The registration process will comprise three main stages: (a) application;[90] (b) examination;[91] and (c) publication and opposition.[92] Interestingly, GI applicants can be not only any "persons who are carrying on an activity as a producer in the geographical area" and the "association of such persons,"[93] but also the competent authorities having responsibility for the geographical indication for which registrations are sought.[94] It is likely that this expanded definition of GI applicant is to allow a large number of foreign registered GIs, such as those owned by producer associations or by national governments and government-controlled entities, to be registered in Singapore.

The 2014 Act additionally will implement a system of substantive examination for GI applications where the application must satisfy all necessary requirements. In particular, Section 39 of the 2014 Act[95] provides that an application for registration of a GI must be done in the prescribed manner and shall specify details such as the name, address, and nationality of the applicant; the capacity in which the applicant is applying for registration; the GI for which registration is sought; the goods to which the GI applies; the geographical area to which the GI applies; and the quality, reputation, or other characteristics of the goods and how they are attributable to the geographical origin. The provision also states that GI registrations may only be made in respect of prescribed categories of goods as set out in the Schedule of the GI Act 2014.[96] Despite the stringent requirements for GI registration, the 2014 Act remains silent on the need to have established bodies, be it governmental entities or the private sector, tasked with quality control in the country of origin. The reason for this is, as previously mentioned, that unlike France and India, Singapore does not have GIs of its own, and the implementation of GI protection, first with the 1999 Act and now the 2014 Act, is primarily the result of trade-related international obligations. Nevertheless, as Singapore is the biggest Asian market in terms of the import-export of GI products, and GI products are routinely sold

[85] TRIPS, *supra* note 13, at Arts. 22–24.
[86] *See* GI Act 1999, *supra* note 82, at section 3(1).
[87] *Id.* at pt. IV, section 17–37.
[88] *Id.* at pt. II.
[89] GI Act 2014, *supra* note 84, at pt. VI.
[90] *Id.* at sections 5–6A.
[91] *Id.* at section 12.
[92] *Id.* at section 13.
[93] *Id.* at section 38(b).
[94] *Id.* at section 38(c).
[95] *Id.* at section 39(1).
[96] *Id.*

by a significant number of retailers, restaurants, and other businesses locally, it remains important to enforce laws which prohibit misleading uses of GIs.

IV Discussion: One Size Does Not Fit All, but a System of (Flexible and Dynamic) Shared Governance Between the State and the Private Sector Would Benefit All

In light of this, we can conclude that, even under a generalized system of *sui generis* GI protection at the national level, the actual level and type of intervention of the state and the private sector can vary considerably from jurisdiction to jurisdiction, and at times also from a specific GI to another GI in the same jurisdiction. To a certain extent, the countries that we have analyzed in Section IV – France, India, and Singapore – have a very diverse system of GI governance. These jurisdictions were intentionally chosen in order to highlight the large spectrum of variations and relevant national interests that can apply in the area of GI governance. Although France's GI tradition and GI governance experience dates back over a century, India and Singapore have implemented GI protection only in the past twenty years as part of their obligation for acceding to the WTO and TRIPS. Nevertheless, both France and India share a common interest in GIs to protect their respective national products. Their position can be contrasted with that of Singapore whose interest in GIs is limited to the imported products that reach its shore and accordingly its GI protection system is catered primarily, if not exclusively, to protecting foreign GIs.

Although these jurisdictions have varied GI governance experiences, their differences serve to capture the complexity, and the possible problems and shortfalls that may befall any system of GI governance involving coordination between the public and private sectors. More importantly, these experiences indicate that, with respect to GI governance, one size cannot fit all and the role that the state and the public sector can play remains highly dependent on the level of maturity – economically, legally, and socially – of the jurisdiction at issue. In particular, different levels of development and national circumstances can justify a diverse framework of GI governance in which the state or the private sector have, respectively, a stronger or lesser role. Moreover, the examples indicate that any system of GI governance should be considered within a specific temporal framework as circumstances change with time, and, in turn, the level of engagement of the state, or the private sector, can also change. Nevertheless, the comparative analysis of these different experiences emphasizes that the state should remain in charge of examining and approving the GI specifications. The state also remains crucial in ensuring that there is no infringement of GIs postregistration.

In France, the role of the state has been diminishing in the past decades, and the initiative for GI application as well as the quality control of GI products is today delegated almost entirely to the producers and third-party organisms of quality control. Yet, French GIs remain amongst the most successful GIs across the globe and are highly valued.[97] Moreover, GI producers in France, as in the EU in general, must implement a stricter

[97] *See* Tanguy Chever, Christian Renault, Séverine Renault, & Violaine Romieu, *Value of Production of Agricultural Products and Foodstuffs, Wines, Aromatised Wines and Spirits Protected by a Geographical Indication (GI)* (2012), an external study commissioned by the EU Commission, https://ec.europa.eu/agriculture/sites/agriculture/files/external-studies/2012/value-gi/final-report_en.pdf (last visited Jul. 20, 2017).

level of quality control compared to other countries worldwide. In other words, the dwindling of the role of the state in France could in part be justified by the fact that the state does not have a specific need to initiate GI registrations and compel producers as a public policy matter. In other words, while the role of the state in France was more prominent in the early stage of establishing GIs (or AOs), state intervention became less relevant once the private sector became stronger and able to defend its interests directly. Today, GI-related initiatives in France can be directly initiated from the ground by the producers. Likewise, there is no longer need for the state to be fully engaged in the sphere of quality control standards, as these controls and quality certification can be proficiently performed by third party private certification bodies, which have been previously certified by the state and its agencies.[98] Nevertheless, the state remains in charge of reviewing GI applications and registering the GIs by reviewing the GI specifications. It also remains in charge of supervising and adjudicating over incidents or complaints related to GIs, and ultimately, ensures the smooth functioning of the French GI governance system through enforcement against GI infringements.[99] Moreover, the French government (in addition to the EU Commission) does contribute to promote GI protection in international markets through EU FTAs.[100] This engagement is certainly the type of role that a state should play in a jurisdiction with a mature system of GI governance like France.

Instead, a more prominent role on the every-day management of GIs would be more common in a jurisdiction where GI protection is still in its infancy. This is certainly the case in India. As in several developing countries, the Indian system of GI governance is today primarily a governmental tool to implement national policies related to agriculture and economic development. Here, GIs are used by the state to protect certain groups of producers and promote their products, nationally and internationally.[101] This system, as previously mentioned, is characterized by a top-down approach, in which the state decides what GIs to register and how these GIs have to be managed. In this system, the framework for product quality control and certification is also often not fully operational, or not operational at all.[102] It is thus unsurprising, as noted by commentators, that India is experiencing problems in the management of several GIs. Hence, this can negatively impact existing GIs, and lead to widespread counterfeit goods.[103] Moreover, it is unclear the extent to which the benefits of GI protection effectively reach the producers and the community living in the GI regions.[104] Consequently, a larger involvement by the private sector could be beneficial in India. Notably, the Indian government and the private sector could collaborate more closely in managing Indian GIs, particularly post-registration, especially in the crucial phases of quality control, marketing, and product management, not to mention ensuring delivery of benefits to the local producers.

[98] *See* discussion *supra* Section IV.
[99] *Id.*
[100] *Id.*
[101] *Id.*
[102] Yogesh Pai & Tania Singla, *supra* note 70, at 357–58.
[103] *Id.*
[104] *Id.*; *see also* Rosemary J. Coombe & S. Ali Malik, *Rethinking the Work of Geographical Indications in Asia: Addressing Hidden Geographies of Gendered Labor*, *in* GEOGRAPHICAL INDICATIONS AT THE CROSSROADS OF TRADE, DEVELOPMENT, AND CULTURE: FOCUS ON ASIA-PACIFIC 87 (Irene Calboli & Ng-Loy Wee Loon eds., 2017); Rangnekar, *Indications of Geographical Origin*, *supra* note 17.

Last but not least, the pragmatic approach taken by Singapore shows that a system of GI governance is closely tied to policies related to national interests. Caught in the middle of the "Old World" versus "New World" dispute without a specific position of its own, Singapore has duly executed its TRIPS obligations but kept GI protection to a necessary minimum and without initially implementing a system of registration. Only the need to negotiate an FTA with the EU later compelled Singapore to strengthen its existing protection regime in a bid to satisfy the EU's demands. Nevertheless, Singapore has carefully balanced its trade interests with the EU with those with "New World" countries, in particular the United States. Overall, the Singapore government's GI strategy is consistent with Singapore's priorities for economic and local development. Specifically, Singapore's interests to comply with international law while advancing the country's trade interest in the international arena point against creating a full-fledged system of GI governance like the one currently existing in France and other countries with direct interests in GI products.[105]

In summary, based on the comparison of the experiences above, GIs can serve a multiplicity of purposes and, in turn, models of GI governance can vary. Accordingly, in order to function efficiently and achieve its public policy objectives, a GI system should be tailored to encompass the level of state intervention that is compatible and best suited for a nation's specific circumstances and level of socioeconomic development. The circumstances to be assessed include the level of development of the national legal system, the existing protection mechanisms for specific GIs, the registration system in place, the national inspection and certification framework, the protection of national GIs abroad, if any, and the level of state engagement in international trade negotiations related to the advancement of the GI protection agenda at the international level. Based on this assessment, the respective roles of the state and the private sector can be specifically designed to better achieve the public policy needs of the respective countries and the producers. Crucially, the state remains paramount in defining GI specifications and, overall, in guaranteeing the fairness of the system, including GI enforcement. Thus, the best framework for GI governance is a system of shared governance between public and private sectors, with different levels and stages of engagement depending on the national circumstances of each individual country.

Conclusion

This chapter provides a brief overview of GI protection and highlights the important roles played respectively by the state and private actors as part of the GI governance framework. Compared to other forms of intellectual property rights, GIs are certainly a more appropriate case study in a framework of closer public–private cooperation due to the more prominent role of the state in the governance of GIs since their inception at the moment of a GI application and registration. In particular, as we have highlighted in this chapter, GIs are different than trademarks, patents, of copyrights, which award and are predominantly governed through private rights. Instead, the unique feature of GIs is that GIs are public goods (or club goods), which protect collective rights and selected communities, and not an individual private stakeholder. Nevertheless, even within *sui generis* system of

[105] *See* discussion *supra* Section IV.

GI protection, that is, a framework in which the state and the private sector closely cooperate with respect to GI governance, it remains unclear which format and degree of cooperation represent an optimal solution for achieving the traditional public policy objectives of GIs.

In this chapter, we have surveyed the French, Indian, and Singaporean experiences, which illustrate a large degree of variations within possible models of national GI governance frameworks. Following from our analysis, we thus conclude that one size does not fit all, and different countries may follow different systems of GI governance, based on their specific national circumstances and the level of maturity of their economic, legal, and social systems. In particular, these varying approaches may involve more, or less, engagement on the part of the state and/or the private sector at different stages of the process of GI governance. Still, we also conclude, based on the problems that we witness in some of our examples, that a combination of shared governance between the state and the private sector remains important to achieve a balanced system of governance, and in turn contribute to the development objectives within the SDGs – which are a primary focus of this book. To the contrary, a governance framework in which either the state or the private sector plays an absolute or largely predominant role may create considerable issues of conflict of interest, and ultimately fail to achieve the public policy objectives of GIs.

On the other side, we also agree that the role of the state, and to a certain extent a large role of the state, remains paramount. In particular, the state should be in charge of supervising the legality of the process of GI application and ultimately registering the GIs. It also should be in charge of supervising the conformity of quality control and certifying, directly or via certified bodies, that the products conform with the GI's specifications. Finally, state involvement is crucial at the level of GI enforcement, as no system of GI protection can be practically successful without a system of enforcement driven by the national public administration and the judiciary.

References

Agdomar, Michelle, *Removing the Greek From Feta and Adding Korbel to Champagne: The Paradox of Geographical Indications in International Law*, 18 FORDHAM INTELL. PROP. MEDIA & ENT. L.J. 541 (2008).

Akaki, Pablo P., *Mexican Agrifood Geographical Indications: Between Productivity and Sustainability*, *in* AC&SD, Agri-Chain and Sustainable Development (2016), https://acsd2016.cirad.fr/content/download/4317/32688/version/1/file/Book+of+abstracts.pdf (last visited Nov. 19, 2017).

Biénabe, Estelle & Delphine Marie-Vivien, *Institutionalizing Geographical Indications in Southern Countries: Lessons Learned from Basmati and Rooibos*, 98 WORLD DEV. 58 (Oct. 2017).

Biénabe, Estelle & Delphine Marie-Vivien, *The Multifaceted Role of the State in the Protection of Geographical Indications: A Worldwide Review*, 98 WORLD DEV. 1 (2017).

Bowen, Sarah, *Embedding Local Places in Global Spaces: Geographical Indications as a Territorial Development Strategy*, 75(2) RURAL SOCIOLOGY 209 (2010).

Bowen, Sarah & Ana Valenzuela Zapata, *Geographical Indications, Terroir, and Socioeconomic and Ecological Sustainability: The Case of Tequila*, 25(1) J. RURAL STUDIES 108 (2009).

Calboli, Irene, *In Territorio Veritas? Bringing Geographical Coherence into the Ambiguous Definition of Geographical Indications of Origin*, 6 WIPO J. 57 (2014).

Calboli, Irene, *Of Markets, Culture, and* Terroir: *The Unique Economic and Culture-Related Benefits of Geographical Indications of Origin, in* INTERNATIONAL INTELLECTUAL PROPERTY: A HANDBOOK OF CONTEMPORARY RESEARCH 433 (Daniel J. Gervais ed., 2015).
Calboli, Irene, *Time to Say Local Cheese and Smile at Geographical Indications? International Trade and Local Development in the United States*, 53 HOUS. L. REV. 373 (2015).
Calboli, Irene & Ng-Loy Wee Loon eds., GEOGRAPHICAL INDICATIONS AT THE CROSSROADS OF TRADE, DEVELOPMENT, AND CULTURE: FOCUS ON ASIA-PACIFIC (2017).
Case C-108/01, Consorzio del Prosciutto di Parma en Salumificio S. Rita SpA v. Asda Stores Ltd. and Hygrade Foods Ltd., 2003 E.C.R. I-5163.
Chever, Tanguy, Christian Renault, Séverine Renault, & Violaine Romieu, *Value of Production of Agricultural Products and Foodstuffs, Wines, Aromatised Wines and Spirits Protected by a Geographical Indication (GI)* (2012), an external study commissioned by the EU Commission, https://ec.europa.eu/agriculture/sites/agriculture/files/external-studies/2012/value-gi/final-report_en.pdf (last visited Jul. 20, 2017).
Coombe, Rosemary J., et al., *Geographical Indications: The Promise, Perils and Politics of Protecting Place-Based Products, in* THE SAGE HANDBOOK OF INTELLECTUAL PROPERTY 207 (Matthew David & Deborah Halbert eds. 2014).
Coombe, Rosemary J. & Nicole Aylwin, *Bordering Diversity and Desire: Using Intellectual Property to a Mark Place-Based Products*, 43 ENV'T AND PLANNING 2027, 2027–29 (2011).
Coombe, Rosemary J. & S. Ali Malik, *Rethinking the Work of Geographical Indications in Asia: Addressing Hidden Geographies of Gendered Labor, in* GEOGRAPHICAL INDICATIONS AT THE CROSSROADS OF TRADE, DEVELOPMENT, AND CULTURE: FOCUS ON ASIA-PACIFIC 87 (Irene Calboli & Ng-Loy Wee Loon eds., 2017).
Council Regulation 2081/92 of 14 Jul. 1992 on the Protection of Geographical Indications and Designations of Origin for Agricultural Products and Foodstuffs, 1992 O.J. (L 208) 1.
Décret-loi du 30 Juillet 1935 Relatif à la Défense du Marché du Vins et au Régime Economique de l'alcool, JOURNAL OFFICIEL DE LA RÉPUBLIQUE FRANÇAISE [J.O.] [Official Gazete of France], Jul. 31, 1935.
Ehring, Lothar, *National Treatment Under the GATT 1994, in* THE PRINCIPLE OF NATIONAL TREATMENT IN INTERNATIONAL ECONOMIC LAW – TRADE, INVESTMENT AND INTELLECTUAL PROPERTY 34 (Anselm Kamperman Sanders ed., 2014).
The EU-Vietnam Free Trade Agreement, EU-Viet. (Aug. 5, 2015), http://trade.ec.europa.eu/doclib/docs/2015/august/tradoc_153674.pdf (last visited Nov. 19, 2017).
EUROPEAN COMMISSION, TRADE, GEOGRAPHICAL INDICATIONS, http://ec.europa.eu/trade/policy/accessing-markets/intellectual-property/geographical-indications/ (last visited Nov. 19, 2017).
EUROPEAN COMMISSION, *European Commission's Trade Policy Portal*, http://ec.europa.eu/trade/policy/accessing-markets/intellectual-property/geographical-indications/ (last visited Nov. 19, 2017).
Gangjee, Dev, *Geographical Indications and Cultural Heritage*, 4 WIPO J. 92 (2012).
Gangjee, Dev, 46 *International Review of Intellectual Property and Competition Law*, Issue No. 7 (2005).
Gangjee, Dev, *Quibbling Siblings: Conflicts Between Trademarks and Geographic Indications*, 82 CHI. KENT L. REV. 1253, 1256–9 (2007).
GANGJEE, DEV, RELOCATING THE LAW OF GEOGRAPHICAL INDICATIONS (2012).
Gangjee, Dev (ed.), RESEARCH HANDBOOK ON INTELLECTUAL PROPERTY AND GEOGRAPHICAL INDICATIONS (2016).
Geographical Indications Act (Cap 117B, 1999 Rev. Ed.) (Sing.).
Geographical Indications Act (No. 19 of 2014) (Sing.).
The Geographical Indications of Goods (Registration & Protection) Act, No. 48 of 1999.

Geographical Indications of Goods (Registration and Protection) Rules, 2002.
Geographical Indication Registry, *State Wise Registration Details of G.I. Applications*, www.ipindia.nic.in/newsdetail.htm?283/State+wise+registration+details+of+GI+applications+15th+September+2003+Till+Date (last visited Aug. 18, 2017).
Giovannucci, Daniele et al., GUIDE TO GEOGRAPHICAL INDICATIONS: LINKING PRODUCTS AND THEIR ORIGINS (2009).
Hughes, Justin, *Champagne, Feta, and Bourbon: The Spirited Debate About Geographical Indications*, 58 HASTINGS L. J. 299 (2006).
INTERNATIONAL CENTRE FOR TRADE AND SUSTAINABLE DEVELOPMENT, *North-South Coalition Sets Out "Draft Modalities" on TRIPS*, www.ictsd.org/north-south-coalition-sets-out-%E2%80%98draft-modalities%E2%80%99-on-trips (last visited Nov. 19, 2017).
Leong, Susanna H.S., *European Union-Singapore Free Trade Agreement: A New Chapter for Geographical Indications in Singapore*, in GEOGRAPHICAL INDICATIONS AT THE CROSSROADS OF TRADE, DEVELOPMENT, AND CULTURE: FOCUS ON ASIA-PACIFIC 33 (Irene Calboli & Ng-Loy Wee Loon eds., 2017).
The Lisbon Agreement for the Protection of Appellations of Origin and their International Registration, 923 U.N.T.S. 205 (Oct. 31, 1958).
Loi du 6 Mai 1919 Relative à la Protection des Appelations d'Origine, JOURNAL OFFICIEL DE LA RÉPUBLIQUE FRANÇAISE [J.O.] [Official Gazette of France], May 8, 1919.
Loi du 1er Août 1905 sur les Fraudes et Falsífications en Matière des Produits ou de Services, JOURNAL OFFICIEL DE LA RÉPUBLIQUE FRANÇAISE [J.O.] [Official Gazete of France], Aug. 5, 1905.
Marie-Vivien, Delphine, *The Role of the State in the Protection of Geographical Indications: from Disengagement in France/Europe to Significant Involvement in India*, 13(2) J. OF WORLD INTELL. 121 (2010).
Marie-Vivien, Delphine, Laurence Bérard, Jean-Pierre Boutonnet, & Francois Casabianca, *Are French Geographical Indications Losing Their Soul? Analyzing Recent Developments in the Governance of the Link to the Origin in France*, 98 WORLD DEV. 24 (Oct. 2015).
Menapace, Luisa & Gian Carlo Moschini, *Quality Certification by Geographical Indications, Trademarks, and Firm Reputation*, 39 EUROPEAN REVIEW OF AGRICULTURAL ECONOMICS 544 (2012).
Menapace, Luisa et al., *Consumers' Preference for Geographical Origin Labels: Evidence from the Canadian Olive Oil Market*, 38 EUR. REV. AGRIC. ECON. 193, (2011).
O'Connor, Bernard, THE LAW OF GEOGRAPHICAL INDICATIONS (2004).
OFFICE OF THE UNITED STATES TRADE REPRESENTATIVE, *The United States Officially Withdraws from the Transpacific-Partnership*, https://ustr.gov/about-us/policy-offices/press-office/press-releases/2017/january/US-Withdraws-From-TPP (last visited Jul. 20, 2017).
Pai, Yogesh & Tania Singla, *"Vanity GIs:" India's Legislation on Geographical Indications and the Missing Regulatory Framework*, in GEOGRAPHICAL INDICATIONS AT THE CROSSROADS OF TRADE, DEVELOPMENT, AND CULTURE: FOCUS ON ASIA-PACIFIC 333 (Irene Calboli & Ng-Loy Wee Loon eds., 2017).
Rangnekar, Dwijen, *Indications of Geographical Origin in Asia: Legal and Policy Issues to Resolve, in* INTELLECTUAL PROPERTY AND SUSTAINABLE DEVELOPMENT: DEVELOPMENT AGENDAS IN A CHANGING WORLD 273 (Ricardo Meléndez-Ortiz & Pedro Roffe eds., 2009).
Ritzert, Margaret, *Champagne Is from Champagne: An Economic Justification for Extending Trademark-Level Protection to Wine-Related Geographical Indicators*, 37 AIPLA Q.J. 191 (2009).
U.N. DEPARTMENT OF ECONOMIC AND SOCIAL AFFAIRS, Sustainable Development Knowledge Platform, *Sustainable Development Goals*, https://sustainabledevelopment.un.org/sdgs (last visited Nov. 20, 2017).

Trans-Pacific Partnership Agreement, Chapter 18: Intellectual Property, *available at* https://ustr.gov/sites/default/files/TPP-Final-Text-Intellectual-Property.pdf (last visited Jul. 20, 2017).

World Intellectual Property Organization, *Diplomatic Conference for the Adoption of a New Act of the Lisbon Agreement – The Geneva Act of the Lisbon Agreement on Appellations of Origin and Geographical Indications* (2015), http://www.wipo.int/meetings/diplomatic_conferences/2015/en/ (last visited Nov. 19, 2017).

World Intellectual Property Organization, The Geneva Act of the Lisbon Agreement on Appellations of Origin and Geographical Indications, WIPO Lex. No. TRT/LISBON/009 (May 20, 2015), *available at* www.wipo.int/wipolex/en/details.jsp?id=15625 (last visited Nov. 19, 2017).

World Trade Organization, Agreement on Trade-Related Aspects of Intellectual Property Rights arts. 22–24 (April 15, 1994), Marrakesh Agreement Establishing the World Trade Organization, Annex 1C, Legal Instruments – Result of the Uruguay Rounds vol. 31, 33 I.L.M. 81 (1994).

World Trade Organization, Complaint by Australia, *EC – Protections of Trademarks and Geographical Indications for Agricultural Products and Foodstuffs*, WTO Doc. WT/DS290/R (adopted April 20, 2005).

World Trade Organization, Complaint by the United States, *EC – Trademarks and Geographical Indications for Agricultural Products and Foodstuffs*, WTO Doc. WT/DS174/R (adopted Apr. 20, 2005).

World Trade Organization, The Ministerial Declaration, WTO Doc. WT/MIN(01)/DEC/1 (adopted in Doha, Qatar, Nov. 14, 2001).

Part IV

Governance and Institutional Design Perspectives

15 Public–Private Partnerships and Technology Sharing: Existing Models and Future Institutional Designs

Padmashree Gehl Sampath*

Introduction

Although public–private partnerships (PPPs) are not an entirely new construct, they have recently acquired an importance on the international level that is arguably novel. Existing for several decades now[1] they are still without a common definition or a consensus understanding as to their functionality or institutional features in different contexts. To address this situation, many recent studies have called for a systematic inquiry of these forms of institutional arrangements from a governance and value-creation perspective.[2] This chapter looks at this challenge of conceptual indeterminacy in the context of international PPPs, namely, those partnerships that have been created at the international level to provide solutions to certain global issues. The analysis focuses on governance issues and institutional design for the future, *from the perspective of technology sharing* (see Box 15.1).

The circumstances that led to the creation of several of these international PPPs (many within the public health policy arena) are well documented in the extant literature, including in other chapters of this volume. Starting from around the time of the WTO and its annex agreements, stronger incentives set out by intellectual property (IP) rights in the Agreement on Trade Related Aspects of Intellectual Property Rights (TRIPS Agreement),[3] widened the existing chasm between private sector rents and the interests of the public particularly in new and promising areas of technology. One concern was that the grant of minimum IP standards could affect the physical supply of products and services in key areas of importance in the developing world such as health or food security. The development community therefore was keen to search for new ways to provide drugs, vaccines, and seed varieties that were needed to ensure the survival and well-being of disadvantaged populations.

* The views expressed in this chapter are the author's personal views.

1 Tony Bovaird, *Public-Private Partnerships: From Contested Concepts to Prevalent Practice*, 70 Int'l Rev. Admin. Sci. 199–215 (2004).

2 *See e.g.* Graeme Hodge & Carsten Greve, *Public–Private Partnerships: An International Performance Review*, 67 Pub. Admin. Rev. 545–558 (2007); Ilze Kivleniece & Bertrand V. Quelin, *Creating and Capturing Value in Public-Private Ties: A Private Actor's Perspective*, 37 Acad. Mgmt. Rev. 272–299 (2012).

3 TRIPS: Agreement on Trade-Related Aspects of Intellectual Property Rights. Part I – General Provisions and Basic Principles, World Trade Organization (Jan. 21, 2017), www.wto.org/english/tratop_e/trips_e/trips_e.htm.

Box 15.1. The importance of "technology sharing" as a goal

The term technology transfer has been in debates for decades, and is often tainted with history and burdened with several connotations of the who, how, when, and through what means. Even if one were to look beyond those stereotypes, the term technology transfer is misleading in the case of a PPP, where the key actors involved should ideally be considered as equal partners in a relatively long-term process, working toward a common goal. Technology transfer is at once not a suitable term since it connotes a technology provider and a technology recipient, and not necessarily technology collaborators. The same is true of other terms such as technology diffusion, technology dissemination, etc. For purposes of the partnership, if one were to provide incentives for access and use of technology, as well as learning, and building upon it, the partners should all be treated as equal and would work toward protecting the knowledge that is common to the PPP. *Technology sharing* therefore is the more apropos term that reflects this kind of equal partnership with an equally important responsibility to contribute and build on the knowledge.

These developments, most of which occurred in the 1990s, are best documented by the variety of legal, ideological, and political disputes that emerged sharply in the context of global health and, to a lesser extent, global food security. In the wake of these disputes, such as the South African public health crises,[4] the developmental community rallied around the delivery of and access to medicines for the treatment of HIV/AIDS, malaria, TB and other tropical diseases. As other chapters in this volume document, this concern was definitely not misplaced, and efforts are still inadequate to meet the growing demand for public goods in these sectors. But the maelstrom around drug delivery or food security was not isolated in itself. It also brought to the forefront a related issue: the critical market failure where the global private sector had little incentive to invest in R&D for the creation of products that disproportionately affected the poor in the developing world.

Given the devastating future consequences of these trends, immediate discussions centred around two important questions: How best to:

(a) provide for products and services in those areas where IP protection could lead to lower supply and/or higher prices of products in the developing world; and,
(b) ensure a steady stream of R&D efforts into products and/or services where the benefits for the global public are not captured by the ability to pay, that is, where common action is clearly needed to make up for the lack of private incentives to invest.

For those trying to discuss and advocate solutions, it became quickly evident that the problem was not simply one of provision of drugs or vaccines or agricultural plant varieties *per se*.[5] Important technologies that were needed to produce existing products to meet those needs, or structure research and development for new products (in areas of neglected diseases or neglected food varieties), were either already privatized or were in

4 Ruth Okediji, *Legal Innovation in International Intellectual Property Relations: Revisiting Twenty-One Years of The Trips Agreement*, 36 U. Pa. J. Int'l L. 191, 193 (2015).

5 *See generally* Soloman Nwaka et al., *Developing ANDI: A Novel Approach to Health Product R&D in Africa*, 7 PLoS Med. (2010), https://doi.org/10.1371/journal.pmed.1000293.

the course of becoming privatized, raising the transaction costs for the production of such products or initiating new R&D ventures.[6] This already skewed distribution of innovation inputs called for new mechanisms that could bridge the gap between private and public interests to ensure production and availability of key outputs in certain sectors, as well as to promote technological ventures and R&D alliances to create a pipeline of products for the future.

Solutions therefore were needed to simultaneously fulfil at least three goals: to (a) engage the global private sector (particularly multinational corporations or other companies) that held the technologies and the R&D capabilities; (b) provide incentives (financial, IP-related, or others) to such actors in order to bridge the gap between private interests and public goals, often in a global context; and (c) piggyback on such arrangements in order to augment existing capacity in developing countries.

PPPs presented two clear advantages over all other existing options. A first was that PPPs were hybrid institutional structures that could be structured as collaborative arrangements between any number of private, public, and other actors. This was of immense appeal to the global community in search of newer models of cooperative action that could be modelled according to need. Secondly, as Hodge and Greve[7] note, PPPs found an intellectual following amongst advocates looking for an alternate perspective to combat concerns on global commodification of knowledge and other assets. By substituting the terms "privatization" and "contracts" with "alternate delivery systems" and "partnerships," PPPs suggested ways that invite broader consensus,[8] and hence were welcomed openly by all stakeholders.

Since then, the policy community has been widely supportive, and sometimes even euphoric, about PPPs, lauding them as a means to foster new forms of collaboration between the private and the public sector for the provision of global public goods.[9] Important examples of PPPs in the public health area include: the International AIDS Vaccines Initiative (IAVI) in 1996 to focus on the development of an AIDS vaccine, Medicines for Malaria Venture (MMV) in 1999, PATH Malaria Vaccines Initiative in 1999, Global Alliance for TB Drug Development (TB Alliance) in 2000, Drugs for Neglected Diseases Initiative (DNDi) in 2003, and the Paediatric Dengue Vaccine Initiative created in 2001[10] for promoting research and development into new kinds of drugs and vaccines. Other notable efforts to increase access to existing medicines and vaccines are not directly related to IP issues but rather to distribution or financing issues for existing technologies: These include the creation of the Global Alliance for

[6] Keith Makus & Jerome Reichman, *The Globalization of Private Knowledge Goods and the Privatization of Global Public Goods*, 7 J. INT'L ECON. L. 279, 317 (2004).

[7] Hodge & Greve, *supra* note 2.

[8] *See* Stephen Linder, *Coming to Terms with the Public-Private Partnership, A Grammar of Multiple Meanings*, 43 AM. BEHAV. SCI. 35–51 (1999); Erik-Hans Klijn & Geert R. Teisman, *Partnership Arrangements: Governmental Rhetoric or Governance Scheme?*, 62 PUB. ADMIN. REV. 197–207 (2002); *see also* Hodge & Greve, *supra* note 2.

[9] Maskus & Reichman, *supra* note 6, at 317; *Science, Technology and Innovation For Sustainable Development in the Global Partnership for Development Beyond 2015: Thematic Think Piece*, UN System Task Team on the Post-2015 UN Development Agenda (2013), www.un.org/en/development/desa/policy/untaskteam_undf/thinkpieces/28_thinkpiece_science.pdf.

[10] Currently, the Dengue Vaccine Initiative continues the work of the PDVI.

Vaccines and Immunisation (GAVI) in 2000 and the Global Fund (to Fight AIDS, Tuberculosis and Malaria) in 2002.

Despite mixed reviews on performance and outcomes,[11] PPPs continue to experience wide appeal. Most critical policy milestones in development in recent times, such as the WHO's Global Strategy and Plan of Action on Public Health, Innovation and Intellectual Property (GSPoA), the 2030 Agenda for Sustainable Development (2030 Agenda)[12] and the Addis Ababa Action Agenda (AAAA) recognise PPPs as important mechanisms to promote international collaboration on common objectives. Particularly, Sustainable Development Goals (SDGs) 17.16 and 17.17 on multi-stakeholder partnerships in the 2030 Agenda call upon the international community to "enhance the global partnership for sustainable development, complemented by multi-stakeholder partnerships that mobilize and share knowledge, expertise, technology and financial resources" and to "[e]ncourage and promote effective public, public–private and civil society partnerships, building on the experience and resourcing strategies of partnerships."[13]

This emphasis makes it timely to address some critical questions that have been building up until now: Given the wide range of loosely structured arrangements that are being clubbed under the term "PPPs", should we be worried that there is no clear definitional consensus on what such a partnership arrangement entails or that there has not been much debate on what institutional models are more suited to problem-solving of this nature than others? In other words, does the lack of clarity on governance issues matter and if so, how? If it does, can there be lessons drawn from this so-called third way to tackle business?[14] What could these lessons be, and how do we build upon them?

In addressing the various challenges and questions arising from the continuing indeterminacy of PPPs, this chapter focuses on international PPPs. Section I looks at the specific features of international PPPs with a view to characterise them in the broader landscape of PPPs, explaining the key aspects that set them apart. The chapter argues that international PPPs should be defined more broadly than other PPPs, as new forms of hybrid institutional models that involve private and the public sectors from both national and international spheres of influence, with handpicked collaborators, tailor-made terms of collaboration, and clear mechanisms for monitoring and control for each of the goals with a fair representation of all interests. Section II then evaluates the current state of empirical information available on these PPPs in the context of technological sharing and capacity building. This is analysed through a bibliometric review of the current state of existing empirical evidence on PPPs, IP, and technology transfer issues. The section narrows down the scope of PPPs relevant to technology transfer and technology sharing,

[11] *See, e.g. World Bank Annual Report*, WORLD BANK GROUP (2014), https://openknowledge.worldbank.org/handle/10986/20093.

[12] Sustainable Development Knowledge Platform, *Transforming our world: the 2030 Agenda for Sustainable Development*, U.N. DEPT. OF ECON. & SOC. AFF., https://sustainabledevelopment.un.org/post2015/transformingourworld.

[13] *See* Sustainable Development Knowledge Platform, SDG 17, U.N. Dept. of Soc. & Econ. Aff., www.un.org/sustainabledevelopment/globalpartnerships/.

SDG 17.16: Enhance the global partnership for sustainable development, complemented by multi-stakeholder partnerships that mobilize and share knowledge, expertise, technology and financial resources, to support the achievement of the sustainable development goals in all countries, in particular developing countries. SDG 17.17: Encourage and promote effective public, public-private and civil society partnerships, building on the experience and resourcing strategies of partnerships.

[14] Hodge & Greve, *supra* note 2.

along with a discussion of the main research policy questions raised by the existing literature. It then presents the results of the bibliometric review and identifies the key strands of analysis that stand out in current empirical research on PPPs.

Drawing on these results, Section III of the chapter critically analyses the treatment of technology transfer in PPPs. It describes an urgent need to understand the ways in which technology-related objectives and achievements of existing PPPs differ and what precise advantages and limitations they could pose in practice, particularly if one were to consider broader goals such as knowledge sharing, expertise development, technological learning, etc., all of which will be important for international PPPs in the future. By comparing experiences through existing analyses, we can not only better understand institutional features that promote technology related objectives, but also reflect on the limitations of these approaches. The section tries to articulate the considerations that might matter for the future in this regard, where the technology challenge in the context of a PPP is considered holistically. Lastly, the chapter raises a set of critical issues on whether existing models and solutions devised thereunder deal with the question of technology transfer in a satisfactory manner, and if not, what issues might be important to consider. It concludes with some suggestions for future institutional design to address capacity-building, technological learning, and technology sharing goals, which the SDGs have prioritized for development.

I Are International PPPs Different and How?

In a lot of ways, the concerns addressed in this chapter are not entirely new or isolated. A large number of studies in recent times have looked at questions of governance in the case of PPPs more broadly, noting the absence of clear definition, institutional parity, and comparative analysis. Despite this, none of the studies have derived a systematic framework to assess the governance structures of PPPs at large, as Kivleniece and Quelin note.[15] In fact, comparing different kinds of PPPs in general, Roehrich et al. find that "[e]xtant literature offers an incoherent picture of PPP outcomes with regards to [their] ... benefits and disadvantages."[16] The situation, however, is much worse when one considers the world only of international PPPs, where not many studies exist on comparative governance and institutional design issues, despite the fact that merging the private rent-seeking nature of some actors and the overall objective of serving the wider public good is even more complex in the latter.

Historically, PPPs had wide usage mainly in the areas of public service delivery and public infrastructure, where they first originated. In the United Kingdom, for example, they were first used in the late 1980s to engage the private sector effectively in the provision of public sector services.[17] Since then, PPPs have been used to finance infrastructure projects such as hospitals, schools, bridges, roads, and even military equipment. They have been used extensively to deliver health infrastructure within countries in the

[15] Kivleniece & Quelin, *supra* note 2, at 273.

[16] Jens Roehrich et al., *Are Public–Private Partnerships A Healthy Option? A Systematic Literature* Review, 113 Soc. Sci. & Med. 110, 113 (2014).

[17] Tobias Krause, A Contingency Framework on Partnership Risk, International Journal of Public Sector Management, Vol. 27, No. 4, 2014, p. 317–333.

form of new technology systems, clinical labs, and so on.[18] PPPs and their use in infrastructure projects are also considerably widespread in the developing world, in countries such as Brazil, Peru, India, and China.[19] More recently, they have also been widely employed in newer areas to give a push toward public policy objectives within countries. A good example is the use of PPPs in large-scale renewable energy projects in some EU countries, such as the Netherlands.[20]

Due to their expanded reach, PPPs are also recognised increasingly as part of the explicit public policy landscape. For example, Boivard[21] notes that PPPs are provided for in urban policy legislation in the United Kingdom and the United States, national industrial policy in France, and economic development policies in Italy, the Netherlands, and the United Kingdom. Other countries such as South Africa, Tanzania, Peru, and India also have national legislations wherein PPPs are recognised.[22]

Remarkably, these varied policy efforts have not resulted in a consensus definition of PPPs. Instead, a wide variety of definitions have been advanced.[23] For example, one study views PPPs as formal collaborations between "public agencies and private sector businesses with the intention of meeting public goals."[24] Another study defines a PPP as "a form of structured cooperation between public and private partners in the planning/construction and/or exploitation of infrastructural facilities in which they share or reallocate risks, costs, benefits, resources and responsibilities."[25] Many of these cases only consider a PPP between a national government and a particular service provider company, although some do take into account other partners. In sum, as Hodge and Greve[26] note, a large number of initiatives are simultaneously clubbed under the term PPP.[27]

[18] James Barlow et al., *Europe Sees Mixed Results From Public-Private Partnerships For Building And Managing Health Care Facilities And Services*, 32 Health Aff. 146–154 (2013); Yongheng Yang et al., *On the Development Of Public-Private Partnerships In Transitional Economies: An Explanatory Framework*, 73 Pub. Adm. Rev. 301–310 (2013).

[19] *See generally* Dexter Whitfield, Global Auction Of Public Assets: Public Sector Alternatives To The Infrastructure Market And Public Private Partnerships (2010).

[20] Maurits Sanders, *Collaborative Enterprise: Next Stage Public-Private Partnerships?*, *in* The Collaborative Enterprise: Creating Values for a Sustainable World 313–334 (2013); Michael Heldeweg and Maurits Sanders, *Toward a Design Framework for Legitimate Public Private Partnerships*, 2014 Euro. Procurement & Pub. Priv. Partnership L. Rev. 187–201 (2014).

[21] Tony Bovaird, *supra* note 1.

[22] Kwame Sundaram Jomo et al., *Public-Private Partnerships and the 2030 Agenda for Sustainable Development: Fit for Purpose?* (DESA Working Paper No. 148, ST/ESA/2016/DWP/148, 2016).

[23] *Id.* (endeavour to provide the numerous definitions of PPPs being advocated in policy circles by agencies such as IMF, World Bank, OECD as well as in-country legislations in an annex to their study).

[24] Justin Waring, Graime Currie, & Simon Bishop, *A Contingent Approach to the Organization and Management of Public–Private Partnerships: An Empirical Study of English Health Care*, 73 Pub. Admin. Rev. 313–326 (2013).

[25] Joop Koppenjan, *The Formation of Public-Private Partnerships: Lessons from Nine Transport Infrastructure Projects in The Netherlands*, 83 Pub. Admin. 135, 137 (2005); *see also* Darrin Grimsey & Mervyn Lewis, Public Private Partnerships: The Worldwide Revolution in Infrastructure Provision and Project Finance 2 (2007).

[26] Hodge & Greve, *supra* note 2.

[27] As another author notes, the extensive literature on PPPs leads us to conclude that there are at least twenty-five different kinds of PPPs. *See* Maria Romero, *What Lies Beneath? A Critical Assessment of PPPs and Their Impact on Sustainable Development*, EURODAD 12 (2015), www.eurodad.org/files/pdf/55cb59060d9d4.pdf.

However, a few particular characteristics differentiate international PPPs from other PPPs at the national, local, or regional levels. To begin with, they are broader, and commonly involve international institutions as well as several national and/or regional agencies, university centres of excellence, the private sector, and public sector institutions from many countries. The permutations and combinations of potential partners vary widely; some PPPs may involve all of these actors while some others may be formed mainly between nonprofit institutions, academia and research institutes. For example, the WHO, the International Vaccine Access Center of Johns Hopkins University, the Sabin Vaccine Centre, and the International Vaccine Centre are all partners of the Dengue Vaccine Initiative. Regardless, the first attribute of international PPPs is the multitude of partners with a regional or international spread, often including a North-South dimension. The North-South dimension is not necessarily a driving factor, but it is increasingly part of the global landscape. Going forward, in the context of the 2030 Agenda or the AAAA, one might expect this to become a regular component of international PPPs.

Secondly, it is not uncommon for international PPPs to embrace multiple social objectives alongside their primary goals. For example, while the primary goal of IAVI is to promote "cross-sector collaboration to expedite the development of broadly effective vaccines and other new prevention options that we need to end AIDS,"[28] it has a number of ancillary goals, such as: (a) engaging with communities that are at highest risk of HIV/AIDS; (b) providing a product development platform for interesting concepts of vaccine development; and (c) capacity building. Similarly, many agricultural PPPs tend to encompass a multitude of related aims, such as efficient management of resources (through economies of scale and scope in research programs), exploiting capabilities across the public and private sectors, and exchanging knowledge amongst all stakeholders.[29] Hence, international PPPs can potentially encompass several objectives at the same time or, alternatively, be structured around a predominant objective that drives the partnership. At the same time, they can include a number of subordinate goals closely intertwined to the main objective. Even where there is only one goal specified, such as in the case of the MMV or the Global TB Alliance, their initiatives often state the overall objective of creating social awareness and socially responsible solutions and/or paradigms.[30] In many international PPPs, therefore, advocacy is a part of the overall objective.

Third, international PPPs are melting pots of actors that come together with different interests, perspectives, and expectations of payoffs. Simply by engaging a wider variety of private and public partners, international PPPs not only mesh the private with the public, as in other kinds of PPPs, but also often bring together actors with varying social, cultural, and knowledge characteristics. Harnessing these diverse attributes in a complementary manner is important to the success of the partnership. Hence, while such PPPs share the

[28] *Mission Statement*, International AIDS Vaccine Initiative, www.iavi.org/about-us.

[29] David Spielman et al., *The Art and Science of Innovation Systems Inquiry: Applications to Sub-Saharan African Agriculture*, 31 Tech. in Soc. 399–405 (2009).

[30] For example, the TB alliance, in the area of innovations, is: "... [m]aking mycolaboratory manuals from ongoing clinical trials publicly available in order to provide a useable template for other TB clinical trial organizations creating their own mycolaboratory manuals, as well as to facilitate comparison of procedures being employed across the field." *Innovations*, TB Alliance, www.tballiance.org/rd/innovations/sharing-lab-manuals.

common issues that concern other national PPPs, such as finance, management, efficiency, and accountability in structuring a partnership between the public and the private sector,[31] the variety of different backgrounds of actors in international PPPs can impose additional transaction costs. The processes of gaining trust and creating a mutual understanding for work among partners are plagued with additional complexities. Creating a common language and work ethic to move toward similar goals may be easier than the task of jointly working toward them and realising these outcomes in capacity constrained environments. Consequently, collaboration within international partnerships takes a lot more effort, and accounts for the varied degrees of successes across PPPs.

International PPPs, therefore, should be defined more broadly than other PPPs. Descriptively, they are new forms of hybrid institutional models that involve private and the public sectors from the national and international spheres of influence, with handpicked collaborators, tailor-made terms of collaboration, clear mechanisms for monitoring and control for each of the goals, and a fair representation of interested parties in every aspect of the partnership. Normatively, such arrangements, agreed and implemented at the international level, should satisfy two important requirements. First, these arrangements must be relatively institutionalized and provide a voice to both public and private sectors in collective decision making from the regions from which they are comprised.[32] Second, they should create synergies to promote collaborative and innovative use of resources to promote the application and management of existing knowledge to attain goals that are beneficial to all parties involved, where such goals could not have materialized in the same way without such a partnership.[33]

II A Survey of Existing Empirical Evidence on International PPPs

Although the literature on PPPs has been growing alongside its applicability,[34] keeping pace with it poses challenges, especially in terms of assessments and pertinent analyses.[35] The kind of information available about PPPs is extensive on the one hand, but highly confusing on the other. To seek some clarity on this topic, this section summarizes the results of a systematic bibliometric search conducted to map existing empirical evidence on the topic. The methodology used for this review was informed by other recent biobliometric analyses of PPPs,[36] which conducted extensive database searches of all peer reviewed articles published using exclusionary criteria in the field of social sciences and natural sciences.

For this review, the search period and search terms were specified and a focus was narrowed down to peer-reviewed publications in journals. Three databases - Scopus,

[31] *See* Roehrich et al., *supra* note 16, for example, who breaks down the general PPP literature into these important topics.

[32] Kent Buse & Andrew Harmer, *Seven Habits of Highly Effective Global Public–Private Health Partnerships: Practice and Potential*, 64 Soc. Sci. & Med. 259 (2007).

[33] Jomo et al., *supra* note 22, at 3.

[34] Roehrich et al., *supra* note 16.

[35] Roehrich et al., *supra* note 16, at 110 (noting that the use of PPPs has expanded fivefold and almost US $4 billion of health PPP contracts were signed worldwide just in the year 2010).

[36] *See, e.g.* Roehrich et al., *supra* note 16; De Pinho Campos et al., *Product Development Public–Private Partnerships for Public Health: A Systematic Review Using Qualitative Data*, 73 Soc. Sci. & Med. 986–994 (2011).

Science Direct, and PubMed – were used to conduct the search. Articles were considered to be relevant only if they:

(a) had been published in any international journal between 2006 and 2016 (i.e., peer-reviewed);
(b) included reference to, and discussions of, any international PPPs on global public goods issues, including through the use of quantitative or qualitative data; and
(c) included any reference to learning, collaboration, technology exchange, or capacity building.

The keywords used for the search included "PPPs" or "public–private partnerships," "technology," "intellectual property," and "capacity building." This resulted in over eight thousand articles in total, which confirmed an observation made by several other recent biobliometric studies of peer reviewed PPP publications, observing an increase in scholarly work on PPPs over the past two decades. From the over eight thousand articles that were shown in the initial bibliographic searches, controlling for several qualifying terms ("international," "technology transfer," "learning," and "capacity building") led to a final compilation of fewer than one thousand articles. After this compilation process, a third step consisted of an arduous method of eliminating publications by considering their abstracts, yielding fewer than fifty full papers that deal with international PPPs and technology issues as their main subject matter. This yield confirmed that the literature on PPPs, IP, and technology issues remains a relatively small set of scholarship operating in the areas of trade, health, agriculture, or development studies and related policy communities.

The resulting articles were then selected for full text consideration on the basis that they addressed some of the aspects of technology (whether directly or indirectly) or referred to issues that could indirectly imply a technology or learning dimension, such as a discussion on capacity building. What follows is an assessment of all these papers in a set of general and technology-specific findings.

A *General Findings*

The general themes of the papers were related to assessing or evaluating results of the particular PPP in question. Some of the papers dealt with cross-PPP evaluations and appraised technology paradigms, mainly in terms of IP management.

All the papers focused on one of three kinds of PPPs: Product development, access, or agricultural PPPs. Product development (PD) PPPs are partnerships for product development, frequently for diseases where there is no automatic market (in terms of a reasonable amount of consumers with the ability to pay, and hence lacking in incentives for investment and risk-taking), such as DNDi.[37] Access PPPs are PPPs structured to

[37] *See, e.g.* Robert G. Ridley *et al.*, *Round Table: A Role of Public–Private Partnerships In Controlling Neglected Diseases*, 79 Bull. World Health Org. 771–777 (2001); Roy Widdus, *Public-Private Partnerships: An Overview*, 99 Trans. Royal Soc. Tropical Med. & Hygiene 1–8 (2005); Richard T. Mahoney, *Product Development Partnerships: Case Studies of a New Mechanism for Health Technology Innovation*, 9 Health Research Policy & Systems 33–42 (2011); de Pinhos Campos, *supra* note 36, among many others.

tackle the other side of disease control, namely promoting access to medicines and/or vaccines to effectively promote public health (and often also focusing on issues of health systems strengthening), such as GAVI.[38] The papers commonly make a distinction between the two kinds of partnerships – that is, they either deal with PD PPPs or access PPPs—with very few papers dealing with issues of technology or institutional design as a common issue for both. A third set of papers examines PPPs related to agricultural biotechnology and/or food security.[39]

A second relevant finding is that the papers were all from different disciplines – a fact that, although not a shortcoming in itself, lends itself poorly to comparability.[40] But often, studies even within the same kind of discipline (say development studies) employed different methodologies: whereas some were simply case studies or opinion pieces backed by a theoretical or research framework, others were a combination of primary studies, opinion pieces, or comparative analysis that were conducted by authors on both PD PPPs and access PPPs. The deficiency of the general PPP literature is mirrored in the case of international PPPs as well, namely that none of the papers focused on proposing a systematic framework to compare the governance or value-creation advantages up until now.[41]

Taken holistically, the existing studies contribute to showing that most international PPPs on topics of global public goods have some important plus points, which could be explained in terms of the following four biases:[42]

- Cooperative bias: Most PPPs are cooperative arrangements of some durability.
- Implicit/ explicit sectoral bias: Most PPPs currently tackle global public goods either in the health sector or in the agricultural sector, although newer PPPs in the context of the 2030 Agenda might plausibly expand this reach into other areas, such as infrastructure.
- Risk sharing bias: Most PPPs enter into the collaborative arrangement to augment deficiencies on the supply side, or demand side, or even both; risk sharing is not only a common feature of the PPPs, but informs how the individual relationships are structured, often serving as the main, if not the only, trigger point for the formation of the PPP.
- A bias toward tangible results: Most PPPs have clear result orientation and articulate clearly the result of the partnership, such as a service (health systems strengthening, vaccine supply), a good, or even a new product like a medicine and/or vaccine.

[38] *See, e.g.*, Buse & Walt, *Global Public–Private Partnerships: Part I – A New Development in Health?* 78 BULL. WORLD HEALTH ORG. 549–561 (2000), www.who.int/bulletin/archives/78(4)549.pdf; Michael Reich, PUBLIC-PRIVATE PARTNERSHIPS FOR PUBLIC HEALTH (2002); Buse & Harmer, *supra* note 32; Stefanie Meredith & Elizabeth Ziemba, A *New Landscape of Partnerships*, 4 GLOBAL F. UPDATE RES. HEALTH 132 (2007); Sania Nishtar, *Public – Private 'Partnerships' In Health – A Global Call To Action*, 2 HEALTH RES. POL. & SYS. 1 (2004).

[39] *See, e.g.*, David Spielman & Klaus von Grebmer, *Public-Private Partner- Ships in International Agricultural Research: An Analysis of Constraints*, 31 J. TECH. TRANSFER 291– 300 (2006).

[40] Kilvenice & Quelin, *supra* note 2, similarly note the fragmentation of current studies in the general PPP literature into different streams such as management, entrepreneurship and economics.

[41] Kilvenice & Quelin, *supra* note 2.

[42] As employed in this paper, the term bias is used in the economic sense, where a bias toward a set of values or objectives shows how something sets itself apart.

Some of these papers contain highly interesting comparisons of PD PPPs,[43] early stage research PPPs,[44] and access PPPs.[45] Beyond this, however, the current literature presents the reader with a mixed, rather confusing picture.

B *Findings Related to Technology Issues*

The existing literature reveals that three common themes are relevant in the context of technology governance and institutional design: ownership structures and funding; definition of innovation; and IP.

1 Ownership Structures and Funding

As recognized by several authors, most PD PPPs today are funded by foundations such as the Bill and Melinda Gates Foundation,[46] and national governments. The PPPs are nongovernmental, nonprofit entities with a range of collaborators, including notably the private sector. At the same time, several access PPPs, especially GAVI and the Global Fund, have attracted significant governmental spending, with a range of donors and representatives from different countries in different capacities in their board structures, although low and middle-income countries are still under-represented to a large extent.[47]

2 Definition of Innovation

Many existing articles and studies view innovation as a very narrow construct relating to that particular initiative: of innovating for the specific product concerned, for example, the production of CoArtem and Lapdap for malaria or Impavido for Leishmaniasis. In some cases, innovation is construed a bit more broadly to include all aspects of capabilities. Mahoney, for example, identifies six determinants of innovation in this regard, which are broader than usual.[48] These include: (a) the design and execution of the R&D programs within the PPP; (b) analysis and planning for the marketing and distribution for new technologies in developing countries that are part of the program; (c) planning for the procurement, and supply of the health technologies in question by the global health community; (d) planning and implementation of manufacturing capabilities; (e) ensuring regulatory systems are in place for products; and finally, (6) the implementation of IP management systems/ strategies.[49]

[43] *See, e.g.*, de Pinhos Campos, *supra* note 36.

[44] *See, e.g.*, Hilde Stevens et al., *Intellectual Property Policies In Early-Phase Research In Public–Private Partnerships*, 34 Nature Biotechnology 504–510 (2016).

[45] *See, e.g.*, Buse and Harner, *supra* note 32.

[46] According to existing estimates in many papers (such as Mahoney *supra* note 37), the Bill and Melinda Gates Foundation remains the single largest donor for PDPs (P. 2 of 9).

[47] Buse & Harmer, *supra* note 32, for example, list twenty-three global health partnerships where they assess board constituencies and conclude that low and middle-income countries are heavily misrepresented in governing bodies with an average of just 17 percent across their sample, whereas the corporate sector had the greatest representation (23%). Although this may have improved since then, new and conclusive figures on such representation across PPPs are not easy to find.

[48] Mahoney, *supra* note 37

[49] *Id.* at 3.

Exceptions to these are some studies conducted in the context of the IAVI, which argue for defining innovation as the ability to develop different problem-solving techniques in complex circumstances.[50] However, these studies do not go into details of the mechanisms that lead to this type of innovation within the PPPs.

3 IP

In most PPPs, issues of technology sharing and technology acquisition are specified in terms of IP provisions, which existing literature suggests is a very important factor in determining the success of a PPP.[51] But as Stevens et al. note,[52] technical outcomes of partnerships remain somewhat unclear even in those PPPs where an IP policy is articulated, and the levels of IP information available about existing partnerships varies a lot. The Stevens study is one of the most comprehensive studies on the topic of IP frameworks of early phase biomedical research PPPs, where the authors provide an in-depth analysis of twenty PPPs that are focused on early stage research.[53] An important conclusion of their paper is to point out the variety of IP frameworks and knowledge-sharing strategies being used currently in PPPs to structure ownership, access, and use issues. Their conclusions are revisited in the chapter by Stevens and Huys in this volume.[54]

Comparing the Stevens et al. paper with other studies that use a similar approach,[55] one finds a three-way categorization of partnership strategies into those that are: (a) partnership focused; (b) open collaboration oriented; and/or (c) hybrid, based on IP management-based institutional arrangements that structure knowledge sharing and use.[56] In general, the following attributes distinguish each of these three kinds of PPP governance structures. Partnership focused PPPs are centered on the presence of certain for-profit firms that are critical for the success of the venture. The background IP (that is, the IP that has been already created and brought into the PPP) is held by the IP owner,

[50] Joanna Chataway & James Smith, *The International AIDS Vaccine Initiative (IAVI): Is It Getting New Science and Technology to the World's Neglected Majority?* 34 World Dev. 16–30 (2006); Alessandro Rosiello, James Smith, & Joanna Chataway, *Public-Private Partnerships In Africa: The Case Of IAVI*, 6 Int'l J. Tech. Mgmt. & Sustainable Dev. 1–3 (2007).

[51] Warren Kaplan et al., *Priority Medicines for Europe and the World 2013 Update*, World Health Organization (2013), www.who.int/medicines/areas/priority_medicines/MasterDocJune28_FINAL_Web.pdf; Richard T. Mahoney, Anatole Krattiger, J. D. Clemens, & R. Curtiss, *The Introduction of New Vaccines into Developing Countries: IV: Global Access Strategies*, 25 Vaccine 4003–4011 (2007).

[52] Stevens et al., *supra* note 44.

[53] Stevens et al., *supra* note 44, start out with a nonexhaustive list of thirty PPPs based on the existing literature, and then narrow down to twenty finally using purposive sampling based on the research stages they cover in the drug discovery and development process, to exclude PPPs engaged in product development or access.

[54] Hilde Stevens and Isabelle Huys, chapter 6, *supra*.

[55] *See, e.g.*, Melvin Reichman & Peter B. Simpson, *Open Innovation in Early Drug Discovery: Roadmaps and Roadblocks*, 21 Drug Discovery Today 779–788 (2016).

[56] Reichman & Simpson, *supra* note 55, also suggest a three-tier classification of the institutional models of PPPs in early drug research, which is slightly different from that of the Stevens et al (2016) paper, namely: traditional joint ventures, partnered innovation and protected open innovation model. Their classification is slightly more orthodox than the Stevens et al., *supra* note 44, study, where the traditional joint venture is a commercial joint venture, and the partnered innovation and protected open innovation models correspond to the partnership approach and the hybrid strategy respectively as Stevens et al. call it, although not on a one-to-one basis.

which explains the emphasis on IP and related license contracts to create a situation of restricted openness. Foreground IP (new IP on knowledge that can be created in the PPP) is allotted to the idea generator. Other alternate mechanisms of knowledge protection are only considered when patenting is not available as an option. A majority of the international PPPs employ this governance model. For instance, the Stevens et al. study[57] shows that over 45 percent of the total PPPs in their sample employ partnership focused governance with IP allocations.[58]

Open collaboration PPPs, on the other hand, fall at the other end of the spectrum in these classifications, where the clear aim is to share the foreground IP resulting from the project with the broader community and/or general public.[59] The sharing is often done through a license signed by the user, but the availability of the research results in the public domain ensures that anyone can gain access to these results subject to the license. Some of these PPPs allow the user to improve, change, or amend the research results for both commercial and non-commercial purposes, but the study notes that this ability to modify research results downstream varies from PPP to PPP, and is not always a given. These authors also find that commercial, for-profit firms may not be willing to invest in open collaboration PPPs given the latter's rather open policy about foreground IP. Agreeing with Stevens et al. that a pure open innovation model with open collaboration might not work in the case of pharmaceutical PPPs that involve commercial partners,[60] Reichman and Simpson suggest a so-called protected open innovation model (a hybrid approach), wherein the proprietary firm offers a so-called consignment right to use all of its IP to all the partners, and receives in turn an option right to develop products based on the leads that result from the work conducted within the PPP.[61]

What stands out from these two recent studies is that a large number of PPPs that chose either a partnership strategy or an open-collaboration strategy are not directed toward research and commercialization of drugs for developing countries, including neglected diseases.[62] These are PPPs that are of a regional nature or those focused on global issues, and where, in a large majority of the cases, commercialization of a medicine/ drug is not a primary objective. For example, the Innovative Medicines Initiative (IMI) is the world's largest PPP in life sciences, founded in 2008 by the European Commission and the European Federation of Pharmaceutical Industries and Associations. The focus of the IMI is on fostering collaboration between companies and universities, rather than focusing on diseases per se. And similarly, many other such PPPs focus on the development of assays or research tools for diseases that are prevalent in the global community, but not specifically for neglected diseases or diseases prevalent in developing countries.

In both studies, only a few focus on neglected diseases or diseases of relevance to the developing world (namely, MMV, DNDi, or WIPO Re:Search). These PPPs employ a

[57] Stevens et al., *supra* note 44.

[58] This is the same as the partnered innovation model proposed by Reichmann & Simpson, *supra* note 55, which is much more of a sponsored joint venture, as they themselves call it, where the pharma company that provides the IP assets receives an up-front payment and where the contractual arrangement clearly specifies all technological stages that might materialize and provides IP options for the IP sponsor.

[59] Stevens et al., *supra* note 44, at 506.

[60] Stevens et al., *supra* note 44, at 506.

[61] Reichman & Simpson, *supra* note 55, at 782

[62] Stevens et al., *supra* note 45; Reichman & Simpson, *supra* note 55.

hybrid governance strategy, where the IP framework is negotiated on a stage-by-stage basis, and access to research results may be available to those outside of the consortium although patenting is possible by partners if within the purview of the consortium.[63] As a result, one leaves the extant literature with the perspective that current approaches to technology in PPPs view them rather narrowly in the context of that particular product or partnership, and often only specify the goals from the perspective of the private sector.

III Limitations in Addressing the Technology Transfer Functions of PPPs

Theoretically, each international PPP faces two specific technological challenges, which are to: (1) align the incentives of the private sector with the other partners; and (2) create and sustain the environment for coinvestment. In other words, the fundamental technology transfer challenge of a PPP is to align the incentives of the private sector with the public interest goals for which the PPP has been set out. For example, if a PDP has been set out to develop a particular drug, then the primary technology transfer challenge is one of ensuring that the private sector party who owns the proprietary information required for the development of such a drug has sufficient incentives to engage in sharing this with the other actors in the PPP. This is where the IP management aspect comes in and acts as an important catalyst.

But if we were to view the issue from a broader perspective, then one is bound to conclude that providing for how background IP is managed and how foreground IP will be allocated does not really help promote technology sharing, transfer, and capacity building in the wider sense. It may not even lead to any form of tacit skills building or know-how transfer, which should be an important aspect of any partnership arrangement, from a maximising value for money perspective. Most such studies do not tackle these questions in any detail.

To look at the first issue raised here, namely the bias toward IP rights as a technology management tool in PPPs, three important explanations can be advanced. Firstly, the PPPs being studied address the broader provision of a good that is available in limited quantities (or not available at all) due to IP stipulations. Hence it can be argued, as many studies do that, in the absence of robust IP provisions within the purview of the arrangement, the partnership would not materialize at all. A second explanation is that a large number of current studies focus on PPPs operating in the pharmaceutical sector, which could then lead to the overarching emphasis on IP.[64] A third explanation is that a large number of international PPPs, despite being international, do not have a very discernible North–South dimension, in the sense of addressing broader global goals of technology sharing, economic development, and so on. One could even perhaps argue that these PPPs are dominated by the interests of the North to a certain extent, because part of the

[63] Stevens et al., *supra* note 45, at 508.

[64] The papers analyzing agricultural biotechnology do not assess IPR issues at such length. Studies cover a large number of such issues, for example, *see Seventh Steering Committee Meeting*, Asia-Pacific Consortium On Agricultural Biotechnology (APCoAB) (2007), www.apcoab.org/documents/pro_7sc.pdf; etc., but these are not peer reviewed. It is also possible that a large number of IPR issues are considered in agricultural biotechnology in the context of Bt varieties, which are not predominantly in use in many countries, and IPR issues are clearly settled.

impetus for their creation has been to ensure a "back door" for the production of goods and/or research that maybe affected by IP.

But even if one were to accept the argument that the IP assets of the proprietary firm need to be protected, and the IP holder needs to have particular incentives to engage in the PPP in the first place, from a broader perspective, one could ask why a PPP, in parallel, should not accommodate the knowledge sharing and learning goals of the other partners of the partnership? Of course, one could always argue that PPPs are established for certain specific goals that partners agree to, and it should be up to the partners to go beyond their original goals. But the more fundamental question is whether the partners have jointly agreed to these goals on the basis of a common understanding of the full developmental outcomes that can materialize from these projects.

The literature review shows that the answer to this, in more cases than not, is negative. The reasons for the narrow focus on IP management in PPPs or, more broadly, what can be called an imbalanced representation of the interests of the different actors within current PPPs, seem to be due to a creation bias. That is, a large number of donors (governments and third-party agencies alike) have a bias toward funding agencies that are based in or are identified with a similar cultural ethic as their own country. Making the same point, Callan and Davies note, in pursuing PPPs with multinational corporations, "donors tend somewhat to favour corporations that are headquartered in, or identified with, their own countries."[65] Over the life time of a PPP, this creation bias then becomes a status-quo bias, to cater to dominant interests due to certain endemic PPP institutional features. These include a constant shortage of funding (that often precludes a PPP from self-reflection on ancillary advantages of its own work), uncertainty over product pipelines and results, as well as rising transaction and coordination costs due to diverging interests, among others. This is exacerbated, as Buse and Harmer point out in their study, by the phenomenon that PPPs are often out of sync in aligning themselves well with partners' and partner countries' priorities.[66]

As a case in point, one of the only PPPs that has integrated technology transfer and capacity building from the start is the IAVI. In the case of IAVI, for example, existing studies document the presence of a capacity building approach as a critical element of the PPP. This is partly due to the structure of IAVI from the start, which set it apart from other such PPPs, namely that: (a) it was mainly comprised of several foundations and only one research institute, apart from boasting of no for-profit private sector entity at all;[67] (b) it relied on creating a series of vaccine development partnerships in the specific regions it worked in; and (c) there was a large NGO presence and reliance.[68] The case of MPP, discussed in a different chapter in this volume,[69] is another such instance.

[65] Margaret Callan & Robin Davies, *When Business Meets Aid: Analysing Public-Private Partnerships for International Development* 2 (The Australian National University, Canberra, Crawford School of Public Policy, Development Policy Centre Discussion Paper 28, 2013), http://devpolicy.anu.edu.au/pdf/papers/DP_28_-_%20When%20business%20meets%20aid%20-%20analysing%20public-private%20partnerships%20for%20international%20development.pdf.

[66] Buse & Harmer, *supra* note 32, at 262.

[67] Chataway & Smith, *supra* note 50, note that as of 2000, IAVI formally listed itself as having only five partners: The Foundation Marcel Merieux, the Francois Xavier Bagnould Foundation, the National AIDS Trust, the AIDS Advocacy Coalition, and the Albert B Sabin Vaccine Institute.

[68] *See* Chataway & Smith, *supra* note 50.

[69] Esteban Burrone, chapter 5, *supra*.

These problems not only are true for PD PPPs, but also are often mentioned in the case of some access PPPs and agriculture PPPs.[70] A potential reason for this is that low and middle-income countries are often not well-represented on boards of PPPs, or do not have an equal voice in negotiating the outcomes or in assessing milestones.[71] Another reason for this is the large-scale private sector dominance of PPPs, for reasons of which Merz suggests that it might be better to call them "private-public partnerships."[72] Either way, in the presence of certain majority interests, PPPs are designed and evaluated in ways that may not accurately reflect the interests of all partners. This may even be true when international organisations are involved, which often play only a moderating role in the process.

PPPs and their successes tend to be tied to the wider institutional environment in which a PPP operates. That is, better and cheaper vaccines cannot be delivered in an efficient way without appropriate measures to strengthen health systems delivery. This is clear in the case of GAVI, for example, which is a PPP that relies extensively on evaluating countries and working with other international agencies with a view to effectively support them to strengthen their health systems while delivering vaccines. Similarly, clinical trials cannot be conducted for important new drug discoveries without promoting the capabilities of the staff in local laboratories, including public health specialists and doctors who may help generate awareness and administer the drugs at the final stages to focus groups. Preliminarily, the review conducted for this paper suggests that as opposed to PD PPPs, which are predominantly structured on IP issues, access PPPs that aim at health sector restructuring and health systems' strengthening are more engaged in effectively building capacity in developing countries as they engage with, and rely more clearly on, national partners for successful delivery outcomes.

IV A Technology Norm Setting for the Future

Notwithstanding their occasional successes, a burning question remains: are PPPs going about the issues correctly from a developmental perspective? Should we have a more balanced perspective on PPPs governance?[73]

Drawing lessons for the future, it is important to look at two separate aspects. On the one hand, PPPs should be evaluated in terms of the services and products they deliver. But at the same time, this should also be weighed against whether there might be greater synergies in delivering these services or products, given the public policy objectives of a country, region, or global community as a whole. Thus, a proper "value for money" exercise should maximise the social benefits of such the partnership, particularly if these partnerships are to achieve developmental impact. In a similar analysis in the context of infrastructure PPPs for 2030 Agenda, Jomo et al. note that the idea that PPPs must

[70] See for example, Buse & Harmer, *supra* note 32, for access PPPs, and agriculture PPPs.

[71] Buse & Harmer, *supra* note 32.

[72] Jon Merz, *Intellectual Property and Product Development Public/Private Partnerships*, Report to the World Health Organization Commission on Intellectual Property Rights, Innovation and Public Health, WHO 1, 16 (2005), www.who.int/intellectualproperty/studies/Merz%20WHO%20report.pdf.

[73] Callan & Davies, *supra* note 65, at 1, note similarly: "However, the potential of public-private partnerships for development is still largely unrealised. Business and development agencies would benefit from a better understanding of what forms of practical partnership might be constructed, for what purposes and with what likely impact."

provide value for money should in fact be interpreted in its widest possible sense, taking into account all efficiency gains and also the social, economic, and other objectives embodied in the 2030 Agenda.[74] Surely an international PPP by nature implies greater heterogeneity and this does not lend itself to a tidy and neat partnership ideal. But if the PPPs are to serve the goals of technological learning and technology transfer, it remains important to consider alternate incentives in such partnerships that account for the longer term needs of all partners.

The different levels of knowledge amongst the partners is one major factor hindering PPPs from functioning effectively in aligning the knowledge incentives of the private sector with its other partners. For example, the level of technological capabilities in any PPP consortium varies from the state of the art, at the one end (typically of the private sector entity), to the most innovation-constrained labs of developing countries, at the other. This raises the question of what the partner with low technological capability (such as a lab, or a university, or even a firm from a low-income country) might stand to gain from institutional structures that focus mainly on protecting background IP and deciding option rights on foreground IP in the contract.

Worse yet, PPPs may be losing the potential to have major breakthroughs in the longer term, by failing to consider more comprehensively the benefits of engaging in collaborative learning for technology. This raises a separate question of how does the PPP engage the private sector, create an environment for co-investment, and promote technological exchange in a better way? A fundamental problem here is the view of technology transfer that continues to taint the discussions between partners even within PPPs (see Box 15.1). Another problem is related to the current institutional designs of technology sharing, which often ignore the cultural and social element of knowledge creation and collaborative learning, and the consequent hurdles for problem solving and trust building.

Scholars in recent times, have tried to articulate the determinants of the boundaries between public and private economic activity and what the implications are of these boundary choices in terms of social and economic value.[75] But these efforts do not take on board the difficulties of merging the private and the public, which is particularly challenging in the case of knowledge goods, with their specific features of non-appropriability and non-excludability. Trading with technological knowledge, and sharing such knowledge for uncertain future outcomes carries along specific risks that need to be borne in mind while creating strategic linkages for technological innovation amongst partners, each of which bring a certain comparative strength to the contract. Not only is this not an easy process,[76] but it also cannot be visualised as a one-shot contract. Such PPPs are therefore better off as relational contracts where all technological stages cannot be *ex ante* specified. That is, governance models have to be fluid enough to allow the parties to engage in repeated collaboration.

[74] Jomo et al., *supra* note 22, at 12.

[75] Kivleniece & Quelin, *supra* note 2; Oliver Hart, *Incomplete Contracts and Public Ownership: Remarks, and an Application to Public-Private Partnerships*, 113 Econ. J. 69–76 (2003); Witold Henisz, *Governance Issues in Public Private Partnerships*, 24 Int'l J. Project Mgmt. 537–538 (2006); Joseph Mahoney, Anita Mcgahan, & Christos Pitelis, *The Interdependence of Private and Public Interests*, 20 Org. Sci. 1034–52 (2009).

[76] Michele Bolten, Roger Maimrose, & William Ouchi, *The Organization of Innovation in the United States and Japan: Neoclassical and Relational Contracting*, 31 J. Mgmt, Stud. 653–679 (1994).

This explains why international PPPs are often structured as hybrid models of relational contracting where the emphasis is on continuing collaboration on a case-by-case basis. Economists have since long advocated that such relational contracting is the better alternative to any other form of arrangement when there are common investments in specialized assets, and when there is a continuous exchange of knowledge with related technology transfer.[77] But such relational contracting needs to be conducted on equal contractual basis, where each partner has the same kind of bargaining power to determine outcomes particularly with relation to technology sharing.

Applying these observations to the current context implies the following changes to existing governance models for international PPPs:

A *A Focus on Collaborative Learning*

Collaborative learning is as much social and cultural as it is technological, and institutions that foster some degree of trust are critical for longer-term success.[78] Developing country institutions need much more engagement and capacity building from such initiatives if they are to really benefit more comprehensively in terms of technological learning.[79] Technological norm setting, with the goal of efficient access to and dissemination of already created knowledge stocks, consists of two parts: (1) agents who hold useful information need incentives to reveal this information (that is IP, as granted to the proprietary owners in the PPP), and (2) efficient mechanisms for the dissemination and use of such information by the other partners in the PPP to ensure learning and longer term capabilities building. The repercussions of the lack of either legal or technology sharing mechanisms are not to be underestimated. In the absence of adequate policy initiatives that allow for both, disputes relating to innovation may become commonplace.

B *Balanced Representation of Partners' Interests from Inception*

PPPs' governance mechanisms in the presence of a North–South dimension must ensure an equal and equitable representation of interests, to make sure that the longer term goals of all partners are well-reflected and built into the contractual arrangement from the start, even if the details are to be specified in instalments over time.

C *Alignment and Recognition of Complementary Skills*

PPPs should be structured with a clear alignment of the roles and responsibilities of all partner institutions. In particular, developing country institutions (where involved) can more actively engage in all stages of the knowledge creation processes (including frontier R&D). Success is more likely if their existing capabilities are nurtured and engaged. The

[77] *See, e.g.* Oliver Williamson, *Transaction-Cost Economics: The Governance of Contractual Relations*, 22 J. L. & Econ. 233–261 (1979); Oliver Hart & John Moore, *Property Rights and the Nature of the Firm*, 98, J. Pol. Econ. 1119–1158 (1990); Arezki et al., *From Global Savings Glut to Financing Infrastructure* 1–39 (Int'l Monetary Fund Working Paper No. WP/16/18 2017) in the context of PPPs.

[78] Leni Wild et al., *Making Sense of the Politics of Delivery: Our Findings So Far*, ODI (2013).

[79] Stevens et al., *supra* note 44, at 505, note that co-ownership of foreground IP creates the PPP to build strong technological basis for all its partners, but find that of all the PPPs that they surveyed in the early development phase, only three PPPS applied a partnership development strategy.

capacity of different actors to contribute to solutions in a more localised way should also be provided for. Simply put, problem solving in complex contexts calls for a multitude of skills, some of which can be brought to the partnership by the developing country partners over time. For example, in the case of a PD PPP, this could include knowledge of local medicinal knowledge and related techniques, knowledge of cheaper production processes (as in the case of generics), and an understanding of local production and distribution networks, etc. However, in an effort to engage the private sector, the particular bias of viewing technological innovation in the context of IP protection might compromise the development of such a comprehensive approach to problem solving.

D *A More Holistic Approach to Technology Sharing and Transfer*

The IP questions and technology transfer challenges can be different in different contexts, challenging the actors to respond differently or modify their approaches over time. But both need to be clearly defined *ex ante* in the ambit of the partnership, with clear board and management guidelines for monitoring over time. Even if these benefits for technology sharing and transfer are recognised as secondary goals, it may be sufficient to ensure that common priorities are better coordinated within PPPs, thereby leading to greater capacity, greater synergy with donor and other partner programs, and better results in the longer run. It would be important for developing country governments and institutions to consider risk-sharing in the PPP itself, to ensure that such an approach to technology materialises.

E *Coordination between PPPs and a Wider Socioeconomic, Technological Paradigm*

From a broader, sustainability perspective, not only do PPPs have synergies with the broader national or regional environment and other initiatives going on therein, but also potentially greater synergies between and among PPPs themselves. In the current context, a large number of PPPs (especially in the health sector) are working alongside each other under a lot of pressure to coordinate their efforts at a bilateral level. Going ahead, and in the context of the 2030 Agenda for Action or other development initiatives,[80] it would be highly relevant to address the questions of how an individual PPP might situate itself within the broader national or regional context. Important questions in this context could be:

- How does the PPP situate itself within the broader technological context of the country, or the region?
- How are the PPP's objectives aligned with national development plans and goals?
- What are the links between the PPP and national donor programmes and local innovation activities?
- How could the PPP interact and engage in promoting technological learning beyond the project?
- What specific contribution to capacity and skills building can be made by the PPP?

[80] These include the AAAA, the WIPO Development Agenda, or the WHO's GSPOA.

Many countries are already far ahead in policy thinking in terms of providing a PPP policy,[81] and this could be a consideration in such a policy context.

Some Concluding Remarks

This chapter has focused on international PPPs and the challenge of providing for technology sharing and transfer therein. Insights from studies on PPPs that are broader in their scope and coverage[82] form the background in discussing the typography of international PPPs, including their structural strengths and weaknesses.

This contribution has sought to provide a clear distinction between international PPPs and a myriad of other such arrangements that are often also called PPPs, with a view to creating a clear nomenclature and understanding. It has suggested a new definition for international PPPs as new forms of hybrid institutional models that involve private and the public sectors from the national and international spheres of influence, with hand-picked collaborators. Normatively, these arrangements should be characterized by: (a) tailor-made terms of collaboration; (b) clear mechanisms for monitoring and control for each of the goals; and (c) fair representation of all interested parties in every aspect of the partnership.

The chapter has also justified why these aspects are important. The review conducted for the chapter shows that economic and other literature has yet to address the question of optimal design of PPPs, including international PPPs. In the case of technological norm setting, most studies on the topic either view it in terms of IP management, with little or no reference to knowledge governance, capacity building, technology transfer, and/or technology sharing. The chapter has also tried to highlight the results of those studies, demarcating the merits of different approaches. A major limitation currently is clearly the lack of a systematic framework in which to study institutional design and governance issues across PPPs.

While acknowledging that all forms of PPPs are not the same, some basis to compare existing evidence is needed. And as the chapter has highlighted, to learn and build upon current experiences in the context of the 2030 Agenda on SDGs and the AAAA calls for a more objective approach to PPPs, one which clearly places the emphasis on value for money. In technological areas of cooperation, this means that the debate on structuring and institutional design of PPPs will invariably move beyond a consideration of IP only. Technological learning and technology transfer is a holistic process, which does not depend on the IP aspect of a transaction only. If partners do not have equal capacity to exploit the information, granting access to IP is not necessarily a technological empowerment in any partnership. It will therefore be important to change the rules of the game in PPPs. Any institutional design and assessment should be cognizant of the limitations imposed by assessing technology in the narrower confines of IP only and constructing PPPs as very narrow technology collaborations. Eliminating these biases will call for a stronger review of the institutional underpinnings of PPPs from the start of the process.

[81] *See, e.g.*, *National Public Private Partnership Policy*, United Republic of Tanzania (2009), https://tanzania.go.tz/egov_uploads/documents/ppp_policy_sw.pdf.

[82] *See, e.g.*, Hodge & Greve, *supra* note 2, that looks at infrastructure PPPs, or Bovaird, *supra* note 1, that considers PPPs to resolve environment, energy, and transport issues.

Finally, a set of guidelines that promote technology sharing as a clear goal (and not as an eventual or incidental outcome) in international PPPs may help increase their effectiveness so far as the SDGs are concerned. Such guidelines have been proposed more recently in the context of infrastructure PPPs for the AAAA,[83] but incorporating the particular characteristics of technological learning and sharing into a similar set of guidelines could well be the next pertinent step.

References

Arezki et al., *From Global Savings Glut to Financing Infrastructure* (Int'l Monetary Fund Working Paper No. WP/16/18 2017).

Barlow, James et al., *Europe Sees Mixed Results from Public-Private Partnerships for Building and Managing Health Care Facilities and Services*, 32 HEALTH AFF. 146–154 (2013).

Bolten, Michele, Roger Maimrose, & William Ouchi, *The Organization of Innovation in the United States and Japan: Neoclassical and Relational Contracting*, 31 J. MGMT, STUD. (1994).

Bovaird, Tony, *Public-Private Partnerships: From Contested Concepts to Prevalent Practice*, 70 INT'L REV. ADMIN. SCI. (2004).

Buse, Kent & Andrew Harmer, *Seven Habits of Highly Effective Global Public–Private Health Partnerships: Practice and Potential*, 64 SOC. SCI. & MED. (2007).

Buse, Kent & G. Walt, *Global Public–Private Partnerships: Part I – A New Development in Health?* 78 BULL. WORLD HEALTH ORG. (2000), www.who.int/bulletin/archives/78(4)549.pdf (last visited Nov. 17, 2017).

Callan, Margaret & Robin Davies, *When Business Meets Aid: Analysing Public-Private Partnerships for International Development* 2 (The Australian National University, Canberra, Crawford School of Public Policy, Development Policy Centre Discussion Paper 28, 2013), http://devpolicy.anu.edu.au/pdf/papers/DP_28_-_%20When%20business%20meets%20aid%20-%20analysing%20public-private%20partnerships%20for%20international%20development.pdf (last visited Nov. 17, 2017).

Chataway, Joanna & James Smith, *The International AIDS Vaccine Initiative (IAVI): Is It Getting New Science and Technology to the World's Neglected Majority?* 34 WORLD DEV. (2006).

De Pinho, Campos et al., *Product Development Public–Private Partnerships for Public Health: A Systematic Review Using Qualitative Data*, 73 SOC. SCI. & MED. (2011).

Grimsey, Darrin & Mervyn Lewis, PUBLIC PRIVATE PARTNERSHIPS: THE WORLDWIDE REVOLUTION IN INFRASTRUCTURE PROVISION AND PROJECT FINANCE (2007).

Hart, Oliver and John Moore, *Property Rights and the Nature of the Firm*, 98, J. POL. ECON. (1990).

Hart, Oliver, *Incomplete Contracts and Public Ownership: Remarks, and an Application to Public-Private Partnerships*, 113 ECON. J. (2003).

Heldeweg, Michael and Maurits Sanders, *Towards a Design Framework for Legitimate Public Private Partnerships*, 2014 EURO. PROCUREMENT & PUB. PRIV. PARTNERSHIP L. REV. (2014).

Henisz, Witold, *Governance Issues in Public Private Partnerships*, 24 INT'L J. PROJECT MGMT. (2006).

Hodge, Graeme & Carsten Greve, *Public–Private Partnerships: An International Performance Review*, 67 PUB. ADMIN. REV. (2007).

International AIDS Vaccine Initiative, *Mission Statement*, www.iavi.org/about-us *(last visited Nov. 17, 2017)*.

[83] *See* Jomo et al., *supra* note 22.

Jomo, Kwame Sundaram et al., *Public-Private Partnerships and the 2030 Agenda for Sustainable Development: Fit for Purpose?* (DESA Working Paper No. 148, ST/ESA/2016/DWP/148, 2016).

Kaplan, Warren et al., *Priority Medicines for Europe and the World 2013 Update*, World Health Organization (2013), www.who.int/medicines/areas/priority_medicines/MasterDocJune28_FINAL_Web.pdf

Kivleniece, Ilze & Bertrand V. Quelin, *Creating and Capturing Value in Public-Private Ties: A Private Actor's Perspective*, 37 Acad. Mgmt. Rev. (2012).

Klijn, Erik-Hans & Geert R. Teisman, *Partnership Arrangements: Governmental Rhetoric or Governance Scheme?*, 62 Pub. Admin. Rev. (2002).

Koppenjan, Joop, *The Formation of Public-Private Partnerships: Lessons from Nine Transport Infrastructure Projects in The Netherlands*, 83 Pub. Admin. (2005).

Krause, Tobias, A Contingency Framework on Partnership Risk, International Journal of Public Sector Management, Vol. 27, No. 4, 2014.

Linder, Stephen, *Coming to Terms with the Public-Private Partnership, A Grammar of Multiple Meanings*, 43 Am. Behav. Sci. (1999).

Mahoney, Joseph, Anita McGahan & Christos Pitelis, *The Interdependence of Private and Public Interests*, 20 Org. Sci. (2009).

Mahoney, Richard T., Anatole Krattiger, J. D. Clemens, & R. Curtiss, *The Introduction of New Vaccines into Developing Countries: IV: Global Access Strategies*, 25 Vaccine (2007).

Mahoney, Richard T., *Product Development Partnerships: Case Studies of a New Mechanism for Health Technology Innovation*, 9 Health Research Pol'y & Sys. (2011).

Maskus, Keith & Jerome Reichman, *The Globalization of Private Knowledge Goods and the Privatization of Global Public Goods*, 7 J. Int'l Econ. L. (2004).

Meredith, Stefanie & Elizabeth Ziemba, *A New Landscape of Partnerships*, 4 Global F. Update Res. Health (2007).

Merz, Jon, *Intellectual Property and Product Development Public/Private Partnerships*, Report to the World Health Organization Commission on Intellectual Property Rights, Innovation and Public Health, WHO 1, 16 (2005), www.who.int/intellectualproperty/studies/Merz%20WHO%20report.pdf (last visited Nov. 17, 2017).

Nishtar, Sania, *Public – Private 'Partnerships' In Health – A Global Call to Action*, 2 Health Res. Pol'y. & Sys. (2004).

Nwaka, Soloman et al., *Developing ANDI: A Novel Approach to Health Product R&D in Africa*, 7 PLoS Med. (2010), https://doi.org/10.1371/journal.pmed.1000293 (last visited Nov. 17, 2017).

Okediji, Ruth, *Legal Innovation in International Intellectual Property Relations: Revisiting Twenty-One Years of The Trips Agreement*, 36 U. Pa. J. Int'l L. (2015).

Reich, Michael, Public-Private Partnerships for Public Health (2002).

Ridley, Robert G. *et al.*, *Round Table: A Role of Public–Private Partnerships In Controlling Neglected Diseases*, 79 Bull. World Health Org. (2001).

Roehrich, Jens et al., *Are Public–Private Partnerships A Healthy Option? A Systematic Literature* Review, 113 Soc. Sci. & Med. (2014).

Romero, Maria, *What Lies Beneath? A Critical Assessment Of PPPs And Their Impact On Sustainable Development*, EURODAD 12 (2015), www.eurodad.org/files/pdf/55cb59060d9d4.pdf (last visited Nov. 17, 2017).

Rosiello, Alessandro, James Smith, & Joanna Chataway, *Public-Private Partnerships In Africa: The Case Of IAVI*, 6 Int'l J. Tech. Mgmt. & Sustainable Dev. (2007).

Sanders, Maurits, *Collaborative Enterprise: Next Stage Public-Private Partnerships?*, *in* The Collaborative Enterprise: Creating Values for a Sustainable World (2013).

Seventh Steering Committee Meeting, Asia-Pacific Consortium On Agricultural Biotechnology (APCoAB) (2007), www.apcoab.org/documents/pro_7sc.pdf (last visited Nov. 17, 2017).

Spielman, David & Klaus von Grebmer, *Public-Private Partner- Ships in International Agricultural Research: An Analysis of Constraints*, 31 J. TECH. TRANSFER (2006).
Spielman, David et al., *The Art and Science of Innovation Systems Inquiry: Applications to Sub-Saharan African Agriculture*, 31 TECH. IN SOC. (2009).
Stevens, Hilde et al., *Intellectual Property Policies in Early-Phase Research in Public–Private Partnerships*, 34 NATURE BIOTECHNOLOGY (2016).
Sustainable Development Knowledge Platform, SDG 17, U.N. Dept. of Soc. & Econ. Aff., www.un.org/sustainabledevelopment/globalpartnerships/ (last visited Nov. 17, 2017).
Sustainable Development Knowledge Platform, *Transforming our world: the 2030 Agenda for Sustainable Development*, U.N. DEPT. OF ECON. & SOC. AFF., https://sustainabledevelopment.un.org/post2015/transformingourworld (last visited Nov. 17, 2017).
TB Alliance, *Innovations*, www.tballiance.org/rd/innovations/sharing-lab-manuals (last visited Nov. 17, 2017).
TRIPS: Agreement on Trade-Related Aspects of Intellectual Property Rights. Part I – General Provisions and Basic Principles, WORLD TRADE ORGANIZATION (Jan. 21, 2017), www.wto.org/english/tratop_e/trips_e/trips_e.htm (last visited Nov. 17, 2017).
UN System Task Team on the Post-2015 UN Development Agenda, *Science, Technology and Innovation for Sustainable Development in the Global Partnership for Development Beyond 2015: Thematic Think Piece* (2013), www.un.org/en/development/desa/policy/untaskteam_undf/thinkpieces/28_thinkpiece_science.pdf (last visited Nov. 17, 2017).
United Republic of Tanzania, *National Public Private Partnership Policy* (2009), https://tanzania.go.tz/egov_uploads/documents/ppp_policy_sw.pdf (last visited Nov. 17, 2017).
Waring, Justin, Graime Currie, & Simon Bishop, *A Contingent Approach to the Organization and Management of Public–Private Partnerships: An Empirical Study of English Health Care*, 73 PUB. ADMIN. REV. (2013).
Whitfield, Dexter, GLOBAL AUCTION OF PUBLIC ASSETS: PUBLIC SECTOR ALTERNATIVES TO THE INFRASTRUCTURE MARKET AND PUBLIC PRIVATE PARTNERSHIPS (2010).
Widdus, Roy, *Public-Private Partnerships: An Overview*, 99 TRANS. ROYAL SOC. TROPICAL MED. & HYGIENE (2005).
Williamson, Oliver, *Transaction-Cost Economics: The Governance of Contractual Relations*, 22 J. L. & ECON. (1979).
Wild, Leni et al., *Making Sense of the Politics of Delivery: Our Findings So Far*, ODI (2013).
WORLD BANK GROUP, *World Bank Annual Report* (2014), https://openknowledge.worldbank.org/handle/10986/20093 (last visited Nov. 17, 2017).
Yang, Yongheng et al., *On the Development of Public-Private Partnerships in Transitional Economies: An Explanatory Framework*, 73 PUB. ADM. REV. (2013).

16 From the MDGs to the SDGs: Cross-Sector Partnerships as Avenues to Development in the UN System

David J. Maurrasse

Introduction

The emergence and proliferation of partnerships such as public–private partnerships (PPPs) demonstrate an important shift in thinking about the roles and responsibilities of the public, private, nongovernmental (NGO), and nonprofit (NPO) sectors. Partnerships such as PPPs bring together the resources of public, private, NGO, and NPO entities with the intent to address a goal or a series of goals that likely could not be adequately resolved without a blend of participants representing different sectors. In these collaborative initiatives, the lines and expectations between the sectors blur, and new institutional models are created.

Some partnerships include multiple participants, such as representatives of corporations, local governments, community-based agencies, private foundations, universities, hospitals, and various other types of institutions. But PPPs can also be represented by a singular corporation and a single government partnering with each other. The term "public–private partnership" can indeed be limiting, as it literally suggests some degree of collaboration between a government entity and a private entity. However, many compelling public–private partnerships involve universities, private foundations, and other types of NPOs in addition to private corporate partners. Therefore, this chapter uses the term "cross-sector partnerships"[1] to be more explicitly inclusive of this reality. Cross-sector partnerships can include but are not limited to PPPs; they refer to the full range of types of partnerships that transcend sectors or fields, especially those that intend to solve social and economic challenges, such as those expressed by the United Nations (UN).

As 2015 approached, it became apparent that the focused call to action championed by the UN through the original Millennium Development Goals (MDGs)[2] required

[1] In a 2014 Research Report, the Canadian-based North-South Institute (NSI) defined 'cross-sector development partnerships' as "commitments between or among public, private, and/or non-profit institutions in which individuals from partner organizations commit various resources and agree to work cooperatively toward common development goals." Shannon Kindornay et al., *The Value of Cross-Sector Development Partnerships*, NSI Research Report, iv (2014), www.nsi-ins.ca/wp-content/uploads/2014/01/The-Value-of-Cross-Sector-Development-Partnerships.pdf.

[2] *The Millennium Development Goals Report 2015*, U.N. (2015), www.un.org/millenniumgoals/2015_MDG_Report/pdf/MDG%202015%20rev%20(July%201).pdf were as follows:

1. Eradicate Extreme Poverty and Hunger
2. Achieve Universal Primary Education
3. Promote Gender Equality and Empower Women

revision and renewed commitment toward a more equitable and just global society. Consequently, the Sustainable Development Goals (SDGs) came into being as part of the 2030 Agenda for Sustainable Development.[3] As with the earlier MDGs (effective between 2000 and 2015), the SDGs have a fifteen-year time horizon, and are intended to be achieved by 2030. Approved unanimously by 193 Heads of State during a UN Summit in September 2015,[4] the global effort toward these substantial goals officially began on January 1, 2016. Among the more notable changes moving from the MDGs to the SDGs are not only the increased number of goals from eight to seventeen, but also the approach to partnerships. Under the SDGs, partnerships are not simply a means to an end, but a preferred means to implementation under SDG 17.[5] Significantly, this implies moving beyond development assistance (and/or decreasing preferential treatment in trade) and towards a "revitalize[d] global partnership for sustainable development."[6]

Throughout this chapter, the role of the cross-sector partnerships, including PPPs, will be examined in light of their influence on the UN SDGs and their former counterpart, the UN MDGs. The chapter first assesses the role that cross-sector partnerships play, reflecting on the potential impact of these partnerships on the realization of the SDGs. It then discusses the lessons learned from the involvement of cross-sector partnerships in the progress made towards the MDGs. In assessing the impact of partnerships on the implementation of both the SDGs and MDGs, the chapter draws primarily on examples from agricultural and rural development for poverty reduction. It concludes by providing thoughts on the future direction of cross-sector partnerships in addressing global development challenges.[7]

I Cross-Sector Partnerships as an Approach to Alleviating Global Disparities

With their ability to leverage a complex array of resources and expertise beyond traditionally defined barriers, cross-sector partnerships emerged as crucial avenues to address the wide range of critical issues in community and economic development included among the previous MDGs and the current SDGs. While some successes are evident in leveraging these partnerships to address both MDGs and SDGs, unique challenges are involved in creating new strategies that effectively force stakeholders to operate outside of their comfort zones. These types of partnerships often bring varying types of public,

4. Reduce Child Mortality
5. Improve Maternal Health
6. Combat HIV/AIDS, Malaria and Other Diseases
7. Ensure Environmental Sustainability
8. Develop a Global Partnership for Development

[3] Sustainable Development Knowledge Platform, *Transforming Our World: The 2030 Agenda for Sustainable Development*, U.N. Dep't of Econ. and Soc. Affairs.

[4] *Sustainable Development Goals Kick Off with Start of New Year*, U.N. (Dec. 30, 2015).

[5] Sustainable Development Knowledge Platform, *Transforming Our World: The 2030 Agenda for Sustainable Development: Topics*, U.N. Dep't of Econ. and Soc. Affairs.

[6] SDG 17, *supra* 4.

[7] This chapter focuses primarily on the historical development and current role of partnerships in sustainable development, and does not address intellectual property issues.

private, and nonprofit institutions together in ways they may never have operated before in innovative institutional collaborations described as "polyglot transnational networks."[8]

In many ways, contemporary social, economic, and political dynamics have blended sectors together, and are increasingly characterized by sheer interdependence. Various shifting social and economic conditions, including shrinking government resources and increasingly complex social problems, illustrated the need for new thinking and strategies. The public sector began to broaden its perspective on influencing civic participation and acquiring revenue. The for-profit sector started finding value beyond their fiscal bottom lines and recognizing symbiosis between financial and societal goals. NPOs continue to be driven by their respective social missions. In recent years, this mission-driven disposition of NPOs has become increasingly prevalent also in for-profit corporations via the human rights-inflected framework of corporate social responsibility. A growing NGO/NPO influence, fueled by the expansion of private financial resources through philanthropy, also constructed new roles for organizations representing civil society. Over recent decades, it has become increasingly apparent that the resources and expertise housed in disparate sectors and industries would have to be coordinated in some fashion to meet our global society's most pressing needs and to eliminate redundancy where possible. These forces have given rise to cross-sector partnerships, including PPPs, as complex but necessary institutional tools to alleviate matters such as poverty, hunger, and health disparities. Cross-sector partnerships accentuate the level of cross-sector communication required for effective implementation of strategies to solve social and economic problems. They are unique applications of the intersecting social and institutional ecosystems in which we all reside.

This is the context around which the UN has considered partnerships as vital to achieving lofty ends around a range of persistent global concerns. To varying degrees of success, cross-sector partnerships have been vehicles to help the UN implement its strategies. And due to their potential, the UN has deliberately, and arguably forcefully, expanded its emphasis on these collaborative approaches.

A *The SDGs and Cross-Sector Partnerships*

The SDGs seek to build on the MDGs and complete what these previous goals did not achieve. The SDGs integrate the three dimensions of sustainable development: the economic, social, and environmental. Most relevant to this chapter is their focus on achieving these new sets of goals through partnerships such as PPPs. As outlined in the 2030 Agenda, all countries and all stakeholders, acting in collaborative partnership, will implement this plan for sustainable development through the SDGs[9]

[8] Margaret Chon, *PPPs in Global IP (public-private partnerships in global intellectual property)*, *in* METHODS AND PERSPECTIVES IN INTELLECTUAL PROPERTY 296 (Graeme B. Dinwoodie ed., 2013).

[9] *See* Sustainable Development Knowledge Platform, *supra* 3. The first fifteen SDGs are as follows:

1. No Poverty: End poverty in all of its forms everywhere.
2. Zero Hunger: End hunger, achieve food security and improved nutrition and promote sustainable agriculture.
3. Good Health and Well Being: Ensure healthy lives and promote well-being for all at all ages.
4. Quality Education: Ensure inclusive and equitable quality education and promote lifelong learning opportunities for all.

The seventeen SDGs include:

16. Peace, Justice, and Strong Institutions: Promote peaceful and inclusive societies for sustainable development, provide access to justice for all and build effective, accountable and inclusive institutions at all levels.
17. Partnerships for the Goals: Strengthen the means of implementation and revitalize the global partnership for sustainable development.

And among the various targets and indicators embedded within Goal 17[10] are:

17.16
Enhance the global partnership for sustainable development, complemented by multi-stakeholder partnerships that mobilize and share knowledge, expertise, technology and financial resources, to support the achievement of the sustainable development goals in all countries, in particular developing countries
17.16.1
Number of countries reporting progress in multi-stakeholder development effectiveness monitoring frameworks that support the achievement of the sustainable development goals
17.17
Encourage and promote effective public, public-private and civil society partnerships, building on the experience and resourcing strategies of partnerships
Data, monitoring and accountability
17.17.1
Amount of United States dollars committed to public-private and civil society partnerships

Although the SDGs clearly elaborate on the shorter list of MDGs, the SDGs add new dimensions to a vision for a more sustainable, equitable, and just global community. For example, Goal 16 ("Peace, Justice, and Strong Institutions") addresses the nature of the societal contexts in which people reside, such as conceptions of social justice and

5. Gender Equality: Achieve gender equality and empower all women and girls.
6. Clean Water and Sanitation: Ensure availability and sustainable management of water and sanitation for all.
7. Affordable and Clean Energy: Ensure access to affordable, reliable, sustainable and modern energy for all.
8. Decent Work and Economic Growth: Promote sustained, inclusive and sustainable economic growth, full and productive employment and decent work for all.
9. Industry, Innovation, and Infrastructure: Build resilient infrastructure, promote inclusive and sustainable industrialization and foster innovation.
10. Reduced Inequalities: Reduce inequality within and among countries.
11. Sustainable Cities and Communities: Make cities and human settlements inclusive, safe, resilient and sustainable.
12. Responsible Consumption and Production: Ensure sustainable consumption and production patterns.
13. Climate Action: Take urgent action to combat climate change and its impacts.
14. Life Below Water: Conserve and sustainably use the oceans, seas and marine resources for sustainable development.
15. Life on Land: Protect, restore and promote sustainable use of terrestrial ecosystems, sustainably manage forests, combat desertification, and halt and reverse land degradation and halt biodiversity loss.

[10] SDG 17 Targets & Indicators, U.N. DEP'T OF ECON. AND SOC. AFFAIRS, https://sustainabledevelopment.un.org/sdg17.

inclusive societies. It stresses the importance of just and peaceful societies and the need for institutional accountability. This goal stands as a noticeable departure from the more issue-oriented goals. The evolution in thinking from the MDGs to the SDGs is reflected in Goals 16 and 17, which both highlight the importance of broader variables beyond singular issues. It is difficult to achieve successful educational progress, for example, in oppressive societies with unaccountable institutions.

The societal and contextual emphasis in Goal 16 is relevant to partnerships, which are the subject of Goal 17. Communities, cities, and regions that promote open institutions and peace provide fertile ground for partnerships. These are likely contexts in which trust and communication across institutional boundaries can be promoted. With rigid boundaries between institutions and sectors, it is difficult to attain healthy collaboration, coordination, and cooperation.

Goal 17 also represents an important evolution in the conception of the specific value and role of partnerships. In the SDG framework, partnerships do not represent an end in themselves; they are a means to an end – a cross-cutting goal relevant to all sixteen of the other goals. Its very name "Partnerships *for the Goals* " (added emphasis) clearly indicates that achieving all of the other goals requires some form of collaboration across multiple institutions and governments. And it makes direct reference to partnerships as "the means to implementation."[11] As stated earlier, the significance of this phrase rests with the notion of moving beyond development assistance and towards overall a "revitalize[d] global partnership for sustainable development"[12] instead.

Thus partnerships, as suggested in Goal 17, are indispensable tools toward delivering the kind of thematic goals that are featured in the SDGs. This assumption represents an understanding and likely learning based on experience with the MDGs. Ambitious intentions such as major reductions in poverty and other manifestations of inequality require a certain degree of common thinking across sectors – a shared belief that poverty reduction and higher levels of equity and development are priorities. Multiple stakeholders across sectors must actively collaborate in order to see demonstrable results. This underlying idea of collaborative partnerships speaks to the nature of processes appropriate for achieving social and economic goals.

While the previous MDGs demonstrated some degree of notable progress in areas like poverty reduction, education, and health, the advent of the SDGs is a recognition of the magnitude of work left to be done. The SDGs are even more ambitious than the MDGs, as the SDGs all constitute results rather than actions. For example, the first MDG emphasized the process of eradicating poverty, whereas the first SDG is simply stated as "No Poverty." While it may be difficult for many to envision a world without poverty in 2030, partnerships are now an indispensable feature in reaching this among other goals, explicitly acknowledging that resources and expertise in various sectors should be tapped in some way in order to address these substantial matters.

Goal 17 of the SDGs not only elevates the role of partnerships in pursuit of global goals, but also highlights a variety of manifestations of collaboration and coordination across institutions and sectors discussed in nineteen accompanying measurable "targets."[13] Many of these targets refer to greater coordination across governments and institutions,

[11] *Id.*
[12] *Id.*
[13] Sustainable Development, *Topics, supra* note 5.

but two of them are very specific to cross-sector partnerships, underneath the subheading of "Multi-stakeholder partnerships."[14] As stated above, Target 17.16 indicates: "Enhance the global partnership for sustainable development, complemented by multi-stakeholder partnerships that mobilize and share knowledge, expertise, technology, and financial resources, to support the achievement of the sustainable development goals in all countries, in particular, developing countries." And Target 17.17 states: "Encourage and promote effective public, *public-private*, and civil society partnerships, building on the experience and resourcing strategies of partnerships."[15]

The language in the targets is very explicit regarding the incorporation of partnerships into the overall framework of the SDGs. The language is also all encompassing in its definition of partnerships. It includes, but also transcends, PPPs, emphasizing partnerships of varying types involving multiple sectors in collaborative pursuits. PPPs in particular stress the inclusion and active participation of the private for-profit sector in collaborative efforts with government. But these are not the only forms of cross-sector or multi-stakeholder partnerships. Some of the most compelling and impactful collaborative pursuits involve entities such as universities, hospitals, and various other NPOs. Thus partnerships can involve multiple stakeholders without necessarily involving private corporations in central roles. On the other hand, some partnerships bring together multiple stakeholders that include a full combination of private corporations, government, universities, and various forms of NPOs. The need to convene resources and expertise from as wide an array of partners as possible has led to the creation of collaboration that involves numerous stakeholders across multiple sectors, representing several fields.

While this section has parsed the language of SDG 17, partnerships function in multiple development contexts. The success or failure of the partnership approach must be evaluated within the specific development domains covered in the other SDGs (1–15). Thus, some examples from the specific area of agricultural development are discussed briefly in the next section.

B *The SDGs and the Example of Sustainable Agricultural Development*

To date, PPP initiatives have been found more frequently in such sectors as infrastructure,[16] health, and education. Their application in the sustainable agriculture sector is relatively new. Within the SDGs, this area is addressed by SDG 2: to "[e]nd hunger, achieve food security and improved nutrition and promote sustainable agriculture."[17]

[14] *See* SDG 17 Targets, *supra* 10.

[15] *Id.* (emphasis added).

[16] An example of an infrastructure PPP comes from the Caribbean where many of the Borrowing Member Countries (BMCs) of the Caribbean Development Bank (CDB) are struggling to improve their infrastructure services – against the challenges of high debt burdens, tight budgets, declining investment and lagging economies. High construction costs and poor quality, together with underinvestment and poor maintenance, have prevented governments from succeeding in their efforts to improve infrastructure services and catalyze economic growth. To find a way around the problems in infrastructure, PPPs have evolved in many countries throughout the Caribbean. Significant investments in transport, water, and sanitation drive public investment in places such as Jamaica where tight budget constraints contribute to under-investment. Jamaica has already pursued a number of PPP options to help close its public investment gap – for example, the concessioning of Sangster airport and the privatization of the electricity sector. *See Public-Private Partnerships in the Caribbean: Building on Early Lessons*, Caribbean Dev. Bank, (May 2014).

[17] Sustainable Development Knowledge Platform, *SDG 2*, U.N., www.un.org/sustainabledevelopment/hunger/.

The Food and Agriculture Organization (FAO) describes new partnership endeavors under the umbrella of the "agri-PPP," which is defined as a "formalized partnership between public institutions and private partners designed to address sustainable agricultural development objectives, where the public benefits anticipated from the partnership are clearly defined, investment contributions and risks are shared, and active roles exist for all partners at various stages throughout the PPP project lifecycle."[18]

One initiative that has already picked up where the MDGs left off is the Core Agriculture Support Program (CASP), consisting of various development partners including: the Asian Development Bank, the Food and Agriculture Organization (FAO), the Nordic Development Funds, and the Greater Mekong Subregion Working Group on Agriculture. The first phase of CASP was implemented in 2006–2010. The second, ongoing phase is now being implemented and builds upon the gains of the first phase of CASP to address emerging challenges to agricultural development, specifically those linked to expanding cross-border trade in agri-food products, climate change adaptation, and food and bioenergy security. The foundation of the strategy includes agricultural research and technology that emphasizes climate-friendly agricultural development, private sector involvement to ensure sustainability, and institutional mechanisms to enhance regional cooperation with incentives to achieve the vision.[19]

Other examples showcase the many ways the SDGs are harnessing the impact of partnerships all around the world to produce sustainable change in agriculture. One example comes from Haiti where conflicts of land ownership, traditional subsistence farming techniques, lack of irrigation, unused farmland, combined with low revenue for rural populations led to many challenges for development in its agricultural sector.[20] Seeing this problem, in 2015 a private company called AGRITRANS, S.A. initiated a project for a plantation of bananas and vegetables with assistance from the Industrial Development Fund, and various ministries (including the Ministry of Trade and Industry, the Ministry of Economy and Finance, and the Ministry of Agriculture, Natural Resources and Rural Development). For this project, the public sector made land available and allocated ad hoc program funding while the private company offered technology, jobs, and marketable products. Now in its second year, the products have been exported to the European market and sold locally, farmers have received 20 percent of the profit in addition to their current salary, and the plantation contributes to soil conservation as well as implementation of regional land policy.[21]

Despite the success of the Haiti project, there were lessons learned and highlighted in the report by the UN Economic Commission for Europe.[22] These are discussed in a later section of this chapter, in conjunction with other observations and suggestions for better leveraging the potential of partnerships. Other agri-PPPs are also described below in the context of the evaluation of the MDGs.

[18] Marlo Rankin, Eva Gálvez Nogales, Pilar Santacoloma, Nomathemba Mhlanga, & Costanza Rizzo, *Public-Private Partnerships for Agribusiness Development: A Review of International Experiences*, Food and Agric. Org. of the U.N. (2016).

[19] United Nations Sustainable Development Goals, *Case Study: Greater Mekong Subregion Core Agriculture Support Program*, U.N. (2016).

[20] *International PPP Forum: Implementing the United Nations 2030 Agenda for Sustainable Development Through Effective, People-First Public-Private Partnerships*, U.N. Econ. Comm'n for Eur. (2016).

[21] *Id.*

[22] *Id.*

C *Thoughts and Reflections on the SDGs and Partnerships*

The United Nations Secretary-General (UNSG) recently published a synthetic report titled "The Road to Dignity by 2030: Ending Poverty, Transforming All Lives and Protecting the Planet" (UNSG 2014 Report).[23] By including "partnerships" as one of six "essential elements," the UNSG further boosts the role of partnerships in Agenda 2030.[24] However, while cross-sector partnerships such as PPPs might have the potential to leverage funding for development, their track record thus far has been mixed. Partnerships involve significant risks and are not right for all projects. Governments therefore need to know how cross-sector partnerships can deliver value for money (VfM),[25] how to structure projects so they deliver these benefits, how to avoid common risks, and in what kind of projects these types of partnerships are most likely to add value.[26] Many factors should be considered. What is the reason for the partnership? What issue is being addressed? Given the issue, who are the appropriate collaborators to convene? Can the issue be resolved without multiple partners?

Partnerships involving private corporations require asking a threshold question regarding whether the issue to be addressed within the area of expertise of the company. Many corporations align their involvement in partnerships with their self-interests. Some PPPs can advance direct financial benefit to corporations. These interests are sometimes directly related to the nature of their goods and/or services. In other instances, a corporation might have a different self-interest, such as the well-being of a geographical area in which the company does business.

A values orientation is useful in striking an appropriate balance between enlightened self-interest and self-dealing. The Anchor Institutions Task Force[27] promotes specific values for institutions in their community partnerships: Equity and Social Justice, Democracy and Democratic Practice, A Commitment to Place, and Partnership and Collaboration. These values encourage collaboration between corporations or other institutions with various stakeholders, but they suggest a particular lens through which institutions can perceive their engagement with partners. There is a distinction between a corporation that engages in collaboration purely to drive profits versus one that pursues mutual benefit among partners. When values overlay partnerships in which a corporation or other institution actually benefits, a certain system of checks and balances is integrated.

The UNSG 2014 Report states that inclusion and dignity are formulas for sustainable development. But this assertion contradicts the results from numerous studies on cross-sector partnerships, which have revealed that disadvantaged groups are rarely included in,

[23] U.N. General Assembly, The road to dignity by 2030: ending poverty, transforming all lives and protecting the planet: Synthesis report of the Secretary-General on the post-2015 sustainable development agenda, at 3, U.N. Doc. A/69/700 (2014).

[24] Jonathan Volt, *Opinion: Why Does United Nations Secretary-General Insist on Placing Public-Private Partnerships in the Heart of the Post 2015 Development Agenda?*, Earth System Governance (Mar. 23, 2015).

[25] For more on the concept, *Value for Money*, see Penny Jackson, *Value for Money and International Development: Deconstructing Myths to Promote a More Constructive Discussion*, OECD (May 2012). In essence, the term refers to an optimal balance between economy, efficiency, and effectiveness. This balance can be determined by a cost-benefit analysis. These conceptions have become increasingly popular in the development arena in order to demonstrate the value of various endeavors.

[26] *Id.*

[27] Anchor Institutions Task Force, www.margainc.com/initiatives/aitf/.

or beneficiaries of, these partnerships (as was also evidenced with the MDGs).[28] Participation in cross-sector partnerships must come with obligations on transparency and accountability. Thus, both a consistent definition of the term "partnerships" and a clear understanding of their role in Agenda 2030 are badly needed.[29] The challenge of clearly articulating the role of partnerships in the implementation of the SDGs may be addressed in part by an assessment of their roles in the prior MDGs, discussed in the next sections.

II Evaluating the Role of Cross-Sector Partnerships in the MDGs

In assessing the potential of cross-sector partnerships to deliver results related to the SDGs, it is important to review the track record of the previous fifteen-year period under the UN MDGs. As stated earlier, beginning in 2000, the UN MDGs established ambitious goals to bring about measurable changes to reduce deep inequities across the globe. It is unlikely that any of the areas identified by the UN for aggressive action could have been adequately addressed without some form of cross-sector collaboration. And, indeed, the UN recognized this reality.

During the time the MDGs were being formed, it was recognized that the only way to bring about sustainable change was to combine resources and establish inclusive, innovative ways of working together. The UNSG stated that "addressing global challenges requires a collective and concerted effort, involving all actors. ... [e]specially through partnerships and alliances, and by pooling comparative advantages, [which] increase our chance of success."[30] This acknowledgement was enshrined in MDG Goal 8, which pledged to "Develop a Global Partnership for Development."[31] As discussed earlier, in its emphasis on partnerships for development, MDG 8 is the apparent precursor to SDG 17. By embedding "[g]lobal [p]artnership[s]"[32] into approaches to pursue the MDGs, the UN attempted to move beyond traditional – often corporate – partnerships and instead focus on what any organization can provide and on the intended outcome of the partnership. This includes incorporating marketing partners, constituency building partners, funding partners, and programmatic partners.[33]

Interestingly, the UN's 2015 report on the MDGs (hereinafter UN 2015 Report) does not suggest a very clear definition of "partnership."[34] Indicators of success in this category include increases in development assistance from developed countries, duty free imports from developed countries, the extent of mobile-cellular coverage, Internet penetration, and other related variables. These indicators point to a very broad definition of partnerships, which involves multiple forms of collaboration between developed and developing

[28] *See* Volt, *supra* note 24.
[29] *Id.*
[30] *A Selection of Partnership Initiatives*, U.N. Office for P'ships (2010).
[31] *Public Private Partnerships: 21st Century Development Models*, GAVI Vaccine All. & The Global Fund to Fight Aids, Malaria and Tuberculosis (Mar. 2013).
[32] Millenium Development Goals and Beyond 2015, *MDG 8*, U.N. (2015).
[33] Kathy Calvin, *Achieving United Nations Millennium Goals: Progress Through Partnerships*, U.N. Found. (n.d.).
[34] *See* The Millennium Development Goals Report 2015, *supra* note 2; Sustainable Development, *Topics*, *supra* note 5.

nations. They also point to the specific development issue of access to technology, which is an area with clear public–private collaborative implications.

The reflections in the UN 2015 report also included some important considerations directly related to cross-sector partnerships. For example, they concluded that gathering data is a "joint responsibility" to be shared across sectors, indicating specific roles for the private sector, civil society, governments, and various international and regional organizations.[35] As data is essential to monitoring progress, the process of data collection is a significant component of the SDGs going forward, and one that requires substantial coordination across sectors.[36]

Despite the fact that the fifteen-year agenda for accomplishing the MDGs ended in 2015, many of the institutional initiatives and mechanisms to support the development of cross-sector partnerships remain in place. For example, the Public–Private Partnerships for Service Delivery (PPPSD) was created as a UNDP program to increase the access of the poor to basic services such as water, waste, energy, education, and health by promoting inclusive partnerships between local government, businesses and communities.[37] Through its work at the local level, PPPSD supported the alleviation of poverty in the context of the MDGs.[38] Additionally, the UN Office for Partnerships (UNOP) was established to promote new collaborations and alliances in furtherance of the MDGs.[39] Presently, the UNOP provides partnership advisory services and outreach to a variety of entities, as well as manages the United Nations Fund for International Partnerships, which serves as the interface in the partnership between the UN system, the UN Foundation, and the UN Democracy Fund, established to support democratization throughout the world.[40] The presence of entities promoting collaboration hardly guarantees the actual effectiveness of partnerships. But the development of institutional infrastructure specifically designated to partnerships demonstrates a conscious effort in the UN system to emphasize the significance of collaboration across sectors.

III The MDGs and Agri-PPPs

In the UN 2015 report, the UN acknowledged uneven progress in all of the MDGs, noting, among other things, continued gender inequality; substantial gaps between the poorest and richest households and rural and urban areas; the role of climate change and environmental degradation in slowing progress; conflict as the most substantial challenge

[35] *Id.*

[36] In a meeting held in Bangkok on October 2015, the Inter-Agency and Expert Group (IAEG-SDGs) as part of its mandate worked to develop an indicator framework by which to monitor the goals and targets of the SDGs. Interestingly, one such proposal for Goal 17 sought to address the "means of implementation" and the inadequacy of the indicators there within. While questioning the inclusion of Public–Private Partnerships in the delivery of any essential resources, services, and so on, civil society organizations suggested that the value of such partnerships should be measured in terms of their contribution to sustainable development, specifically by measuring the percentage of public–private (for profit) partnerships that deliver greater value for achieving the SDGs than public or private finance alone. *See* Barbara Adams, *SDG Indicators and Data: Who collects? Who reports? Who benefits?* GLOB. POL'Y WATCH (2015).

[37] *Public-Private Partnerships for Service Delivery (PPPSD)*, U.N. DEV. PROGRAMME (2016).

[38] *Id.*

[39] U.N. OFFICE OF P'SHIPS (2010), www.un.org/partnerships/.

[40] *Id.*

to human development; and millions still living in poverty and hunger with limited access to basic services.[41]

Yet all of the MDGs can point to significant progress. For example, with respect to Goal 1 ("Eradicate Extreme Poverty and Hunger"), the number of people living in extreme poverty is currently roughly half of what it was in 1990; and the number of under-nourished people in developing countries has been halved since 1990 as well. One of the most glaring aspects of poverty, though perhaps not always acknowledged, is its significantly rural dimension.[42] Between 1993 and 2002, the World Bank estimates that rural poverty reduction contributed more than 45 percent to overall poverty reduction.[43] Given that farming is the main source of income for many rural communities, strengthening the agricultural sector overall will lead to greater economic growth throughout many parts of the world where this activity is prominent.

Several examples under the aegis of the MDGs illustrate the success of agri-PPPs, specifically in addressing the rural challenge. For instance, the year 2007 saw transformative examples of how agricultural programs can transform the lives of small scale farmers. Malawi exported 280,000 tons of maize, and child malnutrition dropped an impressive 80 percent. A major part of this success was due to a fertilizer subsidy program for farmers under a PPP led by the government and funded by the World Bank.[44]

To increase communities' capacities to generate growth, a cross-sector partnership was established in 2006 called the Angola Partnership Initiative with a US$50 million budget to support education, training and small-business development in Angola. This partnership leveraged existing funds and expertise within different organizations in order to promote overall economic and social development.[45] The result was the creation of two programs focused on the public and private sectors in order to impact change at various levels. The first was the Municipal Development Program, which provided support to the Government of Angola to bolster its local institutional capacity. As part of this program, Chevron and USAID established the Enterprise Development Alliance to provide technical assistance and financial support to small enterprises in Angola, with emphasis on the agricultural and water sectors. The second, launched in 2007, was the Agricultural Development and Finance Program also called ProAgro Angola, which aimed to catalyze the value chain of selected agricultural products, from production to processing to marketing, including support for the financial sector along the value chain.[46] This program was a partnership between Chevron which provided funding, USAID, and the Ministry of Agriculture and Rural Development which provided personnel, technical assistance and other resources. In the first two years, the farmers nearly doubled their yields, and connected to the larger global market for their agricultural products. This initiative also increased access to financial services for farmers and agribusinesses, improved the dialogue between agriculture enterprises, the Angolan government and

[41] *See* The Millennium Development Goals Report 2015, *supra* note 2.

[42] David J. Maurrasse, Strategic Public Private Partnerships: Innovation and Development 99 (2013).

[43] *World Development Report 2008 – Agriculture for Development*, World Bank (2007).

[44] *Making the Millennium Development Goals Happen: Perspectives from Global Aid Workers & Development Professionals on Achieving the MDGs*, U.N. Found. & Devex (2010).

[45] *See* Maurrasse, *supra* note 42, at 100.

[46] *See* Maurrasse, *supra* note 42, at 101.

private sector counterparts, as well as helped to strengthen production, processing, buying and selling of agricultural products.

Another example can be drawn from Cuba, where many of the daily foods people eat are grown in intensive organic gardens derived from thousands of poor and underutilized areas, mainly around Havana. For small poor farmers, organic agriculture can also be an effective risk management tool that reduces input costs, diversifies production, and improves local food security – all of which can contribute to poverty reduction.[47] Intensive organic gardens have been developed in urban areas of Cuba since the early 1990s to combat shortage of food in the cities due to the lack of fuel to transport food from rural areas. Nowadays, there are more than seven thousand urban gardens that produce sufficient fruits and vegetables for all Cubans. The productivity of the city has increased from 1.5 kg/m2 to nearly 20 kg/m2, thousands of jobs have been created, and pests are effectively managed due to the area's incredibly high amounts of biodiversity and natural predators.[48] Various cross-sector partners, including the International Federation of Organic Agriculture Movements, the international NGO HIVOS, Oxfam Novib, the "Fund for Sustainable Biodiversity Management" of the Dutch Government, private companies Bio Suisse, Ariza, and others, have contributed to effecting this change.

A final example can be seen in Africa where a 2008 PPP called the Water Efficient Maize for Africa (WEMA) was formed to help smallholder farmers and their families by using advanced plant breeding and biotechnology to develop more drought tolerant maize varieties. Over the last decade, the maize varieties have increased yields as much as 20 to 35 percent. This partnership is comprised of the African Agricultural Technology Foundation (a US tax-exempt Kenyan-based nonprofit organization and registered charity under the laws of England and Wales which facilitates and promotes public–private partnerships) as well as private agricultural companies Monsanto, and Baden Aniline and Soda Factor, or BASF (a German chemical company and largest producer in the world) who provided access to access proprietary germplasm, advanced breeding tools and expertise, and drought-tolerant transgenes for use in WEMA research.[49]

Thus, while the notion of "partnerships" was only mentioned explicitly in one of the eight goals, cross-sector collaborative initiatives, in retrospect, played an important role in achieving progress toward all of the MDGs. As stated earlier, this cross-cutting aspect of partnerships was made explicit via Goal 17 of the SDGs.

IV One Approach to Grassroots Rural Development Under the MDGs

A persistent challenge facing numerous partnerships is building the power and voice of grassroots communities. Ideally, cross-sector partnerships would provide opportunities to expand access and influence for disadvantaged communities.[50] Unfortunately, many

[47] Juan J. Jiménez, *Organic Agriculture and the Millennium Development Goals*, Int'l Fed'n of Organic Agric. Movements (IFOAM) (2007).

[48] Miguel A. Altieri, *The Ecological Role of Biodiversity in Agroecosystems*, 74 Agric., Ecosystems, Env't 19–23 (1999).

[49] *Public-Private Partnerships: A Vital Mechanism for Advancing Agricultural Innovation*, Farming First (2010).

[50] *See* Maurrasse, *supra* note 42, at 37.

partnerships have not yet proven to be consistent with inclusive governance or partnerships. The prevailing standard that any single NGO or organization can represent an entire community or stand in for the wider civil society voice needs to be debunked. Overall, more needs to be done to increase local capacities.

To address this concern, the Millennium Promise attempted to draw upon the resources and expertise of multiple stakeholders across sectors in order to transform select impoverished communities.[51] Established in 2005, the Millennium Promise created the Millennium Villages Project (MVP) to address MDG 1 – to end poverty and hunger. Bringing together various partners, from the UN to host country governments, the MVP developed programs on several critical issues, including agriculture, gender equality, education, community development, environment, infrastructure, and energy, among many others. Each of the sites established across the fourteen host country communities has implemented interventions seeking to improve the performance of subdistrict governments in order to overcome the insufficient capacity of local governments to take full ownership over the projects and activities.[52] Since its establishment, the MVP has had some successes in confronting the challenges faced by impoverished communities; however, future sustained progress will require continued investment and collaboration.

The MVP approach to partnerships is explicitly cross-sector. As indicated on the MVP website, "Our work unites science, business, civil society and government in these efforts by empowering communities and partners alike to become a part of the solution to ending extreme poverty."[53] The reference to science is an important aspect of this framework. While the MVP is an independent entity, it is a project of Columbia University's Earth Institute, an interdisciplinary academic unit. Universities can play a unique role in cross-sector partnerships, capable of leveraging intellectual capital from numerous substantive fields toward problem solving. As the very complex issues highlighted by the UN are in themselves interdisciplinary, the various forms of expertise that can be harnessed through a university are plentiful and significant.

The MVP was formed with the sole intent of creating and advising strategies to achieve the MDGs. The MVP draws resources together to improve rural development in interrelated areas, such as agriculture, business development, health, gender equality, education, and infrastructure. Located in various African countries, each Millennium Village is implemented and funded through NGOs, local and national governments, donors, and the village community. The MVP partners with African governments and other local partners, and draws upon a wide network of corporate, scientific, and nongovernmental organizational partners to help scale up rural development in each locale. Community ownership is a vital component in this framework, as residents in the Villages are involved in shaping projects from the beginning. Indeed, the role of community partners in setting priorities alongside institutions and governments is considered essential to the success of some partnerships.

In Uganda, this approach has helped to expand development in a rural village in Ruhiira. Because of the success of this effort, the Ugandan government, in 2013, scaled up this effort with support from the Islamic Development Bank, which invested

[51] *See id.*, at 135.
[52] *See* Maurrasse, *supra* note 42, at 140.
[53] Millennium Villages, http://millenniumvillages.org/about/overview/ (last visited Jul. 2016).

US$9.75 million in the effort.[54] The Village in Ruhiira began in 2006 has been pursuing an integrated approach to rural development. Through this funding, the effort was expanded from a single village to an entire region. Business development that helps residents generate income is an important component of this effort. And, with additional income, the community has been able to invest in education, health, insurance, and household sanitation.[55]

The MVP represents an innovative approach to meeting MDGs. It brings the pursuit of MDGs to the community level, specifically to small rural areas that are impoverished. It harnesses resources across networks of private resources (corporate and nonprofit) combined with those of local governments and Village residents. With these partnerships, the Villages identify interventions that can, for example, improve residents' ability to generate income – via agribusiness, marketing, etc. While the MVP focuses on rural development, its approach can bring lessons to partnerships in urban settings, particularly at the neighborhood level where local residents can effectively participate in shaping outcomes.

A village by village approach to leveraging cross-sector partnerships to meet ambitious UN goals can certainly change lives. But the challenge is to achieve demonstrable progress at a larger scale. This Ugandan case experienced a multiplier effect in which additional investments were attracted to expand from the local to the regional. With the transition from MDGs to SDGs, scaling up is an important consideration. The full range of types of partnerships (from the smallest scale, time limited, single issue to the most comprehensive and expansive) would have to be employed in order to move the needle substantially toward the numerous UN goals.

V Lessons Learned from the MDGs and Cross-Sector Partnerships

In general, data suggests that setting global development goals was effective in alleviating some of the enormous challenges for which they were designed. The UN 2015 Report referenced above documented improvement across all eight goals which have shaped the development agenda during its fifteen-year tenure. The MDG experience provided compelling evidence that with effective mobilization, the international community can abate complex challenges. Governments, civil society and a wide range of international actors coalesced behind the MDGs in a multi-front battle against poverty and disease.[56]

Of course, while the MDGs were unprecedented in their intentions, some of the goals fell short of their targets. With so many actors and vested interests involved, there is no doubt that convolution and difficulty in implementation occurred. Not all partnerships are strategic, and many attempts to collaborate fail.[57] Indeed, cross-sector partnerships bring together complex organizations that may not always result in effective collaborative efforts. While power dynamics within partnerships can sometimes be a hindrance, larger institutional partners (i.e., multinational corporations) can mitigate this by establishing

[54] *Ugandan Government Launches Scale-up of Millennium Villages Project*, Millennium Villages (Jul. 1, 2013), http://millenniumvillages.org/press-releases/ugandan-government-launches-scale-up-of-millennium-villages-project/.

[55] *Id.*

[56] *Millennium Development Goals Report 2015*, U.N. Dep't of Econ. and Soc. Affairs (Jul. 06, 2015).

[57] *See* Maurrasse, *supra* note 42, at 6.

clear expectations and honest dialogue that serves to leverage their influence uniquely on behalf of the partnerships, particularly with respect to empowering disadvantaged groups.

The shortcomings documented in the 2015 UN Report confirm that despite the successes, the world's poorest and most vulnerable are still being left behind. Gender inequality persists, millions of poor still live without access to basic resources and conflict remains the biggest threat to human development. Moving forward, the various challenges identified with cross-sector partnerships will need to be addressed in order to make Agenda 2030 successful. First, it is critical to secure buy-in from all partners and actors at a partnership initiative's inception. This includes the creation of shared business plans with clear objectives. As Kathy Calvin, the CEO of the UN Foundation stated, "Co-creation is essential."[58] Second, in order to be sustainable, cross-sector partnerships will be most effective when each actor has clearly delineated roles and responsibilities beyond financial support. This is especially crucial when considering government budget constraints, which leave public officials with no choice but to seek out alternative private resources.[59]

Other constraints could hinder the widespread success and implementation of partnerships for development. For example, laws that govern activities of cross-sector partnerships are not always consistent with one another. Furthermore, government policies may be revised with little consideration of the impact on private partners or false promises bestowed on the public.[60] Additionally, the slow pace of deregulation of tariffs for public services could impact project profitability for the private investors. While each country context will be different, there are important advantages and risks to consider. These include: failure to attract qualified bids, poor value for the public sector from lack of competition, hidden fiscal costs, and policy inflexibility (partnership contracts can be difficult and expensive to amend/ terminate).[61]

Outside of the UN system, other organizations such as the OECD have recognized the potential impact of PPPs on SDGs, specifically regarding strategic partnerships' ability to connect decision makers at the global level with the private sector, local governments, and civil society in ways that capitalizes on their specific strengths and balances their weaknesses.[62] Governments are often slow and unreliable, while existing institutions like private corporations and civil society organizations have "on the ground" experience navigating the challenges inherent to their industries. The success of a partnership such as a PPP is determined by inclusivity, local implementation and ownership, transparency, accountability, political engagement, and a strong focus on results.[63] In general, the SDGs focus on more specific goals such as improving infrastructure, conserving oceans,

[58] Calvin, *supra* note 33.

[59] *See* Maurrasse, *supra* note 42, at 9.

[60] *Wastewater Treatment: Case Study of Public-Private Partnerships (PPPs) in Shanghai*, ASIAN DEV. BANK (November 2010).

[61] *Public-Private Partnerships in the Caribbean*, *supra* note 16.

[62] Sophia Wu, *Public-Private Partnerships: The Key to Successfully Implementing the SDGs*, GLOB. PROSPERITY BY THE CTR. FOR GLOB. PROSPERITY (Oct. 2, 2015) (summarizing a talk co-sponsored by The Brookings Institution and the Organization for Economic Co-operation and Development (OECD) on utilizing public–private partnerships (PPPs) in order to effectively implement the UN SDGs following the end of the MDGs in 2015).

[63] *Id.*

and sustaining energy, which leaves room for partnerships to narrow their focus and be potentially more innovative.[64]

Despite its widespread promotion within and outside the UN system, the PPP mechanism is only one of many approaches that can contribute toward the achievement of sustainable development goals, such as those in the area of agriculture and rural development. Cross-sector partnerships such as agri-PPPs may be applicable only in specific circumstances, because they involve high transaction costs and are very complex.[65] Ideally, when deciding whether or not to engage in agri-PPPs, policymakers should make sure that the partnerships will add value by generating greater public benefits than could otherwise have been achieved through any of the alternative modes of public procurement or private investment alone. The success or failure of agri-PPPs, for example, is highly dependent on the enabling environment and the governance strategy designed to support the implementation of these partnerships. In the countries studied by the FAO, the Ministries of Agriculture were generally less prepared than other line ministries, to meet the challenges of partnering with the private sector. Another main challenge is the lack of guidance in the design phase of PPP projects. As a consequence, important issues such as transparency in the selection of private partners, risk sharing and mitigation mechanisms to protect small farmers, as well as conflict resolution strategies have often been overlooked. Inadequate market assessment and feasibility studies during the initial stages of developing the partnership arrangement also contributed to financial challenges encountered during the implementation phase.[66] The agri-PPP project initiated by AGRITRANS in Haiti, and described in a previous section of this chapter, faced obstacles with importing technology, equipment, know-how, specialized workers, and many other key components from the very beginning. In addition, there was a high cost for adjustments due to inappropriate choices and climate hazards. Presumably, with proper cooperation, preparation, and business decisions these pitfalls can be avoided.[67]

VI Thoughts on the Future Direction of Cross-Sector Partnerships

With these lessons in mind, what can be done to improve the positive impact of cross-sector partnerships such as PPPs in the future? First, it is critically important to assess the problem at hand to identify whether a cross-sector partnership is the right pathway to pursue. And, if so, it is important to determine an appropriate scale for the endeavor. Furthermore, there are many manifestations of cross-sector partnerships. They can be agreements between institutions to share information and coordinate. But they may also take form as active collaborations that may even lead to the formation of new organizations to represent the partnership. They might emerge to address specific issues over short time horizons with the intent to dissolve once a defined goal is met. But they might also exist for long term intentions with no expected ending. Once the idea for a partnership surfaces, it is important to take inventory of the menu of possible structures. Furthermore, partners must consider numerous milestones along the way. Intermediate goals can be as significant as end goals. Participants in partnerships are better positioned to sustain

[64] *Id.*
[65] *Id.*
[66] *Public-Private Partnerships for Agribusiness Development: supra* note 18.
[67] *International PPP Forum: supra* note 20.

themselves when they can assess progress intermittently. And demonstrable short-term progress can go a long way in encouraging partners to continue collaborating and informing any necessary refinements. Ultimately, it is easier to actually implement an effective cross-partnership with tangible achievable goals in short term segments.

The Caribbean Development Bank also outlines five separate ideas that could be applied globally to PPPs: First, the CDB highlights the importance of developing policies and processes that serve to set the rules based on affected communities and the parties involved, as well as define the priorities and establish the processes for the development and implementation of PPPs. Second, enabling legal environments need to be created that allow PPPs to be implemented. Third, institutional capacities need to be built in such a way that responsibility for implementation of the PPP policy will be effectively allocated. Fourth, human capacity needs to be developed in order to ensure responsible parties have the skills needed to carry out institutional responsibilities. And finally, fiscal management and accounting frameworks need to be created that produce methods for defining and managing fiscal costs in PPPs, thereby helping governments achieve true VfM.[68]

In general, an institutional capacity to create, manage and evaluate cross-sector partnerships such as PPPs is essential to ensure that they become an effective means of implementation. To reiterate, there is also a need for a common definition of PPPs and internationally accepted guidelines, including uniform accounting and reporting standards.[69]

The UN can and needs to do better in making cross-sector partnerships work. Promoting good governance, accountability, and public acceptability is critical, as well as training of key staff to develop action-oriented partnerships that are economically feasible and can attract the private sector.[70] Given the unique dimensions of cross-sector PPPs, there is a growing need for staff in all sectors to develop competencies to navigate successfully across sectors to solve problems.

Conclusion

The new SDG agenda places a much stronger emphasis on partnerships than did the previous MDG framework. It highlights a central role for the private sector in contributing to sustainable development.[71] Indeed, Goal 17 is intended to strengthen the means of implementation and revitalize the global partnership for sustainable development through specific targets such as mobilization of multi-stakeholder partnerships.[72] If such

[68] *Id.*

[69] Anis Chowdhury et al., *Public-Private Partnerships and the 2030 Agenda for Sustainable Development: Fit for Purpose?* (U.N. Dep't of Econ. and Soc. Affairs, DESA Working Paper No. 148, Feb. 2016).

[70] Geoffrey Hamilton, *Public-Private Partnerships for Sustainable Development*, U. N. Econ. Comm'n for Eur. Rep. (n.d.), *available at* https://sustainabledevelopment.un.org/content/sustdev/csd/csd16/PF/presentations/hamilton.pdf (last visited Feb. 2016).

[71] *Sustainable Development Goals*, International Forum on Public-Private Partnerships for Sustainable Development, U.N. (2015).

[72] *Key Issues: International Forum on Public-Private Partnerships for Sustainable Development*, U.N. PUB.-PRIVATE P'SHIPS (2015), www.un-ppp.org/key-issues ("Encourage and promote effective public, public-private and civil society partnerships, building on the experience and resourcing strategies of partnerships.").

cross-sector partnerships are to catalyze effective approaches to measurable change around the UN development priorities, then it is important to better understand their nature –why they can work, why they might not, and what should be considered in enhancing their viability.

Cross-sector partnerships are unlikely to dissipate from the development landscape any time soon. They are, in fact, likely to continue to spawn and evolve. Given this likelihood, policymakers, researchers, and executives in every industry must build the competency to collaborate beyond narrow fields and sectors, and toward common societal goals that transcend singular institutional goals. Because most specialists are generally unaccustomed to operating outside of highly defined boundaries, it is important to build the relational and respectful capabilities to engage in multi-stakeholder, cross-sector partnerships.

Our expectations of the roles of sectors are undergoing a fundamental transformation. And, indeed, this shift in mindset is necessary if we hope to be able to harness resources and expertise beyond sector boundaries to reduce poverty and other inequities. Cross-sector partnerships have become entities in themselves worthy of focused exploration and investigation. A more robust understanding of why cross-sector partnerships such as PPPs can be effective, why they can fail, and how we can enhance them, will facilitate these important vehicles in solving the pressing development issues highlighted by the MDGs and SDGs.

References

Adams, Barbara, *SDG Indicators and Data: Who collects? Who reports? Who benefits?* Glob. Pol'y Watch (2015), www.globalpolicywatch.org/blog/2015/11/23/sdg-indicators-and-data/ (last visited Nov. 20, 2017).

Altieri, Miguel A., *The Ecological Role of Biodiversity in Agroecosystems*, 74 Agric., Ecosystems, Env't 19–23 (1999).

Anchor Institutions Task Force, www.margainc.com/aitf/ (last visited Nov. 20, 2017).

Asian Dev. Bank, *Wastewater Treatment: Case Study of Public-Private Partnerships (PPPs) in Shanghai* (November 2010), http://adb.org/sites/default/files/pub/2010/urbandev-prc-nov2010-waste.pdf (last visited Nov. 20, 2017).

Calvin, Kathy, *Achieving United Nations Millennium Goals: Progress Through Partnerships*, U.N. Found. [n.d.], www.unfoundation.org/assets/pdf/achieving-un-mdgs-progress-through-partnerships.pdf (last visited Jun. 2016).

Caribbean Dev. Bank, *Public-Private Partnerships in the Caribbean: Building on Early Lessons* (May 2014) www.caribank.org/uploads/2014/05/Booklet-Public-Private-Partnerships-in-the-Caribbean-Building-on-Early-Lessons.pdf (last visited Nov. 20, 2017).

Chon, Margaret, *PPPs in Global IP (public-private partnerships in global intellectual property), in* Methods and Perspectives in Intellectual Property 296 (Graeme B. Dinwoodie ed., 2013).

GAVI Alliance & The Global Fund to Fight Aids, Malaria and Tuberculosis *Public Private Partnerships: 21st Century Development Models* (Mar. 2013), www.gavi.org/library/gavi-documents/advocacy/public-private-partnerships,-21st-century-development-models,-march-2013/ (last visited Nov. 20, 2017).

Jiménez, Juan J., *Organic Agriculture and the Millennium Development Goals*, Int'l Fed'n of Organic Agric. Movements (2007), http://www.feder.bio/files/1529.pdf (last visited Nov. 20, 2017).

Jomo KS, Anis Chowdhury, Krishnan Sharma, & Daniel Platz, *Public-Private Partnerships and the 2030 Agenda for Sustainable Development: Fit for Purpose?* (U.N. Dep't of Econ. and Soc.

Affairs, DESA Working Paper No. 148, Feb. 2016), https://sustainabledevelopment.un.org/content/documents/2288desaworkingpaper148.pdf (last visited Nov. 20, 2017).

Hamilton, Geoffrey, *Public-Private Partnerships for Sustainable Development*, U. N. Econ. Comm'n for Eur. Rep., *available at* https://sustainabledevelopment.un.org/content/sustdev/csd/csd16/PF/presentations/hamilton.pdf (last visited Feb. 2016).

Jackson, Penny, *Value for Money and International Development: Deconstructing Myths to Promote a More Constructive Discussion*, OECD (May 2012), www.oecd.org/development/effectiveness/49652541.pdf (last visited Nov. 20, 2017).

Kindornay, Shannon et al., *The Value of Cross-Sector Development Partnerships*, NSI Research Report, iv (2014), www.nsi-ins.ca/wp-content/uploads/2014/01/The-Value-of-Cross-Sector-Development-Partnerships.pdf (last visited Nov. 20, 2017).

Maurrasse, David J., STRATEGIC PUBLIC PRIVATE PARTNERSHIPS: INNOVATION AND DEVELOPMENT (2013).

MILLENNIUM VILLAGES, http://millenniumvillages.org/about/overview/ (last visited Jul. 2016).

Public-Private Partnerships: A Vital Mechanism for Advancing Agricultural Innovation, FARMING FIRST (2010) https://farmingfirst.org/tag/public-private-partnerships/ (last visited Nov. 20, 2017).

RANKIN MARLO, EVA GÁLVEZ NOGALES, PILAR SANTACOLOMA, NOMATHEMBA MHLANGA, & COSTANZA RIZZO, FOR THE FOOD AND AGRIC. ORG. OF THE U.N., *Public-Private Partnerships for Agribusiness Development: A Review of International Experiences* (2016) Accessed at www.fao.org/3/a-i5699e.pdf (last visited Nov. 20, 2017).

Ugandan Government Launches Scale-up of Millennium Villages Project, MILLENNIUM VILLAGES (Jul. 1, 2013), http://millenniumvillages.org/press-releases/ugandan-government-launches-scale-up-of-millennium-villages-project/ (last visited Nov. 20, 2017).

United Nations [U.N.], Millennium Development Goals and Beyond 2015, *MDG 8* (2015), www.un.org/millenniumgoals/global.shtml (last visited Nov. 20, 2017).

U.N., *The Millennium Development Goals Report 2015* (2015) www.un.org/millenniumgoals/2015_MDG_Report/pdf/MDG%202015%20rev%20(July%201).pdf (last visited Nov. 20, 2017).

U.N., *Sustainable Development Goals Kick Off with Start of New Year* (2015), www.un.org/sustainabledevelopment/blog/2015/12/sustainable-development-goals-kick-off-with-start-of-new-year/ (last visited Nov. 20, 2017).

U.N., *Sustainable Development Goals*, International Forum on Public-Private Partnerships for Sustainable Development (2015), www.un-ppp.org/ (last visited Nov. 20, 2017).

U.N., United Nations Sustainable Development Goals, *Case Study: Greater Mekong Subregion Core Agriculture Support Program* (2016), www.un.org/sustainabledevelopment/blog/2016/06/case-studies/ (last visited Nov. 20, 2017).

U.N. DEPARTMENT OF ECONOMIC AND SOCIAL AFFAIRS [U.N. DEP'T OF ECON. AND SOC. AFFAIRS], *Millennium Development Goals Report 2015* (Jul. 06, 2015), www.un.org/en/development/desa/publications/mdg-report-2015.html (last visited Nov. 20, 2017).

U.N. DEP'T OF ECON. AND SOC. AFFAIRS, SDG 17 Targets, https://sustainabledevelopment.un.org/sdg17 (last visited Nov. 20, 2017).

U.N. DEP'T OF ECON. AND SOC. AFFAIRS, Sustainable Development Knowledge Platform, *SDG 2*, www.un.org/sustainabledevelopment/hunger/ (last visited Nov. 20, 2017).

U.N. DEP'T OF ECON. AND SOC. AFFAIRS, Sustainable Development Knowledge Platform, *Transforming Our World: The 2030 Agenda for Sustainable Development*, https://sustainabledevelopment.un.org/post2015/transformingourworld (last visited Nov. 20, 2017)/ (last visited Nov. 20, 2017).

U.N. ECON. COMM'N FOR EUR.*International PPP Forum: Implementing the United Nations 2030 Agenda for Sustainable Development Through Effective, People-First Public-Private Partnerships*, (2016), www.unece.org/fileadmin/DAM/ceci/documents/2016/PPP/Forum_PPP-SDGs/PPP_Forum_2016-Compendium_All_Presentations.pdf (last visited Nov. 20, 2017).

U.N. Foundation & Devex, *Making the Millennium Development Goals Happen: Perspectives from Global Aid Workers & Development Professionals on Achieving the MDG*, (2010), www.unfoundation.org/assets/pdf/making-the-millennium-development-goals-happen.pdf (last visited Nov. 20, 2017).

U.N. General Assembly, The road to dignity by 2030: ending poverty, transforming all lives and protecting the planet: Synthesis report of the Secretary-General on the post-2015 sustainable development agenda, U.N. Doc. A/69/700 (2014), www.un.org/ga/search/view_doc.asp?symbol=A/69/700&Lang=E (last visited Nov. 20, 2017).

U.N. Office of Partnerships, www.un.org/partnerships/ (last visited Nov. 20, 2017).

U.N. Office for Partnerships, *A Selection of Partnership Initiatives, A Selection of Partnership Initiatives* (2010), http://web.archive.org/web/20100315164054/http://www.un.org/partnerships/partnership_initiatives.html (last visited Nov. 20, 2017).

U.N. Public-Private Partnerships, *Key Issues: International Forum on Public-Private Partnerships for Sustainable Development* (2015), www.un-ppp.org/key-issues (last visited Nov. 20, 2017).

Volt, Jonathan, *Opinion: Why Does United Nations Secretary-General Insist on Placing Public-Private Partnerships in the Heart of the Post 2015 Development Agenda?*, Earth System Governance (Mar. 23, 2015), http://sdg.earthsystemgovernance.org/sdg/news/2015–03–19/opinion-why-does-united-nations-secretary-general-insist-placing-public-private-part (last visited Nov. 20, 2017).

World Bank, *World Development Report 2008 – Agriculture for Development* (2007), http://siteresources.worldbank.org/INTWDR2008/Resources/WDR_00_book.pdf (last visited Nov. 20, 2017).

Wu, Sophia, *Public-Private Partnerships: The Key to Successfully Implementing the SDGs*, Glob. Prosperity by the Ctr. for Glob. Prosperity (Oct. 02, 2015), https://globalprosperity.wordpress.com/2015/10/02/public-private-partnerships-the-key-to-successfully-implementing-the-sdgs/ (last visited Nov. 20, 2017).

17 Sustainable Development through a Cross-Regional Research Partnership

Chidi Oguamanam and Jeremy de Beer

Introduction

Most studies and explorations of public–private partnership (PPP) models focus on specific albeit diverse sectors targeting solutions for cross-border developmental challenges. Studies tend to address problems that classical market economic frameworks and prevailing institutional arrangements, including intellectual property (IP) rights, are unable to fix. For example, they examine the role of PPP in product development, distribution, and procurement, in health,[1] showcasing their relevance, impact, and justification.[2] However, perhaps more germane than the operation of PPPs in specifically enumerated sectors such as global health is their suitability for tackling and negotiating the production, distribution, and/or delivery of the benefits of knowledge as a global public good in the context of what Keith Maskus and Jerome Reichman describe as the "emerging transnational system of innovation."[3]

Rarely explored is how research networks and partnerships not directly associated with specific public interest intervention or product and service delivery for development can help better inform and improve the design of PPPs or partnership building generally. The experience of a research network and partnership strategy dedicated to both empirical and theoretical interrogation of knowledge production and governance dynamics can make a useful contribution to emerging perspectives on collaborative partnerships in general (or even PPPs more specifically) in the areas of IP and knowledge governance.

Accordingly, this chapter examines the Open African Innovation Research (Open AIR) network as a unique cross-regional research platform. It links empirical and theoretical perspectives on PPPs to the key operational elements of Open AIR, including

[1] *See* Chidi Oguamanam, *Patents and Pharmaceutical R&D: Consolidating Public- Private Partnership Approach to Global Public Health Crisis*, 13 J. World Intell. Prop. 4, 556–580 (2010).

[2] *See* Oxfam Briefing Paper, *Ending the R&D Crisis in Public Health: Promoting Pro-Poor Medical Innovation*, Oxfam International (2008), www.oxfam.org/sites/www.oxfam.org/files/file_attachments/bp122-randd-crisis-public-health_3.pdf [hereinafter R&D Crisis in Public Health]; Taiwo A. Oriola, *Strong Medicines: Patents, Markets, and Policy Challenges for Managing Diseases and Affordable Prescription Drugs*, 7 Can. J. L. & Tech. 1, 57–123 (2008) [hereinafter Oriola].

[3] Keith K. Maskus & Jerome H. Reichman, *The Globalization of Private Knowledge Good and Privatization of Global Public Goods*, 7 J. Int'l Econ. L. 2, 279–320 (2004) [hereinafter Maskus & Reichman]; *See also* Joseph E. Stiglitz, *Knowledge as a Global Public Good*, P2PF Wiki (September 15, 2007), https://wiki.p2pfoundation.net/Knowledge_as_a_Global_Public_Good.

its core driving factors relevant to the development gap associated with IP and knowledge governance in Africa. In this regard, the chapter finds that insights from Open AIR's construct and research findings, which flow from its activities as a research-driven rather than a product-driven initiative, can shine light on how PPPs (or cross-sector partnerships in general) can be better exploited and reengineered beyond their current and ad hoc interventionist outlook, in order to make them serve as effective sustainable development vehicles.

The chapter begins with a contextualization of PPPs in global governance generally and their evolution within sustainable development efforts. It then introduces Open AIR. The following section links various elements of Open AIR to potential characteristics of PPPs, emphasizing six features that have resulted in successful interventions: Cross-sector representation; novel approaches to problem-solving; cross-regional approaches; complex methods; networking of networks; interdisciplinary analysis; and a shared vision. The chapter then discusses the nexus of partnerships such as Open AIR to sustainable development, and reflects on policy ramifications, practical lessons, and limitations of the cross-regional research partnership model applicable to development PPPs.

I Contextualizing PPPs for Development

From practical, policy, and theoretical perspectives, there is a conventional understanding of the role of PPPs.[4] They serve as special purpose vehicles for deployment of resources, expertise, technology, knowledge, and various other capabilities that neither the private nor the public sector, or other participants or stakeholders in the partnerships can adequately provide alone.[5] With specific regard to the context of global knowledge governance and its interface with IP rights, PPPs serve as strategic instruments for efficient mobilization of resources to solve R&D problems, promote innovation, and minimize associated transaction costs.

PPPs were proposed as "tools for good governance" in the 1990s, and gained prominence in international relations (IR) literature in the early 2000s.[6] However, PPPs have been understudied with gaps in the literature, stemming from the lack of a cohesive definition, differing schools of thought surrounding the structure and organization of PPPs, and a lack of research to support the hypothesis that PPPs can effectively contribute to the broad issues these partnerships seek to address. Research is only now beginning to recognize this lacuna and explore these issues in more depth.[7]

Public–private partnerships can be defined as:

> any formal relationship or arrangement over a fixed-term/indefinite period of time, between public and private actors, where both sides interact in the decision making

[4] *See* Frank Hartwich et al., Food Security in Practice: Building Public-Private Partnership for Agricultural Innovation (2008).

[5] *Id.*

[6] David J. Maurasse, Strategic public private partnerships: innovation and development 2 (2013).

[7] Rhys Andrews, Marc Esteve, & Tamyko Ysa, *Public-private joint ventures: mixing oil and water?* 35 Pub. Money & Mgmt 4, 265 (2015); Tanja A. Börzel & Thomas Risse (2005). *Public-Private Partnerships. Effective and Legitimate Tools of Transnational Governance?* in Complex Sovereignty: On the Reconstitution of Political Authority in the 21st Century 1 (Edgar Grande & Louis W Pauly eds., 2012).

process, and co-invest scarce resources such as money, personnel, facility and information in order to achieve specific objectives in the area of science, technology and innovation.[8]

Likewise, PPPs can be defined as "collaborative engagements between public, private and not-for-profit actors or institutions."[9] While both definitions mention the cooperative process between actors, the second more recent and less formalized approach includes engagement with civil society represented by nongovernmental or the nonprofit sector.[10] This sector can include "nongovernmental organizations (NGOs) at the community level to large established anchor institutions like universities."[11] With such inclusion, a richer cross-sector collaboration is possible assisting in connecting and harnessing knowledge and creating a unique partnership to assist with developing strategies and tackling transnational issues such as sustainable development. This transnational approach is possible not only because of the unique actors that constitute PPPs, but rather because these partnerships have emerged within "the context of globalization," and have been forged across territorial boundaries.[12] Benefits that derive from these partnerships stem from the "pooling of resources"[13] that occurs between these various sectors and actors. However, such capacity building is only sustained based on relationships of trust and reciprocity, forming a unique "network" organization.[14] Without trust or reciprocity, which the partnership seeks to foster, the exchange of information and resources can be unreliable.

PPPs often share features that include transnationality, public policy objectives, and a network structure.[15] However, not all of the partnerships are created equally, nor do they emerge uniformly across the globe. Partnerships may be more easily forged and/or maintained in certain parts of the world given particular factors (i.e., political, social, and economic) that facilitate their development and contribute to their success in the long term.[16] Although demand for a PPP may be significant in one country or area, the partnership may not emerge simply based on this desire. Instead, one study found that successful partnerships arise in areas that are "already heavily institutionalized and regulated" with a keen eye toward appropriate implementation and oversight.[17] With this

[8] Catherine Moreddu, PUBLIC-PRIVATE PARTNERSHIPS FOR AGRICULTURAL INNOVATION: LESSONS FROM RECENT EXPERIENCES 8 (2016) (citing OECD (2004) "Public/Private Partnerships for Innovations" in OECD Science, Technology and Industry Outlook, 2004, OECD Publishing Paris) http://dx.doi/org/10.1787/sti_outlook-2004-5-en.

[9] William P. Boland & Peter W. B. Phillips, *An Analysis of the Hidden Variables Influencing Challenges and Opportunities of Implementing R&D and Value Chain Agricultural Public-Private Partnerships in the Developing World* (2012) (unpublished manuscript) *available at* www.value-chains.org/dyn/bds/docs/831/Boland_ValueChainPPPs_Final.pdf.

[10] PUBLIC-PRIVATE PARTNERSHIPS FOR SUSTAINABLE DEVELOPMENT: EMERGENCE, INFLUENCE AND LEGITIMACY xi (Philipp H. Pattberg et al. eds., 2012).

[11] *Id.*

[12] Sander Chan & Christina Müller, *Explaining the Geographic, Thematic and Organization Differentiation of Partnerships for Sustainable Development* in PUBLIC-PRIVATE PARTNERSHIPS FOR SUSTAINABLE DEVELOPMENT: EMERGENCE, INFLUENCE AND LEGITIMACY, 44–66, 49 (Philipp H. Pattberg et al. eds., 2012).

[13] David J. Maurasse, *supra* note 6, at 7.

[14] Lea Stradtler, *Designing public-private partnerships for development*, 15 Management 1, 78 (2012).

[15] David J. Maurasse, *supra* note 6, at 3.

[16] *Supra* note 12.

[17] Philipp H. Pattberg et al., *Conclusions: Partnerships for Sustainable Development, in* PUBLIC-PRIVATE PARTNERSHIPS FOR SUSTAINABLE DEVELOPMENT: EMERGENCE, INFLUENCE AND LEGITIMACY 241–242 (Philipp H. Pattberg et al. eds., 2012).

in mind an area that may require more attention is examining how to encourage adequate implementation of the partnership goals within areas where there are limitations in public/private or nonprofit capacity.

PPPs' contribution in reducing transaction costs is a crucial adjunct to the practical realization of PPPs' core mission in the area of IP and knowledge governance in general. Mitigated transaction costs subsidize knowledge production and ensure optimal access to the benefits of innovation, especially by the most vulnerable. Hence, PPPs function as a bridge between private sector-driven hard-edged knowledge production and protection that results in sub-optimal access to innovation and an inclusive public sector-mediated framework that allows for optimal dissemination of benefits of innovation, which in turn has positive effect on development. In a way, a PPP-mediated framework for concerted generation of innovation and delivery of its benefits has the potential to enhance the realization of innovation as a public good in which the instrumentalist mission of intellectual property is advanced in less contentious ways.

Increasingly, PPPs schemes are being deployed in strategic sectors as practical, policy, and theoretical models of R&D, innovation, and social intervention over healthcare delivery, access to essential medicines and vaccines, new technologies and their development, as well as seeds, propagating materials or useful genetic resources for food and agriculture.[18] Perhaps, there is no more visible practical and policy strategies for addressing development gaps[19] and inequity on multi-sectoral levels in the last century than the PPP models and their dynamic configurations, which now includes various categories of actors such as nonprofit and civil society entities.[20] Similarly, not many competitive or imaginative institutional designs for fixing the public interest deficits at the intersection of IP and access to innovation by the most vulnerable exist than the possibilities offered by diverse PPP models.

However, the PPP option is hardly a foolproof public policy intervention strategy.[21] Often PPP models may provide opportunity for private sector capture of the public sector, especially where a PPP is deployed in the execution of mega-infrastructural building, design, and concession projects in partnership with corrupt and weak public partners. This is particularly problematic in less developed countries. Also, the issues of 'equity' and power alignment among partners, the conceptualization of partnerships, and the determination of R&D priorities of PPPs continue to be matters of concern for their effectiveness and their public interest orientations.[22]

[18] *See R&D Crisis in Public Health*, *supra* note 2; International Food Policy Research Institute's (IFPRI), *A Database of Public-Private Partnerships in (PPP) in the CGIAR, 2004*, Harvard Dataverse (2015), *available at* https://dataverse.harvard.edu/dataset.xhtml?persistentId=doi:10.7910/DVN/YHDKKR; *See also* Chidi Oguamanam, *supra* note 1.

[19] *See* Uche Ohia, *Infrastructural Concession in Nigeria: Challenges and Opportunities*, NIGERIANS IN AMERICA (August 16, 2011), *available at* www.nigeriansinamerica.com/infrastructure-concession-in-nigeria-challenges-and-opportunities/; *See also* May Agbamuche-Mbu, *PPPs Key to Our Desired Infrastructure Development*, THIS DAY (September 13, 2016), *available at* www.thisdaylive.com/index.php/2016/09/13/ppps-key-to-our-desired-infrastructure-development/.

[20] For example, of categories of key actors in leading global public health interventionist PPPs, *see* R&D Crisis in Public Health, *supra* note 2.

[21] *See, e.g*, Oxfam, *How a Public-Private Healthcare Partnership Threatens to Bankrupt Lesotho*, OXFAM INTERNATIONAL (April 7, 2014), *available at* www.oxfam.org/en/multimedia/video/2014-how-public-private-healthcare-partnership-threatens-bankrupt-lesotho.

[22] *See* Susan Bragdon, *Reinvigorating the Public Sector: The Case of Food Security, Small-Scale Farmers, Trade and Intellectual Property Rules* (Transnational Institute (TNI), Colloquium Paper No 64, 2016).

Within the United Nations framework, the organization, governance, monitoring, operational modalities of PPPs and the balancing of their development or public interest objectives with the private interests of stakeholders are only evolving and have yet to mature.[23] Certainly, despite gaining traction, PPPs are still embryonic experimentations in development circles and in global governance.[24] PPPs are susceptible to abuse in era of dwindling resources, as governments and development agencies uncritically and conveniently farm out their core responsibilities. The advancement of private agendas at public expense is an inadvertent and possibly inevitable consequence of an uncritical approach to PPPs. Situations like this make continued careful scrutiny of PPPs imperative, and highlight the need to take critics and criticisms seriously, in order to make improvements going forward.[25]

Goal 8 of the 2005 United Nations Millennium Development Goals (MDGs) enunciated the concept of global partnerships for development.[26] Specifically, the MDGs targeted and promoted public sector cooperation with the private sector to ensure affordable access to essential medicines and benefits of new technologies with special emphasis on information and communication technologies (ICTs).[27] The 2015 United Nations Sustainable Development Goals (SDGs)[28] seeks to consolidate the trend through revitalizing and mobilizing global partnerships to support sustainable development. According to the UN,

> A successful sustainable development agenda requires partnerships between governments, the private sector and civil society. These inclusive partnerships built upon principles and values, *a shared vision, and shared goals* that place people and the planet at the centre, are needed at the global, regional, national and local level.[29]

As the UN strengthens the concept of global partnerships as strategic instrument for sustainable development, there is a strong need to explore other ways of imagining partnerships for development via the PPP construct.

II Open AIR: A Peek

Open AIR is a network of dynamic partnerships between academic institutions, national government agencies, philanthropic foundations, civil society groups, intergovernmental organizations, and other unconventional actors.[30] Although these combinations of actors

[23] Barbara Adam & Jen Martens, *Partnerships and 2030 Agenda: Time to Reconsider their Role in Implementation*, Global Policy Forum (May 2016), *available at* www.globalpolicywatch.org/wp-content/uploads/2016/05/On-Partnerships-GPF-input-to-discussion.pdf.

[24] *Id. See also* Michael J. Hatton & Kent Schroeder, *Partnership Theory and Practice: Time for a New Paradigm*, 28 Can. J. Dev. Studies 1, 157–162 (2007).

[25] *Id.*

[26] *See* United Nations Millennium Development Goals, U.N., *available at* www.un.org/millennium goals/ (last visited Oct. 18, 2016).

[27] *Id.*

[28] *Id.*

[29] *See Goal 17: Revitalize the Global Partnership for Sustainable Development*, U.N., *available at* www.un .org/sustainabledevelopment/globalpartnerships/ (last visited Oct. 18, 2016) [emphasis supplied].

[30] For more insights on Open AIR, *see* Open AIR: African Innovation Research, *available at* www.open air.org.za/about-us/ (last visited Oct 18, 2016).

do not directly implicate the private sector in the conventional sense of "for profit" enterprises, they do include nonprofit entities that straddle the private and public spaces in their operations. The network, which we have been privileged to midwife with others, began just before 2007 as a research project aiming to compare the copyright laws, policies, and practices of eight countries in Africa and how they impact on access to educational materials.[31] It expanded and metamorphosed into its current name around 2011 to include researchers in fourteen African countries investigating other areas of IP and innovation from multiple disciplinary perspectives.[32]

Less than a decade after its inception, Open AIR has created a pan-African and global partnership providing a distinct voice to researchers from a continent consistently marginalized in discussions of global knowledge governance. The partnerships span a continent now straddled between the phenomenal opportunity and daunting circumstance of mapping its developmental aspirations within the innovation-driven landscape of the third industrial revolution and the emerging fourth industrial revolution.[33] In 2015, the network took on new challenges by both broadening and deepening connections between researchers across the developed-developing-world divide. Open AIR now contributes to making Africa the centre of attention in a cross-regional network involving multisector partners in North America, Europe and elsewhere, especially Canada.

The Open AIR partnership's current goal is to help explore a problem at the heart of competing visions of the global knowledge governance systems: how to reconcile tensions between appropriation and access, excluding and sharing, and competing and collaborating. Its core aims are to create a better understanding of the ways knowledge-based businesses can scale up to take advantage of global opportunities while simultaneously ensuring that the benefits of innovation are shared inclusively throughout society, more so amongst its most vulnerable. Open AIR's Afrocentric focus calls attention to the importance and sensitivity of context in the making of IP and knowledge governance policy for sustainable development.[34]

Primarily, the Open AIR partnership adopts an empirical approach to obtaining social, economic, cultural, and political insights over developmental issues linked to IP on the African continent. As a unique form of partnership, it attempts to map Africa or the African contexts into the dynamics of the intersection between innovation and intellectual property from a fundamentally development perspective. The research is an initiative that deploys contextual and on-the-ground case studies to provide insights that confront two vastly opposing, but hardly tested, views on the influential role of IP rights in relation to innovation, creativity, and development on the African contexts. One such view is that IP protection is a *sine qua non* to innovation and development.[35] The converse is that rather than promoting innovation, creativity, and development, IP constitutes an

[31] *See* ACCESS TO KNOWLEDGE IN AFRICA: THE ROLE OF COPYRIGHT (Chris Armstrong et al. eds., 2010).

[32] *Id.*

[33] Jeremy Rifkin, THE THIRD INDUSTRIAL REVOLUTION: HOW LATERAL POWER IS TRANSFORMING ENERGY, THE ECONOMY AND THE WORLD (2008). The concept of the third industrial revolution is fast becoming obsolete as the evolution of artificial intelligence is now associated as catalytic of the fourth industrial revolution.

[34] *See, generally*, Jeremy de Beer et al. eds., INNOVATION & INTELLECTUAL PROPERTY: COLLABORATIVE DYNAMICS IN AFRICA (2015).

[35] *Id.*

impediment to free exchange of ideas, and other critical ingredients necessary for the promotion of innovation and creativity, and ultimately development.[36]

The truth may lie somewhere between the two extremes with accommodation given for specific sectoral and contextual characteristics of the interaction between different IP regimes and innovation, creativity, and development in diverse socioeconomic and cultural contexts.[37] Despite the undergirding logic of these polarized views and their persistence, there is still much to be known about how IP dynamics "do or could influence innovation and creativity as a means of development."[38]

Yet from the middle of the twentieth century, the dominant and most influential narrative of IP is one that supports stronger IP protection as the panacea for the challenges of development.[39] As an integral part of the global trade regime, that approach has yielded, in its wake, intense privatization of knowledge and innovation as global public goods.[40] As a consequence, at a time of unprecedented innovation in human history, IP and knowledge governance frameworks are perceived to be complicit in widening access gaps that, in turn, foster sub-optimal impact of innovation on society, especially amongst the most vulnerable. In the late twentieth century a combination of factors, including the embedded and demonstrable capacity of digital technology for collaborative and networked innovation and creativity, unraveled unprecedented pathways to new potentials. But hurried and harried attempts to use IP to police content production in cyberspace unmasked, amplified, and reenforced the potential of IP to constrain creativity and innovation.[41] That heavy-handed privatization and enforcement has helped in no small a measure to support alternative and countervailing narratives around openness and collaboration alongside overzealous IP protection regimes.[42]

Despite the strides toward contested and balanced theories of IP and its interface with development,[43] international IP policy space and institutions tend to continue to operate around the dominant narrative, though there have been significant efforts and initiatives – such as the WIPO Development Agenda – seeking to inject a more development-oriented approach to IP in this space. Against that backdrop, patents, copyrights, and other familiar formal checklists are used to rank the innovative and creative profile of countries.[44]

36 *Id.*

37 *Id.*

38 *See* de Beer et al., *supra* note 34, at 2.

39 *See generally* Peter Drahos and John Braithwaite, Information Feudalism: Who Owns the Knowledge Economy? (2002).

40 *See generally* International Public Goods and Transfer of Technology Under a Globalized Intellectual Property Regime (Keith Maskus & Jerome Reichman eds., 2005).

41 One of the earliest attempts by a major industrialized country, namely, the United States, to extend intellectual property rights protection to cyberspace via the Digital Millennium Copyright Act (DMCA) sparked critical global debate over the potential of intellectual property to undermine creativity on the internet platform resulting in strong interest over a constructive and balanced approach. The DMCA was an attempt to implement two relevant international treaties: WIPO Copyright Treaty (WCT), Dec. 20, 1996, TRT/WCT/001, and the WIPO Performances and Phonograms Treaty (WPPT) Dec. 20, 1996, TRT/WPPT/001.

42 *See generally* Jeremy de Beer and Sara Bannerman, *Access to Knowledge as a New Paradigm for Research on ICTs and Intellectual Property Rights*, in Connecting ICTs to Development: The IDRC Experience (H. Emdon, L. Elder, B. Petrazzini and R. Fuchs, eds., 2013).

43 *See generally* Rami M. Olwan, Intellectual Property and Development: Theory and Practice (2013).

44 *See Intellectual Property Statistics*, WIPO (2015), *available at* www.wipo.int/ipstats/en/.

A country's ability to appropriate the benefits of the free market economy is tied to the extent it protects conventional IP rights.[45] This standard form of IP protection has limited accommodation for social, economic, political, cultural, and other contextual variables. It is a state of affairs totally insensitive and evidently exclusionary to the realities of the African countries. Communities of informal sector actors who thrive in the practice of collaborative knowledge production largely drive innovation on the continent. The standard form of check-listing of specific types of IPs generated is obviously ill suited to and therefore incapable of capturing the dynamics of creativity and innovation that happen on the continent. The irony is that while this artificial matrix relegates African countries to the lowest rung of the innovation, creativity, and development scale,[46] those countries remain under immense economic and political pressure to adopt an IP system that has difficulty grappling with their local contexts and contingencies.[47]

Within the global IP and knowledge governance framework, African countries are neither reckoned nor recognized as innovative. Yet "African policy-makers continue to be offered relatively stale, globalist protection and harmonization-centric IP narratives" with little regard "to nationally or locally contextualized IP realties and imperatives."[48] Setting the cart before the horse, attempts to shore up African IP credentials have focused on formal structures such as laws, IP governance institutions, and bureaucracy that mainly service external interests with little attention paid inwardly to the nature of innovation and creativity and knowledge governance frameworks in Africa.[49]

It is logically tenable that the PPP or other partnership models can be adapted to pull together resources from diverse partners, and to leverage often-untapped local and African diaspora networks of interdisciplinary research expertise. This strategy channels or nudges PPPs or partnership making in a direction that enhances insights on the gaps in international IP as it affects innovation and creativity on the continent and grounds the instrumentality of PPPs outside its conventional application to focus on the policy deficits in the governance of knowledge and innovation. The Open AIR partnership looks at the practical dynamic of innovation and creativity in Africa as an important step to understand what forms of knowledge governance framework would best facilitate, capture, and value the innovation that happens on the continent, as a crucial complement to innovation-driven sustainable development.

III Open AIR as a Partnership Construct

Given the prevailing gap on African voices, realities, and representations in global IP and knowledge governance environment, Open AIR's experience can help inform how to

45 *See* Chidi Oguamanam, *Open Innovation in Plant Genetic Resources for Food and Agriculture*, 13 Chi. Kent J. Intell. Prop. 1, 11–50 (2013).

46 *See e.g.*, Chidi Oguamanam, *Breeding Apples for Oranges: Africa's Misplaced Priority over Plant Breeders' Rights* 18 J of World Intellectual Property 5, 165–195 (2015).

47 *Id.*

48 *See* Jeremy de Beer et al., *supra* note 34, at 6–7.

49 *See generally* Jeremy de Beer & Chidi Oguamanam, *Intellectual Property Training and Education: A Development Perspective*, International Centre for Trade and Sustainable Development (2010) www.ictsd.org/downloads/2010/11/iptrainingandeducation.pdf; *see also* The World Intellectual Property Organization: Resurgence and the Development Agenda (Christopher May ed., 2007)

address this gap in the existing landscape of PPPs. The orthodox (for want of a better expression) approach of using PPPs to deliver products of innovation as global public goods is essentially an *ad hoc* strategy that does not tackle the twisted and top down nature of IP and global knowledge governance in any measured manner. The deliberate composition of Open AIR as a research platform naturally situates it, for the most part, on a grounded theoretical and introspective interrogation of the interface of IP and innovation in the African context. Open AIR's "case study method helps to humanize otherwise abstract information and yields understanding into complex systems of interacting variables"[50] that capture the innovation and creativity that happen in mainly informal and quasi-formal contexts in Africa.

Open AIR's partnership construct unfolds in multiple respects, explored in more detail later in this chapter.

A *Cross-Sector Representation*

First, and most obvious, is the composition of institutional partners and sponsors, which, as indicated earlier, includes academic institutions, national government agencies, philanthropic foundations, civil society groups, intergovernmental organizations, and other unconventional actors. The diversity of the institutional and individual memberships of the partnership is important to inclusively capture the complex dynamic of IP and knowledge governance and its interface with innovation, creativity, and development in Africa.

Open AIR is a form of a cross-regional research consortium, with significant representation of public institutions. The private sector presence is mostly indirect through privately operated academic and research institutional affiliates, including non-governmental organizations, for-profit and not-for-profit advisory groups, consultancies, and think tanks. The key point is that Open AIR reflects a unique combination of state and non-state actors and institutions collaborating to achieve common objectives.

Open AIR consists of mainly African-based and African diaspora and their North American and other geopolitical partners across a diverse range of disciplinary backgrounds. Such an aggregation of grounded human resources with natural familiarity and association with Africa is a departure from usual made-abroad, top-down compliance, and implementation model of IP prescription for the continent.[51]

B *Novel Approach to Problem Solving*

Second, the private sector involvement in Open AIR is indirect, passive, and detached; it thus allows for independent implementation of research in accordance with scholarly tradition. Again, unlike conventional PPPs, Open AIR is not focused on collaborative infrastructure and product development, supply, marketing, or distribution that focuses in one core area designed to fill a development gap or to address a glaring IP-induced social inequity. However, Open AIR's construct addresses both theoretical and practical fissures in IP and the global governance of knowledge that is at the root of a wide range of development gaps that impact negatively on the African continent.

[50] *See* Jeremy de Beer et al., *supra* note 34, at 13.
[51] *See id.*

If Africa's unique contributions to innovation and the on-the-ground cultural, social, economic, and even political contexts in which knowledge produced on the continent are captured and supported, the continent and its peoples are empowered as important actors in innovation and knowledge governance for sustainable development. However, like most PPPs, the Open AIR research partnership is an interventionist project, in that it is engaged in action research designed to have real-world impacts. Perhaps more importantly, its emphasis lies on a unique form of innovation capacity-building, one in which sustainable development is central.[52]

As already indicated, the dominant narratives of IP and knowledge governance favour exclusionary norms and stronger proprietary protection. Formalistic metrics for measuring innovation and creativity are insensitive to African realities. The situation alienates a critical and very creative segment of the human family, resulting in a prescriptive imposition of unsuitable and suspect knowledge protection formulae. Not only does this approach remain antithetical to the continent's capacity for self-determination in knowledge governance for sustainable development, it also deprives the rest of the world of lessons that can be learned from the continent on the subject of knowledge governance. As a multi-stakeholder partnership that has mobilized strategic resources and expertise on African innovation and creativity, Open AIR expands the scope for sharing knowledge necessary to support sustainable development goals.

C *A Cross-Regional Approach*

The third element of Open AIR as a cross-regional construct is its international outlook. IP and global knowledge governance is a subject of regional and global interest,[53] one that requires corresponding consciousness and expertise that the Open AIR network is cultivating. Open AIR recognizes that neither Africa, nor any other continent for that manner, can be engaged in isolation, more so over IP, knowledge governance, and development. After all, recent expansion of IP and its translation in development are incidences of the new global knowledge-based economy in which African innovation, creativity, and development are intertwined. Since the coming into effect of the TRIPS Agreement in 1995 under the WTO framework and other cognate international agreements and policies, global policies on IP and knowledge have continued to exert significant influence at regional and national levels in determined pursuit of international harmonization and a pull toward differentiation.[54] The cross-regional and broader constitution of Open AIR makes it a necessary vehicle to engage a global phenomenon with a regional focus in the manner other PPPs strategies are conventionally deployed, such as in the flagship contexts of access to medicines and new technologies.[55]

[52] On the intersections of capacity-building, development, and human rights *see* Amartya Sen, DEVELOPMENT AS FREEDOM (1999).

[53] Madhavi Sunder, *IP3*, 59 STANFORD L. REV. 2, 257 (2006).

[54] Graham Dutfield and Uma Susthersanen, *Harmonization or Differentiation in Intellectual Property Protection? The Role of History* 23 PROMETHEUS 2, 131–147 (2005); *but see* Maskus & Reichman, *supra* note 3.

[55] *See* R&D Crisis in Public Health, *supra* note 2; Oriola, *supra* note 2; *see also* U.N. MILLENNIUM DEVELOPMENT GOALS, *supra* note 26.

IV Complex Questions and Methods

The fourth feature of Open AIR relates to the inherent complexity of the partnership's subject matter(s). IP and knowledge governance, and its interface with creativity innovation for sustainable development in the African contexts denote a practical, policy, and theoretical research complex that no one entity or stakeholder is equipped to elucidate with any credibility. Not many subject matters engage such complexities and contexts more than IP and knowledge governance in the cultural, social, economic, and political contexts of Africa. Similarly, without foreclosing unexplored options, not many models of inquiry are better suited to grapple with the issues than a cross-regional and open-ended multidisciplinary and interdisciplinary form of research program.

Open AIR takes on a complex practical, theoretical, and policy challenge, namely the alienation or exclusion of, arguably, one of the world's most creative civilizations and peoples from the IP narrative. In seeking to contribute towards asserting Africa into the IP and knowledge governance framework through empirical case studies, grounded theory building, and action-oriented research interventions, Open AIR explores how extant or future IP systems can advance innovation and creativity that drive development on the continent. This broadly framed inquiry logically provides the opportunity to explore and understand how African creators and innovators react, respond to or work around conventional IP frameworks and embedded pressures. As well, Open AIR examines the interplay of the externally prescribed exclusive IP ideology with the culturally oriented collaborative, open, and inclusive knowledge production that happens mainly within Africa's formal-informal dynamic of knowledge production and governance.[56]

This form of complex inquiry not only focuses on Africa with cautious regard to the continent's constitutive diversity and complexity. It also engages IP in its cross-regime and cross-sector, and equally complex contextual unraveling[57] on the African continent. Like a conventional PPP, the research agenda is one that transcends the capacity of any one entity, whether public, private, or other, to grapple.

It is, however, not claimed that Open AIR as presently constituted, or any research consortium for that mater, is in a position to exhaust the open-ended and multifaceted layers of dynamic issues that constitute its *raison d'être*. Rather, Open AIR symbolizes the instrumentality of cross-regional research as an important and unique typology with practical, theoretical, and policy ramifications, in the present case, for IP and knowledge governance and its interface with development.

V Networking of Networks

The fifth feature of Open AIR is the networked model, which it has since developed through strategic recruitments and integration of a diverse range of nodes, including scholars of various levels and categories. Private sector, public sector, and civil society

[56] *See* Dick Kawooya, *Informal-Formal Sector Interactions in Automotive Engineering Kampala*, in Innovation & Intellectual Property: Collaborative Dynamic in Africa 56–76 (2015).

[57] *See* Laurence R. Helfer, *Regime Shifting: The TRIPs Agreement and New Dynamics of International Intellectual Property Making*, 29 Yale J. Int'l L. 1 (2004); *see also* Peter K. Yu, *International Enclosure, the Regime Complex and Intellectual Property Schizophrenia* Mich. L Rev. 1–33 (2007); *see generally*, Chidi Oguamanam, Intellectual Property in Global Governance: A Development Question (2012).

actors as well as resource persons, public/government officials, and collaborators, are all engaged in various capacities in the partnership. Already, we have alluded to the potential or natural morphing of Open AIR in a manner and direction akin to a network of networks.

As Open AIR grows its experience in complex knowledge governance, it continues to make and attract overtures with related research partnerships, building strategic connections and linkages akin to network of networks grounded in a unique partnership framework. For one example, in the area of open data-driven innovation, Open AIR has engaged with the GODAN network, a PPP named for its work on "global open data in agriculture and nutrition."[58] Through GODAN, Open AIR is able to engage organizations ranging from the UN's Food and Agriculture Organization (FAO), to the Consultative Group of International Agricultural Research Centers, now officially known as CGIAR, to the multinational agrochemical company Syngenta.[59] On the topic of human rights, IP, and access to medicines, for example, Open AIR has partnered with the Open Society Foundations (OSF) to create the ASKJustice initiative, "African Scholars for Knowledge Justice."[60] Because of its orientation and dynamism, Open AIR is able to intersect and engage with similar organizations that share common values.

As a crucial foundation of the network strategy, Open AIR leverages the African diaspora and expertise in various fields. Admittedly, Open AIR is not the first or only partnership to tap on the African diaspora as a powerful bridging tool for development and other objectives.[61] However, leveraging the African diaspora serves multiple purposes including, of course, capacity building. But more importantly, it enhances the integrity and legitimacy of grounded and empirical approach to exploring African experiences with IP as opposed to externally driven initiatives and top-down formations that are distanced from Africa's lived experience.

As well, the diaspora appeal supports the transition from the brain drain cliché to the phenomenon of "brain train." The latter recognizes that the interaction between the diaspora and local residents is a positive mutual knowledge translation and knowledge sharing experience. That orientation ties neatly into Open AIR's commitment to use empirical case studies to uncover some of what the rest can learn from Africa's experience with IP and knowledge governance. It is, in a way, a departure from the extant pattern of unidirectional prescription of a top-down and uniform IP model as a panacea for Africa's development problems.

The idea of multidirectional flow and exchange of knowledge in which African insights and experience on IP and knowledge governance are legitimately captured, and taken into consideration in policy formulation, is central to the Open AIR research partnership. Open AIR has continued to re-enforce that imperative through its empirical

[58] *See Global Open Data for Agriculture and Nutrition*, GODAN, *available at* www.godan.info (last visited Jun. 14, 2017).

[59] *See* Jeremy de Beer, Ownership of Open Data: Governance Options for Agriculture and Nutrition (2016).

[60] *See* ASKJustice, ASKJustice RSS, *available at* www.ASKJustice.org (last visited Jun. 14, 2017).

[61] *See, e.g.*, the Carnegie Africa Diaspora Fellowship Program, which leverages African diaspora expertise to support capacity building in curriculum development, collaborative research, and graduate supervision to enhance the quality of higher education on the African continent. Carnegie African Diaspora Fellowship Program, IIE, *available at* www.iie.org/Programs/Carnegie-African-Diaspora-Fellowship-Program (last visited Oct .18, 2016).

case studies and other opportunities within the network. In its latest phase of work, Open AIR has developed cross-regional exchanges of African and other students (both graduate and undergraduate), postdoctoral fellows, a special Open AIR new and emerging researcher group sub-network, and faculty to experience first hand collaborative research in African and other destinations in areas of shared interests under the Open AIR research program.

VI Interdisciplinary Analysis

Sixth, a natural and necessary aspect of the Open AIR is its interdisciplinary composition. The partnership actively supports resource persons and memberships from every possible disciplinary background with perspectives that help understand IP and knowledge governance in the African context. As IP and knowledge governance impact virtually every aspect of human life, the once arcane subject has since ceased to be the exclusive reserve of few disciplines,[62] such as law and economics.

As such, any research partnership that focuses on the complex scope as outlined by the Open AIR program must of necessity not only include diverse disciplinary representations[63] but also ensure that the constitutive or participating disciplinary agents have the benefit of collaborative or interdisciplinary immersion and experience.[64] In addition, such research must be open to leveraging opportune and circumstantial partnerships, outreaches, and connections suited to collaboratively tackling innovation and knowledge governance for sustainable development.

VII A Shared Vision

Finally, like other forms of partnership, an essence of the Open AIR experience is the shared vision and objectives and a convergence among all partners on many counts. For example, partners are united in the hypothesis that the contemporary IP narrative and metrics for measuring innovation not only fails to capture but also alienates Africa's creativity and innovation. All Open AIR partners are convinced on the need for a grounded and empirical approach to investigating African experiences with the extant global IP regime and the need for practical insights into the forms of knowledge governance on the continent. Overall, partners understand that accommodation of context is an important policy building block for progressive IP and knowledge governance policy for sustainable development.

On a more theoretical plane, all categories of Open AIR partners including funders and host research institutions agree on the negative impact of overprotection of IP rights on creativity, innovation, and development. They share the view that despite the mainstream inclination toward stronger IP protection, the extent to which the IP environment influences innovation and creativity has yet to be rigorously interrogated and understood,

[62] Peter K. Yu, *Reconceptualizing Intellectual Property in Human Rights Framework* 40 UC Davis L. Rev. 3, 1039 (2007).

[63] *See* Intellectual Property for the 21st Century: Interdisciplinary Approaches (Courtney B. Doagoo et al. eds., 2014).

[64] *Id.*

especially so in the context of the dynamics of collaborative and openness-oriented innovation in Africa.[65] As a guiding principle, Open AIR partners believe that more and continued inquiries would shed light on pluralistic knowledge governance models. These would include the known and the unknown models with opportunities for understanding how to integrate contexts and sectoral sensitivities or variables while striking a balance between openness or inclusiveness, and various exclusionary frameworks[66].

Like most development-oriented interventionist PPPs, the Open AIR research partnership is interested in how best to optimize the benefits of creativity and innovation to society without undermining the rights of creators. Many PPPs locate the solution to this overarching problem in often ad hoc or temporal bridging of access gaps through schemes that ship ready-made solutions such as the delivery of products and services for those who otherwise cannot afford them. It is a case of giving the fish while neglecting to provide for the manufacturing of the hook and failing to identify how best to optimally fish for creativity in a vast ocean of possibilities on the continent. Open AIR explores a number of African experiences with IP and knowledge governance from the collaborative dynamic of knowledge production. It is an approach that looks at the underlying issues of the practical, theoretical, and policy gaps in the global IP framework. Understanding the negative impact of those gaps in undermining creativity and innovation in Africa provides the foundation or urgency for a context-based framework for bridging access to innovation through grounded perspectives. The results of Open AIR's recent case studies suggest that the outcomes of these insights across sectoral contexts, for example, in music and entertainment,[67] crafts and trade,[68] traditional medicines,[69] as well as food and agriculture,[70] would be helpful to construct and implement more sustainable PPPs not only within the extant conventional models but also to generate new ones across sectoral variables. In all of the above listed sectors, multiple stakeholders (knowledge producers and the consuming public or communities, artists, artisans, traditional medicine practitioners, farmers, etc.) underscore the shared interest of knowledge producers and consumers as a collaborative and mutually reinforcing experience. Symbolically, Egyptian musicians, for example, prefer open distribution and dissemination of their music with little or no IP bottleneck to advance vibrant consumer experience which, in turn, has the effect of reinforcing the artist's professional, social, and economic value.[71]

[65] *See* Jeremy de Beer et al., *supra* note 34.

[66] Colleen Chien, *Opening the Patent System: Diffusionary Levers in Patent Law* 89 S. Calif. L. Rev. 793 (2016); *see also* Jeremy de Beer et al., *supra* note 34.

[67] *See* Nagla Rizk, *From De Facto Commons to Digital Commons? The Case of Egypt's Independent Music Industry, in* Innovation & Intellectual Property: Collaborative Dynamic in Africa 171–202 (2015).

[68] *See, e.g.*, Adebambo Adewopo et al., A *Consideration of Communal Trademarks for Nigerian Leather and Textile Products, in* Innovation & Intellectual Property: Collaborative Dynamic in Africa 109–131 (2015).

[69] *See* Gino Cocchiaro et al., *Consideration of a Legal "Trust" Model for the Kukula Healers' TK Commons, in* Innovation & Intellectual Property: Collaborative Dynamic in Africa 151–170 (2015).

[70] *See, e.g.*, Chidi Oguamanam & Teshager Dagne, *Geographical Indication (GI) Options for Ethiopian Coffee and Ghanian Cocoa, in* Innovation & Intellectual Property: Collaborative Dynamic in Africa 77–108 (2015).

[71] See Rizk, *supra* note 67.

VIII The Sustainable Development Nexus: Some Policy Lessons and Limitations

Most PPPs operate under the conventional knowledge governance framework that links stronger IP protection to development. Hence many PPPs are, essentially, ad hoc and interventionist concessions designed to cushion the effects of stronger IP regimes for developing countries pending such a time they make the magic leap and become like their industrialized counterparts. Therefore, in a way, PPPs are dedicated band-aids or quick fixes for deep-running issues of a skewed framework that has left many countries behind.

One of the flagship legal inspirations for PPPs in the area of access to medicines is the Doha Declaration, which is an adjunct of the much-advertised TRIPS' wiggle room.[72] A prominent aspect of this is compulsory licensing.[73] Despite the practical and legal constraints associated with compulsory licensing, as a proposition, the latter is a source of irrefutable pressure on essential medicine patent holders to cozy up or partner with other public interest actors and proactively bridge the access gap.[74] In such case, PPPs not only help to mitigate the access crisis, but perhaps most importantly, they also ensure the extant IP status quo as well as the impregnable role of the private sector in setting the R & D agenda.[75]

Thus, the operational framework of some PPPs and the legal and policy spaces that have facilitated them focus on the symptom and not on the problem. They are not designed to address the issue of how knowledge production happens in specific sociocultural and economic contexts. As Open AIR has found, that inquiry is important for IP and knowledge governance in the African context. It provides insights that support people to have ownership of their knowledge production process and to insist upon a global IP and knowledge governance policy space that not only recognizes their contribution but also values them as partners, rather than as tacit or docile recipients of IP prescriptions written for all by few in a fixated ideological mindset. It is vision that places people in their cultural and local contexts and at the centre of their own development, which is the essence of sustainable development.

In substance, Open AIR is a large cross-regional research partnership. It is an important vehicle to triangulate the practical, theoretical, and policy ramifications of IP and knowledge governance in Africa. Conceptually, as a research-driven and not a product-driven initiative, insights from Open AIR's research can shine lights, as a foundational matter, on how PPPs can be better exploited and reengineered beyond their current and ad hoc interventionist outlook in order to make them serve as sustainable development vehicles. For example, instead of a PPP to be dedicated to produce a subsidized electric car, green energy technology, or even brand name drugs for Africa's consumption, insights arising from Open AIR inquiries may inspire other PPPs to implement R&D efforts that tap Africa's factor endowments through a combination of on-the-ground practices of open and collaborative innovation, as well as informal and formal interface

[72] *See* World Trade Organization Ministerial Conference, *Declaration on the TRIPs Agreement and Public Health*, WTO Doc, WT/MIN(01)/DEC/W/2 (Nov. 14, 2001), *aviailable at* www.who.int/medicines/areas/policy/tripshealth.pdf?ua=1.

[73] *See* Sara M. Ford, Compulsory Licensing Provision Under the TRIPS Agreement: Balancing Pills and Patents, 15 Am. U. Int'l L. Rev. 4, 941–971 (2000).

[74] *See* Oguamanam, *supra* note 1.

[75] *Id.*

and apprenticeship models, to produce or scale to a substantially African-made version of any of these knowledge products. Such an example represents a model of innovation capacity building as sustainable development.

We have found that despite differences and complexities on the African continent, there are systemic similarities that point to a pattern of collaborative and open innovation models as well as resistances and adaptations as the "continent responds to transformational pressures of market liberalization and global IP norms."[76] African innovation, creativity, and knowledge production and governance models carefully negotiate and vacillate around selective pragmatism and prescriptive orthodoxy.

With innovation occurring in multiple contexts, from a historical continuum and transformation of traditional knowledge to the adaptions of the digital revolution, there is a complex intersection of formal and informal knowledge production and governance frameworks. These uncover opportunities for recalibrated or newer models of public interest partnerships or even business models to optimize the dissemination of the benefits of innovation and creativity. Informed by both practical and theoretical insights, a context-specific approach to IP and knowledge governance that targets the realities of creativity and innovation in the African settings can better inform policy on the use of PPPs to support truly localized sustainable development on the continent in a global knowledge ecosystem. Open AIR is committed to actively studying the IP policies and practices that drive collaborative innovation, a theme that represents an important insight from Africa's knowledge governance experience and practices, which has implications for innovation-driven sustainable development on the continent.

A *Some Policy Lessons from PPPs*

The Open AIR partnership is an ongoing initiative. Building on previous successes, the partnership has continued to expand following the commitment of the partners to continue the research initiatives into the future. As new empirical studies get underway[77] and the network expands, we can draw a few lessons from the partnership experience within the framework of the PPP construct.

The first lessons from Open AIR point to the need for PPPs' objectives to include foundational research, which is separated from the current focus on access to benefits of knowledge and innovation through products and services deliveries. As described above, PPPs remain understudied. In essence, the relevance of research partnerships such as Open AIR lies in their ability to re-imagine and push the envelopes of PPPs with slightly different emphasis. As the UN SDGs get underway there is already a strong consciousness for the creation of innovative partnerships toward accountability and their effective implementation.[78] Certainly from the Open AIR experience, the boundaries of PPPs can be pushed so long as partners have shared goals and objectives.

[76] *See* Jeremy de Beer et al., *Current Realities of Collaborative Intellectual Property in Africa, in* INNOVATION & INTELLECTUAL PROPERTY: COLLABORATIVE DYNAMIC IN AFRICA 373–394 (2015).

[77] *See Research*, OPEN AIR, www.openair.org.za/research/.

[78] *See, e.g.*, the activities of the United Nations Global Compact initiative, which is committed to boosting sustainable and accountable development partnership pursuant to SDGs. *Leading the Way in the SGD Era: Connecting Global Business*, UNITED NATIONS GLOBAL IMPACT, www.unglobalcompact.org/docs/news_events/PSF2016/Leading-the-Way-in-the-SDG-Era.pdf (last visited Oct. 18, 2016).

The second lesson from a cross-regional IP and knowledge governance research partnership is that such initiative is needed to deeply root PPPs in the development agenda.[79] So far, quibbles over the development agenda in IP have built on historic and lingering mistrusts across the developed-developing country geopolitical divide. Even public interest NGOs and regional IGOs are not immune from the vicarious liabilities of these often tense environments for enunciating the development imperative in international IP and global knowledge governance policy.[80] This state of affairs opens an opportunity for a grounded research-based partnership that strategically operates at the intersection of these tensions without being pigeonholed in order to bring evidence-based insights that demonstrate the primacy of sustainability in IP, knowledge governance and development.

A third lesson from the Open AIR experience is that it unravels an uncommon, passive, and indirect form of private sector nesting in a research-driven PPP. Often, the private sector is cast as a self-interested, even opportunistic driver of PPPs. Little consideration is given to fact that some NGOs or ostensible public interest entities benefit from private sector contributions in their operations – in some cases without strings attached. Indirectly related to that, however, is our experience through the partnership in the reaffirmation of the private sector and the notion of entrepreneurship as critical to IP and knowledge governance for development. The private sector and entrepreneurship have remained the operational and constitutive component of PPPs,[81] providing an important plank of that arrangement and assuming as much importance as the public sector and indeed all other partners.

However, in a research-oriented PPP construct such as Open AIR, it became quickly clear that knowledge production in Africa happens at complex interfaces of formal, informal, and semi-formal economies.[82] But little credit is given to the self-evident reality that collaborative knowledge production in Africa happens in the swell of ubiquitous forms of creative entrepreneurships. Open AIR case studies, for example, those that have focused on informal-formal sectors interactions in automotive engineering in Kampala, Uganda,[83] on geographical indications options for Ethiopian Coffee and Ghanaian Cocoa,[84] and on communal trademarks for Nigerian leather and textile products,[85] find that entrepreneurship is a robust site for sustainable development-oriented capacity building on IP and knowledge governance. Open AIR encourages the expansion of its network members to include expertise in knowledge-based industries and grassroots entrepreneurship. The partnership examines the dynamics of IP and knowledge governance model with entrepreneurship and their scalability to leverage hitherto unfathomable opportunities as aspects of sustainable development.

[79] The challenge of how to effectively implement the current phase of WIPO development agenda has engaged policy makers and academics. Open AIR's research preoccupation with a context-specific and responsive innovation system that addresses the needs of the poor and marginalized aligns with the spirit of the development agenda. *See* Peter K. Yu, *A Tale of Two Development Agendas* 35 Ohio N. U. L. Rev 465, 467 (2009).

[80] *See* Oguamanam, *supra* note 57.

[81] *See* de Beer, *supra* note 76.

[82] *See* Kawooya, *supra* note 56.

[83] *Id.*

[84] *See* Oguamanam & Dagne, *supra* note 70.

[85] *See* Adewopo, *supra* note 68.

B *Some Policy Limitations*

As a unique form of partnership, the Open AIR faces wide-ranging limitations in respect of its subject matter but also with regard to the partnership's operational and implementation experience. We have already highlighted the conceptual morass inherent in interfacing IP and knowledge governance with innovation and creativity on a continent that is under external pressure to conform to global IP standards which are not necessarily in sync with the informal-formal dynamic of prevailing collaborative knowledge production. In addition, Africa is a continent of fifty-four countries, comprising a few that are classified as developing countries. Even those in the developing countries category are not at identical levels of development. The same is true throughout the majority of the rest of the continent, which constitute the highest level of least developed countries of any region.

In addition to the variations in the levels of developments, Africa has complex colonial histories that translate in the diversity of its political and legal systems, languages (English, French, Portuguese, and Arabic), and orientations. As such, Africa is neither a unit of analysis, as tempting as it seems, nor is it a site for credible generalizations. As a partnership and network, Open AIR is constantly challenged in its fieldwork and recruitment by the continent's multi-prong diversities and variations in its levels of development. How to adequately tackle these challenges is a constant concern of our partnership. More so, because those considerations are critical to enable us to capture and effectively disseminate for policy impact a broad scope of issues of creativity and innovation on the continent in as much a representative manner as feasible.

Related to the uneven levels of development on the continent is the issue of institutional and social capacities, or lack of them, for effectively partnering in a cross-regional partnership that is funded by multiple agencies that require complex levels of accountability across diverse categories. We have found on the ground that there are uneven levels of gaps across regions, and even among institutions within the same region, in institutional capacity for large-scale grant management, administration, and partnerships.

From the perspective of the sustainability of a research partnership, Open AIR's operational pragmatism identifies the need to support capacity building in grant administration and even in methodologies for conducting interdisciplinary research among institutional and individual members of the network. The ability of African institutions to attract and implement research grants either alone or in partnership is critical to the idea of capacity-building for sustainable development not only in the area of IP and knowledge governance but also in institutional building and social capital development for research. From this experience, Open AIR underscores innovation capacity building as an essential complementary aspect of PPP for sustainable development in Africa's specific context, which is, certainly, relevant to developing countries outside of Africa.

Most conventional PPP models spend time and resources to map, on an extensive scope, the feasibility of the partnerships through, among other things, identifying common interests, organizational designs, benefit-cost analysis, results, and tenure of the partnerships.[86] Even though most of these considerations are relevant to the Open AIR partnership, they are not engaged or explored with the degree of technicality and precision that is pursued

[86] *See* Oguamanam, *supra* note 1.

in business or commercial-oriented PPPs. Pivotal to research partnerships such as Open AIR is, in principle, the idea of common interests in the subject matter(s) of the research shared among funders, partner institutions, and members of the network. However, these are hardly sufficient to engage the issue of commitment at both individual and institutional levels with regard to the implementation of the research and fostering synergy and complementariness across diverse range of subject matters covered in the research. Therefore, there is need for self-assessment and evaluation on continual basis through the progress of the partnership.

Lacking the precision and strict contractual and often narrow orientations of conventional PPPs, the Open AIR partnership navigates through flexible, pragmatic, and often reactive and proactive approaches, to sustain focus on its objectives. That spirit of flexibility and pragmatism is naturally susceptible to discretions and flaws. As a pragmatic matter, decisions are often contingent upon unpredictable variables. Judgment calls on what works and how best to leverage the dynamic of relationships across participating institutional and individual partners represent a steep learning curve that constitute the basis for our experience in growing the partnership. Such a context enables Open AIR to pursue strategies that concurrently focus on institutions and on individuals, including those nested within or without institutions, to ensure that the project is implemented with adequate institutional or individual commitment, or both, in an efficient manner. At times, an individual's commitment may be constrained by institutional factors; at other times institutional assets can be better leveraged by the presence of a specific individual. Such fluidity and flexibility at the intersection of organizational and individual dynamic is a challenge that Open Air has continued to manage. We aim to appraise how such dynamism can be leveraged and its susceptibility for abuse checked as an additional lesson in sustainable development through the Open AIR partnership.

Conclusion

PPPs are understudied and inchoate phenomena that have the potential to be one of the most strategic development tools of the twenty-first century. They can be imaginative institutions for fixing the public interest deficits at the intersection of IP and access to innovation by the most vulnerable. Yet, the paucity of commitment to sustainability is a fundamental flaw of current PPP models. These partnerships are often deployed in an interventionist manner to solve a major access or public interest crises linked to extreme proprietary control of innovation. As *ad hoc* interventionist strategies, PPPs consequently tend to operate under the shadow or suspicion of private capture of the public interest space. Lacking any deliberate commitment to sustainability, PPPs interventions, in some contexts, are perceived as a means of perpetuating the status quo in which extreme proprietary barriers to access to innovation ironically constitute one of the development obstacles of our time.

The current embryonic status of PPP as a form of experimentation in development circles and in global governance presents an opportunity to explore other development oriented and cognate forms of partnership. In this context, we have identified the Open AIR as a cross-regional research network and partnership not directly associated with specific public interest intervention or product and service delivery for development, exploring how such partnership can help better inform and improve the design of PPPs or partnership building generally. In our exploration of Open AIR, we argue that it is typology of a research network and partnership strategy dedicated to both empirical and theoretical interrogation of knowledge production and governance dynamic, which can make a useful contribution to emerging perspectives on PPPs or other partnerships. Its case studies bring forward varied models of innovation and creativity as well as complex and nuanced approaches to IP and knowledge governance in Africa with important ramifications for the continent's overall sustainable development.

References

Adam, Barbara & Jen Martens, *Partnerships and 2030 Agenda: Time to Reconsider Their Role in Implementation*, Global Policy Forum (May 2016), *available at* www.globalpolicywatch.org/wp-content/uploads/2016/05/On-Partnerships-GPF-input-to-discussion.pdf (last visited Nov. 17, 2017).

Adewopo, Adebambo, Helen Chuma Okoro, & Adejoke Oyewunmi, *A Consideration of Communal Trademarks for Nigerian Leather and Textile Products* in INNOVATION & INTELLECTUAL PROPERTY: COLLABORATIVE DYNAMIC IN AFRICA 109–131 (Jeremy de Beer et al. eds. 2015).

Agbamuche-Mbu, May, *PPPs Key to Our Desired Infrastructure Development*, This Day (September 13, 2016), *available at* www.thisdaylive.com/index.php/2016/09/13/ppps-key-to-our-desired-infrastructure-development/ (last visited Nov. 17, 2017).

Andrews, Rhys, Marc Esteve, & Tamyko Ysa, *Public–private joint ventures: mixing oil and water?*, 35 PUB. MONEY & MGMT 4, 265 (2015).

Armstrong, Chris, Jeremy de Beer, Dick Kawooya, Achal Prabhala, & T. Schonwetter, eds., ACCESS TO KNOWLEDGE IN AFRICA: THE ROLE OF COPYRIGHT (2010).

Boland, William P. and Peter W. B. Phillips, *An Analysis of the Hidden Variables Influencing Challenges and Opportunities of Implementing R&D and Value Chain Agricultural Public-Private Partnerships in the Developing World* (2012) (unpublished manuscript) available at: www.value-chains.org/dyn/bds/docs/831/Boland_ValueChainPPPs_Final.pdf (last visited Nov. 17, 2017).

Börzel, Tanja and Thomas Risse, *Public-Private Partnerships. Effective and Legitimate Tools of Transnational Governance? in* COMPLEX SOVEREIGNTY: ON THE RECONSTITUTION OF POLITICAL AUTHORITY IN THE 21ST CENTURY (Edgar Grande & Louis W. Pauly eds., 2012).

Bragdon, Susan, *Reinvigorating the Public Sector: The Case of Food Security, Small-Scale Farmers, Trade and Intellectual Property Rules* (Transnational Institute (TNI), Colloquium Paper No. 64, 2016).

Chan, Sander & Christina Müller, *Explaining the Geographic, Thematic and Organizational Differentiation of Partnerships for Sustainable Development* in PUBLIC-PRIVATE PARTNERSHIPS FOR SUSTAINABLE DEVELOPMENT: EMERGENCE, INFLUENCE AND LEGITIMACY 44–66 (Philipp H. Pattberg et al. eds., 2012).

Chien, Colleen, *Opening the Patent System: Diffusionary Levers in Patent Law*, 89 S. CALIF. L. *Rev*. 793 (2016).

Cocchiaro, Johan Lorenzen, Bernard Maister, & Britta Rutert, *Consideration of a Legal "Trust" Model for the Kukula Healers' TK Commons in South Africa* in INNOVATION & INTELLECTUAL PROPERTY: COLLABORATIVE DYNAMIC IN AFRICA 151–170 (Jeremy de Beer et al. eds., 2015).

de Beer, Jeremy, OWNERSHIP OF OPEN DATA: GOVERNANCE OPTIONS FOR AGRICULTURE AND NUTRITION (2016).

de Beer, Jeremy, Chris Armstrong, Chidi Oguamanam, & Tobias Schonwetter eds., INNOVATION & INTELLECTUAL PROPERTY: COLLABORATIVE DYNAMICS IN AFRICA (2015).

de Beer, Jeremy, and Sara Bannerman, *Access to Knowledge as a New Paradigm for Research on ICTs and Intellectual Property Rights*, in CONNECTING ICTS TO DEVELOPMENT: THE IDRC EXPERIENCE (H. Emdon, L. Elder, B. Petrazzini and R. Fuchs, eds., 2013).

de Beer, Jeremy and Chidi Oguamanam, *Intellectual Property Training and Education: A Development Perspective* (International Centre for Trade and Sustainable Development 2010), www.ictsd.org/downloads/2010/11/iptrainingandeducation.pdf (last visited Nov. 17, 2017).

de Beer, Jeremy, Chris Armstrong, Chidi Oguamanam, & Tobias Schonwetter, *Current Realities of Collaborative Intellectual Property in Africa* in Jeremy De Beer et al., INNOVATION & INTELLECTUAL PROPERTY: COLLABORATIVE DYNAMIC IN AFRICA 373–394 (de Beer et al. eds. 2015).

de Beer, Jeremy, Chidi Oguamanam, & Tobias Schonwetter, *Innovation, Intellectual Property and Development Narratives in Africa*, in Jeremy de Beer et al., INNOVATION & INTELLECTUAL PROPERTY: COLLABORATIVE DYNAMIC IN AFRICA 1–31 (de Beer et al. eds. 2015).

de Beer, Jeremy, Richard Gold, and Mauricio Guaranga, INTELLECTUAL PROPERTY MANAGEMENT: POLICY ISSUES AND OPTIONS (2011).

Doagoo, Courtney B., Mistrale Goudreau, Madelaine Saginur, and Teresa Scassa eds., INTELLECTUAL PROPERTY FOR THE 21ST CENTURY: INTERDISCIPLINARY APPROACHES (2014).

Drahos, Peter and John Braithwaite, INFORMATION FEUDALISM: WHO OWNS THE KNOWLEDGE ECONOMY? (2002).

Dutfield, Graham and Uma Susthersanen, *Harmonization or Differentiation in Intellectual Property Protection? The Role of History*, 23 PROMETHEUS 2, 131–147 (2005).

Ford, Sara M., *Compulsory Licensing Provision Under the TRIPS Agreement: Balancing Pills and Patents*, 15 AM. U. INT'L L. REV. 4, 941–971 (2000

Global Open Data for Agriculture and Nutrition, GODAN, *available at* www.godan.info. (last visited Jun. 14, 2017).

Hartwich, Frank, Jaime Tola, Alejandra Engler, Carolina González, Graciela Ghezan, Jorge M. P. Vázquez-Alvarado, José Antonio Silva, José de Jesús Espinoza, & María Verónica Gottret, FOOD SECURITY IN PRACTICE: BUILDING PUBLIC-PRIVATE PARTNERSHIP FOR AGRICULTURAL INNOVATION (2008) https://core.ac.uk/download/pdf/6388470.pdf (last visited Nov. 17, 2017).

Hatton, Michael J. and Kent Schroeder, *Partnership Theory and Practice: Time for a New Paradigm*, 28 CAN J OF DEVELOPMENT STUDIES 1, 157–162 (2007).

Helfer, Laurence R., *Regime Shifting: The TRIPs Agreement and New Dynamics of International Intellectual Property Making*, 29 YALE J OF INTL L 1 (2004).

Kawooya, Dick, *Informal-Formal Sector Interactions in Automotive Engineering Kampala*, in INNOVATION & INTELLECTUAL PROPERTY: COLLABORATIVE DYNAMIC IN AFRICA 56–76 (Jeremy de Beer et al. eds., 2015).

Maskus, Keith and Jerome Reichman eds., INTERNATIONAL PUBLIC GOODS AND TRANSFER OF TECHNOLOGY UNDER A GLOBALIZED INTELLECTUAL PROPERTY REGIME (2005).

Maurasse, David J, STRATEGIC PUBLIC PRIVATE PARTNERSHIPS: INNOVATION AND DEVELOPMENT (2013).

May, Christopher ed., THE WORLD INTELLECTUAL PROPERTY ORGANIZATION: RESURGENCE AND THE DEVELOPMENT AGENDA (2007).

Moreddu, Catherine, *Public-Private Partnerships for Agricultural Innovation: Lessons from Recent Experiences* (2016), www.oecd-ilibrary.org/agriculture-and-food/public-private-partnerships-for-agricultural-innovation_5jm55j9p9rmx-en (last visited Nov. 17, 2017).

Ohia, Uche, *Infrastructural Concession in Nigeria: Challenges and Opportunities*, Nigerians in America (August 16, 2011), *available at* www.nigeriansinamerica.com/infrastructure-concession-in-nigeria-challenges-and-opportunities/ (last visited Nov. 17, 2017).

Pattberg, Philipp H., Frank Biermann, Sander Chan, and Ayşem Mert eds., PUBLIC-PRIVATE PARTNERSHIPS FOR SUSTAINABLE DEVELOPMENT: EMERGENCE, INFLUENCE AND LEGITIMACY (2012).

Pattberg, Philipp H., Frank Biermann, Sander Chan, and Ayşem Mert, *Conclusions: partnerships for sustainable development* in PUBLIC-PRIVATE PARTNERSHIPS FOR SUSTAINABLE DEVELOPMENT: EMERGENCE, INFLUENCE AND LEGITIMACY 239–248 (Philipp Pattberg et al. eds., 2012).

Oguamanam, Chidi, INTELLECTUAL PROPERTY IN GLOBAL GOVERNANCE: A DEVELOPMENT QUESTION (2012).

Oguamanam, Chidi, *Breeding Apples for Oranges: Africa's Misplaced Priority over Plant Breeders' Rights* 18 J OF WORLD INTELLECTUAL PROPERTY 5, 165–195 (2015).

Oguamanam, Chidi, *Open Innovation in Plant Genetic Resources for Food and Agriculture*, 13 CHICAGO KENT J OF INTELLECTUAL PROPERTY 1, 11–50 (2013).

Oguamanam, Chidi, *Patents and Pharmaceutical R&D: Consolidating Public- Private Partnership Approach to Global Public Health Crisis*, 13 J OF WORLD INTELLECTUAL PROPERTY 4, 556–580 (2010).

Oguamanam, Chidi and Teshager Dagne, *Geographical Indication (GI) Options for Ethiopian Coffee and Ghanian Cocoa* in INNOVATION & INTELLECTUAL PROPERTY: COLLABORATIVE DYNAMIC IN AFRICA 77–108 (Jeremy de Beer et al. eds., 2015).

Olwan, Rami M., INTELLECTUAL PROPERTY AND DEVELOPMENT: THEORY AND PRACTICE (2013).

Oriola, Taiwo A., *Strong Medicines: Patents, Markets, and Policy Challenges for Managing Diseases and Affordable Prescription Drugs*, 7 CAN. J. L. & TECH. 1, 57–123 (2008).

Oxfam, Oxfam Briefing Paper, *Ending the R&D Crisis in Public Health: Promoting Pro-Poor Medical Innovation*, Oxfam International (2008), www.oxfam.org/sites/www.oxfam.org/files/file_attachments/bp122-randd-crisis-public-health_3.pdf (last visited Nov. 17, 2017).

Oxfam, *How a Public-Private Healthcare Partnership Threatens to Bankrupt Lesotho*, Oxfam International (April 7, 2014), *available at* www.oxfam.org/en/multimedia/video/2014-how-public-private-healthcare-partnership-threatens-bankrupt-lesotho (last visited Nov. 17, 2017).

Rifkin, Jeremy, THE THIRD INDUSTRIAL REVOLUTION: HOW LATERAL POWER IS TRANSFORMING ENERGY, THE ECONOMY AND THE WORLD (2008).

Rizk, Nagla, *From De Facto Commons to Digital Commons? The Case of Egypt's Independent Music Industry*, in INNOVATION & INTELLECTUAL PROPERTY: COLLABORATIVE DYNAMIC IN AFRICA 171–202 (Jeremy de Beer et al. eds., 2015).

Sen, Amartya, DEVELOPMENT AS FREEDOM (1999).

Stiglitz, Joseph E., *Knowledge as a Global Public Good*, P2PF Wiki (September 15, 2007), https://wiki.p2pfoundation.net/Knowledge_as_a_Global_Public_Good (last visited Nov. 17, 2017).

Stradtler, Lea, *Designing public-private partnerships for development* 15 MANAGEMENT 1, 78 (2012).

Sunder, Madhavi, *IP3*, 59 STANFORD L REV. 2, 257 (2006).

United Nations Global Impact. *Leading the Way in the SGD Era: Connecting Global Business*, www.unglobalcompact.org/docs/news_events/PSF2016/Leading-the-Way-in-the-SDG-Era.pdf (last visited Oct. 18, 2016).

United Nations Millennium Development Goals, U.N., *available at* www.un.org/millennium goals/ (last visited Oct. 18, 2016).

Yu, Peter K., *A Tale of Two Development Agendas* 35 OHIO NORTHERN UNIV L REV. 465–573 (2009).

Yu, Peter K., *International Enclosure, the Regime Complex and Intellectual Property Schizophrenia*, MICH. L REV. 1–33 (2007).

18 Intellectual Property, Human Rights, and Public–Private Partnerships

Peter K. Yu

Introduction

Since the Agreement on Trade-Related Aspects of Intellectual Property Rights (TRIPS Agreement) of the World Trade Organization (WTO) entered into force in January 1995, policymakers, commentators, advocacy groups, and intergovernmental and nongovernmental organizations have become greatly concerned about the agreement's deleterious effects on human rights protection. Although the lack of access to essential medicines is often cited as a priority human rights concern, especially in light of the HIV/AIDS, malaria, and tuberculosis pandemics in Sub-Saharan Africa,[1] other concerns have included the lack of access to knowledge, educational materials, computer software, information technology, and patented seeds and foodstuffs as well as the inadequate protection of traditional knowledge and traditional cultural expressions.

Catching an equal, if not a greater, amount of attention was the growing – and, for many, undue – influence of transnational corporations (TNCs) on the international trading system, the WTO in particular. After all, these powerful corporations heavily lobbied for the adoption of the TRIPS Agreement. As Susan Sell lamented, "[i]n effect, twelve corporations made public law for the world."[2] Apart from the TRIPS Agreement, TNCs have exerted influence on many other WTO agreements, covering areas such as agriculture, textiles, and services. It is therefore no surprise that the WTO talks in Seattle at the turn of this century collapsed due to antiglobalization protests.

With the rapid expansion of intellectual property rights and the ongoing development of TRIPS-plus bilateral, regional, and plurilateral trade agreements, such as those establishing the Trans-Pacific Partnership, the Regional Comprehensive Economic Partnership, and the Transatlantic Trade and Investment Partnership, TNCs have posed considerable challenges to the international trading and intellectual property systems. These challenges, in turn, have led policymakers, commentators, advocacy groups, and intergovernmental and nongovernmental organizations to actively utilize human rights to curtail the growing expansion of intellectual property rights.

[1] The Global Governance of HIV/AIDS: Intellectual Property and Access to Essential Medicines (Obijiofor Aginam, John Harrington, & Peter K. Yu eds., 2013).

[2] Susan K. Sell, Private Power, Public Law: The Globalization of Intellectual Property Rights 96 (2003).

As if these developments were not complicated enough, public–private partnerships (PPPs) began to appear in the intellectual property arena about two decades ago. With their arrival, new questions have also emerged over their positive and adverse impacts on human rights protection. The establishment of PPPs is attractive because these partnerships "combine the best of both worlds" by "avoid[ing] the often negative effects of either exclusive public ownership and delivery of services . . . or outright privatization."[3] Such establishment can also be problematic because PPPs are hybrid entities that have "status as instruments of the public interest, yet bodies that actively engage private actors."[4] Because of these dual characteristics, the partnerships' human rights responsibilities do not align well with those traditionally assumed by either public or private actors.

This chapter focuses on the roles and responsibilities of intellectual property-related PPPs in the international human rights regime. It begins by debunking two key claims TNCs have advanced in the area intersecting intellectual property and human rights. Although PPPs involve many types of private sector partners, this discussion singles out TNCs because of their frequent and vocal opposition to business and human rights initiatives. Such a focus will underscore the immense challenge of protecting human rights in the private sphere.[5]

This chapter then examines the "protect, respect, and remedy" framework (Ruggie Framework) and the Guiding Principles on Business and Human Rights (Guiding Principles),[6] which John Ruggie presented to the U.N. Human Rights Council in his capacity as the U.N. Secretary-General's Special Representative on the Issue of Human Rights and Transnational Corporations and Other Business Enterprises. These documents are highly relevant to the discussion of the human rights responsibilities of PPPs because they apply to not only States and TNCs, but also other types of private sector partners, such as donor and civil society organizations. After evaluating the strengths and weaknesses of the Ruggie Framework and the Guiding Principles, this chapter will explain why these partnerships should assume greater human rights responsibilities than TNCs.

The chapter concludes with three specific examples illustrating how PPPs can be utilized to foster a more appropriate balance between intellectual property and human rights. These examples are important because striking this balance will require more than efforts in identifying, cataloguing, and clarifying human rights responsibilities. To achieve such a balance, governments, intergovernmental bodies, TNCs, and nongovernmental organizations will also need to pro-actively develop PPPs for human rights (P3s4HR) in the intellectual property arena.

[3] Marek Belka, *Foreword* to UNITED NATIONS ECONOMIC COMMISSION FOR EUROPE, GUIDEBOOK ON PROMOTING GOOD GOVERNANCE IN PUBLIC-PRIVATE PARTNERSHIPS, at iii (2008).

[4] Chris Skelcher, *Governing Partnerships*, *in* INTERNATIONAL HANDBOOK ON PUBLIC-PRIVATE PARTNERSHIPS 292, 292 (Graeme A. Hodge, Carsten Greve, & Anthony E. Boardman eds., 2010) [hereinafter INTERNATIONAL HANDBOOK].

[5] Andrew Clapham, HUMAN RIGHTS IN THE PRIVATE SPHERE (1993); Steven R. Ratner, *Corporations and Human Rights: A Theory of Legal Responsibility*, 111 YALE L.J. 443, 475–88 (2001).

[6] Guiding Principles on Business and Human Rights: Implementing the United Nations "Protect, Respect and Remedy" Framework [hereinafter Guiding Principles], *in Rep. of the Special Representative of the Secretary-General on the Issue of Human Rights and Transnational Corporations and Other Business Enterprises*, Human Rights Council, U.N. Doc. A/HRC/17/31, at 6–27 (Mar. 21, 2011) (by John Ruggie) [hereinafter Ruggie's 2011 Report].

I Corporations Have No Human Rights Obligations

The first claim that TNCs advance often in the area of business and human rights goes as follows: while States take on human rights obligations by entering into international human rights treaties, TNCs are not parties to these treaties and therefore do not have the same obligations. Indeed, States and TNCs have very different missions, values, and objectives. The former also have greater obligations to individual citizens than the latter.

Nevertheless, in the past few decades, commentators, advocacy groups, and intergovernmental and nongovernmental organizations have called on TNCs to strengthen their protection of human rights, including those of their employees and third parties. Efforts to ascertain and catalogue corporate human rights responsibilities can be traced back as early as the mid-1970s.

In December 1974, the U.N. Commission on Transnational Corporations was established to draft a U.N. Code of Conduct on Transnational Corporations.[7] Because the negotiations were launched in the wake of the establishment of the New International Economic Order, "the drive … to deal with [TNCs] and their [foreign direct investment] at the international level … focused on controlling [these corporations]."[8] These negotiations took place until the early 1990s but were eventually abandoned, due largely to the wide disagreement between developed and developing countries.

A few years after the establishment of the U.N. Commission on Transnational Corporations in 1974, the International Labour Organization (ILO) also adopted the Tripartite Declaration of Principles Concerning Multinational Enterprises and Social Policy.[9] Focusing on workers' human rights and covering three distinct groups of actors (governments, employers, and workers), this declaration was adopted in November 1977 and revised in November 2000 and March 2006. The current version of the declaration "offer[s] guidelines to [multinational enterprises], governments, and employers' and workers' organizations in such areas as employment, training, conditions of work and life, and industrial relations."[10]

Although the negotiations on the U.N. Code of Conduct on Transnational Corporations were largely unfruitful, multilateral negotiations in this area resumed in the late 1990s in the wake of the WTO's establishment. In August 1999, a sessional working group was established within the U.N. Sub-Commission on the Promotion and Protection of Human Rights[11] to draft the Norms on the Responsibilities of Transnational Corporations and Other Business Enterprises with Regard to Human Rights (Norms on the Responsibilities of Transnational Corporations).[12] As the U.N. High Commissioner for Human Rights recounted:

[7] Karl P. Sauvant, *The Negotiations of the United Nations Code of Conduct on Transnational Corporations: Experience and Lessons Learned*, 16 J. World Inv. & Trade 11, 13–20 (2015).

[8] *Id.* at 16–17.

[9] International Labour Organization, *Tripartite Declaration of Principles Concerning Multinational Enterprises and Social Policy, reprinted in* International Labour Organization, Tripartite Declaration of Principles Concerning Multinational Enterprises and Social Policy, at 1–10 (2006).

[10] International Labour Organization, *supra* note 9, at v.

[11] David Weissbrodt & Muria Kruger, *Norms on the Responsibilities of Transnational Corporations and Other Business Enterprises with Regard to Human Rights*, 97 Am. J. Int'l L. 901, 903–04 (2003).

[12] Sub-Comm'n on the Promotion & Prot. of Human Rights, *Norms on the Responsibilities of Transnational Corporations and Other Business Enterprises with Regard to Human Rights*, U.N. Doc. E/CN.4/Sub.2/2003/12/Rev.2 (Aug. 26, 2003).

> [These draft norms] attempt to impose direct responsibilities on business entities as a means of achieving comprehensive protection of all human rights – civil, cultural, economic, political and social – relevant to the activities of business. [They] identify specific human rights relevant to the activities of business, such as the right to equal opportunity and non-discrimination, the right to security of persons, the rights of workers, and refer[] to the rights of particular groups such as indigenous peoples. The draft Norms also set out responsibilities of business enterprises in relation to environmental protection and consumer protection. As an initiative of a United Nations expert body, the draft seeks wide territorial coverage.[13]

Although these draft norms were adopted by the U.N. Sub-Commission on the Promotion and Protection of Human Rights in August 2003, they were never adopted by what was then the U.N. Commission on Human Rights (now the Human Rights Council).[14]

Particularly problematic for many TNCs and developed country governments was the drafters' effort to broaden corporate human rights responsibilities. As Paragraph 1 of the draft norms declared:

> Within their respective spheres of activity and influence, transnational corporations and other business enterprises have the obligation to promote, secure the fulfilment of, respect, ensure respect of and protect human rights recognized in international as well as national law, including the rights and interests of indigenous peoples and other vulnerable groups.

Because these norms "would have imposed on companies, within their 'sphere of influence,' the same human rights duties that states have accepted for themselves under treaties they have ratified,"[15] the norms faced strong opposition from TNCs and their supportive developed country governments.

While the drafting of these norms was underway, the United Nations Global Compact (Global Compact) was launched in July 2000 as a PPP between the United Nations and TNCs.[16] This initiative, in its current version, encourages TNCs to

> 1. Do business responsibly by aligning their strategies and operations with Ten Principles on human rights, labour, environment and anti-corruption; and
> 2. Take strategic actions to advance broader societal goals, such as the UN Sustainable Development Goals, with an emphasis on collaboration and innovation.[17]

[13] U.N. High Commissioner for Human Rights, *Rep. of the United Nations High Commissioner on Human Rights on the Responsibilities of Transnational Corporations and Related Business Enterprises with Regard to Human Rights*, ¶ 18, U.N. Doc. E/CN.4/2005/91 (Feb. 15, 2005).

[14] Carlos López, *The "Ruggie Process": From Legal Obligations to Corporate Social Responsibility?*, *in* HUMAN RIGHTS OBLIGATIONS OF BUSINESS: BEYOND THE CORPORATE RESPONSIBILITY TO RESPECT? 58, 62 (Surya Deva & David Bilchitz eds., 2013) [hereinafter HUMAN RIGHTS OBLIGATIONS].

[15] John Gerard Ruggie, JUST BUSINESS: MULTINATIONAL CORPORATIONS AND HUMAN RIGHTS, at xvii (2013).

[16] Surya Deva, *Global Compact: A Critique of the U.N.'s "Public-Private" Partnership for Promoting Corporate Citizenship*, 34 SYRACUSE J. INT'L L. & COM. 107 (2006).

[17] *Our Mission*, UNITED NATIONS GLOBAL COMPACT, www.unglobalcompact.org/what-is-gc/mission (last visited June 12, 2016).

Principle 1 of the Global Compact declares: "Businesses should support and respect the protection of internationally proclaimed human rights . . . "[18] Principle 2 calls on these businesses to "make sure that they are not complicit in human rights abuses." As of December 2014, "over 8,000 companies and 4,000 non-business participants based in over 160 countries" have joined the Global Compact.[19]

In July 2005, U.N. Secretary-General Kofi Annan appointed John Ruggie as his Special Representative on the Issue of Human Rights and Transnational Corporations and Other Business Enterprises. Ruggie oversaw the establishment of the U.N. Global Compact when he served as the Assistant U.N. Secretary-General for Strategic Planning. As Secretary-General Annan's Special Representative, he was charged with developing recommendations for the "identif[ication] and clarif[ication of] standards of corporate responsibility and accountability for transnational corporations and other business enterprises with regard to human rights."[20]

Three years later, Ruggie delivered to the Human Rights Council a report outlining the "protect, respect, and remedy" framework for business and human rights.[21] As he explained, the framework rests on three distinct pillars:

> The first is the State duty to protect against human rights abuses by third parties, including business enterprises, through appropriate policies, regulation, and adjudication. The second is the corporate responsibility to respect human rights, which means that business enterprises should act with due diligence to avoid infringing on the rights of others and to address adverse impacts with which they are involved. The third is the need for greater access by victims to effective remedy, both judicial and non-judicial.[22]

The Council welcomed this framework with enthusiasm and extended Ruggie's mandate for another three years.[23]

In March 2011, before the end of his maximum six-year mandate, Ruggie presented to the Human Rights Council the Guiding Principles, which sought to "operationalize" his earlier framework. Endorsed by the Council by consensus,[24] these principles cover both public and private actors and make clear that States and TNCs have shared responsibilities in advancing human rights protection. Although the Guiding Principles stop short of imposing on private actors the obligation to *protect* human rights, Principle 11 states in no uncertain terms that "[b]usiness enterprises should respect human rights." Principle 13 further identifies two sets of corporate human rights responsibilities:

[18] *The Ten Principles of the UN Global Compact*, UNITED NATIONS GLOBAL COMPACT, www.unglobalcompact.org/what-is-gc/mission/principles (last visited June 12, 2016).

[19] UNITED NATIONS GLOBAL COMPACT, GUIDE TO CORPORATE SUSTAINABILITY: SHAPING A SUSTAINABLE FUTURE 7 (2014).

[20] *Human Rights and Transnational Corporations and Other Business Enterprises*, Human Rights Res. 2005/69, ¶ 1(a) (Apr. 20, 2005).

[21] John Ruggie (Special Representative of the Secretary-General on the Issue of Human Rights and Transnational Corporations and Other Business Enterprises), *Protect, Respect and Remedy: A Framework for Business and Human Rights, in Rep. of the Special Representative of the Secretary-General on the Issue of Human Rights and Transnational Corporations and Other Business Enterprises*, Human Rights Council, U.N. Doc. A/HRC/8/5 (Apr. 7, 2008) [hereinafter Ruggie Framework].

[22] Ruggie's 2011 Report, *supra* note 6, ¶ 6.

[23] Human Rights Council Res. 8/7, ¶¶ 1, 4 (June 18, 2008).

[24] López, *supra* note 14, at 70–71.

(a) Avoid causing or contributing to adverse human rights impacts through their own activities, and address such impacts when they occur;
(b) Seek to prevent or mitigate adverse human rights impacts that are directly linked to their operations, products or services by their business relationships, even if they have not contributed to those impacts.

The first half of the Guiding Principles addresses foundational issues. The rest contains operational details and substantive recommendations. Specifically, Principle 15 calls on TNCs to make a policy commitment to meet their human rights responsibilities, introduce a "human rights due-diligence process to identify, prevent, mitigate and account for how they address their impacts on human rights," and institute "[p]rocesses to enable the remediation of any adverse human rights impacts they cause or to which they contribute." Principles 16–24 then delineate the specific human rights principles governing the operation of these corporations, in areas such as policy commitment, human rights due diligence, remediation, and issues of context.

Apart from these Guiding Principles, human rights guidelines can be found in more specialized areas. A case in point is the *Human Rights Guidelines for Pharmaceutical Companies in Relation to Access to Medicines* (*Guidelines for Pharmaceutical Companies*).[25] Paul Hunt, the former Special Rapporteur on the Right of Everyone to the Enjoyment of the Highest Attainable Standard of Physical and Mental Health, proposed these guidelines in his August 2008 report. As the document made clear in its preamble, "Pharmaceutical companies, including innovator, generic and biotechnology companies, have human rights responsibilities in relation to access to medicines." Such responsibilities are consistent with those outlined by the Committee on Economic, Social and Cultural Rights (CESCR), which stated in its interpretative comment on the right to health that "all members of society – . . . including . . . the private business sector – have responsibilities regarding the realization of the right to health."[26]

Similar to the Guiding Principles, Guideline 1 of the *Guidelines for Pharmaceutical Companies* calls on pharmaceutical companies to "adopt a human rights policy statement which expressly recognizes the importance of human rights generally, and the right to the highest attainable standard of health in particular, in relation to the strategies, policies, programmes, projects and activities of the company." Guideline 2 stipulates that these companies "should integrate human rights . . . into [their] strategies, policies, programmes, projects and activities." Guideline 4 requires pharmaceutical companies to "refrain from any conduct that will or may encourage a State to act in a way that is inconsistent with its obligations arising from national and international human rights law."

Unlike the Guiding Principles, however, the *Guidelines for Pharmaceutical Companies* go beyond what these principles require. The additional requirements may explain

[25] Paul Hunt (Special Rapporteur on the Right of Everyone to the Enjoyment of the Highest Attainable Standard of Physical and Mental Health), *Human Rights Guidelines for Pharmaceutical Companies in Relation to Access to Medicines, in Rep. of the Special Rapporteur on the Right of Everyone to the Enjoyment of the Highest Attainable Standard of Physical and Mental Health*, Human Rights Council, U.N. Doc. A/63/263, at 15–25 (Aug. 11, 2008) [hereinafter *Guidelines for Pharmaceutical Companies*].

[26] Comm. on Econ., Soc. & Cultural Rights, *General Comment No. 14: The Right to the Highest Attainable Standard of Health (Article 12 of the International Covenant on Economic, Social and Cultural Rights)*, ¶ 42, U.N. Doc. E/C.12/2000/4 (Aug. 11, 2000).

why the powerful global pharmaceutical industry has thus far declined to embrace these industry-specific guidelines. Specifically, Guideline 26 calls on pharmaceutical companies to "make and respect a public commitment not to lobby for more demanding protection of intellectual property interests than those required by TRIPS, such as additional limitations on compulsory licensing." Guidelines 27–29 declare that these companies should respect the Doha Declaration on the TRIPS Agreement and Public Health and the extensions on transition periods provided by the TRIPS Agreement. Guideline 30 states that pharmaceutical companies "should issue non-exclusive voluntary licences with a view to increasing access, in low-income and middle-income countries, to all medicines." Guidelines 31 and 32 focus on problems caused by the development of data exclusivity regimes and the "evergreening" of patents.

When all of these initiatives are taken together, the past few decades have seen policymakers, commentators, advocacy groups, and intergovernmental and nongovernmental organizations working together to push TNCs to shoulder greater human rights responsibilities. Considerable efforts have also been devoted to identifying, cataloguing, and clarifying these responsibilities. Although TNCs still do not have the same obligations as States or other public actors, they do have responsibilities to respect human rights, including the introduction of preventive and remedial measures. Thus, it is somewhat misleading for these powerful corporations to insist that they have no human rights obligations.

II Corporations Have Human Rights Too

Another claim that TNCs have advanced increasingly frequently in the area of business and human rights is that, to the extent that human rights should be discussed in the intellectual property context, these corporations should also have human rights. After all, article 15(1)(c) of the International Covenant on Economic, Social and Cultural Rights (ICESCR) requires state parties to "recognize the right of everyone ... to benefit from the protection of the moral and material interests resulting from any scientific, literary or artistic production of which he [or she] is the author."[27] Similar language can also be found in article 27(2) of the Universal Declaration of Human Rights (UDHR).[28]

In Europe, the position that corporations should have human rights has been greatly strengthened by the European Court of Human Rights' interpretation of Article 1 of the Protocol No. 1 to the European Convention of Human Rights.[29] In *Anheuser-Busch, Inc. v. Portugal*, for instance, the Court's Grand Chamber extended the protection of "the peaceful enjoyment of ... possessions" to cover both registered trademarks and

[27] International Covenant on Economic, Social and Cultural Rights art. 15(1)(c), Dec. 16, 1966, 993 U.N.T.S. 3.

[28] Article 27(2) provides: "Everyone has the right to the protection of the moral and material interests resulting from any scientific, literary or artistic production of which he [or she] is the author." Universal Declaration of Human Rights art. 27(2), G.A. Res. 217A, U.N. GAOR, 3d Sess., 1st plen. mtg., U.N. Doc A/810 (Dec. 10, 1948).

[29] Article 1 provides: "Every natural or legal person is entitled to the peaceful enjoyment of his possessions. No one shall be deprived of his possessions except in the public interest and subject to the conditions provided for by law and by the general principles of international law." Protocol to the Convention for the Protection of Human Rights and Fundamental Freedoms art. 1, *opened for signature* Mar. 20, 1952, 213 U.N.T.S. 262.

trademark applications of a multinational corporation.[30] The language "[i]ntellectual property shall be protected" can also be found in the right to property provision in Article 17(2) of the Charter of Fundamental Rights of the European Union, which entered into force in December 2009.[31]

In previous articles, I have already explained in great depth why intellectual property rights held by corporations should not be equated with human rights held by authors, inventors, and other individuals.[32] Although this section does not intend to repeat these explanations, it will summarize three key rebuttals to the claim that TNCs should also have human rights.

The first rebuttal concerns the norms articulated in the European Convention of Human Rights and the Charter of Fundamental Rights of the European Union. Because these norms are regional by nature, they do not reflect an international consensus. Nor do they possess a universal appeal. Indeed, it remains unclear thus far how much the existing international and regional human rights instruments have recognized the right to the own *private* property. Due to cold-war politics and concerns raised by Socialist countries, neither the International Covenant on Civil and Political Rights (ICCPR) nor the ICESCR includes a provision on the right to own private property.[33]

The UDHR does contain a provision on the right to own property, but wide disagreement existed, and continues to exist, over whether that provision should focus on *private* property. At the time of drafting, concerns were raised by not only the Soviet Union and other Eastern bloc countries, but also Latin American countries and the United Kingdom's Labour Party government.[34] In the end, article 17(1) of the UDHR "omitt[ed] the word private" and was reduced to "a high level of generality."[35] This provision, which "openly acknowledge[s] both the capitalist and communist way of organizing a national economy,"[36] now reads: "Everyone has the right to own property alone as well as in association with others." How the phrase "in association with others" is to be interpreted, however, remains open to debate.

The second rebuttal concerns the wide disagreement within the international human rights community concerning whether it was appropriate for the European Court of

[30] *Anheuser-Busch, Inc. v. Portugal*, 45 Eur. Ct. H.R. 36 (2007) (Grand Chamber).

[31] Charter of Fundamental Rights of the European Union art. 17(2), Dec. 7, 2000, 2000 O.J. (C 364) 1.

[32] For the author's earlier articles on intellectual property and human rights, see Peter K. Yu, *The Anatomy of the Human Rights Framework for Intellectual Property*, 69 SMU L. REV. 37 (2016); Peter K. Yu, *Digital Copyright Enforcement Measures and Their Human Rights Threats*, *in* RESEARCH HANDBOOK ON HUMAN RIGHTS AND INTELLECTUAL PROPERTY 455 (Christophe Geiger ed., 2015); Peter K. Yu, *Intellectual Property and Human Rights in the Nonmultilateral Era*, 64 FLA. L. REV. 1045 (2012) [hereinafter Yu, *Nonmultilateral Era*]; Peter K. Yu, *Reconceptualizing Intellectual Property Interests in a Human Rights Framework*, 40 U.C. DAVIS L. REV. 1039 (2007) [hereinafter Yu, *Reconceptualizing Intellectual Property Interests*]; Peter K. Yu, *Ten Common Questions About Intellectual Property and Human Rights*, 23 GA. ST. U. L. REV. 709 (2007) [hereinafter Yu, *Ten Common Questions*].

[33] Yu, *Reconceptualizing Intellectual Property Interests*, *supra* note 32, at 1085 n.179.

[34] Mary Ann Glendon, A WORLD MADE NEW: ELEANOR ROOSEVELT AND THE UNIVERSAL DECLARATION OF HUMAN RIGHTS 182 (2001); Johannes Morsink, THE UNIVERSAL DECLARATION OF HUMAN RIGHTS: ORIGINS, DRAFTING, AND INTENT 139–52 (1999); Audrey R. Chapman, *Core Obligations Related to ICESCR Article 15(1)(c)*, *in* CORE OBLIGATIONS: BUILDING A FRAMEWORK FOR ECONOMIC, SOCIAL AND CULTURAL RIGHTS 305, 314 (Audrey Chapman & Sage Russell eds., 2002).

[35] Glendon, *supra* note 34, at 183.

[36] Morsink, *supra* note 34, at 147.

Human Rights to extend human rights protection beyond individuals to cover corporations, such as Anheuser-Busch, Inc.[37] Such an extension is inconsistent with the CESCR's authoritative interpretation of article 15(1)(c) of the ICESCR. As *General Comment No. 17* declared:

> [O]nly the "author", namely the creator, whether man or woman, individual or group of individuals, of scientific, literary or artistic productions, such as, inter alia, writers and artists, can be the beneficiary of the protection of article 15, paragraph 1(c) ... Under the existing international treaty protection regimes, legal entities are included among the holders of intellectual property rights. However, ... their entitlements, because of their different nature, are not protected at the level of human rights.[38]

In her report entitled *Copyright Policy and the Right to Science and Culture*, Farida Shaheed, the former Special Rapporteur in the Field of Cultural Rights, also noted:

> Corporate rights holders play an essential role in the cultural economy. They innovate ways of delivering cultural works to consumers, provide income to artists, offer much-needed capital to finance high-budget cultural productions and can free artists from many of the burdens of commercializing their work. Nonetheless, their economic interests do not enjoy the status of human rights.[39]

Because "[t]he right to protection of authorship is the right of the human author(s) whose creative vision gave expression to the work," corporate rights holders, in her view, "must not be presumed to speak for the interests of authors."[40] The lack of such a presumption is important because "the material interests of [these] rights holders do not always coincide with those of authors."[41]

The third rebuttal concerns the claim that TNCs have aggregated the disparate human rights interests of their individual shareholders. Although one could make a strong argument that these corporations should be allowed to file lawsuits on behalf of these shareholders, giving them legal standing to bring human rights claims on behalf of these individuals is not the same as allowing them to claim violations of their own "human" rights.[42] As Jack Donnelly rightly reminded us: "Collectivities of all sorts have many and varied rights. But these are not – cannot be – human rights, unless we substantially recast the concept."[43]

In sum, even though the European Convention of Human Rights has thus far granted TNCs human rights-like protection, these powerful corporations do not have human rights as recognized by the UDHR, the ICCPR, and the ICESCR – or, for that matter, many other international and regional human rights instruments. In the

[37] Yu, *Nonmultilateral Era*, *supra* note 32, at 1066–70.

[38] Comm. on Econ., Soc. & Cultural Rights, *General Comment No. 17: The Right of Everyone to Benefit from the Protection of the Moral and Material Interests Resulting from Any Scientific, Literary or Artistic Production of Which He Is the Author (Article 15, Paragraph 1(c), of the Covenant)*, ¶ 7, U.N. Doc. E/C.12/GC/17 (Jan. 12, 2006) [hereinafter *General Comment No. 17*].

[39] Farida Shaheed (Special Rapporteur in the Field of Cultural Rights), *Copyright Policy and the Right to Science and Culture: Rep. of the Special Rapporteur in the Field of Cultural Rights*, ¶ 41, Human Rights Council, U.N. Doc. A/HRC/28/57 (Dec. 24, 2014).

[40] *Id.* ¶ 99.

[41] *Id.* ¶ 42.

[42] Yu, *Ten Common Questions*, *supra* note 32, at 730.

[43] Jack Donnelly, Universal Human Rights in Theory and Practice 25 (2d ed. 2003).

intellectual property context, the CESCR has been very clear that the rights found in trade and intellectual property agreements should not be equated with the human right recognized in article 15(1)(c) of the ICESCR.[44] As the Committee explained:

> Human rights are fundamental as they are inherent to the human person as such, whereas intellectual property rights are first and foremost means by which States seek to provide incentives for inventiveness and creativity, encourage the dissemination of creative and innovative productions, as well as the development of cultural identities, and preserve the integrity of scientific, literary and artistic productions for the benefit of society as a whole.[45]

Thus, TNCs have gone too far to claim that they have human rights, too. Such a position is simply not supported by international and regional human rights instruments.

III The Ruggie Framework and the Guiding Principles

After debunking the two key claims TNCs have advanced to deny or reduce their human rights responsibilities, this chapter moves on to explore the human rights responsibilities of TNCs and other private actors, including potential PPP participants. Because the Ruggie Framework and the Guiding Principles remain the most authoritative U.N. documents on business and human rights and represent "the first corporate human rights responsibility initiative ever to be approved by the [United Nations],"[46] this section discusses the rationales behind the development of this framework and the ensuing principles. It further examines their strengths and weaknesses.

To better understand these documents, it is important to put them in their formative contexts. Despite the adoption by the U.N. Sub-Commission on the Promotion and Protection of Human Rights of the draft Norms on the Responsibilities of Transnational Corporations in August 2003, TNCs and their supportive developed country governments remained adamantly opposed to accepting new human rights obligations outlined in the draft norms. Their reactions were unsurprising, considering that all the major initiatives on business and human rights that existed at the time involved voluntary action. These initiatives included the ILO Tripartite Declaration, the Global Compact, and the *OECD Guidelines for Multinational Enterprises*.[47] In the view of TNCs, asking them to shoulder responsibilities that had traditionally belonged to States was an unacceptable, radical restatement of international human rights principles and obligations.

To move the debate on corporate human rights responsibilities forward, Ruggie therefore did not return to the draft norms. Instead, he advanced a new "protect, respect, and remedy" framework, which sought to "defin[e] the specific responsibilities of companies with regard to all rights," as opposed to providing "a limited list of rights linked to imprecise and expansive responsibilities."[48]

44 *General Comment No. 17*, *supra* note 38, ¶ 3.
45 *Id.* ¶ 1.
46 Surya Deva, *Treating Human Rights Lightly: A Critique of the Consensus Rhetoric and the Language Employed by the Guiding Principles*, *in* HUMAN RIGHTS OBLIGATIONS, *supra* note 14, at 78, 103 [hereinafter Deva, *Treating Human Rights Lightly*].
47 ORG. FOR ECON. CO-OPERATION & DEV., OECD GUIDELINES FOR MULTINATIONAL ENTERPRISES 7–25 (2008).
48 Ruggie Framework, *supra* note 21, ¶ 51.

To underscore the differentiated but complementary human rights responsibilities within his framework, Ruggie relied on three core principles: "the State duty to protect against human rights abuses by third parties, including business; the corporate responsibility to respect human rights; and the need for more effective access to remedies."[49] As he explained:

> Each principle is an essential component of the framework: the State duty to protect because it lies at the very core of the international human rights regime; the corporate responsibility to respect because it is the basic expectation society has of business; and access to remedy, because even the most concerted efforts cannot prevent all abuse, while access to judicial redress is often problematic, and non-judicial means are limited in number, scope and effectiveness. The three principles form a complementary whole in that each supports the others in achieving sustainable progress.[50]

Although the Ruggie Framework has remained somewhat controversial within the human rights circle, the framework and the ensuing principles are important to fostering a dialogue between TNCs on the one hand and policymakers, commentators, advocacy groups, and intergovernmental and nongovernmental organizations on the other. By "assigning responsibilities to relevant actors," this framework facilitates the determination of whether a specific group of actors has appropriately discharged its human rights obligations.[51]

Even better, the Ruggie Framework and the Guiding Principles isolate the corporate responsibility to respect human rights from the "States' abilities and/or willingness to fulfil their own human rights obligations."[52] In doing so, these documents avoid the "the slippery distinction between 'primary' State and 'secondary' corporate obligations – which in any event would invite endless strategic gaming on the ground about who is responsible for what."[53]

Moreover, the Guiding Principles are attractive from a business standpoint. The requirements on human rights due diligence, including those on disclosure, monitoring and audits, are not only written in a language familiar to business leaders,[54] but are likely requirements that are already found in the laws and regulations in many jurisdictions.[55] Some investors have also demanded information concerning the TNCs' social and environmental performance.[56]

49 *Id.* ¶ 9.

50 *Id.*

51 *Id.* ¶ 10.

52 Guiding Principles, *supra* note 6, Principle 11, commentary.

53 Ruggie Framework, *supra* note 21, ¶ 55.

54 Deva, *Treating Human Rights Lightly*, *supra* note 46, at 92; Radu Mares, *"Respect" Human Rights: Concept and Convergence*, *in* LAW, BUSINESS AND HUMAN RIGHTS: BRIDGING THE GAP 3, 16 (Robert C. Bird, Daniel R. Cahoy, & Jamie Darin Prenkert eds., 2014) [hereinafter LAW, BUSINESS AND HUMAN RIGHTS].

55 Ruggie Framework, *supra* note 21, ¶ 56; Stephen Kim Park, *Human Rights Reporting as Self-Interest: The Integrative and Expressive Dimensions of Corporate Disclosure*, *in* LAW, BUSINESS AND HUMAN RIGHTS, *supra* note 54, at 48.

56 *Statement by Socially Responsible Investors to the Eighth Session of the Human Rights Council on the Third Report of the Special Representative of the UN Secretary-General on Business and Human Rights*, BUS. & HUM. RTS. RESOURCE CENTRE (June 3, 2008), https://business-humanrights.org/sites/default/files/reports-and-materials/SRI-letter-re-Ruggie-report-3-Jun-2008.pdf.

In addition, the operational principles are written with typical management functions in mind, covering such functions as "human resources, security of assets and personnel, supply chains, and community engagement."[57] Because the Guiding Principles do not require TNCs to take on new human rights obligations,[58] they greatly alleviate the concerns these powerful corporations and their supportive developed country governments expressed during the drafting of the Norms on the Responsibilities of Transnational Corporations.

Notwithstanding these various strengths, human rights advocacy groups have remained dissatisfied with the Ruggie Framework and the Guiding Principles.[59] As Ruggie recounted in his book, *Just Business*:

> Some of the international human rights NGOs were less enthusiastic. In a joint statement at the time of any final presentation to the Council, several leading advocacy groups acknowledged that the [Guiding Principles] "do address a range of topics in a useful manner; however some important issues that merit attention are not adequately reflected or addressed," chief among them being an international legal instrument covering business and human rights. A number of NGOs also felt leery about operational-level grievance mechanisms, arguing that these would reflect the power imbalance between companies and rights-holders and fearing that they might become substitutes for judicial processes – though both of these issues are specifically addressed in the [Guiding Principles'] provisions for how such processes should be structured. A group of anticorporate-antiglobalization NGOs actually urged the Council to reject the [principles] on grounds of their "insufficiencies."[60]

IV Applying the Guiding Principles to PPPs

Despite the continued dissatisfaction of human rights advocacy groups over the Ruggie Framework and ensuing principles, the problems they identify will pose less of a challenge to PPPs than to TNCs, as these partnerships involve public actors as much as they involve private actors. As such, they should be held to a much higher human rights standard than private actors alone, lest States have perverse incentives to avoid human rights obligations by outsourcing their operations to PPPs.

The main distinction in the Ruggie Framework is that "states must protect [while] companies must respect."[61] Nevertheless, the Guiding Principles seem to have defined the obligation to respect broader than what States usually assume when that obligation is analyzed separately under the traditional "respect, protect, and fulfill" framework.[62] As Radu Mares observed:

> [In international human rights law], *respect* refers to the harmful conduct of the state while *protect* refers to the harmful conduct of third parties. Protect is based on the failure of a state to adopt legislative and other measures to prevent and hold third parties

[57] Ruggie Framework, *supra* note 21, ¶ 52.

[58] As the preamble of the Guiding Principles declares: "Nothing in these Guiding Principles should be read as creating new international law obligations . . ."

[59] E.g., Human Rights Obligations, *supra* note 14.

[60] Ruggie, *supra* note 15, at 120–21.

[61] *Id.* at xxi.

[62] *General Comment No. 17*, *supra* note 38, ¶ 28.

> accountable when they harm others. Thus, the way in which the [Guiding Principles] use *respect* in [Principle 13(b)] covers responsibility for third parties' conduct, which is precisely what [international human rights law] covers with its use of *protect*.[63]

Thus, even though the Guiding Principles do not create in private actors a duty to protect against human rights abuses, their responsibility to respect those rights does cover their own harmful conduct as well as those of third parties.

Under the Ruggie Framework, private actors have the lightest human rights responsibilities. Because these responsibilities form the baseline expectations for these actors, PPPs will assume at least the same level of responsibilities. Specifically, PPPs "should avoid infringing on the human rights of others and should address adverse human rights impacts with which they are involved" (Principle 11). They should also provide remedies to any human rights injuries that they have caused or contributed to through their operations, products, or services.

These responsibilities are consistent with those provided by the *Guidelines for Pharmaceutical Companies*, which provide as follows:

> 42. When participating in a public-private partnership, a [pharmaceutical] company should continue to conform to these Guidelines.
> 43. If a company joins a public-private partnership, it should disclose any interest it has in the partnership's decisions and activities.
> 44. So far as these Guidelines bear upon the strategies, policies, programmes, projects and activities of public-private partnerships, they shall apply equally to such partnerships.
> 45. A company that joins a public-private partnership should take all reasonable steps to ensure that the partnership fully conforms to these Guidelines.[64]

Although Guidelines 42–45 remain some of the rare provisions covering PPPs, they do not fully delineate the partnerships' human rights responsibilities. After all, the focus of these guidelines is on the responsibilities of pharmaceutical companies in their role as the PPPs' public sector partners. This distinction is important because these partnerships involve both public and private actors. Any guidelines that focus only on the partnerships' private sector partners – or worse, a single type of private sector partner, such as pharmaceutical companies – are necessarily incomplete.

To fully delineate the human rights responsibilities of PPPs, we need to take account of both the public and private aspects of these partnerships. Because we have already covered the human right responsibilities of TNCs and other private actors, we now turn to the public aspects of PPPs. Analyzing these aspects is complicated because a PPP not only involves public and private actors, but also exists as an independent entity. As a result, the partnership has to be analyzed in terms of its constituent partners – both public and private – as well as its existence as an independent entity.

As far as public sector partners are concerned, States do not avoid human rights obligations by establishing PPPs. For instance, when they establish PPPs to provide access to essential medicines, they continue to hold obligations emanating from the right to

[63] Mares, *supra* note 54, at 12.
[64] *Guidelines for Pharmaceutical Companies*, *supra* note 25, Guidelines 42–45.

health and the right to life. In addition to these obligations, States may assume additional obligations imputed to them by virtue of their participation in PPPs, such as when they "fail[] to exercise due diligence with respect to the [harmful] acts of these partnerships."[65] As public sector partners, they may be held responsible for the partnerships' distribution of harmful drugs or vaccines if they "have known, or should have known, that there was a real and immediate risk of breaches of human rights, and failed to take appropriate measures which might be expected to avoid this risk."[66]

Thus far, international organizations, regional bodies, and national courts have imputed responsibility to States based on factors such as functionality, organizational or governance structure, management or financial control, dependency on the State, and public interest needs.[67] Although the scope and length of this chapter do not allow me to discuss in greater detail the different ways of imputing human rights responsibility to the relevant State,[68] or a multitude of States,[69] the key takeaway of this truncated discussion is that States cannot avoid human rights obligations by outsourcing their operations to PPPs.

As independent entities, PPPs will have a distinct set of human rights responsibilities that are somewhat different from those assumed by their constituent partners – whether public or private. These responsibilities will also exist irrespective of the latter's obligations. For example, a PPP will still have its own human rights responsibilities even though a court has already imputed similar responsibilities to the State by virtue of its participation in this PPP.

Given the wide variations in missions, designs, and structures, PPPs will assume different levels of human rights responsibilities. Nevertheless, because of their hybrid nature and dual characteristics, virtually all partnerships will shoulder greater responsibilities than private actors. How similar these responsibilities are to those of public actors, however, will depend on how closely they resemble public actors and what nexus they have with those actors.

There are at least four reasons why PPPs should assume greater responsibilities than private actors. First, PPPs bear a strong resemblance to public actors; they often have public-oriented missions, focusing on the provision of public goods and services. They also do not focus on profit maximization the same way private actors do. For instance, the mission of Global Alliance for TB Drug Development (TB Alliance) is "dedicated to the discovery and development of better, faster-acting, and affordable tuberculosis drugs that are available to those who need them."[70] Likewise, the mission of the International AIDS Vaccine Initiative (IAVI) is "to ensure the development of safe, effective, accessible, preventive HIV vaccines for use throughout the world."[71] Given these public-oriented missions, it is understandable why PPPs will have to take on additional human rights responsibilities. As John Ruggie reminded us in his 2008 report:

[65] Lisa Clarke, Public-Private Partnerships and Responsibility Under International Law: A Global Health Perspective 103 (2014).
[66] *Id.* at 119.
[67] Christopher Bovis, Public-Private Partnerships in the European Union 36–41 (2014).
[68] Clarke, *supra* note 65, at 102–69.
[69] *Id.* at 141.
[70] *Our Mission*, TB Alliance, www.tballiance.org/about/mission (last visited June 13, 2016).
[71] *About Us*, Int'l AIDS Vaccine Initiative, www.iavi.org/who-we-are/leaders/about-us (last visited June 13, 2016).

> There are situations in which companies may have additional responsibilities – for example, where they perform certain public functions, or because they have undertaken additional commitments voluntarily. But the responsibility to respect is the baseline expectation for all companies in all situations.[72]

Second, many PPPs have more resources and capabilities than private actors, including even many TNCs. In economic terms, they are therefore closer to public actors than private actors. In the areas of public health and food security, for instance, some commentators estimated that "billions of dollars [now flow] through PPPs aiming to improve the health of the global poor or to alleviate hunger through the development of new farming techniques."[73] As these partnerships become bigger and more powerful, it is only logical that they be treated more like public actors. Although Principle 14 states that the Guiding Principles apply "regardless of . . . size, sector, operational context, ownership and structure," that principle acknowledges that "the scale and complexity of the means through which enterprises meet that responsibility may vary according to these factors and with the severity of the enterprise's adverse human rights impacts."

Third, many PPPs involve a significant linkage between their public and private sector partners. Focusing on the "state-business nexus," Principle 4 declares:

> States should take additional steps to protect against human rights abuses by business enterprises that are owned or controlled by the State, or that receive substantial support and services from State agencies . . . , including, where appropriate, by requiring human rights due diligence.

The explanatory commentary on this principle further provides: "[T]he closer a business enterprise is to the State, or the more it relies on statutory authority or taxpayer support, the stronger the State's policy rationale becomes for ensuring that the enterprise respects human rights." Because PPPs heavily involve public actors, they are by definition close to the State – and in some cases, many different States. The State's policy rationale in the Guiding Principles therefore should logically apply, and such application should vary according to the partnership's nexus with the State.

Finally, PPPs should not be able to avoid human rights responsibilities when they have been complicit in human rights abuses[74] – for example, whether they have been "involve[d] . . . in human rights abuses committed by another party, including government agents."[75] Corporate complicity in human rights abuses remains a highly challenging issue. It is also a key driver behind many existing initiatives on business and human rights. Among the abuses that have sparked these initiatives were ITT Corp.'s alleged involvement in the plot to overthrow a democratically elected socialist government in Chile, Dow Chemical's potential contribution to Union Carbide's pesticide plant disaster in Bhopal, India, and Royal Dutch Shell's controversial oil production operations in

[72] Ruggie Framework, *supra* note 21, ¶ 24.

[73] Emmanuel B. Omobowale et al., *Addressing Conflicts of Interest in Public Private Partnerships*, 10 BMC Int'l Health & Human Rights 19 (2010), http://bmcinthealthhumrights.biomedcentral.com/articles/10.1186/1472-698X-10-19.

[74] John Ruggie (Special Representative of the Secretary-General on the Issue of Human Rights and Transnational Corporations and Other Business Enterprises), *Clarifying the Concepts of "Sphere of Influence" and "Complicity,"* Human Rights Council, U.N. Doc. A/HRC/8/16 (May 15, 2008).

[75] Ruggie, *supra* note 15, at 11–12.

Ogoniland, Nigeria.[76] While complicity in human rights abuses is unlikely to arise to the same extent in the intellectual property context, a fair question can be raised about whether a PPP is complicit in these abuses when it willfully ignores its technology transfer-related obligations, especially those stipulated in contracts with developing country governments or businesses.[77]

V The Human Rights Obligations of PPPs

The previous section has explained why PPPs should be held to a higher human rights standard than private actors, but probably a lower standard than States or other public actors. Because the Guiding Principles do not provide clear guidelines on the human rights responsibilities of these partnerships, this section offers some suggestions on what the responsibilities may entail and how PPPs can appropriately discharge them.

Like TNCs, PPPs will have to make a policy commitment to meet their human rights responsibilities, introduce a "human rights due-diligence process to identify, prevent, mitigate and account for how they address their impacts on human rights," and institute "[p]rocesses to enable the remediation of any adverse human rights impacts they cause or to which they contribute" (Principle 15). As part of human rights due diligence, they "should identify and assess any actual or potential adverse human rights impacts with which they may be involved either through their own activities or as a result of their business relationships" (Principle 18). They should also be "prepared to communicate ... externally [how they are to address their human rights impacts], particularly when concerns are raised by or on behalf of affected stakeholders" (Principle 21).

Notwithstanding these principles, not all PPPs will raise human rights concerns. The PPPs discussed in this chapter, for instance, will have very positive human rights impacts. They are what I have described as P3s4HR – partnerships that have been established to promote human rights protection. Although the Guiding Principles will still apply to them, such application will not be problematic. After all, the missions of these partnerships already reflect strong policy commitments to meet their human rights responsibilities. They also do not have any adverse human rights impacts that require identification, prevention, mitigation, or remediation.

While the comparison with TNCs provides the baseline expectations for PPPs, these partnerships are hybrid entities with dual characteristics as both public and private actors. Their human rights responsibilities therefore include those assumed by not only the former, but also the latter. Although PPPs do not have the same regulatory power or the same ability to develop adjudicatory, grievance, or remedial mechanisms as States, they can induce their public and private sector partners to better respect or protect human rights. For example, similar to States, they can "[p]rovide effective guidance to [their constituent partners] on how to respect human rights throughout their operations" (Principle 3(c)). They can also encourage these partners "to communicate how they address their human rights impacts" (Principle 3(d)). Such communication "can range from informal engagement with affected stakeholders to formal public reporting" (Principle 3, Explanatory Commentary).

[76] *Id.* at 6–14; Tagi Sagafi-Nejad & John H. Dunning, The UN and Transnational Corporations: From Code of Conduct to Global Compact 41–44 (2008).

[77] Thanks to Chidi Oguamanam for making this helpful suggestion.

As stated in the Guiding Principles, PPPs "should exercise adequate oversight in order to meet the[] international human rights obligations [of the public sector partner] when [the latter] contract[s] with, or legislate[s] for, business enterprises to provide services that may impact upon the enjoyment of human rights" (Principle 5). As the explanatory commentary on this principle further declares: "the relevant service contracts . . . should clarify the [public sector partner]'s expectations that these enterprises respect human rights." PPPs "should [also] ensure that they can effectively oversee the enterprises' activities, including through the provision of adequate independent monitoring and accountability mechanisms" (Principle 5, Explanatory Commentary).

In addition, drawing on Principle 8 of the Guiding Principles, PPPs should ensure that their public and private sector partners be "aware of and observe the [public sector partner]'s human rights obligations when fulfilling their respective mandates, including by providing them with relevant information, training and support." As noted in the explanatory commentary on this principle, attention should be paid to both vertical and horizontal coherence. While the former covers "the necessary policies, laws and processes to implement . . . international human rights law obligations," the latter concerns the ability of internal departments, agencies, or other subunits "to be informed of and act in a manner compatible with [these] obligations."

Finally, we should not forget that some PPPs will take on the same level of human rights obligations that States or other public actors assume. Such heightened responsibilities can be attributed to the close nexus between these partnerships and the participating States as well as the way the partnerships have been governed, financed, or supervised. Just as international organizations, regional bodies, and national courts may impute human rights responsibility to States by virtue of their participation in PPPs, these bodies may also apply to these partnerships higher human rights standards that traditionally apply to States or other public actors.

VI Three Illustrations of P3s4HR

Although PPPs should be held to higher human rights standards than private actors, it is insufficient to focus on their human rights responsibilities alone. If we are to strike a more appropriate balance between human rights and intellectual property, PPPs should be proactively designed to promote human rights protection in the intellectual property arena. The more the missions of these partnerships are aligned with such protection, the less we need to subject them to heightened human rights scrutiny – based on either the Guiding Principles or other guidelines.

To highlight the wide variety of P3s4HR that can be established, this section focuses on three illustrative examples. The first one concerns an operational partnership[78] between a developed country government and a private corporation (or a number of governments and a group of private corporations). This type of partnership is often found in the public health arena. Among the early examples involving drug and vaccine

[78] On the various types of PPPs, see Benedicte Bull & Desmond McNeill, Development Issues in Global Governance: Public-Private Partnerships and Market Multilateralism 12–20 (2007); Benedicte Bull, *Public-Private Partnerships: The United Nations Experience*, *in* International Handbook, *supra* note 4, at 479, 483–87.

development are the TB Alliance, IAVI, and the Medicines for Malaria Venture.[79] Other notable examples in the public health arena are the Global Alliance for Vaccines and Immunization (GAVI), the Global Fund for AIDS, Tuberculosis and Malaria, the Global Partnership to Stop Tuberculosis and the Roll Back Malaria Partnership. As the U.K. Commission on Intellectual Property Rights described in its final report:

> A number of [PPPs] have developed [intellectual property] strategies that seek to reconcile the interests of patent owners with the objective of making products available at affordable prices in the developing world. These usually involve contractual arrangements relating to any intellectual property that might be created. For instance, rights to commercialise in the developed world market may be assigned to a commercial partner in return for a royalty-free licence to the developing world for the PPP entity. Numerous other strategies can be considered to balance the objectives of the PPP entity against the need to provide meaningful incentives to the commercial partner.[80]

Whether it is for research and development, product procurement, or service delivery, an operational partnership will enable the State to leverage the expertise, technologies, resources, and other contributions of pharmaceutical manufacturers.[81] Meanwhile, the partnership will provide the participating private actors with demands for their products or services. The partnership will also provide political legitimacy and public recognition while enabling the constituent partners to maximize efficiency, reallocate risks, and capitalize on their competitive or comparative advantages. The overall cooperative arrangement will therefore create a win-win solution that promotes access to essential medicines. In human rights terms, this arrangement will ensure the respect and protection of the right to health – and, in life-threatening situations, also the right to life.

The second example concerns an advocacy or norm-setting partnership between the government in a developing country on the one hand and academics, policy experts, the media, and civil society organizations in developed countries on the other. This type of North–South partnership has been particularly helpful in pushing for greater protection of human rights in the international intellectual property regime. Efforts drawn from this type of partnership range from human rights advocacy in international trade and intellectual property arenas to assistance in efforts to challenge inappropriate laws and policies through the WTO dispute settlement process.[82]

As I noted in a previous article, this type of partnership can be beneficial in three ways.[83] First, the partnership will help advance the developing country's cause by serving

[79] Craig Wheeler & Seth Berkley, *Initial Lessons from Public-Private Partnerships in Drug and Vaccine Development*, 79 Bull. World Health Org. 728, 729 (2001).

[80] Comm'n on Intellectual Prop. Rights, Integrating Intellectual Property Rights and Development Policy: Report of the Commission on Intellectual Property Rights 130 (2002).

[81] B. Guy Peters & Jon Pierre, *Public-Private Partnerships and the Democratic Deficit: Is Performance-Based Legitimacy the Answer?*, *in* Democracy and Public-Private Partnerships in Global Governance 41, 44 (Magdalena Bexell & Ulrika Mörth eds., 2010); Marco Schäferhoff, Sabine Campe, & Christopher Kaan, *Transnational Public-Private Partnerships in International Relations: Making Sense of Concepts, Research Frameworks and Results* 11 (SFB-Governance, Working Paper Series No. 6, 2007), www.ciaonet.org/attachments/317/uploads.

[82] Gregory C. Shaffer, Defending Interests: Public-Private Partnerships in WTO Litigation (2003). Although Shaffer's book focuses on the partnerships between developed country governments and transnational corporations in WTO litigation, the norm-shaping outcomes for the partnerships in the book are the same as the strategic outcomes for the advocacy or norm-setting partnerships discussed in this example.

[83] Peter K. Yu, *A Tale of Two Development Agendas*, 35 Ohio N.U. L. Rev. 465, 552–53 (2009).

as Northern allies within the domestic political contexts in the developed world.[84] Second, the academics and policy experts in this partnership can help identify policy choices and negotiating strategies that will enhance the country's development potential.[85] Third, these experts, along with the supportive mass media, can help reframe the public debate, which in turn will make the debate more favorable to the cause of the developing country at issue.[86]

Although the two earlier examples cover partnerships that aim to promote human rights protection – sometimes at the expense of intellectual property protection – PPPs can also be established to promote the protection of both human rights and intellectual property. Such establishment is particularly feasible in situations implicating the intellectual property interests of developing countries or indigenous populations, as opposed to those of developed countries.

A good illustration of this type of situation is a partnership between a bio-rich developing country government and a TNC. At the time of writing, the most widely cited example remains the research collaborative agreement signed by the Costa Rican government and Merck in the early 1990s.[87] Although the Instituto Nacional de Biodiversidad (INBio) created out of this agreement has since faced significant financial and operational challenges[88] and has now been taken over by the National Natural History Museum in Costa Rica,[89] the arrangement embodied in this agreement illustrates how such a partnership, if fairly negotiated and effectively managed, can promote the protection of both human rights and intellectual property rights.

Under INBio's research collaborative agreement, Merck obtained permission to collect biological samples in conservatories set up in Costa Rica and thereafter conduct research and develop commercial products based on these samples.[90] In return, INBio, and by extension Costa Rica, received an advance payment as well as royalties generated from these commercial products. The development of this access and benefit-sharing

[84] Gregory Shaffer, *Recognizing Public Goods in WTO Dispute Settlement: Who Participates? Who Decides? The Case of TRIPS and Pharmaceutical Patent Protection*, 7 J. Int'l Econ. L. 459, 479 (2004); Antonio Ortiz Mena L.N., *Getting to "No:" Defending Against Demands in NAFTA Energy Negotiations*, *in* Negotiating Trade: Developing Countries in the WTO and NAFTA 177, 212 (John S. Odell ed., 2006) [hereinafter Negotiating Trade]; J.P. Singh, The Evolution of National Interests: New Issues and North-South Negotiations During the Uruguay Round, *in* Negotiating Trade, *supra*, at 41, 47.

[85] Andrea Koury Menescal, *Changing WIPO's Ways? The 2004 Development Agenda in Historical Perspective*, 8 J. World Intell. Prop. 761, 762 (2005).

[86] Carolyn Deere, The Implementation Game: The TRIPS Agreement and the Global Politics of Intellectual Property Reform in Developing Countries 173 (2009); Duncan Matthews, Intellectual Property, Human Rights and Development: The Role of NGOs and Social Movements 202–05 (2011); John S. Odell & Susan K. Sell, *Reframing the Issue: The WTO Coalition on Intellectual Property and Public Health, 2001*, *in* Negotiating Trade, *supra* note 84, at 85, 87.

[87] Rodrigo Gamez, *The Link Between Biodiversity and Sustainable Development: Lessons from INBio's Bioprospecting Programme in Costa Rica*, *in* Biodiversity and the Law: Intellectual Property, Biotechnology and Traditional Knowledge 77, 82–83 (Charles R. McManis ed., 2007).

[88] Edward Hammond, *Costa Rica's INBio, Nearing Collapse, Surrenders Its Biodiversity Collections and Seeks Government Bailout*, TWN Info Serv. on Biodiversity & Traditional Knowledge (Apr. 20, 2013), www.twn.my/title2/biotk/2013/biotk130401.htm.

[89] Edward Hammond, *Amid Controversy and Irony, Costa Rica's INBio Surrenders Biodiversity Collections and Lands to the State*, TWN Info Serv. on Biodiversity & Traditional Knowledge (Apr. 2, 2015), www.twn.my/title2/biotk/2015/btk150401.htm.

[90] Gamez, *supra* note 87, at 82–83.

arrangement not only enabled Costa Rica to control and benefit from its own biological resources, but also respected the human rights of Costa Ricans. These protected rights included the right to self-determination, the right to take part in cultural life, the right to enjoy the benefits of scientific progress and its applications, and the right to the protection of the interests resulting from intellectual productions.

Although INBio's research collaborative agreement was set up specifically between a TNC and a Southern government, its access and benefit-sharing arrangement can be modified to suit other needs. For instance, if one fears that the government would not deliver the proceeds to the relevant population, such as the local indigenous population, or if one is concerned about the usual corruption, mismanagement, or infrastructural problems commonly found in the developing world,[91] the agreement can be designed to enable the proceeds to go directly to the relevant population, as opposed to the national government. Thus, instead of directly following INBio's model, a PPP can be set up between a TNC and the public governing body of the local indigenous population.

Conclusion

The development of PPPs has provided countries with wide-ranging opportunities to strike a more appropriate balance between human rights and intellectual property. Nevertheless, if these opportunities are to fully materialize, we will have to acquire a deeper understanding of the human rights responsibilities of intellectual property-related PPPs. We will also have to pay greater attention to the different ways in which P3s4HR can be developed in the intellectual property arena.

The three illustrative examples provided at the end of this chapter are only some of the many partnership possibilities. Hopefully, they will inspire governments, intergovernmental bodies, TNCs, and nongovernmental organizations to think more creatively about the use of P3s4HR to improve the existing intellectual property system. Such creative use, in turn, will enable us to achieve broader societal goals beyond just the intellectual property arena, such as the Sustainable Development Goals outlined in the United Nations' 2030 Agenda for Sustainable Development.

References

Aginam, Obijiofor, John Harrington, and Peter K. Yu eds., THE GLOBAL GOVERNANCE OF HIV/AIDS: INTELLECTUAL PROPERTY AND ACCESS TO ESSENTIAL MEDICINES (2013).

Anheuser-Busch, Inc. v. Portugal, 45 Eur. Ct. H.R. 36 (2007) (Grand Chamber).

Belka, Marek, *Foreword* to UNITED NATIONS ECONOMIC COMMISSION FOR EUROPE, GUIDEBOOK ON PROMOTING GOOD GOVERNANCE IN PUBLIC-PRIVATE PARTNERSHIPS (2008).

Bovis, Christopher, PUBLIC-PRIVATE PARTNERSHIPS IN THE EUROPEAN UNION (2014).

Bull, Benedicte & Desmond McNeill, DEVELOPMENT ISSUES IN GLOBAL GOVERNANCE: PUBLIC-PRIVATE PARTNERSHIPS AND MARKET MULTILATERALISM (2007).

Bull, Benedicte, *Public-Private Partnerships: The United Nations Experience, in* INTERNATIONAL HANDBOOK, INTERNATIONAL HANDBOOK ON PUBLIC-PRIVATE PARTNERSHIPS 292 (Graeme A. Hodge, Carsten Greve, & Anthony E. Boardman eds., 2010).

[91] Peter K. Yu, *Cultural Relics, Intellectual Property, and Intangible Heritage*, 81 TEMP. L. REV. 433, 469 (2008).

Chapman, Audrey R., *Core Obligations Related to ICESCR Article 15(1)(c)*, *in* CORE OBLIGATIONS: BUILDING A FRAMEWORK FOR ECONOMIC, SOCIAL AND CULTURAL RIGHTS 305 (Audrey Chapman & Sage Russell eds., 2002).

Charter of Fundamental Rights of the European Union, Dec. 7, 2000, 2000 O.J. (C 364) 1.

Clapham, Andrew, HUMAN RIGHTS IN THE PRIVATE SPHERE (1993).

Clarke, Lisa, PUBLIC-PRIVATE PARTNERSHIPS AND RESPONSIBILITY UNDER INTERNATIONAL LAW: A GLOBAL HEALTH PERSPECTIVE (2014).

COMM'N ON INTELLECTUAL PROP. RIGHTS, INTEGRATING INTELLECTUAL PROPERTY RIGHTS AND DEVELOPMENT POLICY: REPORT OF THE COMMISSION ON INTELLECTUAL PROPERTY RIGHTS (2002).

Deere, Carolyn, THE IMPLEMENTATION GAME: THE TRIPS AGREEMENT AND THE GLOBAL POLITICS OF INTELLECTUAL PROPERTY REFORM IN DEVELOPING COUNTRIES (2009).

Deva, Surya, *Global Compact: A Critique of the U.N.'s "Public-Private" Partnership for Promoting Corporate Citizenship*, 34 SYRACUSE J. INT'L L. & COM. 107 (2006).

Deva, Surya, *Treating Human Rights Lightly: A Critique of the Consensus Rhetoric and the Language Employed by the Guiding Principles*, *in* HUMAN RIGHTS OBLIGATIONS OF BUSINESS: BEYOND THE CORPORATE RESPONSIBILITY TO RESPECT? 58 (Surya Deva & David Bilchitz eds., 2013).

Donnelly, Jack, UNIVERSAL HUMAN RIGHTS IN THEORY AND PRACTICE (2d ed. 2003).

Gamez, Rodrigo, *The Link Between Biodiversity and Sustainable Development: Lessons from INBio's Bioprospecting Programme in Costa Rica*, *in* BIODIVERSITY AND THE LAW: INTELLECTUAL PROPERTY, BIOTECHNOLOGY AND TRADITIONAL KNOWLEDGE 77 (Charles R. McManis ed., 2007).

Glendon, Mary Ann, A WORLD MADE NEW: ELEANOR ROOSEVELT AND THE UNIVERSAL DECLARATION OF HUMAN RIGHTS (2001).

Guiding Principles on Business and Human Rights: Implementing the United Nations "Protect, Respect and Remedy" Framework, *in Rep. of the Special Representative of the Secretary-General on the Issue of Human Rights and Transnational Corporations and Other Business Enterprises*, Human Rights Council, U.N. Doc. A/HRC/17/31 (Mar. 21, 2011).

Hammond, Edward, *Amid Controversy and Irony, Costa Rica's INBio Surrenders Biodiversity Collections and Lands to the State*, TWN INFO SERV. ON BIODIVERSITY & TRADITIONAL KNOWLEDGE (Apr. 2, 2015), www.twn.my/title2/biotk/2015/btk150401.htm (last visited Nov. 18, 2017).

Hammond, Edward, *Costa Rica's INBio, Nearing Collapse, Surrenders Its Biodiversity Collections and Seeks Government Bailout*, TWN INFO SERV. ON BIODIVERSITY & TRADITIONAL KNOWLEDGE (Apr. 20, 2013), www.twn.my/title2/biotk/2013/biotk130401.htm (last visited Nov. 18, 2107).

Human Rights and Transnational Corporations and Other Business Enterprises, Human Rights Res. 2005/69 (Apr. 20, 2005).

Human Rights Council Res. 8/7 (June 18, 2008).

Hunt, Paul (Special Rapporteur on the Right of Everyone to the Enjoyment of the Highest Attainable Standard of Physical and Mental Health), *Human Rights Guidelines for Pharmaceutical Companies in Relation to Access to Medicines*, *in Rep. of the Special Rapporteur on the Right of Everyone to the Enjoyment of the Highest Attainable Standard of Physical and Mental Health*, Human Rights Council, U.N. Doc. A/63/263, at 15–25 (Aug. 11, 2008).

Int'l AIDS Vaccine Initiative, About Us, www.iavi.org/who-we-are/leaders/about-us (last visited June 13, 2016).

International Covenant on Economic, Social and Cultural Rights, Dec. 16, 1966, 993 U.N.T.S. 3.

International Labour Organization, *Tripartite Declaration of Principles Concerning Multinational Enterprises and Social Policy*, *reprinted in* INTERNATIONAL LABOUR ORGANIZATION,

TRIPARTITE DECLARATION OF PRINCIPLES CONCERNING MULTINATIONAL ENTERPRISES AND SOCIAL POLICY (2006).

López, Carlos, *The "Ruggie Process": From Legal Obligations to Corporate Social Responsibility?*, *in* HUMAN RIGHTS OBLIGATIONS OF BUSINESS: BEYOND THE CORPORATE RESPONSIBILITY TO RESPECT? 58 (Surya Deva & David Bilchitz eds., 2013).

Mares, Radu, *"Respect" Human Rights: Concept and Convergence*, *in* LAW, BUSINESS AND HUMAN RIGHTS: BRIDGING THE GAP 3 (Robert C. Bird, Daniel R. Cahoy, & Jamie Darin Prenkert eds., 2014).

Matthews, Duncan, INTELLECTUAL PROPERTY, HUMAN RIGHTS AND DEVELOPMENT: THE ROLE OF NGOS AND SOCIAL MOVEMENTS (2011).

Mena L.N., Antonio Ortiz, *Getting to "No:" Defending Against Demands in NAFTA Energy Negotiations*, *in* NEGOTIATING TRADE: DEVELOPING COUNTRIES IN THE WTO AND NAFTA 177 (John S. Odell ed., 2006).

Menescal, Andrea Koury, *Changing WIPO's Ways? The 2004 Development Agenda in Historical Perspective*, 8 J. WORLD INTELL. PROP. 761 (2005).

Morsink, Johannes, THE UNIVERSAL DECLARATION OF HUMAN RIGHTS: ORIGINS, DRAFTING, AND INTENT (1999).

Odell, John S. & Susan K. Sell, *Reframing the Issue: The WTO Coalition on Intellectual Property and Public Health, 2001*, *in* NEGOTIATING TRADE: DEVELOPING COUNTRIES IN THE WTO AND NAFTA 85 (John S. Odell ed., 2006).

ORG. FOR ECON. CO-OPERATION & DEV., OECD GUIDELINES FOR MULTINATIONAL ENTERPRISES (2008).

Omobowale, Emmanuel B. et al., *Addressing Conflicts of Interest in Public Private Partnerships*, 10 BMC INT'L HEALTH & HUMAN RIGHTS 19 (2010), http://bmcinthealthhumrights.biomedcentral.com/articles/10.1186/1472-698X-10-19 (last visited Nov. 18, 2017).

Park, Stephen Kim, *Human Rights Reporting as Self-Interest: The Integrative and Expressive Dimensions of Corporate Disclosure*, *in* LAW, BUSINESS AND HUMAN RIGHTS: BRIDGING THE GAP (Robert C. Bird, Daniel R. Cahoy, & Jamie Darin Prenkert eds., 2014).

Peters, B. Guy and Jon Pierre, *Public-Private Partnerships and the Democratic Deficit: Is Performance-Based Legitimacy the Answer?*, *in* Democracy and Public-Private Partnerships in Global Governance 41 (Magdalena Bexell & Ulrika Mörth eds., 2010).

Protocol to the Convention for the Protection of Human Rights and Fundamental Freedoms, *opened for signature* Mar. 20, 1952, 213 U.N.T.S. 262.

Ratner, Steven R., *Corporations and Human Rights: A Theory of Legal Responsibility*, 111 YALE L.J. 443 (2001).

Ruggie, John (Special Representative of the Secretary-General on the Issue of Human Rights and Transnational Corporations and Other Business Enterprises), *Clarifying the Concepts of "Sphere of Influence" and "Complicity,"* Human Rights Council, U.N. Doc. A/HRC/8/16 (May 15, 2008).

Ruggie, John (Special Representative of the Secretary-General on the Issue of Human Rights and Transnational Corporations and Other Business Enterprises), *Protect, Respect and Remedy: A Framework for Business and Human Rights*, *in Rep. of the Special Representative of the Secretary-General on the Issue of Human Rights and Transnational Corporations and Other Business Enterprises*, Human Rights Council, U.N. Doc. A/HRC/8/5 (Apr. 7, 2008).

Ruggie, John Gerard, JUST BUSINESS: MULTINATIONAL CORPORATIONS AND HUMAN RIGHTS (2013).

Sagafi-Nejad, Tagi & John H. Dunning, THE UN AND TRANSNATIONAL CORPORATIONS: FROM CODE OF CONDUCT TO GLOBAL COMPACT (2008).

Sauvant, Karl P., *The Negotiations of the United Nations Code of Conduct on Transnational Corporations: Experience and Lessons Learned*, 16 J. WORLD INV. & TRADE 11 (2015).

Schäferhoff, Marco, Sabine Campe, & Christopher Kaan, *Transnational Public-Private Partnerships in International Relations: Making Sense of Concepts, Research Frameworks and Results* (SFB-Governance, Working Paper Series No. 6, 2007), *available at* www.ciaonet.org/attachments/317/uploads.

Sell, Susan K., PRIVATE POWER, PUBLIC LAW: THE GLOBALIZATION OF INTELLECTUAL PROPERTY RIGHTS (2003).

Shaffer, Gregory C., DEFENDING INTERESTS: PUBLIC-PRIVATE PARTNERSHIPS IN WTO LITIGATION (2003).

Shaffer, Gregory, *Recognizing Public Goods in WTO Dispute Settlement: Who Participates? Who Decides? The Case of TRIPS and Pharmaceutical Patent Protection*, 7 J. INT'L ECON. L. 459 (2004).

Shaheed, Farida (Special Rapporteur in the Field of Cultural Rights), *Copyright Policy and the Right to Science and Culture: Rep. of the Special Rapporteur in the Field of Cultural Rights*, Human Rights Council, U.N. Doc. A/HRC/28/57 (Dec. 24, 2014).

Singh, J.P., THE EVOLUTION OF NATIONAL INTERESTS: NEW ISSUES AND NORTH-SOUTH NEGOTIATIONS DURING THE URUGUAY ROUND, *in* NEGOTIATING TRADE: DEVELOPING COUNTRIES IN THE WTO AND NAFTA 41 (John S. Odell ed., 2006).

Skelcher, Chris, *Governing Partnerships*, *in* INTERNATIONAL HANDBOOK ON PUBLIC-PRIVATE PARTNERSHIPS 292 (Graeme A. Hodge, Carsten Greve, & Anthony E. Boardman eds., 2010).

Statement by Socially Responsible Investors to the Eighth Session of the Human Rights Council on the Third Report of the Special Representative of the UN Secretary-General on Business and Human Rights, BUS. & HUM. RTS. RESOURCE CENTRE (June 3, 2008), https://business-humanrights.org/sites/default/files/reports-and-materials/SRI-letter-re-Ruggie-report-3-Jun-2008.pdf.

Sub-Comm'n on the Promotion & Prot. of Human Rights, *Norms on the Responsibilities of Transnational Corporations and Other Business Enterprises with Regard to Human Rights*, U.N. Doc. E/CN.4/Sub.2/2003/12/Rev.2 (Aug. 26, 2003).

TB ALLIANCE, *Our Mission*, www.tballiance.org/about/mission (last visited June 13, 2016).

U.N. Comm. on Econ., Soc. & Cultural Rights, *General Comment No. 14: The Right to the Highest Attainable Standard of Health (Article 12 of the International Covenant on Economic, Social and Cultural Rights)*, U.N. Doc. E/C.12/2000/4 (Aug. 11, 2000).

U.N. Comm. on Econ., Soc. & Cultural Rights, *General Comment No. 17: The Right of Everyone to Benefit from the Protection of the Moral and Material Interests Resulting from Any Scientific, Literary or Artistic Production of Which He Is the Author (Article 15, Paragraph 1(c), of the Covenant)*, U.N. Doc. E/C.12/GC/17 (Jan. 12, 2006).

UNITED NATIONS GLOBAL COMPACT, GUIDE TO CORPORATE SUSTAINABILITY: SHAPING A SUSTAINABLE FUTURE (2014).

UNITED NATIONS GLOBAL COMPACT, *Our Mission*, www.unglobalcompact.org/what-is-gc/mission (last visited June 12, 2016).

UNITED NATIONS GLOBAL COMPACT, *The Ten Principles of the UN Global Compact*, www.unglobalcompact.org/what-is-gc/mission/principles (last visited June 12, 2016).

U.N. High Commissioner for Human Rights, *Rep. of the United Nations High Commissioner on Human Rights on the Responsibilities of Transnational Corporations and Related Business Enterprises with Regard to Human Rights*, U.N. Doc. E/CN.4/2005/91 (Feb. 15, 2005).

Universal Declaration of Human Rights, G.A. Res. 217A, U.N. GAOR, 3d Sess., 1st plen. mtg., U.N. Doc A/810 (Dec. 10, 1948).

Weissbrodt, David & Muria Kruger, *Norms on the Responsibilities of Transnational Corporations and Other Business Enterprises with Regard to Human Rights*, 97 AM. J. INT'L L. 901 (2003).

Wheeler, Craig & Seth Berkley, *Initial Lessons from Public-Private Partnerships in Drug and Vaccine Development*, 79 BULL. WORLD HEALTH ORG. 728 (2001).

Yu, Peter K., *The Anatomy of the Human Rights Framework for Intellectual Property*, 69 SMU L. Rev. 37 (2016).
Yu, Peter K., *Cultural Relics, Intellectual Property, and Intangible Heritage*, 81 Temp. L. Rev. 433 (2008).
Yu, Peter K., *Digital Copyright Enforcement Measures and Their Human Rights Threats, in* Research Handbook on Human Rights and Intellectual Property 455 (Christophe Geiger ed., 2015).
Yu, Peter K., *Intellectual Property and Human Rights in the Nonmultilateral Era*, 64 Fla. L. Rev. 1045 (2012).
Yu, Peter K., *Reconceptualizing Intellectual Property Interests in a Human Rights Framework*, 40 U.C. Davis L. Rev. 1039 (2007).
Yu, Peter K., *A Tale of Two Development Agendas*, 35 Ohio N.U. L. Rev. 465 (2009).
Yu, Peter K., *Ten Common Questions About Intellectual Property and Human Rights*, 23 Ga. St. U. L. Rev. 709 (2007).

Conclusion

19 The Triple Interface: Findings and Future Directions

Margaret Chon

The foregoing chapters explore and analyze key areas of public–private partnership (PPP) involvement across a variety of development fields – or what we have termed the 'triple interface' of PPPs, intellectual property (IP), and the sustainable development goals (SDGs). They represent diverse perspectives on the ways in which this triple interface can advance both public and private interests toward the realization of the SDGs, on multiple levels: practical, policy, and conceptual.

This final chapter provides a partial synthesis, situating the contributions within a global *knowledge governance* framework: evaluating whether and how PPPs encourage innovation, build innovation capacity, engage in technology transfer or sharing, or otherwise ensure wide dissemination and diffusion of innovation results across borders to advance the progress of the SDGs. Based on the evidence presented in this book, this chapter summarizes findings according to four thematic sections and illustrates these findings with references to specific chapters: (1) aligning with public policy objectives; (2) coordinating with other knowledge governance efforts; (3) managing the partnership boundaries; and (4) enhancing sustainable development. Because so many of the book's contributions touch upon all four themes, any references are meant to be illustrative rather than comprehensive. After this thematic tour, the chapter concludes with suggestions for a future policy and research agenda.

I Aligning with Public Policy Objectives

The public policy objectives of knowledge governance include not only the generation of IP-protected inventions and works but also the dissemination and diffusion of these innovations, and the knowledge embedded within them. These are not just goals in and of themselves, but also function to further other public policy ends, such as promoting better health, education, or climate conditions. PPPs implement these various policies through the IP management and choices of private partners as well as through the regulatory and public policies of public partners.

A *IP Management and Policies*

A number of authors touch upon IP licensing issues as a key subset of IP management and choices. These include licensing models (exclusive and nonexclusive licensing), approaches (humanitarian and dual licensing), and policies (e.g., global access policies, as well as the transparent licensing policy discussed in the case of the Medicines Patent Pool (MPP)).[1] Not surprisingly, this discussion about IP licensing is most developed in the public health section of the book.[2] For example, the case study of the MPP outlines its approaches with respect to IP management, with origins in the practical application of access-oriented licensing to HIV, and subsequent expansion into hepatitis C and TB. Its current policy of transparent voluntary licenses with industry arguably can be replicated in other areas of pharmaceutical research and development (R&D).[3] The examination of the World Intellectual Property Organization (WIPO) Re:Search partnership offers 'Guiding Principles' for pharmaceutical R&D PPPs.[4] And the study of the Innovation Medicines Initiative (IMI) explains the various ways in which background and foreground IP can be licensed and managed to promote collaborative R&D, especially in the precompetitive biomedical research space.[5]

Also notable in this regard is the case study of the Health InterNetwork Access to Research Information (HINARI), which is the World Health Organisation's (WHO) PPP for providing access to scientific information to researchers in least developed countries. This initiative has been able to address multiple issues of for-profit publishers in making their works more accessible to developing country researchers. In this PPP, for-profit publishers are incentivized to participate enthusiastically in initiatives directed at scientists in least developed countries, in part by ensuring that profitable markets are fenced off from areas of nonprofit access to scientific information.[6]

In bilateral clean energy research partnerships such as the US–China Clean Energy Research Centre, IP agreements have been concluded between the partners. In the case of this specific PPP, a 'Technology Management Plan' for each sector fleshes out IP arrangements for technologies developed by each partner separately and jointly.[7] As the discussion of WIPO GREEN documents, by contrast, its licensing agreements are entirely left to the individual technology providers and seekers.[8] Citing to a plethora of recent humanitarian licensing guidelines and proposals, another chapter focusing on climate change-related technologies advances a crucial framework for PPPs of innovation

[1] See Esteban Burrone, chapter 5, *supra*.
[2] See Frederick M. Abbott, chapter 2, *supra*; cf. Peter K. Yu, chapter 18, *supra*.
[3] Esteban Burrone, chapter 5, *supra* at 93 ("MPP is the first patent pool in public health designed to enhance access to affordable medicines in developing countries through the negotiation of access-oriented and transparent voluntary licences with the pharmaceutical industry.").
[4] Anatole Krattiger et al., chapter 3, *supra* at 64 ("Members will provide royalty-free licenses for R&D related to NTDs, malaria, and tuberculosis; Members will provide a royalty-free license for any product developed through WIPO Re:Search that is used and sold in LDCs; Members will consider the issue of access and affordability to these products for all developing countries, including those that do not qualify as LDCs; and Users will retain ownership of any new IP developed, but are encouraged to make new inventions available to other Members of WIPO Re:Search.")
[5] Hilde Stevens & Isabelle Huys, chapter 6, *supra*.
[6] Jens Bammel, chapter 7, *supra*.
[7] Ahmed Abdel-Latif, chapter 11, *supra*.
[8] Abdel-Latif, *id.*, at 233 ("It is thus interesting to note that WIPO GREEN has no specific prescriptive licensing arrangements or terms in place (though offers a Licensing Checklist; see later). The technologies uploaded to the WIPO GREEN database remain the property of the rights holder. It is then up to them and the collaborating parties to structure agreements in the manner they feel is most appropriate and effective.")

policy and management, viewing private management mechanisms to be as important as the public policy levers wielded by public partners.[9]

These and other chapters raise the vital question of how to further foster the uptake of a broader range of key IP policy and management levers, such as IP licensing practices, across different sectors in order to facilitate progress towards the numerous public policy goals set forth by the SDGs.

B *Technology Sharing and Innovation Capacity-Building*

Technology transfer is an important part of knowledge governance from the perspective of many developing countries. The chapter reviewing existing models and future institutional designs contributes to a conceptual understanding of this critical activity by coining the term 'technology sharing' to denote a less unilateral relationship between partners in international PPPs.[10] Yet with a few exceptions, most international PPPs described in the extant literature are not particularly oriented either toward technology sharing or innovation capacity building. This observation corroborates the findings of a study of climate change and related partnerships, based upon PPPs formed after the 2002 World Summit on Sustainable Development (post-WSSD PPPs).[11] And the on-going absence of robust mechanisms for 'technology transfer' (now understood to include technology collaboration and facilitation) is still apparent in the green technology space under the United Nations Framework Convention on Climate Change (UNFCCC)[12] as well as the climate change goals under the 2030 Agenda.

These converging observations raise the obvious question of what more can be done to implement technology sharing and innovation capacity building goals more broadly and effectively throughout the SDGs and within PPPs. These include not just the clearly related goals of SDG 9 and SDG 17, but other SDGs as well.

C *The 'Three A's' of Accessibility, Availability, and Affordability*

Dissemination and diffusion activities of knowledge governance are critical to sustainable development and could be described as the 'three A's' of accessibility, availability, and affordability. The global debate over the importance of the three 'A's' to IP policy

9 Joshua D. Sarnoff & Margaret Chon, *supra* at 271–72 (suggesting that "upstream owners [] retain the power to authorize experimental uses (to the extent that any jurisdiction lacks such restrictions on patent rights) and []permit "humanitarian" uses (at low or no cost) for climate mitigation and adaptation needs . . ." and changing "the default resort from exclusive to non-exclusive licensing (unless the former has been demonstrated to be needed)."

10 Padmashree Gehl Sampath, chapter 15, *supra* at 334. According to her, "if one were to provide incentives for access and use of technology, as well as learning, and building upon it, the partners should all be treated as equal and would work towards protecting the knowledge that is common to the PPP. *Technology sharing* therefore is the more apropos term that reflects this kind of equal partnership with an equally important responsibility to contribute and build on the knowledge.").

11 Ayşem Mert & Philipp Pattberg, chapter 13, *supra*.

12 Ahmed Abdel-Latif, chapter 11, *supra* at 227 ("a Technology Facilitation Mechanism (TFM) was launched to support the implementation for the SDGs ... [and] is tasked with facilitating multi-stakeholder collaboration and partnerships through the sharing of information, experiences, best practices and policy advice among Member States, civil society, the private sector, the scientific community, and United Nations entities "); see also Joshua D. Sarnoff & Margaret Chon, chapter 12, *supra*.

underlies each of the contributions in the public health section, all of which address the question of access to R&D or the fruits of R&D on poverty-related neglected diseases (PRNDs).

Outside of the global health arena, advocates of greater access to knowledge point to digitization as a crucial technological development underpinning the potentially inexpensive, rapid, and geographically inclusive dissemination of many works, whether under copyright or in the public domain. For instance, the analysis of the WIPO Accessible Books Consortium (ABC) looks at the advantages of an initiative that promotes partnerships with for-profit publishers to provide materials to communities of visually impaired persons (VIPs).[13] This chapter, however, documents the very real challenges in providing digital works in accessible formats, which require accompanying and compatible software, hardware, and/or technical know-how. Similarly, the HathiTrust case study asserts that this US-based PPP has increased not only accessibility of works to all readers, including VIPS in other countries, but also furthered preservation and therefore availability of works that might otherwise have been lost due to degradation of the paper medium on which they were stored.[14]

This aspect of global knowledge governance is often framed in terms of simply increasing the 'public domain' or encouraging 'open access' models over proprietary models of knowledge transfer. Yet these and other pieces in the book show that barriers to dissemination could be defined and addressed with more granularity. They raise the issue of how to encourage more PPPs to include explicit goals addressing the 'three A's.' Furthermore, they illustrate how dissemination might potentially be furthered by harnessing knowledge governance goals to the private sector's resources and cross-border reach.

II Coordinating with Other Knowledge Governance Efforts

PPPs often contend with the IP-intensive nature of knowledge governance activities. And knowledge governance is often conflated simply with IP. But innovation activities go much further than simply generating IP (whether patents, copyrights, or other formal kinds of IP) and/or licensing IP. This section links the activities of PPPs, including the IP management and policies described above, with other knowledge governance efforts – particularly those in multilateral treaty frameworks such as those administered by WIPO or the WTO. And given the emphasis on goals, targets, and indicators within the current sustainable development paradigm, it also addresses the kind of metrics appropriate to measure progress in these efforts.

A *Relationship to Other Forms of Regulatory Coordination, Harmonization, and Oversight within IP Legal Regimes*

Within the public health domain, the WIPO Re:Search initiative illustrates some mechanisms for collaborative governance and regulatory coordination, specifically between an intergovernmental organization (INGO) such as WIPO and other PPP stakeholders.

[13] Susan Isiko Štrba, chapter 9 (describing the Marrakesh Treaty to Facilitate Access to Published Works for Persons Who Are Blind, Visually Impaired, or Otherwise Print Disabled (VIP Treaty)).

[14] Melissa Levine, chapter 10, *supra*.

On the one side is the partnership hub – BIO Ventures for Global Health (BVGH) – that functions to organize and promote the activities of various R&D efforts;[15] on the other side is the INGO – WIPO – that engages in evaluation, oversight, and possible steering of partnership.[16] Important to note in the public health arena, moreover, is the relationship of PPPs to compulsory licensing provisions in multilateral agreements; the activities of these PPPs are not necessarily intended to be a substitute for these harmonized multilateral licensing mechanisms.[17]

Likewise, in the arena of education and libraries, the activities of WIPO's ABC are viewed as complements to rather than substitutes for exceptions and limitations to copyright such as those authorized by multilateral treaties because even PPPs affiliated with an INGO such as WIPO are limited in their impact compared to the potential reach of INGOs through their treaty-making activities.[18] And as argued in the case study of HathiTrust, the multilateral treaty framework for copyright exceptions and limitations is crucial to facilitate increased cross-border access to copyrighted works and therefore should be expanded to increase harmonization for public domain works.[19]

Similarly, with green technologies, international efforts to encourage the development and diffusion of new technologies under the UNFCCC are intertwined with national (including private) efforts. However, much more work is needed to develop the role of PPPs within the institutional framework of the UNFCCC. Bilateral collaborative PPPs may provide models for further efforts at collaborative partnerships.[20]

A comparative case study on geographical indications (GIs) finds no optimal degree or balance of involvement by the public sector *vis-à-vis* the private sector in partnerships. Both sectors operate necessarily hand-in-hand, and its authors conclude that jurisdictions should choose the correct balance according to national goals, culture, customs, and agricultural practices.[21]

Thus, experts across different development domains posit that optimal knowledge governance necessarily involves coordination between public and private sectors, as well as across local, national, and multinational levels. The question is how to make this cross-cutting and multi-level coordination involving PPPs more consistent and effective.

B *Effectiveness Metrics, Such as Demonstrated Output, Outcomes, and Impact on the Production and Distribution of Knowledge Goods*

Work in biomedical R&D PPPs such as IMI suggests a large number of metrics other than formal IP to evaluate the effectiveness of these PPPs;[22] similarly, the WIPO

[15] Katy M. Graef et al., chapter 4, *supra*.
[16] Anatole Krattiger et al., chapter 3, *supra*.
[17] Esteban Burrone, chapter 5, *supra*.
[18] Susan Isiko Štrba, chapter 9, *supra*.
[19] Melissa Levine, chapter 10, *supra*.
[20] Ahmed Abdel-Latif, chapter 11, *supra*.
[21] Irene Calboli & Delphine Marie-Vivien, chapter 14, *supra*.
[22] Hilde Stevens & Isabelle Huys, chapter 6, *supra* at 132 ("Performance of scientific research, and in particular the evaluation of IP in PPPs, is quantitatively demonstrated by key performance indicators (KPIs), often tangible deliverables such as number and impact of publications, number of citations, or number of patents. However, a patent application is far from being the only value-critical step in drug R&D ... KPIs should also capture the development of, and access to technologies, capability, and talent, as well as the provision of improved rules for decision making or to reduce costs (impact on R&D

Re:Search activities including the development of indicators and metrics to measure progress in knowledge governance, in lieu of standard IP metrics such as patent filings.[23] Many authors also point to the value of networking *per se* in the advancement of knowledge generation and, ultimately, innovation: for example, the growing support of individual research scientists who travel to other laboratories in order to conduct collaborative research.[24] And as observed with respect to IMI, "knowledge gathered in the different IMI projects exceeds pure scientific results" and can also include standardized templates and protocols as well as other ways to maximize cooperation across separate laboratories.[25] The case study of Open Air also underlines the importance of providing a platform for a continent-wide research network, and asserts that this approach is superior to a top-down approach for generating R&D from the actual needs and capacities of those affected.[26]

Not only do the SDGs enumerate goals, but they also articulate targets and indicators. Sustainable development is now overtly a goal-driven process based on measurable progress. In that context, it is important to continue to develop metrics for knowledge governance that do not over-rely on IP filings and that instead acknowledge and cover a more capacious range of knowledge generation and dissemination activities.

C *Relationship to Overall Global Governance Theory and Practice, Including Accountability, Inclusivity, and Transparency*

Arguably the most thorough discussion of global governance theory is presented in the chapter on post-WSSD PPPs. This contribution studies "three hypothetical global governance deficits that partnerships are supposed to address"[27] and its findings indicate

productivity).). They further note that "[s]ome researchers have identified seven domains to monitor different types of organizations' progress: a) funding, b) talent, c) dissemination, d) collaboration, e) output, f) validation, and g) external uptake. (citing Robert Pozen & Heather Kline, *Defining Success for Translational Research Organizations*, 3 Sci. Translational Med. 94cm20, 3–4 (2011)).

[23] Katy M. Graef et al., chapter 4, *supra* at 88 (For example, the WIPO Re:Search collaboration guidelines require partners to report "(1) Research milestones achieved; (2) Publications and presentations arising from the collaboration; (3) Grants applied for and any funding received; [and] (4) Number of students or postgraduates that received training as part of the collaboration.").

[24] Anatole Krattiger et al., chapter 3, *supra* (Appendix).

[25] Hilde Stevens & Isabelle Huys, chapter 6, *supra* at 131 ("An enormous number of templates, harmonized protocols, and standardization endeavors for information exchange has been developed within and between consortia. It took the consortium members considerable efforts and time to come to these harmonized and standardized templates and protocols. Therefore any assessment of effectiveness should valorize these knowledge assets.").

[26] Chidi Oguamanam & Jeremy De Beer, chapter 17, *supra* at 390–91 ("insights arising from Open AIR inquiries may inspire other PPPs to implement R&D efforts that tap Africa's factor endowments through a combination of on-the-ground practices of open and collaborative innovation, as well as informal and formal interface and apprenticeship models, to produce or scale to a substantially African-made version of any of these knowledge products. Such an example represents a model of innovation capacity building as sustainable development.")

[27] Ayşem Mert & Philipp Pattberg, chapter 13, *supra* at 300 ("... [T]he regulatory deficit, the implementation deficit, and participatory deficit. First, partnerships are expected to confront the regulatory deficit in current sustainability governance by providing avenues for cooperation and joint problem-solving in areas where intergovernmental regulation is largely non-existent. A second deficit that partnerships are believed to fill is an implementation deficit in sustainability governance. That is, partnerships could help implement intergovernmental regulations that do exist but that are only poorly implemented, if at all. Third,

that post-WSSD PPPs did not effectively address these deficits. On the other hand, a number of contributions point to evolving practices of accountability, inclusivity, and transparency within PPPs. One example from the pharmaceutical R&D space is the WIPO Re:Search Guiding Principles, as well as its collaboration guidelines for partners.[28]

HINARI, the PPP supported by the WHO, also illustrates how issues among partners can be handled relatively openly and informally despite the absence of any detailed agreements.[29] And while demonstrating that PPPs can be transparent regarding their governing legal frameworks, the HathiTrust initiative reinforces the importance of clear contractual mechanisms between participating partners, within a national US context.[30]

Within knowledge governance practice, legitimate concerns have been voiced among observers regarding the degrees of accountability, inclusivity, and transparency within PPPs – and some pieces in this book echo these concerns. This is true, for example, of the case study of the WIPO's Access to Research for Development and Innovation (ARDI) initiative.[31] As with global governance more generally, these profound challenges are certain to continue in search of viable solutions, based upon ongoing evaluation and revision of the policies and practices of PPPs.

III Managing the Partnership Boundaries

As hybrid arrangements, PPPs are necessarily complex. The degree of alignment among partners can vary within and across PPPs, with respect to either partners' incentives, interests, or goals. Within a global knowledge governance framework, the internal and external dynamics and decision making within PPPs can be viewed as a type of joint governance or co-governance toward shared goals. As the introductory chapter notes, global knowledge governance is a two- or even three-dimensional process: partnerships require some type of effective internal governance or management to coordinate the differing approaches of partners internally, and they also require mechanisms to manage boundaries with external stakeholders within their networks. Finally, individual PPPs are stakeholders themselves within decentralized governance models; as such, they necessarily interact with are constrained by both national and multilateral funding and regulatory institutions. The interaction of the various actors, whether partners or stakeholders, are expected to result in specified outcomes. In that regard, it is important to discern what attributes of PPPs result in successful collaboration towards intended goals, and what mechanisms fruitful PPPs use to manage their relationships. This aspect of the triple interface deserves careful attention.

partnerships are often expected to assist in solving a participation deficit in global governance. In this view, intergovernmental negotiations are seen as dominated by powerful governments and international organizations, while partnerships, by contrast, might ensure higher participation of less privileged actors.").

[28] Anatole Krattiger et al., chapter 3, *supra*; Katy M. Graef et al., chapter 4, *supra*.

[29] Jens Bammel, chapter 7, *supra*.

[30] Melissa Levine, chapter 10, *supra*.

[31] Sara Bannerman, chapter 8, *supra*.

A *Relationships among Various Partner and Stakeholder Goals, e.g., Mission, Profit, and Public Policy*

Almost all of this book's contributions grappled with the challenges of managing hybridity within PPPs, but some were more explicit than others in addressing this foundational issue. Some case studies identify ingredients for such success in balancing the differing agendas of public and private partners. For example, the study of collaborative engagement within the pre-competitive pharmaceutical research partnerships, such as the IMI, finds that trust and flexibility are essential qualities in responding to uncertainties within the PPP relationship.[32] As the case study of Open AIR shows, collaborative knowledge governance should include mechanisms for inclusion and participation by a broad range of stakeholders; specific attributes contribute to the success of this partnership (in the view of its main architects), which operates with an expansive geographic scope such as the African continent.[33]

On the other hand, the case study on post-WSSD PPPs shows that many of these PPPs fell short of expectations to achieve consensus regarding the partnership goals in public policy areas prioritized within multilateral environmental governance. While documenting efforts that fell short of goals rather than successes, this chapter also suggests best practices for PPPs moving forward such as screening mechanisms for accountability.[34]

Internal governance arrangements ideally should lower transaction costs among partners. Various contributions to the book highlight partners engaged in constructive and ongoing relationships accompanied by relatively transparent expectations of the shared partnership goals, and dynamic management of potentially conflicting or competing public and private interests through contractual or other mechanisms. They raise the possibility of disseminating best practices for PPPs, based upon documented successes and lessons learned from failures.

B *Inclusivity of Partnerships*

The post-WSSD PPPs not only often suffered from a lack of clarity regarding the nature of the relationship between the partners as well as the expected output from the partners' efforts but also only took symbolic and limited gestures towards ensuring full participation by partners in developing countries.[35] Similarly, the case study of the ARDI partnership housed within WIPO finds that this PPP requires greater inclusivity and participation by a broader range of stakeholders than is currently the case.[36] Along the

[32] Hilde Stevens & Isabelle Huys, chapter 6, *supra* at 119 (the "level of trust among stakeholders will determine the capability of precompetitive PPPs to become effective networking platforms. . . . Flexible arrangements, whereby room to renegotiate well-defined issues when pre-defined milestones have been reached or certain deliverables have been accomplished is provided, can anticipate uncertainties in the negotiation process. This stepwise approach, also sometimes referred to as the stage-gate process, could facilitate trust building.").

[33] Chidi Oguamanam & Jeremy De Beer, chapter 17, *supra* (discussing multiple attributes).

[34] Ayşem Mert & Philipp Pattberg, chapter 13, *supra* at 305 ("We want to stress in particular the necessity for a critical screening mechanism that could ensure transparency, accountability, co-benefits, and fit with the 2030 Agenda, as well as ensuring adequate levels of participation for marginalized actors in this multi-stakeholder institutional framework.")

[35] Ayşem Mert & Philipp Pattberg, chapter 13, *supra*.

[36] Sara Bannerman, chapter 8, *supra*.

same lines, the chapter examining effective partnerships implementing the Millennium Development Goals (MDGs) emphasizes that cross-sector PPPs can and should be more intentionally inclusive of the developing country (public) partners that often constitute the end beneficiaries of a partnership's efforts.[37]

These contributions, among others, caution us that PPPs may fall short of full inclusivity of potential partners and stakeholders without careful and intentional processes to facilitate coordination and inclusion. Integral to the question of accomplishing this partner inclusion, in addition to accommodating the potentially different approaches of partners within PPPs, is the specific blueprint of a PPP's governance mechanisms, including those for partner match-making, participation, and ongoing evaluation.

C *Funding Models, Including Evaluation of Long-Term Sustainability*

The role and extent of public funding of development efforts relative to private investment, whether through PPPs or other institutions, is a controversial topic, which is far from resolved. In the interim, however, nonprofit stakeholders have catalysed and subsidized many PPPs in the public health space. For example, the study addressing PPPs as models for new drug R&D builds upon the role and out-sized presence of foundation-funded PPPs in the public health arena. It posits that such PPPs could lead to a sustainable alternative funding model of pharmaceutical R&D, by forming a bridge from a profit-driven model to one that would broadly delink profits from R&D.[38]

A different contribution emphasizes that public sector funding remains essential to the operation of climate change-related PPPs, and it outlines a comprehensive range of approaches to public sector support and funding, which the authors consider to be integral to innovation policy choices within PPPs.[39] These studies and others demonstrate that much more work can and should be done to elucidate different funding models and their impact on the sustainability of PPPs' efforts within knowledge governance.

IV Enhancing Sustainable Development

The coverage of Agenda 2030 is ambitious and holistic. Knowledge governance arguably contributes to the realization of all the SDGs. The links between the PPPs described in this book and the SDGs are occasionally quite obvious. For example, SDG 3, which is to "[e]nsure healthy lives and promote well-being for all at all ages"[40] has a specific target 3B, which addresses the multilateral IP framework and states that R&D should be "in accordance with the Doha Declaration on the TRIPS Agreement and Public Health, which affirms the right of developing countries to use to the full the provisions in the Agreement on Trade-Related Aspects of Intellectual Property Rights regarding flexibilities to protect public health, and, in particular, provide access to medicines

[37] David J. Maurrasse, chapter 16, *supra*.
[38] Frederick M. Abbott, chapter 2, *supra*.
[39] Joshua D. Sarnoff & Margaret Chon, chapter 12, *supra*.
[40] Sustainable Development Goal 3: Ensure Healthy Lives and Promote Well-Being for All at All Ages, SUSTAINABLE DEVELOPMENT KNOWLEDGE PLATFORM, https://sustainabledevelopment.un.org/sdg3 (last visited Nov. 16, 2017).

for all."[41] In many other instances, the links between the SDGs and knowledge governance are less evident and are still in the process of being discerned and integrated within the work of PPPs.

A *Extent to which Partnership Framework within Knowledge Governance Adds Value or Contributes to Other Sustainable Development Goals*

All of the chapters address the SDGs in some way, shape, or form. At the same time, many of the authors felt challenged in making the connections more salient. Arguably this is because of the relative lack of policy discourse or scholarly literature to support the linkage of knowledge governance activities to global governance via the SDGs. The study on PPPs and technology sharing, for example, systematically addresses the published literature on the impact of PPPs on technology transfer and development, and finds very little work to date.[42] This finding shows that the relevant linkages are in need of much greater understanding, both in the policy arenas and scholarly communities.

B *Differences in Approaches within and toward Least Developed Countries, Middle-Income Countries, and Industrialized Countries*

Agenda 2030 is intended to deemphasize the previous MDGs' dichotomy between developed and developing countries. Yet in the global health discussions, the very term 'PRND' implies a unilateral approach, in which the countries that are rich in R&D, technological capacity, and advanced markets will confer knowledge upon those countries lacking those attributes. The efforts described on the WIPO Re:Search initiative are attempts to overcome this typical construct by emphasizing the inclusion and participation of developing country partners. And the study on PPP models for new drug development takes this impulse several steps further, by positing a major restructuring of the global model for pharmaceutical R&D.[43]

In the copyright-related PPPs described in the book, beneficiaries are often located in developing countries. As noted, for example, one challenge in the WHO's HINARI is the transition "from aid to trade."[44] A different challenge facing WIPO's ARDI is the greater inclusion of beneficiary stakeholders within the PPP's governance structure and decision-making processes.[45] And, as also documented, is the difficulty facing WIPO's

41 *Id.* ("Support the research and development of vaccines and medicines for the communicable and non-communicable diseases that primarily affect developing countries, provide access to affordable essential medicines and vaccines, in accordance with the Doha Declaration on the TRIPS Agreement and Public Health, which affirms the right of developing countries to use to the full the provisions in the Agreement on Trade-Related Aspects of Intellectual Property Rights regarding flexibilities to protect public health, and, in particular, provide access to medicines for all.") Similar concerns has been raised by the UN Secretary-General's High Level Panel on Access to Medicines, Promoting Innovation and Access to Health Technologies, 2016. U.N. Secretary-General's High-Level Panel on Access to Medicines, *Report of the U.N. Secretary-General's High-Level Panel on Access to Medicines: Promoting Innovation and Access to Health Technologies* (Sep. 14, 2016), www.unsgaccessmeds.org/final-report/.

42 Padmashree Gehl Sampath, chapter 15, *supra*; David J. Maurrasse, chapter 16, *supra*.

43 Frederick M. Abbott, chapter 2, *supra*.

44 Jens Bammel, chapter 7, *supra* at 144.

45 Sara Bannerman, chapter 8, *supra*.

ABC, particularly that developing countries may lack technology required to access texts in so-called 'accessible formats.'[46]

In the comparison of three different jurisdictions varying in development status (France, Singapore, and India), the case study of GIs claims that a one size fits all approach to co-governance does not exist.[47] This and other contributions illustrate that distinctions among levels of development remain relevant and persistent.

C *Relation to Human Rights, Intergenerational Equity, and Distributive Justice*

The SDGs incorporate a number of human rights measures, which in turn raise the critical question of whether and how private sector partners (particularly those operating for-profit) can be subject to human rights obligations. The study on PPP and human rights surveys three examples to make the case for "PPPs for human rights (P3s4HR) in the intellectual property arena."[48] In doing so, the chapter's author reiterates that the human rights discourse in knowledge governance has become a critical part of the IP policy equation, while acknowledging at the same time that asking for-profit partners to adopt human rights obligations is fraught with obstacles.

Intergenerational equity is profoundly embedded within the concept of sustainable development.[49] The contributions on climate change-related technologies include intergenerational equity as their implicit or explicit baseline. In the case of climate change, moreover, major distributional justice issues are implicated across geographic sectors,[50] which in turn affect the goals of technology sharing and innovation capacity building. Arguably, global geographic disparity in knowledge governance inputs and outcomes affects many development sectors beyond those addressing climate change.

Essential to the work envisioned by Agenda 2030, the concepts of human rights, intergenerational equity, and distributional justice need much more elucidation within the accompanying knowledge governance framework examined in this book.

V Suggestions for a Policy and Research Agenda

The various contributions to this book urge us to consider more deeply the extent and quality of involvement of PPPs in knowledge governance toward the SDGs. They raise numerous issues, including but not limited to:

46 Susan Isiko Štrba, chapter 9, *supra*.
47 Irene Calboli & Delphine Marie-Vivien, chapter 14, *supra*.
48 Peter K. Yu, chapter 18, *supra*.
49 The foundational Brundtland Report defined sustainable development as "development that meets the needs of the present without compromising future generations to meet their own needs." U.N. World Commission on Environment and Development, Our Common Future (1987). SDGs 10 and 16 refer to "Reduced Inequalities" and "Peace, Justice and Strong Institutions," respectively. Sustainable Development Knowledge Platform, *Sustainable Development Goal 10*, U.N. Dep't of Econ. of Soc. Affairs, www.un.org/sustainabledevelopment/inequality/; Sustainabe Development Knowledge Platform, *Sustainable Development Goal 16*, U.N. Dep't of Econ. of Soc. Affairs, www.un.org/sustainabledevelopment/peace-justice/.
50 Joshua D. Sarnoff & Margaret Chon, chapter 12, *supra*.

- fostering the uptake of a broader range of key IP policy and management levers, including licensing practices, across different sectors to facilitate progress towards the SDGs;
- implementing technology sharing and innovation capacity building goals more widely and effectively throughout the SDGs, and not just with regard to Goals 9 and 17;
- encouraging more PPPs to include goals involving dissemination aspects of knowledge governance and policy, including the 'three A's' of accessibility, availability, and affordability;
- coordinating between INGO partners and other partners more consistently and effectively;
- developing metrics for knowledge governance that do not over-rely on IP filings and that include a more capacious range of knowledge generation and dissemination activities;
- promoting accountability, inclusivity, and transparency both within PPPs and with regard to their external stakeholders;
- encouraging the implementation of best practices for PPP internal management and external relations;
- generating information regarding internal governance attributes and mechanisms of PPPs, including those for promoting full participation by partners and stakeholders;
- evaluating different funding models and their impact on PPP sustainability and/or the sustainability of their underlying goals;
- documenting better how PPPs operate within knowledge governance to contribute to the SDGs through technology transfer, technology sharing, or other means;
- understanding when degrees of development and/or differences in cultural perceptions, economic systems, and political priorities matter in the joint governance or co-governance models of PPPs; and
- internalizing the SDG's concepts of human rights, intergenerational equity, and distributive justice within knowledge governance PPPs.

The case studies, policy analyses, and scholarly work in this book represent pioneering efforts at analysing the triple interface, which is at its early stages of description and evaluation. Relatedly, this emerging area of policy analysis and scholarly research faces numerous challenges. Because many PPP initiatives are new, it is difficult to explore them thoroughly or even sometimes to gather preliminary data at this point. Moreover, the hybrid nature of PPPs can throw a cloak of privacy over their operations, and the diversity and range of PPPs can make it impossible to generalize across them. Transnational lawmaking practices via PPPs are types of informal regulation or 'soft law' and therefore difficult to document and analyze. The various challenges associated with this stream of policy analysis and scholarly research could be viewed by some as a deterrent. Yet others might see the presence of so many unanswered questions about these relatively new and untested "means of implementation"[51] as ripe with possibilities for further policy analysis and scholarly inquiry.

As stated in the introductory chapter to this book, one certainty is that the knowledge gaps about the triple interface far outweigh what is known. The continuing definitional

[51] Sustainable Development Knowledge Platform, *Sustainable Development Goal 17*, U.N. Dep't of Econ. of Soc. Affairs, www.un.org/sustainabledevelopment/globalpartnerships/.

and functional ambiguities around PPPs involved in global knowledge governance have reflected lack of consensus around basic goals and implementation practices. Yet the analyses and case studies provided by the various contributors herein arguably provide evidence of an emerging if tentative consensus toward some common themes, shared goals, and acknowledged best practices. Considered together, the chapters begin to coalesce towards a clearer picture of the overall framework of the knowledge governance PPPs currently involved in sustainable development. And these contributions not only describe the current situation but also provide normative suggestions for future directions about this triple interface from either a policy or an academic standpoint. Looking forward, the hope is that they can provide a springboard for further inquiry along these and other lines, in order to "transform[] our world"[52] for the benefit of ourselves and our coming generations.

[52] Sustainable Development Knowledge Platform, *Transforming Our World: The 2030 Agenda for Sustainable Development*, U.N. Dep't of Econ. and Soc. Affairs, https://sustainabledevelopment.un.org/post2015/transformingourworld.